1999 FOOD & WINE

THE COMPLETE COLLECTION OF RECIPES
FROM THE 1998 ISSUES OF
AMERICA'S FAVORITE FOOD MAGAZINE

Carrot Gnocchi (p. 129)

1999 FOOD & WINE

THE COMPLETE COLLECTION OF RECIPES FROM THE 1998 ISSUES OF AMERICA'S FAVORITE FOOD MAGAZINE

FOOD & WINE
B O O K S

American Express Publishing Corporation
New York

FOOD & WINE MAGAZINE
EDITOR IN CHIEF: Dana Cowin
CREATIVE DIRECTOR: Stephen Scoble
FOOD EDITOR: Tina Ujlaki

FOOD & WINE BOOKS
EDITOR IN CHIEF: Judith Hill
ART DIRECTOR: Nina Scerbo
MANAGING EDITOR: Terri Mauro
PROJECT EDITOR: Barbara A. Mateer
DESIGNER: Leslie Andersen
COPY AND PRODUCTION EDITOR: Amy Schuler
ASSISTANT EDITOR: Dana Speers
PRODUCTION MANAGER: Yvette Williams-Braxton

VICE PRESIDENT, CONSUMER MARKETING: Mark V. Stanich
VICE PRESIDENT, BOOKS AND INFORMATION SERVICES: John Stoops
MARKETING DIRECTOR: Bruce Rosner
SENIOR MARKETING MANAGER: Mary V. Cooney
OPERATIONS MANAGER: Doreen Camardi
BUSINESS MANAGER: Joanne Ragazzo

COVER PHOTO: Quentin Bacon (Orecchiette with Broiled Feta, Peppers and Sausage, p. 140)
BACK PHOTOS: TOP—Beatriz Da Costa (Braised Lamb Shanks with Peppers and Garlic, p. 279);
William Abranowicz (Island Salad with Shallot-Soy Vinaigrette, p. 88);
BOTTOM—Simon Watson (Macadamia and Polenta–Crusted Cambozola, p. 22)
Beatriz Da Costa (Bittersweet Chocolate Tart, p. 395)

AMERICAN EXPRESS PUBLISHING CORPORATION
©1999 American Express Publishing Corporation

ISBN 0-916103-52-8 (hardcover)   ISSN 1097-1564

Published by American Express Publishing Corporation
1120 Avenue of the Americas, New York, New York 10036

Manufactured in the United States of America

contents

p. 150

p. 441-42

Bittersweet Chocolate Tart (p. 394)

foreword

1998 was a momentous year for FOOD & WINE magazine: we marked our twentieth anniversary. It was a time to celebrate but also to reflect on where we've been and where we're headed. And so you'll find our past, present and even a glimpse of our future represented in this terrific annual collection.

As part of our anniversary celebration, we scoured two decades' worth of issues to find our twenty favorite recipes. (Our very favorite of the favorites—Joël Robuchon's elegant Bittersweet Chocolate Tart—is pictured opposite.) Looking at this list of twenty next to the five-hundred-plus recipes that ran in 1998, we realized just how far we've all come. Many of the ingredients that we consider essential and take for granted today were virtually unavailable in 1978 when the magazine published its first issue. Extra-virgin olive oil, heirloom fruits and vegetables from local farmers' markets, fresh cilantro and basil weren't easy to find back then—if they could be found at all. But we didn't think twice about using them in any of the wonderful recipes that we ran this year.

As our access to more ingredients grows, so does our eagerness to experiment with new dishes. In the past twelve months alone, we've ventured to Australia, South Africa, Greece and France for delicious meals. You can be sure that this spirit of exploration will remain a hallmark of FOOD & WINE in 1999 and for many fantastic years—and recipes—to come.

Dana Cowin

EDITOR IN CHIEF
FOOD & WINE MAGAZINE

Judith Hill

EDITOR IN CHIEF
FOOD & WINE BOOKS

Sake-Marinated Beef Ribs (p. 267)

KEY TO SYMBOLS

Some special recipes have been marked with colorful symbols so that you can easily find the dishes that fall in the categories below. Complete lists of these recipes begin on page 448.

* **Quick recipes** that appeared in the Cooking Fast column during 1998.

* **Health-conscious recipes** that include nutritional breakdowns.

* **Recipes from this year's winners** of the FOOD & WINE America's Best New Chefs awards.

* **FOOD & WINE's choice of the twenty best recipes** that have run in the magazine during its twenty years of existence.

AND PLEASE NOTE

Beginning this year, due to reader requests, we have identified our annual FOOD & WINE collection by the year in which it's released, in this case 1999, rather than by the year in which the magazine issues were published. This means you can always be certain that you are getting the most up-to-date edition.

Hence this year's book, published in January of 1999, is titled 1999 FOOD & WINE and is a compilation of the recipes from the 1998 magazines. Whereas last year's book was called 1997 FOOD & WINE and included the recipes from the 1997 magazines. If you have been collecting the annuals and have the 1997 and 1999 volumes, you have a complete set; there is no book labeled 1998.

CHAPTER 1 hors d'oeuvres

A Smoked Salmon and Leek Tartlet (p. 29).

Summer Vegetable Pickles

Summer Vegetable Pickles

MAKES 2 TO 3 QUARTS

Here is a great way to use whatever you have too much of in your garden. The pickles taste best when they're made the same day that the vegetables are picked.

About 6 cups water

3   cups white wine vinegar
½   cup sugar
15 whole black peppercorns
12 garlic cloves, peeled
3   tablespoons sea salt
1   tablespoon fennel seeds
3   medium fennel bulbs— trimmed, halved lengthwise, cored and cut into ½-inch lengthwise wedges
3   small zucchini, cut into 5-by-½-inch matchsticks
½   medium cauliflower, cut into 1-inch florets
5   medium red onions, quartered lengthwise
½   cup extra-virgin olive oil
½   cup balsamic vinegar

1. In a large saucepan, combine 6 cups of the water with the white wine vinegar, sugar, peppercorns, garlic, sea salt and fennel seeds and bring to a boil over high heat. Boil vigorously for 2 minutes and then add the fennel wedges and cook until just tender, about 5 minutes. Using a slotted spoon, transfer the fennel to a large bowl. Add the zucchini to the vinegar mixture and cook until crisp-tender, about 1 minute, and then add to the fennel in the bowl. Repeat the process with the cauliflower, cooking it for about 3 minutes, and then the red onions, cooking them for about 2 minutes.

2. Divide the vegetables among 2 or 3 large heatproof jars with tight-fitting lids. Add the oil and balsamic vinegar to the cooking liquid and let cool slightly. Divide the cooking liquid among the jars, adding water if necessary to cover the vegetables. Let cool completely and then cover and refrigerate overnight. Serve the pickles chilled or at room temperature. —*Mario Batali*

MAKE AHEAD The pickles can be refrigerated for up to 1 month.

Raita with Crispy Radishes

MAKES 1½ CUPS RAITA

Radish roses make a pretty accompaniment for this cucumber-yogurt dip, but other vegetables and flat breads work well too.

¾   cup plain whole-milk yogurt
½   cup finely chopped seeded cucumber
¼   cup sour cream
¼   cup finely shredded mint leaves
3   tablespoons finely chopped red onion
1½ teaspoons rice vinegar
1   teaspoon fresh lime juice
1   teaspoon finely chopped jalapeño
½   teaspoon minced fresh ginger
½   teaspoon finely grated lime zest
½   teaspoon kosher salt
24 radishes, stems trimmed

1. Combine all the ingredients except the radishes in a medium bowl and refrigerate for up to 3 hours.

2. Cut a deep X in the bottom of each radish. Transfer them to a bowl of ice water and refrigerate until they open up, at least 1 hour. Drain the radishes and serve with the raita.

—*Mary Barber and Sara Corpening*

Radishes with Chive Butter

MAKES 16 HORS D'OEUVRES

These whimsical hors d'oeuvres can be served as sandwiches: slice the radishes and arrange them on thin squares of white or whole wheat bread that have been spread with the chive butter.

16 medium radishes, trimmed and halved crosswise
4   tablespoons unsalted butter, softened

Roasted Beet Crostini with Zucchini Flowers

1   tablespoon plus 1 teaspoon minced chives
Kosher salt

Arrange the radishes, cut side up, on a serving plate. In a bowl, blend the butter with 1 tablespoon of the chives and season with kosher salt. Transfer the chive butter to a small pastry bag fitted with a small star tip and pipe a star onto each radish half; or use a small spoon to dollop the butter on the radishes. Sprinkle with the remaining 1 teaspoon of chives and serve.

—*Clifford Harrison and Anne Quatrano*

Roasted Beet Crostini with Zucchini Flowers

MAKES 8 CROSTINI

Zucchini flowers add a peppery fragrance, but can be omitted if you can't find them at the market. If you've got your grill going for other dishes, by all means use it to toast the bread.

4   medium beets (about 1 pound), preferably a mixture of red and yellow
¼   cup extra-virgin olive oil
2   tablespoons balsamic vinegar

1 teaspoon finely chopped
  rosemary
¼ teaspoon crushed red pepper
Salt and freshly ground black pepper
Eight ¾-inch-thick slices of Italian
  country bread
6 large zucchini flowers, torn into
  ½-inch-wide strips

ı. Preheat the oven to 450°. Loosely wrap the beets in aluminum foil and roast for about 1 hour, or until tender. Let cool slightly and then peel the beets and cut them into ½-inch dice.

Pumpkin-Parmesan Toasts with Herb Pesto

Combine the beets with 2 tablespoons of the oil, the vinegar, rosemary, red pepper and a generous pinch each of salt and black pepper.

2. Heat a grill pan. Lightly brush the bread on both sides with the remaining 2 tablespoons of oil and grill until crisp and golden. Fold the zucchini flowers into the beet mixture, divide evenly among the grilled bread slices and serve. —*Mario Batali*

MAKE AHEAD The peeled beets can be refrigerated for up to 2 days.

Pumpkin-Parmesan Toasts with Herb Pesto

MAKES 30 TOASTS

1 loaf 7-grain bread—crusts
  trimmed, bread sliced ⅓ inch
  thick and cut into thirty
  3-by-1½-inch rectangles
¼ cup walnuts
1½ cups plus 2 tablespoons
  freshly grated Parmesan
  cheese
1 cup canned unsweetened
  pumpkin puree
1 teaspoon ground cumin
Salt and freshly ground black pepper
1 cup flat-leaf parsley leaves
1 cup (loosely packed) cilantro
  leaves
½ cup pure olive oil
2 tablespoons dill sprigs
¼ teaspoon cayenne pepper

ı. Preheat the oven to 400°. On a baking sheet, toast the bread for about 12 minutes, or until lightly browned. Let cool. In a cake pan, toast the walnuts for 3 to 4 minutes, or until browned. Let cool.

2. Preheat the broiler. In a medium bowl, combine 1 cup of the Parmesan with the pumpkin puree and ½ teaspoon of the cumin. Season with salt and black pepper.

3. In a food processor, pulse ½ cup of the Parmesan, the parsley, cilantro, oil, dill and toasted walnuts until minced. Add the cayenne and the remaining ½ teaspoon of cumin and season with salt and black pepper. Spread each of the toasts with 1 heaping teaspoon of the herb pesto and top with 1½ heaping teaspoons of the pumpkin-Parmesan mixture.

4. Arrange the toasts on a baking sheet and sprinkle with the remaining 2 tablespoons of Parmesan. Broil for 1 to 2 minutes, or until lightly browned on top. Serve warm or at room temperature. —*Rori Spinelli*

Skillet Cheddar Toasts

MAKES 8 TOASTS

1 tablespoon curry powder
Vegetable oil
8 large rye or whole-grain crackers, such as Ryvita
8 oil-packed sun-dried tomato halves, cut into thin strips
Salt
Eight ¼-inch-thick slices of Cheddar cheese (about 6 ounces)
1 scallion, thinly sliced

In a medium skillet, toast the curry powder over moderate heat, stirring, until fragrant, about 1 minute. Transfer the curry powder to a plate to cool and wipe out the skillet. Rub the skillet lightly with oil and set 2 rye crackers in the pan. Arrange one-eighth of the sun-dried tomato strips on each cracker and season with salt. Top each with a slice of Cheddar, a few scallion slices and 1 to 2 large pinches of curry powder. Cover the skillet and cook over moderately low heat until the cheese has melted, about 4 minutes. Serve hot from the skillet. Repeat with the remaining ingredients.—*Marcia Kiesel*
WINE A glass of Chardonnay, such as the 1996 Geyser Peak, would be welcome with these open-faced snacks; a nonvintage brut sparkling wine from California, such as the Scharffenberger or Roederer Estate, would lend a touch of luxury.

White Bean Crostini with Rosemary

MAKES 12 CROSTINI

2½ teaspoons extra-virgin olive oil
2 small garlic cloves, minced
Salt and freshly ground black pepper
Twelve ¼-inch-thick baguette slices
⅔ cup rinsed and drained cannellini beans (from a 14-ounce can)
¼ teaspoon finely chopped rosemary
Large pinch of crushed red pepper

1. Preheat the oven to 375°. In a small bowl, combine 2 teaspoons of the oil with half of the garlic and season with salt and black pepper. Brush the baguette slices on one side with the garlic oil and arrange them, oiled side down, on a baking sheet. Toast the baguette slices for about 7 minutes, or until they are lightly browned and crisp.

2. Meanwhile, in a food processor, combine the cannellini beans, rosemary and crushed red pepper. Add the remaining garlic and ½ teaspoon of oil, season with salt and process until smooth. Spoon the bean puree onto the toasts and serve.—*Ferdinand Metz*
ONE CROSTINI Calories 55 kcal, Total Fat 1.5 gm, Saturated Fat 0.2 gm

Roasted Garlic Butter Crostini with Tomato Confit

MAKES 8 CROSTINI

This recipe makes more than enough garlic butter for the crostini. Use the leftovers for sublime garlic bread or toss it with roasted vegetables and pasta.

1 tablespoon olive oil
2 medium tomatoes—peeled, seeded and quartered
Salt and freshly ground pepper
4 thyme sprigs
4 medium garlic heads, top thirds cut off
6 tablespoons unsalted butter, softened
8 Crostini Toasts (p. 17)

1. Preheat the oven to 250°. Spread ½ tablespoon of oil on a baking sheet. Arrange the tomatoes on the baking sheet and drizzle with the remaining ½ tablespoon of oil. Season with salt and pepper and top with the thyme sprigs. Bake for about 2 hours, or until the tomatoes are dry and firm but still pliable. Carefully transfer the tomatoes to a plate. Discard the thyme sprigs. Raise the oven temperature to 325°.

Skillet Cheddar Toasts

2. Set the garlic heads, cut side up, on a large piece of aluminum foil. Spread 2 tablespoons of the butter on the cut sides of the garlic and season with salt and pepper. Seal the garlic in the foil and bake for about 1 hour, or until very soft. Let cool.

3. Squeeze the garlic from the skins into a mini-processor. Add the remaining 4 tablespoons of butter and process until smooth. Transfer the garlic butter to a bowl and season with salt and pepper.

4. Spread each Crostini Toast with about 1 teaspoon of the garlic butter, top each with a confit tomato quarter and serve.—*Joseph and Thomas Keller*
MAKE AHEAD The garlic butter can be refrigerated for 5 days; the tomato confit can be refrigerated for 2 days. Let them return to room temperature before using.

Olive Tapenade Toasts

MAKES 8 TOASTS

Use the leftover tapenade as a garnish for roasted chicken.

4 anchovy fillets
½ cup milk

½ cup Niçoise olives (4 ounces),
   pitted
¼ teaspoon Dijon mustard
3 tablespoons extra-virgin olive oil
8 Crostini Toasts (opposite page)

In a small bowl, cover the anchovy fillets with the milk and let soak for 30 minutes. Drain the anchovies and add them to a food processor along with the olives and mustard. Process to a paste. With the machine on, slowly pour in the oil to make a smooth puree. Top each Crostini Toast with a heaping teaspoon of tapenade.

—*Joseph and Thomas Keller*

MAKE AHEAD The tapenade can be refrigerated for up to 1 week.

Caramelized Onion and Cheese Toasts

MAKES 8 TOASTS

2 tablespoons extra-virgin
   olive oil
1 small onion, thinly sliced
Salt
¼ cup water
8 Crostini Toasts (opposite page)
2 ounces Taleggio or Reblochon
   cheese, cut into 8 thin slices

I. Heat the oil in a medium skillet. Add the onion, season with salt and cook over moderate heat, stirring, until the onion begins to brown, about 8 minutes. Add the water and cook until it has evaporated and the onion is very tender and caramelized, about 10 minutes. Season with salt and let cool.

2. Preheat the oven to 350°. Put the Crostini Toasts on a baking sheet and top each with a slice of cheese. Bake for about 4 minutes, or just until the cheese melts. Top with the onion and serve. —*Joseph and Thomas Keller*

MAKE AHEAD The caramelized onion can be refrigerated for up to 5 days. Let the onion return to room temperature before using it.

Roasted Eggplant Caviar Crostini

MAKES 8 CROSTINI

Make the topping a day ahead to allow the flavor to develop. The extra eggplant caviar can be used on a pizza or as filling for a fluffy omelet.

2 large eggplants (about 1 pound
   each), halved lengthwise
Kosher salt
2 tablespoons extra-virgin olive oil
I small garlic clove, minced
½ teaspoon Dijon mustard
Freshly ground pepper
8 Crostini Toasts (recipe follows)

I. Score the cut sides of the eggplants in a crisscross pattern and sprinkle with 1 tablespoon of kosher salt. Arrange the halves, cut side down, on a large platter, cover with a baking sheet and weight down with cans. Let stand for 1 hour to press the moisture from the eggplants.

2. Preheat the oven to 375°. Spread 1 tablespoon of the oil on a baking sheet. Pat the eggplants dry with paper towels and set them, cut side down, on the baking sheet. Bake the eggplants for about 1 hour, or until very soft. Let the eggplants cool slightly and then remove the skin and seeds and finely chop the pulp. Put the pulp in a strainer and press out as much moisture as possible.

3. Transfer the eggplant to a food processor. Stir in the garlic and mustard,

LEFT TO RIGHT: **Roasted Eggplant Caviar Crostini and Olive Tapenade Toasts.**

some pepper and the remaining 1 tablespoon of oil. Refrigerate the eggplant caviar overnight. Let it return to room temperature. Spread each Crostini Toast with a heaping teaspoon of the eggplant caviar and serve.

—Joseph and Thomas Keller
MAKE AHEAD The eggplant caviar can be refrigerated for up to 5 days.

Crostini Toasts

MAKES 32 TOASTS

1 medium baguette, cut into thirty-two ¼-inch-thick slices

About ¼ cup olive oil, for brushing

Preheat the oven to 350°. Arrange the bread on 2 large baking sheets and brush each slice on both sides with some of the oil. Bake for about 7 minutes, or until golden brown. Let the toasts cool completely.

—Joseph and Thomas Keller
MAKE AHEAD The toasts can be stored in an airtight container for up to 3 days.

Walnut Kisses

MAKES 20 KISSES

40 dried cranberries (about ¼ cup)

¼ cup ruby port

¼ to ½ cup mousse de foie gras (see Note)

40 walnut halves

1. Put the cranberries and the port in a small saucepan. Bring to a simmer and cook for 5 minutes. Remove from the heat, cover and let cool. Drain the cranberries.

2. Spread approximately 1 teaspoon of mousse de foie gras on each of the the walnut halves. Top the foie gras with 2 of the steeped cranberries and sandwich with another walnut half.

—Marcia Kiesel
NOTE Mousse de foie gras is available at supermarket delicatessen counters and by mail order from D'Artagnan, 800-327-8246.

Mashed Avocado with Lily Bulbs and Lotus Root Chips

8 SERVINGS

Sweet, salty, creamy, crisp, juicy—this dish offers a wonderful variety of tastes and textures. The mashed avocado can be served on a platter surrounded by the marinated lily bulbs and the chips. Or the avocado can be served atop the lotus chips and garnished with the salad as an hors d'oeuvre. A mandoline makes easy work of slicing the lotus root thinly.

Corn oil, for frying

One ½-pound firm lotus root, peeled and very thinly sliced crosswise (see Note)

Salt

½ pound fresh lily bulbs (see Note), layers separated and cut into fine julienne, or jicama, peeled and cut into matchsticks

2½ tablespoons fresh lemon juice

1 teaspoon white wine vinegar

1 teaspoon olive oil

3 ripe Hass avocados, halved and pitted

2 scallions, thinly sliced

½ cup finely diced tomato

1 teaspoon chopped cilantro

Dash of Tabasco

Freshly ground pepper

1. In a medium saucepan, heat 1 inch of oil to 350°. Fry the lotus root slices, 4 or 5 at a time, until golden brown and crisp, about 2 minutes. Drain on paper towels and sprinkle with salt. Repeat until all of the slices have been fried.

2. In a bowl, toss the lily bulbs with ½ tablespoon of the lemon juice, the vinegar and oil. Season with salt and refrigerate.

3. Scoop the avocado flesh into a large bowl, add the remaining 2 tablespoons of lemon juice and mash with a fork to a chunky puree. Stir in the scallions, diced tomato, cilantro and Tabasco. Season with salt and pepper.

Mashed Avocado with Lily Bulbs and Lotus Root Chips

four fast hors d'oeuvres

• Spread narrow wedges of green apple with crème fraîche mixed with a little horseradish. Top each with a piece of smoked trout.

• Slather thin toasts with mild blue cheese and sprinkle with coarsely chopped spiced pecans.

• Top Yukon Gold potato chips with small dollops of chive-studded sour cream, and then garnish with caviar.

• Mix plain yogurt with grated, seeded cucumber, chopped cilantro, salt and cayenne. Serve the mixture as a dip with steamed shrimp.

4. Spoon the mashed avocado onto a serving platter and surround with the marinated lily bulbs. Serve the lotus chips on the side. *—Alan Tardi*
NOTE Fresh lotus roots and lily bulbs are available at Asian markets. Be sure to buy firm, unblemished roots and bulbs.

WINE Try a sparkling Prosecco (those of Nino Franco and Zardetto are terrific), on its own or mixed with a couple of tablespoons of freshly squeezed blood orange juice.

Potato Chips
Cooked in Duck Fat

MAKES ABOUT 40 CHIPS

- 1 8-ounce baking potato, peeled
- 6 tablespoons duck fat (see Note), melted
- 2 tablespoons salt

1. Preheat the oven to 400°. Cut the potato into thin slices using a mandoline or a very sharp knife.

2. Pour 3 tablespoons of the duck fat onto each of 2 large baking sheets. Place half of the potato slices on each sheet in a single layer, turning to coat in fat. Sprinkle with the salt. Bake for about 15 minutes, or until the slices are brown all over. Drain the chips on paper towels. —*Marcia Kiesel*

NOTE Duck fat is available by mail order from D'Artagnan, 800-327-8246.

Paprika Chips

MAKES ABOUT 5 DOZEN CHIPS

These spiced pita chips are good with all kinds of dips.

- ½ teaspoon hot or sweet paprika
- ½ teaspoon ground fennel seeds
- ½ teaspoon onion powder
- ¼ teaspoon cinnamon
- ¼ teaspoon salt
- 4 pocket pitas, each split into 2 rounds
- ¼ cup vegetable oil

Preheat the oven to 350°. In a small bowl, combine the paprika, fennel seeds, onion powder, cinnamon and salt. Brush the rough sides of the pita rounds with the oil and sprinkle with the spice mixture. Stack the rounds and cut them into 8 wedges. Unstack and arrange the wedges on 2 large rimmed baking sheets, spiced side up, and bake on the upper and middle racks of the oven for about 9 minutes, or until crisp and golden. Switch the baking sheets halfway through for even toasting.—*Mary Barber and Sara Corpening*

MAKE AHEAD The chips can be stored in an airtight container at room temperature for up to 2 days.

Cumin Seed Crackers

MAKES 2 DOZEN CRACKERS

Serve these buttery salt- and spice-accented crackers with cheese or just on their own.

- 7 tablespoons cold unsalted butter
- 1 cup finely chopped sweet onion, preferably Vidalia
- 2 cups all-purpose flour
- 1 teaspoon sugar
- ½ teaspoon kosher salt
- ¼ teaspoon freshly ground pepper
- About ¼ cup ice water
- 1 large egg white, beaten with 1 tablespoon of water
- 1½ tablespoons cumin seeds
- 1 tablespoon coarse sea salt

1. Heat 1 tablespoon of the butter in a nonstick medium skillet. Add the onion and cook over moderate heat, stirring, until browned, 8 to 10 minutes. Let cool.

2. In a medium bowl, mix the flour with the sugar, kosher salt and pepper.

Work in the remaining 6 tablespoons of butter, rubbing it into the flour with your fingertips until the mixture resembles coarse meal. Mix in the onion. Stir in 3 tablespoons of the ice water and shape the dough into a ball; if necessary, add more ice water, 1 tablespoon at a time. Divide the dough in half and pat into two 4-inch squares. Wrap each square in plastic and refrigerate until the dough is chilled, at least 1 hour.

3. Preheat the oven to 350°. Line 2 large baking sheets with parchment paper. On a lightly floured surface, roll out 1 dough square to a 12-by-9-inch rectangle, about ⅛ inch thick. Cut the dough into 3-inch squares and transfer to 1 of the baking sheets. Brush with some of the egg-white wash and sprinkle with half of the cumin seeds and sea salt. Bake for about 20 minutes, or until the crackers are golden brown and crisp. Let cool completely on a rack. Meanwhile, repeat with the remaining dough, egg-white wash, cumin seeds and sea salt.
—*Clifford Harrison and Anne Quatrano*

MAKE AHEAD The dough can be refrigerated for up to 2 days. The baked crackers can be kept in an airtight container overnight.

Benne Wafers

MAKES ABOUT 100 WAFERS

Benne wafers are a Carolina Low Country favorite. Benne comes from the Nigerian word for sesame seeds, which slaves considered lucky. Be sure to bake the wafers to a rich brown to bring out their flavor. Like cheese straws, they are good with soups and salads, and they're delicious with Shrimp Paste (p. 26) and other savory spreads.

- 1 cup sesame seeds (5 ounces)
- 3 cups unbleached all-purpose flour

LEFT TO RIGHT: **Roasted Pepper, Almond and Cilantro Pesto (p. 358) and Paprika Chips.**

1 teaspoon cream of tartar

½ teaspoon baking soda

Salt

⅔ cup chilled lard or vegetable shortening

⅔ cup cold milk

1. Preheat the oven to 425°. Toast the sesame seeds in a pie pan in the oven for 4 minutes, stirring occasionally, until deep golden. Transfer to a plate and let cool.

2. In a large bowl, sift the flour with the cream of tartar, baking soda and 1 teaspoon of salt. Cut in the lard until the mixture resembles coarse meal. Stir in the sesame seeds and the milk and mix until blended.

3. Turn the dough out onto a lightly floured surface and knead briefly. Divide the dough in half. Roll out 1 piece of dough as thinly as possible (at most ⅛ inch thick). Prick the dough all over with a fork and stamp out 2-inch rounds. Transfer the rounds to a large baking sheet and sprinkle with salt. Bake for about 14 minutes, or until deep golden brown. Let cool slightly and then transfer to a rack. Repeat with the remaining dough. Serve the wafers warm or at room temperature.

—*Edna Lewis and Scott Peacock*

MAKE AHEAD The wafers can be stored in an airtight container for up to 1 week. Rewarm before serving.

Cheese Straws

MAKES 4 DOZEN CHEESE STRAWS

In the South, cheese straws are almost always present at celebrations. They're perfect with cocktails and can also be served with salads and certain soups. Unlike many baked goods, cheese straws improve in flavor when they're made a day before they're served.

1⅔ cups unbleached all-purpose flour

1¼ teaspoons dry mustard

1 teaspoon salt

¼ teaspoon cayenne pepper

½ pound extra-sharp Cheddar cheese, coarsely grated (2½ cups)

1 stick (4 ounces) unsalted butter, at room temperature

2 tablespoons water

1. Sift the flour, mustard, salt and cayenne into a medium bowl. Using an electric mixer, beat the cheese and butter on low speed until well blended. Gradually beat in the flour mixture until completely incorporated. Add the water and beat for 1 minute.

2. Turn the dough out onto a lightly floured surface and knead it 5 times. On a large sheet of wax paper, roll the dough into a 12-by-9-inch rectangle. Slide this onto a cookie sheet and refrigerate until chilled, about 15 minutes.

3. Preheat the oven to 425°. Cut the dough in half crosswise, then cut it into 6-by-¼-inch strips. Transfer the strips to 2 cookie sheets. Bake 1 sheet at a time for about 14 minutes, or until the cheese straws are golden brown and crisp. Let cool slightly and then transfer to a rack to cool completely.

—*Edna Lewis and Scott Peacock*

MAKE AHEAD The Cheese Straws can be stored in an airtight container for up to 1 week.

Blue Cheese Straws

MAKES 2 DOZEN CHEESE STRAWS

It takes a light touch to roll this delicate dough thin enough to make straws. An alternative is to make coins: Shape the dough into a one-inch-thick log, roll the log in poppy seeds and chill and then slice the log a quarter inch thick. Bake the coins for 15 minutes, or until crisp.

4½ ounces Maytag or other sharp blue cheese (½ cup packed)

¼ cup plus 2 tablespoons all-purpose flour

Cheese Straws

3 tablespoons cornstarch

2½ tablespoons unsalted butter, softened

⅛ teaspoon kosher salt

⅛ teaspoon freshly ground pepper

¾ teaspoon poppy seeds

1. In a food processor, combine the blue cheese, flour, cornstarch, butter, kosher salt and pepper and pulse until the dough just comes together. Transfer the dough to a sheet of plastic wrap and shape it into a 4-inch disk. Wrap the disk and refrigerate it until firm, about 1 hour, or for up to 1 day.

2. Preheat the oven to 375°. Line a baking sheet with parchment paper. On a well-floured surface, roll out the dough to a 12-by-6-inch rectangle about ⅛ inch thick. Sprinkle the poppy seeds over the dough and press lightly to help them adhere. Cut the dough into 6-by-½-inch strips and transfer them to the baking sheet; twist the ends of the strips in opposite directions to make spirals. Bake the cheese straws for about 15 minutes, or until they are crisp and brown. Let the

Blue Cheese Straws

cheese straws cool on the baking sheet before serving.

—*Mary Barber and Sara Corpening*
MAKE AHEAD The Blue Cheese Straws can be frozen for up to 1 month; recrisp them in a 350° oven.

Oniony Cheese Puffs

MAKES ABOUT 30 PUFFS
Bread cubes dipped into a savory cheese mixture and baked until golden make an easy hors d'oeuvre.

- 1 stick (4 ounces) unsalted butter, softened
- ⅓ cup finely chopped onion

Salt and freshly ground pepper
- 4 ounces cream cheese, softened
- ⅓ cup packed grated Jarlsberg cheese (2 ounces)
- 3 tablespoons dehydrated minced onion
- 3 tablespoons chopped chives
- 2 large egg whites
- ¾ pound challah, crusts removed, bread cut into ¾-inch cubes

1. Preheat the oven to 350°. Line a large baking sheet with parchment paper. In a small skillet, melt 1 tablespoon of the butter. Add the chopped onion, season with salt and pepper and cook over moderate heat until the onion is softened but not browned, about 4 minutes.

2. In a medium saucepan, combine the cream cheese, Jarlsberg and dehydrated onion. Set the pan over simmering water and stir until melted. Remove the cheese mixture from the heat and stir in the remaining 7 tablespoons of butter along with the chives and sautéed onion.

3. Beat the egg whites until they hold stiff peaks. Stir one-quarter of the egg whites into the warm cheese mixture and then fold in the remaining whites. Coat the bread cubes with the cheese mixture, a few cubes at a time.

Warm Figs with Feta and Basil

4. Transfer the cubes to the prepared baking sheet. Bake for 15 minutes, or until golden. Serve hot.

—*Mary Barber and Sara Corpening*
MAKE AHEAD The puffs can be prepared through Step 3 and frozen for up to 1 week.

Warm Figs with Feta and Basil

MAKES 16 HORS D'OEUVRES
This hors d'oeuvre offers a wonderful combination of sweet, tangy and herbal flavors and contrasting textures.

- 2 tablespoons red wine vinegar
- 2 tablespoons honey
- 16 black Mission figs
- 16 large basil leaves
- 2 ounces feta cheese, cut into 16 equal pieces

1. Light a grill or heat a grill pan over moderately high heat. In a small saucepan, bring the vinegar and honey to a simmer. Set aside.

2. Grill the figs, turning, until they are warmed through, about 4 minutes. Transfer the figs to a large platter. Using a small sharp knife, split open each of the figs. Fold a basil leaf around each piece of feta and tuck the cheese and basil into a fig. Pour the warm vinegar-honey mixture over the figs and serve. —*Tony Najiola*

Macadamia and Polenta–Crusted Cambozola

MAKES ABOUT 16 PIECES

Cambozola, a German cheese that tastes like a combination of creamy Brie and potent Gorgonzola, is the base of these luxurious warm hors d'oeuvres. If you can't find Cambozola, you can use Brie instead with excellent results. Before frying, be sure to coat the pieces of cheese completely with the polenta-nut crumbs to seal them well.

¾ pound Cambozola, chilled
2 large eggs
¼ cup milk
1 cup unsalted macadamia nuts (about 4½ ounces)
¾ cup polenta (about 4 ounces)
About ½ cup all-purpose flour
1 tablespoon vegetable oil

Macadamia and Polenta–Crusted Cambozola

1. Cut the cheese into 1¼-by-¾-inch rectangles. In a shallow bowl, beat the eggs with the milk. In a food processor, pulse the macadamia nuts until coarsely ground. Add the polenta and pulse to a coarse powder. Transfer the nut mixture to a plate. Spread the flour on another plate.

2. Lightly dredge the cheese rectangles in flour. Coat with the egg mixture and then with the polenta-nut crumbs.

3. Heat the oil in a large nonstick skillet. Working in batches, fry the cheese rectangles over high heat, turning once, until browned, about 30 seconds per side. Transfer the rectangles to paper towels to drain. Let cool slightly before serving. —*Theodora van den Beld*

MAKE AHEAD The recipe can be prepared through Step 2 and refrigerated for up to 8 hours.

Goat Cheese Quesadillas

MAKES 2 DOZEN WEDGES

Guests will appreciate the extra work it takes to make these quesadillas bite-size. The salsa is also good as a quick, light sauce for pasta.

SALSA

3 large plum tomatoes, seeded and finely chopped
⅛ teaspoon kosher salt
⅓ cup Calamata olives (2 ounces), pitted and finely chopped
1 tablespoon finely chopped flat-leaf parsley
1 tablespoon finely chopped red onion
1 tablespoon balsamic vinegar
2 teaspoons fresh lime juice
1 teaspoon hot sauce
½ teaspoon minced garlic
¼ teaspoon dried oregano

QUESADILLAS

Eight 6-inch flour tortillas
4 ounces goat cheese, softened
4 small scallions, thinly sliced
Freshly ground pepper
2 tablespoons vegetable oil
Kosher salt

1. MAKE THE SALSA: In a strainer set in the sink, toss the tomatoes with the kosher salt and let drain for 10 minutes. Transfer the tomatoes to a bowl and add the olives, parsley, onion, vinegar, lime juice, hot sauce, garlic and oregano. Mix well.

2. MAKE THE QUESADILLAS: Cut the tortillas into 4-inch rounds, using a small saucer as a template. Spread the tortillas with the goat cheese and sprinkle with the scallions and pepper; sandwich to make 4 quesadillas.

3. In a large skillet, heat the vegetable oil. Add the quesadillas and cook over moderately high heat until golden and crisp, about 1 minute per side. Transfer the quesadillas to a cutting board and cut each one into 6 wedges. Sprinkle with kosher salt and top each

wedge with 1 teaspoon of the salsa. Serve immediately, passing the remaining salsa separately.

—*Mary Barber and Sara Corpening*

MAKE AHEAD The quesadillas can be prepared through Step 2 and refrigerated for up to 1 day.

Goat Cheese Heart

6 SERVINGS

- ½ **cup soft goat cheese (3½ ounces), at room temperature**
- ½ **baguette, thinly sliced and toasted**

Set a 2½ to 3 inch heart-shaped cookie cutter or coeur à la crème mold on a plate. In a bowl, beat the cheese with a fork until smooth. Pack the cheese into the cookie cutter and smooth the top. Cover and refrigerate until cold, at least 1 hour and up to 3 days. Gently unmold the cheese onto the center of a plate. Serve with the baguette toasts. —*Alice Harper*

Goat Cheese and Almond Torte

16 SERVINGS

- 1 **cup whole blanched almonds (about 5 ounces)**

Vegetable oil, for frying

- 30 **medium sage leaves**
- 11 **ounces mild goat cheese, softened**
- ½ **pound cream cheese, softened**
- ½ **teaspoon freshly ground pepper**

Toasted croutons, for serving

1. Preheat the oven to 350°. Spread the almonds on a baking sheet and toast for about 10 minutes, or until golden. Let cool and then coarsely chop the nuts.
2. Heat ½ inch of vegetable oil in a skillet. Fry the sage leaves in 2 batches until crisp, about 30 seconds. Transfer to paper towels to drain. Let cool and then crumble.
3. In a bowl, combine the goat cheese and cream cheese and beat with a

wooden spoon until smooth. Stir in the pepper. Line an 8-inch round cake pan with plastic wrap, leaving a 5-inch overhang; smooth out any large wrinkles. Spread half of the cheese mixture evenly in the cake pan and sprinkle with two-thirds of the almonds; press them down lightly. Scatter the sage on top and then cover with the remaining cheese; don't dislodge the almonds. Fold the overhanging plastic onto the cheese and refrigerate until firm, at least 1 hour or overnight.

4. Unwrap the torte and invert onto a large plate; discard the plastic. Pat the remaining almonds around the edge of the torte and let return to room temperature. Serve the croutons on the side. —*Theodora van den Beld*

Bocaditos

MAKES ABOUT
20 HORS D'OEUVRES

These delicious potato and cheese fritters are party food from Oaxaca, Mexico. The recipe has been adapted from *The Food and Life of Oaxaca* (Macmillan) by Zarela Martinez of Zarela in New York City.

- 2 **large baking potatoes (about 1 pound), peeled and cut into chunks**
- 1 **cup crumbled cotija, ricotta salata or feta cheese (4 ounces)**
- 2 **large eggs, lightly beaten**
- ½ **teaspoon salt**

Freshly ground pepper
Vegetable oil, for frying

1. Cook the potatoes in a medium saucepan of boiling salted water until just tender, about 12 minutes; drain. Transfer the potatoes to a bowl and mash. Using a wooden spoon, beat in the cheese and eggs. Season the mixture with the salt and a large pinch of pepper. With wet hands, shape the potato mixture into round cakes, 2½ inches across. Put the potato cakes

TOP: **Goat Cheese Quesadillas.** ABOVE: **Bocaditos.**

on a large baking sheet and refrigerate until they are chilled and firm, at least 30 minutes.

2. In a medium nonstick skillet, heat ½ inch of oil. Carefully add 4 cakes at a time and fry over moderately high heat until lightly browned, about 4 minutes per side. Drain on paper towels and keep warm in a low oven until all are fried. Serve hot. —*Zarela Martinez*

MAKE AHEAD The shaped potato cakes can be refrigerated, covered, for up to 1 day.

WINE A 1997 Quinta da Aveleda Vinho Verde or a nonvintage Roederer Estate Brut.

Shrimp with Rice Vinegar Dipping Sauce

Deviled Eggs

MAKES 1 DOZEN HORS D'OEUVRES

- 1 dozen large eggs

Fine sea salt

- ½ cup mayonnaise
- 2 tablespoons heavy cream
- 1 teaspoon sugar
- 1 tablespoon white wine vinegar
- 2 teaspoons snipped chives and chervil

1. Put the eggs in a large saucepan with water to cover by 2 inches. Add 1 tablespoon of sea salt and bring to a rolling boil over high heat. Immediately remove the pan from the heat, cover and let stand for 10 minutes. Pour off the hot water and fill the saucepan with cold water. Gently crack the eggs in the water to loosen the shells.

2. Shell the eggs. Cut a very thin slice from the bottom of each egg so the eggs will stand up. Slice off the top third of each egg and scoop the yolks into a coarse strainer; reserve the whites. Press the egg yolks through the strainer into a bowl. Blend in the mayonnaise, cream, sugar and vinegar. Season with sea salt.

3. Using a teaspoon or a pastry bag fitted with a star tip, generously fill the egg whites. Arrange the eggs on a plate, sprinkle with the chives and chervil and serve.

—*Edna Lewis and Scott Peacock*

MAKE AHEAD The stuffed eggs can be refrigerated for up to 4 hours. Sprinkle with herbs just before serving.

Crab and Pea Salad in Celery Ribs

MAKES ABOUT 5 DOZEN
HORS D'OEUVRES

Another way to serve this spring salad is to spoon it onto challah toasts.

- 8 wide celery ribs, trimmed
- ¼ cup cream cheese (2 ounces), softened
- 2 tablespoons mayonnaise
- 1 tablespoon plus 1 teaspoon fresh lemon juice
- 1 tablespoon finely chopped basil
- 2 teaspoons finely chopped tarragon
- 2 teaspoons finely chopped flat-leaf parsley
- ½ teaspoon finely grated lemon zest
- ½ pound lump crabmeat, picked over and well drained
- ½ cup frozen baby peas, thawed
- ¼ cup finely chopped fennel bulb, plus fennel fronds, for garnish
- 3 tablespoons finely chopped red onion

Kosher salt and freshly ground pepper

Peel the celery ribs so they sit flat and then cut them on the diagonal into 1-inch lengths. In a medium bowl, combine the softened cream cheese with the mayonnaise, lemon juice, basil, tarragon, parsley and lemon zest. Add the crabmeat, peas, fennel bulb and onion and stir gently until just combined. Season with kosher salt and pepper. Spoon 1 teaspoon of the crab salad onto each piece of celery and garnish with a bit of fennel frond.

—*Mary Barber and Sara Corpening*

MAKE AHEAD The crab salad can be refrigerated for up to 1 day.

Shrimp with Rice Vinegar Dipping Sauce

MAKES 2 DOZEN HORS D'OEUVRES

To boost the shrimp flavor, shell and devein the shrimp after boiling them.

- ½ cup rice vinegar
- ½ cup water

One 4-inch piece of lemongrass, inner white bulb only, cut into strips

One 1-inch piece of fresh ginger, peeled and cut into matchsticks

- 1 tablespoon fresh lime juice
- 1 teaspoon finely grated lime zest

Crab and Pea Salad in Celery Ribs

- ¼ teaspoon crushed red pepper

Pinch of kosher salt

Pinch of sugar

- 24 medium shrimp (about ¾ pound), shelled but with tails left intact, then deveined

1. In a small stainless-steel saucepan, combine all of the ingredients except the shrimp and bring to a boil. Transfer to a bowl and let cool and then refrigerate until chilled or for up to 1 day.

2. Prepare an ice water bath. Cook the shrimp in a medium saucepan of boiling salted water, stirring occasionally, until pink, about 2 minutes. Drain the shrimp and plunge into the ice bath; drain again and pat dry. Transfer the shrimp to a platter and serve with the dipping sauce.

—*Mary Barber and Sara Corpening*

Ginger Shrimp in Napa Cabbage

MAKES ABOUT 2 DOZEN
HORS D'OEUVRES

One unpeeled 4-inch piece of fresh ginger

- 1 teaspoon salt
- 4 cups water
- 24 medium shrimp, shelled and deveined

Ginger Shrimp in Napa Cabbage

12 Napa cabbage leaves, halved lengthwise, ribs removed

2 teaspoons Asian black bean–chili sauce

½ cup daikon sprouts, roots trimmed

1. In a food processor, finely chop the ginger. Transfer to a saucepan, add the salt and water and bring to a boil. Simmer over moderate heat for 10 minutes. Strain the ginger broth through a fine sieve, discarding the ginger. Return the broth to the saucepan and bring to a boil. Add the shrimp and cook over high heat just until opaque, about 1 minute. Remove the shrimp to a plate with a slotted spoon and let cool. Let the cooking liquid cool too, and then add the shrimp and refrigerate until chilled, at least 30 minutes. Drain the shrimp and pat dry.

2. In a large pot of boiling water, cook the cabbage until tender, about 2 minutes. Drain and let cool under running water. Dry the cabbage leaves thoroughly with paper towels.

3. Cut the cabbage into 6-by-1-inch strips. Set a shrimp at one end of a cabbage strip, top with a scant ⅛ teaspoon of the black bean–chili sauce and a few of the daikon sprouts and roll up the shrimp in the cabbage strip. Repeat with the remaining ingredients. Serve the shrimp chilled or at room temperature.

—*Theodora van den Beld*

MAKE AHEAD The recipe can be prepared through Step 2 up to 6 hours ahead. Refrigerate the shrimp; leave the black bean sauce and cabbage at room temperature.

WINE DeLille Chaleur Estate Blanc or Chateau Ste. Michelle Sauvignon Blanc.

Shrimp Paste

MAKES 2¼ CUPS

This dip from the Carolina Low Country is really just an extravagant compound butter, highly flavored and, of course, very rich. Serve it with Benne Wafers (p. 18) or, for a treat at brunch, stir it into hot grits. It's also delicious in rice or mashed potatoes.

2 sticks (½ pound) unsalted butter

1 pound medium shrimp, shelled and deveined

Salt and freshly ground black pepper

¼ cup cream sherry

2 tablespoons fresh lemon juice

¼ teaspoon cayenne pepper

1. In a large skillet, melt 6 tablespoons of the butter until it foams. Add the shrimp and ½ teaspoon each of salt and black pepper. Cook over high heat, stirring, until the shrimp are pink and cooked through, about 5 minutes. Using a slotted spoon, transfer the shrimp to a food processor.

2. Return the skillet to high heat. Add the sherry, lemon juice and cayenne and cook until reduced to 3 tablespoons, 2 to 3 minutes. Pour the liquid over the shrimp and process until very smooth.

3. With the machine on, add the remaining butter, 1 tablespoon at a time, and process until smooth and silky. Transfer the shrimp paste to a serving bowl and let cool. Press a piece of plastic wrap directly onto the surface and refrigerate for at least 1 day. Bring the Shrimp Paste to room temperature before serving.

—*Edna Lewis and Scott Peacock*

MAKE AHEAD The Shrimp Paste can be refrigerated for up to 1 week.

Curried Scallops on Pumpkin Polenta Cakes

MAKES ABOUT
32 HORS D'OEUVRES

½ cup canned unsweetened
    pumpkin puree
1½ cups water
 2 tablespoons heavy cream
 1 tablespoon unsalted butter
½ tablespoon honey
Salt
½ cup polenta (not instant)
¼ cup vegetable oil, plus more
    for frying
½ tablespoon curry powder
16 medium sea scallops
Cilantro leaves, for garnish

1. In a medium saucepan, combine the pumpkin with the water and bring to a boil. Add the cream, butter, honey and a generous pinch of salt. Add the polenta in a thin stream, whisking constantly. Cook over moderate heat, stirring with a wooden spoon, until thickened and tender, about 20 minutes. Scrape the polenta into a 9-inch-square pan and refrigerate until firm.
2. In a small saucepan, heat the ¼ cup of vegetable oil with the curry powder. Pour the curry oil into a small bowl and let cool. Spoon off the yellow oil and discard the curry powder.
3. Run a knife around the sides of the pan and unmold the polenta. Cut it into 1½-inch squares; you should have about 32. Heat ½ inch of oil in a large nonstick skillet until shimmering. Fry the polenta cakes in batches, turning once, until deep golden and crisp, about 2 minutes per side. Transfer to a rack set over a baking sheet to drain.
4. In a large skillet, heat 2 tablespoons of the curry oil until shimmering. Season the scallops with salt. Add 8 scallops to the skillet and cook over high heat until browned, about 2 minutes per side. Transfer to a plate and repeat with the remaining scallops and curry

oil. Let the scallops cool and then cut in half crosswise.
5. Arrange the scallop halves on the polenta cakes, cut side down, garnish with cilantro and drizzle very lightly with the remaining curry oil. Serve immediately. —*Theodora van den Beld*
MAKE AHEAD The recipe can be prepared through Step 3 and kept at room temperature for up to 6 hours.

Grilled Oysters with Fennel Butter

MAKES 16 HORS D'OEUVRES
Be extra careful when lifting the grill cover, as the oyster shells can pop from the intense heat. Partially cooked oysters are easy to pry open, but use oven mitts when handling them; the shells get very hot.

 1 teaspoon fennel seeds
 5 tablespoons unsalted butter,
    softened
 1 tablespoon minced shallots
 1 tablespoon minced fennel
    fronds or parsley
 1 teaspoon coarsely ground pepper
½ teaspoon kosher salt
16 medium oysters

1. Light a grill or preheat the oven to 500°. In a small skillet, toast the fennel seeds over moderately high heat until fragrant, about 1 minute. Transfer to a plate to cool. Pound the seeds to a coarse powder in a mortar. In a bowl, blend the butter with the ground fennel seeds, shallots, fennel fronds, pepper and kosher salt.
2. Arrange the oysters on the grill, cover and cook for 3 to 5 minutes, just until they start hissing and releasing their juices but are not wide open. Transfer the oysters to a large baking sheet. Alternatively, arrange the oysters on a large rimmed baking sheet and roast in the oven for 3 to 5 minutes, until they start hissing.
3. Using an oyster knife, pry each of

the oysters open at the hinge, loosen the meat and discard the flat shell. Top each oyster with ½ teaspoon of the fennel butter. Serve hot. —*Tony Najiola*
MAKE AHEAD The fennel butter can be frozen for up to 1 week. Bring to room temperature before using.
SERVE WITH Toast points spread with the remaining fennel butter.

Fried Bass Fingers

8 SERVINGS
Even finicky children can't refuse these homemade fish sticks. They're ideal for summer buffets.

½ cup all-purpose flour
Salt and freshly ground pepper
 3 large eggs
 2 cups fine cracker crumbs
1½ pounds skinless striped bass
    fillets, cut into 3-by-½-inch
    strips
Vegetable oil, for frying
Lemon wedges

1. Put the flour in a shallow bowl and season it generously with salt and pepper. Crack the eggs into another

Spiced Pork Tenderloin with Corn Salsa (p. 34) and Curried Scallops on Pumpkin Polenta Cakes.

shallow bowl and beat them well. Put the cracker crumbs in a third shallow bowl and season them with salt and pepper.

2. Dredge the fish strips in the flour. Dip the strips in the beaten eggs and then coat completely with the seasoned cracker crumbs. Arrange the fish fingers on a large baking sheet, cover them with plastic wrap and then refrigerate them for at least 1 hour or overnight.

3. In a medium saucepan, heat 2 inches of oil to 375°. Fry the fish fingers 4 or 5 at a time until they are golden brown and just cooked through, about 3 minutes. Using a slotted spoon, transfer the fried fish to paper towels to drain. Serve at once with lemon wedges. —*Mark Gottwald*

Flat Bread with Smoked Salmon and Crème Fraîche

Cured Salmon Tartare with Cilantro

8 SERVINGS

Try using brown sugar to cure the salmon for a sweeter flavor. Be sure to allow a day and a half for the salmon to cure.

- 1 pound skinless salmon fillet
- 1½ cups coarse salt
- ½ cup sugar
- 1 medium red onion, thinly sliced
- 1 bunch of cilantro (about 4 ounces)
- Zest of 1 lemon, cut into 2-inch-long strips
- 1 small red bell pepper, finely chopped
- 1 medium jalapeño, seeded and finely chopped
- ½ cup plus 3 tablespoons finely chopped chives
- 3 tablespoons sour cream
- 1 tablespoon fresh lemon or lime juice
- Fine salt and freshly ground black pepper
- Toast points, for serving

1. Put the salmon in a glass or ceramic baking dish and spread ¾ cup of the coarse salt on top. Refrigerate for 4 hours. Turn the fish over, coat with the remaining ¾ cup of coarse salt and refrigerate for 4 hours longer. Rinse the salt off the salmon and rub both sides with the sugar.

2. Wipe out the baking dish and line it with a large piece of plastic wrap. Spread half of the onion, cilantro and lemon zest in the baking dish and set the salmon on top. Cover with the remaining onion, cilantro and zest and wrap the fish snugly in the plastic. Refrigerate the fish in the baking dish and let it cure for 12 hours. Pour off any liquid from the dish. Turn the salmon package and refrigerate it for 12 hours longer.

3. Unwrap the salmon. Scrape the onion, cilantro and lemon zest off the fish and finely chop enough of this onion mixture to yield ¼ cup; discard the rest. Cut the salmon into ½-inch dice and transfer it to a medium bowl. Add the chopped onion mixture, the red pepper and jalapeño and toss to combine.

4. Stir ½ cup of the chives, the sour cream and lemon juice into the tartare and season with fine salt and black pepper. Sprinkle with the remaining 3 tablespoons of chives. Serve the tartare with toast points. —*Melissa Kelly*

MAKE AHEAD The salmon tartare can be prepared through Step 3 and refrigerated for up to 1 day. Let the tartare return to room temperature before serving.

Flat Bread with Smoked Salmon and Crème Fraîche

MAKES 24 HORS D'OEUVRES

¾ cup crème fraîche
½ cup finely chopped red onion
1 tablespoon finely chopped dill, plus 24 tiny sprigs, for garnish
2 teaspoons prepared horseradish
Salt and freshly ground pepper
Twenty-four 3-inch triangles cut from ¾ pound flat bread (such as pita or Afghan bread)
½ pound thinly sliced smoked salmon
2 ounces salmon roe

In a small bowl, combine the crème fraîche, onion, chopped dill and horseradish. Stir well and season with salt and pepper. Cover each bread triangle with smoked salmon, trimming it to fit. Top each triangle with 2 teaspoons of the sauce, a little salmon roe and a dill sprig. —*Christer Larsson*
WINE A nonvintage Mumm Cordon Rouge Brut or the 1995 Kerpen Wehlener Sonnenuhr Riesling Kabinett.

Jasmine Rice Cakes with Wasabi and Smoked Salmon

MAKES ABOUT 3 DOZEN RICE CAKES

1½ cups jasmine rice (about 10 ounces)
1¾ cups plus 1 tablespoon water
Salt
3 tablespoons unsweetened coconut milk
1 tablespoon wasabi powder
4 ounces thinly sliced smoked salmon, cut into 2-by-½-inch strips
4 large arugula leaves, finely shredded

I. In a medium saucepan, combine the rice with 1¾ cups of the water and 1 teaspoon of salt and bring to a boil over moderately high heat. Cover, reduce the heat to very low and cook without stirring until all of the water is absorbed and the rice is tender, about 25 minutes. Fluff the rice with a fork and stir in the coconut milk. Transfer the rice to a baking sheet and spread it out to a 9-inch square, about ½ inch thick. Press a piece of plastic wrap directly on the rice and refrigerate until chilled.

2. In a small bowl, combine the wasabi powder with the remaining 1 tablespoon of water and mix to a paste. Using a 1½-inch round cookie cutter, cut the rice into individual cakes. Spread a scant ⅛ teaspoon of the wasabi paste on each and arrange a strip of smoked salmon on top. Garnish with the arugula and serve at room temperature. —*Theodora van den Beld*
MAKE AHEAD The salmon-topped rice cakes can be refrigerated for up to 3 hours. Let them return to room temperature and garnish with the arugula just before serving.

Smoked Salmon and Leek Tartlets

MAKES 24 TARTLETS

As a richer alternative to phyllo dough, try making these little hors d'oeuvres with buttery pâte brisée.

2½ teaspoons unsalted butter, 1½ teaspoons melted
1½ teaspoons extra-virgin olive oil
3 sheets of phyllo dough, plus more in case of tearing
3 large leeks, white and tender green, thinly sliced
Salt and freshly ground pepper
2 ounces thinly sliced smoked salmon, cut into twenty-four 1-inch-square pieces
Chopped chives, for garnish

I. Preheat the oven to 375°. In a small bowl, combine the melted butter and oil. Lightly brush two 12-cup mini-muffin tins with a little of the butter-oil mixture. Lay a sheet of phyllo on a work

A Jasmine Rice Cake with Wasabi and Smoked Salmon.

surface and brush lightly with a little of the butter-oil mixture. Top with the remaining 2 sheets of phyllo brushed with the butter-oil mixture.

2. Using a 2¼-inch round biscuit cutter, cut out 24 phyllo rounds. Press the rounds, buttered side up, into the muffin cups. Bake for about 4 minutes, or until golden and crisp; don't let the phyllo burn. Let the phyllo cups cool slightly and then carefully transfer to a rack to cool completely.

3. Melt the remaining 1 teaspoon of butter in a large skillet. Add the leeks and a large pinch of salt and pepper. Cook over moderate heat, stirring, until the leeks are tender but still slightly green, 8 to 10 minutes.

4. Just before serving, spoon the leeks into the phyllo cups. Top each of the cups with a piece of smoked salmon and a sprinkling of chives and serve immediately. —*Georges Perrier*
MAKE AHEAD The phyllo cups can be kept covered in the muffin tins overnight at room temperature.
ONE TARTLET Calories 25 kcal, Total Fat .1 gm, Saturated Fat .3 gm
WINE The nonvintage Diebolt-Vallois Blanc de Blancs, a 100 percent Chardonnay Champagne from a small

A Smoked Salmon and Leek Tartlet.

domaine located in Cramant, has the elegance and complexity to make a wonderful aperitif. Another excellent choice: the nonvintage Jacquesson Brut Perfection.

Heart-Shaped Caviar Canapés

MAKES 12 CANAPÉS

Red pepper gives caviar some valentine color in an easy-to-make canapé.

- 1 tablespoon unsalted butter, melted
- 6 slices white bread
- ½ red bell pepper
- 2 tablespoons crème fraîche
- 1½ ounces osetra caviar
- 12 chervil leaves

I. Preheat the oven to 350°. Lightly brush a baking sheet with some of the butter. Lightly brush 1 side of each of the bread slices with the remaining butter. Using a 2-inch heart-shaped cookie cutter, cut 2 hearts from each slice of bread and set them on the baking sheet, buttered side up. Toast the hearts for 10 minutes, or until pale golden and crisp. Let the hearts cool.

2. Flatten the red pepper on a cutting board. Cut out 12 hearts using a ½-inch heart-shaped aspic cutter.

3. Spoon ½ teaspoon of crème fraîche and ½ teaspoon of caviar onto each toast. Garnish with a pepper heart and a chervil leaf.   —Alice Harper

WINE Nonvintage Taittinger Cuvée Prestige Brut Champagne.

Phyllo Spring Rolls with Chicken and Chanterelles

MAKES 32 HORS D'OEUVRES

If you happen to have leftover cooked chicken breast in your refrigerator, you can use one cup of shredded meat to fill the spring rolls.

- 2 tablespoons extra-virgin olive oil
- 2 skinless, boneless chicken breast halves (½ pound total), pounded ¾ inch thick

Salt and freshly ground pepper

- 4 ounces fresh chanterelles, rinsed well and quartered
- 2 shallots, thinly sliced
- 3 tablespoons dry sherry or dry white wine
- 1 teaspoon finely chopped sage
- 1 teaspoon finely chopped thyme
- 2 ounces chilled Brie with the rind removed, cut into ½-inch cubes
- 8 phyllo sheets

About 4 tablespoons unsalted butter, melted

I. In a large skillet, heat 1 tablespoon of the oil just until smoking. Season the chicken on both sides with salt and pepper and cook over moderately high heat until browned, about 4 minutes. Turn

and sear until just cooked through, 2 to 3 minutes. Transfer to a work surface and cut across the grain into thin strips.

2. Heat the remaining 1 tablespoon of oil in the skillet. Add the mushrooms and cook over moderately high heat, stirring occasionally, until tender and browned around the edges, about 7 minutes. Add the shallots and cook, stirring, until tender, about 3 minutes. Add the sherry, sage and thyme and cook, scraping up any brown bits, until the liquid has evaporated. Season the mushrooms with salt and pepper and transfer to a bowl. Add the chicken and Brie and stir until the Brie has melted.

3. Lay a sheet of phyllo on a work surface with a long edge toward you.

Heart-Shaped Caviar Canapés

Brush the phyllo with some of the melted butter and top with a second phyllo sheet. Cut the sheets in half lengthwise. Spoon ¼ cup of the filling along the short edge of one phyllo rectangle. Shape the filling into a 6-inch log and roll up one complete turn. Fold in the sides and continue rolling to form a tight cylinder. Fill and roll the second phyllo half. Brush the rolls with some of the butter and transfer to a baking sheet. Repeat with the remaining phyllo and filling. Refrigerate the rolls until chilled.

4. Preheat the oven to 375°. Bake the phyllo rolls in the upper third of the oven for about 30 minutes, or until golden brown and heated through. Let cool and then transfer to a cutting board. Cut each roll in half and then in half again diagonally. Set the spring rolls upright on a tray and serve immediately.   —Theodora van den Beld
MAKE AHEAD The uncooked spring rolls can be refrigerated for up to 8 hours.

Shredded Chicken Tinga
MAKES ABOUT 2 DOZEN
HORS D'OEUVRES
This chicken tinga, or chicken hash, has been adapted from Zarela Martinez's *Food from My Heart,* published by Macmillan. Here the hash is rolled in flour tortillas and sliced so that it can be served as finger food. The hash can also be used as a dip with fried tortilla chips.

- 2 tablespoons vegetable oil
- 1 medium onion, thinly sliced
- 2 large garlic cloves, finely chopped
- 1 large ripe tomato—peeled, seeded and diced
- 2 canned chipotle chiles in adobo, finely chopped
- 1 teaspoon ground cumin
- ½ teaspoon freshly grated nutmeg

- 3 cups shredded cooked chicken (about ¾ pound)
- Salt and freshly ground pepper
- Six 8-inch flour tortillas
- Cilantro sprigs, for garnish

1. In a medium skillet, heat the oil. Add the onion and garlic and cook over moderately high heat, stirring, until slightly softened, about 3 minutes. Add the tomato, chipotles, cumin and nutmeg and cook, stirring, for 3 minutes. Add the chicken and cook over moderate heat, stirring occasionally, until most of the liquid has evaporated, about 10 minutes. Season with salt and pepper.

2. Heat a griddle or cast-iron skillet over moderate heat. Add the flour tortillas, 1 at a time, and cook until warmed through. Arrange the tortillas on a work surface and spread the filling on them in an even layer. Roll up the tortillas and cut each crosswise on the diagonal into 1½-inch pieces. Discard the ends and serve the neat pieces warm or at room temperature, garnished with cilantro sprigs.   —Zarela Martinez
WINE A 1995 Codice Rioja or a 1996 Farnese Montepulciano d'Abruzzo.

Lemongrass Chicken Satay
MAKES 16 SATAYS
Marinate chicken in a sweet lemongrass marinade before grilling for an easy-to-prepare hors d'oeuvre.

- 2 tablespoons minced fresh lemongrass (see Note)
- 2 tablespoons minced fresh ginger
- 2 tablespoons minced garlic
- 2 tablespoons honey
- ½ teaspoon Asian sesame oil
- ½ teaspoon Asian fish sauce, or to taste
- ½ teaspoon five-spice powder
- ¼ teaspoon salt
- ¼ teaspoon white pepper
- 8 skinless, boneless chicken thighs

- Vegetable oil, for brushing
- 4 lettuce leaves

1. In a medium bowl, combine the lemongrass, ginger, garlic, honey, sesame oil, fish sauce, five-spice powder, salt and white pepper. Gently pound the chicken thighs to an even thickness and then cut the thighs lengthwise into 1½-inch-wide strips. Add the chicken to the marinade and stir to coat. Cover and refrigerate for 1 hour. Meanwhile, soak 16 mini bamboo skewers in water.

2. Light a grill or preheat the broiler. Thread each chicken strip onto a skewer and lightly brush the chicken with vegetable oil. Grill for about 6 minutes, or until browned on both sides and just cooked through. Serve on a platter lined with the lettuce leaves.   —Jeem Han Lock
NOTE To prepare lemongrass, cut off the green stalks and discard any tough leaves before mincing the white inner bulb.
MAKE AHEAD The marinade and chicken strips can be prepared and refrigerated separately overnight.
WINE Serve a 1996 Gran Feudo Navarra Rosado, 1996 Sokol Blosser Müller-Thurgau or 1996 Ca'del Solo Big House Red.

Chunky Chicken Liver Pâté
8 SERVINGS
- 2 tablespoons olive oil
- 1 pound chicken livers, trimmed
- Salt and freshly ground pepper
- 3 tablespoons finely chopped shallots
- ½ cup port
- ¼ cup heavy cream
- 2 tablespoons finely chopped chives
- Baguette toasts, for serving

1. In a skillet, heat the oil until shimmering. Season the chicken livers with salt and pepper, add to the skillet and

cook over high heat, turning once, until crisp and browned but still slightly pink in the center, about 5 minutes. Using a slotted spoon, transfer the livers to a plate.

2. Add the shallots to the skillet and cook over high heat until softened, about 1 minute. Add the port and cook, scraping up any brown bits, until the mixture is reduced to a thick syrup, about 2 minutes. Add the cream and boil until thickened, about 2 minutes. Return the livers to the skillet and toss to coat with the cream. Transfer to a bowl and coarsely chop the livers with a fork. Add the chives and season with salt and pepper. Refrigerate the pâté until slightly chilled before serving on the toasts. —*Sascha Lyon*

MAKE AHEAD The chicken liver pâté can be refrigerated for up to 3 days.

Vietnamese Spring Rolls

MAKES 20 ROLLS

These fresh and fragrant rolls from Jeem Han Lock of Wild Ginger in Seattle are not fried. Shrimp, pork, rice vermicelli and herbs are wrapped in softened Asian rice papers and eaten at room temperature.

- 20 medium shrimp, shelled and deveined
- 6 ounces rice vermicelli

Twenty 8-inch round Asian rice papers
- 20 thin slices of Chinese roasted or barbecued pork
- 20 small basil sprigs, large stems discarded
- 20 small cilantro sprigs, large stems discarded
- 20 small mint sprigs, large stems discarded
- 5 lettuce leaves, thinly sliced

Hoisin Dipping Sauce (recipe follows)

1. In a medium saucepan of boiling salted water, cook the shrimp until bright pink and loosely curled, about 30 seconds; drain. Halve the shrimp

TOP TO BOTTOM: **Chunky Chicken Liver Paté (in glass bowl), Charcuterie with Horseradish Cream (p. 35) and Cinnamon-Spiced Duck with Sweet-Sour Shallots (p. 66).**

lengthwise, cover and refrigerate.

2. In another medium saucepan of boiling water, cook the rice vermicelli, stirring constantly, until al dente, about 1 minute. Drain and rinse with cold water until completely cooled. Let the vermicelli dry in the colander, tossing occasionally, for about 20 minutes.

3. Dip each rice paper in a bowl of cool water to wet it thoroughly. Set the paper on a work surface to soften; the paper will become opaque, pliable and slightly stretchy. Put 2 shrimp halves, cut side up, on the lower third of each

rice paper. Top with 1 slice of pork, 1 sprig of each herb, a little lettuce and a little of the rice vermicelli. Press to flatten the filling slightly. Pull the rice paper up and over the filling and roll up tightly, folding in the sides as you go. Serve with the Hoisin Dipping Sauce.

MAKE AHEAD The spring rolls can be covered with damp paper towels and plastic wrap and refrigerated for up to 3 hours.

WINE Try serving a nonvintage Moët & Chandon White Star or 1996 Pine Ridge Chenin Blanc.

Autumn Antipasto

HOISIN DIPPING SAUCE

MAKES ABOUT 1 CUP

- ½ cup hoisin sauce
- ½ cup Asian bean sauce
- ¼ cup water
- 1 to 2 tablespoons Asian chile-garlic sauce
- 2 tablespoons finely chopped peanuts

In a small bowl, stir together the hoisin sauce, bean sauce and water. Stir in the chile-garlic sauce. Sprinkle the peanuts over the top.—*Jeem Han Lock*

MAKE AHEAD The sauce can be refrigerated for up to 1 day. Bring to room temperature before serving.

Spiced Pork Tenderloin with Corn Salsa

MAKES ABOUT 2½ DOZEN
HORS D'OEUVRES

Combining coriander-coated pork with a juicy corn salsa and sweet plantain chips makes a satisfying hors d'oeuvre. Look for yellow plantains with some black spots—ripe, but not too ripe—to make the crisp chips.

- ½ teaspoon ground coriander
- Salt and freshly ground pepper
- 1 pork tenderloin (about ¾ pound)
- Vegetable oil, for frying
- 2 ripe plantains, peeled and sliced diagonally ⅛ inch thick
- 1½ tablespoons canola oil
- ¼ cup fresh or frozen corn kernels
- ¼ cup finely diced red onion
- ¼ cup finely diced tomato
- 2 tablespoons finely chopped cilantro
- 1 tablespoon fresh lime juice

1. In a small bowl, combine the coriander with 1 teaspoon each of salt and pepper. Rub the pork tenderloin all over with the spice mixture. Let the tenderloin stand at room temperature for 3 hours.

2. Meanwhile, heat ¾ inch of vegetable oil in a large deep skillet until shimmering. Add about 10 plantain slices and fry over moderately high heat, turning, until uniformly golden, 2 to 3 minutes. Using a slotted spoon, transfer the plantains to a wire rack to drain. Pry apart or unfold the chips as necessary; the plantains will crisp as they cool. Continue to fry the remaining plantains in batches.

3. Preheat the oven to 350°. Heat 1 tablespoon of the canola oil in a large ovenproof skillet. Add the pork and cook over high heat until brown and crusty all over, about 6 minutes. Transfer the skillet to the oven and roast the pork for about 10 minutes, or until an instant-read thermometer inserted in the thickest part registers 135°. Transfer the pork to a cutting board and let cool completely.

4. Heat the remaining ½ tablespoon of canola oil in a small skillet. Add the corn and cook over moderate heat until tender, about 2 minutes. Transfer to a bowl and let cool. Add the onion, tomato, cilantro and lime juice and season with salt and pepper.

5. Thinly slice the pork. Arrange a pork slice on each plantain chip, top with a teaspoon of the corn salsa and serve.   —*Theodora van den Beld*

MAKE AHEAD The recipe can be prepared through Step 3 up to 1 day ahead; store the chips in an airtight container and refrigerate the pork.

Autumn Antipasto

8 SERVINGS

This virtually instant hors d'oeuvre allows guests to assemble their own combinations of contrasting flavors.

- 1 cup roasted natural almonds (about 5 ounces)
- 1 pound large, moist dates, preferably Medjool, split in half and pitted

½ pound Parmigiano-Reggiano cheese, broken into ¾-inch chunks

½ pound thinly sliced prosciutto, halved

Mound the almonds on a large platter or put them in a bowl. Arrange the halved dates, Parmigiano-Reggiano chunks and prosciutto slices around the almonds and serve.

—*Nancy Verde Barr*

MAKE AHEAD The assembled antipasto platter can be covered with plastic wrap and kept at room temperature for up to 6 hours before serving.

Charcuterie with Horseradish Cream

8 SERVINGS

A variety of cured meats, pickles and olives makes a welcome hors d'oeuvre in no time at all.

1 cup sour cream or crème fraîche

3 tablespoons freshly grated horseradish or drained bottled horseradish

1 tablespoon finely chopped chives

½ teaspoon freshly ground pepper

Salt

2 pounds assorted sliced cured meats, such as prosciutto, coppa, spicy coppa, bresaola, rosette and spicy Hungarian salami

Cornichons, olives and assorted mustards, for serving

Grilled bread or croutons, for serving

1. Combine the sour cream, horseradish, chives and pepper in a small bowl. Season with salt to taste and refrigerate the sour cream mixture until chilled.

2. Arrange the meats on a large platter and serve with the horseradish cream, cornichons, olives, mustards and grilled bread. —*Sascha Lyon*

Prosciutto Spirals

MAKES 20 SLICES

3 very thin slices prosciutto

¼ cup mousse de foie gras (see Note)

2 medium apples, cut into thin wedges

1. Arrange the prosciutto slices, overlapping, to form a 7-by-5-inch rectangle. Spread the prosciutto with the mousse de foie gras.

2. Starting at one short end, roll the prosciutto up snugly. Wrap in plastic and refrigerate until very firm, about 1 hour, or overnight.

3. Cut the prosciutto log into ¼-inch-thick slices. Set each slice on a thin apple wedge. —*Marcia Kiesel*

NOTE Mousse de foie gras is available at supermarket delicatessen counters and by mail order from D'Artagnan, 800-327-8246.

Roast Beef Grissini with Remoulade

MAKES 2 DOZEN HORS D'OEUVRES

Roast beef goes well with the strong flavors of arugula and remoulade.

REMOULADE SAUCE

½ cup mayonnaise

1 hard-cooked egg, finely chopped

2 tablespoons minced gherkins

1 tablespoon plus 1 teaspoon Dijon mustard

1 tablespoon drained finely chopped capers

1 tablespoon finely chopped flat-leaf parsley

1 tablespoon finely chopped dill

2 teaspoons finely chopped chives

1 teaspoon minced garlic

Freshly ground pepper

GRISSINI

2 garlic cloves, thinly sliced

Roast Beef Grissini with Remoulade

2 tablespoons olive oil

½ pound thinly sliced rare roast beef, cut into twenty-four 6-by-1½-inch strips

Salt and freshly ground pepper

24 arugula leaves, stemmed

8 to 10 grissini (about ½ inch thick) or breadsticks, broken into 4-inch lengths

1. **MAKE THE REMOULADE:** In a bowl, combine all of the ingredients and refrigerate until chilled or for up to 1 day.

2. **PREPARE THE GRISSINI:** In a small saucepan, cook the garlic in the oil over moderate heat until golden. Using a slotted spoon, discard the garlic slices; let the garlic oil cool completely.

3. Spread the roast beef strips on a work surface and lightly brush them with the garlic oil; sprinkle with salt and pepper and cover each beef strip with an arugula leaf slightly larger than the strip. Roll 1 roast beef strip tightly around 1 end of each grissini. Arrange on a platter and serve with the remoulade sauce.

—*Mary Barber and Sara Corpening*

MAKE AHEAD The assembled grissini can be refrigerated for up to 1 hour.

Marinated Beef Wraps with Pepper Relish

MAKES ABOUT 4 DOZEN
HORS D'OEUVRES

¼ cup plus 1 tablespoon olive oil
¼ cup Worcestershire sauce
¼ cup red wine vinegar
1 pound flank steak
2 red bell peppers, cut into
 2-inch-long matchsticks
1 medium onion, thinly sliced
1 teaspoon finely chopped sage
1 teaspoon finely chopped
 rosemary
Salt and freshly ground black pepper
Six 8-inch flour tortillas
⅓ cup mayonnaise
12 green leaf lettuce leaves

1. In a sturdy resealable plastic bag, combine ¼ cup of the oil with the Worcestershire sauce and 2 tablespoons of the vinegar. Add the meat. Seal the bag and marinate the meat at room temperature for 2 hours.

2. Heat the remaining 1 tablespoon of oil in a large skillet. Add the red peppers and onion. Cook over moderate heat, stirring, until tender and browned, about 10 minutes. Add the remaining 2 tablespoons of vinegar along with the sage and rosemary and cook until the vinegar has evaporated, about 2 minutes. Season the bell pepper mixture with salt and black pepper.

3. Preheat the broiler and position a rack 8 inches from the heat. Remove the flank steak from the marinade. Season with salt and black pepper and broil for about 4 minutes per side for medium rare. Transfer the steak to a cutting board, cover loosely with aluminum foil and let stand for 5 minutes. Thinly slice the steak against the grain.

4. Spread a tortilla with a thin layer of the mayonnaise and top with 8 to 10 slices of steak in a single layer. Season with salt and black pepper and then add 2 lettuce leaves and 2 tablespoons of the pepper relish. Roll up the steak in the tortilla and seal the roll with a little mayonnaise if necessary. Cut off the ends to make a neat roll and cover with plastic wrap. Repeat with the remaining ingredients. Slice the rolls ¾ inch thick and serve.

—*Theodora van den Beld*

MAKE AHEAD The filled rolls can be refrigerated for up to 3 hours. Slice them just before serving.

Curried Lamb "Cigars"

MAKES 3 DOZEN
HORS D'OEUVRES

The curried goat at Gloria's Roti Shop in Brooklyn, New York, inspired this recipe. Caribbean roti is a kind of burrito, and nobody's surpasses Gloria's.

2 tablespoons canola oil
1 pound ground lamb
1 small onion, finely chopped
2 garlic cloves, minced
3 tablespoons curry powder
1 cup unsweetened coconut milk
1 cup canned low-sodium chicken broth

Lamb Skewers with Grainy Mustard Dipping Sauce

party tactics

1. **Count eight hors d'oeuvres per person** per hour when you're not serving a meal.
2. **Balance the menu:** offer hot kebabs alongside room-temperature dips, rich cheese straws with low-fat poached shrimp, spicy quesadillas beside delicate crab salad.
3. **Provide at least one vegetarian offering** unless you're sure your crowd is carnivorous.
4. **Consider your kitchen equipment.** If you have only a standard range, don't limit yourself to stovetop dishes—serve a mix of stovetop, baked, raw, room-temperature and cold foods.
5. **Choose a few make-ahead dishes** so there's less to do on the day of the party.
6. **Stay away from dips** if you're worried about stains on your carpet.
7. **Decorate platters with whole spices** or colorful dried bean compositions. But don't be surprised when some guests think the garnishes are edible. People have even been known to eat decorative pebbles.

1 small sweet potato, peeled and cut into ½-inch dice
2 small tomatoes, diced
2 whole star anise pods
1 bay leaf
1 teaspoon habanero sauce, plus more for serving
Salt and freshly ground pepper
Sugar
⅓ cup crumbled feta cheese
36 triangular sheets of yufka (see Note and "Phyllo and Its Relatives," p. 435)
Vegetable oil, for frying

1. In a large skillet, heat the canola oil. Add the lamb and cook over high heat,

stirring occasionally, until no trace of pink remains, about 7 minutes. Using a slotted spoon, transfer the meat to a plate. Add the onion and garlic to the skillet and cook, stirring, until softened but not browned, 2 to 3 minutes.

2. Return the meat to the skillet and add the curry powder. Cook, stirring, until fragrant, about 2 minutes. Add the coconut milk and chicken broth and bring to a boil. Add the sweet potato, tomatoes, star anise, bay leaf, the 1 teaspoon of habanero sauce and a generous pinch each of salt, pepper and sugar. Simmer over moderately low heat until the sweet potato is tender and the liquid is absorbed, about 20 minutes. Transfer the filling to a bowl and let cool. Discard the star anise and bay leaf. Stir in the feta.

3. Lightly brush both sides of 1 yufka triangle with water. Set it on a work surface with the pointed end away from you. Keep the remaining pastry covered with plastic wrap. Spread 1 tablespoon of the filling along the bottom edge of the triangle. Roll the pastry up from the bottom, folding in the sides as you go. Transfer to a platter, seam side down. Repeat with the remaining yufka and filling.

4. Heat 2 inches of vegetable oil in a large deep skillet. Fry the cigars in batches, 6 at a time, turning, until golden and crisp, about 3 minutes. Drain on a rack set over a baking sheet. Serve immediately with habanero sauce.   —*Grace Parisi*

NOTE Yufka is available at Middle Eastern grocery stores and by mail from Adriana's Caravan, 800-316-0820. Asian spring roll wrappers (not egg roll wrappers) are the best substitute.

MAKE AHEAD The uncooked cigars can be frozen in an airtight container between layers of wax paper for several weeks. Don't defrost them before frying.

Tandoori Lamb Kebabs

MAKES 2 DOZEN KEBABS

Neela Paniz of Los Angeles's Bombay Cafe adds green papaya to the marinade, which makes the lamb especially tender.

½ cup chopped green papaya or green mango
8 garlic cloves, chopped
One 2-inch piece of fresh ginger, peeled and chopped
2 tablespoons plain yogurt
1 tablespoon tomato paste
1 tablespoon ground coriander
½ tablespoon ground cumin
1 teaspoon salt
½ teaspoon garam masala
1 pound boneless leg of lamb, trimmed and cut into ¾-inch cubes
1 tablespoon vegetable oil

1. In a mini-processor, puree the papaya with the garlic and ginger. Add the yogurt, tomato paste, coriander, cumin, salt and garam masala and process to combine.

2. In a medium bowl, coat the lamb cubes with the oil. Add the marinade and turn the meat to coat. Cover and refrigerate the meat for at least 3 hours or up to 1 day. Meanwhile, soak 24 mini bamboo skewers in water for 1 hour.

3. Light a grill or preheat the broiler. Thread 2 lamb cubes on each skewer. Grill or broil the skewers for about 2 minutes per side for medium rare. Serve hot.   —*Neela Paniz*

WINE A 1995 Rosenblum Contra Costa Zinfandel or 1996 Rosemount Shiraz will go well with the kebabs.

Lamb Skewers with Grainy Mustard Dipping Sauce

MAKES 30 HORS D'OEUVRES

Here the lamb is marinated and sautéed, then served warm with a piquant sauce.

¼ cup vegetable oil
¼ cup finely chopped onion
2 tablespoons red wine
2 tablespoons rosemary leaves
2 garlic cloves, smashed
1 tablespoon Dijon mustard
¾ pound boneless trimmed lamb loin, halved lengthwise
¼ cup whole-grain mustard
3 tablespoons crème fraîche or heavy cream
1½ teaspoons honey
Cayenne pepper
Freshly ground black pepper
1 tablespoon extra-virgin olive oil
Salt

1. In a blender or mini-processor, combine the vegetable oil, onion, wine, rosemary, garlic and Dijon mustard and blend until smooth. Transfer the marinade to a resealable plastic bag, add the loin of lamb and refrigerate overnight.

2. In a small bowl, combine the whole-grain mustard, crème fraîche, honey and a pinch each of cayenne and black pepper; whisk until smooth.

3. Remove the lamb from the bag and scrape off the marinade. Heat the olive oil in a skillet. Season the lamb with salt and black pepper and add it to the skillet. Cook the lamb over high heat until browned, about 3 minutes on each side for medium rare. Transfer the lamb to a cutting board, cover it with aluminum foil and let stand for 10 minutes.

4. Thinly slice the lamb, fold the pieces and spear them on wooden picks. Transfer the lamb skewers to a platter and serve immediately with the mustard dipping sauce.

—*Mary Barber and Sara Corpening*

CHAPTER 2 first courses

Broiled Clams (p. 53)

Grilled Asparagus with Mozzarella

Grilled Asparagus with Mozzarella

8 SERVINGS

2 tablespoons fresh lemon juice

1 medium shallot, finely chopped

1 tablespoon coarsely chopped chervil or flat-leaf parsley

½ teaspoon kosher salt

¼ teaspoon coarsely cracked black pepper

¼ cup plus 1 tablespoon extra-virgin olive oil

32 large asparagus stalks (about 2 pounds), peeled

½ pound lightly salted fresh mozzarella, cut into eight ½-inch-thick slices

Chive blossoms, for garnish

1. In a medium bowl, whisk together the lemon juice, shallot, chervil, kosher salt and black pepper. Gradually whisk in 3 tablespoons of the oil.

2. In a large skillet of boiling water, blanch the asparagus for 1 minute. Using tongs, transfer the asparagus stalks to a plate and toss them with the remaining 2 tablespoons of oil.

3. Heat a grill pan over moderately high heat. Working in batches, grill the asparagus stalks, turning, until just tender and lightly browned, about 4 minutes. Divide the asparagus among 8 large plates and top each serving with a slice of mozzarella. Drizzle with the chervil vinaigrette, sprinkle with chive blossoms and serve.

—*Clifford Harrison and Anne Quatrano*

MAKE AHEAD The recipe can be prepared through Step 2 up to 4 hours ahead. Let the dressing and asparagus stand separately at room temperature.

Leeks with Truffle Vinaigrette

6 SERVINGS

Leeks tend to be quite gritty and sandy. To clean them, split the green portions lengthwise and soak them in several changes of cold water, rinsing the leeks thoroughly between soakings. To clean the truffle, scrape off any encrusted dirt and then use a vegetable brush. Wipe any remaining dirt from the truffle with a damp paper towel.

18 small leeks, white and tender green—trimmed, split, soaked and rinsed

2 tablespoons sherry vinegar

2 tablespoons truffle juice (see Note)

1 tablespoon balsamic vinegar

Sugar

Salt and freshly ground white pepper

¼ cup vegetable oil

¼ cup extra-virgin olive oil

One 2- to 3-ounce fresh black truffle (see Note)

1. In a steamer basket, steam the leeks over boiling water until tender, about 10 minutes; pat dry. Arrange the leeks on salad plates or a platter.

2. In a medium bowl, combine the sherry vinegar with the truffle juice, balsamic vinegar, a pinch of sugar and a generous pinch each of salt and white pepper. Gradually whisk in the vegetable and extra-virgin olive oils. Pour the vinaigrette over the leeks. Thinly shave the truffle over all and serve the leeks immediately.   —*Betsy Bernardaud*

NOTE Fresh truffles and truffle juice are available at specialty food shops.

MAKE AHEAD The leeks can be steamed several hours ahead and kept covered at room temperature.

Yukon Potato and Bacon Tart

4 SERVINGS ✺

¼ cup olive oil

2 small onions, thinly sliced

4 thick bacon slices

Flaky Tart Pastry (recipe follows)

Salt and freshly ground pepper

⅓ cup (packed) grated Fontina cheese

3 Yukon Gold or red potatoes, thinly sliced

½ teaspoon minced rosemary

1 large egg yolk mixed with ½ teaspoon water

1. Preheat the oven to 450°. In a large skillet, heat 2 tablespoons of the oil. Add the onions and cook over moderately high heat, stirring, until softened and lightly browned, about 5 minutes. Transfer the onions to paper towels and blot dry.

2. Cook the bacon in the skillet over moderate heat until crisp, about 8 minutes. Drain the bacon on paper towels and then crumble into small pieces.

3. On a lightly floured sheet of parchment paper, roll out the pastry to a 13-inch round. Transfer the pastry and parchment paper to a baking sheet. Spread the onions on the pastry, leaving a 1-inch border. Season with salt and pepper; sprinkle with the cheese and bacon. Arrange the potato slices in a single layer on top and season with salt and pepper. Garnish with the rosemary and drizzle on the remaining 2 tablespoons of oil. Fold the edge of the pastry over onto the topping and brush the rim with the egg wash.

4. Bake the tart for about 20 minutes, or until the pastry is golden. Let cool slightly before serving

FLAKY TART PASTRY

MAKES ONE 13-INCH TART SHELL

This buttery pastry, which is also used in the recipes for Asparagus and Goat Cheese Tart (p. 42), Smoked Salmon and Onion Tart (p. 60) and Smoked Chicken and Cheese Tart with Olives (p. 64), is easily doubled. Shape the dough into two disks and freeze one for future use.

1 cup all-purpose flour

¼ teaspoon sugar

Large pinch of salt

6 tablespoons cold unsalted butter, cut into bits

About 2½ tablespoons ice water

In a food processor, combine the flour, sugar and salt. Add the bits of butter and pulse until the mixture resembles coarse meal. Add 2½ tablespoons of the water and pulse just until the pastry dough comes together; add more water if necessary. On a lightly floured surface, shape the pastry dough into a disk, wrap the disks in plastic and refrigerate them until chilled, about 30 minutes. —*Peggy Smith*

MAKE AHEAD The pastry can be refrigerated for up to 2 days or frozen for up to 1 month.

Eggs with Spicy Onion Sauce
8 SERVINGS

This dish of hard-cooked eggs is called egg roast in Kerala, India, where the term *roast* describes a process in which food, typically some type of fowl, is cooked, whole or in large pieces, in a covered pan. If it's the main course, as it often is, it serves four.

8 extra-large eggs
Water
2 tablespoons ground coriander
1 teaspoon fennel seeds, ground in a spice mill or mortar
½ teaspoon ground cumin
¼ teaspoon turmeric
⅛ teaspoon cayenne pepper
⅛ teaspoon freshly ground black pepper
⅛ teaspoon cinnamon
⅛ teaspoon ground cloves
⅛ teaspoon ground cardamom
3 tablespoons vegetable oil
½ teaspoon mustard seeds
10 curry leaves, or 2 bay leaves
1 dried red chile
2 medium onions, thinly sliced
1 teaspoon salt
1 cup chopped tomatoes
¼ cup canned unsweetened coconut milk

1. In a large saucepan, cover the eggs with water and bring to a boil. Simmer for 9 minutes and then drain and cool in a bowl of cold water. Peel the eggs.

2. In a small bowl, combine the coriander, fennel, cumin, turmeric, cayenne, black pepper, cinnamon, cloves and cardamom with ⅓ cup of water to make a paste.

3. In a large nonstick skillet, warm the oil over moderately high heat and add the mustard seeds. When the seeds begin to pop, add the curry leaves and dried red chile and cover. After most of the mustard seeds have popped, uncover, add the onions and cook, stirring occasionally, until softened and lightly browned, about 6 minutes. Add the spice paste and salt and cook over moderate heat for 5 minutes, adding a few tablespoons of water if the pan is dry. Add the tomatoes and ¾ cup of water and simmer over low heat, stirring occasionally, until the tomatoes are soft and the gravy is thick. Add the coconut milk and the eggs, spooning the sauce over the eggs. Bring to a simmer, cover and cook over low heat until the eggs are heated through. Serve at once. —*Maya Kaimal*

SERVE WITH Pal Appam (p. 290).

WINE The mild heat that the mustard and chiles give to this egg dish needs a simple, not-quite-dry white for contrast. Chenin Blanc–based wines, such as the 1996 Hogue Cellars from Washington State or the 1995 Gaston Huet Le Mont Sec Vouvray from France, would work particularly well here.

Asparagus and Goat Cheese Tart
4 SERVINGS ✺

Flaky Tart Pastry (p. 41)
½ pound soft goat cheese
10 pencil-thin asparagus stalks, cut into 1-inch pieces
2 teaspoons olive oil
1 small roasted red pepper, cut into thin strips
Salt and freshly ground black pepper
1 large egg yolk mixed with ½ teaspoon water
3 prosciutto slices, torn into pieces

1. Preheat the oven to 450°. On a lightly floured sheet of parchment paper, roll out the pastry to a 13-inch round. Transfer the pastry and parchment to a baking sheet.

2. Spread the goat cheese on the pastry, leaving a 1-inch border. Toss the asparagus with the oil and arrange on the tart with the red pepper strips; season with salt and black pepper. Fold the edge of the pastry over onto the topping and brush the rim with the egg wash. Bake for about 20 minutes, or until the pastry is golden. Let the tart cool slightly, scatter the prosciutto on top and serve. —*Peggy Smith*

Goat Cheese Soufflé with Thyme
2 SERVINGS

2 tablespoons freshly grated Parmesan cheese
2 tablespoons unsalted butter
¼ cup all-purpose flour
½ cup milk
2 tablespoons dry white wine
½ teaspoon dry mustard
½ teaspoon anchovy paste
3½ ounces goat cheese, crumbled
1½ teaspoons thyme leaves
Salt and freshly ground pepper
2 large eggs, separated, plus 3 large egg whites
¼ cup grated sharp white Cheddar
Mixed Greens with Papaya (p. 78)

1. Preheat the oven to 375°. Butter a 1-quart soufflé dish. Add the Parmesan and turn the dish to coat it with the cheese.

2. In a medium saucepan, melt the butter over low heat. Add the flour and cook, whisking, until blended. Whisk in

Yukon Potato and Bacon Tart

Goat Cheese Soufflé with Thyme, with Mixed Greens with Papaya (p. 78).

the milk, wine, mustard and anchovy paste and cook, whisking, until the sauce is smooth and thick, about 8 minutes. Remove from the heat and stir in the goat cheese and 1 teaspoon of the thyme. Season with salt and pepper and stir in the egg yolks. Scrape the soufflé mixture into a large bowl; press a piece of plastic wrap directly on the surface.

3. In a large stainless steel bowl, beat the egg whites with a pinch of salt until soft peaks form. Using a rubber spatula, fold one-third of the beaten whites into the soufflé mixture; fold in the remaining whites until just a few streaks remain.

4. Gently scrape the soufflé mixture into the prepared dish. Sprinkle the top with the Cheddar, the remaining ½ teaspoon of thyme and some pepper. Bake the soufflé in the middle of the oven for about 25 minutes, or until it is nicely risen and browned on top. Serve the soufflé at once with Mixed Greens with Papaya. —*Janie Master*

NOTE You can also prepare this soufflé in two 2-cup ramekins. Be sure to reduce the cooking time slightly.

MAKE AHEAD The soufflé can be prepared through Step 2 and refrigerated overnight. Bring the mixture to room temperature before proceeding.

WINE A 1996 Bonny Doon Vin Gris de Cigare—the wine's lovely, dry fruitiness will stand up to the cheese.

Roquefort-Walnut Terrine with Apple Salad

8 SERVINGS

2 **cups walnuts (about 7 ounces)**
1 **pound Roquefort cheese, at room temperature**
1 **cup crème fraîche or sour cream**
4 **medium Granny Smith apples**
2 **tablespoons plus 2 teaspoons fresh lemon juice**

Roquefort-Walnut Terrine with Apple Salad

¼ **cup pure olive oil**
2 **tablespoons Dijon mustard**
1 **tablespoon plus 1 teaspoon balsamic vinegar**
Salt and freshly ground pepper
Crusty bread, for serving

1. Preheat the oven to 350°. Spread the walnuts on a baking sheet. Toast for about 10 minutes, or until the nuts are lightly browned and fragrant. Let cool.

2. Line a 7-by-5-inch loaf pan with plastic wrap, leaving 3 inches of overhang all around. In a large bowl, break up the Roquefort with a fork until slightly chunky. Add the toasted walnuts and the crème fraîche and mix thoroughly. Scrape the Roquefort mixture into the loaf pan, smooth the top and cover with

the overhanging plastic wrap. Refrigerate the terrine until very firm, at least 6 hours or overnight.

3. Peel, core and thinly slice the apples. In a medium glass or stainless-steel bowl, toss the apples with 2 tablespoons of the lemon juice. In a small glass or stainless-steel bowl, combine the remaining 2 teaspoons of lemon juice with the oil, mustard and balsamic vinegar. Season with salt and pepper. Pour the vinaigrette over the apples and toss well.

4. Unmold the Roquefort terrine and discard the plastic wrap. Run a thin knife under hot water, wipe it off and then cut the terrine into ¾-inch-thick slices, rinsing and drying the knife

Grilled Shrimp with Fennel and Lemon

after each cut. Arrange the slices on small plates and serve with the apple salad and bread.   —*Marcia Kiesel*

WINE The dominating saltiness of the Roquefort and the unctuousness of the walnuts make an ideal contrast for the 1989 Château Lafaurie-Peyraguey Sauternes or the 1988 Château Sigalas Rabaud Sauternes.

Grilled Shrimp with Fennel and Lemon

4 SERVINGS

Watermelon adds unexpected sweetness to the vibrant salsa that accompanies the grilled shrimp. To make a more substantial first course, double the recipe.

- 8 large shrimp, shelled and deveined
- 3 tablespoons extra-virgin olive oil
- 1 large fennel bulb—halved lengthwise, cored and thinly sliced crosswise
- 1 tablespoon finely chopped unsalted pistachios
- 1 tablespoon fresh lemon juice
- 1 teaspoon finely grated lemon zest
- ½ teaspoon fennel seeds

Salt and freshly ground pepper
Pinch of sugar

- 2 teaspoons finely chopped shallot
- 2 tablespoons finely chopped peeled tomato
- 2 tablespoons finely chopped watermelon
- ½ tablespoon finely chopped basil, preferably purple

1. Soak eight 8-inch bamboo skewers in warm water for 30 minutes; drain. Insert 2 bamboo skewers through 2 shrimp so the skewers form an X; repeat with the remaining shrimp. Rub the skewered shrimp with 1 teaspoon of the oil.

2. In a medium bowl, combine the sliced fennel, pistachios, lemon juice, lemon zest and 2½ tablespoons of the oil. In a small dry skillet, toast the fennel seeds over moderately high heat, stirring, until fragrant, about 3 minutes. Add the toasted fennel seeds to the fennel salad. Season with salt, pepper and the sugar.

3. Heat the remaining ½ teaspoon of oil in the small skillet. Add the shallot and cook over moderately high heat, stirring, until softened. Remove from the heat and stir in the tomato and watermelon. Transfer to a small glass or stainless-steel bowl and stir in the chopped basil.

4. Heat a grill pan. Season the shrimp with salt and pepper. Grill the shrimp over high heat until they are opaque throughout, about 2 minutes per side. Spoon the fennel salad onto plates. Set the shrimp skewers on the fennel and top with a spoonful of the salsa. Serve at once.   —*Gray Kunz*

Spiced Shrimp and Calamari Sauté

8 SERVINGS

This lemony, garlicky sauté is a lovely alternative to standard deep-fried shellfish. For a more substantial first course, serve it with whole pan-seared shrimp.

- 4 garlic cloves, minced
- 1½ tablespoons kosher salt
- ½ teaspoon ground coriander
- ½ teaspoon ground cardamom

¼ teaspoon paprika

¾ pound medium shrimp—
shelled, deveined and cut into
½-inch dice

¾ pound cleaned small squid,
bodies cut into ¼-inch rings,
tentacles halved

¼ cup plus 1 tablespoon olive
oil

1 medium onion, finely chopped

1 serrano or jalapeño chile,
seeded and finely chopped

3 tablespoons fresh lemon juice

2 tablespoons coarsely chopped
mint

1 teaspoon finely grated lemon
zest

1. In a small bowl, combine the garlic, kosher salt, coriander, cardamom and paprika. Put the shrimp and squid in separate bowls; sprinkle them with the seasoning mixture. Add 1 tablespoon of the oil to each bowl and toss to coat.

2. Heat the remaining 3 tablespoons oil in a large heavy skillet. Add the onion and chile; cook over moderate heat, stirring, until golden brown, 8 to 10 minutes. Using a slotted spoon, transfer the onion mixture to a large bowl. Add the lemon juice, mint and lemon zest.

3. Reheat the oil in the skillet. Add the shrimp and stir-fry over high heat until opaque, 2 to 3 minutes. Using a slotted spoon, transfer the shrimp to the onion mixture. Add the squid to the hot oil. Stir-fry until opaque, 2 to 3 minutes; add to the large bowl and toss well. Serve warm or at room temperature.

—*Christer Larsson*

Grilled Shrimp with Fresh Papaya Blatjang

8 SERVINGS

Blatjang (Malay for chutney) is usually cooked, but a few versions are served raw, like salsa. This one makes a wonderfully light and refreshing dipping sauce for seafood and poultry.

BLATJANG

2 ripe medium papayas, halved
and seeded

2 scallions, white only, minced

1 tablespoon minced fresh ginger

1 garlic clove, minced

2 teaspoons fresh lemon juice

½ teaspoon ground cumin

¼ teaspoon salt

¼ teaspoon freshly ground white
pepper

2 tablespoons minced cilantro

¼ teaspoon crushed red pepper

SHRIMP

1½ pounds medium shrimp, shelled
and deveined

2 tablespoons fresh lemon juice

2 tablespoons olive oil

1 scallion, chopped

1 garlic clove, crushed

One ½-inch piece of fresh ginger,
peeled and chopped

½ teaspoon ground coriander

1 tablespoon chopped cilantro

1. MAKE THE BLATJANG: Scoop the flesh from the papaya into a food processor. Add the scallions, ginger, garlic, lemon juice, cumin, salt and white pepper to the food processor and pulse until chunky. Transfer the blatjang to a bowl, cover and refrigerate for at least 1 hour. Stir the cilantro and crushed red pepper into the blatjang just before serving.

2. PREPARE THE SHRIMP: Light the grill or preheat the broiler. Soak eight 8-inch bamboo skewers in water. Double skewer the shrimp on 4 pairs of parallel skewers. In a mini-processor, combine the lemon juice, oil, scallion, garlic, ginger and coriander and process to a fine paste. Spread the paste on both sides of the skewered shrimp. Grill or broil the shrimp skewers for 3 to 4 minutes, or until the shrimp are pink on both sides. Sprinkle the grilled shrimp with the cilantro and then serve with the blatjang. —*Jenna Holst*

Altherr's Shrimp with Pineapple on Naan

4 SERVINGS ♛

Oliver Altherr, of Hoku's restaurant in Honolulu, recommends that when you want to serve something hot from the oven and baking time is short (as it is for this naan), you have all the other components of the dish assembled in advance.

1½ cups all-purpose flour

1½ teaspoons baking powder

½ teaspoon sugar

½ teaspoon salt

1 large egg yolk

3 tablespoons water

2 tablespoons milk

2 tablespoons plain yogurt

1 tablespoon vegetable oil

¼ cup plus 1 tablespoon crème
fraîche

1½ tablespoons plus 1 teaspoon
fresh lime juice

1½ tablespoons coarsely chopped
dill

1 tablespoon prepared white
horseradish

1 tablespoon mayonnaise

¾ cup finely chopped fresh
pineapple

1 tablespoon extra-virgin
olive oil

Salt and freshly ground pepper

4 cups baby greens (about
2 ounces)

12 cooked medium shrimp, or
16 very thin slices smoked
salmon

1. In a medium bowl, toss the flour with the baking powder, sugar and salt. In a small bowl, whisk together the egg yolk, water, milk, yogurt and vegetable oil. Stir the liquid into the flour mixture with a wooden spoon. Transfer the dough to a lightly floured work surface and knead briefly until smooth. Divide the dough into 4 pieces and shape each piece into an

Altherr's Shrimp with Pineapple on Naan

oval disk. Wrap each dough disk in plastic wrap; refrigerate until chilled, about 4 hours or overnight.

2. In a small bowl, stir together 1 tablespoon of the crème fraîche, 1 tablespoon of the lime juice, 1 tablespoon of the chopped dill and the horseradish and mayonnaise. Fold in the pineapple. Refrigerate the pineapple mixture until chilled, about 2 hours.

3. Set a large pizza stone in the bottom third of the oven. Preheat the oven to 500° for at least 40 minutes. In a small bowl, combine the remaining ¼ cup of crème fraîche with the ½ tablespoon of the lime juice and the remaining ½ tablespoon of chopped dill.

4. On a lightly floured work surface, roll out each piece of dough to a 9-by-7-inch oval. Set the ovals on the pizza stone and bake for about 3½ minutes, or just until golden and puffed.

5. Meanwhile, in a bowl, whisk the olive oil with the remaining 1 teaspoon of lime juice; season with salt and pepper. Add the greens and toss to coat.

6. Set a hot naan on each of 4 plates and top with the greens. Cover with the pineapple, half of the dill cream and the shrimp. Spoon the remaining dill cream on top; serve at once. —*Oliver Altherr*

WINE An herbaceous Sauvignon Blanc makes a refreshing foil for the fruity-sweet shrimp on naan.

revolutionary fare

"Johny or hoe cake, hot from the fire, is better than a Yorkshire muffin," Benjamin Franklin wrote in a 1776 letter to the *London Gazetteer* lauding the virtues of American corn bread. There were other fine Yankee dishes as well:

Philadelphia pepper pot According to legend, this peppercorn-flavored tripe soup was created for George Washington at Valley Forge during the winter of 1777.

Shad A member of the herring family, the fish was ubiquitous in Revolutionary times. It was even included in the rations that Washington's troops received.

Spoon bread This custardy dish made with cornmeal is eaten with a spoon, but it may actually owe its name to the Native American word for porridge, *suppawn*.

Succotash The Colonial stew of corn and lima beans was a version of the Narrganset Indians' *misickquatash*.

Curried Lobster Salad on Johnnycakes

10 SERVINGS

- 1 tablespoon vegetable oil
- 1 celery rib, coarsely chopped
- ½ small onion, coarsely chopped
- 1½ tablespoons Madras curry powder
- 1 teaspoon thyme leaves
- ½ teaspoon crushed red pepper
- 2 cups dry white wine

Three 1½-pound live lobsters
- ¾ cup crème fraîche

Fresh lemon juice
- 2 tablespoons chopped chives

Johnnycakes (recipe follows)

Curried Lobster Salad on Johnnycakes

49

Poached Scallops with Tarragon Vinaigrette

how low can you go?

Here are two vinaigrette tips to help cut back on fat.

Shake up the traditional ratio of three or four parts oil to one part vinegar by replacing half the oil with reduced chicken or vegetable stock.

Use warm vinaigrettes, thickened with arrowroot or cornstarch, as elegant alternatives to cream or butter sauces.

—Ferdinand Metz

JOHNNYCAKES

MAKES TWENTY 2½-INCH CAKES

- 1 cup all-purpose flour
- 1 cup yellow cornmeal
- 1½ tablespoons baking powder
- 1½ teaspoons salt
- 2 large eggs
- 1½ cups buttermilk
- 3 tablespoons unsalted butter, melted

Vegetable oil

1. In a large bowl, sift together the flour, cornmeal, baking powder and salt. In a small bowl, whisk the eggs with the buttermilk. Stir the buttermilk mixture into the dry ingredients and then fold in the melted butter. Refrigerate for at least 20 minutes and up to several hours. The batter should have the consistency of heavy cream; thin with water if necessary.

2. Heat a griddle; grease lightly with the oil. For each cake, pour 2 tablespoons of batter onto the griddle and cook over moderate heat until golden brown on the bottom, about 30 seconds. Flip and cook until browned on the second side, about 30 seconds. —*Brendan Walsh*

MAKE AHEAD The Johnnycakes can be set on a baking sheet, brushed with melted butter and refrigerated, covered, overnight. Rewarm in a hot oven.

1. In a stockpot, heat the vegetable oil. Add the celery, onion, curry powder, thyme and crushed red pepper and cook over moderate heat, stirring, until the vegetables soften, about 6 minutes. Add the wine and bring to a boil over high heat. Plunge the lobsters into the pot head first, cover tightly and cook until they turn bright red, 15 to 20 minutes. Transfer the lobsters to a bowl to cool; reserve the cooking liquid.

2. Working over a large bowl to catch the juices, twist the lobster tails off the bodies. Using poultry shears, split the tail shells lengthwise and carefully remove the meat; pull out and discard the black intestinal veins. Crack the claws and knuckles and remove the meat. Cut the tails into ½-inch medallions and the remaining meat into small pieces.

3. Strain the lobster cooking liquid and any lobster juices into a small saucepan, pressing hard on the solids. Boil the liquid gently until it is reduced to ⅓ cup, about 10 minutes. Remove the pan from the heat and stir in the crème fraîche and some lemon juice. Fold in the lobster meat and 1 tablespoon of the chives. Set 2 of the Johnnycakes on each plate and then spoon the warm lobster salad on top. Garnish the lobster salad with the remaining chives and serve.

MAKE AHEAD The lobster salad can be refrigerated overnight. Rewarm the salad gently before serving.

WINE The 1991 Taittinger Comtes de Champagne Rosé Brut would be an excellent choice to accompany the lobster salad.

Poached Scallops with Tarragon Vinaigrette

4 SERVINGS ❋ ⚜

- 1 cup dry white wine
- 1 cup fish stock, or ½ cup bottled clam juice mixed with ½ cup water
- 1 small shallot, minced
- 1 pound sea scallops, muscles discarded
- ½ teaspoon arrowroot dissolved in 1 teaspoon cold water
- 3 tablespoons extra-virgin olive oil
- 2 tablespoons tarragon vinegar or white wine vinegar
- Salt and freshly ground pepper
- 1 pound green beans
- 1 medium tomato—peeled, seeded and finely chopped
- 2 teaspoons finely chopped tarragon

1. In a skillet, bring the wine, fish stock and shallot to a boil. Add the scallops in a single layer and simmer over moderate heat, turning once, until cooked through, about 5 minutes. Transfer the scallops to a plate and keep warm.

2. Bring ½ cup of the poaching liquid to a boil in a saucepan. Whisk in the dissolved arrowroot. Cook over moderate heat until slightly thickened. Remove from the heat. Whisk in the oil and vinegar; season with salt and pepper.

3. In a large pot of boiling salted water, cook the green beans just until tender, about 6 minutes. Drain.

4. Spread the green beans on 4 plates. Thickly slice the scallops and set them on the green beans. Drizzle with the vinaigrette, garnish with the tomato and tarragon and serve.

—Ferdinand Metz

ONE SERVING Calories 241 kcal, Total Fat 11.6 gm, Saturated Fat 1.6 gm

WINE A California Sauvignon Blanc will balance the bite of the vinaigrette. Look for the 1996 Groth or the 1996 Dry Creek.

Seared Scallops in Black Bean—Orange Vinaigrette

4 SERVINGS

- ¼ cup extra-virgin olive oil
- 2 tablespoons mirin (sweet rice wine)
- 1 tablespoon fermented black beans, rinsed and coarsely chopped
- 1 tablespoon light soy sauce
- 1 shallot, minced
- 1 garlic clove, minced
- 2 teaspoons minced fresh ginger
- 2 teaspoons rice vinegar
- 1 teaspoon finely grated orange zest
- Salt and freshly ground white pepper
- 16 sea scallops
- One 8-inch-square sheet of nori (pressed seaweed), cut with scissors into 4-by-½-inch strips (optional)
- 2 tablespoons cilantro leaves

1. In a small glass or stainless-steel bowl, whisk 3 tablespoons of the oil with the mirin, black beans, soy sauce, shallot, garlic, ginger, rice vinegar and orange zest. Season the vinaigrette with salt and white pepper.

2. In a large nonstick skillet, heat ½ tablespoon of the oil until smoking. Season the scallops with salt and white pepper. Add 8 scallops to the skillet; cook over high heat until well browned

Seared Scallops in Black Bean—Orange Vinaigrette

Broiled Clams

but still slightly translucent in the center, about 2 minutes per side. Transfer to a plate and keep warm. Repeat with the remaining oil and scallops.

3. Divide the nori strips among 4 dinner plates and top each portion with 4 of the scallops. Spoon the vinaigrette over the scallops, garnish with the cilantro and serve at once. —*Tetsuya Wakuda*

WINE The 1996 Howard Park Chardonnay from Australia and the 1996 Edna Valley Paragon Chardonnay from California are Chablis-style wines that won't overpower the scallops.

Broiled Clams

8 SERVINGS

Under the broiler, a thin slice of compound butter becomes a lightly garlicky herbed crumb topping for the clams.

  1 stick (¼ pound) unsalted butter, at room temperature
  ⅓ cup cracker crumbs
  ¼ cup finely chopped mixed herbs, such as parsley, chives, oregano and thyme
  1 small egg yolk
1½ teaspoons minced garlic
  ¼ teaspoon Tabasco
Rock salt
  4 dozen freshly shucked littleneck clams, on the half shell

1. In a medium bowl, combine the butter, cracker crumbs, herbs, egg yolk, garlic and Tabasco. Scrape the butter onto a sheet of plastic wrap and roll it into a 6-inch log. Refrigerate until firm.

2. Preheat the broiler. Spread rock salt on a large rimmed baking sheet; set the clams on the salt. Top each clam with a ⅛-inch-thick slice of the butter. Broil the clams 8 inches from the heat for about 10 minutes, shifting the pan as necessary, until deep golden and bubbling. Serve at once. —*Mark Gottwald*

MAKE AHEAD The herb butter can be refrigerated for 3 days or frozen for 1 week.

Shellfish Bruschetta

Shellfish Bruschetta

4 SERVINGS ❋

Paul Bertolli, chef and owner of Oliveto in Oakland, California, recommends a firm, rustic bread for his bruschetta. Day-old bread is even better for soaking up the delicious shellfish broth.

  4 large ½-inch-thick slices of sourdough bread
Fruity extra-virgin olive oil, for brushing and drizzling
  1 large garlic clove, halved, plus 1 teaspoon minced garlic
  ¾ cup dry white wine
  1 large shallot, minced

  3 bay leaves
1½ pounds Manila clams or cockles, scrubbed
1½ pounds small mussels, scrubbed and debearded
  2 tablespoons chopped flat-leaf parsley

1. Preheat the oven to 375°. Lightly brush the bread on both sides with oil and toast for about 10 minutes, or until golden. Rub each slice generously with the halved garlic clove.

2. In a large heavy saucepan, combine the wine, shallot, minced garlic and bay leaves and bring to a boil over high heat. Add the shellfish, cover and cook, shaking the pan often, until the clams and mussels open, about 5 minutes. Remove from the heat and discard any shellfish that haven't opened. Stir in the parsley.

3. Put the toasts in bowls and top with the clams and mussels; discard the bay leaves. Spoon the shellfish broth over the toasts. Drizzle a little oil over all and serve. —*Paul Bertolli*

WINE Mussels, clams, garlicky toasts: this shellfish stew needs the sharp contrast of a tart, crisp white. Look for California Sauvignon Blanc bottlings, such as the 1997 Cakebread or the 1997 Quivira.

Salt Cod Cakes with Herbed Mayonnaise

Salt Cod Cakes with Herbed Mayonnaise

8 TO 12 SERVINGS

Serve this appetizer at dinner parties; it's always popular. Cod is used instead of the more standard crab because the dried fish has a more potent flavor— and it's inexpensive. Allow time for the cod to soak overnight.

MAYONNAISE

- 1 cup mayonnaise
- 1 tablespoon coarsely chopped tarragon
- 1 tablespoon coarsely chopped flat-leaf parsley
- 1 tablespoon coarsely chopped chives

COD CAKES

- 1 pound skinless salt cod fillet
- 3 cups milk
- 2 cups diced (1-inch) peeled Idaho potatoes (about 3 medium)
- 2 tablespoons olive oil
- 1 cup thinly sliced scallions (about 1 bunch)
- 1/3 cup heavy cream
- 2 tablespoons coarsely chopped tarragon
- 1 tablespoon coarsely chopped flat-leaf parsley

Salt and freshly ground pepper
All-purpose flour, for dusting
Vegetable oil, for frying

1. MAKE THE MAYONNAISE: Combine all of the ingredients in a medium bowl and refrigerate.

2. MAKE THE COD CAKES: In another bowl, cover the cod with water. Soak the cod overnight in the refrigerator, changing the water once or twice. Drain and rinse the fish and transfer to a large saucepan. Add the milk and simmer over moderate heat until the cod flakes easily, about 10 minutes. Drain the cod and discard the milk. Coarsely flake the fish and transfer it to a large bowl.

3. Meanwhile, in a medium saucepan, cover the potatoes with water. Bring to a boil and cook the potatoes until just tender, about 10 minutes. Drain well and let cool slightly. Using your hands, mix the potatoes with the cod; the mixture should be chunky.

4. Heat the olive oil in a medium skillet. Add the scallions and cook over moderately low heat until tender, about 4 minutes. Add the scallions to the cod mixture along with the cream, tarragon and parsley. Season with salt and pepper. Shape into 3-inch cakes, about 3/4 inch thick. Lightly flour the cakes and set them on a baking sheet.

5. Heat 1/2 inch of vegetable oil in a large skillet. Working in batches, fry the

54

cod cakes, turning once, until they are golden brown and crisp, 3 to 4 minutes. Drain on paper towels and keep warm while you cook the remaining cakes. Serve the cod cakes with the herbed mayonnaise. —*Sascha Lyon*

MAKE AHEAD The mayonnaise and the fried cod cakes can be refrigerated for up to 2 days. Rewarm the cod cakes in a 325° oven.

WINE Both the nonvintage Billecart-Salmon Grande Marqué Rosé Champagne and the 1995 Domaine Ernest Burn Tokay Pinot Gris from Alsace are light, easy to drink wines that stand up well to the cod cakes—the Champagne because of its effervescence, the Pinot Gris because of its characteristic acid.

Seared Salmon with Nasturtiums and Saffron Vinaigrette

8 SERVINGS

Flash-seared salmon with a confetti of peppers and a shower of flowers is a beautiful dish. If you don't have a long, sharp knife at home, ask the fishmonger to slice the salmon for you.

- 2   tablespoons dry white wine
- 1   teaspoon minced onion

Pinch of saffron threads

- 1   tablespoon fresh lemon juice
- ½   teaspoon Dijon mustard
- ½   cup extra-virgin olive oil

Salt and freshly ground black pepper

- 2   pounds skinless salmon fillet, cut on a very wide diagonal into eight ⅓-inch-thick slices
- ½   teaspoon ground coriander
- ½   teaspoon cayenne pepper
- 2   tablespoons finely diced red bell pepper
- 2   tablespoons finely diced yellow bell pepper
- ¼   cup finely shredded nasturtium leaves
- 1   teaspoon finely chopped chives
- ¼   cup nasturtiums or pansies

1. In a small saucepan, combine the wine, onion and saffron and bring to a simmer; let cool. Transfer the mixture to a blender, add the lemon juice and mustard and blend until smooth. Gradually blend in the oil in a thin stream. Transfer the vinaigrette to a glass or stainless-steel bowl and season with salt and black pepper.

2. Spread the salmon out on a baking sheet. In a bowl, combine the coriander, cayenne and a pinch of salt. Lightly brush the top side of the salmon with vinaigrette and sprinkle liberally with the spice mixture.

3. Heat 2 nonstick skillets. When the pans are hot, add 2 salmon slices to each, spiced side down, and cook over high heat until the salmon is opaque around the edges but slightly rare in the center, about 2 minutes. Flip the salmon onto 4 dinner plates, cooked side up, and then repeat with the remaining fish.

4. Scatter the red and yellow peppers, nasturtium leaves and chives over the salmon. Drizzle with some of the vinaigrette and garnish with the flowers. Serve the salmon warm or at room temperature. —*Alan Tardi*

Seared Salmon with Sweet Corn, Shiitakes and Spinach

6 SERVINGS ★★★ 1992

This salmon from Michael Romano, executive chef and partner at Union Square Cafe in New York City, was the restaurant's most popular dish in 1992. The recipe can easily be doubled to serve six as a main course.

- 1½   sticks (6 ounces) unsalted butter
- 1   cup thinly sliced red onion
- ¼   pound shiitake mushrooms— stems removed and reserved, caps quartered
- 1   medium tomato, coarsely chopped

Seared Salmon with Sweet Corn, Shiitakes and Spinach

- 3   garlic cloves—2 thinly sliced, 1 whole
- 1   teaspoon whole black peppercorns
- 1   bay leaf
- ⅓   cup balsamic vinegar
- ⅓   cup water

Salt and freshly ground pepper

- 3   tablespoons olive oil
- 1   pound fresh spinach—stemmed, washed and patted dry
- 2   cups fresh corn kernels
- 1   pound center-cut salmon fillet, sliced crosswise into 6 strips
- 3   tablespoons finely chopped chives

1. Cut 6 tablespoons of the butter into ½-inch dice and chill. In a medium saucepan, melt 2 tablespoons of the remaining butter and add the onion, shiitake stems, tomato, sliced garlic, peppercorns and bay leaf. Cook over moderately low heat until the vegetables are soft but not browned, about 12 minutes. Add the vinegar and water and cook over moderately high heat, stirring occasionally, until the liquid is almost syrupy, about 4 minutes.

2. Reduce the heat to low and whisk in the 6 tablespoons of chilled diced butter, 2 to 3 pieces at a time. When all

the chilled butter has been added, season the sauce with salt and pepper. Strain the sauce through a very fine sieve into a saucepan and keep warm; discard the solids.

3. Spear the whole garlic clove securely with a dinner fork. In a large skillet, heat 2 tablespoons of the oil over high heat until just beginning to smoke. Very carefully add the spinach and stir with the garlic clove–tipped fork until wilted. Season the spinach with salt and pepper and drain.

4. Wipe the skillet clean. Add 3 tablespoons of the butter. Add the shiitake caps and cook over moderate heat, stirring, until softened, about 3 minutes. Stir in the corn kernels and cook until they are tender, about 3 minutes. Season the vegetables with salt and pepper and transfer them to a bowl; keep warm.

5. In the same skillet, melt the remaining 1 tablespoon of butter in the remaining 1 tablespoon of oil over high heat. Season the salmon with salt and pepper and sear the pieces in the hot pan, turning once, until browned but barely cooked through, about 3 minutes per side.

6. Mound the spinach in the center of 6 plates and surround with the corn and shiitakes. Set the salmon on the spinach and then spoon the balsamic sauce on top. Garnish with the chives and serve. —*Michael Romano*

Salmon Terrine with Roasted Poblano Cream

Smoked Salmon Salad with Orange Vinaigrette

4 SERVINGS

The citrusy vinaigrette makes a lively dressing for the rich smoked salmon or for canned fish. Serve the salad with boiled potatoes, white rice or lentils as a light supper. Or, as a lunch, you can serve it with crackers.

- 3 tablespoons fresh orange juice
- 2 tablespoons olive oil
- 1 tablespoon fresh lemon juice
- ½ teaspoon finely chopped orange zest

Salt and freshly ground pepper

- ½ pound sliced smoked salmon, cut into thick strips, or two 5½- to 6-ounce cans of fish, drained and broken up (see Note)
- 1 small red onion, thinly sliced

In a medium glass or stainless-steel bowl, combine the orange juice, oil, lemon juice and orange zest. Season the vinaigrette with salt and pepper. Add the salmon and red onion and toss to coat them with the dressing. Arrange the salmon salad on 4 plates and serve. —*Marcia Kiesel*

NOTE Use water-packed salmon or tuna, or try the delicious and delicate smoked whitefish that's available by mail from Minnesota's Ojibwe Foods, 218-335-8312.

WINE The oily richness of smoked salmon is a classic match with the lemony-dry tartness of Champagne. Look for nonvintage bruts from Taittinger or Perrier-Jouët.

Salmon Terrine with Roasted Poblano Cream

20 SERVINGS

In order to set up properly, this delicious terrine needs a day of chilling.

Two 8-ounce skinless salmon fillets

- 3 large poblano or Anaheim chiles
- 1 pound cream cheese, softened

½ cup chopped cilantro

3 tablespoons fresh lemon juice

1 large garlic clove, minced

Salt

½ pound thinly sliced smoked salmon

Freshly ground pepper

Mixed salad greens, for garnish

1. Fill a large skillet with salted water and bring to a boil. Add the salmon fillets and poach over low heat until they are just opaque throughout, about 4 minutes. Transfer the fillets to a platter, cover loosely with aluminum foil and let cool.

2. Roast the chiles directly over a gas flame until charred all over. Transfer them to a bowl and cover with plastic wrap for 5 minutes to loosen the skins. Rub off the skins and remove the seeds and ribs. Rinse and then coarsely chop the chiles.

3. In a food processor, combine the chiles, cream cheese, cilantro, 2 tablespoons of lemon juice and the garlic and process to blend coarsely. Transfer the poblano cream to a bowl and season with salt.

4. Line two 8-by-4-inch loaf pans with plastic wrap, leaving a 4-inch overhang on all sides. Line the bottom and sides of each pan with one-fourth of the smoked salmon slices, slightly overlapping them. Add ¾ cup of poblano cream and spread in an even layer. Season the salmon fillets with salt, pepper and the remaining lemon juice; center a fillet on the cream in each pan. Spread half the remaining poblano cream over each salmon fillet and cover with half the remaining smoked salmon. Fold the overhanging plastic up and over the top of the terrine and refrigerate until firm, at least 6 hours and up to 12 hours.

5. Peel back the plastic and unmold the terrines onto a cutting board. Using a sharp knife, slice them crosswise.

Arrange the slices of salmon terrine on a platter, garnish with the mixed greens and serve. —*Marcia Kiesel*

Gravlax

12 SERVINGS ★★★ **1989**

Gravlax has always been featured on Christer Larsson's menus, first at New York City's Aquavit when he was the executive chef there, and now at his own restaurant, Christer's, also in New York. In the days before refrigeration, Swedes buried cured salmon in the ground to keep it through the long winter: hence the name gravlax, Swedish for "salmon from the grave."

¼ cup kosher salt

¼ cup sugar

1 tablespoon crushed white peppercorns

1¾ pounds center-cut salmon fillet with skin

2 large bunches of dill, 12 sprigs set aside for garnish

Lemon wedges, for serving

1. In a small bowl, combine the kosher salt, sugar and peppercorns. Rub a handful of the seasoning mixture on both sides of the salmon fillet. Set the salmon fillet in a glass or ceramic dish, skin side down, and sprinkle the rest of the seasoning mixture on top. Place the dill bunches on the salmon fillet and cover with plastic wrap. Let the salmon stand at room temperature for 6 hours and then refrigerate for 24 hours.

2. Scrape off the dill and seasonings and pat the fish dry. Using a long sharp knife, thinly slice the salmon fillet on the diagonal; do not slice through the skin. Cut off the gray triangle at the bottom of each slice. Arrange the salmon on a large platter, overlapping the slices slightly. Cover tightly with plastic wrap and refrigerate for up to 6 hours.

3. Cut the salmon skin crosswise into 12 strips. Set a large cast-iron skillet over moderately high heat. When hot,

add the salmon-skin strips and fry until lightly browned, about 45 seconds per side. Drain on paper towels.

4. Set one of the dill sprigs in the center of each of the strips of salmon skin and then roll up the strips. Garnish the gravlax platter with the rolls and serve with lemon wedges.—*Christer Larsson*

Tourondel's Semi-Smoked Salmon with Apple Broth

4 SERVINGS ♛

Laurent Tourondel is chef at the Palace Court in Las Vegas. His luscious apple broth relies on fresh apple juice; you'll need a juicer to make this dish. You'll also need about one cup of hardwood chips, preferably applewood.

Four 7-ounce skinless center-cut salmon fillets

Salt and freshly ground white pepper

2 medium Granny Smith apples, cut into small wedges, plus ¼ cup julienned Granny Smith apple tossed with ½ teaspoon fresh lemon juice

4½ tablespoons unsalted butter

½ teaspoon Dijon mustard

7 ounces pea shoots or well-trimmed watercress sprigs

1 large garlic clove, minced

1 ounce caviar, preferably Beluga

¼ cup julienned Red Delicious apple tossed with ½ teaspoon fresh lemon juice

¼ cup daikon or radish sprouts

1. Soak the wood chips in warm water to cover for 20 minutes and then drain. Light a small charcoal fire or prepare a stovetop smoker following the manufacturer's instructions. Add the wood chips and heat until smoking. Season the salmon fillets on both sides with salt and white pepper and set them on the rack. Cover and smoke for about 10 minutes, or until fragrant but still very rare in the center. Transfer the salmon to a plate. ➤

Tourondel's Semi-Smoked Salmon with Apple Broth

2. Heat a large nonstick skillet. Add the salmon and cook over moderately high heat until the fillets are browned and barely cooked through, about 2 minutes per side. Remove from the heat and keep warm.

3. Meanwhile, juice the Granny Smith apple wedges. In a small saucepan, bring the apple juice to a boil. Over low heat, whisk in 4 tablespoons of the butter and the mustard until incorporated. Strain the apple broth through a fine sieve, return it to the saucepan and season with salt and white pepper.

4. Melt the remaining ½ tablespoon of butter in a large skillet. Add the pea shoots and garlic; cook over high heat, tossing, until wilted, about 4 minutes. Season with salt and white pepper and transfer to 4 shallow soup plates.

5. Arrange the salmon fillets on the pea shoots and top each fillet with a small dollop of caviar. Scatter the julienned Granny Smith and Red Delicious apples all around the salmon fillets and garnish with the daikon sprouts. Whisk the apple broth over high heat until it is foamy and then pour it around the salmon fillets and serve.

—*Laurent Tourondel*

WINE A Gewürztraminer has the character and acidity to match the salmon and the fruity apple broth.

Indian-Spiced Phyllo and Smoked Salmon Napoleons

6 SERVINGS

Crisp sheets of phyllo dough make a lower-fat alternative to the buttery puff pastry typically used in napoleons.

1½ **cups plain yogurt**
4 **tablespoons unsalted butter**
1 **teaspoon pure chile powder**
½ **teaspoon ground cumin**
¼ **teaspoon ground coriander**
⅛ **teaspoon cayenne pepper**
5 **sheets of phyllo dough, thawed**
¼ **cup cilantro leaves**

Indian-Spiced Phyllo and Smoked Salmon Napoleons

2 **tablespoons snipped chives**
2 **tablespoons mint leaves**
4 **large radishes—3 cut into matchsticks, 1 thinly sliced**
⅓ **cup finely diced red onion**
1 **large jalapeño, seeded and minced**
½ **cup heavy cream**
Salt
½ **pound thinly sliced smoked salmon**

1. Drain the yogurt in a coffee filter in the refrigerator for at least 3 hours or overnight.

2. Preheat the oven to 375°. In a small saucepan, melt the butter. Let it cool slightly and then pour the butter into a small bowl, leaving the milk solids behind. Stir in the chile powder, cumin, coriander and cayenne.

3. Cut the phyllo sheets in half crosswise. Working with 3 sheets at a time and keeping the rest covered with plastic wrap and a kitchen towel, brush the sheets with some of the spiced butter. Stack them in three separate 3-layer piles; discard the remaining half sheet. Trim any ragged edges. Cut 1 stack into six 3½-inch squares. Transfer all the phyllo to 2 baking sheets, re-forming the cut rectangle, and bake for about 10 minutes, or until golden; let cool.

4. In a blender, puree the yogurt with the cilantro, chives and mint. Transfer to a small bowl and stir in the radish matchsticks, onion and jalapeño. Whip the cream until it holds firm peaks and fold it into the herbed yogurt. Season with salt. Reserve ½ cup of the yogurt mixture for garnish. ➤

5. Set 1 of the large phyllo stacks on a work surface; top with half the salmon and half the remaining herbed yogurt. Cover with the second large phyllo stack, the remaining salmon and the rest of the remaining yogurt. Top with the phyllo squares, re-forming the rectangle. Using a very sharp knife, cut the napoleons, between the squares, wiping the knife blade after each cut. Set each napoleon on a plate and top with a dollop of the reserved yogurt mixture. Garnish with the radish slices and serve. —*Grace Parisi*

MAKE AHEAD The recipe can be prepared through Step 4 up to 1 day ahead. Wrap the phyllo stacks on the 2 baking sheets tightly with plastic and store at room temperature. Refrigerate the herbed yogurt. Recrisp the phyllo in a 325° oven before proceeding if necessary.

SERVE WITH A mesclun salad.

Smoked Salmon and Onion Tart

Smoked Salmon and Onion Tart

4 SERVINGS

Here the bite of onion sets off the rich smoked salmon and the tangy crème fraîche.

Flaky Tart Pastry (p. 41)
- 1 large white onion, thinly sliced

Salt and freshly ground pepper
- 1 large egg yolk mixed with ½ teaspoon water
- 4 ounces thinly sliced smoked salmon, cut into thin strips
- 3 tablespoons crème fraîche or sour cream
- 1 tablespoon chopped parsley
- 1 teaspoon finely chopped dill

Juice of ½ lemon

1. Preheat the oven to 450°. On a lightly floured sheet of parchment paper, roll out the pastry to a 13-inch round. Transfer the pastry and parchment to a baking sheet.

2. Spread the onion slices on the tart in a single layer, leaving a 1-inch border. Season with salt and pepper. Fold the edge of the pastry over onto the onion and brush the rim with the egg wash. Bake for about 20 minutes, or until the pastry is golden. Let cool.

3. Arrange the salmon on the tart. With a warm fork, stir the crème fraîche and drizzle it over the tart. Sprinkle the parsley, dill and lemon juice on top and serve. —*Peggy Smith*

Fried Sardines with Bacon and Shiso

4 SERVINGS

Shiso is a Japanese herb with a slightly sweet and peppery flavor. Lemony-flavored sansho is ground Szechwan peppercorns.

- 3 large eggs, lightly beaten
- ¼ cup plus 1 tablespoon all-purpose flour, plus more for dredging
- ¼ cup plus 1 tablespoon arrowroot or rice flour
- ⅔ cup water
- 1 teaspoon sansho (Japanese pepper) or freshly ground white pepper

Salt and freshly ground white pepper
- 6 fresh sardines (½ pound each), filleted, or four 6-ounce mackerel fillets, cut into 4-by-2-inch strips
- 6 slices of bacon, halved crosswise
- 6 shiso leaves, halved lengthwise, or 12 basil leaves
- 3 tablespoons fresh lemon juice
- 1 teaspoon finely grated lemon zest
- ¼ cup grapeseed oil or vegetable oil, plus more for frying
- 2 medium Granny Smith apples, peeled and cut into matchsticks
- 4 Belgian endives, cored and cut into long thin strips

Fried Sardines with Bacon and Shiso

1. In a bowl, beat the eggs with the all-purpose flour and arrowroot. Mix in the water just until blended; do not over-mix. Let stand for 30 minutes. In a small bowl, combine the sansho with 1 teaspoon of salt and ¼ teaspoon of white pepper.

2. Set the sardine fillets on a work surface, skin side down; season with salt and white pepper. Top each fillet with a half slice of bacon and a shiso leaf half. Roll up the fillets, starting at the wider end, and secure with a toothpick.

3. In a large bowl, combine the lemon juice and zest with ¼ cup of the oil. Season with salt and white pepper. Add the apples, toss to coat and refrigerate for up to 1 hour.

4. Preheat the oven to 300°. In a medium saucepan, heat 2 inches of oil to 350° or until a bread cube turns golden in 1 minute. Dredge each sardine roll in flour; shake off the excess. Dip 4 rolls in the batter and fry until golden brown and crisp all over, about 4 minutes. Transfer to a rack set over a large baking sheet to drain. Keep warm in the oven. Repeat with the remaining rolls.

5. Add the endives to the apple salad and toss well. Arrange the salad on 4

plates and set 3 sardine rolls beside each salad. Dust with the sansho mixture and serve. —*Tetsuya Wakuda*

WINE Rosé has the right balance of flavor and body to complement the sardines. Try the 1997 Charles Melton's Rose of Virginia Rosé of Grenache from Australia or the 1996 Domaine Tempier Bandol Rosé from France.

Marinated Tuna Tartare with Goat Cheese

4 SERVINGS

This sublime first course boasts the unlikely combination of rich tuna and smooth goat cheese. Getting the balance right requires both the very best quality tuna and fresh goat cheese that's not too strongly flavored.

- ½ pound sushi-grade tuna, cut into ½-inch dice
- 1 tablespoon olive oil

Pinch of freshly ground white pepper

- 3 ounces fresh goat cheese (⅓ cup)
- ½ tablespoon soy sauce
- ½ tablespoon mirin (sweet rice wine)
- ½ small garlic clove, minced
- ½ teaspoon minced ginger

Pinch of cayenne pepper
Salt

- 1 tablespoon minced chives
- 1 cup (lightly packed) small arugula leaves

1. In a shallow glass baking dish, drizzle the tuna with the oil and season with the white pepper. Cover with plastic wrap and refrigerate until chilled, or for up to 2 hours.

2. In a bowl, mash the goat cheese with the soy sauce, mirin, garlic, ginger and cayenne; season with salt. Gently toss the tuna with the goat-cheese mixture and the chives until well-coated. Mound the tuna on plates, top with the arugula and serve. —*Tetsuya Wakuda*

WINE When choosing a white wine to accompany this dish, look for fresh

fruit with lively acidity to match the fresh goat cheese and the buttery tuna. The 1997 Katnook Estate Sauvignon Blanc from Australia and the 1997 Geyser Peak Sonoma County Sauvignon Blanc are just right.

Aromatic Snails

8 SERVINGS

- 1 cup dry white wine
- 1 cup water
- 8 large garlic cloves, chopped
- 3 large thyme sprigs
- 2 strips orange zest
- 2 large shallots, chopped
- 2 tablespoons Cognac

Four 8.75-ounce cans large snails (see Note), drained and rinsed

- 1 tablespoon coarse sea salt

Freshly ground pepper
About 48 snail shells, for serving

1. In a medium saucepan, combine the wine, water, garlic, thyme sprigs, orange zest, shallots and Cognac. Cover and simmer over low heat for 10 minutes.

2. Add the snails, sea salt and a few grindings of pepper to the saucepan, cover and simmer for 5 minutes. Remove from the heat and let stand, covered, for 20 minutes. Transfer the snails to the shells and serve.
—*Nancy Harmon Jenkins*

NOTE Snails and their shells are available at specialty food shops.

MAKE AHEAD The snails can be refrigerated in their aromatic liquid for up to 2 days. Reheat gently before serving.

Smoked Chicken and Winter Squash Blintzes

4 SERVINGS

Blintzes are traditionally stuffed with sweetened fresh cheese or potatoes, but this inviting cold-weather recipe proves the value of innovation.

FILLING

- 1 medium winter squash, such as butternut, halved lengthwise and seeded (about 1½ pounds)
- 1 tablespoon extra-virgin olive oil
- 2 leeks, white and tender green, thinly sliced
- ½ pound smoked chicken breast, skinned and cut into ⅓-inch dice
- 1 tablespoon maple syrup, plus more for serving
- 1 teaspoon thyme

Salt and freshly ground pepper

BLINTZES

- ¾ cup all-purpose flour
- ¼ teaspoon salt
- 4 large eggs, lightly beaten
- 1 tablespoon finely chopped flat-leaf parsley
- 1 cup milk
- 5 tablespoons unsalted butter, 3 melted

Sour cream or yogurt, for serving

1. MAKE THE FILLING: Preheat the oven to 350°. Set the squash, cut side down, on a lightly oiled baking sheet and bake for about 45 minutes, or until tender when pierced. Let cool and then scoop out 2 cups of squash.

2. Heat the oil in a medium skillet. Add the leeks and cook over moderate heat, stirring, until softened, about 5 minutes. Stir in the squash, chicken, 1 tablespoon of the maple syrup and the thyme. Season generously with salt and pepper. Cover and set aside.

3. MAKE THE BLINTZES: In a bowl, whisk together the flour and salt; whisk in the eggs and parsley and then whisk in the milk to form a smooth batter. Add the melted butter to the batter and mix thoroughly.

4. Heat a lightly oiled 8-inch skillet. Pour in 3 tablespoons of the batter and quickly tilt the skillet in a circular motion to spread the batter evenly. Cook over moderate heat until the blintz is lightly browned on the bottom, 1 to 2

Aromatic Snails

minutes. Transfer the blintz, cooked side up, to a plate. Repeat to make 11 more blintzes.

5. Spread about ¼ cup of the filling along 1 edge of the cooked side of the blintz. Fold in 2 sides of each blintz and then roll it up like a burrito; flatten slightly. Set the rolled blintzes, seam side up, on a lightly oiled baking sheet.

6. In a large heavy skillet, melt 1 tablespoon of the remaining butter over moderately low heat. Add 6 of the blintzes, seam side up, and cook them until golden brown, about 2 minutes. Turn the blintzes and cook them on the other side until golden brown. Transfer the blintzes to a warmed platter and repeat with the remaining but-

ter and blintzes. Serve the blintzes at once, with maple syrup and dollops of sour cream. *—Jesse Cool*

MAKE AHEAD The blintzes can be prepared through Step 5 and refrigerated, covered, for up to 1 day. Bring to room temperature before proceeding.

SERVE WITH Buttered beet greens or red chard.

WINE Smoked chicken is an easy match with just about any wine, but leeks, maple syrup and squash add a sweetness best matched by a light, fruity Pinot Noir, such as the 1996 Fetzer Barrel Select from California or the 1994 Henry Estate Barrel Select from Oregon.

Smoked Chicken and Winter Squash Blintzes

Smoked Chicken and Cheese Tart with Olives

4 SERVINGS 🎇

Flaky Tart Pastry (p. 41)

- 2 small red onions, thinly sliced
- 9 oil-cured black olives, pitted and coarsely chopped
- 1 large egg yolk mixed with ½ teaspoon water
- 1 cup shredded smoked chicken (about 3 ounces)
- ¾ cup (packed) grated Monterey Jack cheese (about 3 ounces)
- 1 tablespoon chopped parsley

tart whites

A dry white wine is ideal with the buttery tart above and those on pages 41, 42 and 60. Look for one with enough acidity to underline the contrasting notes from the olives and onions. Crisp Sauvignon Blanc is an obvious choice, but a deep-flavored Chardonnay-based wine, such as the 1996 Château de Maligny Chablis Premier Cru Fourchaume from France or the 1995 Byron Santa Barbara, would be more interesting.

1 tablespoon finely chopped
   chives

1. Preheat the oven to 450°. On a lightly floured sheet of parchment paper, roll out the pastry to a 13-inch round. Transfer the pastry and parchment to a baking sheet.

2. Spread the onions on the pastry in a single layer, leaving a 1-inch border. Sprinkle the olives all over the onion topping. Fold the edge of the pastry over onto the onions and brush the rim with the egg wash. Bake the tart for 10 minutes.

3. Spread the shredded chicken on the tart and sprinkle with the cheese. Bake the tart for about 10 minutes longer, or until the pastry is golden and the cheese has melted. Let the tart cool slightly. Just before serving, sprinkle the parsley and chives on top. Serve warm.   —*Peggy Smith*

Marie Boulud's Chicken Liver and Parsley Custard

6 SERVINGS

Chef Daniel Boulud's mother, Marie, learned this version of the rich and delicious classic from the countryside near Lyons from *her* mother, Francine.

  1 tablespoon unsalted butter
  2 shallots, finely chopped
10 ounces firm white mushrooms, finely chopped
Salt and freshly ground white pepper
  ¾ pound chicken livers, well-trimmed and finely chopped
  ½ cup finely chopped parsley
  2 cups heavy cream
  4 large eggs

1. Preheat the oven to 325°. Butter a 9-by-12-inch oval gratin dish that's about 2 inches deep. Melt the butter in a large skillet. Add the shallots; cook over low heat, stirring, until softened but not browned, about 4 minutes. Add the mushrooms and cook over moderate heat until they release their liquid and then absorb it again, about 8 minutes. Season the mushrooms with salt and white pepper and transfer to a bowl to cool.

2. Add the chicken livers and parsley to the mushrooms and season with salt and white pepper. In another bowl, whisk the cream with the eggs and season with ¾ teaspoon of salt and ¼ teaspoon of white pepper. Stir the custard into the chicken liver mixture and pour into the prepared gratin dish. Bake for about 30 minutes, or until the custard is just set. Serve the custard warm.   —*Daniel Boulud*

MAKE AHEAD The baked custard can be refrigerated overnight. Cover tightly with aluminum foil and rewarm in a 300° oven for about 25 minutes.

WINE A dry mineral wine will enrich this dish with its slight zing. Try the 1993 Edna Valley Reserve Chardonnay from California or the 1996 Domaine du Closel Savennières from France.

Foie Gras Terrine with Caramelized Apples

12 SERVINGS

The key to working with fresh foie gras is controlling its temperature. Make sure the foie gras is at room temperature when removing the veins so it's pliable and then chill before cooking so it doesn't start to melt. Allow time for the foie gras terrine to refrigerate for at least one day before serving.

  2 Grade A foie gras lobes (see Note), about 1 pound each, at room temperature
1½ cups Sauternes or other sweet dessert wine
  ¾ cup ruby port
Salt and freshly ground pepper
Pinch of freshly grated nutmeg
  2 tablespoons unsalted butter
  4 medium Granny Smith apples— peeled, halved, cored and cut into ½-inch wedges
  1 tablespoon sugar
Walnut Bread (p. 287) or brioche, toasted, for serving

1. Line an 8-by-4-inch glass or ceramic loaf pan with 4 layers of plastic wrap, leaving a 4-inch overhang all around.

2. Using your hands, gently pull open each lobe of foie gras at its natural separations and remove the network of veins with a thin sharp knife; if the lobes break apart, the pieces can be pressed back together. Set the foie gras in a large baking dish and pour the Sauternes and port over it. Cover with plastic wrap and refrigerate for 2 hours.

3. Drain off the marinade from the foie gras, season generously with salt and pepper and then sprinkle with the nutmeg. Arrange one of the foie gras lobes in the prepared loaf pan, set the second lobe on top and press firmly to pack the 2 lobes together in the pan. Cover the foie gras with the overhanging plastic wrap and then cover the pan tightly with aluminum foil.

4. Set the loaf pan in a small flameproof roasting pan and add enough water to the roasting pan to reach three-quarters of the way up the sides of the loaf pan. Remove the loaf pan and bring the water to a simmer on the stove. Return the loaf pan to the water and simmer gently over low heat until an instant-read thermometer inserted in the foie gras registers 130°, about 15 minutes. Transfer the foie gras terrine to a rack and let cool to room temperature. Remove the aluminum foil. Top the foie gras terrine with another loaf pan weighted down with canned goods and refrigerate the terrine for at least 24 hours.

5. Melt the butter in a large skillet. Add the apple wedges and toss to coat. Sprinkle with the sugar and cook over moderate heat until the apples are browned on the bottom, about 4 minutes. Raise the heat to high, turn the apples and cook until they are browned on the bottom but still slightly crisp, about 3 minutes.

6. Unwrap and unmold the terrine onto a platter. To serve, run a thin sharp knife under hot water and wipe dry. Cut the terrine into 1/2-inch-thick slices, rinsing the knife under hot water and drying it between cuts. Set each slice on a plate; serve with the sautéed apple wedges and toasted Walnut Bread.

—*The Point, Lake Saranac, New York*

NOTE Fresh foie gras is available by mail order from D'Artagnan, 800-327-8246. The company also sells prepared foie gras terrine in case you'd rather not make it yourself.

MAKE AHEAD The cooked terrine can be refrigerated for up to 1 week.

WINE A dry, spicy, lush and aromatic Alsace Gewürztraminer, such as the 1995 Zind Humbrecht Wintzenheim or the 1995 Clos St Landelin, would not only complement the richness of the foie gras terrine but would provide contrast as well. Alternatively, serve a California Gewürztraminer, such as the 1997 De Loach or 1997 Navarro.

Cinnamon-Spiced Duck with Sweet-Sour Shallots

8 SERVINGS

The duck must marinate overnight in the cinnamon oil, so be sure that you plan accordingly.

SHALLOTS

1 cup thinly sliced shallots
1/2 cup sherry vinegar
1/4 cup light brown sugar

DUCK

1/2 cup olive oil
1 tablespoon cinnamon
2 boneless duck breast halves (2 1/2 pounds total)

Salt and freshly ground pepper

I. PREPARE THE SHALLOTS: Combine the shallots, vinegar and sugar in a medium saucepan and bring to a boil. Simmer over moderately low heat until the liquid is syrupy and the shallots are softened, about 30 minutes. Transfer to a bowl.

2. PREPARE THE DUCK: In a sturdy resealable plastic bag, combine the oil and cinnamon. Add the duck breasts, seal and refrigerate overnight.

3. Preheat the oven to 450°. Remove the duck from the marinade, scraping off as much cinnamon oil as possible. Season with salt and pepper. Heat a large ovenproof skillet. Add the duck breasts, skin side down, and cook over low heat, without turning, until the skin is deep golden and most of the fat has been rendered, about 25 minutes; spoon off the fat as it accumulates. Transfer the skillet to the oven and roast the duck for about 13 minutes, or until medium rare. Transfer the duck to a plate and refrigerate until chilled.

4. Thinly slice the duck against the grain; remove the skin if you like. Arrange the slices on a platter and serve with the shallots. —*Sascha Lyon*

MAKE AHEAD The shallots can be refrigerated for 1 week. The duck can be refrigerated overnight; slice before serving.

Spiced Sausage Patties

8 SERVINGS

An essential component of many *braais,* or South African barbecues, the distinctive coriander-spiced sausages known as *boerewors* are sold in virtually every South African butcher shop, supermarket and grocery; local competitions are held to determine the best. Traditionally the meat is seasoned and then stuffed into sausage casings, but patties are easier to make.

1 tablespoon whole coriander seeds
1 pound ground beef
1/2 pound ground pork or lamb
2 tablespoons cider vinegar

1/2 teaspoon freshly ground pepper
1/4 teaspoon freshly grated nutmeg
1/8 teaspoon ground cloves
Kosher salt

I. In a small dry skillet, toast the coriander seeds over moderately low heat, shaking the pan, until fragrant, about 2 minutes. Let cool and then transfer the seeds to a spice grinder or mortar and grind until fine.

2. In a medium bowl, mix the beef and pork with the ground coriander seeds, vinegar, pepper, nutmeg and cloves. Cover and refrigerate the meat mixture for at least 3 hours and up to 2 days to allow the flavors to blend.

3. Light the grill or preheat the broiler. Form the meat mixture into 16 patties and season on all sides with kosher salt. Grill or broil the patties, turning them as they brown, for 10 to 12 minutes, or until the meat is no longer pink. Serve at once. —*Jenna Holst*

Pernot's Tamales Cubano with Sun-Dried Cherry Mojo

4 SERVINGS ♛

Guillermo Pernot, chef at the Vega Grill in Philadelphia, recommends using very coarse polenta to give tamales a better texture.

PORK TAMALES

1 1/4 pounds trimmed boneless fresh pork shoulder or butt
2 1/2 cups water
1 1/2 cups Chicken Stock (p. 117) or canned low-sodium broth
1 medium onion, quartered
1 medium carrot, quartered
1 medium celery rib, quartered
1 bay leaf

Salt

1/4 teaspoon whole black peppercorns
1/4 cup milk
3/4 cup coarse cornmeal (about 4 ounces)
1/3 cup masa harina

⅓ cup lard or vegetable shortening

½ teaspoon crushed red pepper

2 tablespoons shredded culentro (see Note), or 3 tablespoons shredded cilantro

CHERRY MOJO

¾ cup fresh orange juice

½ cup cherry juice or mixed-berry juice

⅓ cup fresh lime juice

⅓ cup finely chopped red onion

1 teaspoon minced garlic

¼ cup olive oil

½ cup dried cherries

Salt and freshly ground pepper

SALAD

1 large bunch of watercress, large stems removed

3 scallions, cut into 1½-inch long julienne

Salt and freshly ground pepper

Pernot's Tamales Cubano with Sun-Dried Cherry Mojo

I. MAKE THE PORK TAMALES: In a medium saucepan, cover the pork with the water and stock. Add the onion, carrot, celery, bay leaf, ½ teaspoon of salt and the peppercorns and bring to a simmer. Reduce the heat to low, cover and simmer, skimming occasionally, until the meat is very tender when pierced with a knife, about 2¼ hours. Transfer the meat to a plate. Let cool completely and then coarsely shred with 2 forks. Strain the stock and refrigerate until chilled; discard the vegetables, bay leaf and peppercorns. Discard the fat from the stock and then boil the stock over high heat until reduced to 1½ cups.

2. In a large saucepan, bring the stock and milk to a simmer. Whisk in the cornmeal, masa harina, lard, crushed red pepper and 1 teaspoon of salt. Stir over moderately low heat until thick and smooth, about 5 minutes. Remove from the heat. Stir in the pork and culentro; let cool. Shape the mixture into 8 ovals. Wrap each in a rectangle of aluminum foil, twisting the ends securely.

3. MAKE THE CHERRY MOJO: In a medium saucepan, combine the orange, cherry and lime juices with the onion. Bring to a boil over moderate heat and cook until reduced to ¾ cup, about 12 minutes. In a small skillet, cook the garlic in the oil over moderate heat until very lightly browned, about 3 minutes. Whisk the garlic oil into the reduced juices, add the dried cherries and season with salt and pepper. Let cool, and then refrigerate until chilled, about 1 hour.

4. Spread the tamales in a single layer in a steamer. Cover and steam over several inches of boiling water until the cornmeal is no longer gritty, about 30 minutes. Add more boiling water to the steamer halfway through cooking.

5. MAKE THE SALAD: In a bowl, toss the watercress, scallions and ½ cup of the cherry mojo and season with salt and pepper. Mound the salad on 4 plates. Unwrap the tamales; arrange 2 on each plate next to the salad. Spoon the remaining mojo onto the plates and serve. —*Guillermo Pernot*

NOTE Culentro, a jagged-leaf herb from Central America, is similar in flavor to cilantro, but stronger. It is available at Latin American markets.

MAKE AHEAD The tamales and the cherry mojo can be prepared through Step 3 and refrigerated overnight.

WINE A Sauvignon Blanc has enough acid to match the tart cherry mojo

Stuffed Grape Leaves

Stuffed Grape Leaves

8 SERVINGS

Lots of tart lemon juice and vibrant fresh herbs in the braising liquid for the veal and rice filling make for a satisfying mouthful. The stuffed grape leaves could also be cut in half and served on a platter with a bowl of yogurt for an excellent hors d'oeuvre.

- 1 stick (4 ounces) unsalted butter
- 2 large red onions, minced
- 1½ pounds ground veal
- 1 cup medium-grain rice, such as Valencia
- ¼ cup chopped dill
- ¼ cup chopped flat-leaf parsley
- ½ teaspoon salt
- ¼ teaspoon freshly ground pepper
- One 16-ounce jar brined grape leaves, rinsed
- 2 cups water
- ½ cup fresh lemon juice
- Cilantro sprigs, for garnish
- Plain yogurt, for serving

1. In a large skillet, melt 4 tablespoons of the butter over moderately low heat. Add the onions and cook, stirring occasionally, until they are softened but not browned, about 8 minutes. Scrape the onions into a large bowl and let them cool to room temperature. Add the veal, raw rice, dill, parsley, salt and pepper and stir with a fork until thoroughly combined.

2. Spread all of the grape leaves, vein side up, on a work surface. Piece together the smaller leaves, overlapping the edges, to approximate the size of the larger leaves. Set 2 tablespoons of the veal mixture in the center of each leaf. Pull one side of the leaf up and over the filling and roll up, folding in the ends as you go.

3. Put the remaining 4 tablespoons of butter, the water and lemon juice in a large saucepan over moderately high heat. As soon as the butter melts, remove the pan from the heat.

4. Snugly arrange the rolls in the pan in a spokelike pattern in 2 layers. Set a heatproof plate on the rolls to keep them submerged. Cover and cook over moderately high heat for 20 minutes and then simmer over low heat until all of the liquid has been absorbed, about 10 minutes.

5. Serve the grape leaves hot or warm, garnished with coriander sprigs. Pass the yogurt separately. —*Fany Boutari*

MAKE AHEAD The Stuffed Grape Leaves can be refrigerated for 1 day before serving.

CHAPTER 3 salads

Beet Salad with Endives and Walnuts (p. 73)

Endive-Watercress Salad with Candied Walnuts

Endive-Watercress Salad with Candied Walnuts

8 SERVINGS

1½ cups walnut halves (about
    5 ounces)
½ tablespoon water
2 tablespoons light brown sugar
Kosher salt
3 tablespoons red wine vinegar
¼ teaspoon freshly ground
    pepper
3 tablespoons extra-virgin
    olive oil
2 tablespoons walnut oil
4 large Belgian endives—halved
    lengthwise, cored and cut into
    thirds crosswise
3 bunches of watercress, large
    stems trimmed

I. Preheat the oven to 350°. Toast the walnuts for about 8 minutes, or until lightly browned. Gently rub off any large pieces of skin and transfer the nuts to a bowl. Add the water and toss to moisten the nuts and then add the brown sugar and a large pinch of kosher salt and toss to coat.

2. Spread the sugar-coated walnuts on a baking sheet lined with parchment paper. Bake for about 10 minutes, stirring a few times, until the walnuts are browned and crisp. Transfer the candied walnuts to a plate to cool.

3. In a small glass or stainless-steel bowl, whisk the vinegar with ½ teaspoon of kosher salt and the pepper. Stir in the olive oil and walnut oil. In a large bowl, combine the endives and watercress. Just before serving, toss the salad with the dressing and scatter the candied walnuts over the top.

—Joseph and Thomas Keller

WINE The core of golden fruit in the 1995 Pahlmeyer Chardonnay, coupled with its smokiness, will marry well with the nutty dressing and candied walnut garnish. An alternative: the 1996 Araujo Eisele Vineyard Sauvignon Blanc; its ripe concentrated fruit will be a perfect balance for the slight bitterness of the endive.

Grilled Endives with Tarragon Oil

8 SERVINGS

Pepato, a semidry sheep's-milk cheese studded with black peppercorns, lends salt and spice to the pleasant bitterness of the grilled endives. If you can't find it, substitute shavings of Pecorino Romano or ricotta salata.

1 cup tarragon leaves
¾ cup plus 3 tablespoons
    extra-virgin olive oil
Salt
3 tablespoons red wine vinegar
Freshly ground pepper
8 large Belgian endives (about
    2 pounds), halved lengthwise
One 4-ounce piece of Pepato cheese

I. Bring a small saucepan of water to a boil. Plunge the tarragon into the water and cook just until wilted but still bright green. Drain the tarragon and refresh under cold water. Pat the tarragon dry with paper towels and transfer to a blender or food processor. Add ¾ cup of the oil and a pinch of salt and blend until smooth.

2. Meanwhile, light a grill or heat a grill pan. Combine the remaining 3 tablespoons of oil with the vinegar and add a generous pinch each of salt and pepper. Brush the endives with the oil and vinegar mixture. Grill over a medium-low fire for about 12 minutes, turning, until softened and slightly charred. Arrange the endives on a serving platter.

3. Pour the tarragon oil over the endives. Using a vegetable peeler, shave the Pepato over the endives. Serve the salad warm or at room temperature.

—Mario Batali

MAKE AHEAD The grilled endives and tarragon oil can stand separately at room temperature for up to 3 hours.

Beet Salad with Endives and Walnuts

4 SERVINGS

To save time, roast the beets for both the salad and the dressing (below) together. The recipe is from *The French Culinary Institute's Salute to Healthy Cooking* (Rodale).

2 large beets, washed and
    patted dry
1 ounce Roquefort cheese,
    crumbled
1 tablespoon chopped flat-leaf
    parsley
1 teaspoon minced thyme
½ garlic clove, minced
3 Belgian endives, cut crosswise
    into 2-inch pieces
8 walnut halves, lightly toasted
    and coarsely chopped
Beet Vinaigrette (recipe follows)

I. Preheat the oven to 450°. Wrap the beets in a large sheet of aluminum foil. Set the packet on a baking sheet and roast for 1 hour, or until the beets are just tender when pierced. Unwrap the beets, let cool and then peel. Cut the beets into 2-inch-long matchsticks.

2. In a small bowl, toss the Roquefort with the parsley, thyme and garlic. Arrange the endives on plates. Scatter the beets, Roquefort mixture and nuts on top. Spoon the vinaigrette over the salads; serve at once.

MAKE AHEAD The beets can be roasted up to 4 days ahead.

ONE SERVING Calories 177 kcal, Total Fat 8 gm, Saturated Fat 2 gm

BEET VINAIGRETTE

MAKES ¾ CUP

1 medium beet, washed and
    patted dry
½ cup defatted chicken stock or
    canned low-sodium broth
1 teaspoon olive oil
1 teaspoon red wine vinegar
Salt and freshly ground pepper

Beet Salad with Endives and Walnuts

1. Preheat the oven to 450°. Wrap the beet in a large sheet of aluminum foil. Set the packet on a baking sheet and roast for 45 minutes, or until the beet is just tender when pierced. Unwrap the beet and let cool.

2. Peel and chop the beet. In a blender, combine the beet with the stock, oil and vinegar; blend until completely smooth. Season with salt and pepper.

—*Jacques Pépin, Alain Sailhac, André Soltner and Jacques Torres*

MAKE AHEAD The vinaigrette can be refrigerated for up to 3 days.

ONE-QUARTER CUP Calories 22 kcal, Total Fat 1 gm, Saturated Fat .2 gm

Roasted Beet Salad with Orange Dressing

4 SERVINGS

- 3 medium beets, preferably a mix of red and golden beets
- ¼ cup fresh orange juice
- 1½ teaspoons finely grated orange zest
- 1½ teaspoons honey
- 1½ teaspoons balsamic vinegar
- 1 teaspoon Dijon mustard
- ½ teaspoon extra-virgin olive oil
- Salt and freshly ground pepper
- 4 cups mixed salad greens, such as arugula, mâche and radicchio
- ½ cup thinly sliced red onion

1. Preheat the oven to 350°. Wrap the beets in foil and roast for about 1¼ hours, or until tender. Let cool and then peel the beets. Cut into ¼-inch dice.

2. In a glass or stainless-steel bowl, whisk together the orange juice, zest, honey, vinegar, mustard and oil; season with salt and pepper. Add the beets. Toss to coat. Top the greens with the beets and onion.

—*Betsy Nelson and Jim Kyndberg*

MAKE AHEAD The roasted beets can be refrigerated for up to 2 days.

ONE SERVING Calories 64 kcal, Total Fat .8 gm, Saturated Fat .1 gm

Heartbeet Salad

Heartbeet Salad

6 SERVINGS

- 2½ pounds medium beets, trimmed
- 3 tablespoons extra-virgin olive oil
- 1 tablespoon fresh lemon juice
- ¼ teaspoon salt
- ¼ teaspoon freshly ground pepper
- 1 bunch of arugula (4 ounces), large stems discarded
- 1 head of frisée (4 ounces), cored
- 1 tablespoon snipped chives

1. Preheat the oven to 375°. Wrap the beets in a large piece of aluminum foil and bake for 1 to 1½ hours, or until tender. Let cool slightly and then peel and slice ¼ inch thick. Using a 1-inch heart-shaped cookie cutter, cut out as many hearts as possible from each slice.

2. In a large glass or stainless-steel bowl, whisk the oil with the lemon juice, salt and pepper. Add the arugula, frisée and heart-shaped beet cut-outs and toss. Mound the salad on plates. Sprinkle the salads with the chives and serve. —*Alice Harper*

MAKE AHEAD The beet hearts can be refrigerated for up to 1 day.

Frisée Salad with Warm Bacon Vinaigrette

2 SERVINGS

- 2 tablespoons extra-virgin olive oil
- 1½ tablespoons red wine vinegar
- Salt and freshly ground pepper
- 2 thick-cut bacon slices, cut crosswise into ½-inch strips

1 small shallot, finely chopped

4 ounces frisée, torn into small
pieces

I. In a glass or stainless-steel bowl, whisk together the oil, vinegar and a pinch each of salt and pepper.

2. In a skillet, cook the bacon over moderately high heat until browned and crisp, about 5 minutes. Add the shallot and cook, stirring, until softened, 1 to 2 minutes. Pour off all but 1 tablespoon of the fat from the skillet and stir in the vinaigrette, scraping up any brown bits from the bottom of the pan. Pour the hot dressing into a large bowl, add the frisée and toss well. Serve immediately. —*Jan Newberry*

BELOW: **Zuni Caesar Salad.** BOTTOM: **Greek Salad.**

Herbed Fresh Cheese with Frisée

6 SERVINGS

This fresh cheese enlivened with minced shallots, fresh herbs and vinegar is typically served in *bouchons,* or bistros, throughout the Lyonnais.

HERBED CHEESE

¾ pound fromage blanc (1½ cups), or 11 ounces soft goat cheese mixed with 2 tablespoons milk

1 tablespoon finely chopped chives

1 tablespoon finely chopped flat-leaf parsley

1 teaspoon finely chopped tarragon

1½ teaspoons minced shallots

1 tablespoon extra-virgin olive oil

1½ teaspoons red wine vinegar

Salt and freshly ground pepper

SALAD

1 pound frisée (3 heads)

2 tablespoons extra-virgin olive oil

2 teaspoons red wine vinegar

Salt and freshly ground white pepper

I. MAKE THE HERBED CHEESE: Combine the cheese, chives, parsley, tarragon, shallots, oil and vinegar in a medium glass or stainless-steel bowl. Mix with a wooden spoon until thoroughly blended. Season with salt and pepper.

2. MAKE THE SALAD: In a large serving bowl, toss the frisée with the oil and vinegar and season with salt and white pepper. Make a well in the center of the frisée salad, spoon in the herbed cheese and serve. —*Daniel Boulud*

MAKE AHEAD The herbed cheese can be refrigerated for up to 8 hours.

SERVE WITH Garlic-rubbed sourdough toast.

Zuni Caesar Salad

6 SERVINGS

Judy Rodgers of Zuni in San Francisco offers two pieces of advice on composing this salad: use the best ingredients you can find and taste each element every step of the way.

4 ounces country-style bread, cut into ¾-inch dice (4 cups)

⅓ cup plus ¼ cup mild olive oil

Sea salt

½ tablespoon red wine vinegar

1 salt-packed anchovy—rinsed, filleted and finely chopped

2 small garlic cloves, minced

3 tablespoons fresh lemon juice

2 very fresh large eggs (see Note)

¼ cup plus 2 tablespoons freshly grated Parmigiano-Reggiano cheese

Freshly ground pepper

1½ pounds romaine lettuce hearts, cored, leaves separated

1. Preheat the oven to 400°. In a pie pan, toss the bread cubes with ¼ cup of the oil and season with sea salt. Toast the bread in the oven for about 6 minutes, or until golden brown. Let cool to room temperature.

2. In a large glass or stainless-steel bowl, combine the vinegar with the anchovy, garlic and lemon juice; stir in the remaining ⅓ cup of oil. Beat in the eggs and 1 tablespoon of the cheese and season with sea salt and pepper. Add the lettuce and toss well. Sprinkle the croutons and the remaining 5 tablespoons of cheese over the salad and serve at once. — *Judy Rodgers*

NOTE If you prefer to avoid raw eggs, add an additional tablespoon of oil in their place.

WINE Something dry and fun to drink will work best here—like a fresh white wine, such as the 1996 Kris Pinot Grigio, or a crisp rosé with stony fruit, such as the 1997 Domaine de Fontsainte Gris de Gris.

Greek Salad

12 SERVINGS

½ cup extra-virgin olive oil

3 tablespoons red wine vinegar

3 tablespoons lemon juice

2 tablespoons chopped oregano

1 tablespoon chopped mint

Salt and freshly ground pepper

4 romaine hearts, torn

6 medium tomatoes, cored and cut into wedges

6 kirby cucumbers, peeled and sliced ½ inch thick

½ pound feta cheese, crumbled (about 1½ cups)

1 cup Gaeta olives, pitted (6 ounces)

In a small glass or stainless-steel bowl, whisk together the oil, vinegar, lemon juice, oregano and mint. Season with salt and pepper. In a large salad bowl, combine the romaine, tomatoes, cucumbers, cheese and olives. Toss the salad with the dressing and serve at once. — *Grace Parisi*

Greek Easter Salad

8 SERVINGS

Eggs, the symbol of renewal, make this salad especially appropriate for Easter.

1 large head Romaine lettuce, torn into bite-size pieces

1 cucumber, peeled and thinly sliced

8 radishes, thinly sliced

2 scallions, thinly sliced

¼ cup plus 2 tablespoons extra-virgin olive oil

¼ cup red wine vinegar

Salt and freshly ground pepper

4 hard-cooked eggs, halved

Dill sprigs, for garnish

In a large salad bowl, combine the lettuce, cucumber, radishes and scallions. In a small glass or stainless-steel bowl, whisk the oil with the vinegar; season with salt and pepper. Add the dressing to the salad and toss well. Top with the eggs, garnish with dill and serve immediately. — *Fany Boutari*

Spinach Salad with Prosciutto, Portobellos and Cheese Fondue

8 SERVINGS

4 large Portobello mushrooms (about 1 pound), stemmed

¾ cup plus 3 tablespoons extra-virgin olive oil

Salt and freshly ground black pepper

2 red or yellow bell peppers

¼ cup sherry vinegar

4 garlic cloves, crushed

2 thyme sprigs

1 basil sprig

½ cup dry white wine

¾ cup heavy cream

1½ cups shredded Italian Fontina cheese (5 ounces), plus 4 ounces thinly sliced

8 cups lightly packed baby spinach

8 thin slices of prosciutto (4 ounces)

1. Light a grill or heat a grill pan. Coat the mushroom caps with 3 tablespoons of the oil and season with salt and black pepper. Grill the mushrooms until deeply browned and crisp, about 5 minutes per side. Transfer to a large shallow dish to cool. Cut the caps in half and then thinly slice them crosswise; return the mushrooms to the dish.

2. Grill the bell peppers until charred all over. Transfer them to a bowl, cover with plastic wrap and let steam for 5 minutes. Remove the charred skins, seeds and stems. Cut the peppers into ½-inch strips, removing the ribs, and add to the mushrooms.

3. In a glass or stainless-steel bowl, combine the remaining ¾ cup of oil with the vinegar, 3 of the garlic cloves, the thyme, basil and 2 teaspoons of black pepper. Pour all but ¼ cup of the marinade over the mushrooms and bell peppers and season lightly with salt and black pepper. Let marinate at room temperature for 1 to 3 hours. Drain before using.

4. In a small saucepan, boil the wine with the remaining 1 garlic clove until reduced to 2 tablespoons, about 7 minutes. Add the cream; bring to a boil. Remove the pan from the heat; stir in the shredded cheese. Whisk over moderate heat until the fondue is smooth. Season with salt and black pepper.

5. In a large glass or stainless-steel bowl, toss the spinach with the reserved ¼ cup of marinade and mound on plates. Arrange the mushrooms,

Spring Salad with Baby Carrots

roasted peppers and prosciutto along-side and top with the sliced Fontina. Briefly reheat the fondue, whisking constantly until smooth. Drizzle the spinach with the fondue and serve the salad at once. —*Tony Najiola*

Spring Salad with Baby Carrots

4 SERVINGS

Baby carrots and radishes combined with greens make a beautiful salad. Don't use the carrots that come already peeled in plastic bags; they have no flavor.

- ¼ cup extra-virgin olive oil
- 2 tablespoons red wine vinegar
- 1 medium shallot, thinly sliced
- ¾ teaspoon salt
- 12 baby carrots, peeled
- 4 small radishes

- 8 cups salad greens, such as arugula, dandelion, red oak leaf lettuce and frisée, torn into bite-size pieces
- 12 chives, cut into 1-inch lengths

1. In a large glass or stainless-steel bowl, combine the oil, vinegar, shallot and salt.

2. In a small saucepan of boiling salted water, blanch the baby carrots for 2 minutes. Refresh the carrots in cold water and pat dry. Transfer the carrots to a small glass or stainless-steel bowl, add the radishes and toss with 2 table-spoons of the vinaigrette.

3. Add the salad greens and chives to the large bowl and toss with the remaining vinaigrette. Garnish the salad with the baby carrots and radishes and serve. —*Alice Waters*

Arugula Salad

6 SERVINGS

If an all-arugula salad is too spicy for you, use half arugula and half spinach.

- 3 tablespoons extra-virgin olive oil
- 1 tablespoon white wine vinegar

Salt and freshly ground pepper

Four 6-ounce bunches of arugula

In a large salad bowl, whisk together the oil and vinegar; season with salt and pepper. Add the greens and toss to coat. Serve immediately. —*Ed Giobbi*

Mixed Greens with Papaya

2 SERVINGS

This light and refreshing salad, with its oil-free citrus dressing, would also be delicious with grilled chicken, shrimp or pork tenderloin.

- ¼ cup fresh orange juice
- 1 teaspoon Dijon mustard
- 1 teaspoon balsamic vinegar

Salt

Cayenne pepper

Chili powder

- ½ ripe papaya—peeled, seeded and thinly sliced
- 4 loosely packed cups arugula and frisée, torn into bite-size pieces

In a medium glass or stainless-steel bowl, whisk together the orange juice, mustard, vinegar and a pinch each of salt, cayenne and chili powder. Add the papaya and let stand for 10 minutes. Add the greens to the bowl, toss lightly and serve. —*Janie Master*

Arugula, Mushroom and Walnut Salad

8 SERVINGS

The dressing here won't clash with wine because it *is* wine, not vinegar or lemon juice, along with oil.

- 1 cup walnut pieces (4 ounces)
- ¼ cup extra-virgin olive oil
- 3 tablespoons full-bodied red wine
- ¾ teaspoon kosher salt
- ¼ teaspoon freshly ground pepper

16 cups packed arugula leaves
(¾ pound)

½ pound white or cremini
mushrooms, stems trimmed,
thinly sliced

1. Preheat the oven to 400°. In a pie plate, toast the nuts for about 6 minutes, or until golden brown. Let cool.

2. In a small glass or stainless-steel bowl, whisk the oil with the wine. Add the kosher salt and pepper. In a large glass or stainless-steel bowl, combine the arugula, mushrooms and walnuts. Add the dressing; toss to coat. Serve on salad plates. *—Umberto Creatini*

Arugula and Chanterelle Salad with Vacherin Croutons

6 SERVINGS

Vacherin, a rich but runny cheese, is available from fall through early spring. If you can't find Vacherin, Edel de Cléron, Brie or Camembert can be used in its place.

VINAIGRETTE

1 tablespoon red wine vinegar

1 tablespoon raspberry vinegar

1 teaspoon minced shallot

¼ teaspoon sugar

3 tablespoons canola oil

1 tablespoon hazelnut oil

1 teaspoon thyme leaves

1 teaspoon minced chives

½ teaspoon kosher salt

¼ teaspoon freshly ground pepper

SALAD

6 baguette slices cut on the
diagonal about ⅓ inch thick

1½ tablespoons olive oil

¼ cup hazelnuts

1 pound haricots verts

1 tablespoon unsalted butter

1 pound small chanterelle
mushrooms, stems trimmed

Salt and freshly ground pepper

1 tablespoon minced shallots

1 small garlic clove, minced

½ tablespoon chopped parsley

Arugula, Mushroom and Walnut Salad

½ tablespoon thyme leaves

6 ounces Vacherin cheese without
the rind

6 cups (packed) arugula leaves

1. MAKE THE VINAIGRETTE: In a glass or stainless-steel bowl, whisk the vinegars with the shallot and sugar; whisk in the remaining ingredients.

2. MAKE THE SALAD: Preheat the oven to 350°. Brush the baguette slices with the olive oil and arrange on a baking sheet. Bake the croutons for about 10 minutes, or until lightly toasted.

3. In a pie pan, toast the hazelnuts in the oven until browned, about 10 minutes. Transfer the nuts to a kitchen towel and rub well to remove the skins. Coarsely chop the nuts.

4. In a saucepan of boiling salted water, cook the haricots verts until they are

just tender, about 3 minutes. Drain and then rinse under cold running water until cool; pat dry.

5. In a large skillet, melt the butter over moderately high heat. Add the chanterelles and reduce the heat to moderately low. Cook the mushrooms slowly, allowing any exuded juices to evaporate, about 4 minutes. Increase the heat to high, season the mushrooms with salt and pepper and cook until lightly browned, about 3 minutes. Add the shallots, garlic, parsley and thyme leaves and cook, stirring, until fragrant, about 1 minute.

6. Spread the Vacherin on the croutons. In a large glass or stainless-steel bowl, toss the arugula and haricots verts with the vinaigrette. Mound the salad on plates. Spoon the mushrooms

Arugula and Chanterelle Salad with Vacherin Croutons

on top and garnish with the hazelnuts. Set a crouton beside each salad, sprinkle with pepper and serve.

—Eleven Madison Park, New York City

MAKE AHEAD The salad can be prepared through Step 4 early in the day. Reheat the croutons before proceeding with the recipe.

WINE The dynamic 1995 Albert Boxler Grand Cru Riesling Sommerberg is able to bridge the gap between the earthy chanterelles and the creamy Vacherin.

Warm Escarole and Radicchio Slaw with Sunflower Seeds

4 SERVINGS

This dish showcases four members of the Compositae family: radicchio, escarole, tarragon and sunflowers. Escarole tends to be sandy, so wash it well.

- 1 medium head of radicchio (about ½ pound), cored and cut crosswise into ¼-inch ribbons
- 1 small head of escarole (about ½ pound), cored and cut crosswise into ¼-inch ribbons
- ¼ cup salted sunflower seeds
- 2 tablespoons chopped tarragon
- 3 tablespoons peanut oil
- ¼ cup coarsely chopped pancetta (2 ounces)
- 1 Granny Smith apple—peeled, cored and cut into 2-by-¼-inch matchsticks
- 1 large shallot, thinly sliced
- 3 tablespoons sherry vinegar

Salt and freshly ground pepper

1. In a large glass or stainless-steel bowl, toss the radicchio, escarole, sunflower seeds and tarragon.

2. In a medium skillet, heat the oil. Add the pancetta and cook over moderately high heat, stirring occasionally, until browned, about 3 minutes. Using a slotted spoon, transfer the pancetta to a plate. Add the apple and shallot to the skillet. Cook over high heat, stirring, until softened and lightly browned, 2

Warm Escarole and Radicchio Slaw with Sunflower Seeds

to 3 minutes. Add the vinegar and boil. Pour the hot dressing over the greens, add the pancetta and toss well. Season the slaw with salt and pepper and serve immediately. *—Grace Parisi*

Salad of Smoked Trout, Pink Grapefruit and Radicchio with Walnuts

6 SERVINGS ★★★
1995

This elegant first-course salad, from Daniel Boulud of Restaurant Daniel in New York City, offers a symphony of tastes and textures.

- 1 cup cubed (½ inch) firm-textured white bread
- 1 garlic clove, minced
- 1 tablespoon olive oil or walnut oil
- 1 large pink grapefruit
- ⅓ cup heavy cream
- 2 tablespoons sherry vinegar

Salt and freshly ground pepper

- ¾ pound radicchio, 12 large outer leaves reserved, the rest cut into ¼-inch strips

Two smoked trout fillets, skinned and cut into ½-inch dice

- ½ cup coarsely chopped walnuts

Salad of Smoked Trout, Pink Grapefruit and Radicchio with Walnuts

salad with the croutons, cilantro leaves and whole grapefruit sections. Drizzle the salad with the remaining dressing and serve.　　　—Daniel Boulud

Asparagus Salad with Roasted Bell Peppers

8 SERVINGS

Best-quality olive oil and balsamic vinegar are essential to make this simple salad vibrant; they combine with the sweet pepper juices to make a fruity dressing. Be sure to serve the dish warm.

- 2　medium red bell peppers, halved lengthwise
- 2　medium yellow bell peppers, halved lengthwise
- ¼　cup extra-virgin olive oil, plus more for brushing
- 2　garlic cloves, minced

Salt and freshly ground black pepper

- 1½　pounds asparagus, trimmed and cut into 3-inch lengths
- 1　tablespoon balsamic vinegar

1. Preheat the oven to 400°. Brush the bell pepper skins lightly with oil and set them, cut side down, on a baking sheet. Bake the bell peppers for about 15 minutes, or until the skins are blistered. Remove the skins and seeds and cut the roasted peppers into long thin strips. In a bowl, combine the roasted peppers with the ¼ cup of oil and the garlic and season with salt and black pepper.

2. In a large pot of boiling salted water, cook the asparagus until just tender, about 4 minutes. Drain the asparagus, refresh under cold running water and then pat the asparagus dry with paper towels.

3. Preheat the oven to 450°. Spread half of the roasted peppers in a baking dish. Arrange the asparagus over the roasted peppers and season with salt and black pepper. Top with the remaining roasted peppers and spoon

- 2　teaspoons chopped cilantro, plus additional leaves for garnish
- 3　small scallions, white part only, thinly sliced

1. Preheat the oven to 350°. On a baking sheet, toss the bread cubes with the garlic and oil. Toast for about 7 minutes, or until golden.

2. Using a sharp stainless steel knife, peel the grapefruit, removing all the bitter white pith. Working over a glass or stainless-steel bowl, cut in between the membranes to release the sections. Set aside 6 sections; cut the

remaining sections into ½-inch pieces.

3. In a small glass or stainless-steel bowl, combine the cream and vinegar and season with salt and pepper. In a large glass or stainless-steel bowl, toss the radicchio strips with three-quarters of the dressing. Add the smoked trout, walnuts, chopped cilantro, scallions and cut-up grapefruit sections. Season with salt and pepper and toss gently but thoroughly.

4. Arrange 2 radicchio leaves on each of 6 plates and mound the salad in the center of the leaves. Garnish the

Green Bean Salad with Seared Ham

the dressing on top. Bake for about 15 minutes, or until bubbling. Drizzle with the balsamic vinegar and serve warm.

—*Joseph and Thomas Keller*

MAKE AHEAD The salad can be prepared through Step 2 and refrigerated overnight; store the roasted peppers and the asparagus separately. Bring both to room temperature before proceeding.

Green Bean Salad with Seared Ham

4 FIRST-COURSE SERVINGS ✳

- 1 pound haricots verts or young green beans
- 4 ounces thickly sliced cured ham, such as Bayonne ham or prosciutto, cut into thin strips
- 2 tablespoons sherry vinegar
- ⅛ teaspoon kosher salt
- ⅛ teaspoon freshly ground white pepper
- 3 tablespoons extra-virgin olive oil
- 2 tablespoons snipped chives
- 1 tablespoon finely chopped shallot
- 1 tablespoon small basil leaves
- 1 cup firm sheep's-milk cheese shavings, such as P'tit Basque, or Gruyère (about 2½ ounces)

Green Bean and Fennel Salad with Shaved Parmesan

1. In a pot of boiling salted water, cook the beans until tender, about 8 minutes. Drain the beans and rinse in cold running water. Spread the beans on paper towels to dry.

2. Heat a large nonstick skillet. Add the ham and cook over high heat just until slightly crisp, about 1 minute. Transfer the ham to paper towels to drain.

3. In a large glass or stainless-steel bowl, combine the vinegar, kosher salt and white pepper. Whisk in the oil. Add the chives, shallot and basil and mix well. Add the beans, ham and cheese shavings to the bowl; toss gently. Serve the salad at once. —*Gerald Hirigoyen*

Green Bean and Fennel Salad with Shaved Parmesan

4 SERVINGS

Look for green beans that are tender and fresh. In the German tradition, a pinch of sugar can be added to the vinaigrette to make it a little less harsh; judge for yourself. If you happen to own a mandoline, use it to slice the fennel thinly and evenly. If you don't, be sure to use a sharp knife.

- 1 pound green beans
- ¼ cup extra-virgin olive oil
- 2 tablespoons fresh lemon juice
- Salt and freshly ground pepper
- 2 small fennel bulbs (about 1 pound)
- ⅔ cup shaved Parmesan cheese (about 3 ounces)

1. Cook the beans in a large saucepan of boiling salted water until nearly tender, about 6 minutes. Drain them in a colander and refresh under cold running water. Drain well.

2. In a medium glass or stainless-steel bowl, combine the oil and lemon juice; season with salt and pepper. Thinly slice the fennel lengthwise, add it to the bowl and toss. Transfer the fennel to a platter or individual plates with a slotted spoon. Add the green beans to the bowl. Toss the beans with the remaining dressing and then transfer the beans to the platter or plates. Add a pile of Parmesan shavings and serve. —*Eberhard Müller*

Fennel and Goat Cheese Salad

4 SERVINGS

What I admire in this chastely white-on-white salad from the restaurant Al Cacciatore, in Friuli, Italy, is the refreshing juxtaposition of the flavors and textures of its two components.

- 1 large fennel bulb (1½ pounds), trimmed and very thinly sliced crosswise
- Salt
- 4 ounces fresh creamy goat cheese, cut into ¼-inch slices
- Coarsely ground pepper
- 3 tablespoons extra-virgin olive oil

Soak the fennel in cold water for 10 minutes and then drain and pat thoroughly dry. Spread the fennel on a platter and sprinkle lightly with salt. Arrange the goat cheese on top, sprinkle the salad with pepper, drizzle with the oil and serve. —*Marcella Hazan*

WINE The herby, bracing acidity of Sauvignon Blanc is a classic foil for tangy goat cheese. Look for Italian examples (especially those from Friuli), notably the 1996 Jermann or the 1995 Schiopetto.

Prosciutto and Fennel Salad with Persimmon Vinaigrette

8 SERVINGS

Sweet juicy pears complement the crisp fennel and salty prosciutto in this perfumed salad. Select a persimmon that is pudding-soft for the dressing.

- ½ pound thinly sliced prosciutto, trimmed of visible fat
- 1 very ripe persimmon—peeled, seeded and coarsely chopped, with its juice
- 1 small shallot, minced
- 3 tablespoons white wine vinegar
- ¼ cup plus 3 tablespoons olive oil
- Salt and freshly ground pepper
- 2 ripe Anjou pears—peeled, cored and thinly sliced
- 1 large fennel bulb, cored and thinly sliced
- ½ pound frisée, torn into pieces

Arrange the prosciutto around the edge of a platter. In a large glass or stainless-steel bowl, combine the persimmon, shallot and vinegar. Whisk in ¼ cup plus 2 tablespoons of the oil and then season the dressing with salt and pepper. Add the pears, fennel and frisée to the dressing and toss well. Mound the salad in the middle of the platter. Drizzle the prosciutto with the remaining 1 tablespoon of oil, sprinkle with pepper and serve. —*Melissa Kelly*

Avocado and Radish Salad

12 SERVINGS

Serve this refreshing salad with Tortilla Pie (p. 190).

- ½ cup fresh lemon juice
- ½ cup olive oil
- Salt and freshly ground pepper
- 6 firm ripe Hass avocados—halved, peeled and sliced ⅓ inch thick
- 3 scallions, thinly sliced
- 6 bunches of white and red radishes (3 pounds), thinly sliced
- ¼ cup chopped cilantro

In a glass or stainless-steel bowl, whisk the lemon juice and oil. Season with salt and pepper. In another glass or stainless-steel bowl, combine the avocados and scallions with half of the dressing and toss. Arrange the avocados around a large platter or shallow bowl. Add the radishes to the remaining dressing and toss. Mound the radishes in the center of the avocados. Sprinkle the cilantro over the salad and serve. —*Marcia Kiesel*

BELOW: **Summertime Tomato and Leek Salad.**
BOTTOM: **Yellow Tomato, Watermelon and Arugula Salad.**

Yellow Tomato, Watermelon and Arugula Salad

8 SERVINGS

- 2 cups seeded and diced (½ inch) watermelon
- ¼ cup balsamic vinegar
- Salt and freshly ground pepper
- ½ cup extra-virgin olive oil
- 6 ounces arugula leaves, large stems removed (4 cups)
- 5 yellow tomatoes (about 2 pounds), sliced crosswise ¼ inch thick

1. In a medium glass or stainless-steel bowl, toss the watermelon cubes with 1 tablespoon of the vinegar; season with salt and pepper. Let the watermelon cubes stand for 5 minutes, then drain.

2. In a small glass or stainless-steel bowl, whisk the remaining 3 tablespoons of vinegar with the oil. In another glass or stainless-steel bowl, gently toss the arugula with 3 tablespoons of the dressing. Fan the tomato slices on 8 plates and sprinkle with salt. Scatter the arugula over the tomato slices and top with the watermelon cubes. Drizzle the remaining dressing over the salads and serve them at once.   —*Brendan Walsh*

Custer's Tomato Salad with Grilled Greens and Stilton

6 SERVINGS 👑

Danielle Custer is the chef of Laurels restaurant in the Sheraton Park Central Hotel in Dallas. She recommends grilling greens in a clump; if you spread them too thinly, they burn.

- 3 tablespoons pine nuts
- 1½ pounds medium yellow tomatoes, thinly sliced
- 1½ pounds medium red tomatoes, thinly sliced
- 3 tablespoons Meyer lemon—flavored olive oil (see Note), or extra-virgin olive oil mixed with 2 teaspoons fresh lemon juice
- Salt and freshly ground pepper
- 1 cup purple basil sprigs, plus 1 tablespoon finely shredded leaves
- 1 cup green basil sprigs, plus 1 tablespoon finely shredded leaves
- 1 tablespoon finely chopped chives
- ¼ cup light olive oil
- 2 tablespoons fresh lemon juice
- 1 large bunch watercress (about 6 ounces), tough stems discarded
- 1 cup (packed) baby spinach leaves

1 cup (packed) tender arugula, tough stems discarded

½ cup crumbled Stilton cheese (2 ounces)

1. Preheat the oven to 350°. Spread the pine nuts in a pie plate and toast for about 8 minutes, or until golden.

2. Arrange the tomato slices in a ring, alternating yellow and red, on each of 6 large plates. Drizzle with the lemon-flavored olive oil and season with salt and pepper. Scatter the shredded basil and chopped chives on top.

3. Heat a large cast-iron skillet. In a glass or stainless-steel bowl, whisk the light olive oil with the lemon juice and a generous pinch each of salt and pepper. Add the basil sprigs and watercress and toss well. Add the dressed greens to the skillet; cook over moderately high heat, tossing frequently, until the greens are charred and lightly wilted, 1 to 2 minutes.

4. Return the greens to the bowl, add the spinach and arugula and toss until wilted. Add the Stilton and pine nuts, season with salt and pepper and toss. Mound the salad in the centers of the plates and serve. —*Danielle Custer*

NOTE Meyer lemon–flavored olive oil is available at specialty shops and by mail from O Olive Oil, 415-460-6598.

WINE A floral Sauvignon Blanc will balance the saltiness of the cheese.

Custer's Tomato Salad with Grilled Greens and Stilton

Summertime Tomato and Leek Salad

4 SERVINGS

This is a sharp dish, with several different levels of acidity and pungency. But if you begin with good tomatoes, it's also sweet.

8 thin leeks (about 2 pounds), white and tender green, split almost in half lengthwise and rinsed thoroughly

3 small tomatoes, cored and cut into wedges

¼ cup extra-virgin olive oil

¼ cup red wine vinegar

Salt and freshly ground pepper

Flat-leaf parsley sprigs or minced chives, for garnish

1. In a large skillet, cook the leeks in boiling salted water until tender, 10 to 12 minutes. Drain the leeks in a colander, refresh them under cold running water and drain on paper towels.

2. In a medium glass or stainless-steel bowl, combine the tomato wedges with the oil and vinegar and toss to coat. Season the tomatoes with salt and pepper and let them stand for 10 minutes. Transfer the leeks to a platter and spoon the tomatoes and vinaigrette over the leeks. Serve the salad garnished with parsley sprigs.

—*Eberhard Müller*

Jade Broccoli with Pecans

Cherry Tomato Salad

8 SERVINGS

Cherry tomatoes make an excellent summery salad even in the dead of winter when other tomatoes taste like cotton balls. If you can find them, add a few sweet little yellow pear tomatoes.

- 2 tablespoons balsamic vinegar
- 1 tablespoon red wine vinegar
- 1 large shallot, minced
- 1 teaspoon minced garlic
- ¼ cup plus 2 tablespoons extra-virgin olive oil

Salt and freshly ground pepper

- 3 pints cherry tomatoes, halved
- ⅓ cup finely shredded basil

In a large glass or stainless-steel bowl, whisk together the vinegars, the shallot and garlic. Whisk in the oil in a thin stream and season with salt and pepper. Add the tomatoes and basil to the dressing and toss. Season with salt and pepper and serve. *—Melissa Kelly*

Jade Broccoli with Pecans

4 SERVINGS ★★★ 1982

Shirley Sarvis was conducting food-and-wine-pairing seminars when she developed this unusual warm salad made with peeled broccoli stalks. Shred the broccoli stalks with the shredding blade of a food processor or on the large holes of a box shredder.

- 3½ tablespoons unsalted butter
- ⅓ cup chopped pecans
- 2½ cups peeled and shredded broccoli stalks (from 3 pounds broccoli)
- ½ teaspoon salt
- 4 very thin slices of prosciutto

1. In a small skillet, melt ½ tablespoon of the butter over low heat. Add the pecans and sauté until lightly browned, 2 to 3 minutes. Transfer the pecans to a plate to cool.

2. Steam the broccoli until just tender, about 3 minutes. Drain well and toss with the remaining 3 tablespoons of butter and the salt. Mound the broccoli on plates or in bowls and sprinkle the toasted pecans on top. Arrange a slice of prosciutto alongside the broccoli and serve. *—Shirley Sarvis*

WINE A Brut Champagne.

Island Salad with Shallot-Soy Vinaigrette

6 SERVINGS

This salad, inspired by the island of Mustique in the Caribbean, is based on a dish created by Eric Ripert, the executive chef at Le Bernardin in New York City.

- ¼ medium onion, coarsely chopped
- 3 tablespoons balsamic vinegar
- 1 large shallot, coarsely chopped
- 1½ tablespoons soy sauce
- 1 teaspoon finely grated fresh ginger
- 3 tablespoons grapeseed or other mild oil
- 1 tablespoon finely chopped cilantro

Salt and freshly ground black pepper

- ¼ pound haricots verts or thin green beans
- ½ pound mesclun
- ½ Hass avocado, thinly sliced
- ½ mango, peeled and thinly sliced
- 1 small red bell pepper, thinly sliced
- ½ medium cucumber, peeled and thinly sliced

1. In a blender, combine the onion with the vinegar, shallot, soy sauce and ginger and puree. Add the oil and blend

Island Salad with Shallot-Soy Vinaigrette

until smooth. Transfer to a small bowl, add the cilantro and season with salt and black pepper.

2. Cook the beans in boiling salted water until barely tender, 5 to 7 minutes. Drain and rinse under cold water.

3. In a large glass or stainless-steel bowl, toss the mesclun with the avocado, mango, red pepper, cucumber, beans and the dressing. Mound the salad on plates and serve.   —*Sylvia Fernandez*

Cabbage and Green Bean Salad

12 SERVINGS

1½ **pounds green beans, split lengthwise**

⅓ **cup white wine vinegar**

4 **small garlic cloves, minced**

3 **tablespoons light olive oil**

1 **tablespoon finely grated fresh ginger**

1 **tablespoon chopped thyme**

¾ **teaspoon salt**

¼ **teaspoon freshly ground pepper**

One 2½-pound head green cabbage, **finely shredded**

2 **medium tomatoes, cut into 1-inch dice**

1. In a large saucepan of boiling salted water, cook the beans until al dente, about 4 minutes. Drain and refresh under cold running water, then pat dry.

2. In a small glass or stainless-steel bowl, combine the vinegar, garlic, oil, ginger, thyme, salt and pepper. In a large glass or stainless-steel bowl, toss the cabbage with the tomatoes and beans. Add the dressing, toss to coat and serve.   —*Marcia Kiesel*

MAKE AHEAD The green beans can be cooked and refrigerated for 1 day.

Vietnamese Salad with Chile-Mint Dressing

4 SERVINGS ★★★ 1987

Associate Test Kitchen Director Marcia Kiesel's fascination with Vietnamese food led to the creation of this salad, which is composed in the Vietnamese style, with a little meat and a lot of vegetables. If you want to double the meat, cook it in two pans and double the dressing too.

½ **pound boneless pork shoulder, trimmed of excess fat and cut into ¼-inch strips**

2 **large garlic cloves, minced**

2 **tablespoons mushroom soy sauce**

1 **tablespoon peanut oil**

1 **medium onion, thinly sliced**

⅓ **cup water**

1½ **tablespoons cider vinegar**

1½ **tablespoons fresh lime juice**

1½ **tablespoons chopped mint, plus 1½ tablespoons shredded mint**

2 **teaspoons Asian fish sauce**

¼ **teaspoon sugar**

¼ **teaspoon salt**

¼ **teaspoon crushed red pepper**

2 **large white turnips, peeled and shredded**

2 **large carrots, shredded**

3 **cups finely shredded romaine lettuce**

3 **cups finely shredded cabbage**

⅓ **cup chopped unsalted peanuts**

1. Preheat the oven to 350°. In a medium bowl, toss the pork with half of the garlic and 1 tablespoon of the soy sauce. Set aside to marinate at room temperature for 1 hour.

Vietnamese Salad with Chile-Mint Dressing

2. In a medium ovenproof skillet, heat 2 teaspoons of the oil. Add the onion; cook over moderately high heat, stirring occasionally, until evenly browned, about 5 minutes. Transfer the skillet to the oven and cook, stirring occasionally, until the onion is dry and deep brown, about 25 minutes. Remove the onion from the skillet and set aside.

3. In a medium glass or stainless-steel bowl, whisk the water with the remaining garlic and the vinegar, lime juice, chopped mint, fish sauce, sugar, salt and red pepper. In a glass or stainless-steel bowl, toss the turnips and carrots with 6 tablespoons of the dressing.

4. In a large skillet, heat the remaining 1 teaspoon of peanut oil over high heat. Add the pork strips in an even layer and cook, without stirring, until browned on the bottom, about 2 minutes. Turn and cook until browned on the second side, about 2 minutes longer. Add the remaining 1 tablespoon of soy sauce to the skillet; stir to coat the meat. Transfer the meat to a plate and let cool.

5. In a salad bowl, toss the lettuce, cabbage, shredded mint and pork. Add the remaining dressing and any excess dressing from the turnips and carrots. Arrange the turnips and carrots on each of 4 plates and mound the pork salad in the center. Sprinkle the browned onion and chopped peanuts over all. —*Marcia Kiesel*

Grilled Shrimp Salad with Savoy Cabbage

8 SERVINGS

A mixture of crisp cabbage, tart apple, sweet fried shallots and grilled shrimp makes an exciting salad. Any leftover basil oil can be used to make vinaigrette for other salads, as an accent for grilled white-fleshed fish, in pastas or on pizza.

- 2 cups (packed) basil leaves, coarsely chopped
- ½ cup pure olive oil, plus more for brushing
- 1½ tablespoons fresh lemon juice
- Kosher salt and freshly ground pepper
- Peanut or canola oil, for frying
- 8 medium shallots, thinly sliced and separated into rings
- 24 large shrimp, shelled and deveined
- 1 large Cortland apple
- 6 cups (packed) baby tatsoi or arugula leaves (about 3 ounces)
- 4 cups (packed) finely shredded Savoy cabbage (about ½ head)

1. In a blender, puree the basil with the ½ cup of olive oil. Pour the basil puree into a small bowl and let stand at room temperature for about 20 minutes, or until the oil separates from the solids. Skim ¼ cup of the basil oil into a clean glass or stainless-steel bowl, leaving the solids behind. Stir in the lemon juice and season the dressing with ¾ teaspoon of kosher salt and ¼ teaspoon of pepper.

2. In a medium saucepan, heat ½ inch of peanut oil over moderate heat until shimmering. Add half of the shallots and stir well. Reduce the heat to moderately low and fry the shallots, stirring once or twice, until they are lightly browned and crisp, about 15 minutes. Remove the shallots to paper towels with a slotted spoon. Repeat with the remaining shallots.

3. Light a grill or heat a grill pan. Brush the shrimp with olive oil and season with kosher salt and pepper. Grill the shrimp for about 2 minutes per side, or until opaque throughout.

4. Cut the apple into matchsticks. In a salad bowl, toss the tatsoi, Savoy cabbage, apple matchsticks and shallots. Add the basil dressing and toss well. Arrange the salad on 8 plates, top each salad with 3 of the grilled shrimp and serve. —*Normand Laprise*

MAKE AHEAD The recipe can be prepared through Step 2 up to 2 days ahead. Refrigerate the basil dressing and store the fried shallots at room temperature.

WINE Serve a not-too-fruity Chardonnay from central California, such as Calera's Central Coast version.

Seven-Vegetable Slaw with Citrus Dressing

10 SERVINGS

DRESSING

- 1 cup fresh orange juice
- 1 cup rice wine vinegar
- 3 tablespoons sugar
- 2 tablespoons salt
- 1½ teaspoons freshly ground pepper

SLAW

- 1 small head of cabbage (about 1½ pounds), finely chopped
- 3 small zucchini (about ¾ pound total), halved lengthwise and seeded
- 2 medium yellow squash (about ½ pound total), halved lengthwise and seeded
- 4 medium carrots
- 1 jicama (about 1 pound)
- 1 medium red bell pepper
- 1 medium yellow bell pepper

1. MAKE THE DRESSING: In a medium glass or stainless-steel bowl, whisk all the ingredients together until the sugar is dissolved.

2. MAKE THE SLAW: Put the cabbage in a large salad bowl. Cut the remaining vegetables into fine julienne strips, add them to the bowl and toss. Add the dressing and toss again. Serve the salad at once with tongs.

—*Brendan Walsh*

MAKE AHEAD The dressing and the vegetables can be refrigerated separately for up to 1 day.

Cantaloupe, Mango and Asian Pear Slaw

Cantaloupe, Mango and Asian Pear Slaw

4 SERVINGS

- 1 tablespoon sugar
- 2 tablespoons fresh lime juice
- 1 tablespoon minced cilantro
- 1 tablespoon Asian fish sauce
- ½ tablespoon chile sauce, preferably Sriracha
- 1 garlic clove, minced
- 2 cups julienned cantaloupe
- 1 cup julienned carrot
- ½ cup julienned mango
- ½ cup julienned Asian pear

In a glass or stainless-steel bowl, dissolve the sugar in the lime juice. Stir in the cilantro, fish sauce, chile sauce and garlic. In another glass or stainless-steel bowl, combine the julienned cantaloupe, carrot, mango, and Asian pear. Add the dressing, toss and refrigerate until cold. —*Norman Van Aken*

SERVE WITH Grilled chicken, tuna, swordfish or salmon.

ONE SERVING Calories 89 kcal, Total Fat .8 gm, Saturated Fat .1 gm

Celery Root and Pear Remoulade with Walnuts

6 SERVINGS

Traditionally, remoulade sauce is made with raw egg yolks. If you'd prefer to avoid raw eggs, you can use three-quarters of a cup of prepared mayonnaise doctored with lemon juice and Dijon mustard in place of the homemade sauce base.

- 2 large egg yolks, at room temperature
- 1 tablespoon water
- 1½ teaspoons Dijon mustard
- Salt and freshly ground white pepper
- ¾ cup vegetable oil
- 6 tablespoons fresh lemon juice
- 1 large hard-cooked egg, finely chopped
- 1 tablespoon finely chopped cornichons or sour gherkins

FRONT: **Celery Root and Pear Remoulade with Walnuts.** BACK: **Marinated Mackerel and Yukon Gold Potato Salad (p. 166).**

- 1 tablespoon finely chopped capers
- 1 tablespoon finely chopped parsley
- 1½ teaspoons chopped tarragon
- 1 small garlic clove, minced
- ½ cup walnuts
- 1½ pounds celery root, peeled
- 3 firm Bosc pears, peeled
- ½ cup celery leaves from the heart

I. In a heavy glass or ceramic bowl, whisk the egg yolks with the water, mustard and a pinch each of salt and white pepper. Whisk in the oil in small drops until the sauce starts to thicken. Whisk in the remaining oil in a thin, steady stream; when all of the oil has been added, the sauce should be thick. Whisk in 1 tablespoon of the lemon juice. Fold in the egg, cornichons, capers, parsley, tarragon and garlic. Season with salt and white pepper and refrigerate.

2. Preheat the oven to 400°. In a cake pan, toast the walnuts for about 4 minutes, or until fragrant and deep brown.

3. Bring a medium saucepan of salted water to a boil. Shred the celery root on the largest holes of a box grater; toss

Potato Salad with Bacon

immediately with 1 tablespoon of the lemon juice. Add 3 tablespoons of the lemon juice to the saucepan. Add the celery root; blanch until crisp-tender, about 2 minutes. Drain and plunge into a bowl of ice water to stop the cooking. Drain again and pat thoroughly dry.

4. Grate the pears into a salad bowl; toss with the remaining 1 tablespoon of lemon juice. Add the celery root, remoulade and walnuts. Toss well. Season with salt and white pepper; garnish with the celery leaves. —*Daniel Boulud*

MAKE AHEAD The recipe can be prepared through Step 3 up to 1 day ahead.

Red, White and Blue Potato Salad

10 SERVINGS

Inspired by the wide variety of new potatoes at an upstate farm stand, this salad looks prettiest when all the potatoes measure about two and a half inches in diameter.

10 small red-skinned potatoes (about 1 pound)
10 small Yukon Gold or white new potatoes (about 1 pound)
10 small blue potatoes (about 1 pound)
1 cup extra-virgin olive oil
3 tablespoons red wine vinegar
Salt and freshly ground pepper

1. Using a mandoline or sharp knife, slice the potatoes ⅛ inch thick. Put each kind of potato in a separate bowl of cold water.

2. In a small glass or stainless-steel bowl, whisk the oil with the vinegar and season with salt and pepper.

3. In a medium saucepan, cook the red potatoes in boiling salted water until just tender, about 5 minutes. Using a slotted spoon, transfer the potatoes to a bowl of ice water to stop the cooking; remove and pat thoroughly dry. Put the potatoes in a medium bowl, add 2 tablespoons of the vinaigrette

and toss. Repeat the process first with the Yukon Gold potatoes and then with the blue potatoes, putting each in a separate bowl.

4. Arrange the potatoes on a large platter, keeping the 3 kinds separate. Drizzle with some of the remaining vinaigrette. —*Brendan Walsh*

MAKE AHEAD The potato salad can be refrigerated for up to 4 hours. Bring to room temperature before serving.

Potato Salad with Bacon

4 SERVINGS

The smaller the potatoes you choose for this salad, the better they'll taste; but don't overcook them. Toss them in the stock mixture while they're still warm so they'll absorb all the flavors.

1½ pounds small new potatoes
One ¼-pound piece of slab bacon, sliced ¼ inch thick and cut into 1-inch strips
¼ cup chicken stock (p. 117) or canned low-sodium broth
1 tablespoon finely chopped shallots
1 tablespoon sherry vinegar
1 tablespoon Dijon or grainy mustard
2 tablespoons olive oil
Salt and freshly ground pepper
Chives, for garnish

1. Cook the new potatoes in boiling salted water until tender, 12 to 15 minutes, and then drain them.

2. Meanwhile, in a medium skillet, cook the bacon, stirring occasionally, over moderately high heat until crisp, about 4 minutes. Drain on paper towels.

3. Peel the potatoes as soon as they're cool enough to handle. Toss the potatoes with the stock, shallots, vinegar and mustard and let stand for 1 hour, tossing occasionally. Add the bacon and oil, season with salt and pepper and toss. Garnish with chives. Serve at room temperature. —*Eberhard Müller*

Red, White and Blue Potato Salad

2. In a large pot, cover the potatoes with water and bring to a boil. Add salt and simmer over high heat until tender, about 25 minutes. Drain the potatoes, let cool and then halve them.

3. In a medium salad bowl, combine the mayonnaise, onion, lemon juice and mustard; season with 1½ teaspoons of salt and the pepper. Fold in the lobster and potatoes and refrigerate until chilled or for up to 3 hours. Serve cold.   —*Mark Gottwald*

Michelena's Crab Salad with Homemade Potato Chips

4 SERVINGS

Rene Michelena is chef at La Bettola in Boston. To make sure oil is hot enough to fry potato slices, he says to drop one in—bubbles should form around it.

- **4 ounces large shiitake mushrooms, stems discarded, caps thinly sliced**
- **¼ cup plus 2 teaspoons extra-virgin olive oil**

Salt and freshly ground pepper

- **3 medium Yukon Gold potatoes, peeled**
- **1½ cups vegetable oil, for frying**
- **1½ tablespoons sherry vinegar**
- **2½ cups coarsely chopped frisée**
- **12 cherry tomatoes, halved**
- **1 scallion, thinly sliced**
- **1 small shallot, finely chopped**
- **6 ounces Dungeness crabmeat or jumbo lump crabmeat, picked over and cut into 1-inch pieces (about 1½ cups)**

1. Preheat the oven to 350°. On a medium baking sheet, toss the sliced mushrooms with 2 teaspoons of the olive oil and season with salt and pepper; spread out in a single layer. Bake for about 17 minutes, turning occasionally with a spatula, until browned and crisp.

2. Slice the potatoes ⅛ inch thick with a mandoline or a thin knife. Rinse the

Michelena's Crab Salad with Homemade Potato Chips

Potato and Lobster Claw Salad

8 SERVINGS

Here's a way to use up lobster claws after the tails have been used for another recipe, such as Grilled Lobster Tails with Sorrel-Sauternes Sauce (p. 178).

- **16 uncooked lobster claws**
- **4 pounds medium red potatoes, scrubbed but not peeled**

Salt

- **1 cup mayonnaise**
- **1 sweet onion, finely chopped**
- **¼ cup plus 2 tablespoons fresh lemon juice**
- **3 tablespoons Dijon mustard**
- **½ teaspoon freshly ground pepper**

1. Bring a large saucepan of water to a boil. Add the lobster, cover and bring to a boil. Uncover and boil over moderate heat for 6 minutes. Drain, let cool and then refrigerate until cold. Crack the claws; remove the meat in one piece.

slices in a bowl of cold water, changing the water twice, to remove the potato starch; drain. Spread the slices in a single layer between paper towels and pat dry.

3. In a large skillet, heat the vegetable oil until almost smoking. Add half of the potato slices and cook them over moderately high heat, turning once, until they are golden and crisp, about 7 minutes. Remove the potato chips with a slotted spoon and transfer to paper towels to drain. Repeat with the remaining potato slices.

4. In a large glass or stainless-steel bowl, whisk the remaining ¼ cup of olive oil with the sherry vinegar and ½ teaspoon of salt; season with pepper. Add the frisée, tomatoes, scallion, shallot, shiitakes and potato chips and toss well. Let the salad stand for 15 minutes for the flavors to combine. Add the crab, divide the salad among 4 plates and serve.   —*Rene Michelena*
WINE Pinot Grigio, or any light, crisp white, is lovely with the fresh taste of this crab and potato salad.

Pasta with Dandelion Stems
4 SERVINGS
- ½ pound linguine
- 2 tablespoons olive oil
- 2 ounces pancetta or bacon, coarsely chopped
- Dandelion stems from 2 pounds of greens, cut into 1½-inch pieces
- 2 garlic cloves, thinly sliced
- 1 tablespoon fresh lemon juice
- Crushed red pepper
- Salt
- Freshly grated Parmesan cheese

1. Cook the linguine in a large pot of boiling salted water until al dente.
2. Meanwhile, in a large skillet, heat the oil. Add the pancetta; cook over moderately high heat until crisp. Transfer to a plate. Add the dandelion stems to the skillet and cook until crisp-tender,

about 5 minutes. Add the garlic; cook until lightly browned, about 2 minutes.
3. Drain the linguine. In a large warmed glass or stainless-steel bowl, toss the pasta with the dandelion stems, lemon juice and a large pinch of crushed red pepper. Season with salt, top with the pancetta and serve. Pass the Parmesan at the table.   —*Grace Parisi*
WINE The dandelion stems and the classic Italian flavors—olive oil, garlic, Parmesan and pancetta—call for a fruity, tart, dry Italian white. The best choice would be a Gavi, perhaps the 1995 Michele Chiarlo or the 1995 La Scolca Villa Scolca.

Couscous Salad with Dried Fruit and Olives
4 SERVINGS
The tartness of the lemony dressing makes a lovely counterpoint to the sweet fruit and salty olives.
- ¼ cup slivered blanched almonds
- 1 cup fresh orange juice
- ⅓ cup extra-virgin olive oil
- ¼ cup fresh lemon juice
- Salt and freshly ground pepper
- 1⅓ cups couscous (about 10 ounces)
- 2 cups boiling water
- 6 dried apricots, coarsely chopped
- 5 pitted dates, coarsely chopped
- ½ cup green Picholine olives, pitted and coarsely chopped
- 3 tablespoons coarsely chopped parsley

1. Preheat the oven to 350°. Toast the almonds in a pie plate for about 6 minutes, or until golden.
2. In a small saucepan, boil the orange juice over high heat until reduced to ¼ cup. Transfer to a glass or stainless-steel bowl and let cool. Whisk in the oil and lemon juice and season with salt and pepper.
3. Put the couscous in a large glass or stainless-steel bowl. Stir in the boiling water and ½ teaspoon of salt. Add the

apricots and dates, cover with plastic wrap and let stand for about 15 minutes. Fluff the couscous with a fork. Stir in the olives, almonds, orange juice dressing and 2 tablespoons of the parsley. Cover the couscous and let stand for 1 hour. Fluff the couscous again, transfer to a platter and sprinkle with the remaining 1 tablespoon of parsley.   —*Matthew Kenney*

Israeli Couscous and Corn Salad
8 SERVINGS
Peppercorn-sized Israeli couscous, corn, red bell pepper and a lime-honey dressing combine in a summery salad.
- 1½ cups Israeli couscous (about ½ pound) (see Note)
- 3 cups boiling water
- Salt
- 1 tablespoon olive oil
- 2 cups fresh or thawed frozen corn kernels
- 1 medium onion, finely chopped
- 1 teaspoon ground coriander
- ¼ teaspoon caraway seeds
- 1 red bell pepper, finely chopped
- 2 jalapeños, seeded and minced
- 2 scallions, thinly sliced
- 3 tablespoons finely chopped mint
- ⅓ cup fresh lime juice
- ¼ cup canola oil
- 2 tablespoons rice wine vinegar
- 1 tablespoon honey
- ½ teaspoon finely grated lime zest
- Freshly ground black pepper

1. Put the couscous in a bowl and add the boiling water. Stir in 2 teaspoons of salt, cover tightly with plastic wrap and let the couscous stand, stirring once, until the grains are plump and tender, about 1 hour.
2. Meanwhile, in a large skillet, heat the olive oil. Add the corn kernels, onion, coriander and caraway. Cook over moderately low heat, stirring occasionally, until the onion is softened,

about 8 minutes. Transfer to a large glass or stainless-steel bowl; let cool.

3. Add the couscous to the bowl along with the red pepper, jalapeños, scallions and mint. In a glass or stainless-steel bowl, whisk together the lime juice, canola oil, rice wine vinegar, honey and lime zest. Add the dressing to the couscous and toss to combine. Season with salt and black pepper and serve. —*Christer Larsson*

NOTE Israeli couscous is available at Middle Eastern groceries or by mail-order from Kalustyan's, 212-685-3451.

MAKE AHEAD The recipe can be prepared through Step 2 and refrigerated overnight. Let return to room temperature before proceeding.

Quinoa and Winter Fruit Salad

6 SERVINGS

1⅓ cups quinoa (about ½ pound), rinsed

1½ cups water

 2 kumquats—halved, seeded and coarsely chopped

 2 tablespoons coarsely chopped cilantro

¼ cup pure olive oil

2½ tablespoons fresh lemon juice

½ teaspoon kosher salt

 1 large Bosc pear—peeled, cored and cut into ½-inch dice

 1 medium cucumber—peeled, seeded and cut into ½-inch dice

 1 cup coarsely chopped stemmed watercress

1. In a medium saucepan, combine the quinoa and water and bring to a boil. Simmer over low heat, stirring often, until the quinoa is just tender, about 12 minutes; the grains should be separate and intact. Drain the quinoa and let cool completely.

2. In a small glass or stainless-steel bowl, combine the kumquats and cilantro with the oil, lemon juice and kosher salt and let steep for 5 minutes.

3. In a large salad bowl, toss together the quinoa, pear and cucumber. Add the dressing and toss well. Add the watercress and toss again. Serve the salad at once. —*Marcia Kiesel*

Olive and Dried Tomato Lentil Salad

4 SERVINGS

This lemony two-lentil salad travels well. Pack it in containers for a picnic lunch and serve it as a side dish with anything from pan-fried trout to steak.

 1 cup Vertes du Puy lentils (about ½ pound)

½ cup red lentils (about 4 ounces)

 3 scallions, thinly sliced

¼ cup chopped drained oil-packed sun-dried tomatoes

 2 tablespoons chopped pitted brine-cured olives

 2 tablespoons fresh lemon juice

 2 tablespoons olive oil

Salt and freshly ground pepper

In a medium saucepan of boiling water, cook the Vertes du Puy lentils over moderately high heat until almost tender, about 15 minutes. Add the red lentils and continue cooking until all the lentils are tender, about 8 minutes longer. Drain the lentils. Return them to the saucepan and let cool to room temperature. Stir in the scallions, sun-dried tomatoes, olives, lemon juice and oil. Season with salt and pepper and serve. —*Marcia Kiesel*

MAKE AHEAD The salad can stand at room temperature for up to 4 hours.

Crab and Fennel Salad

6 SERVINGS

Although the Ristorante al Bersagliere is located in Mantua, in northern Italy, chef Massimo Ferrari's salad here packs the punch of southern Italy.

 2 navel oranges

 3 tablespoons lemon juice

 1 tablespoon balsamic vinegar

 2 hard-cooked egg yolks, mashed

Salt

Cayenne pepper

 6 tablespoons extra-virgin olive oil

 2 medium fennel bulbs—halved, cored and thinly sliced, some fronds minced for garnish

¼ cup drained capers

 1 pound jumbo lump crabmeat

1. Using a sharp knife, peel both the oranges, removing all of the white pith. Working over a strainer set over a bowl, cut in between the membranes to release the orange sections; quarter the sections. Squeeze the membranes over the strainer.

2. In a blender, combine 2 tablespoons of the orange juice with the lemon juice, vinegar, egg yolks and a pinch each of salt and cayenne. Blend until smooth and then blend in the oil.

3. In a large glass or stainless-steel bowl, toss the fennel and capers with the oranges and ¼ cup of the dressing. Season with salt and put on plates. In another glass or stainless-steel bowl, toss the crab with 3 tablespoons of the dressing. Mound the crab on the fennel, garnish with the fronds and serve with the remaining dressing. —*Massimo Ferrari*

WINE Look for the 1996 Bollini Reserve Pinot Grigio or 1995 Livio Felluga Pinot Grigio.

Grilled Marinated Trout and Fennel Salad

8 SERVINGS

If you're short on time, skip Steps 1 and 2 and use smoked trout fillets instead.

 4 filleted brook trout with skin (about ½ pound each)

 2 cups vegetable oil or light olive oil, plus more for grilling

Salt and freshly ground black pepper

 1 cup thickly sliced shallots (about 4 large)

Olive and Dried Tomato Lentil Salad

½ cup thickly sliced garlic cloves (1 medium head)

2 cups white wine vinegar

3 sage sprigs

2 medium red bell peppers

2 medium yellow bell peppers

¼ cup olive oil

1½ tablespoons sherry vinegar

1½ teaspoons Dijon mustard

3 bunches of arugula, stemmed

2 large fennel bulbs—halved, cored and thinly sliced crosswise

1 pint small cherry tomatoes

I. Light a grill or heat a grill pan. Rub the trout fillets with a little vegetable oil and season with salt and black pepper. Grill the trout fillets, skin side down, until cooked around the edges but still raw on top. Arrange the trout fillets in a large baking dish, skin side down, in a single layer.

2. Combine the 2 cups of vegetable oil with the shallots and garlic in a medium saucepan. Cook the shallots over high heat until they are barely softened but not colored, about 5 minutes. Add the vinegar and sage, bring the marinade to a boil and cook for 5 minutes. Let the marinade cool slightly and then pour it evenly over the trout fillets. Let the trout marinate at room temperature for 2 hours.

3. Meanwhile, roast the bell peppers over a gas flame or under a broiler until charred all over and softened. Transfer the bell peppers to a bag and let steam for 20 minutes. Peel, seed and core the roasted peppers and then cut them into ¼-inch strips.

4. In a large glass or stainless-steel bowl, whisk the olive oil with the vinegar and mustard until blended. Season with salt and black pepper. Add the arugula, fennel, tomatoes and roasted peppers and toss them gently to coat. Mound the salad on a large platter. Arrange the marinated trout on top of the salad and serve immediately.

—Sascha Lyon

MAKE AHEAD The recipe can be prepared through Step 3; drain the trout and refrigerate it for up to 1 day. Refrigerate the roasted red and yellow peppers separately.

WINE The 1996 Domaine Fournier Sancerre and the 1996 Didier Dague-neau Pouilly-Fumé are both made with the Sauvignon Blanc grape, giving them the crisp, clean acidity to stand up to the power of the marinade. The smoky flavor of the Fumé also accents the grilled trout.

Chicken, Bacon and Tomato Salad

4 SERVINGS ✳

Chicken tenders, small breast meat "tenderloins," are widely available at supermarkets. If you can't find them, you can cut one pound of skinless, boneless chicken breasts into two-inch-wide strips.

4 bacon strips, coarsely chopped

1 pound chicken tenders

Salt and freshly ground pepper

½ pint small cherry tomatoes, halved

Chicken, Bacon and Tomato Salad

6 scallions, white and tender
   green, coarsely chopped
2 tablespoons red wine vinegar
1 large bunch of watercress,
   large stems discarded

1. Heat a large skillet. Add the bacon and cook over high heat until crisp, about 4 minutes. Transfer the bacon to a plate. Season the chicken tenders with salt and pepper, add them to the skillet and turn to coat with the bacon fat. Cook the tenders, turning once or twice, until they are brown on the outside and white throughout, about 5 minutes. Add the chicken tenders to the bacon.

2. Add the cherry tomatoes, scallions and vinegar to the skillet and boil for 1½ minutes. Return the tenders and the bacon to the pan, stir well and season the chicken salad with salt and pepper. Arrange the watercress on 4 plates, top with the chicken salad and serve. —*Jan Newberry*

WINE A round, ripe Chardonnay would be the perfect accompaniment for this chicken salad.

---

make-ahead tips

Here are a few things to keep in mind when storing food:

Select nonreactive containers, made of materials like glass or plastic, to store cooked food in the refrigerator. Aluminum can react, especially with acidic ingredients, and make the whole thing taste bad.

Cover prepared food securely, either with a tight-fitting lid or plastic wrap, before refrigerating.

Don't use aluminum foil to cover dishes made with such acidic ingredients as tomatoes, wine, vinegar and citrus fruits.

Use the coldest part of the refrigerator, usually at the back, to store already cooked food.

CHAPTER 4 soups

Lobster Bisque with Armagnac (p. 112)

Cucumber-Watercress Soup

Cucumber-Watercress Soup

4 SERVINGS ✳

Using a blender instead of a food processor makes this refreshing soup especially velvety and light. To chill it quickly, set the bowl in a larger bowl of ice water for about 30 minutes, stirring the soup occasionally.

  4 large cucumbers (about 3½ pounds)—peeled, seeded and cut into chunks
  1 cup (packed) watercress sprigs
 10 dill sprigs
  2 tablespoons white wine vinegar
  1 tablespoon extra-virgin olive oil, plus more for drizzling
Salt
1½ cups plain yogurt
Freshly ground pepper
  4 radishes, finely chopped
  2 scallions, finely chopped

1. In a blender, puree the cucumbers, a handful at a time, until smooth. Add the watercress, 6 of the dill sprigs, the vinegar, 1 tablespoon of the oil and 1 teaspoon of salt and puree until smooth.

2. Transfer the soup to a bowl and stir in the yogurt. Refrigerate until chilled, about 2 hours. Season with salt and pepper and pour into bowls. Garnish with the radishes, scallions and the remaining 4 dill sprigs. Drizzle with a little olive oil and serve. —Jan Newberry

MAKE AHEAD The soup can be refrigerated overnight. Garnish before serving.

Cold Cucumber and Yogurt Soup with Dill

4 SERVINGS

Try to get small, slender, crisp cucumbers when they're in season; they have fewer seeds and more flavor. Off-season, use the long European cucumbers. Leaving some of the skin on adds color, texture and flavor to the soup. Salad burnet is a gray-green herb that tastes like cucumbers.

  1 pound unwaxed cucumbers, plus 8 thin cucumber slices, for garnish
  1 tablespoon sherry vinegar
  2 teaspoons kosher salt
  2 cups whole-milk yogurt
  ½ cup heavy cream
  2 tablespoons coarsely chopped dill
  4 salad burnet sprigs, for garnish

1. Using a vegetable peeler, peel half of the whole cucumbers; leave the skin on the rest. Halve all of the cucumbers lengthwise; scoop out and discard the seeds. Coarsely chop the cucumbers. In a bowl, toss the cucumbers with the vinegar and kosher salt and let stand for 30 minutes.

2. Using a slotted spoon, transfer the marinated cucumbers to a blender or food processor, reserving the liquid. Add 2 tablespoons of the cucumber liquid and the yogurt, cream and dill to the cucumbers and blend until smooth. Add 1 to 2 tablespoons of the reserved cucumber liquid to thin the soup if needed. Refrigerate until cold, about 1 hour or up to 1 day. Ladle into bowls, garnish with cucumber slices and salad burnet and serve. —Eberhard Müller

Watercress and Sorrel Soup

4 SERVINGS ✳

Tangy sorrel gives a refreshing edge to this smooth soup, while the croutons add crunch. If you can't find sorrel, use another bunch of watercress and one tablespoon of lemon juice instead.

  ¼ cup plus 2 tablespoons olive oil
  ⅓ medium baguette, crusts removed, bread cut into 1-inch cubes (about 1 cup)
  ½ cup minced onion
  ½ pound yellow Finn or red potatoes, peeled and quartered
3½ cups chicken stock (p. 117), vegetable stock or canned low-sodium chicken broth

Cold Cucumber and Yogurt Soup with Dill

  1 pound watercress, tough stems discarded
  ½ pound sorrel, stems discarded
Salt and freshly ground pepper

1. Heat ¼ cup of the oil in a skillet until almost smoking. Add the bread cubes and fry over moderately high heat, stirring, until well browned, about 5 minutes. Transfer the croutons to paper towels to drain.

2. Heat the remaining 2 tablespoons of oil in a large saucepan. Add the onion and cook over moderate heat, stirring, until softened, about 5 minutes. Add the potatoes and stock and bring to a boil. Reduce the heat to low, cover and simmer until the potatoes are tender, about 15 minutes.

3. Stir in the watercress and sorrel, cover and simmer over low heat until the watercress and sorrel are wilted, about 5 minutes. Working in batches, puree the soup in a blender. Return the soup to the saucepan and rewarm it over moderately high heat; season the soup with salt and pepper. Ladle the soup into bowls and garnish with the croutons. —Alice Waters

Radish Greens Soup

Radish Greens Soup

6 SERVINGS

Be sure to pick bunches of radishes with very fresh-looking leaves for this earthy, slightly bitter soup.

- 6 tablespoons unsalted butter
- 12 cups radish greens (from 4 large bunches of radishes), coarsely chopped
- ½ pound scallions, white and tender green, cut into 1-inch lengths
- 4½ cups water
- Salt and freshly ground white pepper
- Croutons (recipe follows)

I. In a large saucepan, melt 3 tablespoons of the butter over moderately high heat. Add the radish greens and scallions and cook, stirring occasionally, until wilted, about 4 minutes. Add the water, bring to a boil and simmer until the vegetables are tender, about 10 minutes. Let cool slightly. Puree the soup in batches in a blender, about 2 minutes per batch.

2. Gently reheat the soup in a clean saucepan. Swirl in the remaining 3 tablespoons butter; season with salt and white pepper. Serve in shallow soup plates, garnished with the Croutons.

MAKE AHEAD The soup can be prepared through Step 1 and refrigerated for up to 8 hours.

CROUTONS

MAKES 12 CROUTONS

Three ½-inch-thick slices of firm-textured white bread, crusts trimmed

3 tablespoons unsalted butter

Cut the bread crosswise into ¾-inch strips. Melt the butter in a medium skillet. Add the bread and sauté over moderately high heat until browned all over, about 5 minutes. Drain on paper towels. —*Betsy Bernardaud*

MAKE AHEAD The Croutons can be stored in an airtight container for up to 2 days.

Chilled Zucchini Bisque with Stuffed Zucchini Blossoms

8 SERVINGS

- 2 quarts water
- 4 medium zucchini (1¾ pounds)— halved lengthwise, seeded and cut into 2-inch pieces
- 1 small onion, coarsely chopped
- Salt
- 2 cups spinach leaves
- 2 tablespoons heavy cream
- 1 tablespoon fresh lemon juice
- 8 mint leaves
- Freshly ground pepper
- 8 large zucchini blossoms
- 4 ounces mild fresh goat cheese, at room temperature
- ¼ cup tomato juice
- 1 tablespoon extra-virgin olive oil
- 1 cup finely diced yellow tomatoes

I. In a large saucepan, bring the water to a boil. Add the zucchini, onion and 1 teaspoon of salt and cook over moderate heat until the zucchini are tender, about 15 minutes. Drain, reserving the cooking liquid. Let cool.

2. In a blender, combine the cooked vegetables with the spinach, cream, lemon juice and mint; pulse until finely chopped. With the machine on, gradually add about 2 cups of the reserved

cooking liquid and blend until smooth. Season with salt and pepper and refrigerate until chilled.

3. Meanwhile, gently open the zucchini blossoms and remove the yellow stamen. Cut off any spiky leaves at the base of the blossoms.

4. In a small bowl, beat the goat cheese with salt and pepper. Using a small spoon, fill the zucchini blossoms with the goat cheese. Gently twist the tips of the blossoms around the filling. Set them on a baking sheet and refrigerate until firm.

5. Preheat the oven to 350°. Bake the zucchini blossoms just until warmed through, about 6 minutes.

6. In a small bowl, whisk the tomato juice with the oil. Season with salt and pepper. Ladle the soup into 8 shallow soup plates. Set a stuffed blossom in the center of each. Garnish with the diced tomatoes and a drizzle of the tomato juice mixture. —*Alan Tardi*

WINE A light- to medium-bodied white, crisp and with pronounced floral overtones, is ideal for this soup. Try one of the excellent Alsace Pinot Blancs from Trimbach or Hugel. A good Beaujolais, such as a Michel Tête Juliénas, would do nicely too.

Cauliflower Soup with Pan-Seared Mushrooms

6 SERVINGS

- 3 tablespoons unsalted butter
- 3 onions, halved and thinly sliced
- 3 pounds cauliflower, separated into florets and coarsely chopped
- 4 cups chicken stock (p. 117) or water
- ¾ cup heavy cream

Salt and freshly ground white pepper
- 4 medium matsutake mushrooms or small Portobellos, stemmed and halved crosswise
- 2 tablespoons olive oil

1. Melt the butter in a heavy saucepan. Add the onions and cook over moderately low heat, stirring occasionally, until very soft but not browned, about 15 minutes.

2. Add the cauliflower and stock and bring to a boil. Cover and simmer over moderately low heat, stirring once, until the cauliflower is very soft, about 30 minutes. Let cool slightly.

3. Working in batches, puree the soup in a blender. Return the soup to the saucepan, stir in the cream and season with salt and white pepper. If necessary, add a few tablespoons of water to thin the soup.

4. Preheat the oven to 325°. Heat a large ovenproof skillet. Brush the mushrooms with the oil, season with salt and white pepper and add them to the skillet. Sear over moderately high heat, turning once, just until tender, 6 to 8 minutes. Transfer the skillet to the oven and bake for 3 to 4 minutes, or until

Chilled Zucchini Bisque with Stuffed Zucchini Blossoms

Callaloo

1. In a large saucepan, melt the butter in the oil. Add the onion and cook over moderate heat until softened, about 3 minutes. Add the garlic and cook, stirring, until softened but not browned, about 2 minutes. Add the bacon and cook, stirring frequently, until the fat is rendered, about 5 minutes. Add the callaloo, basil, parsley and celery leaves and cook over moderately high heat, stirring occasionally, until the greens are wilted and barely tender, about 7 minutes.

2. Add the water and bring to a boil. Cover and cook over moderate heat until the greens are soft, about 10 minutes. Puree the soup in batches in a blender until perfectly smooth. Return the soup to the saucepan, add the cream and season with salt and pepper. Bring to a simmer and serve in soup plates.　—*Sylvia Fernandez*

NOTE Callaloo leaves are available in West Indian and Asian markets.

MAKE AHEAD The soup can be refrigerated for up to 1 day.

WINE A simple, dry white, like the 1995 Chalk Hill Sauvignon Blanc, pairs well with the fresh taste of the greens.

the mushrooms are very tender. Thinly slice the mushrooms.

5. Rewarm the soup over moderate heat; ladle into shallow bowls. Garnish the soup with the sliced mushrooms and serve.　—*Normand Laprise*

Callaloo

6 SERVINGS

Callaloo is the name of this traditional West Indian soup as well as of the large fan-shaped leafy greens—sometimes called dasheen leaves or taro root leaves—that are its chief component. The greens taste like a cross between spinach and cabbage.

- 2　tablespoons unsalted butter
- 2　tablespoons vegetable oil
- 1　medium onion, coarsely chopped
- 2　tablespoons coarsely chopped garlic
- 4　slices of bacon, coarsely chopped
- ½　pound callaloo (see Note) or spinach, stemmed, leaves cut into ½-inch ribbons
- ¼　cup plus 2 tablespoons basil
- ¼　cup flat-leaf parsley leaves
- 2　tablespoons celery leaves
- 4　cups water
- ½　cup heavy cream

Salt and freshly ground pepper

Grilled Corn Soup

8 SERVINGS

Brendan Walsh first tasted this soup when he was cooking at an event with Stephen Pyles, the chef at Star Canyon in Dallas. Its smoky quality makes it a favorite.

- 1　dozen ears of corn, shucked
- 2　tablespoons corn oil
- 1　large onion, finely chopped
- 1　large carrot, finely chopped
- 1　celery rib, finely chopped
- 4　garlic cloves, smashed
- 1　bay leaf
- ½　teaspoon crushed red pepper
- ¼　teaspoon ground coriander

Pinch of ground cloves

- 3　cups water

3 cups chicken stock (p. 117) or canned low-sodium broth

Salt and freshly ground black pepper

ı. Light a grill. Grill the corn, turning the ears frequently, until the kernels are well browned. Alternatively, pan-roast the corn in a cast-iron skillet over low heat. Cut the kernels off the cobs.
2. Heat the oil in a large saucepan. Add the onion, carrot, celery and garlic, cover and cook over low heat, stirring frequently, until softened, about 15 minutes. Add the bay leaf, crushed red pepper, coriander and cloves and cook for 2 minutes. Add the corn, water and stock and bring to a boil. Reduce the heat to moderately low, cover partially and simmer for 40 minutes.
3. Discard the bay leaf. Transfer the soup to a blender or food processor and puree until smooth. Strain the soup into a large saucepan, pressing hard on the solids; thin with water if necessary. Reheat and season with salt and black pepper. Ladle the soup into bowls and serve.   *—Brendan Walsh*
MAKE AHEAD The soup can be refrigerated for up to 3 days.
WINE The 1996 Archery Summit Vireton, an Oregon wine in the Alsatian style, has all the spirit of its European brothers. The 1995 Chalone Pinot Blanc is a less floral, sturdier wine, but it is terrific too.

Silky Squash and Celery Root Soup

4 SERVINGS

1 tablespoon canola oil
1 medium onion, finely chopped
½ medium Kabocha squash (about 2 pounds)—peeled, seeded and cut into 1-inch cubes
1 celery root (about 1 pound), peeled and cut into 1-inch cubes
2 shallots, minced
4 cups Vegetable Stock (recipe follows)

¼ teaspoon freshly grated nutmeg
Salt and freshly ground pepper
4 chervil sprigs for garnish (optional)

ı. Heat the oil in a large heavy saucepan. Add the onion and cook over moderately low heat until golden brown. Add the squash, celery root and shallots and cook until lightly browned around the edges, about 5 minutes. Add the stock, nutmeg and a generous pinch each of salt and pepper and bring to a boil. Reduce the heat to moderately low, cover partially and cook until the vegetables are tender, about 30 minutes.

Silky Squash and Celery Root Soup

2. Working in batches, puree the soup in a blender or food processor. Season with salt and pepper and float a chervil sprig on top of each serving.
MAKE AHEAD The soup can be refrigerated overnight. Rewarm before serving.
ONE SERVING Calories 183 kcal, Total Fat 4.4 gm, Saturated Fat .4 gm

VEGETABLE STOCK

MAKES 4 CUPS

2 celery ribs, coarsely chopped
1 medium onion, coarsely chopped
1 carrot, coarsely chopped

Silken Turnip and Potato Soup

1 tomato, coarsely chopped
6 dried shiitake mushrooms,
   broken into 1-inch pieces
2 tablespoons tomato paste
1 teaspoon fennel seeds
3½ quarts water

Combine all of the ingredients in a stock pot and bring to a boil over moderately high heat. Reduce the heat to moderately low and simmer for 2 hours. Strain the stock and boil until reduced to 4 cups.

—*Betsy Nelson and Jim Kyndberg*
MAKE AHEAD The stock can be frozen for up to 2 months.
ONE CUP Calories 35 kcal, Total Fat .2 gm, Saturated Fat 0

Silken Turnip and Potato Soup

8 SERVINGS

A wonderful use for an underutilized root vegetable, the soup tastes rich and creamy but is surprisingly light. It contains no milk or cream, and so makes a fine starter for an elaborate meal.

6 tablespoons unsalted butter
4 medium onions, thinly sliced
3 pounds turnips, peeled and
   thinly sliced
1½ pounds baking potatoes, peeled
   and thinly sliced
Salt
6 cups chicken stock (p. 117) or
   canned low-sodium broth

¼ teaspoon freshly grated
   nutmeg
¼ cup finely shredded basil,
   for garnish

1. In a large heavy stockpot or casserole, melt the butter until it foams. When the foam subsides, add the onions and cook over moderate heat until softened but not browned, about 5 minutes. Add the turnips and potatoes and stir to coat with the butter. Add 2 teaspoons of salt, cover and cook over low heat, stirring occasionally, until the vegetables are tender, about 20 minutes.
2. Stir in the chicken stock and bring to a simmer. Cover partially and cook over moderate heat until the vegetables are very tender, about 10 minutes.
3. Working in batches, puree the soup in a blender until perfectly smooth. Return the soup to the pot and season with salt and the nutmeg. Ladle the soup into shallow bowls and garnish with the basil before serving.

—*Edna Lewis and Scott Peacock*
MAKE AHEAD The soup can be refrigerated overnight.

Silken Bread and Parmesan Soup

10 SERVINGS

Thickened with fresh bread crumbs, this chicken soup tastes rich thanks to the addition of cheese and egg yolks.

10 cups chicken stock (p. 117) or
   canned low-sodium broth
10 slices (10 ounces) firm-textured
   white bread, crusts removed,
   bread torn into large pieces
6 ounces Parmesan cheese, diced
   (about 1¼ cups)
2 large egg yolks, lightly beaten
Extra-virgin olive oil, for drizzling
Freshly ground pepper

1. In a large saucepan, heat the stock until bubbles appear around the edge. Drop the bread into a food processor and pulse until coarse crumbs form. Add the Parmesan and pulse until it is finely chopped. Transfer the bread and cheese mixture to a large saucepan and gradually whisk in 8 cups of the stock. Cook over moderate heat, stirring constantly with a wooden spoon, just until the soup begins to simmer. Keep warm over very low heat.

2. Gradually whisk the remaining 2 cups of stock into the egg yolks and then whisk this mixture into the soup. Using an immersion blender, blend the soup until it is smooth and frothy. Alternatively, carefully puree the soup in batches in a blender. Ladle the soup into warmed soup plates and garnish with a drizzle of oil and a sprinkling of freshly ground pepper.

—*Frédérick Hermé*

Swiss Chard, Barley and Cannellini Bean Soup

4 SERVINGS

A Friulian cook will rarely pass up the opportunity to add a fistful of barley to a soup; its chewy consistency gives marvelous body to every mouthful.

  1 **pound Swiss chard**
 ¼ **cup extra-virgin olive oil**
  1 **cup finely chopped onion**
 ½ **cup finely chopped carrot**
 ½ **cup finely chopped celery**
 ⅓ **cup chopped canned Italian plum tomatoes with their juice**
Salt
  5 **cups water**
 ½ **cup pearl barley**
1½ **cups canned cannellini beans, drained (19-ounce can)**
Freshly ground pepper
Freshly grated Parmigiano-Reggiano cheese

1. Soak the Swiss chard in cold water for 10 minutes and then drain and wash well. Slice the Swiss chard stalks crosswise ⅛ inch thick. Cut the leaves into ¼-inch-wide strips.

2. Put the oil and onion in a large heavy casserole and cook over moderate heat, stirring occasionally, until the onion is light gold, about 5 minutes. Add the carrot and celery and cook for 7 minutes, stirring occasionally. Add the tomatoes and their juices and cook, stirring now and then, until all the vegetables are softened, about 6 minutes. Stir in the chard and 1 teaspoon salt. Cover and cook over very low heat for 40 minutes, stirring once or twice.

3. Meanwhile, in a medium saucepan, bring the water to a boil. Add the barley and simmer over moderately low heat until tender, about 35 minutes. Drain the barley, reserving the cooking water.

4. Add the barley and beans to the chard, stir well and cook for 2 minutes. Stir in 2½ cups of the barley water, season with salt and pepper and bring the soup just to a simmer. Ladle the soup into bowls and pass the cheese at the table.   —*Marcella Hazan*

MAKE AHEAD The soup can stand at room temperature for up to 8 hours. Thin the soup with water if it seems too thick when reheated.

WINE Swiss chard's attractive, sweet, green note harmonizes with light, dry,

Silken Bread and Parmesan Soup

Swiss Chard, Barley and Cannellini Bean Soup

fruity whites. Try the 1996 Livio Felluga Pinot Grigio from Friuli or the 1997 Ceretto Blange Arneis from Piedmont.

Lobster Bisque with Armagnac

8 SERVINGS

The easiest way to split live lobsters open is to ask your fishmonger to do the job for you; he can also remove the claws and tails. Start making the bisque as soon after the lobsters are cut as possible.

- 3 quarts water
- Four 1½-pound live lobsters, split lengthwise
- ¼ cup pure olive oil
- 1 pound fennel bulbs—halved, cored and coarsely chopped
- 2 medium celery ribs, coarsely chopped
- 1 medium carrot, coarsely chopped
- 1 medium onion, coarsely chopped
- 1 medium leek, halved lengthwise and coarsely chopped
- 1 unpeeled head of garlic, halved crosswise
- ½ cup all-purpose flour
- 2 tablespoons tomato paste
- 2 cups dry white wine
- 3 tablespoons Armagnac or Cognac, plus more for serving
- 1 thyme sprig
- 1 bay leaf
- Large pinch of saffron threads
- 1 cup heavy cream
- Salt and freshly ground pepper
- 8 small parsley sprigs

1. In a large stockpot, bring the water to a boil. Twist the claws and tails from the lobster bodies and set aside the bodies. Add the claws and tails to the boiling water. Simmer the tails until just cooked, about 3 minutes, and the claws until they turn bright red all over, about 8 minutes; transfer the pieces to a large bowl as they are done and reserve the cooking liquid. Let the lobster cool slightly. Crack the claws; remove the meat from the tails and claws and then cover and refrigerate.

2. Twist the legs from the lobster bodies and cut the bodies into large pieces. Heat the oil in a large enameled cast-iron casserole. Add the fennel, celery, carrot, onion, leek and garlic and cook over moderately high heat, stirring frequently, until the vegetables are browned, about 8 minutes.

3. Add the lobster legs and body pieces to the casserole and cook over high heat, stirring, until the shells start to brown, about 8 minutes. Sprinkle the flour evenly over the shells and stir well. Add the tomato paste and cook, stirring, until it starts to brown, about 3 minutes. Stir in the wine and Armagnac and simmer for 3 minutes. Stir in the thyme, bay leaf, saffron and the reserved lobster cooking liquid until well blended.

4. Simmer the broth over low heat, skimming occasionally, until very flavorful, about 1½ hours. Strain the broth through a coarse sieve, pressing on the solids to extract as much liquid as possible, and then return the broth to the casserole.

5. Add the heavy cream to the casserole and simmer for 5 minutes. Season

Lobster Bisque with Armagnac

Shrimp and White Bean Stew

the bisque with salt and pepper. Cut the reserved lobster tail and claw meat into 1-inch pieces. Add the lobster meat to the simmering bisque and cook until just heated through, about 1 minute. Add a splash of Armagnac to 8 soup plates. Ladle the bisque into the soup plates, garnish with the parsley and serve.

—*The Point, Lake Saranac, New York*
MAKE AHEAD The recipe can be prepared through Step 4 and refrigerated for up to 1 day. Rewarm the broth before proceeding with the bisque.

Tamarind Shrimp Soup

10 SERVINGS
10 cups water
½ cup (4 ounces) tamarind pulp with seeds (see Note)
1 tablespoon vegetable oil
1 pound medium shrimp, shelled and deveined, shells reserved
2 small red onions—1 coarsely chopped, 1 minced
1 tablespoon tomato paste
1½ cups cubed fresh pineapple (½-inch cubes)

½ jalapeño chile, seeded and minced
Salt and freshly ground pepper
1. In a small saucepan, bring 2 cups of the water to a boil. Remove from the heat and add the tamarind pulp. Cover and let stand until softened, about 30 minutes. Pass the mixture through a coarse strainer; discard the seeds.
2. Meanwhile, in a large saucepan, heat the oil. Add the shrimp shells and cook over high heat, stirring, until pink, about 3 minutes. Add the coarsely chopped onion and cook over moderately high heat, stirring, until softened and starting to brown, about 3 minutes. Add the tomato paste and cook, stirring, until it starts to caramelize, about 2 minutes. Add the remaining 8 cups of water and bring to a simmer, scraping up the brown bits on the bottom of the pan. Simmer over low heat for 30 minutes. Strain the broth and return it to the saucepan.
3. Add the minced onion and the pineapple to the broth. Cover and simmer over low heat for 10 minutes. Stir in the tamarind puree and return to a simmer. Add the shrimp and cook over moderately high heat until opaque throughout, about 3 minutes. Add the jalapeño and season with salt and pepper. Serve hot. —*Marcia Kiesel*
NOTE Tamarind pulp is available at Asian, Latin and Caribbean markets.
MAKE AHEAD The recipe can be prepared through Step 2 up to 2 days ahead. Refrigerate the broth and tamarind puree separately.

Shrimp and White Bean Stew

4 SERVINGS ✳ 🌷
Is this a fish soup or stew? In the tradition of bouillabaisse and cioppino, classification is difficult. We call it a stew but eat it like soup.
2 tablespoons olive oil
1 medium onion, finely chopped

3 garlic cloves, crushed
3 cups cooked cannellini beans, drained and rinsed if canned
One 14-ounce can whole peeled tomatoes, drained and crushed
1 teaspoon salt
½ teaspoon dried rosemary
½ teaspoon freshly ground pepper
4 cups fish stock or bottled clam broth
1 pound medium shrimp, shelled and deveined
¼ cup finely chopped flat-leaf parsley
1. Heat the oil in a large enameled cast-iron casserole. Add the onion and garlic and cook over moderately high heat, stirring frequently, until the onion softens, about 5 minutes. Stir in the cannellini beans, tomatoes, salt, rosemary and pepper.
2. Add the stock and bring to a boil. Reduce the heat to moderately low and simmer until the stew is slightly thickened, about 15 minutes. Add the shrimp and simmer just until cooked through, about 2 minutes. Stir in the parsley and serve. —*Jan Newberry*
ONE SERVING Calories 372 kcal, Total Fat 9.3 gm, Saturated Fat 1.4 gm
WINE A rich, full-bodied California Chardonnay can wrap around the flavors of the sweet shrimp and hearty white beans in this tomato-based stew. Consider the 1995 Chateau St. Jean Robert Young Vineyard or the 1995 Arrowood.

Turkey Escarole Soup with Parmesan

6 SERVINGS ✳
Twelve ½-inch-thick slices of Italian bread
¼ cup freshly grated Parmesan cheese, plus more for serving
2 tablespoons unsalted butter
1 large onion, coarsely chopped
2 large garlic cloves, minced

1 small head of escarole (about
   1 pound), thinly sliced crosswise
Salt and freshly ground pepper
6 cups Turkey Stock (p. 117)
2 cups diced cooked turkey
   (about ½ pound)

1. Preheat the oven to 350°. Arrange the bread on a baking sheet, sprinkle the ¼ cup Parmesan on top and toast for about 10 minutes, or until the bread is golden and the cheese is bubbling.
2. Melt the butter in a large saucepan. Add the onion and garlic and cook over moderately low heat, stirring occasionally, until tender, about 10 minutes. Stir in the escarole, ¾ teaspoon of salt and ¼ teaspoon of pepper. Add the stock and bring to a boil. Reduce the heat to moderately low and cook until the escarole is tender, about 7 minutes.
3. Add the turkey and cook just until heated through. Spoon the soup into bowls, add the Parmesan toasts and serve the soup with additional grated cheese.   —*Jan Newberry*
WINE Escarole gives the mild, straightforward soup an attractive edge best matched by a tart, herbaceous California Sauvignon Blanc, such as the 1997 Brander or the 1997 Iron Horse Fumé Blanc.

Mexican Turkey-Tomato Soup with Chipotles

6 SERVINGS ❋

A sprinkling of silky diced avocado, a squeeze of fresh lime juice and a spoonful of tangy sour cream all help balance the smoky heat that chipotle chiles bring to this lively soup.

2 tablespoons pure olive oil
1 large onion, coarsely chopped
2 large garlic cloves, minced
1 teaspoon salt
¼ teaspoon freshly ground pepper
2 cups canned whole peeled tomatoes with their juice
4 cups Turkey Stock (p. 117)

2 chipotle chiles in adobo, finely chopped
1 teaspoon dried oregano
2 cups diced cooked turkey (about ½ pound)
¼ cup coarsely chopped cilantro
1 large avocado, diced, for serving
Lime wedges, sour cream and tortilla chips, for serving

1. Heat the oil in a large saucepan. Add the onion, garlic, salt and pepper and cook over moderately low heat, stirring occasionally, until the onion is tender, about 10 minutes.
2. Add the tomatoes, breaking them up against the side of the pot. Add the stock, chipotles and oregano and bring to a boil over moderate heat. Reduce the heat to moderately low and cook until the tomatoes begin to break down and the soup is flavorful, about 10 minutes.
3. Add the turkey and cilantro and cook just until the turkey is heated through. Ladle the soup into bowls and top with the avocado. Serve lime wedges, sour cream and tortilla chips on the side.   —*Jan Newberry*
WINE The smoky chipotle and tomato flavors in this soup call for a dry but

Turkey Escarole Soup with Parmesan

Mexican Turkey-Tomato Soup with Chipoltes

fragrant and fruity white wine to provide an attractive contrast. Viognier would be an ideal choice: look for the 1997 Jepson or the 1997 Preston from California or the 1996 Domaine de Montine from France.

Turkey Rice Soup with Sausage

6 SERVINGS ✳

Make this super-quick gumbo when you crave the hearty flavors of the Cajun classic but don't have time to make the roux.

- 2 tablespoons vegetable oil
- 1 large onion, coarsely chopped
- 1 large green bell pepper, coarsely chopped
- 3 medium celery ribs, coarsely chopped
- 2 large garlic cloves, minced
- ¾ cup long-grain rice (about 4½ ounces)
- 2 bay leaves
- ¾ teaspoon dried thyme
- ⅛ teaspoon crushed red pepper

Salt

- 4 cups Turkey Stock (p. 117)

One 28-ounce can whole peeled tomatoes with their juice

- 1 tablespoon tomato paste
- ½ pound andouille sausage, cut into ½-inch slices
- 2 cups diced cooked turkey (about ½ pound)

1. Heat the oil in a large saucepan. Add the onion, green pepper, celery and garlic and cook over moderately high heat, stirring occasionally, until softened, about 10 minutes.

2. Add the rice, bay leaves, thyme, crushed red pepper and 1 teaspoon of salt and stir to coat the rice with the oil. Add the stock, tomatoes and tomato paste, breaking up the tomatoes against the side of the pot. Bring to a boil, cover and cook over moderately low heat until the rice is almost tender, about 15 minutes.

3. Meanwhile, heat a medium skillet. Add the andouille and cook over high heat until browned, 2 to 3 minutes per side. Add the andouille and turkey to the soup and cook until the turkey is heated through and the rice is tender.

Discard the bay leaves and season the soup with salt. Ladle the soup into bowls and serve. —*Jan Newberry*

WINE All that this meaty, spicy soup needs to wrap up the flavors is a full-bodied Chardonnay, such as the 1996 Cuvaison Carneros from California or the 1996 Fortant Réserve from France.

Beef and Lettuce Congee

6 SERVINGS

Although the soothing, simple rice soup known as congee is most often served unseasoned, with flavors that are added as you eat, some versions are flavored while they cook. There are yam and pumpkin congees, fish congees and sweet bean congees—all wonderful collections of contrasting tastes and textures. In this version, flavor and texture are added in the form of thin slices of marinated beef, sliced scallions and ribbons of crisp romaine lettuce. The soup should be served with chile paste and freshly ground white or black pepper.

- 1 tablespoon Chinese cooking wine, dry white wine or dry sherry
- 1 tablespoon soy sauce
- 1 teaspoon cornstarch
- 6 ounces beef round, thinly sliced
- 1 cup medium-grain Chinese, Japanese or Korean white rice
- 8 cups cold water
- 4 scallions, sliced ¼ inch thick
- ½ pound romaine lettuce leaves, cut crosswise into 1-inch ribbons (6 cups)
- 1 teaspoon salt

Hot Chile Paste (recipe follows)
Freshly ground pepper

1. In a medium bowl, combine the wine, soy sauce and cornstarch. Add the beef and turn to coat. Let marinate at room temperature for 30 minutes.

2. Wash the rice thoroughly until the water runs clear. Put the rice in a large saucepan and wash again until the water runs clear; drain. Cover the rice with the 8 cups of cold water and bring to a vigorous boil. Lower the heat and simmer until the rice is very tender, about 20 minutes.

3. About 5 minutes before serving, bring the congee to a vigorous boil. Stir in the meat and its marinade and the scallions and remove from the heat. Stir in the lettuce and salt. Serve immediately in large bowls, and pass chile paste and freshly ground pepper at the table so guests can season their congee as they wish.

MAKE AHEAD The recipe can be prepared through Step 2 up to 2 hours ahead. The congee will thicken as it stands, so you may have to add up to 1 cup of water to ensure a soupy texture.

WINE One way to match the underlying heat of chile paste is to serve an equally assertive, spicy wine, such as the 1995 Robert Mondavi Zinfandel; alternatively, offer a cool, refreshing beer, such as Japan's Asahi.

HOT CHILE PASTE
MAKES ABOUT ¾ CUP

There is no single chile paste (*lajiao jiang*) in China, any more than there is a single salsa in Mexico. It serves as an ingredient in the kitchen and as a condiment at the table. Having tried many bottled versions over the years, we can assure you that by far the best chile paste is the one you make yourself.

- 1 cup loosely packed dried red chiles (1 ounce), rinsed
- ¾ cup boiling water
- 1 teaspoon salt
- 1 teaspoon sugar
- 1 tablespoon peanut oil
- ¼ cup minced shallots
- 1 teaspoon cider vinegar or rice vinegar

1. In a heatproof bowl, cover the chiles with the boiling water. Place a small plate on the chiles to keep them submerged and soak until pliable, at least 20 minutes or up to 2 hours.

2. Transfer the chiles and their soaking liquid to a blender and puree. Blend in the salt and sugar.

3. Set a wok over moderately high heat. When it's very hot, add the oil and swirl to coat the wok. Add the shallots and stir-fry until softened, about 2 minutes. Add the chile puree and stir-fry for about 20 seconds and then remove the wok from the heat and stir in the vinegar. Transfer the chile paste to a bowl to cool and then store in a glass jar.

—*Jeffrey Alford and Naomi Duguid*

MAKE AHEAD The chile paste can be refrigerated for up to 3 months.

Chicken Stock
MAKES 2 QUARTS

- 6 pounds chicken bones, backs, legs or wings
- 3 celery ribs, cut into 2-inch pieces
- 2 medium carrots, cut into 2-inch pieces
- 2 medium unpeeled onions, quartered
- 3 quarts water

1. Combine all the ingredients in a small stockpot and bring to a boil over high heat. Simmer over moderate heat for 20 minutes, skimming frequently. Reduce the heat to low and cover partially, leaving only a small opening. Simmer 2½ hours.

2. Strain the stock into a large bowl and press on the solids to extract all the liquid. Wipe out the pot, return the stock to it and boil until reduced to 2 quarts. Let cool completely before refrigerating.

MAKE AHEAD The stock can be refrigerated for up to 3 days or frozen for up to 2 months.

Turkey Stock
MAKES ABOUT 3 QUARTS

- 1 carcass from a large turkey, cut or broken into 4-inch pieces
- 4 quarts water
- 3 carrots, cut into 2-inch pieces
- 3 celery ribs, cut into 2-inch pieces
- 2 medium onions, quartered
- 4 unpeeled garlic cloves
- 5 thyme sprigs
- 1 small bunch of flat-leaf parsley
- 2 bay leaves, broken

1. Put the turkey bones in a large stockpot, cover with the water and bring to a boil, skimming occasionally. Add the carrots, celery, onions, garlic, thyme, parsley and bay leaves and cook over low heat, partially covered, for 2 hours.

2. Strain the stock into a large bowl and press down on the solids to extract all the liquid. —*Jan Newberry*

MAKE AHEAD The turkey stock can be refrigerated for up to 3 days or frozen for up to 2 months.

Turkey Rice Soup with Sausage

CHAPTER 5 pasta

Hefter's Artichoke and Goat Cheese Agnolotti with Truffles (p. 122)

Ziti with Spicy Pesto Pantesco

Ziti with Spicy Pesto Pantesco

8 FIRST-COURSE SERVINGS

Pantesco means in the style of Pantelleria, an island off the coast of Sicily. Capers grow well there, so they are a major source of flavor in the sauce.

- 4 ripe plum tomatoes (about ¾ pound), cut into ½-inch pieces
- ⅓ cup extra-virgin olive oil
- ¼ cup finely chopped flat-leaf parsley
- 2 tablespoons finely chopped mint
- 2 tablespoons finely chopped basil
- 1 tablespoon capers, rinsed
- 1 garlic clove, minced
- ½ teaspoon crushed red pepper
- ¼ to ½ teaspoon freshly ground black pepper

Sea salt

- 1 pound ziti
- ¼ cup freshly grated Pecorino Romano

1. In a large serving bowl, combine the tomatoes, olive oil, parsley, mint, basil, capers, garlic, crushed red pepper and black pepper. Season with sea salt.

2. Meanwhile, bring a large pot of water to a boil. Add 2 tablespoons of sea salt, add the pasta and cook, stirring occasionally, until al dente. Drain the pasta and add to the serving bowl. Toss well, sprinkle with the cheese and toss again before serving.   —*Mario Batali*

Pasta with Oven-Dried Tomatoes and Spicy Greens

4 FIRST-COURSE SERVINGS

Oven-dried tomatoes add both sweet and tart notes to this meal in a bowl.

- 10 ounces dried fettuccine or linguine
- 2 cups packed stemmed arugula or mustard greens

Oven-Dried Tomatoes in Herbed Oil (p. 311), herbs discarded

- ½ cup coarsely grated Parmesan cheese

Pasta with Oven-Dried Tomatoes and Spicy Greens

Salt and freshly ground pepper

- 2 tablespoons chopped mixed herbs, such as basil, chives and parsley

In a large pot of boiling salted water, cook the pasta until al dente. Drain the pasta and transfer it to a large warmed bowl. Add the arugula, the tomatoes in oil and the cheese. Season the pasta with salt and pepper and toss to coat. Sprinkle the herbs over the pasta and serve at once.   —*Odessa Piper*

WINE The 1997 Bonny Doon Vin Gris de Cigare from California or the 1994 Koehler-Ruprecht Kallstadter Saumagen Riesling Spätlese from Germany.

Pasta Risotto with Crunchy Sprouts

4 FIRST-COURSE SERVINGS

Sprouts bring refreshing crispness to this savory risotto made with tiny macaroni, which can be served as either a first course or a side dish. "Crunchy sprouts," a packaged combination of lentil, green pea and adzuki bean sprouts sold in health-food stores, are particularly good here, but any one of the three will work.

- 1½ cups crunchy sprouts
- 1¼ cups tubettini (about ½ pound)
- 2 tablespoons butter
- 1 teaspoon olive oil

Pasta Risotto with Crunchy Sprouts

1 medium onion, finely chopped
¼ pound shiitake mushrooms, stemmed, caps thinly sliced
Salt and freshly ground pepper
1½ cups chicken stock (p. 117), vegetable stock or canned low-sodium chicken broth
¼ cup freshly grated Parmesan cheese (1 ounce)
1½ teaspoons fresh lemon juice

1. Bring a large saucepan of salted water to a boil. Add the bean sprouts and cook until crisp-tender, about 5 minutes. Using a slotted spoon, transfer the sprouts to a bowl of cold water and then drain. Add the tubettini to the boiling water and cook until barely al dente, about 4 minutes. Drain well.
2. In the same saucepan, melt 1 teaspoon of the butter in the oil. Add the onion; cook over moderately high heat, stirring, until softened but not browned, about 4 minutes. Add the mushrooms and cook, stirring, until softened, about 5 minutes. Season with salt and pepper

and stir in the tubettini. Reduce the heat to moderate and add ½ cup of the stock. Cook, stirring gently, until the liquid is absorbed, about 2 minutes. Add the bean sprouts. Add the remaining stock ½ cup at a time, stirring, until the pasta is al dente and most of the stock is absorbed. Stir in the remaining 1 tablespoon plus 2 teaspoons of butter, the Parmesan and the lemon juice and serve.   —*Grace Parisi*
ONE SERVING Calories 364 kcal, Total Fat 10.6 gm, Saturated Fat 5.2 gm
WINE The mushrooms here echo the flavors of a California Chardonnay; look for the 1995 J. Phelps Carneros or the 1995 Chateau Montelena.

Curly Pasta with Spinach and Chickpeas

8 FIRST-COURSE SERVINGS
This simple pasta was conceived as part of a multi-course meal, so the portions are small. If you're serving it as a main dish, the recipe will feed four.

1½ pounds fresh spinach, stemmed and washed well, or three 8-ounce packages frozen whole-leaf spinach, thawed and squeezed dry
¼ cup extra-virgin olive oil
2½ ounces pancetta, cut into thin strips
4 large garlic cloves, coarsely chopped
1 pound curly spaghetti or fusilli col buco, broken in half
One 19-ounce can chickpeas, drained and rinsed
Salt and freshly ground pepper

1. Heat a large skillet. Gradually add the fresh spinach and cook over moderately high heat, stirring between additions, until it is wilted. Transfer the spinach to a colander, rinse under cold water and then gently squeeze the spinach fairly dry. Coarsely chop the fresh or frozen spinach.

2. In the same skillet, heat the oil. Add the pancetta and garlic. Cook over low heat, stirring, until the garlic is lightly browned, about 12 minutes.
3. In a large pot of boiling salted water, cook the pasta until al dente. Reserve ¾ cup of the cooking water and drain the pasta. Transfer it to a large bowl.
4. Return the spinach to the skillet and cook over high heat, stirring, until it is heated through. Add the chickpeas and the reserved pasta water; simmer for 3 minutes. Pour over the pasta and toss well. Season with salt and pepper and serve at once.   —*Umberto Creatini*

Hefter's Artichoke and Goat Cheese Agnolotti with Truffles

4 FIRST-COURSE SERVINGS
For even more flavor, Lee Hefter, chef at Spago Beverly Hills, recommends partially cooking the pasta in boiling water and then finishing it in the sauce.
FILLING
½ lemon
2 large artichokes
½ cup heavy cream
1 garlic clove, thinly sliced
¼ cup mascarpone or softened cream cheese
¼ cup fresh goat cheese (2 ounces)
Salt and freshly ground white pepper
PASTA
1 cup plus 2 tablespoons all-purpose flour
¼ cup semolina, plus more for dusting
½ teaspoon olive oil
½ teaspoon salt
2 large eggs
SAUCE
1 cup Chicken Stock (p. 117)
2 thyme sprigs
2 tablespoons unsalted butter
Salt and freshly ground white pepper
1 tablespoon freshly grated Parmesan cheese

Curly Pasta with Spinach and Chickpeas

Hefter's Artichoke and Goat Cheese Agnolotti with Truffles

1 small black or white truffle, thinly shaved, or 1 teaspoon truffle oil (see Note)

4 baby artichokes, split and grilled (optional)

I. MAKE THE FILLING: Squeeze the lemon juice into a medium bowl of water; add the lemon. Working with 1 artichoke at a time, snap off the tough outer leaves. Using a sharp knife, cut off the yellow leaves at the top of the heart and all but 1 inch of the stem; trim the dark green stubs and fibers from the artichoke bottom and stem. Using a melon baller or spoon, scoop out the furry choke. Thinly slice the artichoke heart and put it in the acidulated water.

2. Drain the artichoke hearts and put them in a saucepan. Add the heavy cream and garlic and cook over moderately low heat until the artichoke hearts are tender and the cream thickens, about 15 minutes; add a few tablespoons of water if the cream gets too thick. Using a slotted spoon, transfer the artichoke hearts to a food processor and puree until smooth. Transfer the puree to a bowl. Stir in the mascarpone, goat cheese and a generous pinch each of salt and white pepper. Refrigerate until chilled.

3. MAKE THE PASTA: In a food processor, pulse the flour, semolina, oil and salt to combine. Add the eggs and process just until the mixture resembles wet crumbs. Transfer the dough to a board and knead until silky, about 1 minute. Wrap the dough in plastic and let rest at room temperature for 30 minutes.

4. Cut the dough into 4 pieces. Using a hand-cranked pasta machine, roll 1 piece of the dough through successively narrower settings until you reach the thinnest setting. Lay the sheet of pasta on a work surface, cover with a kitchen towel and then repeat with the remaining dough, layering it between towels. Using a 2¼-inch round biscuit cutter, cut out rounds from the sheets of pasta dough and arrange the rounds without touching between layers of plastic wrap.

5. Working with 6 rounds at a time, brush each one lightly with water. Set a heaping ¼ teaspoon of the filling in the center of each round and fold the dough over to form half-moons. Crimp and seal the edges, pressing out the air. Arrange the agnolotti in a single layer, without touching, on a baking sheet dusted with semolina. Continue making agnolotti with the remaining dough and filling.

6. MAKE THE SAUCE: In a medium nonstick saucepan, boil the stock with the thyme sprigs until reduced to ¼ cup; discard the thyme. Reduce the heat to low and whisk in the butter. Season with salt and white pepper and remove from the heat.

7. In a large pot of boiling salted water, cook the agnolotti, stirring gently, until just al dente, about 2 minutes. Drain the agnolotti and add them to the saucepan, turning to coat them with the sauce. Sprinkle the agnolotti with the Parmesan cheese. Using a slotted spoon, transfer the agnolotti to 4 shallow soup plates and spoon any sauce on top. Garnish the agnolotti with the truffle shavings and the optional grilled baby artichokes and serve.

—*Lee Hefter*

NOTE Truffle oil is available at specialty food stores and by mail from Urbani Truffles, 800-281-2330.

MAKE AHEAD The agnolotti can be prepared through Step 5 and frozen for up to 1 month; freeze them on the baking sheet and then transfer to an airtight container. Do not thaw the agnolotti before cooking.

WINE A Sauvignon Blanc will stand up to the richness of the agnolotti.

Petal-Printed Pasta with Summer Vegetable Ragout

8 FIRST-COURSE SERVINGS

½ pound fresh peas, shelled

2 large ripe tomatoes, cored

1½ tablespoons extra-virgin olive oil

2 ears of corn, shucked, kernels cut from the cob

4 large scallions, white and tender green thinly sliced, dark green tops finely chopped

1 large artichoke—stem, leaves and hairy choke removed, heart finely chopped

2 large garlic cloves, minced

¾ cup chicken stock (p. 117) or canned low-sodium broth

3 asparagus spears, peeled and cut into ¼-inch dice

Salt and freshly ground pepper

¼ cup coarsely chopped basil

8 Petal-Printed Pasta sheets (recipe follows)

¼ cup freshly grated Parmigiano-Reggiano cheese (optional)

picking flowers

WHAT TO DO

Buy organically grown flowers from greenmarkets, farm stands and specialty produce stores.

Use flowers quickly. They look and taste their best when they've just been picked.

Know your flowers; some of them just are not palatable, and others have inedible or even poisonous parts. A good reference guide is Cathy Wilkinson Barash's *Edible Flowers: From Garden to Palate,* published by Fulcrum.

WHAT TO AVOID

Stay away from florist's shops, where flowers are often treated with pesticides.

Don't clip roadside blossoms—fumes from passing cars can contaminate them.

Don't pat washed flowers dry; it can bruise them. Air-dry flowers instead.

1. Bring a medium saucepan of water to a boil. Add the peas and cook just until tender, about 5 minutes. Using a slotted spoon, transfer the peas to a bowl of cold water. Drain well.

2. Return the water in the saucepan to a boil and add the tomatoes. Cook for 10 seconds and then transfer to a bowl of cold water. Peel the tomatoes and halve them horizontally. Working over a strainer set over a bowl, scrape out the seeds with a spoon. Press on the seeds to extract all the juice; discard the seeds. Finely chop 1 of the tomatoes and add it to the juice. Cut the other tomato into ¾-inch pieces.

3. Heat 1 tablespoon of the oil in a large skillet. Add the corn, sliced scallions, artichoke, garlic and peas and cook over moderate heat, stirring, until softened slightly. Add the stock and asparagus and cook until the liquid has reduced by half, about 5 minutes. Stir in the finely chopped tomato with its juice and a pinch each of salt and pepper. Cook over moderate heat until the liquid is nearly evaporated, about 3 minutes. Off the heat, stir in the basil, scallion greens and the remaining tomato.

4. In a large pot of boiling salted water, cook the pasta, stirring occasionally, until al dente, about 5 minutes. Drain well. Spoon the ragout into 8 warmed shallow soup plates and top with the pasta. Lightly brush the pasta with the remaining ½ tablespoon of olive oil. Sprinkle with the Parmigiano-Reggiano, if using, and serve at once.

WINE Rosé, which often combines the fruit and body of a red with the freshness and acidity of a white, is a great floral accompaniment. Try a Bandol rosé from France, an Italian rosé from Regaleali (Sicily) or Zeni (Veneto) or a Swanson rosé (made from the Sangiovese grape) from California.

PETAL-PRINTED PASTA

MAKES 12 SHEETS

Making this pasta sounds like more work than it actually is. You will, however, need to use a hand-cranked pasta machine.

- 2 cups all-purpose flour
- Pinch of salt
- 3 large eggs, beaten
- 1 teaspoon olive oil
- 1 cup packed small, flat edible flowers, such as pansies and nasturtiums, and flat herbs, such as chives, dill, cilantro, chervil and flat-leaf parsley

1. In a food processor, pulse the flour and salt. With the machine on, add the eggs and oil and process until the dough forms a ball. Transfer the pasta dough to a lightly floured work surface and knead until smooth; the dough should be firm but not dry. Wrap the pasta dough in plastic and set aside for 30 minutes.

2. Cut the pasta dough into 4 pieces. Working with 1 piece at a time, and keeping the rest covered, run the dough through successively narrower settings on a pasta machine until you reach the thinnest. You should have a 2-foot-long sheet of pasta. Cut the sheet in half crosswise.

Petal-Printed Pasta with Summer Vegetable Ragout

3. Lay 1 sheet of the pasta dough on a lightly floured work surface; cover the other sheet with plastic wrap. Scatter ¼ cup of the flowers and leaves evenly over the pasta sheet, leaving a ¼-inch border. Cover with the second pasta sheet and then use a rolling pin to press the 2 sheets together. Roll the sheets through the narrowest setting on the pasta machine one more time. Cut the pasta into 3 even pieces. Set the pasta on a floured baking pan in a single layer and cover with plastic wrap. Repeat with the remaining dough, flowers and herbs.   —*Alan Tardi*

MAKE AHEAD The pasta sheets can be refrigerated overnight.

Buckwheat Noodles with Ginger-Sautéed Squid

4 FIRST-COURSE SERVINGS

- 6 ounces buckwheat noodles (soba)
- 1 tablespoon grapeseed oil or vegetable oil
- ½ cup chicken stock (p. 117) or canned low-sodium broth
- 2 tablespoons soy sauce
- 2 tablespoons olive oil
- 1 tablespoon Asian fish sauce
- 1 tablespoon mirin (sweet rice wine)
- 1 teaspoon minced ginger
- ½ teaspoon Chinese oyster sauce
- ½ garlic clove, minced

Pinch of sugar

Freshly ground white pepper

- 8 large snow peas, thinly sliced lengthwise
- 1 tablespoon minced scallion
- ½ pound cleaned squid, bodies cut into thin rings, tentacles cut into short strips
- 2 medium tomatoes—peeled, seeded and finely chopped
- 1½ tablespoons finely chopped cilantro

Salt

Sothy with Rice Noodles

One 8-inch square sheet of nori (pressed seaweed), cut with scissors into 4-by-½- inch strips

- 1 tablespoon finely chopped flat-leaf parsley

1. In a large saucepan of boiling salted water, cook the buckwheat noodles until just tender, about 3 minutes. Drain and rinse the noodles under cold water and drain again. Toss the noodles with the grapeseed oil and set aside.

2. In a bowl, stir together the stock, soy sauce, olive oil, fish sauce, mirin, ginger, oyster sauce, garlic, sugar and a pinch of white pepper. Transfer to a large skillet and bring to a simmer over high heat. Add the snow peas and scallion and cook, stirring, for 1 minute. Add the squid, tomatoes and cilantro and stir until the squid is just tender, about 2 minutes. Add the buckwheat

noodles and toss until heated through. Season with salt and white pepper and transfer to 4 plates. Top the noodles with the nori strips and parsley and serve.   —*Tetsuya Wakuda*

WINE A medium-weight Chardonnay, such as the 1997 Dromana Estate Australia or the 1996 Beringer Napa Valley, goes with this lively combination of ginger, soy sauce and cilantro.

Sothy with Rice Noodles

4 SERVINGS

This traditional Sri Lankan dish is usually served with homemade rice noodles called *iddyappam,* but rice sticks make a simple substitute. It's important, however, to get the rice sticks as thick as angel hair pasta, between vermicelli and fine spaghetti. If possible, make this dish with fresh curry leaves.

Carrot Gnocchi

1½ cups canned unsweetened coconut milk

½ cup thinly sliced shallots

2 serrano or Thai chiles, cut in half lengthwise

⅛ teaspoon turmeric

14 curry leaves

Salt

Water

8 ounces rice sticks (see Note)

1 tablespoon vegetable oil

¼ teaspoon mustard seeds

1 dried red chile

1 tablespoon fresh lime juice

I. In a medium saucepan, combine 1 cup of the coconut milk with the shallots, serrano chiles and turmeric. Add 8 of the curry leaves, ½ teaspoon of salt and 1 cup of water and simmer over moderate heat until the sauce is thick and the shallots are softened, about 15 minutes. Add the remaining ½ cup of coconut milk and bring just to a simmer. Cover and remove from the heat.

2. Meanwhile, bring a large pot of water to a boil. Add the rice sticks and ½ teaspoon of salt, return to a boil and cook, stirring occasionally, until al dente, about 5 minutes. Drain well and divide the noodles among 4 bowls.

3. In a small skillet, combine the oil, mustard seeds, dried red chile and the remaining 6 curry leaves. Cover and cook over moderately high heat until the mustard seeds pop. Stir the spice mixture into the sauce along with the lime juice and a generous pinch of salt. Spoon the sauce over the noodles. Serve immediately.   —Maya Kaimal

NOTE Rice sticks are available at Southeast Asian groceries and large supermarkets.

Carrot Gnocchi

4 FIRST-COURSE SERVINGS

½ pound carrots

1 tablespoon finely chopped onion

3 tablespoons butter

¼ cup freshly grated Parmigiano-Reggiano cheese

3 tablespoons all-purpose flour

1 large egg yolk

Salt and freshly ground pepper

Freshly grated nutmeg

3 sage leaves

I. Boil the carrots until tender, about 16 minutes. Drain and slice them into 1-inch rounds.

2. In a medium skillet, cook the onion in 1 tablespoon of the butter over moderate heat, stirring, until pale gold. Add the carrots; cook for 6 minutes, stirring occasionally. Transfer the carrot mixture to a food processor and puree until smooth. Scrape the puree into a bowl and let cool completely.

3. Add 3 tablespoons of the cheese, the flour and the egg yolk to the carrot puree. Season with salt, pepper and a pinch of nutmeg; mix thoroughly.

4. Preheat the oven to 400°. Bring a wide shallow saucepan of water to a boil and add 2½ tablespoons of salt. Prepare a bowl of ice water.

5. Using 2 soup spoons, shape the carrot mixture into neat 3-sided ovals by gently scooping a portion between the spoons. Once the gnocchi are shaped, slide 4 at a time into the boiling water and cook just until they rise to the surface, 7 to 10 seconds. When the gnocchi are done, transfer them to the ice water with a slotted spoon.

6. Lightly butter a baking dish large enough to hold the gnocchi in a single layer without crowding. Drain the gnocchi and arrange them in the baking dish. Tear the sage leaves into small pieces and scatter them on top of the gnocchi. Sprinkle the gnocchi with the remaining 1 tablespoon of cheese and dot with the remaining butter. Bake the gnocchi on the top shelf of the oven for 10 minutes. Serve at once.

—Gianfranco Marcolin and Antonino Venica

Pasta with Peas, Garlic and Ricotta Salata

Pasta with Peas, Garlic and Ricotta Salata

4 SERVINGS

½ cup extra-virgin olive oil

4 large garlic cloves, thinly sliced

1 cup fresh baby peas (1 pound unshelled)

1 pound linguine

Salt and freshly ground pepper

1 tablespoon coarsely chopped marjoram

½ cup crumbled or shaved ricotta salata or feta cheese (about 2 ounces)

I. Heat the oil in a medium skillet. Add the garlic and cook over low heat, stirring, until very soft and golden, about 3 minutes. Remove from the heat.

2. In a large saucepan of boiling salted water, blanch the peas in a strainer until just tender, about 3 minutes. Transfer the peas to a bowl.

3. Add the linguine to the saucepan and boil until al dente. Drain the linguine, reserving ¼ cup of the cooking water. Return the cooked linguine to the saucepan and then toss with the garlic oil, the peas and the reserved

pasta water. Season with salt and pepper and sprinkle with the marjoram. Top the linguine with the cheese and serve at once. —*Alice Waters*

WINE The pasta suggests a sophisticated dry white from California, but one with an aromatic, fruity character that can play off the sweetness of the peas and fresh marjoram. Viognier—the 1995 Arrowood or the 1996 Calera—would be an attractive match.

Spaghetti Primavera

6 SERVINGS ★★★ 1978

Sirio Maccioni's classic, from FOOD & WINE's premier issue, was a signature dish at New York City's Le Cirque. And it's still made the same way today at Le Cirque 2000.

- ⅓ cup pine nuts
- ¼ cup plus 2 tablespoons olive oil
- 2 medium tomatoes, coarsely chopped
- ¼ cup plus 1 tablespoon finely chopped flat-leaf parsley
- ¼ cup minced basil
- 1 teaspoon finely minced garlic

Salt and freshly ground pepper
- 2 cups broccoli florets, cut into 1-inch pieces
- ½ pound snow peas, trimmed and halved crosswise
- 2 small zucchini, quartered lengthwise and sliced ¼ inch thick
- 6 asparagus stalks, peeled and sliced ¼ inch thick
- 1 pound imported spaghetti
- ½ pound mushrooms, thinly sliced
- 1 cup thawed frozen baby peas
- ¼ cup chicken stock (p. 117) or canned low-sodium broth
- 1 to 1½ cups freshly grated Parmesan cheese
- ⅔ cup heavy cream
- 6 tablespoons butter, cut into small pieces

1. Preheat the oven to 300°. Spread the pine nuts in a pie plate and toast for about 12 minutes, or until golden.

2. In a small skillet, heat 2 tablespoons of the oil. Add the tomatoes, ¼ cup of the parsley, the basil and ½ teaspoon of the garlic and cook over moderate heat, stirring, until the tomatoes soften, 2 or 3 minutes. Season with salt and pepper.

3. Bring a large pot of water to a boil. Add the broccoli, snow peas, zucchini and asparagus, bring back to a boil and blanch for 30 seconds. Using a slotted spoon, quickly transfer the vegetables to a colander. Rinse under cold running water to stop the cooking. Drain and pat dry.

4. Return the water to a boil and add salt. Add the spaghetti and boil until al dente, about 11 minutes.

5. Meanwhile, in a large skillet, heat the remaining ¼ cup of oil. Add the mushrooms and the remaining 1 tablespoon of parsley and ½ teaspoon of garlic. Cook over moderately high heat, stirring occasionally, until the mushrooms are lightly browned. Add the blanched vegetables and the baby peas and toss over high heat until most of the liquid has evaporated and the vegetables are just tender.

6. Reheat the tomato sauce. Drain the spaghetti and return it to the pot. Add the chicken stock, Parmesan, cream and butter and stir over low heat until the cheese melts. Add the vegetables, season with salt and pepper and toss thoroughly. Transfer the spaghetti to 6 plates, top with the tomato sauce and pine nuts and serve. —*Sirio Maccioni*

Fettuccine with Roasted Spring Vegetables and Ham

Fettuccine with Roasted Spring Vegetables and Ham

12 SERVINGS

3 pounds thin asparagus, trimmed and cut on the diagonal into 1½-inch lengths

1½ pounds leeks, white and tender green, halved lengthwise and sliced crosswise 1½ inches thick

12 scallions, cut into 1½-inch lengths

⅓ cup extra-virgin olive oil

3 tablespoons fresh lemon juice

Salt and freshly ground pepper

2 cups heavy cream

¼ cup chopped dill

2 pounds dried fettuccine

¾ pound smoked ham, cut into 2-by-¼-inch strips

Freshly grated Parmesan cheese

I. Preheat the oven to 450°. In a large roasting pan, combine the asparagus, leeks, scallions, oil and half the lemon juice; season with salt and pepper. Roast the vegetables, tossing once or twice, for 20 minutes, or until tender.

2. In a small saucepan, combine the cream and dill; season with salt and pepper. Bring to a boil and then remove from the heat, cover and keep warm.

3. Cook the pasta in a large pot of boiling salted water until al dente. Drain well, reserving 1 cup of the cooking water. Return the pasta to the pot; add the vegetables, ham, cream mixture and the remaining 1½ tablespoons lemon juice. Toss over low heat; add some of the cooking water if the pasta seems dry. Season with salt and pepper, transfer to a platter and serve. Pass the cheese separately. —*Grace Parisi*

WINE A rich Chardonnay.

Summer Vegetable Pasta

4 SERVINGS

Delicious and simple, this vegetable packed pasta dish is perfect on a hot summer day.

1 cup fresh peas (about 1 pound in the pod) or thawed frozen peas

Salt

¾ pound penne, orecchiette or medium shells

2 tablespoons extra-virgin olive oil

1 cup fresh or thawed frozen corn kernels

1 cup halved cherry tomatoes

½ cup torn basil leaves

2 tablespoons unsalted butter

Freshly ground pepper

½ cup freshly grated Parmesan cheese (about 1½ ounces)

I. In a small saucepan of boiling water, cook the fresh peas until just tender, about 4 minutes. Drain and rinse the cooked peas under cold water.

2. In a large saucepan of boiling salted water, cook the pasta, stirring occasionally, until al dente. Drain well and transfer to a large bowl.

3. Add the oil to the large saucepan and then add the peas and corn. Cook over moderate heat until the vegetables are tender but not browned, about 5 minutes. Add the cherry tomatoes and basil and cook just until warmed through. Remove the sauce from the heat and stir in the butter; season with salt and pepper. Add the pasta, tossing to coat with the sauce. Return to the bowl, add the Parmesan and serve immediately.   —*Emily Luchetti*

SERVE WITH A tossed green salad.

WINE A clean, lean Pinot Grigio from Italy, such as the 1997 Doro Princic or 1996 Santa Margherita, is all the contrast the sweet corn and peas and tangy tomatoes in this pasta need.

Farfalle with Wild Mushrooms

2 SERVINGS

1 head of garlic

¼ cup extra-virgin olive oil

4 plum tomatoes, quartered

Salt and freshly ground pepper

¼ cup dried porcini (scant ½ ounce)

½ cup boiling water

½ pound assorted fresh mushrooms, such as chanterelles and stemmed shiitakes, halved or quartered if large

1 large shallot, minced

2 tablespoons dry Marsala

½ pound farfalle

1½ tablespoons unsalted butter

½ cup shaved Parmesan cheese

6 basil leaves, finely shredded

I. Preheat the oven to 425°. Cut 1 inch off the top of the garlic and set the head on a piece of aluminum foil, cut side up. Pour 1 teaspoon of the oil over the cut garlic, wrap it in the foil and roast for about 1 hour or until very tender. Squeeze the roasted garlic from the skins into a small bowl and mash well. Cover with plastic wrap.

2. Meanwhile, on a rimmed baking sheet, toss the tomato wedges with 2 teaspoons of the oil and season with salt and pepper. Lay the wedges on their side and roast for about 30 minutes, or until tender and browned on the bottom. Using a spatula, transfer the tomatoes to a plate.

3. In a small heatproof bowl, cover the porcini with the boiling water and set aside to soften, about 20 minutes. Remove the mushrooms from the liquid and rinse them under running water to remove any grit; reserve the liquid.

4. In a large skillet, heat 2 tablespoons of the oil. Add the fresh mushrooms in an even layer, season with salt and pepper and cook over moderately high heat, without stirring, until deep brown on the bottom, about 4 minutes. Stir the mushrooms and continue to cook until tender, about 4 minutes longer. Transfer to a plate.

5. Add the remaining 1 tablespoon of oil and the shallot to the skillet and

Farfalle with Wild Mushrooms

cook over moderate heat until translucent, about 3 minutes. Add the Marsala and simmer until reduced by half. Pour in the reserved mushroom soaking liquid, stopping when you reach the grit at the bottom. Add the porcini and the roasted garlic puree.

6. Cook the farfalle in a large pot of boiling salted water until al dente, about 10 minutes. Meanwhile, rewarm the roasted tomatoes and the mushroom sauce. Add the sautéed fresh mushrooms to the sauce and swirl in 1 tablespoon of the butter. Season with salt and pepper.

7. Drain the pasta and toss it with the remaining ½ tablespoon of butter. Add the sauce and toss well. Mound the pasta in 2 shallow bowls and top with the roasted tomato wedges, Parmesan shavings and basil.

—Mel's Bar & Grill, Denver

WINE The dish shouts out for a hearty, rich Southern Italian red, such as the 1990 Dr. Cosimo Taurino Notarpanaro.

Spaghetti Rotolo with Zucchini and Bacon

6 SERVINGS

The kitchen at Casa Shangri-La, a small Italian resort in Friuli, Italy, serves deftly executed dishes that could be described as generically Italian. For this one, each portion of pasta is rolled up on a long fork to make what resembles a skein of wool.

- 1 **pound fresh young zucchini**
- 2 **tablespoons vegetable oil**
- 2 **tablespoons butter**
- 3 **garlic cloves**

One 6-inch rosemary sprig

Salt and freshly ground pepper
- 3 **ounces bacon, cut crosswise into fine julienne (½ cup)**
- ½ **cup dry white wine**
- 1 **pound imported spaghetti**
- ⅔ **cup freshly grated Parmigiano-Reggiano cheese (2½ ounces)**

1. Soak the zucchini in a bowl of cold water for 20 minutes. Using a vegetable brush, scrub the zucchini under running water. Trim off the ends and finely shred the zucchini in a food processor or on a box grater.

2. In large deep skillet, combine the oil, butter, garlic and rosemary and cook over moderately high heat until fragrant; do not let the garlic brown. Discard the garlic and rosemary. Add the zucchini; season with salt and pepper. Cook, stirring, until thoroughly coated, about 1 minute. Stir in the bacon and cook for 1 minute. Add the wine and simmer over moderate heat until the sauce is creamy, about 6 minutes.

3. Meanwhile, bring a large pot of water to a boil. Add 1½ tablespoons of salt and when the water returns to a boil, add the spaghetti. Cook, stirring occasionally, until al dente. Add 3 tablespoons of the pasta cooking water to the sauce and then drain the spaghetti well. Add the spaghetti to the skillet and stir once or twice over high heat. Remove from the heat, stir in the grated cheese and toss the spaghetti rapidly until thoroughly coated.

4. Spear one-sixth of the pasta with a long-tined meat fork and hold it a few inches above the plate. Working quickly, twirl the fork to form a coil about 2 inches wide by 5 inches long; it may help to hold your other hand at the tine end to keep the pasta from slipping off. Transfer the coil to a warmed platter and repeat with the remaining pasta, lining up the coils side by side. Spoon any remaining sauce around the pasta. Serve at once. *—Marcella Hazan*

WINE An earthy white, such as Pinot Grigio, would work well with this savory pasta, but Tocai Friulano, an Italian white with more character, would match the smoky bacon particularly well. Consider the 1996 Doro Princic or the 1996 Livio Felluga.

Spinach-Ricotta Cavatelli with Tomato Sauce

8 SERVINGS

You can substitute one and three-quarter pounds of store bought fresh or frozen cavatelli or potato gnocchi for the homemade cavatelli.

CAVATELLI
- 1¼ **cups low-fat ricotta cheese (12 ounces)**
- ¼ **cup thawed frozen spinach, squeezed dry and chopped**
- 1 **large egg yolk**
- 1 **tablespoon olive oil**
- 1¾ **cups all-purpose flour**
- 1 **cup semolina**
- 1 **tablespoon salt**
- ½ **teaspoon freshly ground white pepper**

SAUCE
- ½ **cup sun-dried tomatoes (not packed in oil)**
- 2 **teaspoons olive oil**
- 2 **pounds plum tomatoes, cored and quartered**
- 4 **garlic cloves, smashed**
- 1 **cup finely chopped basil**
- ½ **cup chicken stock (p. 117) or canned low-sodium broth**

Salt and freshly ground black pepper
- 2 **tablespoons plus 2 teaspoons freshly grated Parmesan cheese**

1. MAKE THE CAVATELLI: Put the ricotta, spinach, egg yolk and 1 tablespoon of oil in a food processor and process to a paste. Add the flour, semolina, salt and white pepper; process until the mixture comes together to form a ball. Scrape the dough out onto a lightly floured work surface and knead briefly. Wrap in plastic. Let stand at room temperature for 30 minutes.

2. MAKE THE SAUCE: Cover the sun-dried tomatoes with hot water and let soak until plumped, about 25 minutes. Drain well and coarsely chop and then transfer to a mini-processor and puree. ➤

Red Tortelli with Five Cheeses

3. Heat the 2 teaspoons of oil in a saucepan. Add the plum tomatoes and the garlic and cook over moderate heat, stirring, until the tomatoes release their juices, about 3 minutes. Add the basil and stock. Cover and simmer over low heat until the tomatoes are very soft, about 5 minutes. Strain the sauce, pressing on the tomatoes to extract as much sauce as possible. Stir in the sun-dried tomatoes and season the sauce with salt and black pepper.

4. Cut the cavatelli dough into 10 equal pieces. On a lightly floured work surface, using both hands, roll out each piece of dough into a ½-inch-thick rope. With a fork, cut the rope into ½-inch pieces. Press the side of the fork lengthwise into the center of each piece. Set the cavatelli on a lightly floured baking sheet.

5. In a large pot of boiling salted water, cook the cavatelli in batches, stirring, until they rise to the surface, about 4 minutes. Drain the cavatelli and divide them among 8 shallow bowls. Pour ½ cup of the hot tomato sauce over each portion and then sprinkle each with 1 teaspoon of the Parmesan.
—*Francesco Martorella*

MAKE AHEAD The cavatelli can be shaped and then frozen, uncooked, for up to 1 month.

ONE SERVING Calories 312 kcal, Total Fat 6.8 gm, Saturated Fat 2.2 gm

Farfalle alla Primavera
6 SERVINGS
The sauce for this dish can be prepared in the time it takes to boil the pasta. Ripe farm-stand tomatoes and buffalo mozzarella make all the difference here.

1 pound imported farfalle
2 pounds ripe tomatoes, halved and seeded
½ cup coarsely chopped flat-leaf parsley, plus 2 tablespoons for sprinkling
½ cup coarsely chopped basil
4 garlic cloves, coarsely chopped
Salt and freshly ground pepper
¾ pound buffalo mozzarella, cut into ½-inch dice
¼ cup extra-virgin olive oil, plus more for drizzling

1. Cook the pasta in a large pot of boiling salted water, stirring occasionally, until al dente.

2. Meanwhile, in a food processor, puree half the tomatoes with ½ cup of the parsley, the basil and garlic and season with salt and pepper. Transfer the puree to a large glass or stainless-steel bowl. Cut the remaining tomatoes into ½-inch dice and add them to the bowl, along with the mozzarella and ¼ cup of the oil.

3. Drain the pasta, add it to the bowl and toss to coat. Season with salt and pepper. Serve the pasta at once, drizzling each plate with oil and sprinkling with chopped parsley.   —*Ed Giobbi*

Red Tortelli with Five Cheeses
6 SERVINGS
Store-bought fresh pasta sheets can be used in place of the Tomato Pasta in this *tortelli rossi*.

½ cup freshly grated Parmigiano-Reggiano cheese
½ cup plus 2 tablespoons fresh ricotta cheese
¼ cup robiola cheese
3 tablespoons Gorgonzola cheese
2 tablespoons freshly grated Pecorino Romano cheese
Tomato Pasta (recipe follows)
2 tablespoons unsalted butter, melted
Freshly ground pepper

Farfalle alla Primavera

1. In a bowl, mix ¼ cup of the Parmigiano-Reggiano with the ricotta, robiola, Gorgonzola and Pecorino cheeses. Refrigerate.

2. Cut the pasta into 4 pieces and flatten slightly. Wrap 3 of the pieces in plastic. Using a hand-cranked pasta machine, roll the fourth piece of dough through successively narrower settings until you reach the thinnest. Cut the dough into 4-inch squares and cover with plastic wrap. Repeat with the remaining pieces of dough; you will need 18 squares total.

3. Working with 3 squares at a time, lightly moisten the edges. Place 1 tablespoon of the cheese filling in the center of each square and fold in half to make a triangle; press around the edges to seal. Transfer the tortelli to a baking sheet dusted with cornmeal and cover them with a kitchen towel. Repeat with the remaining pasta dough and cheese filling.

4. Cook the tortelli in a large pot of boiling salted water, stirring once or twice, until al dente, about 6 minutes

Spaghetti with Fried Capers and Anchovies

from the time they rise to the surface. Drain the tortelli gently and toss them with the melted butter. Transfer 3 of the tortelli to each plate and top with the remaining Parmigiano-Reggiano. Season with pepper and serve.

WINE The 1993 Prunotto Barbaresco or 1990 Rainoldi Sassella Riserva.

TOMATO PASTA

MAKES ABOUT 1¼ POUNDS

- 2½ cups all-purpose flour
- 2 large eggs plus 1 egg yolk
- ⅓ cup tomato paste
- 2 teaspoons extra-virgin olive oil
- ½ teaspoon salt

Put the flour in a large bowl and make a well in the center. Add the eggs, egg yolk, tomato paste, oil and salt to the well and stir to blend. Gradually work in the flour until the dough masses together and pulls away from the side of the bowl; it should be soft, pliable and slightly sticky. Turn the dough out onto a lightly floured surface and knead until it is smooth and elastic, 8 to 10 minutes. Form the pasta dough into a ball, wrap the ball in plastic and let the dough rest at room temperature for 30 minutes.   —*Romano Tamani*

Cavatappi with Shrimp, Sugar Snaps and Artichokes

12 SERVINGS

- Two 9-ounce packages frozen artichoke hearts, thawed and patted dry
- 6 garlic cloves—2 lightly smashed, 4 thinly sliced
- ¾ cup plus 2 tablespoons extra-virgin olive oil
- 1 tablespoon fresh lemon juice
- Salt and freshly ground pepper
- 1 pound sugar snap peas
- 1½ pounds fava beans, shelled
- 2 pounds dried cavatappi (long corkscrew pasta tubes)
- 2 fresh red chiles, thinly sliced

- 2¼ pounds medium shrimp— shelled, deveined and halved lengthwise
- 4 scallions, thinly sliced
- 2 tablespoons chopped tarragon
- ½ cup dry white wine

1. In a glass or stainless-steel bowl, combine the artichoke hearts with the smashed garlic, 2 tablespoons of the olive oil and the lemon juice; season with salt and pepper. Refrigerate the artichoke hearts for 2 hours or up to 1 day. Discard the garlic.

2. Cook the sugar snap peas in boiling water until just tender, about 5 minutes. Using a slotted spoon, transfer them to a colander set under cold running water; drain. Repeat with the fava beans, cooking them for 2 minutes. Peel the beans and then add them to the peas.

3. Heat a 12-inch skillet. Add the artichokes in a single layer and cook over high heat, turning once or twice, until golden, about 8 minutes. Transfer the artichokes to a large bowl. Repeat with the snap peas and fava beans, cooking them for 3 minutes; add to the artichoke hearts.

4. Cook the cavatappi in a large pot of boiling salted water until al dente. Drain well, reserving ½ cup of the cooking water, and then add the cavatappi to the vegetables.

5. Meanwhile, heat the remaining ¾ cup of oil in the skillet. Add the chiles and sliced garlic and cook over high heat, stirring, for 2 minutes. Add the shrimp, scallions and tarragon, season with salt and pepper and cook, stirring, just until the shrimp turn pink. Add the wine and cook, stirring, for 2 minutes and then pour the sauce over the pasta and toss. Add some of the cooking water if the pasta looks dry. Season the pasta with salt and pepper and serve.   —*Grace Parisi*

WINE An elegant Chianti Classico.

Spaghetti with Fried Capers and Anchovies

4 SERVINGS

The fried capers described in Peggy Knickerbocker's outstanding book *Olive Oil,* published by Chronicle Books, were the inspiration for this dish. The capers add a wonderful bite to the lemon-spiked pasta.

- ⅓ cup olive oil (see Note)
- ½ cup drained nonpareil capers, rinsed
- 1 pound spaghetti
- 6 anchovy fillets, coarsely chopped
- 1 garlic clove, minced
- 1 tablespoon finely grated lemon zest
- ½ cup finely chopped flat-leaf parsley
- ⅓ cup extra-virgin olive oil (see Note)
- 2 tablespoons fresh lemon juice
- ½ teaspoon crushed red pepper

1. In a small skillet, heat the olive oil until shimmering. Add the capers and fry over high heat, stirring occasionally, until browned and shriveled, about 4 minutes. Strain the capers and discard the oil.

2. Cook the pasta in a large pot of boiling salted water until al dente. Meanwhile, in a mortar or mini-processor, combine the anchovies, garlic and lemon zest and pound or process to a thick paste. Transfer to a large glass or stainless-steel bowl; stir in the parsley, extra-virgin olive oil, lemon juice, red pepper and fried capers.

3. Drain the spaghetti and add it to the fried caper mixture. Toss to coat and serve.   —*Jan Newberry*

NOTE Use a mild-flavored olive oil to fry the capers; look for a peppery or pungent extra-virgin olive oil to pick up the tangy pasta sauce.

WINE This salty, savory pasta points to a white with a fairly high level of acidity. Try the herby, flavorful 1996 Cakebread Sauvignon Blanc or the 1996 Dry Creek Fumé Blanc Reserve, both from California.

Tom's Spicy Macaroni with Clams and Sausage

6 SERVINGS

Tom Valenti, the chef at Manhattan's Butterfield 81, has a knack for transforming a classic dish with one or two powerful flavors.

- 2 tablespoons olive oil
- 1½ cups coarsely chopped Spanish onion
- 1 celery rib, finely chopped
- 3 garlic cloves, thinly sliced
- 2 tablespoons tomato paste
- One 28-ounce can peeled whole plum tomatoes
- 1 teaspoon finely chopped thyme
- 1 teaspoon finely chopped marjoram
- 1 bay leaf
- 1 pound hot Italian sausages, casings removed, sausages cut into 1-inch pieces
- 1 pound short tubular pasta, such as ditalini or tubetti
- ¼ cup dry white wine
- 2 dozen small clams, scrubbed and rinsed
- 1 teaspoon crushed red pepper

Salt and freshly ground black pepper

- ¼ cup chopped flat-leaf parsley

1. Heat the oil in a large saucepan. Add the onion, celery and half of the garlic and cook over moderate heat, stirring, until tender, 8 to 10 minutes. Add the tomato paste and cook, stirring, for 3 minutes. Stir in the tomatoes, thyme, marjoram and bay leaf, cover partially and simmer over low heat for 1 hour.

2. Heat a large skillet and add the sausages. Cook over moderate heat, stirring, until browned and cooked through, 8 to 10 minutes. Transfer the sausages to a dish.

3. In a large saucepan of boiling salted water, cook the pasta until al dente. Drain, rinse under cold running water and drain again.

4. In a large saucepan, heat the wine with the remaining garlic and then add the clams. Cover and cook the clams over moderately high heat until they open, 4 to 5 minutes. Using a slotted spoon, transfer the clams to a bowl, discarding any that do not open. Strain the cooking liquid, leaving behind any grit.

5. Reheat the tomato sauce in a large saucepan. Add the sausages and cook them over moderate heat until warmed through, about 5 minutes. Stir in the pasta, clam liquid and red pepper and reheat the pasta thoroughly, about 8 minutes. Add the clams. Season the pasta with salt and black pepper. Remove the bay leaf. Sprinkle with the parsley and serve. —*Tom Valenti*

MAKE AHEAD The recipe can be prepared through Step 4. Refrigerate the clams in their cooking liquid and the other components separately for up to 1 day.

Al Cacciatore's Mlinci with Blasut's Chicken Thigh Ragù

6 SERVINGS

On the plate, *mlinci* looks something like *pane frattau,* the pasta dish Sardinians make with briefly boiled pieces of *carta musica,* their wafer-thin bread. The taste and texture of *mlinci,* however, are entirely different and, in fact, unique—more reminiscent of corn tortillas than of any Italian pasta. This recipe was inspired by the *mlinci* at Al Cacciatore, in Friuli, Italy. The traditional sauce for *mlinci* would be made with boar, hare or wild duck, but it's delicious with a chicken thigh sauce flavored with herbs, tomatoes, white wine and lemon zest.

- 1½ cups all-purpose flour
- ⅔ cup fine polenta or cornmeal

- 3 extra-large eggs, at room temperature
- Salt
- Blasut's Chicken Thigh Ragù (recipe follows)

1. In a food processor, combine the flour, polenta and eggs; process just until a dough forms. Transfer to a lightly floured work surface. Knead until smooth and elastic, 2 to 3 minutes. Cover and set aside for 10 minutes.

2. Cut the dough into 8 pieces and flatten each piece. Set a hand-cranked pasta machine on the widest setting and roll each piece of dough through the machine, working through successively narrower settings until you reach the smallest. Cut each pasta sheet into pieces that will fit your cast-iron griddle and set them on a work surface lined with clean kitchen towels; be sure the pieces don't overlap.

3. Set the griddle over moderately high heat and place a single layer of pasta sheets on the hot griddle. Hold the sheets flat using a metal spatula and toast the pasta until it is firm and speckled with brown, about 1 minute on the first side, a little less on the second. Set aside to cool. Repeat with the remaining pasta.

4. Bring a large pot of water to a boil and add 2 tablespoons of salt. Break the pasta into 2-inch pieces and boil until tender, about 1 minute. Drain, toss with the ragù and serve.

WINE Chicken thigh meat, toasted pasta, rosemary and sage all point to a full-flavored but medium-bodied red, such as Merlot. Naturally, Italy offers a variety of excellent choices, including the 1994 Plozner.

BLASUT'S CHICKEN THIGH RAGU

MAKES ABOUT 2 CUPS

Dante Bernardis, a.k.a. Blasut at the eponymous Blasut's restaurant in Friuli, Italy, makes this pasta sauce with young roosters, which are tastier than hens. Chicken thighs, the tastiest part of the bird, are used here. The liberal use of herbs, unusual in most Italian cooking, makes this sauce intensely aromatic and endows it with a depth of flavor that one generally associates with game. The ragù is excellent on any sturdy pasta, such as penne.

1½ pounds chicken thighs—
   skinned, boned and trimmed of
   visible fat
3 tablespoons butter
2 tablespoons vegetable oil
⅓ cup finely chopped onion
⅓ cup finely chopped carrot
½ cup finely chopped celery
½ cup dry white wine
1 tablespoon finely chopped mint
Salt and freshly ground pepper
2 cups canned Italian plum
   tomatoes with their juices,
   chopped
3 strips lemon zest, minced
2 teaspoons finely chopped sage
½ teaspoon finely chopped
   rosemary

1. In a meat grinder fitted with a fine blade, grind the chicken thighs. Alternatively, pulse the chicken in a food processor until finely chopped.

2. In a medium skillet, combine the butter and oil. Add the onion and cook over moderately high heat, stirring, until light gold. Add the carrot and celery and cook, stirring, for 1 minute.

3. Add the chicken to the skillet. Cook over high heat for 7 minutes, stirring frequently. Add the wine and mint and season with salt and pepper. Cook, stirring occasionally, until the wine has bubbled away, about 7 minutes. Stir in the tomatoes and their juices, reduce the heat to moderate and simmer for 30 minutes, stirring occasionally. Stir in the lemon zest, sage and rosemary and simmer for 10 minutes longer. Season to taste and serve. —*Marcella Hazan*

Tom's Spicy Macaroni with Clams and Sausage

Trenne Pasta with Giblet-Mushroom Sugo

8 SERVINGS

In southern Italy, the term *sugo* refers to pasta sauce enriched with meat; it's basically what would be called a ragù in Bologna or points north. Judy Rodgers, of Zuni restaurant in San Francisco, makes a dozen versions, using seasonal mushrooms and bits of beef (skirt, oxtail, cheek), poultry (duck, squab) or rabbit. This one she tosses with trenne—big, chewy triangular pasta tubes; you can also use penne, rigatoncini or wide egg noodles. Rodgers salts the giblets (or any other meat she is using) and refrigerates them for twenty-four hours before cooking.

1 pound duck gizzards and hearts
   (see Note)
Sea salt
½ cup plus 3 tablespoons olive oil
4 ounces pancetta, minced
2 large carrots, finely diced
2 large celery ribs, finely diced
1 medium onion, finely diced
3 cups drained canned chopped
   tomatoes, preferably organic
4 garlic cloves, coarsely chopped
1 dried red chile
1 bay leaf
2 cups hearty red wine, such as a
   Salice Salentino
1 pound mixed wild mushrooms,
   tough stems discarded, caps
   and tender stems finely
   chopped

Orecchiette with Broiled Feta, Peppers and Sausage

1 tablespoon chopped flat-leaf
   parsley

1¾ pounds trenne (see Note)

Freshly ground pepper

1. Sprinkle the giblets with 1½ tea-spoons of sea salt. Cover and refriger-ate for 24 hours.

2. The next day, rinse and dry the giblets and cut them into fine dice. In a large saucepan, heat ½ cup of the oil. Add the giblets and pancetta and cook over low heat, stirring, until the meats have lost their raw look, about 5 minutes.

3. Add the carrots, celery and onion to the saucepan. Cover and cook, stirring occasionally, until the vegetables are tender, about 30 minutes. Stir in the tomatoes, garlic, chile and bay leaf and bring the sauce to a boil over moderate heat. Add the wine, reduce the heat to low and simmer uncovered until the sauce is rich and thick, about 40 minutes.

4. In a large skillet, heat the remaining 3 tablespoons of oil. Add the mush-rooms and cook over moderate heat for 5 minutes. Add the mushrooms to the sauce along with the parsley. Sea-son with sea salt and simmer for 10 minutes longer.

5. In a large pot of boiling salted water, cook the pasta until al dente, about 12 minutes. Reserve 1 cup of the pasta cooking water; drain the trenne and return it to the pot. Add the sauce to the pasta and toss. Season with sea salt and pepper; add some of the pasta cooking water if the pasta seems dry. Remove the bay leaf and serve the pasta at once.   —*Judy Rodgers*

MAKE AHEAD The giblet-mushroom sugo can be refrigerated for up to 5 days. Reheat it gently and season with salt if needed.

NOTE One pound of duck breast can be used in place of the giblets and treated similarly, but the sauce will not be as richly flavored. The trenne pasta can be ordered from Virtual Vineyards at www.virtualvin.com.

WINE Where pasta is the central dish, stick with an Italian wine, such as the classic Barbarescos 1990 Produttori del Barbaresco or 1990 Giuseppe Cortese. You can serve the 1995 San Felice Chianti Classico if a lighter wine seems more appropriate to your menu. Or if you'd prefer a Californian wine, try a medium-weight Zinfandel, such as the 1990 Clos du Val or the 1996 Nalle; both wines have clear varietal fruit without being too oaky or too high in alcohol.

Penne with Spicy Sausage and Chard

4 SERVINGS ✳

Joanne Weir, a cooking teacher and the author of *You Say Tomato,* published by Broadway Books, often treats her guests to this homey pasta—because, as she says, "Everybody likes pasta."

1½ cups chicken stock (p. 117) or
   canned low-sodium broth

3 tablespoons extra-virgin olive oil

¾ pound hot Italian sausage,
   casings removed

2 garlic cloves, minced

1 pound Swiss chard, ribs
   discarded, leafy greens cut into
   1-inch strips

¾ pound penne or fusilli

½ pound ricotta salata or mild feta,
   crumbled

1 tablespoon minced oregano

1 tablespoon coarsely chopped
   flat-leaf parsley

Salt and freshly ground pepper

1. In a medium saucepan, boil the stock over high heat until reduced to ¾ cup, about 6 minutes.

2. In a large skillet, heat 1 tablespoon of the oil. Add the sausage, breaking it up with a spoon, and sauté over mod-erately high heat until cooked through and beginning to brown, about 10 min-utes. Add the garlic and stir until fra-grant, about 1 minute.

3. Transfer the sausage to a platter and pour off all but 1 tablespoon of the fat. Add the chard, cover and cook, stirring occasionally, until tender, about 7 minutes.

4. Meanwhile, in a large pot of boiling salted water, cook the pasta until al dente. Drain the pasta and return it to the pot. Stir in the sausage mixture, chard, ricotta salata, reduced stock, oregano and parsley and season with salt and pepper; toss well. Drizzle with the remaining 2 tablespoons of olive oil and serve.   —*Joanne Weir*

WINE This savory Italian-inspired dish needs a tart, equally savory Italian-inspired red wine, such as a Sangio-vese from California, for contrast. Look for the 1996 Iron Horse or the 1995 Atlas Peak.

Orecchiette with Broiled Feta, Peppers and Sausage

12 SERVINGS

Whole cherry tomatoes look pretty in this dish, but it will actually taste better if you halve or even chop them so that the juices blend with the oil and herbs to make a light sauce.

3 pints red or yellow cherry
   tomatoes

½ cup extra-virgin olive oil

⅓ cup thinly sliced mint leaves

2½ tablespoons chopped oregano

Salt and freshly ground black pepper

2 large red bell peppers

¾ pound feta, sliced ¾ inch thick

2 pounds sweet and hot sausages

2 pounds dried orecchiette

1. In a large glass or stainless-steel bowl, toss the tomatoes with 7 table-spoons of the oil, the mint and 2 table-spoons of the oregano; season with salt and black pepper. Let stand at room temperature for up to 2 hours. ➤

Pasta al Ducale

feta and toss both with the orecchiette; add some of the pasta cooking water if the pasta seems dry. Season with salt and black pepper and serve immediately. —*Grace Parisi*

WINE An aromatic Pinot Gris.

Pasta al Ducale

6 SERVINGS

This is reminiscent of the Mantuan peasant dish that was traditionally made at the time of the pig slaughter.

- ½ cup dried borlotti or other dried beans, soaked overnight and drained
- 4 cups water
- Salt
- 2 sweet Italian sausages
- 2 tablespoons olive oil
- 1 medium onion, finely chopped
- 2 garlic cloves, minced
- 2½ tablespoons tomato paste dissolved in ⅔ cup water
- Freshly ground pepper
- 1 pound rigatoni
- 1 tablespoon finely chopped parsley
- 1 tablespoon finely chopped basil
- 1 tablespoon unsalted butter
- Freshly grated Grana Padano or Parmigiano-Reggiano cheese

I. Put the dried beans in a saucepan, add the water and bring to a boil. Cover and cook over low heat until the beans are tender, about 1 hour; after 50 minutes, add 1½ teaspoons of salt. Drain the beans, reserving ½ cup of their cooking liquid.

2. In a small pan of boiling water, simmer the sausages until they are cooked through, about 8 minutes; drain. When the sausages are cool, remove the casings and finely crumble the meat.

3. Heat the oil in a large skillet. Add the onion, garlic and sausage; cook over moderately high heat, stirring, until the onion softens. Stir in the dissolved

2. Preheat the broiler. Roast the red peppers under the broiler, turning, until charred. Transfer the peppers to a plastic bag and let them steam for 15 minutes. Peel the roasted peppers, discarding the cores, ribs and seeds; cut the peppers into ¼-inch strips.

3. Brush the slices of feta with the remaining 1 tablespoon of oil. Sprinkle the slices with black pepper and the remaining 1½ teaspoons of oregano and broil them until the cheese is golden on both sides.

4. Broil the sausages, turning, until cooked through. Transfer to a cutting board and cover with aluminum foil.

5. Cook the orecchiette in a large pot of boiling salted water until al dente. Drain well, reserving 1 cup of the pasta cooking water. Add the orecchiette to the tomatoes and add the red pepper strips. Slice the sausage, crumble the

tomato paste and cook until slightly thickened. Add the beans and 3 tablespoons of the reserved bean cooking liquid. Season the sauce with salt and pepper.

4. Meanwhile, cook the rigatoni in a large pot of boiling salted water until al dente. Drain the pasta and return it to the pot. Add the sauce and stir over moderate heat for 1 minute; if the pasta seems dry, add a little of the reserved bean cooking liquid. Stir in the parsley, basil and butter. Serve the pasta at once. Pass the grated cheese.

—Aquila Nigra, Mantua, Italy

WINE The 1993 Travaglini Gattinara or 1990 Marchesi di Gresy Martinenga Barbaresco.

Pastitsio

12 SERVINGS

Pastitsio is a taverna favorite made with layers of noodles, a deeply flavored lamb and tomato sauce and a savory custard.

  2 quarts milk
  1 stick (4 ounces) unsalted butter

Pastitsio

½ cup plus 2 tablespoons
all-purpose flour
Salt and freshly ground pepper
Freshly grated nutmeg
4 pounds boneless lamb
shoulder, cut into ½-inch
pieces
5 tablespoons olive oil

best bottles

Here are the finest of the premium
olive oils from California.

McEvoy of Marin Olive Oil Fresh
and harmonious, with herbal flavors and
a slight, pleasant bitterness in the finish.

DaVero Extra Virgin Well-balanced,
with fresh green fruit flavors and a
pleasant pungency.

Lila Jaeger's Olive Oil From an old
orchard of 100-year-old trees, soft,
sweet, rather buttery, with clean fruit
flavors and a pleasantly bitter edge.

Frantoio Soft, sweet, with lushly
fruity flavors.

Stutz 1997 Mission Reserve Unfiltered
single-varietal with light fruit flavors and a
hint of almonds—contradicting the belief
that Mission olives can't produce a fine oil.

B.R. Cohn Sonoma Estate Smooth,
soft, lightly fruity, but a trifle bland, in a
hand-etched bottle.

Mail-order sources
Oakville Grocery, 800-455-2305
Strictly Olive Oil, 800-930-0077

1 large onion, finely chopped
1¼ teaspoons cinnamon
¼ teaspoon allspice
¼ cup tomato paste
1 cup dry red wine
One 35-ounce can whole peeled
Italian tomatoes, chopped,
with their liquid
One 8-ounce can tomato sauce
2 teaspoons dried oregano
2 teaspoons sugar
1½ pounds ziti, preferably uncut
1½ cups freshly grated Pecorino-
Romano cheese (4½ ounces)
4 large egg yolks

1. In a medium saucepan, heat the milk
until bubbles appear around the edge.
In a large saucepan, melt the butter.
Add the flour and whisk over moderately high heat until light golden, about
1 minute. Gradually whisk in the hot
milk and bring to a boil. Reduce the
heat to moderately low and cook, stirring, until the sauce is thick, about 8
minutes. Season with 2 teaspoons of
salt, ¼ teaspoon of pepper and ½ teaspoon of nutmeg. Press plastic wrap
directly on the sauce and let cool.

2. Season the lamb with salt and pepper and brown it in 4 batches: for each
batch, heat 1 tablespoon of the oil in a
large heavy casserole. Add one-fourth
of the lamb and brown over high heat;
transfer the lamb to a large platter as
it's browned.

3. Add the remaining 1 tablespoon of
oil and the onion to the casserole. Cook
over moderate heat until the onion is
softened but not browned, about 3
minutes. Stir in the cinnamon, allspice
and ¼ teaspoon of nutmeg and then
the tomato paste. Add the wine and
cook, stirring, until the wine is nearly
evaporated. Add the lamb along with
the tomatoes and their liquid, the tomato sauce, oregano and sugar. Season the lamb mixture with salt and
pepper and bring to a boil. Cover and

cook over low heat until the lamb is
tender, about 1 hour.

4. Meanwhile, cook the ziti in a large
pot of boiling salted water until barely
al dente, about 10 minutes. Drain well,
blot the pasta dry with paper towels
and let cool.

5. Preheat the oven to 375°. Lightly
butter two 13-by-9-inch baking dishes.
Line the bottom of each dish with one-
fourth of the ziti. Spread 2 cups of the
white sauce on top of each and then
cover with the lamb sauce. Sprinkle
each with ¼ cup of the cheese and
top with the remaining ziti. Stir the egg
yolks into the remaining white sauce
and spread the sauce over the ziti.
Sprinkle with the remaining cheese
and bake for 40 minutes, or until the
edges of the ziti are golden and the
sauce is bubbling. Let the Pastitsio
stand for 20 minutes before cutting.
—*Grace Parisi*

MAKE AHEAD The Pastitsio can be
refrigerated for 3 days and reheated in
a 325° oven.

WINE Try the 1996 Casal Thaulero
Orsetto Oro Montepulciano d'Abruzzo.

Madame Hermé's Spaetzle

MAKES 10 SIDE-DISH SERVINGS
Pierre Hermé's recipe for this Alsatian
specialty—a cross between dumplings
and pasta—comes from his mother.

3 cups all-purpose flour
2 cups semolina flour (see Note)
6 large eggs, lightly beaten
1½ cups water
Salt
2 tablespoons unsalted butter

1. Sift the flours into a large bowl and
make a well in the center. Add the
eggs, water and 1 teaspoon of salt to
the well. Using a fork, gradually incorporate the flour, tossing and stirring to
blend; the dough should be smooth
and very soft. Cover and refrigerate for
1 hour.

2. Bring a large pot of salted water to a boil. Working with about ½ cup of the dough at a time, pat each portion into a 3-inch square on a small cutting board with a handle or on the back of a cake pan.

3. Using a moistened metal spatula, a pastry scraper or a chef's knife, cut and scrape ¼-inch strips of dough into the simmering water. Cook the spaetzle, stirring, until they float to the surface, about 2 minutes. Using a slotted spoon, transfer the spaetzle to a colander. Repeat with the remaining dough, moistening the spatula whenever the dough begins to stick.

4. In a large skillet, melt the butter. Add all of the spaetzle and sauté until it is lightly browned. Season the spaetzle with salt and serve hot.

—Pierre Hermé

N O T E Semolina flour is available at specialty food shops.

Spiced Golden Couscous

6 SIDE-DISH SERVINGS

- 1 teaspoon cumin seeds
- 2 cups water
- 1 teaspoon salt
- ½ teaspoon turmeric
- ¼ teaspoon crushed red pepper

Small pinch of saffron threads

- 1½ cups couscous

I. In a saucepan, stir the cumin seeds over moderately high heat until they are toasted. Add the water, salt, turmeric, crushed red pepper and saffron and bring to a boil. Stir in the couscous. Cook, stirring, until the couscous absorbs all of the water that is visible on top.

2. Remove the couscous from the heat, cover and let stand until all the liquid is absorbed, about 15 minutes. Fluff with a fork and serve.

—Betsy Nelson and Jim Kyndberg

ONE SERVING Calories 263 kcal, Total Fat .6 gm, Saturated Fat .1 gm

Mango Couscous

4 SIDE-DISH SERVINGS

- 1½ cups water

Salt

- 1 cup couscous
- ⅓ cup fresh orange juice
- ¼ cup thinly sliced scallions
- ¼ cup finely diced mango
- 2 tablespoons finely chopped red bell pepper
- 2 tablespoons coarsely chopped cilantro
- 1 tablespoon olive oil
- 1 tablespoon rice-wine vinegar

Freshly ground black pepper

In a medium saucepan, bring the water to a boil. Add a pinch of salt and the couscous, cover and remove from the heat; fluff with a fork after 10 minutes. Transfer the couscous to a medium glass or stainless-steel bowl. Add the remaining ingredients, toss gently and serve. *—Oliver Saucy*

ONE SERVING Calories 222 kcal, Total Fat 3.7 gm, Saturated Fat .5 gm

CHAPTER 6 fish shellfish

Romesco of Shellfish and Salted Cod (p. 175)

Foshee's Striped Bass with Caramelized Onion Sauce

Foshee's Striped Bass with Caramelized Onion Sauce

6 SERVINGS

Trey Foshee, chef at the Tree Room in Sundance, Utah, suggests that if you can't find fresh morels, you can substitute reconstituted dried ones.

- 5 pounds fresh fava beans, shelled
- 1 stick (4 ounces) unsalted butter
- ½ cup finely chopped onion, plus 2 medium onions, thinly sliced

Salt and freshly ground white pepper

- 4 garlic cloves, thinly sliced
- 4 cups Chicken Stock (p. 117)
- 2 thyme sprigs
- ¼ cup balsamic vinegar
- 12 baby leeks or large scallions, trimmed, leeks rinsed well
- 3 tablespoons extra-virgin olive oil
- 24 fresh morels (about 4 ounces), rinsed well and patted dry
- 2 teaspoons coarsely chopped chives
- 1 teaspoon minced shallot

Six 6-ounce striped bass fillets, with skin, about 1¼ inches thick

- 1 teaspoon white truffle oil (see Note)

1. In a large saucepan of boiling water, cook the fava beans for 2 minutes. Drain and refresh under cold running water. Peel off and discard the tough bean skins.

2. In a large deep skillet, melt 2 tablespoons of the butter. Add the chopped onion; cook over moderate heat, stirring, until softened, about 7 minutes. Add all but ½ cup of the fava beans and cook for 2 minutes. Transfer to a food processor. Blend until smooth, adding a little water if the puree is too stiff. Add 1 tablespoon of the butter and process until incorporated. Season with salt and white pepper.

3. Melt 2 tablespoons of the butter in the skillet. Add the sliced onions; cook over moderately high heat, stirring, until soft and caramelized, about 20 minutes. Add the garlic and cook until softened, 2 to 3 minutes. Add the stock and thyme and boil until reduced by half, about 17 minutes. Add the vinegar and simmer for 5 minutes. Strain the sauce into a medium saucepan, pressing on the solids. Boil the sauce until reduced to 1 cup.

4. Heat a grill pan. Pat the leeks dry with towels and toss with 1 tablespoon of the olive oil. Season with salt and white pepper and grill over moderate heat until tender and charred all over, about 8 minutes.

5. Heat 1 tablespoon of the butter in a medium skillet until lightly browned. Add the morels and cook over moderately high heat until softened, about 5 minutes. Add the reserved ½ cup of fava beans, 1 teaspoon of the chives and the shallot and cook for 1 minute. Season with salt and white pepper.

6. Preheat the oven to 400°. In each of 2 ovenproof skillets, preferably nonstick, heat 1 tablespoon of the olive oil until shimmering. Season the bass fillets with salt and white pepper and add them to the pans, skin side down. Cook over high heat just until opaque around the edges, about 3 minutes. Transfer the skillets to the oven. Roast the fish for about 11 minutes, or until the flesh flakes at the thickest part.

7. Meanwhile, bring the sauce to a simmer over low heat. Whisk in the remaining 2 tablespoons of butter and 1 teaspoon of chives. Whisk in the truffle oil and season with salt and white pepper; keep warm but do not boil. Rewarm the fava bean puree and sautéed morels on top of the stove and the grilled leeks in the oven.

8. Spoon the morels onto 6 warmed plates. Set the bass fillets, skin side up, on the morels and top with the leeks. Spoon the fava bean puree alongside, pour the sauce around the fish and then serve.   —*Trey Foshee*

NOTE Truffle oil is available at specialty food stores and by mail from Urbani Truffles, 800-281-2330.

MAKE AHEAD The fava bean puree, onion sauce and leeks can be prepared through Step 4. Refrigerate overnight.

WINE Pinot Noir has the fruitiness to stand up to the rich onion sauce and the mushrooms but is light enough to balance the striped bass.

Roasted Whole Sea Bass with Bay Leaves

6 SERVINGS

- 1 tablespoon coarse sea salt
- 4 tablespoons unsalted butter, cut into ½-inch pieces
- 20 bay leaves, preferably fresh

One 4½- to 5-pound sea bass or red snapper, cleaned and scaled

1. Preheat the oven to 500°. On a large rimmed baking sheet, sprinkle ½ tablespoon of the sea salt roughly in the shape of the fish. Scatter half of the butter pieces and 8 of the bay leaves over the salt. Set the fish on the salt and stuff 6 bay leaves into the cavity. Top the fish with the remaining

Roasted Whole Sea Bass with Bay Leaves

butter, ½ tablespoon of sea salt and 6 bay leaves.

2. Bake the fish in the middle of the oven for about 30 minutes, or until it is cooked through. Use 2 large spatulas to transfer the fish to a platter.

—*Betsy Bernardaud*

Black Bass with Grilled Celery Root and Ginger

4 SERVINGS

Here is an easy-to-prepare but surprisingly complex dish that matches nutty celery root and grilled bass with a light soy-ginger sauce. Red snapper can be substituted for the black bass.

1½ pounds celery root, peeled and thinly sliced
¼ cup corn oil
Salt and freshly ground pepper
Four 8-ounce black bass fillets, with skin
2 tablespoons minced shallots
2 tablespoons minced peeled fresh ginger
2 tablespoons soy sauce
2 tablespoons coarsely chopped cilantro

1. Heat a grill pan. Toss the celery root with 1 tablespoon of the oil and season with salt and pepper. Grill the celery root over moderately low heat, turning occasionally, until tender and browned, 6 to 8 minutes. Transfer the celery root to a large platter, cover loosely with aluminum foil and keep warm.

2. Heat 1 tablespoon of the oil in a nonstick skillet. Season the fish with salt and pepper and cook over high heat just until the flesh flakes easily, about 3 minutes per side. Set on the celery root, skin side up, and cover loosely with aluminum foil.

3. Heat the remaining 2 tablespoons oil in a small skillet. Add the shallots and cook over high heat until golden. Add the ginger; cook just until fragrant and then add the soy sauce. Pour the sauce over the fish, scatter the cilantro on top and serve immediately. —*Gray Kunz*

Steamed Whole Fish with Scallions and Ginger

4 SERVINGS

In this classic southern Chinese dish, a whole fish is flavored lightly with salt, ginger, scallions, wine and sesame oil, placed on a plate and then steamed for less than twenty minutes. Any leftovers are very tasty cold.

One 2-pound red snapper, black sea bass or salmon trout, cleaned and scaled
Sea salt
2 tablespoons minced fresh ginger
2 tablespoons soy sauce
2 tablespoons Chinese cooking wine, dry white wine or dry sherry
1 teaspoon Asian sesame oil
8 scallions—halved crosswise, finely julienned and then cut into 1-inch lengths
1 tablespoon peanut oil or vegetable oil

1. Wash the fish in cold water; wipe dry. Make 3 parallel diagonal 2-inch-long slashes on each side, slicing through to the bone. Rub the fish all over with 1 teaspoon of sea salt. Lay it on a heat-proof plate large enough to hold it.

2. In a mortar, pound the ginger to a paste with a pinch of sea salt. Take one-third of the ginger paste and stuff a little into each of the slashes in the fish. In a small glass or stainless-steel bowl, mix the remainder of the ginger paste with the soy sauce, wine and ½ teaspoon of the sesame oil. Spoon the sauce into the cavity and on top of the fish; let marinate for 10 to 20 minutes.

3. Tuck one-fourth of the scallions into the cavity of the fish. Spoon any marinade from the plate over the fish and top with the remaining scallions.

4. Pour about 3 cups of water into a large wok and bring to a boil over high heat. Set the plate with the fish in a metal or bamboo steamer and cover tightly with a lid or with aluminum foil. When the water is boiling vigorously, put on oven mitts and carefully place the steamer in the wok; the water should not touch the plate. Steam the fish until it is opaque throughout and flakes easily when pulled with a fork, 15 to 18 minutes. Carefully remove the steamer from the wok.

5. When the fish is almost done, heat the peanut oil and the remaining ½ teaspoon of sesame oil in a small skillet until very hot. Remove the plate with the fish from the steamer. Pour the hot oil over the fish to glaze it (steaming often leaves a very matte finish); serve the fish immediately from the plate. Guests can lift pieces off the plate with chopsticks as they eat or they can be served formal portions. Be sure to serve a little of the sauce with the fish.

—*Jeffrey Alford and Naomi Duguid*

WINE Ginger and soy sauce accent the snapper's mild flavor, but this dish

Steamed Whole Fish with Scallions and Ginger

still calls for a lighter white, such as a fragrant but dry Riesling from Alsace. Look for the 1994 Trimbach or the 1996 Lucien Albrecht.

Tomato-Crusted Snapper with Artichokes and Olives

4 SERVINGS

Chef Alfonso Contrisciani's restaurant at the Philadelphia Art Alliance, Opus 251, serves some of the best food in Philadelphia. You can prepare a double batch of the sun-dried tomato powder and keep it on hand in an airtight container to sprinkle on pasta, risotto and potatoes.

- 10 sun-dried tomato halves (not packed in oil)
- ½ lemon
- 3 large artichokes
- 2 tablespoons olive oil
- 1 tablespoon minced shallots
- ½ teaspoon minced garlic
- 1 small fennel bulb—halved, cored and thinly sliced
- ¼ cup finely chopped onion
- ¼ cup dry white wine

- ¾ cup chicken stock (p. 117) or canned low-sodium broth
- 2 tablespoons unsalted butter
- 12 Calamata olives, pitted and coarsely chopped
- ½ tablespoon finely chopped basil
- ¼ teaspoon finely chopped thyme
Salt and freshly ground pepper
Four 7-ounce red snapper fillets, with skin
- 1 tablespoon canola oil

1. Preheat the oven to 225°. Arrange the sun-dried tomatoes on a wire rack set on a baking sheet. Bake the tomatoes in the oven for about 2 hours, or until completely dry; let cool. Finely grind the tomatoes in a mortar or food processor.

2. Bring a small saucepan of water to a boil. Squeeze the lemon juice into a bowl of water. Working with one of the artichokes at a time, snap off the outer leaves and trim off all but ½ inch of the stem. Using a sharp knife, cut off the yellow leaves at the top of the heart and trim the base and stem. Using a spoon or a melon baller, scoop out the

furry choke. Cut the heart into 1-inch wedges and add to the lemon water. Drain the artichoke hearts and add them to the boiling water. Cook, stirring occasionally, until tender, about 12 minutes; drain and transfer to a bowl.

3. Heat the olive oil in a deep medium skillet. Add the shallots and garlic and cook over moderate heat just until golden. Add the fennel and onion and cook, stirring, until tender, about 5 minutes. Add the artichoke hearts and cook until heated through. Add the wine and cook until reduced by half, about 3 minutes. Add the stock and cook until it is reduced by two-thirds, about 5 minutes. Swirl in the butter until melted and then stir in the olives, basil and thyme. Season with salt and pepper and keep warm.

4. Preheat the oven to 350°. Season the red snapper with salt and pepper and sprinkle each fillet, on the flesh side only, with ½ teaspoon of the sun-dried tomato powder.

5. Heat the canola oil in a large non-stick skillet until shimmering. Add the fish fillets, skin side down, and cook over high heat until browned and crisp, about 3 minutes. Turn and cook until lightly browned, about 2 more minutes. Transfer the fillets to a rimmed baking sheet, skin side down, and bake for 12 to 14 minutes, or until opaque throughout. Transfer the fillets to 4 large plates, spoon the artichoke-olive sauce on top and serve. —*Alfonso Contrisciani*
SERVE WITH Mashed potatoes that have been flavored with pesto.

Panamanian-Style Red Snapper

4 SERVINGS

This colorful fish dish is a specialty of Miami's Las Molas restaurant; the Panamanian name is *pescado boca-toreno,* after the coastal town of Bocas del Toro. The fish gets a triple blast of flavor—from the marinade, the stuffing

Tomato-Crusted Snapper with Artichokes and Olives

and the sauce. Rosario Salas McNish, the chef and owner of Las Molas, uses whole snapper, but you can use thick fish steaks instead; cut a pocket in the side for the stuffing. Culentro is a Central American herb with a jagged-edged leaf and a flavor similar to that of cilantro. The herb is available at Latin American markets; if you can't find it, double the amount of cilantro.

STUFFED FISH

Two 2-pound whole red snappers, cleaned and scaled

3 garlic cloves, minced

1 teaspoon sea salt

½ teaspoon freshly ground pepper

¼ cup fresh lime juice

1 cup all-purpose flour

2½ tablespoons finely chopped flat-leaf parsley

2½ tablespoons finely chopped cilantro

2½ tablespoons finely chopped scallions

1½ tablespoons minced celery leaves

2 culentro leaves, finely chopped

¼ Scotch bonnet chile, seeded and minced

2 tablespoons vegetable oil

PEPPER SAUCE

¼ cup olive oil

1 medium onion, thinly sliced

1 medium green bell pepper, thinly sliced lengthwise

1 medium red bell pepper, thinly sliced lengthwise

3 garlic cloves, thinly sliced

1 celery rib, thinly sliced

1 teaspoon dry mustard

½ teaspoon Madras curry powder

½ teaspoon dried oregano

½ teaspoon freshly ground black pepper

¾ cup water

½ cup canned tomato puree

Table salt

Lime wedges, for serving

I. MAKE THE STUFFED FISH: Rinse the snappers and pat dry. Make 3 diagonal slashes to the bone on both sides of each fish. Sprinkle the fish with the garlic, sea salt and pepper and rub them into the slashes and cavities of the fish. Set the fish on a platter, pour the lime juice on top and let marinate in the refrigerator for 1 hour, turning once or twice.

2. Preheat the oven to 400°. Spread the flour on a plate. In a small bowl, combine the parsley, cilantro, scallions, celery leaves, culentro and Scotch bonnet. Work as much of this herb stuffing as possible into the slashes in the red snappers; spread the rest in the cavities.

3. Heat 1 tablespoon of the vegetable oil in each of 2 large ovenproof skillets. Dredge the snappers in the flour. Fry until golden and crisp, about 3 minutes per side. Transfer the pans to the oven and bake the snappers for about 25 minutes, or until the fish is cooked through.

4. MAKE THE PEPPER SAUCE: Meanwhile, heat the olive oil in a medium skillet. Add the onion, green and red peppers, garlic and celery and cook over high heat until crisp-tender and aromatic, about 3 minutes. Stir in the mustard, curry powder, oregano and black pepper and cook until fragrant, about 1 minute. Stir in the water, the tomato puree and any juices from the cooked fish and gently simmer the sauce over moderately low heat until thickened, about 10 minutes. Season with salt.

5. Transfer the fish to a large platter. Spoon the sauce around the fish, garnish with lime wedges and serve.

—*Rosario Salas McNish*

WINE For this zesty dish, stick with an equally assertive Chilean Sauvignon Blanc, such as the 1996 Carmen Reserve or the 1996 Casa Lapostolle.

Haddock Fillets in Rice Paper with Shallot-and-Soy Sauce

4 SERVINGS

Rice papers form crisp shells for the moist seared fish. Cut into smaller portions, these make good appetizers; use the sauce as a dip. The recipe has been adapted from *Jacques Pépin's Table,* published by KQED Books & Tapes.

Four 8½-inch rice paper rounds

1 teaspoon finely chopped tarragon leaves

½ teaspoon salt

½ teaspoon freshly ground pepper

Four 7-ounce skinless haddock or cod fillets, with skin, cut 1 inch thick

¼ cup soy sauce

3 tablespoons rice vinegar

2 large shallots, finely chopped (3 tablespoons)

2 tablespoons chopped chives

1 garlic clove, minced (1 teaspoon)

1 teaspoon sugar

¼ teaspoon Tabasco

1 tablespoon canola or corn oil

I. Using a pastry brush, lightly moisten the rice paper rounds on both sides with water and set them aside for 5

---

the rice paper rap

The rice paper rounds used to wrap the fish for Haddock Fillets in Rice Paper with Shallot-and-Soy Sauce are made from a dough of rice flour, water and salt that's been rolled out paper-thin and dried on bamboo mats.

When buying the rounds, look for the whitest ones you can find. They are available at Asian groceries and some supermarkets.

When using the rounds, begin by moistening them with water to render them pliable. They can then be used raw to wrap cold foods, or filled and steamed, sautéed or deep-fried.

Haddock Fillets in Rice Paper with Shallot-and-Soy Sauce

minutes to soften. In a small bowl, mix the tarragon, salt and pepper; sprinkle on both sides of the haddock fillets.

2. Place 1 piece of haddock in the center of each rice paper round and then fold the wrappers around the pieces of fish to enclose them securely.

3. In a glass or stainless-steel bowl, combine the soy sauce, vinegar, shallots, chives, garlic, sugar and Tabasco.

4. Heat the oil in a large nonstick skillet. Set the fish packages in the pan, seam side down; cook over moderate heat until lightly browned, about 3 minutes. Turn the fish packages, cover and cook until lightly browned, about 3 minutes longer. Remove from the heat and set aside to steam, covered, for 4 minutes. Transfer the wrapped fish to plates and serve with the sauce.

—Jacques Pépin

MAKE AHEAD The fish packages can be assembled and refrigerated in a single layer, seam side down, for up to 4 hours before cooking. The shallot-and-soy sauce can be prepared 1 day in advance.

ONE SERVING Calories 238 kcal, Total Fat 4.6 gm, Saturated Fat .5 gm **WINE** The spicy, salty sauce needs the balance of a soft, fruity white, such as the 1996 Alexander Valley Vineyards Dry Chenin Blanc from California.

Fish Cooked with Fresh Green Chutney

6 SERVINGS ★★★ **1980**

When Madhur Jaffrey wrote her first book, *An Invitation to Indian Cooking,* published by Knopf in 1973, Indian flavors were exotic to Americans. When this recipe was published in the magazine, fresh chiles and cilantro were hard to find.

1 teaspoon cumin seeds
½ cup (packed) chopped cilantro
¼ cup fresh lemon juice
¼ cup water

3 garlic cloves
1 jalapeño, seeded and chopped
1½ cups coarsely grated fresh coconut (about ½ coconut)
2 teaspoons sugar
Salt
3 pounds skinless halibut fillet, cut into six 1-inch-thick pieces
Freshly ground pepper
6 tablespoons unsalted butter, cut into 12 pieces and softened
Chopped flat-leaf parsley, for garnish
Lemon wedges, for serving

1. In a small dry skillet, toast the cumin seeds over moderately high heat until they are fragrant, about 30 seconds. Let the seeds cool and then grind them in a mortar or spice mill.

2. Preheat the oven to 500°. In a food processor or a blender, combine the cilantro, lemon juice, water, garlic and jalapeño; process to a smooth paste. Transfer the paste to a bowl and stir in the coconut, sugar, ground cumin and ½ teaspoon of salt.

3. Lightly season the halibut with salt and pepper. Cut six 12-by-10-inch rectangles of aluminum foil. Butter each rectangle with 1 piece of the butter. Spread 1 heaping tablespoon of the coconut chutney on the foil and top with a piece of fish. Cover each fillet with another heaping tablespoon of chutney and a piece of butter. Seal the foil around the fish, leaving room for steam to build up.

4. Set the packets on a baking sheet. Bake on the bottom rack of the oven for 10 minutes. Open the packets; sprinkle the fish with parsley. Serve at once with lemon wedges. *—Madhur Jaffrey*

Halibut Steaks with Moroccan Spiced Oil

4 SERVINGS

Almost any fish steaks are lovely with this fragrant, lightly spicy oil; try it with tuna or sea bass.

1 teaspoon coriander seeds
1 teaspoon cumin seeds
½ teaspoon fennel seeds
⅛ teaspoon crushed red pepper
2½ tablespoons extra-virgin olive oil
   (see Note)
Four ½-pound halibut steaks, about
   1 inch thick
Salt and freshly ground black pepper

ɪ. In a small skillet, toast the coriander, cumin and fennel seeds over moderate heat, shaking the skillet, just until fragrant, about 3 minutes. Transfer the seeds to a spice grinder or mortar, add the crushed red pepper and grind to a powder. Return the ground spices to the skillet. Add 2 tablespoons of the oil and cook over low heat just until warmed through. Pour the oil through a very fine strainer or a tea strainer and keep warm.

2. In a large nonstick skillet, heat the remaining ½ tablespoon of oil until shimmering. Season the halibut with salt and black pepper and cook over moderately high heat until browned on the bottom, about 5 minutes. Turn and cook the other side until browned and the fish is just cooked through, about 3 more minutes. Transfer the halibut to warmed plates, drizzle with the spiced oil and serve. —*Jan Newberry*

NOTE A nutty extra-virgin olive oil complements the fish; a peppery oil adds depth to the sauce.

WINE When halibut steaks are dressed in oil, the wine needs to have plenty of richness to compensate. Look for a weighty California Chardonnay, such as the 1996 Beringer Private Reserve or the 1996 Alexander Valley Vineyards.

Le Grand Aïoli

8 SERVINGS

The feast known as Le Grand Aïoli is a rather simple meal consisting of boiled fish and vegetables; the aïoli—that golden garlic-scented mayonnaise—is what turns the meal into a gastronomic celebration, the very symbol of Provençal cuisine. Ideally, a *grand aïoli* should feature at least six components. Feel free to use fewer; just serve more of them.

2 pounds white fish fillets, such as
   cod or grouper, with skin, about
   1 inch thick
Coarse sea salt
1 cup dried chickpeas (7 ounces)—
   picked over, rinsed, soaked
   overnight and drained
2 bay leaves
2 garlic cloves
1½ pounds medium beets
8 medium yellow-fleshed
   potatoes, such as Yellow Finn
   or Yukon Gold
1½ pounds medium carrots, peeled
1 cauliflower, cut into large
   florets
1 pound green beans
8 medium artichokes
½ lemon
8 large hard-cooked eggs, peeled
Aromatic Snails (p. 62)
Classic Aïoli (p. 354) or Aïoli-Style
   Mayonnaise (p. 354)

LEFT: **Fish Cooked with Fresh Green Chutney.**
BELOW: **Le Grand Aïoli.**

1. Sprinkle the fish fillets on both sides with 2 tablespoons of sea salt. Arrange the fish fillets on a wire rack set over a pan to catch any juices. Cover the fish fillets with aluminum foil and refrigerate overnight.

2. The next day, rinse the fish fillets thoroughly. Bring a large deep skillet of water to a simmer. Add the fish fillets and poach them gently over low heat until just cooked through, about 8 minutes. Transfer the fish fillets to a large platter and pat it dry.

3. In a saucepan, combine the chickpeas with the bay leaves and garlic. Add water to cover and bring to a simmer over moderate heat. Cover and cook gently until the chickpeas are tender, 1 to 2 hours, adding more water if necessary. Drain and discard the bay leaves and garlic.

4. In a saucepan, cover the beets with salted water and bring to a boil. Turn the heat down to moderate and simmer the beets for 30 minutes, or until you can pierce them with a knife. Drain and set aside. Meanwhile, in another saucepan, cover the potatoes with salted water and boil over high heat cook for 20 minutes. Drain and set aside. At the same time and in the same way, in a different saucepan, boil the carrots. Drain and set aside.

5. Fill a saucepan two-thirds full with salted water. Bring to a boil and add the cauliflower. Boil for 8 minutes, drain and set aside. Meanwhile, fill another saucepan two-thirds full with salted water and bring to a boil. Add the green beans and boil for 4 minutes. While they are cooking, fill a large bowl with ice and water. Drain the beans and plunge them into the ice water. Remove the beans when they have cooled and set aside.

6. Trim the stems from the artichokes and snap off the tough leaves. Cut off the top third of each artichoke and rub the artichokes all over with the lemon. In a large saucepan of boiling salted water, simmer the artichokes over moderate heat until the bottoms are tender when pierced with a knife, about 15 minutes. Drain the artichokes and, when cool enough to handle, pull out the inner leaves. Using a teaspoon, scrape out the hairy chokes. Quarter the artichokes.

7. To serve, arrange the fish, eggs, vegetables and snails on platters and put the chickpeas and aïoli in bowls.

—*Lucie Romana Martin*

MAKE AHEAD The vegetables, eggs and chickpeas can all be refrigerated overnight. Serve chilled or at room temperature.

Paprika-Coated Cod with Cilantro-Walnut Sauce

4 SERVINGS ✳

⅓ cup walnut halves
1 large egg
1 teaspoon vegetable oil
Salt
¼ cup all-purpose flour
1 teaspoon sweet paprika
1 teaspoon hot paprika
Four 6-ounce skinless cod fillets, about ¾ inch thick
1½ cups packed cilantro leaves and tender stems
3 tablespoons fresh lemon juice
¼ cup plus 2 tablespoons extra-virgin olive oil

1. Preheat the oven to 400°. Toast the walnuts for about 5 minutes, or until fragrant. In a small bowl, beat the egg with the vegetable oil and a large pinch of salt. On a plate, combine the flour with the sweet paprika and ½ teaspoon of the hot paprika.

2. Dip each fish fillet in the beaten egg, letting the excess drip off. Coat the fillets with the seasoned flour and arrange them on a wire rack set over a baking sheet. Refrigerate the fish until the coating has set, about 20 minutes.

3. Meanwhile, in a blender or food processor, combine the cilantro with the lemon juice, walnuts and the remaining ½ teaspoon of hot paprika; pulse to combine. With the machine on, slowly add all but 1 tablespoon of the olive oil and process until blended. Transfer the sauce to a bowl and season with salt.

4. Heat the remaining 1 tablespoon of olive oil in a large skillet. Add the fish and fry over moderately high heat until the coating is crisp and the fish is cooked though, about 3 minutes per side. Transfer to plates and serve with the cilantro-walnut sauce.

—*Jan Newberry*

WINE The tender cod gets dual kicks from the paprika batter and the tangy sauce. Serve a chilled, fragrant California Viognier, such as the 1995 Kunde or the 1995 Arrowood.

Pan-Seared Cod with Duck Confit

4 SERVINGS

At Les Platanes in Biarritz, Arnaud Daguin blends seafood from his adopted home with the specialties of his native Gascony. Here, rich duck fat and confit lend the fish a meaty flavor.

Four 7-ounce skinless cod fillets, 1¼ inches thick
Salt and freshly ground pepper
All-purpose flour
2 tablespoons duck fat (see Note)
1 duck leg confit (see Note), boned, skin and meat finely diced
⅓ cup minced shallots
½ cup dry white wine
1 tablespoon unsalted butter
2 tablespoons finely chopped flat-leaf parsley

1. Preheat the oven to 375°. Season the cod on both sides with salt and pepper and dust with flour. In a large

Pan-Seared Cod with Duck Confit

nonstick skillet, melt the duck fat over high heat. Add the cod, skinned side up, and cook until golden on the bottom, about 4 minutes. Carefully transfer the fish to a baking sheet, browned side up, and bake until the fillets are opaque throughout, about 5 minutes.
2. Meanwhile, pour off half of the fat from the skillet. Add the confit to the skillet and cook over moderate heat, stirring, until the skin is crisp and the meat is hot, 3 to 5 minutes; transfer to a plate. Add the shallots to the skillet and cook over low heat, stirring, until softened, about 2 minutes. Add the shallots to the confit. Add the wine to the skillet and cook over moderately high heat until reduced by half. Swirl in the butter and then stir in the parsley.
3. Transfer the fish to warmed dinner plates. Spoon the sauce over the fish, top with the confit and shallots and serve.   —*Arnaud Daguin*
WINE Try a regional match—a white Graves from Bordeaux, such as the 1994 Château Carbonnieux; or serve the 1995 Clos Uroulat Jurançon Sec.
NOTE The duck fat and duck leg confit are available by mail-order from D'Artagnan, 800-327-8246.

Heart and Sole

a valentine's day menu

**Heart-Shaped Caviar Canapés
(p. 31)**

NONVINTAGE TAITTINGER CUVEE
PRESTIGE BRUT CHAMPAGNE

—

**Heartbeet Salad (p. 75)
Goat Cheese Heart (p. 23)**

—

Lobster Ravioli in Broth (p. 177)

—

Heart and Sole (p. 159)

1996 GIOVANNI ALMONDO
ROERO ARNEIS

—

**Chocolate Mousse Cake
with Raspberry Sauce (p. 380)**

1988 CHATEAU RIEUSSEC
SAUTERNES

Moroccan-Spiced Turbot Roasted on Marrow Bones

10 SERVINGS

Although it seems unusual, fish and beef marrow is a delicious combination now appearing on menus all over Paris. Soaking the marrow bones in salted water for two days whitens the marrow. Set out marrow spoons or other small spoons so that marrow lovers can scoop out every bite.

Twenty 2-inch-long beef marrow
    bones (see Note)
Kosher salt
  2 large carrots, thinly sliced
One 5- to 6-pound pan-dressed
    turbot or halibut
  2 tablespoons olive oil
  4 tablespoons unsalted butter,
    cut into small pieces
Fragrant Chicken Jus (recipe follows)

1. In a large bowl, cover the marrow bones with water, add 3 tablespoons of kosher salt and refrigerate the bones for 2 days, changing the salted water several times.

2. Preheat the oven to 425°. Bring a large pot of salted water to a boil. Cover 1 end of each marrow bone with a carrot slice; secure the carrot slices with kitchen string. Add the marrow bones to the pot. Simmer very gently over low heat for 10 minutes, and then remove the pot from the heat and let stand for 5 minutes. Transfer the marrow bones, carrot side down, to a large roasting pan.

3. Rub the turbot with the oil and season with kosher salt. Set the fish on the bones and dot with 2 tablespoons of the butter. Roast the fish for about 50 minutes, or until the flesh is opaque throughout. Remove from the oven, cover loosely with aluminum foil and let stand for 10 minutes.

4. In a small saucepan, heat the Fragrant Chicken Jus over moderately low heat. Gradually whisk in the remaining 2 tablespoons of butter and keep warm over low heat.

5. Using 2 large serving forks, remove the top skin from the fish and then loosen the fillet on each side of the backbone. Cut the fish into servings, set on warmed plates and spoon some of the sauce on top. Untie the marrow bones and set 2 of them on each plate. Serve immediately.

NOTE Beef marrow bones can be ordered from any butcher.

FRAGRANT CHICKEN JUS

MAKES ABOUT 2 CUPS

This sauce would also give a Moroccan flair to chicken, quail or lamb.

  2 tablespoons olive oil
2½ pounds chicken parts, such as
    wings, necks and drumsticks
Salt and freshly ground pepper
  ⅛ teaspoon turmeric
  2 medium onions, coarsely
    chopped
  ½ cup cured green and black
    olives
One 3-inch piece of fresh ginger,
    peeled and thickly sliced
  2 garlic cloves, smashed
  4 cilantro sprigs, coarsely
    chopped
  1 preserved lemon, flesh
    discarded, skin thickly sliced
    (see Note)

Thick strips of zest from 1 fresh
　　lemon
1　dried red chile
1/8　teaspoon ground cumin
6　cups water

1. In a large casserole, heat 1 tablespoon of the oil. Add half of the chicken parts, season with salt and pepper and brown over moderately high heat, about 3 minutes per side. Sprinkle half of the turmeric over the chicken, stir well and transfer the chicken to a plate. Repeat with the remaining chicken and turmeric, using the oil already in the casserole.

2. Add the remaining 1 tablespoon of oil to the casserole and stir in the onions, olives, ginger, garlic, cilantro, preserved lemon, lemon zest, chile and cumin. Cook, stirring, until the onions soften slightly, about 3 minutes.

3. Return the chicken parts to the casserole, add the water and bring to a boil. Cover partially and simmer over low heat for 1 hour. Remove the chicken parts and simmer the sauce over moderately low heat until reduced to 2 cups, about 50 minutes. Remove and discard the chile. Refrigerate the jus for 3 hours and up to 2 days. Spoon off any fat before using.

　　　　　　　　　　—*Frédérick Hermé*

NOTE Preserved lemons are available from Middle Eastern groceries.

Heart and Sole

6 SERVINGS

Serve this delicate sole on Valentine's Day; the parchment pouch is shaped like a heart. Or enjoy it as a delicious light main course on any occasion.

6　tablespoons unsalted butter,
　　softened
1/4　cup mixed chopped herbs, such
　　as parsley, chives and mint
2　tablespoons fresh lemon juice
1　teaspoon grated lemon zest
Salt and freshly ground pepper

Olive oil, for brushing
2 1/4　pounds sole fillets
One 9-ounce package frozen
　　artichoke hearts—thawed,
　　patted dry and halved
　　lengthwise

1. In a small bowl, mash the butter with the herbs, lemon juice, lemon zest, 1/2 teaspoon of salt and 1/4 teaspoon of pepper. Refrigerate the herb butter, covered, for at least 1 hour and up to 3 days.

2. Preheat the oven to 450°. Cut 6 hearts, 20 inches wide and 12 inches long, out of parchment paper. Brush the top of the paper with oil. Evenly divide the sole fillets among the paper hearts, placing the fish on the right side of each heart. Season the fish with salt and pepper and top with the artichoke hearts and 1 tablespoon of the herb butter. Fold the papers over to enclose the fish. Crimp the edges of the papers to seal.

3. Arrange the fish packages on 2 large baking sheets and brush lightly with oil. Bake for 10 minutes, or until the packages are puffed and lightly browned. Transfer the fish packages to plates and serve.

WINE The 1996 Giovanni Almondo Roero Arneis.

Baked Trout with Shiitake Mushroom Pesto

4 SERVINGS

Chef Jim Kyndberg, of the Aveda Spa Retreat in Osceola, Wisconsin, developed this simple, savory dish to spotlight organic midwestern trout. Have the fishmonger prepare the fish for you.

1 1/2　cups dried shiitake mushrooms
2　tablespoons tamari or soy sauce
　　mixed with 2 cups boiling water
3　tablespoons coarsely chopped
　　flat-leaf parsley
2　garlic cloves
1　medium shallot
1　tablespoon plus 1 teaspoon
　　olive oil
Salt and freshly ground pepper
4　trout (about 10 ounces each)—
　　heads removed, fish cleaned
　　and boned, fillets left attached
　　to the skin
Vegetable oil cooking spray

Baked Trout with Shiitake Mushroom Pesto, on Spiced Golden Couscous (p. 145).

Brodetto alla San Benedettese

season with salt and pepper. Spread one-quarter of the pesto in a thin layer on each trout. Spoon the leeks on top and bake for about 10 minutes, or just until the trout is cooked through.

—*Jim Kyndberg*

ONE SERVING Calories 327 kcal, Total Fat 14 gm, Saturated Fat 2 gm

Pan-Fried Monkfish with Shiitakes

4 SERVINGS

- 1 pound spinach, large stems discarded
- 3 tablespoons olive oil
- 2 tablespoons finely chopped lean bacon
- 1 large shallot, finely chopped
- 3 cups chicken stock (p. 117) or canned low-sodium broth
- 6 fresh shiitake mushrooms, stems discarded, caps finely chopped
- 2 small tomatoes—peeled, seeded and finely chopped
- 2 teaspoons soy sauce
- 1½ pounds well-trimmed monkfish fillets, cut into sixteen ½-inch-thick medallions

Salt and freshly ground white pepper
- 2 teaspoons finely chopped chives
- 1 teaspoon finely chopped tarragon
- 2 tablespoons cold unsalted butter, divided in half

One 8-inch square sheet of nori (pressed seaweed), cut with scissors into 4-by-½-inch strips

1. Heat a large skillet. Add the spinach by the handful and cook over moderately high heat, tossing with tongs, until wilted. Transfer to a colander, rinse under cold running water and gently squeeze out the excess water.

2. Heat 2 tablespoons of the olive oil in a large skillet. Add the bacon and shallot and cook over moderate heat, stirring occasionally, until the bacon is

- 2 large leeks, white and tender green, thinly sliced
- 2 tablespoons dry white wine

Juice of 1 lemon

1. In a bowl, soak the shiitakes in the tamari-spiked boiling water until softened, about 30 minutes. Drain the shiitakes, reserving 2 tablespoons of the soaking liquid. In a food processor, pulse the shiitakes and the reserved soaking liquid with the parsley, garlic and shallot until finely chopped. With the machine on, slowly add 1 tablespoon of the oil. Transfer the shiitake pesto to a small bowl and season with salt and pepper.

2. Place the trout on a work surface. Using tweezers, remove the fine pin bones that run along the center of each trout fillet. Coat a large nonstick baking sheet with cooking spray. Arrange the trout fillets, skin side down, on the baking sheet.

3. Heat the remaining 1 teaspoon of oil in a skillet. Add the leeks and cook over moderately high heat until just wilted, about 3 minutes. Add the wine, season with salt and pepper and cook until the liquid has evaporated, 1 to 3 minutes.

4. Preheat the oven to 400°. Sprinkle the trout fillets with the lemon juice;

browned and the shallot is softened, about 4 minutes. Add the stock and mushrooms and simmer over moderate heat until the mushrooms soften, about 7 minutes. Add the tomatoes and soy sauce and cook over high heat until the liquid is reduced by one-third, about 4 minutes.

3. In a large nonstick skillet, heat ½ tablespoon of the olive oil until almost smoking. Season the monkfish with salt and white pepper and add 8 of the medallions to the skillet. Cook the medallions over moderately high heat until nicely browned on the bottom, about 3 minutes. Turn the medallions and cook until just opaque throughout, about 1 minute. Transfer the medallions to a warm platter, cover them with aluminum foil and repeat with the remaining monkfish and oil. Wipe out the skillet and add the cooked spinach. Cook the spinach over high heat, stirring, until warmed through. Season with salt and white pepper.

4. Bring the mushroom sauce to a simmer. Add the chives and tarragon and whisk in the butter, 1 tablespoon at a time. Season with salt and white pepper. Mound the spinach in the center of 4 warm plates; top each mound with 4 monkfish medallions. Spoon the sauce over the fish, sprinkle with the nori strips and serve.

—*Tetsuya Wakuda*

WINE The 1997 Tyrrell's Vat 47 Chardonnay and the 1996 Morgan Monterey Chardonnay have the full flavor to stand up to the butter-thickened sauce served with this fish.

Brodetto alla San Benedettese

6 SERVINGS

Along Italy's Adriatic coast, *brodetto* means fish stew. This one from San Benedetto, northeast of Rome, uses white wine vinegar and tomatoes that are more green than red.

Six ¾-inch-thick slices of Tuscan or peasant bread, halved

¼ cup plus 2 tablespoons extra-virgin olive oil

2 medium red bell peppers, cut lengthwise into ½-inch strips

2 medium red onions, thinly sliced

6 garlic cloves, finely chopped

½ cup white wine vinegar

½ cup coarsely chopped basil

½ cup coarsely chopped flat-leaf parsley

4 unripe medium tomatoes— halved, seeded and diced

2¼ pounds skate, dark skin removed, cut into 6 pieces

2¼ pounds monkfish fillets, skinned and cut into 6 pieces

Salt and freshly ground black pepper

2 pounds littleneck clams, scrubbed

1 pound large shrimp, shelled and deveined

1. Preheat the oven to 400°. Brush the bread with 2 tablespoons of the oil. Arrange the slices on a baking sheet and bake for 8 minutes, or until crisp.

2. In a large casserole or roasting pan, heat the remaining ¼ cup of oil. Add the red peppers and cook over moderate heat until lightly browned, about 5 minutes. Add the onions and cook until lightly browned, about 4 minutes. Add the garlic and cook for 2 minutes. Add the vinegar, cover and cook over low heat for 5 minutes. Stir in the basil and parsley and cook over high heat for 1 minute. Add the tomatoes, cover and bring to a boil and then reduce the heat to low and cook for 10 minutes.

3. Add the skate and monkfish, season with salt and black pepper and bring to a boil. Cover and cook over moderate heat until the fish is opaque throughout, about 12 minutes. Using a slotted spoon, transfer the fish to a large deep platter, leaving the vegetables and broth behind; loosely cover the platter with aluminum foil. Add the clams to the pot, cover and cook until most are open, about 12 minutes. Add the shrimp and cook until pink, about 2 minutes longer. Transfer the clams and shrimp to the platter; discard any clams that haven't opened.

4. Boil the broth over high heat for 5 minutes to concentrate the flavor. Season with salt and black pepper. Serve the fish and broth and pass the toasts separately. —*Ed Giobbi*

MAKE AHEAD The recipe can be prepared through Step 2 and left at room temperature for up to 2 hours.

WINE The dish's tomato and red pepper flavors suggest a tart, Sangiovese-based red. Look for the 1996 Castello di Gabbiano Vino Rosso di Toscana or the 1996 Antinori Santa Christina.

Mango-Jerk Tuna with Couscous

4 SERVINGS

Mango, pureed for a marinade, gives the tuna a lush, sweet flavor. Jerk sauce is available at specialty food stores.

1 small mango, peeled and coarsely chopped

1 small shallot, quartered

2 tablespoons prepared jerk sauce

2 tablespoons fresh lime juice

1 teaspoon honey

Four ⅓-inch-thick 7-ounce slices of sushi-quality tuna

Salt and freshly ground pepper

Mango Couscous (p.145)

1. In a food processor, combine the mango, shallot, jerk sauce, lime juice and honey. Process until smooth and transfer to a medium glass or stainless-steel bowl. Add the tuna and turn to coat. Cover and refrigerate the tuna for 3 hours.

2. Preheat the grill or broiler. Remove the tuna from the mango marinade and season with salt and pepper. Grill

Mango-Jerk Tuna with Couscous

the tuna on a lightly oiled rack or broil-er pan for 1 to 1½ minutes per side, for very rare, or slightly longer for medium. Serve the grilled tuna with the Mango Couscous. —*Oliver Saucy*
ONE SERVING Calories 339 kcal, Total Fat 9.8 gm, Saturated Fat 2.5 gm
WINE With the meaty tuna, try a round, fat-textured, fruity California Chardonnay, such as the 1995 Mark West or the 1995 St. Francis.

Symon's Herb-Crusted Walleye with Lobster Pierogi

4 SERVINGS ♛

If you haven't got the time to make the pierogi dough, you can always substi-tute store-bought spring-roll wrappers, advises Michael Symon, chef at Lola restaurant in Cleveland.

- 2 cups Chicken Stock (p. 117)
- 3 tablespoons truffle butter (see Note)
- 1 tablespoon unsalted butter
- ⅓ cup plus 1 tablespoon coarsely chopped chives

Salt and freshly ground pepper
- ¾ cup (loosely packed) flat-leaf parsley leaves
- ¾ cup (loosely packed) basil leaves
- ⅓ cup light olive oil, plus more for brushing
- ¾ cup coarse stale bread crumbs

Four 1/2-pound skinless walleye pike fillets, about 1 inch thick, or thick grouper, red snapper or sea bass fillets, with skin

12 Lobster Pierogi (recipe follows)

1. In a saucepan, boil the stock over moderately high heat until reduced to 2/3 cup. Reduce the heat to low and whisk in the butters, 1 tablespoon at a time, until incorporated. Stir in 1 tablespoon of the chives and season with salt and pepper.

2. Preheat the oven to 475°. In a blender or food processor, combine the remaining 1/3 cup of chives with the parsley, basil and the 1/3 cup of oil; blend until minced. Transfer the herb puree to a bowl and stir in the bread crumbs. Season with salt and pepper.

3. Line a baking sheet with parchment and brush it with oil. Set the fish on the baking sheet, skinned side down, and season with salt and pepper. Top the fillets with the herb mixture, pressing it down lightly with your fingers. Bake the fish for 12 to 14 minutes, or until it flakes easily at the thickest part.

4. Meanwhile, in a large saucepan of boiling salted water, cook the pierogi until al dente, about 3 minutes. Drain well and return to the pan. Rewarm the sauce and toss 1/4 cup of it with the pierogi. Arrange 3 pierogi on each of 4 large plates and pour the remaining truffle butter sauce over them. Set the fish alongside or on top and serve.

NOTE Truffle butter is available at specialty food stores and by mail from Urbani Truffles, 800-281-2330.

WINE Because Viognier is aromatic, it goes nicely with the rich truffle butter sauce and the mixed herb crust.

LOBSTER PIEROGI

MAKES ABOUT 2 1/2 DOZEN

 1/2 cup sour cream
  6 tablespoons unsalted butter, softened

  1 large egg, lightly beaten
  1 tablespoon minced chives
Freshly ground pepper
  2 cups all-purpose flour
  1 large Yukon gold potato (1/2 pound)
  2 tablespoons half-and-half or heavy cream
  4 ounces cooked lobster meat, cut into 1/4-inch pieces
Salt

1. In a medium bowl, combine the sour cream with 4 tablespoons of the

butter, the egg, chives and 1 teaspoon of pepper. Using your hands, work in the flour. Turn the dough out onto a work surface and knead until smooth and elastic. Shape the dough into two 6-inch disks, wrap in plastic and let rest at room temperature for 30 minutes.

2. Meanwhile, in a medium saucepan, boil the potato in water to cover until tender, about 20 minutes; drain. Peel and press through a ricer or sieve into a medium bowl. Stir in the remaining 2 tablespoons of butter and the half-

Symon's Herb-Crusted Walleye with Lobster Pierogi

and-half and then add the lobster meat. Season with salt and pepper and let cool completely.

3. On a lightly floured work surface, roll out 1 piece of the dough to a 15-inch round about ⅛ inch thick. Using a 3-inch biscuit cutter or a glass, cut out 12 to 15 rounds. Brush each round lightly with water and spoon 1 scant tablespoon of the lobster filling in the center. Fold the dough over the filling to form half moons, pressing out the air; press and crimp the edges to seal. Arrange the finished pierogi so that they don't touch on a baking sheet lined with wax paper. Repeat with the remaining dough and filling.

—Michael Symon

MAKE AHEAD The pierogi can be refrigerated overnight or frozen for up to 1 month; don't thaw before cooking.

Fish Curry with Green Mango

4 SERVINGS

The green (unripe) mango adds a tangy note to this excellent fish curry.

- 1 **cup finely grated dried unsweetened coconut**
- ¼ **cup finely chopped onion**
- 16 **curry leaves**
- ½ **teaspoon ground coriander**
- ¼ **teaspoon cayenne pepper**
- ⅛ **teaspoon turmeric**
- 1 **cup water**
- ¾ **teaspoon salt**
- 1½ **pounds swordfish steaks (1 inch thick), skinned and cut into cubes**
- ¾ **cup slivered green mango with skin**
- 1 **serrano or Thai chile, thinly sliced**

I. In a food processor or blender, combine the coconut, onion and 8 of the curry leaves with the coriander, cayenne and turmeric. Add ½ cup of the water and process to a paste.

2. In a large deep skillet, combine the coconut paste and the salt with the remaining ½ cup of water. Add the swordfish in a single layer and bring to a boil. Add the mango, the chile and the remaining 8 curry leaves, tucking them between the cubes of fish. Gently turn each piece of fish and simmer over low heat until just cooked through, about 10 minutes. Serve the fish curry immediately. *—Maya Kaimal*

MAKE AHEAD The coconut paste can stand at room temperature for up to 3 hours.

SERVE WITH Boiled rice.

WINE A round-textured, ripe-flavored California Chardonnay, such as the 1995 Laurier or the 1996 Meridian, would provide the ideal fruity backdrop.

Herb Roasted Salmon with Creole Vegetables

Herb Roasted Salmon with Creole Vegetables

6 SERVINGS

Alexander Smalls rounds out his salmon with a side of spicy skillet vegetables and roasted sweet potatoes.

SALMON

- 1 **tablespoon olive oil**
- 1 **small onion, minced**
- 1 **medium celery rib, minced**
- 2 **garlic cloves, minced**

One 2½-pound skinless salmon fillet

- ¼ **teaspoon freshly grated nutmeg**

Salt and freshly ground pepper

- 6 **sage leaves**

Leaves from 1 large rosemary sprig

CREOLE VEGETABLES

- ¼ **cup plus 2½ tablespoons olive oil**
- 3 **large sweet potatoes, peeled and cut into 1-inch chunks**
- 5 **garlic cloves, minced**
- 2 **shallots, minced**
- 1 **teaspoon thyme leaves**
- ¼ **teaspoon freshly grated nutmeg**

Pinch of cayenne pepper
Salt and freshly ground black pepper
½ pound small okra, halved
     lengthwise
½ pound shiitake mushrooms,
     stems discarded, caps halved
½ fresh cayenne chile, or
     1 jalapeño, seeded and minced

1. PREPARE THE SALMON: Preheat the oven to 450°. Coat a large roasting pan with ½ tablespoon of the oil. Add the onion, celery and garlic and stir to combine. Set the salmon on the vegetables, skinned side down, and rub with the remaining ½ tablespoon of oil. Season the salmon with the nutmeg and salt and pepper. Sprinkle the sage and rosemary all over the salmon and roast in the upper third of the oven for about 25 minutes, or until nicely glazed and just cooked through. Keep warm.

2. MEANWHILE, PREPARE THE CREOLE VEGETABLES: Spread ¼ cup of the oil on a large rimmed baking sheet. Add the sweet potatoes, 3 of the garlic cloves, the shallots, thyme and nutmeg and toss well. Season with the cayenne pepper and salt and black pepper and roast in the lower third of the oven with the salmon, stirring a few times, for about 25 minutes, or until well browned.

3. Heat 1 tablespoon of the oil in a cast-iron skillet until almost smoking. Add the okra, season with salt and black pepper and cook over high heat, stirring, until lightly charred, about 2 minutes. Transfer the okra to a bowl; keep warm.

4. Reduce the heat to moderate. In a bowl, toss the shiitake mushrooms with the cayenne chile and the remaining 1½ tablespoons of oil and season with salt and black pepper. Add the shiitakes to the skillet and cook, stirring, until tender, about 5 minutes. Add the remaining 2 garlic cloves and

cook until the shiitakes begin to crisp, about 2 minutes. Stir the okra into the shiitakes and cook for 1 minute.

5. Cut the salmon into 6 pieces and place on 6 large plates. Spoon the vegetables around the fish and serve at once. —*Alexander Smalls*

Pan-Roasted Salmon with Savoy Cabbage, Cider and Bacon

2 SERVINGS

Don't be put off by the vanilla in this luscious salmon dish from Ben Davis at Mel's Bar and Grill in Denver; it adds a lovely aromatic note to the cider-sauced cabbage.

½ pound Savoy cabbage, shredded
1 cup apple cider
1 vanilla bean, split
2 slices of bacon, cut into ½-inch
     dice
1 cup dry white wine
2 shallots, thinly sliced
1 tablespoon white wine vinegar
8 whole black peppercorns
2 small tarragon sprigs, leaves
     removed, stems reserved
½ bay leaf
1 tablespoon vegetable oil
Two 6-ounce salmon fillets, with skin
Salt and freshly ground pepper
4½ tablespoons cold unsalted
     butter, cut into pieces
1 tablespoon minced chives

1. In a medium saucepan of boiling salted water, blanch the cabbage until it is barely tender, about 30 seconds. Plunge the cabbage into a bowl of ice water to stop the cooking. Drain and pat the cabbage dry.

2. In a medium saucepan, boil the cider with the vanilla bean until reduced to ¼ cup, about 10 minutes. Remove from the heat.

3. Preheat the oven to 400°. Scatter the bacon in a pie pan and roast for 15 minutes, or until the bacon is crisp and

most of the fat has been rendered. Transfer the bacon to a plate. Leave the oven on.

4. Meanwhile, in a small saucepan, combine the wine with the shallots, vinegar, peppercorns, tarragon stems and bay leaf. Boil until the liquid has reduced to 2 tablespoons, about 12 minutes. Strain the sauce into a small saucepan.

5. In a large ovenproof skillet, heat the oil until almost smoking. Season the salmon with salt and pepper and set the fillets in the skillet, skin side up. Cook over moderately high heat until the fillets are browned on the bottom, about 2 minutes. Turn the fillets and cook for 2 minutes longer and then transfer the skillet to the oven and roast the fish until just cooked through, about 6 minutes.

6. Bring the wine reduction to a simmer and swirl in 4 tablespoons of the cold butter until smooth. Remove from the heat, add the tarragon leaves and chives and season with salt and pepper. In a medium saucepan, reheat the reduced cider over moderately high heat; discard the vanilla bean. Add the cabbage and bacon and cook until warmed through. Season with salt and pepper and swirl in the remaining ½ tablespoon of butter.

7. Spoon the cabbage onto 2 large warmed dinner plates. Set the salmon alongside, spoon the herb butter sauce on the fish and serve.

—*Mel's Bar & Grill, Denver*

MAKE AHEAD The recipe can be prepared through Step 4 up to 1 day ahead. Refrigerate the components separately and rewarm them before proceeding.

WINE Look for the 1996 Cain Vineyard Musqué Sauvignon Blanc. The Sauvignon's characteristics cut the richness of the salmon and intrigue the palate.

Alan's Grilled Salmon Burritos with Chipotle Cream

6 SERVINGS

The Alan here is Alan Harding, chef and owner of Patois in Brooklyn, New York. If you're using an outdoor grill, throw some soaked hardwood chips on the fire and close the lid so that the smoke flavors the fish as it cooks.

- 1 cup fresh or frozen corn kernels
- 1 cup cooked white rice
- 1 cup cooked drained black beans
- ½ cup sour cream
- ½ cup plain yogurt
- 2 tablespoons finely chopped canned chipotle chiles in adobo
- 2 ripe Hass avocados
- 2½ tablespoons fresh lime juice

Salt and freshly ground pepper

- 3 medium red onions, thickly sliced
- 2 tablespoons pure olive oil, plus more for the grill

Six 6-ounce skinless salmon fillets

- ¼ teaspoon ground cumin
- ¼ teaspoon ground coriander

Six 12-inch flour tortillas

1. In a small saucepan of boiling water, cook the corn until tender, about 4 minutes; drain and let cool. Put the corn in a medium bowl and add the rice and beans. In a small bowl, stir together the sour cream, yogurt and chipotles.

2. Halve the avocados and scoop the flesh into a bowl. Add the lime juice and mash until smooth. Season the mashed avocado with salt and pepper and cover with plastic wrap.

3. Light a grill or heat a grill pan. Brush the onion slices with the 2 tablespoons of oil and season with salt and pepper. Grill the onions over a low fire for about 20 minutes, turning once, until nicely caramelized; transfer to a plate.

4. Brush the grill or grill pan with oil and season the fillets with the cumin, coriander and salt and pepper. Put the fillets on the grill and cover. Alterna-tively, arrange the fillets on the grill pan and cover tightly. Grill over a low fire for 8 to 10 minutes, or until cooked through. Transfer the fish to a plate.

5. Warm the tortillas on the grill for a few seconds, just until pliable. For each burrito, spread some of the grilled on-ions on a tortilla and top with a salmon fillet, some of the rice mixture and the mashed avocado and 2 heaping table-spoons of chipotle cream. Fold in the bottom, sides and top of the tortilla to enclose the filling and serve.

—*Alan Harding*

Parsnip Pancakes with Smoked Fish and Caper Sour Cream

4 SERVINGS

The sweetness of the parsnips is com-plemented by the saltiness of the smoked fish, but it's the caper sour cream that makes this whole dish come together.

- ¾ cup sour cream
- ½ cup plus 2 tablespoons grated red onion, plus 2 tablespoons minced red onion, for garnish
- 2 tablespoons chopped dill
- 2 tablespoons drained capers
- 4 large parsnips, peeled and grated
- 1 large baking potato, peeled and grated
- 1 large egg, beaten
- 2 tablespoons all-purpose flour
- ¾ teaspoon baking powder
- ½ teaspoon salt
- ¼ teaspoon freshly ground pepper

Vegetable oil, for frying

- 6 to 8 ounces sliced smoked fish, such as sable or salmon

1. In a small bowl, combine the sour cream with 2 tablespoons of the grat-ed onion, 1 tablespoon of the dill and the capers; cover and refrigerate.

2. In a colander set in the sink, com-bine the remaining ½ cup of grated onion with the parsnips and potato. Let stand for 15 minutes and then squeeze to remove any excess liquid. Transfer the vegetables to a medium bowl and add the egg, flour, baking powder, salt and pepper. Mix thoroughly.

3. Preheat the oven to 300°. Heat ⅛ inch of oil in a large cast-iron skillet. Drop rounded tablespoons of the pan-cake batter into the skillet, spacing them evenly and pressing lightly to flatten. Cook the pancakes over mod-erate heat until browned and crisp, about 4 minutes per side. Drain the pancakes on a paper towel–lined plat-ter and then transfer them to a baking sheet and keep warm in the oven.

4. Arrange 4 pancakes on each plate. Place 1½ to 2 ounces of the smoked fish and a dollop of caper sour cream alongside. Top with the remaining dill and minced onion and serve.

—*Jesse Cool*

MAKE AHEAD The sour cream top-ping can be refrigerated for up to 1 day.

SERVE WITH A salad of romaine let-tuce with tomatoes and olives.

WINE Tangy sour cream and smoked fish dominate here, pointing to a crisp, savory, acerbic white wine as the best accompaniment. A Sauvignon Blanc, such as the 1996 Morgan from Cali-fornia or the 1996 Michel Lynch from France, would be perfect.

Marinated Mackerel and Yukon Gold Potato Salad

6 SERVINGS

- 1¼ pounds mackerel fillets, with skin, cut into 6 pieces

Salt and freshly ground white pepper

- 1 bottle dry white wine
- ½ cup white wine vinegar
- 4 shallots, thinly sliced
- 2 carrots, thinly sliced
- 2 celery ribs, thinly sliced
- 1½ lemons, cut into 12 wedges
- 2 bay leaves
- 2 thyme sprigs
- ¼ teaspoon black peppercorns

Parsnip Pancakes with Smoked Fish and Caper Sour Cream

Baked Mackerel Marie-Louise

¼ teaspoon coriander seeds

3 whole cloves

Yukon Gold Potato Salad with Leeks, for serving (recipe follows)

I. Season the mackerel with salt and white pepper and arrange the pieces in a 9-by-13-inch glass or ceramic baking dish, skin side down.

2. In a large saucepan, combine all of the remaining marinade ingredients with 1½ tablespoons of salt and bring to a boil. Reduce the heat to moderately low and simmer until the vegetables are just tender, about 20 minutes. Immediately pour the marinade over the mackerel, spreading the vegetables in an even layer. Cover tightly with plastic wrap and let cool to room temperature, then refrigerate overnight.

3. Transfer the mackerel fillets to plates, skin side up. Top with some of the vegetables and a drizzle of the marinade; serve the potato salad alongside.

MAKE AHEAD The mackerel can be refrigerated for up to 2 days.

WINE A rich wine with floral overtones will offset the acidity of the mar-

inated mackerel and add depth to the dish. Try the 1995 Albert Mann Grand Cru Furstentum Gewürztraminer from France or the 1997 Joseph Phelps Vin du Mistral Viognier from California.

YUKON GOLD POTATO SALAD WITH LEEKS

6 SERVINGS

1½ pounds Yukon Gold potatoes, peeled and cut into ¼-inch dice

2 small leeks, white part only, cut into ¼-inch dice

⅔ cup crème fraîche

1 tablespoon sherry vinegar

2 tablespoons minced chives

Salt and freshly ground white pepper

I. Bring a large saucepan of salted water to a boil. Add the potatoes and cook until barely tender, about 2 minutes. Add the leeks and cook until the potatoes are tender, about 2 to 3 minutes longer. Drain the potatoes and leeks and cool under running water. Drain again and pat thoroughly dry with paper towels.

2. In a medium glass or stainless-steel bowl, whisk the crème fraîche with the vinegar and chives and season with salt and white pepper. Fold in the potatoes and leeks and serve.

—*Daniel Boulud*

MAKE AHEAD The potato salad can be refrigerated for up to 1 day. Bring to room temperature before serving.

Baked Mackerel Marie-Louise

4 SERVINGS

Whole fish cooked on the bone is always more flavorful than fillets. You can use another fish of equal size if mackerel is not available. Whiting, small red snapper and cod would all be good substitutes. The recipe has been adapted from *Jacques Pépin's Kitchen: Encore with Claudine,* published by KQED Books & Tapes.

1¾ pounds red potatoes, peeled and thinly sliced

2 medium onions, thinly sliced

2 tablespoons extra-virgin olive oil

1 tablespoon finely chopped savory

Salt and freshly ground pepper

½ cup chicken stock (p. 117) or canned low-sodium broth

2 large ripe tomatoes (1 pound), sliced ½ inch thick

¼ cup dry white wine

Two 1¼-pound mackerel—cleaned, heads and tails removed, fish cut in half crosswise

½ teaspoon herbes de Provence

2 tablespoons finely chopped parsley

I. Preheat the oven to 400°. Put the potatoes in a colander and rinse under cool running water for 1 minute. Drain and pat dry.

2. In a large bowl, toss the potatoes with the onions, oil, savory and ½ teaspoon each of salt and pepper. Spread the vegetables in a 2½-quart gratin dish or a 13-by-9-inch glass baking dish and pour the stock over them. Arrange the tomato slices in a single layer on top and bake until the potatoes are tender, about 1 hour. Remove from the oven and pour the wine over the gratin.

3. Preheat the broiler. Make three ¼-inch-deep slashes through the skin on each side of each piece of mackerel. Season with salt and the herbes de Provence. Set the fish on the tomatoes and broil 10 inches from the heat for about 10 minutes, or until browned and cooked through. Sprinkle with the parsley and serve immediately.

—*Jacques Pépin*

WINE Mackerel is oily and assertive; an oak-aged Chardonnay has the flavor and the bite to cut the fattiness. Try the 1996 Benziger Reserve or the 1996 Estancia Reserve.

Shrimp with Lemon and Dill

12 SERVINGS

- 3 pounds large shrimp, shelled and deveined, tails left on

Salt and freshly ground pepper

- 1 cup extra-virgin olive oil
- ½ cup fresh lemon juice
- ¼ cup coarsely chopped dill
- ¾ cup water

Warm pita bread, for serving

I. Season the shrimp with salt and pepper and cook in 3 batches: for each batch, heat ⅓ cup of the oil in a large deep skillet and add one-third of the shrimp. Cook over high heat, turning once, until golden, about 3 minutes. Add 2 tablespoons of the lemon juice and 1 tablespoon of the dill and toss to coat. Transfer the shrimp as they're cooked to a large deep serving platter. Add ¼ cup of the water to the skillet after cooking each batch of shrimp and boil over high heat, scraping up any brown bits from the bottom of the skillet, until the juices are reduced to 2 tablespoons; add to the platter with the cooked shrimp.

2. Add the remaining 2 tablespoons of lemon juice and 1 tablespoon of dill to the shrimp and season with salt and pepper. Toss well. Serve the shrimp warm or at room temperature, with the warm pita bread. —*Grace Parisi*

MAKE AHEAD The cooked shrimp can be refrigerated for 3 hours. Bring to room temperature before serving.

Lemon-Bay Shrimp

4 SERVINGS ✳

- 6 cups water
- 8 bay leaves, crushed
- 5 garlic cloves, crushed
- 1 lemon
- 1½ teaspoons salt
- 1½ pounds medium shrimp in their shells

I. In a medium pot, bring the water, bay leaves, garlic, ¼ of the lemon, and the salt to a boil. Cover, reduce the heat and simmer 10 minutes.

2. Using scissors, snip the backs of the shrimp; remove the dark veins. Put the shrimp in the pot, cook for 4 minutes and then drain and peel. Serve with lemon wedges cut from the remaining ¾ of the lemon. —*Jan Newberry*

Grilled Shrimp on Skewers

6 SERVINGS

When shelling the shrimp, separate the three little tail shells, snap each one slightly and then wriggle the shrimp out with the deep pink, feathery portion of the tail intact.

- 2 pounds large shrimp, shelled and deveined

Grilled Shrimp on Skewers

- ⅔ cup fine dry bread crumbs
- 3½ tablespoons extra-virgin olive oil
- 3½ tablespoons vegetable oil
- 2 teaspoons minced parsley
- ½ teaspoon minced garlic

Salt and freshly ground pepper

I. Rinse the shrimp thoroughly in cold water and pat completely dry. Put the shrimp in a large bowl. Add the bread crumbs and both oils; toss lightly to evenly coat the shrimp. Add the parsley and garlic, season with salt and pepper and toss again. Set aside to marinate at room temperature for at least 30 minutes and up to 2 hours.

2. Light a charcoal grill or preheat the broiler. Curl each shrimp around its

Pan-Roasted Shrimp with Orange, Arugula and Tarragon

feathery tail and thread it onto a skewer; be sure to pierce each shrimp at three points to anchor it securely and prevent it from sliding around when you turn the skewers. Grill or broil the shrimp as close to the heat source as possible, turning once, until a thin, golden crust forms on both sides, about 3 1/2 minutes. Serve the shrimp immediately.   —*Marcella Hazan*

Pan-Roasted Shrimp with Orange, Arugula and Tarragon

4 SERVINGS

There's no orange wasted in this warm winter salad. It makes use of every part of the fruit but the pith.

- 2 large seedless oranges
- 16 jumbo shrimp (about 2 pounds), shelled and deveined
- 1/4 cup olive oil
- 2 tablespoons tarragon leaves
- 1 teaspoon kosher salt
- 1/2 teaspoon freshly ground pepper
- 1/2 teaspoon minced garlic
- 1/2 cup fresh orange juice
- 2 tablespoons Champagne or white wine vinegar
- 2 bunches arugula, trimmed
- 1 small red onion, sliced into rings

1. Preheat the oven to 425°. Finely grate the zest of 1 orange. Using a sharp knife, peel both oranges, removing all of the bitter white pith. Thinly slice the oranges crosswise; set aside. In a large bowl, toss the shrimp with 2 tablespoons of the oil, 1 tablespoon of the tarragon and the kosher salt, pepper and garlic.

2. Heat a large ovenproof skillet. Add the shrimp in a single layer and cook over moderately high heat, stirring, for 1 minute. Remove from the heat.

3. Roast the shrimp in the oven for 2 minutes. Using tongs, turn the shrimp and add the orange juice and zest. Roast for another 1 to 2 minutes, or until the shrimp are opaque throughout.

4. Meanwhile, in a large glass or stainless-steel bowl, whisk the vinegar into the remaining 2 tablespoons of oil. Whisk in the juices from the shrimp. Add the arugula and toss; transfer the salad to plates. Arrange the shrimp, orange slices and onion on the salads, garnish with the remaining tarragon and serve.   —*Allen Susser*

ONE SERVING Calories 419 kcal, Total Fat 17.7 gm, Saturated Fat 2.5 gm

WINE Look for a simple, fruity-but-tart white that won't compete with the dish, such as the 1996 Jekel Johannisberg Riesling from California or the 1996 Hogue Cellars Dry Johannisberg Riesling from Washington State.

Sautéed Shrimp with Arugula

4 SERVINGS

The strong flavorings here—garlic, lemon, pepper and arugula—make a neutral background best. Serve the shrimp with white rice or orzo.

- 1 large garlic clove
- 2 teaspoons finely grated lemon zest
- 1/2 teaspoon whole black peppercorns

Salt

- 1/4 cup fresh lemon juice
- 1/4 cup plus 1 teaspoon extra-virgin olive oil (see Note)
- 1 pound medium shrimp, shelled and deveined
- 1/2 pound arugula, large stems discarded

1. In a mortar, combine the garlic, lemon zest, peppercorns and a pinch of salt and mash to a coarse paste. Stir in the lemon juice and then 1/4 cup of the oil.

2. In a large skillet, heat the remaining 1 teaspoon of oil. Add the shrimp and cook over moderately high heat, stirring, until they are beginning to curl, about 3 minutes. Add the arugula and stir until it is wilted and the shrimp is

Sautéed Shrimp with Arugula

Grilled Shrimp with Tomato Jam, on Lemon Tabbouleh with Red Pepper (p. 345).

cooked through, about 2 minutes. Add the lemon mixture. Toss well; season with salt. Serve hot. —*Jan Newberry*

NOTE A buttery extra-virgin olive oil adds richness to the shrimp; a peppery oil gives the sauce bite.

WINE The sweet shrimp require a simple, crisp, dry white, such as an Italian Pinot Grigio. Try the 1996 Zemmer or the 1996 Lungarotti.

Shrimp Creole

4 SERVINGS ★★★ 1985

Before "Bam!" and long before *The Essence of Emeril,* Emeril Lagasse was the executive chef at the legendary Commander's Palace in New Orleans, where he developed this recipe. Any leftover Creole seasoning can be stored in an airtight container.

SEASONING

- 2 teaspoons salt
- 2 teaspoons hot paprika
- 1½ teaspoons garlic powder
- 1½ teaspoons black peppercorns
- 1 teaspoon onion powder
- ¾ teaspoon cayenne pepper
- ¾ teaspoon dried thyme
- ¾ teaspoon dried oregano

SHRIMP

- 2 tablespoons unsalted butter
- 1 medium onion, finely chopped
- 1 green bell pepper, finely chopped
- 2 celery ribs, finely chopped
- 5 garlic cloves, minced
- 4 bay leaves
- 1 teaspoon hot paprika
- ⅛ teaspoon cayenne pepper
- 1¼ cups chicken stock (p. 117) or canned low-sodium broth
- One 28-ounce can Italian peeled tomatoes, drained and coarsely chopped
- 3 scallions, thinly sliced
- 1 tablespoon Worcestershire sauce
- 1 teaspoon hot sauce
- ½ teaspoon salt
- 2 tablespoons vegetable oil
- 1½ pounds medium shrimp, shelled and deveined

Steamed rice, for serving

1. MAKE THE SEASONING: Combine all of the ingredients in a spice mill and process them to a fine powder.

2. PREPARE THE SHRIMP: Melt the butter in a large skillet. Add the onion, green pepper, celery and garlic and cook over moderately high heat, stirring occasionally, until the vegetables are softened but not browned, about 5 minutes. Add 2 teaspoons of the Creole seasoning, the bay leaves, paprika and cayenne and cook for 30 seconds. Add the stock, bring to a boil and simmer until slightly reduced, about 5 minutes. Add the tomatoes and cook for 10 minutes, stirring occasionally. Add the scallions, Worcestershire sauce, hot sauce and salt, reduce the heat to low and cook until thickened, about 10 minutes.

3. Heat the oil in a large skillet. When it begins to shimmer, add the shrimp and 2 teaspoons of the Creole seasoning. Cook over moderately high heat, stirring occasionally, until the shrimp are barely pink, about 30 seconds. Add the tomato sauce and cook over moderate heat until the shrimp are just cooked through, about 2 minutes. Remove the bay leaves and serve at once over steamed rice.

—*Emeril Lagasse*

Grilled Shrimp with Tomato Jam

4 SERVINGS

Sweet, spicy tomato jam is a popular Moroccan condiment, but the jam can also be used for a marinade, as it is in this recipe.

- 1 tablespoon unsalted butter
- 2 tablespoons finely grated fresh ginger
- 2 garlic cloves, minced
- ¼ cup cider vinegar
- 1 cinnamon stick
- One 35-ounce can imported peeled tomatoes—drained, seeded and coarsely chopped
- ¼ cup light brown sugar
- 1 teaspoon ground cumin
- ¼ teaspoon cayenne pepper
- ⅛ teaspoon ground cloves
- ¼ cup honey
- Salt and freshly ground black pepper
- 1 pound medium shrimp, shelled and deveined

1. Melt the butter in a saucepan. Add the ginger and garlic and cook over moderately high heat, stirring, until fragrant. Add the vinegar and cinnamon stick and cook until reduced to a glaze, about 1 minute. Stir in the tomatoes, brown sugar, cumin, cayenne and cloves. Reduce the heat to low and cook, stirring occasionally, until the liquid has evaporated, about 1 hour. Discard the cinnamon stick.

2. Stir in the honey and season with salt and black pepper. Transfer the mixture to a food processor and puree until smooth. Let the tomato jam cool.

3. Light a grill or preheat the broiler. In a medium glass or stainless-steel bowl, coat the shrimp with the tomato jam and let marinate at room temperature for 30 minutes.

4. Grill the shrimp for about 2 minutes per side, or until lightly charred on the outside and opaque throughout.

—*Matthew Kenney*

MAKE AHEAD The tomato jam can be refrigerated for up to 4 days. Let the jam return to room temperature before using.

WINE Try the 1996 Alban Vineyards Central Coast Viognier. This Viognier has a bright, beautiful nose, good fruit and just the right dose of acid to complement the shrimp.

Steamed and Seared Shellfish in Coconut Broth

Coconut Curried Shrimp with Mung Bean Sprouts

4 SERVINGS

Serve these sweet-spicy shrimp with jasmine rice or rice noodles. Red curry paste is available at Asian markets and at most supermarkets.

- ⅓ cup canned unsweetened coconut milk
- 2 tablespoons chicken stock (p. 117) or canned low-sodium broth
- ½ teaspoon red curry paste
- 2 teaspoons peanut oil
- 1 pound medium shrimp, shelled and deveined
- Salt
- 1½ teaspoons finely chopped fresh ginger
- ½ medium red onion, thinly sliced
- ½ pound mung bean sprouts
- ½ teaspoon cornstarch dissolved in 1 tablespoon water
- 2 tablespoons cilantro leaves
- Lime wedges, for serving

1. In a small bowl, combine the coconut milk, stock and curry paste. Heat a wok and add 1 teaspoon of the oil, swirling to coat the bottom of the wok. Add the shrimp and stir-fry over high heat just until opaque throughout, about 3 minutes. Season the shrimp with salt and transfer to a plate.

2. Wipe out the wok and set it over high heat. Add the remaining 1 teaspoon of oil. Add the ginger and stir-fry until fragrant, about 15 seconds. Add the onion; stir-fry just until brown around the edges, about 30 seconds, and then add the bean sprouts. Cook just until heated through. Transfer to a plate.

3. Return the wok to high heat, add the coconut milk mixture and cook until small bubbles appear around the edge. Stir the cornstarch mixture, add it to the wok and stir until the sauce thickens slightly. Return the shrimp to the wok and toss to coat. Add the bean sprouts and cilantro and toss. Serve with lime wedges.

—*Grace Parisi*

ONE SERVING Calories 185 kcal, Total Fat 8.2 gm, Saturated Fat 4.3 gm

WINE An aromatic, dry Riesling, such as the 1996 Trefethen White from California, would complement the mild spice of this sweet shrimp dish.

Steamed and Seared Shellfish in Coconut Broth

8 SERVINGS

- 2 teaspoons canola oil
- 2 large fresh shiitake mushrooms, coarsely chopped
- 2 shallots, coarsely chopped
- 2 tablespoons coarsely chopped fresh ginger
- 2 stalks of fresh lemongrass, tops discarded, bulbs cut into 1-inch lengths, or one 2-inch strip of lemon zest
- 2 sprigs of basil
- 2 sprigs of cilantro
- 1½ cups chicken stock (p. 117) or canned low-sodium broth
- 1½ cups bottled clam juice

½ cup unsweetened coconut milk

¼ teaspoon Asian sesame oil

Salt and freshly ground pepper

8 large sea scallops (about 6 ounces)

8 large shrimp, shelled and deveined (about 6 ounces)

8 small bok choy leaves

Two 1½-pound cooked lobsters—shelled, tails halved lengthwise, claw meat left whole

2 plum tomatoes, each cut into 4 slices

1. Heat 1 teaspoon of the canola oil in a medium saucepan. Add the mushrooms, shallots and ginger and cook over moderate heat, stirring, until fragrant, about 2 minutes. Add the lemongrass, basil, cilantro, stock and clam juice and bring to a boil. Reduce the heat to low and simmer the broth for 25 minutes.

2. Strain the broth and return it to the saucepan. Boil the broth over high heat until reduced to 1 cup, about 10 minutes. Add the coconut milk and simmer for 3 minutes. Stir in the sesame oil, season with salt and pepper and keep warm.

3. In a skillet, heat the remaining 1 teaspoon of canola oil until it is almost smoking. Season the scallops with salt and pepper and sear over high heat until browned on the bottom, about 3 minutes. Turn the scallops; cook until browned and almost cooked through, about 2 minutes.

4. In a steamer over a pan of simmering water, cook the shrimp and bok choy until the shrimp are just cooked through and the boy choy is bright green, about 1 minute. Transfer to a plate. Add the lobster tails and claws and steam until heated through, about 30 seconds.

5. Transfer the coconut broth to a blender and blend for 30 seconds. Put a tomato slice in each of 8 warmed soup plates and then set a scallop on each tomato slice. Arrange 1 shrimp, 1 bok choy leaf and 1 lobster claw or tail half alongside each shrimp. Spoon about 2 tablespoons of the coconut broth into each plate and serve.

—*Francesco Martorella*

ONE SERVING Calories 126 kcal, Total Fat 5.3 gm, Saturated Fat 3 gm

WINE The rich shellfish pairs well with the 1985 Prince Poniatowski Aigle Blanc Cuvée Katharine Vouvray, a special cuvée that exhibits beautiful honeyed aromatics. As an alternative, try the 1996 Domaine Pelaquié Tavel, a rosé from southern France.

Romesco of Shellfish and Salted Cod

4 SERVINGS

Don't feel obliged to use exactly the seafood called for in the recipe for this grand and showy dish. Judy Rodgers, the chef at Zuni Café, in San Francisco, sometimes braises sea bass, fresh cod and whole spot prawns in the sauce. In Catalonia, home of romesco sauce, hake is the fish of choice. The cod here is refrigerated for twenty-four hours, so plan accordingly.

½ pound Eastern or Alaskan cod fillet, about ½ inch thick

Coarse sea salt

1 tablespoon extra-virgin olive oil

1 sweet onion, such as Vidalia, coarsely chopped

2 cups Romesco (recipe follows)

2 cups lightly salted chicken stock or fish stock

¼ cup dry white wine

16 mussels, scrubbed and debearded

16 littleneck clams, scrubbed

16 large shrimp, shelled and deveined

Crusty bread, for serving

1. Put the cod fillet on a rack set over a plate and sprinkle liberally on both sides with sea salt. Cover loosely and refrigerate for 24 hours.

2. Rinse the cod and cut it into 2-inch chunks. Soak the cod in a bowl of cold water for 1 hour. Drain and pat dry.

3. Preheat the oven to 500°. Heat the oil in a large saucepan. Add the onion and cook over moderate heat until translucent, about 6 minutes. Add the Romesco and cook, stirring, for 1 minute. Whisk in the stock and wine and bring to a boil. Simmer over moderately high heat, whisking occasionally, until the sauce is slightly thickened, about 10 minutes.

4. Put the mussels and clams in a shallow baking dish that is large enough to hold them in a single layer. Pour in the sauce and bring to a simmer. Add the cod and shrimp, nestling them between the mussels and clams. Bake in the oven for about 10 minutes, or until the clams and mussels open. Serve the shellfish immediately, with plenty of crusty bread.

WINE This dish needs a big young white wine with a full, lively flavor. Either the 1996 Bodega Morgadio Albariño or the 1997 Duckhorn Vineyards Sauvignon Blanc would be very good choices.

ROMESCO

MAKES 4 CUPS

This Romesco is a bit labor-intensive, but it will keep for up to one week, and it actually improves as the flavors mingle. At Zuni Café, Rodgers makes a large batch and uses it in different ways during the following week. The sauce is traditionally served with grilled fish or chicken.

3 ancho chiles

½ cup hazelnuts

¾ cup extra-virgin olive oil

One 1-inch-thick slice of chewy, crusty white country bread (2 ounces)

Romesco of Shellfish and Salted Cod

6 garlic cloves

4 cups drained chopped tomatoes
(from three 35-ounce cans)

About 3 tablespoons red wine
vinegar

2 tablespoons Spanish paprika

Salt

1. Soak the ancho chiles in a bowl of hot water until softened, about 20 minutes. Drain the chiles and discard the stems, cores and seeds.

2. Meanwhile, preheat the oven to 350°. Put the hazelnuts in a pie pan and toast for about 12 minutes, or until they are fragrant and the skins blister. Transfer the hazelnuts to a sturdy kitchen towel and rub them together to remove the skins; let cool. Leave the oven on.

3. Heat ¼ cup of the oil in a medium skillet. Add the bread and fry over moderately high heat until golden, about 4 minutes. Drain on paper towels and let cool and then tear into 1-inch pieces.

4. In a food processor, combine the ancho chiles with the hazelnuts, fried bread and garlic and process until minced, scraping down the side of the bowl as necessary. Add the tomatoes and process to a fine paste. Transfer the paste to a bowl and stir in the 3 tablespoons of vinegar, the paprika and the remaining ½ cup of oil. Season the Romesco with salt and additional vinegar.

5. Spread the Romesco in a 1-inch layer in a shallow baking dish and bake for 15 minutes, or until the top is just brown and a bit dry. Stir the Romesco, spread it in an even layer and bake for 45 minutes longer, stirring and spreading it out again every 15 minutes; the Romesco will have the consistency of tomato paste.

—*Judy Rodgers*

MAKE AHEAD The Romesco can be refrigerated for up to 1 week.

Lobster Ravioli in Broth

Lobster Ravioli in Broth

6 SERVINGS

1 steamed lobster (about
2 pounds), shelled, coral and
shells reserved separately

10 cups water

3 medium leeks, white and tender
green, thinly sliced

2 carrots, coarsely chopped

1 celery rib, thickly sliced

10 parsley stems

2 garlic cloves, crushed

Salt and freshly ground pepper

1 cup thinly sliced Napa cabbage

24 heart-shaped lobster ravioli
(see Note)

1 tablespoon snipped chives

1. Cut the lobster tail and claw meat into 1-inch pieces; refrigerate. Coarsely chop the shells. In a large saucepan, combine the shells with the water, leeks, carrots, celery, parsley, garlic,

1 teaspoon of salt and ½ teaspoon of pepper. Bring to a boil and then simmer over moderate heat until reduced to 3 cups, about 40 minutes.

2. Strain the lobster broth into a medium saucepan. Add the Napa cabbage and lobster meat and bring to a boil. Simmer over moderately low heat until the cabbage is tender, about 5 minutes. Stir in the lobster coral and season with salt and pepper.

3. Meanwhile, cook the lobster ravioli in a large pot of boiling salted water until al dente, about 10 minutes, and drain. Arrange the ravioli in soup plates and then ladle the lobster and cabbage broth on top. Sprinkle the lobster ravioli with the chives and serve.

—*Alice Harper*

NOTE Heart-shaped lobster ravioli can be ordered December through February from The Ravioli Store, 212-925-1737.

Steamed Lobsters with Seared Wild Mushrooms

4 SERVINGS ✳

Mark Franz, chef and co-owner of Farallon, in San Francisco, likes to start his lobster dinner with oysters on the half shell. You can ask your fishmonger to halve the lobsters for you, but then you'll need to use them immediately. Or skip the flavored steaming liquid in Step 2 and simply cook the whole lobsters in a pot of boiling water and split them in half before serving.

Two 2-pound live lobsters, halved lengthwise
¼ cup plus 1 tablespoon extra-virgin olive oil
1½ teaspoons minced garlic
Salt and freshly ground pepper
¾ cup dry white wine
Juice of ½ lemon
8 juniper berries, crushed
2 bay leaves
1 teaspoon chopped thyme plus 5 thyme sprigs

1 pound assorted wild mushrooms, stems trimmed and mushrooms thinly sliced
Large slices of sourdough bread, toasted

1. Rub the cut sides of the lobster tails with 1 tablespoon of the oil and ½ teaspoon of the garlic. Season the lobster with salt and pepper.

2. In a large steamer, combine ½ cup of the wine with the lemon juice, juniper berries, bay leaves and thyme sprigs. Add 2 inches of water and then the lobsters, cut side up, in a steamer basket and cover tightly. Steam the lobsters over high heat about 8 minutes, or until the tails are cooked through and the claws are red.

3. Meanwhile, in a large skillet, heat the remaining ¼ cup of oil until shimmering. Add the mushrooms and cook over high heat until they are tender and just beginning to brown, about 8 minutes. Add the remaining 1 teaspoon of garlic and the chopped thyme and cook until fragrant, about 1 minute. Add the remaining ¼ cup of wine and cook until almost evaporated. Season with salt and pepper.

4. Transfer the lobster to 4 large plates. Spoon the mushrooms onto the toasts and serve alongside.   —*Mark Franz*

WINE A dry, fruity white is the perfect complement to the garlicky mushrooms and sweet lobster meat. Consider an elegant, crisp Riesling, such as the 1997 Trefethen Dry Riesling from California or the 1996 Hugel Jubilee Riesling Réserve Personnelle from Alsace.

Grilled Lobster Tails with Sorrel-Sauternes Sauce

8 SERVINGS

The creamy, slightly tangy and slightly sweet sorrel sauce is an ideal foil for smoky grilled lobster. If you buy whole live lobsters, have the fishmonger split

the tails for you. Save the claws for Potato and Lobster Claw Salad (p. 96) and the tomalley and roe for Lobster Butter (p. 354).

1 cup plus 2 tablespoons Sauternes
1 small shallot, minced
2 cups heavy cream
8 uncooked lobster tails, split lengthwise
2 tablespoons light olive oil
Salt and freshly ground black pepper
1 bunch watercress (3 ounces), large stems removed
½ pound sorrel, large stems removed
Pinch of cayenne pepper

1. Light a grill. In a medium saucepan, boil 1 cup of the Sauternes with the shallot until reduced by one-third, about 4 minutes. Add the cream and simmer over moderate heat, stirring occasionally, until reduced to 1½ cups, about 15 minutes. Remove from the heat.

---

menu

1996 CAKEBREAD CELLARS
SAUVIGNON BLANC

Broiled Clams (p. 53)

Mussels with Curry Yogurt (p. 182)

Fried Bass Fingers (p. 27)

Grilled Lobster Tails with Sorrel-Sauternes Sauce (p. 178)

Potato and Lobster Claw Salad (p. 96)

Lobster Butter on grilled corn (p. 354)

Wilted Spinach with Shallot Vinaigrette (p. 305)

Lentils with Thyme (p. 327)

—

Almond Berry Cakes (p. 412)

2. Rub the cut side of the lobster tails with the oil and season with salt and black pepper. Grill the tails over a hot fire, cut side down, until nicely charred, about 3 minutes. Turn the tails and grill for about 4 minutes longer, or until the meat is just cooked through and the juices are bubbling. Transfer the lobster to a platter and cover with aluminum foil to keep warm.

3. Add the remaining 2 tablespoons of Sauternes to the sauce and bring to a simmer. Working in 3 batches, pour one-third of the sauce into a blender and add one-third of the watercress and sorrel; blend until smooth and then pour the sorrel sauce into a clean saucepan. Reheat the sauce and then season with salt, black pepper and cayenne. Serve at once with the lobster tails. —*Mark Gottwald*

Moroccan-Spiced Crab Cakes
4 SERVINGS
These succulent crab cakes are accompanied by a refreshing cilantro dressing.

- 1 tablespoon olive oil
- ¼ cup finely chopped red bell pepper
- ¼ cup finely chopped celery
- 2 scallions, white and tender green, thinly sliced
- ½ teaspoon minced fresh ginger
- ½ teaspoon ground cumin
- ½ teaspoon turmeric
- ⅛ teaspoon ground cardamom
- ½ cup heavy cream
- ½ pound jumbo lump crabmeat, picked over
- 1 cup Japanese bread crumbs (panko) or coarse stale bread crumbs
- 2 tablespoons finely chopped parsley
- 2 tablespoons chopped chives
- ½ teaspoon finely grated lemon zest

Pinch of cayenne pepper
Salt
- ¼ cup canola oil
Cilantro-Orange Dressing (p. 355)

1. Heat the olive oil in a nonstick skillet. Add the red pepper and celery and cook over moderately high heat, stirring, until the vegetables are just softened, about 2 minutes. Add the scallions and ginger and cook until the scallions are wilted, 1 to 2 minutes. Stir in the cumin, turmeric and cardamom and cook until fragrant, about 1 minute. Add the cream; boil until reduced by half, about 6 minutes. Transfer to a bowl and let cool slightly.

2. Add the crab to the cream mixture along with ¼ cup plus 1 tablespoon of the bread crumbs, 1½ tablespoons each of the parsley and chives, and the lemon zest. Season the crab mixture with cayenne and salt and mix gently but thoroughly.

3. With moistened hands, shape the crab mixture into 8 cakes, using a scant ⅓ cup for each; the cakes should be about 3 inches wide and ¾ inch thick. Spread the remaining bread crumbs on a large plate. Coat the crab cakes with the bread crumbs and then transfer them to a baking sheet lined with wax paper. ➤

Moroccan-Spiced Crab Cakes.

Fennel, Mushroom and Arugula Salad with Seared Scallops

4. Heat 2 tablespoons of the canola oil in a medium nonstick skillet. Add half of the crab cakes; cook until browned and crisp, about 3 minutes per side. Transfer to a platter. Repeat with the remaining canola oil and crab cakes. Arrange the crab cakes on plates and drizzle with the Cilantro-Orange Dressing. Garnish the crab cakes with the remaining ½ tablespoon each of the parsley and chives.—*Matthew Kenney*

Sautéed Scallops with Lime

4 SERVINGS

3 tablespoons olive oil
1½ pounds sea scallops
2 tablespoons finely chopped cilantro
1 garlic clove, minced
1 teaspoon fresh lime juice
Salt and freshly ground pepper
Crusty bread, for serving

Heat the oil in a large nonstick skillet until almost smoking. Add the scallops and cook over moderately high heat until browned on the bottom, about 2 minutes. Turn the scallops and cook until just opaque throughout, about 2 minutes longer. Add the cilantro, garlic and lime juice, season with salt and pepper and toss to combine. Serve with bread. —*Jan Newberry*

WINE A crisp Sauvignon Blanc.

Fennel, Mushroom and Arugula Salad with Seared Scallops

2 SERVINGS

This recipe is adapted from one from Christian "Goose" Sorensen, executive chef and co-owner of Starfish, in Denver. The scallops make the salad a substantial main course. If you can't find fresh chanterelles, quartered shiitake caps make a fine substitute.

¼ cup extra-virgin olive oil
2 tablespoons fresh lemon juice
1 teaspoon balsamic vinegar
Kosher salt and freshly ground pepper

½ pound small chanterelles
2 tablespoons unsalted butter
½ pound sea scallops
4 cups arugula, torn into pieces
1 fennel bulb—halved, cored and very thinly sliced
½ cup cherry tomatoes
Small chunk of Parmesan cheese
Truffle oil (optional; see Note)

1. In a small glass or stainless-steel bowl, combine 2 tablespoons of the olive oil with the lemon juice, vinegar and ¼ teaspoon each of kosher salt and pepper.

2. In a large skillet, heat 1 tablespoon of the olive oil. Add the chanterelles and 1 tablespoon of the butter and season with kosher salt and pepper. Spread the mushrooms in an even layer and cook over moderately high heat, without stirring, until deeply browned on the bottom, about 4 minutes. Stir the mushrooms and continue cooking until tender, about 3 minutes longer. Transfer to a plate.

3. Return the skillet to high heat and add the remaining 1 tablespoon of olive oil. Season the scallops with kosher salt and pepper. When the oil is hot, add the scallops to the skillet along with the remaining 1 tablespoon of butter; tilt the pan to coat the undersides of the scallops with butter. Cook, without stirring, until the scallops are deep brown on the bottom, about 3 minutes. Turn the scallops and cook until browned on the second side and just cooked through, about 3 minutes longer.

4. In a medium glass or stainless-steel bowl, toss the arugula and fennel with 3 tablespoons of the dressing. Transfer the salad to 2 large plates. Add the tomatoes and mushrooms to the bowl and toss with the remaining dressing; scatter over the salads along with the scallops. Shave thin slices of Parmesan

cheese on top and season the salad with pepper. Drizzle with truffle oil and serve at once.

—*Mel's Bar & Grill, Denver*

NOTE Truffle oil is available at specialty food stores and by mail from Urbani Truffles, 800-281-2330.

WINE The 1995 A. et P. de Villaine Bourgogne Aligoté de Bouzeron—the Aligoté de Bouzeron has weight and fruit but is not as overwhelming as a big Chardonnay.

Mussels à la Cagouille

2 SERVINGS

Oh so simple, this dish was inspired by the mussels served at La Cagouille, a wonderful little Parisian restaurant.

2 large baking potatoes, scrubbed
3 pounds mussels, scrubbed and debearded
1 teaspoon chopped thyme leaves
1 stick (4 ounces) unsalted butter
Juice of ½ lemon
Coarse salt

1. Preheat the oven to 400°. Bake the potatoes until they are tender, about 40 minutes.

2. Shortly before the potatoes are done, set a large cast-iron skillet over high heat. When it starts to smoke, add the mussels and sprinkle with the thyme. Cover and cook, shaking the pan occasionally, until the mussels open, about 4 minutes; discard any that haven't opened. Transfer the mussels to a platter and cover them with aluminum foil to keep warm.

3. Boil the mussel juices in the skillet for 2 minutes to concentrate the flavor and then whisk in 4 tablespoons of the butter to make a rich pan sauce. Melt the remaining 4 tablespoons of butter in a small saucepan and then add the lemon juice.

4. Split the potatoes and pinch from both ends at once to make the insides mound up. Pour the pan sauce into

Mussels à la Cagouille

the potatoes and sprinkle with coarse salt. Serve the potatoes surrounded by the mussels, with the lemon butter alongside for dipping.

—*Mel's Bar & Grill, Denver*

WINE The 1996 Tortoise Creek Chardonnay-Viognier blend from Languedoc would be an excellent choice. This crisp, fresh, fragrant wine is a perfect foil to shellfish.

Mussels with Curry Yogurt
4 SERVINGS

- 2 teaspoons vegetable oil
- 1 medium onion, finely chopped
- 1 tablespoon plus 1 teaspoon Madras curry powder
- 1 cup dry white wine
- 1 cup whole-milk yogurt
- 1 teaspoon honey
- **Salt**

- 2 pounds mussels, scrubbed and debearded
- 1 cup water

1. Heat the oil in a small skillet. Add the onion; cook over moderately low heat, stirring, until translucent, about 8 minutes. Add the curry powder and cook, stirring, for 2 minutes longer. Add 2 tablespoons of the wine and cook until the liquid evaporates.

2. Transfer the curry mixture to a blender and let cool slightly. Add 2 tablespoons of the yogurt and the honey and blend until smooth. Pour the sauce into a bowl. Stir in the remaining yogurt and season with salt. Refrigerate until chilled.

3. In a large pot, combine the mussels with the remaining wine and the water. Cover and cook over high heat until the mussels open, about 5 minutes; discard any mussels that don't open. Using a slotted spoon, transfer the mussels to a large platter and let cool. Serve the mussels with the curry sauce on the side.   —*Mark Gottwald*

MAKE AHEAD The curry sauce can be refrigerated for up to 2 days.

Thai Curried Clams

4 SERVINGS ✳

Curry paste punches up the rich coconut broth here. Asian fish sauce and a variety of curry pastes are available at Asian groceries and many supermarkets.

    1   garlic clove, minced
    1   tablespoon peanut oil
One 14-ounce can unsweetened
        coconut milk
    ½   cup fish stock, or ¼ cup bottled
        clam juice diluted with ¼ cup
        water
    2   tablespoons Asian fish sauce
    1   tablespoon green, red or yellow
        curry paste
    1   tablespoon sugar
    3   pounds small clams, scrubbed
        and rinsed
    ½   cup frozen petite peas
    2   tablespoons finely chopped basil
Lime wedges

I. In a large deep skillet, cook the garlic in the oil over moderately high heat just until fragrant, about 1 minute. Stir in the coconut milk, fish stock, fish sauce, curry paste and sugar and then cover and bring to a boil.

2. Add the clams to the skillet. Cover and cook over moderately high heat just until the clams open, 3 to 4 minutes. Add the peas; cook until warmed through, about 1 minute. Remove from the heat and sprinkle with the basil. Serve the clams in bowls with lime wedges.   —*Jan Newberry*

SERVE WITH Steamed rice.

WINE A sweet but crisp Riesling.

Baked Kamut with Chorizo and Clams

4 SERVINGS

    2   cups kamut
    9   cups water
    ½   cup dry white wine
Scant ½ teaspoon lightly packed
        saffron threads
    I   tablespoon unsalted butter
    1   tablespoon olive oil
    2   medium carrots, cut into 1-inch
        dice
    1   large onion, coarsely chopped
    2   ounces chorizo or other smoked
        spicy sausage, cut into ½-inch
        dice
    1   large garlic clove, minced
Salt and freshly ground pepper
    3   dozen littleneck clams,
        scrubbed

I. In a large saucepan, combine the kamut and 6 cups of the water and bring to a boil. Cover and cook over low heat until almost tender, about 45 minutes. Drain the kamut. Meanwhile, in a small saucepan, heat the wine. Remove from the heat, crumble in the saffron and let steep for at least 20 minutes.

2. Preheat the oven to 400°. In a heavy 13-by-9-inch roasting pan set over low heat, melt the butter in the oil. Add the carrots and onion and cook, stirring, until softened, about 4 minutes. Add the saffron-infused wine and bring to a boil. Add the kamut and the remaining 3 cups of water and bring to a boil.

Cover tightly with aluminum foil and bake for 1¾ hours.

3. Raise the oven temperature to 450°. Stir the chorizo, the garlic and a pinch each of salt and pepper into the kamut. Arrange the clams, hinges down, in the kamut. Cover tightly with aluminum foil and bake in the bottom of the oven for about 15 minutes, or until the clams have opened. Discard any that don't open. Serve the clams at once.   —*Marcia Kiesel*

CHAPTER 7 chicken other birds

Cornish Hens with Pomegranate and Lemon (p. 219)

Kearney's Chicken Stuffed with Garlic and Preserved Lemon, served on Stewed Flageolets with Thyme (p. 330).

Kearney's Chicken Stuffed with Garlic and Preserved Lemon

4 SERVINGS ♕

Anne Kearney, the chef at Peristyle restaurant in New Orleans, suggests chilling the stuffing before tucking it under the chicken skin. This makes it easier to handle and keeps it from expanding in the oven. Kearney sometimes serves the dish with steamed spinach as shown here.

15 large garlic cloves, peeled
¾ cup vegetable oil
2 tablespoons coarse stale bread crumbs
2½ tablespoons unsalted butter, softened
1 tablespoon finely chopped preserved lemon rind (see Note)
1 teaspoon finely chopped flat-leaf parsley
Salt and freshly ground white pepper
1 quart Chicken Stock (p. 117)
½ cup dry white wine
2 tablespoons Champagne vinegar
Four 5-ounce boneless chicken breast halves, with skin
Stewed Flageolets with Thyme (p. 330)

1. In a small saucepan, cook the garlic in the vegetable oil over low heat, turning the cloves, until golden and softened, about 10 minutes. Let the garlic cool in the oil and then drain. Finely chop the garlic; reserve 2 tablespoons of the garlic oil and save the rest for another use.

2. In a bowl, combine 3 tablespoons of the chopped roasted garlic with the bread crumbs, 1½ tablespoons of the butter, the preserved lemon rind, parsley and a pinch each of salt and white pepper. Chill the filling until firm.

3. Boil the stock over high heat until reduced to 1 cup. Add the wine, vinegar and 2 tablespoons of the chopped garlic and boil until reduced to ¾ cup. Season with salt and white pepper.

Strain the sauce in a fine sieve, pressing through as much garlic as possible; whisk to incorporate.

4. Preheat the oven to 400°. Using your fingers, loosen the skin from the chicken breasts. Shape the preserved lemon filling into 4 short ropes and stuff one under the skin of each chicken breast, pressing gently to flatten it. Season the chicken with salt and white pepper.

5. Heat 2 tablespoons of the reserved garlic oil in a large ovenproof skillet. Add the chicken breasts, skin side down, and cook over high heat until crisp and golden, 5 to 6 minutes. Turn the chicken, transfer the skillet to the oven and roast for about 10 minutes, or until cooked through.

6. Spoon the Stewed Flageolets with Thyme onto 4 warmed dinner plates and top with the chicken breasts. Pour any accumulated pan juices into the sauce and rewarm. Whisk in the remaining 1 tablespoon of butter. Spoon the sauce over and around the chicken and serve. —*Anne Kearney*

MAKE AHEAD The stuffed chicken recipe can be prepared through Step 3 and refrigerated overnight.

NOTE Preserved lemons are available in specialty food stores.

SERVE WITH Steamed spinach.

WINE Contrast the savory chicken and beans with a light Pinot Noir from Oregon.

Pot au Feu of Chicken with Winter Vegetables

8 SERVINGS ♕

8 cups chicken stock (p. 117)
24 baby carrots, halved lengthwise
24 baby turnips, halved lengthwise
24 thin scallions, cut into 4-inch lengths
½ pound assorted small fresh wild mushrooms, such as shiitakes, chanterelles and hon shimeji, shiitake stems removed

menu

Smoked Salmon and Leek Tartlets (p. 29)

NONVINTAGE DIEBOLT-VALLOIS
BLANC DE BLANCS

———

Steamed and Seared Shellfish in Coconut Broth (p. 174)

1985 PRINCE PONIATOWSKI
AIGLE BLANC
CUVEE KATHARINE VOUVRAY

———

Spinach-Ricotta Cavatelli with Tomato Sauce (p. 133)

Pot au Feu of Chicken with Winter Vegetables (p. 187)

1984 DOMAINE ROBERT AMPEAU
LA PIECE SOUS LE BOIS BLAGNY

———

Fruit Soup with Caramel Meringues (p. 420)

Eight 5-ounce boneless chicken breast halves with skin
Salt and freshly ground pepper

1. In a large saucepan, bring the stock to a simmer. Add the carrots and cook over moderate heat until tender, about 10 minutes. Using a slotted spoon, transfer the carrots to a plate. Add the turnips to the stock and cook until tender, about 6 minutes. Add to the plate of carrots. Simmer the scallions for 5 minutes and add them to the plate. Simmer the mushrooms just until tender, about 4 minutes, and add them to the plate.

2. Add the chicken breasts to the simmering stock and poach at a bare simmer until just cooked through, about 12 minutes. Transfer the chicken to a plate and let rest for 5 minutes. Return the vegetables to the stock to reheat them; season with salt and pepper.

3. Remove the skin from the chicken and discard. Slice each chicken breast

low-fat cooking tips

Georges Perrier and Francesco Martorella, chefs at Le Bec–Fin in Philadelphia, share some tricks of the trade.

1. **Cook poultry** with its skin to keep the meat moist; discard the skin before serving.

2. **Puree sauces** in a blender before serving to give them a creamy texture.

3. **Use a nonstick pan** and a drop or two of oil to sauté ingredients.

4. **Grill** whatever, whenever you can.

diagonally ⅓ inch thick. Divide the vegetables among 8 shallow bowls and then arrange the chicken over them. Add the hot broth. —*Georges Perrier*

ONE SERVING Calories 244 kcal, Total Fat 3.4 gm, Saturated Fat 1.2 gm

WINE Look for an elegant, mature red Burgundy, such as the 1984 Domaine Robert Ampeau La Pièce Sous le Bois Blagny. Its earthy edge will complement this refined country-cuisine dish. The 1984 Domaine Robert Ampeau Santenots Volnay is earthier yet.

Raspberry-Glazed Chicken Breasts

8 SERVINGS

This super-easy low-fat preparation has a tangy, fruity flavor. The best way to bring it out is to marinate the chicken breasts overnight.

- 2 cups raspberries
- 2 garlic cloves, minced
- 2 tablespoons honey
- 1 tablespoon olive oil
- ½ tablespoon Dijon mustard
- ½ teaspoon kosher salt
- Eight 8-ounce whole skinless, boneless chicken breasts, trimmed and pounded to an even thickness

1. In a food processor, puree the raspberries. Strain the puree through a fine sieve into a bowl. Stir in the garlic, honey, oil, mustard and kosher salt. In

a large glass or ceramic dish, pour the raspberry marinade over the chicken and turn to coat. Cover and refrigerate for at least 8 hours or overnight.

2. Light a grill or preheat a grill pan. Grill the chicken breasts over high heat until they are lightly charred and just cooked through, about 4 minutes per side. Serve hot.   —*Marcia Kiesel*

ONE SERVING Calories 298 kcal, Total Fat 4.7 gm, Saturated Fat 1 gm

SERVE WITH Baby beet, escarole and goat cheese salad.

WINE The raspberry glaze gets an added kick from mustard and garlic, but the honey underscores its sweetness. The fruit points to a big, fruity California Chardonnay with a sweet oaky flavor that echoes that of the dish. Try the 1996 Simi Sonoma County or the 1996 Mark West Russian River.

Chicken Breasts with Pesto and Summer Vegetables

8 SERVINGS

- ⅓ cup olive oil, plus more for rubbing
- 3 medium zucchini, cut into 1-inch dice
- 3 medium summer squash, cut into 1-inch dice
- 3 medium red bell peppers, cut into 1-inch dice
- 3 medium yellow bell peppers, cut into 1-inch dice
- 1 large sweet onion, cut into 1-inch dice
- Salt and freshly ground black pepper
- 2 tablespoons fresh lemon juice
- Handmade Pesto (recipe follows)
- Sixteen 4-ounce skinless, boneless chicken breast halves, trimmed and pounded to an even thickness
- Lemon wedges

1. Preheat the oven to 425°. In a large roasting pan set over 2 burners, heat ⅓ cup of the oil. Add the zucchini,

summer squash, red and yellow peppers and onion, season lightly with salt and black pepper and stir to coat with oil. Roast the vegetables in the oven for 25 minutes, or until tender. Transfer the vegetables to a bowl and let cool to room temperature. Stir in the lemon juice and pesto.

2. Light a grill or preheat a grill pan. Rub the chicken breasts with olive oil and season with salt and black pepper. Grill the chicken over high heat until lightly charred and just cooked through, about 4 minutes per side. Serve hot, topped with the pesto vegetables. Pass the lemon wedges separately.

WINE Peppers, onions and pesto call for a light, fruity red. Pick a Beaujolais and serve it slightly chilled. Top choices include the 1997 Georges Duboeuf Chiroubles and the 1997 Georges Duboeuf Julienas.

HANDMADE PESTO

MAKES ABOUT 1½ CUPS

Pounding the ingredients in a mortar produces a pesto of incomparable texture: silky basil leaves and olive oil bind coarser bits of garlic and Parmesan.

- ¾ cup pine nuts or coarsely chopped macadamia nuts (6 ounces)
- 5 cups basil leaves, chilled and perfectly dry
- 6 small garlic cloves, quartered
- ⅓ cup freshly grated Parmesan cheese
- ¾ cup extra-virgin olive oil, plus more for sealing
- Kosher salt and freshly ground pepper

1. Preheat the oven to 400°. Toast the pine nuts on a baking sheet for about 4 minutes, or until lightly browned.

2. Coarsely chop the basil leaves. In a large mortar, combine the basil and garlic and pound to a coarse paste. Add the pine nuts and pound until a smooth paste forms. Stir in the Parmesan and then ¾ cup of the oil. Transfer the pesto to a bowl and season with kosher salt and pepper. Smooth the surface and pour a little olive oil on top to seal.   —*Marcia Kiesel*

Chicken Francese

8 SERVINGS

Here the chicken is dipped in flour and eggs and then sautéed and served with a piquant sauce.

6   large eggs
½   cup plus 2 tablespoons extra-virgin olive oil
¼   cup plus 2 tablespoons finely grated Pecorino Romano cheese
Eight 8-ounce whole skinless, boneless chicken breasts, trimmed and pounded to an even thickness
Salt and freshly ground pepper
All-purpose flour, for dredging
1   cup dry white wine
½   cup fresh lemon juice
3   tablespoons large salt-packed capers, rinsed (see Note)
4   tablespoons cold unsalted butter

1. Preheat the oven to 350°. In a large, shallow bowl, beat the eggs. Stir in 2 tablespoons of oil and the cheese. Season the chicken with salt and pepper.
2. In a large skillet, heat ¼ cup of the oil. Working with half the chicken breasts, dredge 1 breast at a time in the flour, shaking off the excess. Dip it in the beaten egg and add it to the skillet. Sauté over moderate heat until golden brown, about 2 minutes per side; transfer to a large baking sheet. Add the remaining ¼ cup oil to the skillet and repeat with the remaining chicken breasts. Transfer the baking sheet to the oven to finish cooking the chicken, 3 to 5 minutes more.
3. Drain the oil from the skillet; wipe the skillet clean. Add the wine and boil

Chicken Breasts with Pesto and Summer Vegetables

until reduced by half, about 4 minutes. Add the lemon juice and capers and simmer for 2 minutes. Remove the skillet from the heat and whisk the butter into the sauce 1 tablespoon at a time. Season with salt and pepper. Transfer the chicken to a platter, pour the sauce over it and serve.   —*Marcia Kiesel*

NOTE Salt-packed capers, available at specialty food stores and some supermarkets, have more depth of flavor than the brined variety.

SERVE WITH A green vegetable, such as steamed broccoli florets.

WINE The caper, wine and lemon sauce calls for a sharp California white, such as the 1996 Quivira Sauvignon Blanc Reserve or the 1997 Iron Horse Vineyards Fumé Blanc.

Chicken and Polenta Stew

4 SERVINGS ☀ ❀

For a delicious vegetarian dish, omit the chicken from the following recipe.

2   tablespoons olive oil
1   medium onion, finely chopped
2   garlic cloves, minced
½   teaspoon dried thyme
Salt and freshly ground pepper
1   pound kale, stems discarded, leaves cut into thin strips
8   cups chicken stock (p. 117) or canned low-sodium broth
1   cup yellow polenta (not instant)
1½   pounds skinless, boneless chicken breasts, cut crosswise into thin strips

1. Heat the oil in a large enameled cast-iron casserole. Add the onion,

garlic, thyme, 1 teaspoon of salt and ½ teaspoon of pepper and cook over moderately high heat, stirring often, until the onion softens, about 5 minutes. Stir in the kale, cover and cook until wilted, about 8 minutes.

2. Add the stock to the casserole and bring to a boil over high heat. Gradually add the polenta in a thin steady stream, stirring constantly. Lower the heat to moderate and cook, stirring occasionally, until the polenta thickens, 20 to 25 minutes.

3. Stir in the chicken and simmer until cooked through, 3 to 5 minutes. Season with salt and pepper and serve.

—*Jan Newberry*

ONE SERVING Calories 434 kcal, Total Fat 12.3 gm, Saturated Fat 3 gm

WINE The kale adds a green note to this thick chicken stew, suggesting a dry white wine with an assertive edge of its own—ideally a Pinot Grigio. Look for the 1996 Campanile or the 1995 Baron Fini.

Tortilla Pie

12 SERVINGS

For this one-dish feast, corn tortillas are layered with sliced poached chicken breasts, cilantro, two kinds of cheese and a smoky chile sauce.

- 10 large ancho chiles
- 2 large dried chipotle chiles
- 2 cups boiling water
- 10 large garlic cloves, unpeeled
- 1 large Spanish onion (1½ pounds), cut into thick wedges
- Twelve 5-ounce skinless, boneless chicken breast halves
- 6 cups water
- About ½ cup vegetable oil
- 1½ cups chopped cilantro
- ½ teaspoon ground cloves
- ¼ teaspoon ground cinnamon
- Salt and freshly ground pepper
- Twenty-four 6- or 8-inch corn tortillas
- 2 cups shredded Cheddar cheese (6 ounces)
- 2 cups shredded Monterey Jack cheese (6 ounces)
- 2 cups sour cream

1. Set a lightly oiled large cast-iron skillet over moderately high heat. Add half of the chiles and cook, pressing occasionally, until lightly toasted, about 2 minutes per side. Transfer to a plate. Repeat with the remaining chiles. Let cool slightly. Remove the stems and seeds and rinse the chiles.

2. In a large bowl, combine the chiles with the 2 cups of boiling water and let them soak until softened, about 20 minutes; use a plate to keep the chiles submerged.

3. Meanwhile, lightly oil the cast-iron skillet again. Add the garlic and onion wedges; cook over low heat until lightly charred, about 20 minutes. Transfer the garlic and onion to a food processor. Add the chiles with their soaking liquid and puree. Strain the puree through a coarse sieve, pressing hard on the solids with a rubber spatula.

4. In a large pot, cover the chicken breasts with the 6 cups of water and simmer over low heat until just cooked through, about 15 minutes. Transfer the chicken breasts to a large plate and let cool and then slice crosswise ¼ inch thick; reserve 3 cups of the poaching liquid.

5. In a large skillet, heat 1 tablespoon of the oil. Add the chile puree and 1 cup of the cilantro and cook over moderate heat for about 10 minutes, stirring frequently. Scrape the sauce into a large bowl and add the cloves and cinnamon. Season the sauce with 2½ teaspoons of salt and ½ teaspoon of pepper. Stir the reserved poaching liquid into the sauce.

6. In a medium skillet, heat ¼ cup of the oil over moderate heat. Fry 1 tortilla at a time until it starts to puff up but is still pliable, about 30 seconds per side. Transfer the fried tortillas to a large baking sheet; add more oil to the skillet as needed.

7. Preheat the oven to 350°. In a 15-by-12-inch shallow baking dish, spread 1 cup of the chile sauce. Cover with 8 slightly overlapping tortillas, half of the chicken and ¼ cup of the cilantro. Season with salt and pepper. Cover with 2 cups of the sauce and sprinkle with ¾ cup of each cheese. Continue layering with 8 more tortillas and the remaining chicken and cilantro; press lightly. Season with salt and pepper. Add 2 more cups of sauce and sprinkle with another ¾ cup of each cheese. Finally, press the remaining tortillas onto the pie and top with the remaining sauce and cheese.

8. Cover the pan tightly with aluminum foil, making sure that the foil does not touch the cheese. Bake in the center of the oven for about 1 hour and 20 minutes, or until the pie is hot and bubbling. Serve hot with the sour cream.

—*Marcia Kiesel*

MAKE AHEAD The Tortilla Pie can be prepared through Step 5 up to 2 days ahead.

WINE A hearty Zinfandel is one of the few red wines with enough fruit and spice to match the intensity and rustic flavors of this pie. Go for the 1995 Cline or the 1994 Rosenblum Napa.

Soupy Chicken with Mushrooms

2 SERVINGS

The texture makes this ideal for serving alongside a crunchy vegetable stir-fry. The dish has a depth of flavor that you'd think could come only from good stock and a long simmer, but the dish needs neither—just thirty minutes for the chicken to marinate and the mushrooms to soak and then five minutes of cooking and it's done.

CHICKEN

- 1 tablespoon Chinese cooking wine, dry white wine or dry sherry
- 1 teaspoon cornstarch
- ½ egg white
- ½ teaspoon salt
- 10 ounces skinless, boneless chicken breast, cut into ¼-inch dice

STIR-FRY

- 6 dried black or shiitake mushrooms
- 3 cups hot water
- 2 tablespoons soy sauce
- 1 tablespoon Chinese cooking wine, dry white wine or dry sherry
- ½ teaspoon sugar
- ½ teaspoon salt
- 2 tablespoons peanut oil
- 1 tablespoon minced garlic
- ¼ pound white mushrooms, quartered
- 1 medium green bell pepper, cut into ½-inch dice
- 1 teaspoon Asian sesame oil
- 1 teaspoon cornstarch mixed with 1 tablespoon cold water

Freshly ground black or white pepper

I. PREPARE THE CHICKEN: In a medium bowl, combine the wine, cornstarch, egg white and salt. Add the chicken and turn to coat thoroughly. Cover and let stand for 30 minutes.

2. MAKE THE STIR-FRY: In a small bowl, cover the dried mushrooms with 1 cup of the hot water and let soak until softened, about 30 minutes. Discard the mushroom stems and quarter the caps; reserve the soaking liquid.

3. In another bowl, combine the remaining 2 cups of hot water with the soy sauce, wine, sugar and salt.

4. Set a large wok over high heat. Add the peanut oil. When the oil is very hot, add the chicken. Stir-fry until the chicken turns opaque, about 30 seconds.

Transfer the chicken to a plate with a slotted spoon.

5. Add the garlic to the wok and stir-fry for 25 seconds. Add the fresh mushrooms and stir-fry for 1 minute. Add the soaked dried mushrooms, green pepper and chicken; stir-fry for 30 seconds. Pour in the reserved mushroom soaking liquid, stopping when you reach the grit at the bottom. Add the soy sauce mixture and bring to a boil. Add the sesame oil and the cornstarch mixture and simmer until slightly thickened, about 1 minute. Transfer to a serving bowl, season with ground pepper and serve immediately.

—*Jeffrey Alford and Naomi Duguid*

MAKE AHEAD The chicken can be prepared through Step 1 and refrigerated for up to 8 hours. Bring to room temperature before cooking.

Tortilla Pie

WINE The green pepper and mushrooms are clues that Bordeaux and similar reds will work here. Try the 1994 Château La Louvière Rouge or the 1995 St. Francis Merlot from California.

Spicy Lemon Chicken with Cashews

4 SERVINGS

This dish is a study in contrasts: the sweet and spicy sauce is a lovely counterpoint to the mild, tender chicken.

SAUCE

- 1 teaspoon minced fresh ginger
- 1 large garlic clove, minced
- 2 tablespoons soy sauce
- 2 tablespoons dry Vermouth or dry sherry
- 2 tablespoons chicken stock (p. 117) or canned low-sodium broth

Spicy Lemon Chicken with Cashews

until golden and just cooked through, about 3 minutes. Add the chicken to the cashews in the bowl.

5. Heat the remaining 1½ teaspoons of sesame oil and the chili oil in the wok. Add the bell peppers and stir-fry over high heat for 30 seconds. Add the snow peas and stir-fry until all the vegetables are crisp-tender, about 2 minutes. Return the chicken and nuts to the wok. Stir the sauce and then add it to the wok. Stir-fry until the sauce is clear, about 2 minutes. Spread the lettuce on a platter, spoon the chicken stir-fry on top and serve at once.

—*Susan G. Purdy*

ONE SERVING Calories 364 kcal, Total Fat 15 gm, Saturated Fat 2.8 gm

SERVE WITH Steamed white rice.

WINE A crisp, herby California Sauvignon Blanc, such as the 1996 Wente or the 1996 Cakebread.

Saigon Chicken Breasts

4 SERVINGS ✳

A potent lemongrass marinade infuses the chicken breasts before grilling and doubles as the sauce for the rice noodles.

1½ tablespoons sugar

3 tablespoons fresh lemon juice

1 teaspoon finely grated lemon zest

⅛ teaspoon crushed red pepper

Pinch of cayenne pepper

1½ teaspoons cornstarch dissolved in 2 tablespoons cold water

STIR-FRY

1½ pounds skinless, boneless chicken breasts

1½ tablespoons cornstarch

Scant ½ cup unsalted dry-roasted cashews (2 ounces)

1 tablespoon peanut oil

2½ teaspoons Asian sesame oil

½ teaspoon Asian chili oil

2 medium bell peppers, preferably 1 red and 1 yellow, cut into 1-inch pieces

7 ounces snow peas or sugar snap peas, halved diagonally

2 cups finely shredded iceberg lettuce

I. MAKE THE SAUCE: Combine all of the sauce ingredients except the dissolved cornstarch in a small bowl; then stir in the dissolved cornstarch.

2. MAKE THE STIR-FRY: Slice the chicken across the grain into ¼-inch strips. Transfer to a bowl and toss with the cornstarch.

3. Heat a large wok. Add the cashews and toss over high heat until they begin to brown, about 15 seconds; transfer the nuts to a medium bowl.

4. Heat the peanut oil and 1 teaspoon of the sesame oil in the wok. Add the chicken, spreading the strips in a single layer, and stir-fry over high heat

1 pound dried rice noodles

3 tablespoons finely chopped lemongrass, white inner bulb only

3 tablespoons sugar

2 garlic cloves, coarsely chopped

One 1-inch piece of fresh ginger, peeled and coarsely chopped

1 serrano chile, coarsely chopped

1 tablespoon peanut oil

¼ cup fresh lime juice

¼ cup Asian fish sauce

Four 5-ounce skinless, boneless chicken breast halves, pounded ¼ inch thick

¼ cup water

¼ cup coarsely chopped cilantro

¼ cup coarsely chopped roasted peanuts

1. In a large bowl, cover the rice noodles with water and let stand until pliable, about 20 minutes.

2. In a mini-processor, combine the lemongrass, sugar, garlic, ginger, chile and oil and process to a paste. Scrape the paste into a bowl and then stir in the lime juice and fish sauce. Put the chicken breasts in a large shallow bowl and add ¼ cup of the lemongrass mixture, turning to coat the chicken. Marinate the chicken for 20 minutes. Stir the water and cilantro into the remaining lemongrass mixture.

3. Light a grill. Cook the rice noodles in a pot of boiling water, stirring, until just tender, about 2 minutes. Drain and return the noodles to the pot. Rinse the noodles with cold water and drain again and then rinse and drain once more. Let the rice noodles dry, lifting them to separate the strands.

4. Grill the chicken over a medium-hot fire or in a preheated grill pan for 3 to 4 minutes per side. Let the chicken cool for 1 to 2 minutes and then cut the breasts into thick strips. Toss the rice noodles with the lemongrass dressing and the peanuts, top with the chicken breast strips and serve.

—*Jan Newberry*

Chicken Paillards in Papaya Syrup with Papaya-Poblano Salsa

4 SERVINGS

Paillards are boneless pieces of meat pounded thin for quick cooking.

½ cup finely diced papaya
¼ cup finely diced yellow bell pepper
¼ cup finely diced red onion
¼ cup seeded and finely diced poblano chile
2 tablespoons minced cilantro
1½ tablespoons fresh lime juice
⅛ teaspoon cinnamon
Salt and freshly ground black pepper

Four 5-ounce skinless, boneless chicken breast halves, pounded ⅓ inch thick
1 tablespoon vegetable oil
Papaya Syrup (recipe follows)

1. In a medium bowl, combine the papaya, bell pepper, onion, poblano, cilantro, lime juice and cinnamon. Season with salt and black pepper and let stand for 30 minutes.

2. Season the chicken on both sides with salt and black pepper. Divide the oil between 2 large nonstick skillets and heat. Add the chicken paillards and cook over high heat until browned on the bottom, about 2 minutes. Turn and cook until done, about 2 minutes longer. Transfer the chicken paillards to warmed plates and top with the salsa and Papaya Syrup.

ONE SERVING Calories 236 kcal, Total Fat 5.6 gm, Saturated Fat 1 gm

WINE The fruity, fragrant, spicy salsa makes these sautéed chicken breasts a natural for a fragrant but dry white such as Viognier. Consider the 1996 Smith & Hook from California.

PAPAYA SYRUP

4 SERVINGS

1 large ripe papaya—peeled, seeded and cut into ½-inch dice
¾ cup unsweetened pineapple juice
¾ cup water
⅓ cup sugar
3 tablespoons fresh lime juice
2 dried red chiles
6 black peppercorns
2 allspice berries
3 inches of cinnamon stick
¼ teaspoon fennel seeds
¼ teaspoon coriander seeds
1 teaspoon cornstarch dissolved in 2 tablespoons water

1. In a medium saucepan, combine the papaya, pineapple juice, water, sugar, lime juice, chiles, peppercorns, allspice, cinnamon stick, fennel seeds and coriander seeds; bring to a boil. Reduce the heat to moderately low and cook, stirring occasionally, until the papaya just begins to fall apart, about 20 minutes.

2. Strain the papaya syrup through a fine sieve, pressing on the fruit to puree it. Return the syrup to the saucepan and add the cornstarch mixture. Bring the papaya syrup to a boil and then cook over moderate heat until the syrup is thick, about 5 minutes.

—*Robbin Haas*

MAKE AHEAD The syrup can be refrigerated for up to 1 week.

ONE SERVING Calories 146 kcal, Total Fat .8 gm, Saturated Fat .1 gm

Curried Chicken Moghlai

12 SERVINGS ★★★ 1993

Ann Chantal Altman, who is now the executive chef for the Joseph Seagram Company, developed this curry recipe for an Indian client when she was working at Donald Bruce White Caterers in New York City.

Twelve 5-ounce skinless, boneless chicken breast halves
Salt and freshly ground black pepper
All-purpose flour, for dredging
1 stick (4 ounces) unsalted butter
5 medium onions, finely chopped
6 garlic cloves, minced
1 tablespoon finely grated fresh ginger
½ teaspoon ground cumin
½ teaspoon cumin seeds
½ teaspoon turmeric
½ teaspoon caraway seeds
Cayenne pepper
One 35-ounce can Italian peeled tomatoes, coarsely crushed, with their liquid
2 cups chicken stock (p. 117) or canned low-sodium broth
3 cups sour cream
½ cup (packed) light brown sugar

1 tablespoon tomato paste

1 teaspoon crushed red pepper

1 teaspoon loosely packed saffron threads

½ teaspoon ground cardamom

¼ teaspoon ground cloves

¼ teaspoon freshly grated nutmeg

Cilantro sprigs, for garnish

Cooked basmati rice, for serving

1. Season the chicken breasts with salt and black pepper and then coat them lightly with flour, shaking off the excess. Melt 4 tablespoons of the butter in a large skillet. Add 6 of the chicken breasts and cook over moderately high heat, turning once, until the chicken is golden, about 4 minutes on each side. Transfer the chicken breasts to a large plate and repeat with the remaining 6 breasts.

2. Melt the remaining 4 tablespoons of butter in the skillet. Add the onions and cook over moderate heat, stirring, until softened, about 10 minutes. Stir in the garlic and ginger and cook until slightly softened, about 3 minutes. Add the ground cumin, cumin seeds, turmeric, caraway seeds and ¼ teaspoon of cayenne and cook for 1 minute. Stir in the crushed tomatoes and stock. Transfer the mixture to an enameled cast-iron casserole.

3. Add the chicken breasts to the casserole. Simmer over moderately low heat for 10 minutes and then stir in the sour cream, brown sugar, tomato paste, crushed red pepper, saffron, cardamom, cloves and nutmeg. Cover and cook over low heat for 30 minutes. Uncover and cook, stirring occasionally, until the sauce is thickened, about 45 minutes longer; the sauce will not be completely smooth. Season with salt and cayenne and spoon the chicken breasts and the sauce onto plates. Garnish with cilantro sprigs and serve with basmati rice.

—Ann Chantal Altman

Chicken Breasts with Guacamole and Fried Prosciutto

8 SERVINGS

4 ripe Hass avocados—halved, pitted and peeled

¼ cup plus 2 tablespoons fresh lemon juice

¼ cup chopped cilantro

2 garlic cloves, minced

2 jalapeños, seeded and minced

1 small red onion, finely chopped

Salt and freshly ground pepper

3 tablespoons olive oil

1 tablespoon unsalted butter

¼ pound cold thinly sliced prosciutto, cut crosswise into ½-inch strips

Eight 8-ounce whole skinless, boneless chicken breasts, trimmed and pounded to an even thickness

2 ripe medium tomatoes, chopped

1. In a large bowl, coarsely mash the avocados with a fork. Add the lemon juice, cilantro, garlic, jalapeños and onion and mix well. Season with salt and pepper and smooth the surface. Press plastic wrap directly on the guacamole and refrigerate.

2. In a large skillet, heat 1 tablespoon of the oil with the butter. Add the prosciutto in a single layer and cook over moderately high heat, stirring often, until lightly browned, about 3 minutes. Drain on paper towels.

3. Light a grill or preheat a grill pan. Rub the chicken breasts with the remaining 2 tablespoons of oil and then season with salt and pepper. Grill the chicken breasts over high heat until they are lightly charred and just cooked through, about 4 minutes per side. Serve the chicken breasts hot, topped with the guacamole, prosciutto and tomatoes. *—Marcia Kiesel*

MAKE AHEAD The guacamole and fried prosciutto can be refrigerated separately for up to 1 day. Serve them at room temperature.

WINE The strips of fried prosciutto and the tomatoes tilt the flavors toward a light red with character, such as a Rioja. Stick with such younger, brighter bottlings as the 1994 Conde de Valdemar Crianza and the 1994 Marqués de Riscal.

Award-Winning Chili

6 SERVINGS

This white chili, made with Great Northern beans, chicken and Monterey Jack cheese, took the prize at a Kansas City cook-off. The recipe appears in *John Madden's Ultimate Tailgating,* by Peter Kaminsky and John Madden. The beans have to soak overnight, so be sure to plan accordingly.

1 pound dried Great Northern or other white beans (about 2½ cups), picked over and rinsed

1½ pounds skinless, boneless chicken breast halves

1 quart chicken stock (p. 117) or canned low-sodium broth

1 tablespoon pure olive oil

2 medium onions, finely chopped

Two 4-ounce cans chopped green chiles

4 garlic cloves, minced

2 teaspoons ground cumin

¼ teaspoon cayenne pepper

1¼ pounds Monterey Jack cheese, shredded (7 cups)

Salt

3 to 4 jalapeños—halved, seeded and coarsely chopped

Sour cream, for serving

1. In a large saucepan, cover the beans with 2 inches of water and let soak overnight. Drain the beans and return them to the saucepan; add enough water to cover by 2 inches. Bring to a boil over moderate heat and simmer until the beans are tender, about 1 hour. Drain the beans.

Award-Winning Chili

2. Meanwhile, put the chicken breasts in a saucepan and add the stock; if necessary, add a little water to cover the chicken. Bring to a simmer and cook over low heat until the chicken is just opaque throughout, about 15 minutes. Transfer the breasts to a plate to cool and then shred. Boil the stock over high heat until reduced to 2½ cups, about 4 minutes.

3. Heat the oil in a large saucepan. Add the onions and then cook over moderate heat, stirring, until translucent, about 4 minutes. Add the canned chiles, garlic, cumin and cayenne and cook, stirring, for 3 minutes. Add the beans, chicken, reduced stock and 4 cups of the cheese and simmer for 10 minutes. Season with salt.

4. Ladle the chili into large bowls and top each with ¼ cup of cheese and a generous sprinkling of the chopped jalapeños. Serve the sour cream and the remaining cheese and chiles on the side. —*Nancy Walters*

MAKE AHEAD The recipe can be prepared through Step 2 and refrigerated overnight.

Fragrant Steamed Chicken
12 SERVINGS
Steaming the chicken on the bone over an aromatic mixture produces incredibly succulent meat and richly flavored pan juices, which are the base for the sauce. Serve the chicken on a bed of rice.

¼   **cup plus 2 teaspoons soy sauce**
2½ **teaspoons Asian sesame oil**
Six **1-pound whole chicken breasts on the bone with skin**
1   **cup dry sherry**

Caramelized Black Pepper Chicken

2 tablespoons extra-virgin olive oil
1 tablespoon minced rosemary
1 teaspoon kosher salt
1 teaspoon freshly ground pepper
16 chicken drumettes
Romesco Sauce (recipe follows)

1. In a large shallow bowl, combine the oil, rosemary, kosher salt and pepper. Using a small sharp knife, cut around the bone at the small end of each drumette to release the meat. Scrape the meat down the bone to form a fat nugget at the other end. Add to the marinade and stir to coat. Cover and refrigerate for 4 hours or overnight.
2. Light a grill or preheat the broiler. Grill or broil the drumettes, turning often, for about 15 minutes, or until well browned and cooked through. Serve hot with the Romesco Sauce.

ROMESCO SAUCE

MAKES ABOUT 1 CUP

1 medium tomato, halved crosswise and seeded
1 small red bell pepper
¼ cup plus 2 tablespoons extra-virgin olive oil
3 tablespoons sliced almonds
1 garlic clove, minced
1 teaspoon crushed red pepper
3 tablespoons coarse dry bread crumbs
2 tablespoons sherry vinegar
Salt and freshly ground black pepper

1. Preheat the broiler and broil the tomato and red pepper until the skins are charred. Transfer the red pepper to a bowl, cover with plastic wrap and let steam for 5 minutes. Peel the vegetables and discard the charred skins, seeds and stem. Coarsely chop the tomato and roasted pepper and add them to a food processor along with any accumulated juices.
2. In a small skillet, heat the oil. Add the almonds and cook over moderate heat, stirring, until the nuts are slightly golden, about 3 minutes. Add the garlic and crushed red pepper and cook for 1 minute. Stir in the bread crumbs and remove from the heat. Scrape the mixture into the food processor and puree until smooth. Blend in the vinegar. Scrape the sauce into a bowl and season with salt and black pepper.
—*Tony Najiola*

MAKE AHEAD The sauce can be refrigerated for up to 3 days. Serve at room temperature.

Caramelized Black Pepper Chicken

2 SERVINGS

Charles Phan, the chef and owner of The Slanted Door in San Francisco, uses bone-in chicken pieces for this sweet and hot Vietnamese dish, but skinless, boneless pieces cook faster. Because fish sauces vary in their saltiness, Phan advises adding the fish sauce to taste. The chicken is good on a bed of steamed jasmine rice.

½ cup dark brown sugar
¼ cup water
3 tablespoons rice vinegar
1 teaspoon minced garlic
1 teaspoon finely grated fresh ginger
1 teaspoon coarsely ground pepper
2 fresh Thai chiles, halved, or dried red chiles
About ¼ cup fish sauce (nam pla)
1 tablespoon canola oil
1 shallot, thinly sliced
1 pound skinless, boneless chicken thighs, cut into 1-inch pieces
4 cilantro sprigs

1. In a small bowl, combine the brown sugar, water, vinegar, garlic, ginger, pepper, chiles and fish sauce to taste.
2. Heat the oil in a large deep skillet. Add the shallot and cook over moderate heat until softened, about 4 minutes. Add the fish sauce mixture and the chicken and simmer over high heat until the chicken is cooked through, about 10 minutes. Transfer to a serving bowl, garnish with the cilantro and serve.
—*Charles Phan*

WINE An oaky, round and ripe Napa Valley Chardonnay, such as the 1996 Shafer Red Shoulder Ranch or the 1996 Marcelina, will balance the pepper-sweet sauce of this chicken dish.

Bay Leaf–Braised Chicken with Chickpeas

4 SERVINGS

Turkish bay leaves are some of the best in the world. Most of the year, the bay trees that grow on the mountains of western Turkey benefit from the moist air of the Mediterranean and Aegean seas. During the late summer the air turns drier, a phenomenon that helps to quickly dehydrate the leaves and concentrate their flavor.

¼ cup olive oil
8 bay leaves
8 chicken thighs (about 3 pounds)
Salt and freshly ground black pepper
1 medium onion, coarsely chopped
2 garlic cloves, minced
¼ cup dry white wine

One 15-ounce can of chickpeas,
      drained and rinsed
About ¾ cup chicken stock (p. 117)
      or canned low-sodium broth
  1 large roasted red pepper, cut
      into thin strips
  ¼ cup coarsely chopped flat-leaf
      parsley

1. In a large skillet, heat 2 tablespoons
of the oil until almost smoking. Add the
bay leaves. Season the chicken thighs
with salt and black pepper, add to the
skillet and cook over moderately high
heat until well-browned, about 5 minutes per side. Transfer the chicken to
a plate and pour off all but 1 tablespoon of the fat from the pan; leave
the bay leaves in the pan.

2. Heat the remaining 2 tablespoons
of oil in the skillet. Add the onion and
cook over moderately high heat, stirring occasionally, until softened, about
5 minutes. Stir in the garlic and cook
until fragrant, about 1 minute. Add the
wine and cook, scraping up any brown
bits from the bottom of the pan, until
almost evaporated, about 2 minutes.

3. Return the chicken thighs to the
skillet. Add the chickpeas and ¾ cup
of the chicken stock. Cover and cook
over moderately low heat until the
chicken thighs are tender, 17 to 20
minutes. Discard the bay leaves and
remove the chicken thighs. Stir the
red pepper strips and parsley into the
chickpeas and season with salt and
black pepper; add a little chicken stock
to the chickpeas if they seem dry.
Spoon the chickpea mixture into bowls
and top with the chicken thighs.
      —*Jan Newberry*

WINE With chicken, the preparation
dictates the wine choice. Here, the
bay leaves and the roasted red peppers call for a fruity, herbaceous white.
Try a California Sauvignon Blanc, such
as the 1996 Silverado or the 1996 Dry
Creek.

Bay Leaf—Braised Chicken with Chickpeas

Coq au Vin

10 SERVINGS

Marinating the chicken overnight considerably deepens the flavor.

 10 whole chicken legs (6½ pounds
      in all), cut into drumsticks and
      thighs
  1 bottle dry red wine, preferably
      Burgundy
  2 medium onions, coarsely
      chopped
  2 carrots, coarsely chopped
  ½ cup Cognac or other brandy
  2 tablespoons olive oil
  2 garlic cloves, halved
 10 whole black peppercorns
Salt
 2½ cups dried porcini mushrooms
      (3 ounces)
  4 cups boiling water
 10 ounces slab bacon, sliced
      ¼ inch thick, then cut crosswise
      into ½-inch strips
Freshly ground pepper
  ¼ cup plus 2 tablespoons
      all-purpose flour

Skillet Fried Chicken

keep the chicken at a steady sizzle. Transfer the chicken pieces to a rack set over a sheet pan to drain and then serve them hot with lemon wedges.

—*Marcia Kiesel*

WINE This juicy, lemon-accented chicken can be dramatically set off with a lighter Sauternes from the Barsac appellation, such as the 1989 Château Coutet or the 1988 Château Doisy Daëne.

Poulet au Riz

4 SERVINGS

This recipe makes more broth than is needed to complete the dish; you can use whatever's leftover to make soup. The recipe was adapted from *Jacques Pépin's Kitchen: Encore with Claudine,* published by KQED Books & Tapes.

6 carrots, peeled and halved crosswise
6 small white turnips, halved
3 parsnips, peeled and halved crosswise
3 small onions, halved
2 large or 4 small leeks, white and green, split lengthwise and washed well
Bouquet garni made with 12 parsley stems, 1 celery rib, 1 large sage sprig, 1 large rosemary sprig and 2 bay leaves
3¼ teaspoons salt
4 quarts water
One 4-pound chicken, neck and gizzard reserved
1½ cups jasmine rice (10½ ounces)
8 small scallions, coarsely chopped

1. In a stockpot, combine the carrots, turnips, parsnips, onions, leeks, bouquet garni and 2¼ teaspoons of salt. Add the water and bring to a boil over high heat. Reduce the heat to low, cover and simmer the vegetables for 10 minutes.

2. Add the chicken to the pot, breast down; rearrange the vegetables, if necessary, to keep the chicken submerged. Add the neck and gizzard and bring to a boil over high heat, skimming as necessary. Reduce the heat to moderately low, cover and simmer for 15 minutes. Remove from the heat and let stand, covered, for 30 minutes; the chicken will finish cooking in the hot broth.

3. Using a large, heavy-duty wire skimmer, transfer the chicken to a platter and the vegetables to a large, deep gratin dish and discard the bouquet garni. Skim the fat from the surface of the chicken broth. Reserve 6 cups of the broth and keep warm; strain and refrigerate or freeze the remaining broth for future use.

4. In a medium saucepan, combine the rice with the scallions, the remaining 1 teaspoon of salt and 3 cups of the reserved broth. Bring to a boil over high heat, stirring occasionally. Cover, reduce the heat to low and cook until the rice is tender and all of the liquid has been absorbed, about 18 minutes.

5. Meanwhile, when the chicken is cool enough to handle, remove all of the skin and bones, keeping the meat in large pieces. Add the chicken meat to the vegetables in the gratin dish and pour the remaining 3 cups of reserved warm broth over all; cover and keep warm.

6. When the rice is done, fluff it with a fork. Spoon a generous mound of rice in the center of each of 4 soup plates. Arrange the chicken and vegetables around the rice, moisten them with

Poulet au Riz

some of the broth from the gratin dish and serve. —*Jacques Pépin*

SERVE WITH Dijon mustard, cornichons, a green salad and some crusty French bread.

WINE An off-dry white, such as the 1995 Château de Montfort Vouvray from France or the 1996 Pine Ridge La Petite Vigne Chenin Blanc Sur Lie from California

Roasted Chicken with Bread Salad

4 SERVINGS

Be sure not to substitute a large roaster for the two and three-quarter pound free-range chicken called for here. Roasters are too lean. For perfect results, salt the bird and wait at least twenty-four hours before roasting it. Salt draws out the succulent juices

One 2¾-pound free-range
    chicken
4 thyme sprigs
4 small garlic cloves, lightly
    crushed and peeled
2 teaspoons fine sea salt
Freshly ground pepper
Bread Salad with Currants and
    Pine Nuts (recipe follows),
    for serving

Roasted Chicken with Bread Salad

1. Slide your fingers under the skin of the chicken and spread the thyme and the garlic over the breasts and thighs. Sprinkle the sea salt all over the chicken breasts and thighs and then season with pepper. Cover the chicken and refrigerate for at least 24 hours.

2. Preheat the oven to 500°. Choose a heavy cast-iron skillet that is just large enough to hold the chicken and preheat it in the oven for 5 minutes; this prevents the chicken skin from sticking. Put the chicken in the hot skillet, breast up, and roast for 30 minutes. Turn the chicken breast down and roast for about 15 minutes longer, or until the juices run clear when a thigh is pierced. Transfer the chicken to a cutting board and let rest for 10 minutes before carving.

3. Skim the fat from the juices in the skillet. Arrange the bread salad on plates and top with the chicken. Pour the pan juices over all and serve the chicken at once.

WINE A not-too-oaky Italian Barbera with good fruit and medium weight will complement the chicken. Consider the 1995 Bersano Barbera d'Asti or the 1996 Corino Barbera d'Alba. A young California Pinot Noir with clear varietal fruit, such as the 1996 Saintsbury Garnet, would also work well.

BREAD SALAD WITH CURRANTS AND PINE NUTS

4 SERVINGS

- 1 tablespoon currants
- 1 tablespoon warm water
- 1 teaspoon red wine vinegar
- 2 tablespoons Champagne vinegar
- ½ cup plus 2½ tablespoons olive oil

Fine sea salt

Freshly ground pepper

- ½ pound stale, chewy Italian-style bread, cut into large chunks
- 1 tablespoon pine nuts
- 4 scallions, thinly sliced crosswise
- 3 garlic cloves, slivered
- 4 cups (lightly packed) small arugula leaves

1. Preheat the oven to 450°. In a small glass or stainless-steel bowl, soak the currants in the warm water and red wine vinegar until they are soft and plump, about 10 minutes. Drain the currants well in a small sieve.

2. In another small glass or stainless-steel bowl, combine the Champagne vinegar with ½ cup of the oil. Season the Champagne vinaigrette with ¾ teaspoon of sea salt and ¼ teaspoon of pepper.

3. On a rimmed baking sheet, toss the chunks of bread with 2 tablespoons of the oil. Bake for about 5 minutes, or until the bread is lightly toasted. Let cool and then tear the bread into irregular bite-size pieces. In a bowl, toss the toasted bread with three-quarters of the Champagne vinaigrette and let marinate for 30 minutes.

4. Put the pine nuts in a pie pan and warm them in the oven for 2 minutes. Leave the oven on.

5. In a small skillet, heat the remaining ½ tablespoon of oil. Add the scallions and garlic and cook over moderate heat until softened, about 2 minutes. Transfer the scallions and garlic to a large glass or stainless-steel bowl. Add the currants, toasted bread, pine nuts and the remaining Champagne vinaigrette and toss well.

6. Spoon the bread salad into a shallow 1-quart baking dish and cover it loosely with aluminum foil. Bake the bread salad for about 15 minutes, or until it is heated through. Uncover the bread salad and bake for a few minutes longer to dry out the top and brown the bottom. Transfer the bread salad to a platter and toss with the arugula. Serve the bread salad at once.

—*Judy Rodgers*

Provençal Herb and Lemon Roasted Chicken

4 SERVINGS

The juicy herb-stuffed chicken bakes with a splash of lemon juice, which also spikes the rich pan sauce.

- 2 tablespoons finely chopped thyme, plus 6 sprigs
- 1 tablespoon finely chopped rosemary, plus 1 small sprig
- 1 teaspoon lavender leaves, preferably flowering, plus 1 small sprig
- ¼ cup extra-virgin olive oil

Salt and freshly ground pepper

One 3½- to 4-pound chicken, wing tips removed

- 1 lemon, preferably Meyer— halved, juice squeezed into a bowl, halves reserved
- 6 unpeeled garlic cloves, lightly smashed
- 1 cup water

1. Preheat the oven to 450°. In a small bowl, combine the chopped thyme and rosemary and the lavender leaves with 2 tablespoons of the oil, 1 teaspoon of salt and ½ teaspoon of pepper.

2. Carefully loosen the skin over the chicken breast and legs; don't tear the skin. Gently work the herb paste under the skin, spreading it all over the breast and legs. Season the cavity with salt and pepper and stuff with the reserved lemon halves, garlic cloves and herb sprigs.

3. Set the chicken in a medium roasting pan and rub the skin with the remaining 2 tablespoons of oil. Drizzle with half of the lemon juice and season generously with salt and pepper. Roast the chicken for 20 minutes. Drizzle with the remaining lemon juice and then reduce the oven temperature to 350° and roast for about 40 minutes longer, or until the juices run clear when a thigh is pierced; baste once or twice during cooking. Cover

the bird loosely with aluminum foil if it browns too quickly. Transfer the chicken to a cutting board and let rest for 15 minutes before carving.

4. Spoon off the fat from the roasting pan and set the pan on 2 burners over moderately high heat. Add the water and bring to a boil, scraping up any brown bits from the bottom of the pan. Boil the sauce until reduced to ¾ cup and then strain and serve with the chicken.   —*Maria Helm*

WINE The sun-dried cherry, orange spice and sweet, slightly smoky oak flavors of the 1996 Robert Sinskey Vineyards Pinot Noir Los Carneros make it an elegant companion for the herbed chicken. If you can't find it, consider an Italian wine, such as the Castello di Cacchiano Chianti Classico Riserva.

Hakka Salt-Baked Chicken

4 SERVINGS ★★★ **1983**

Barbara Tropp, a scholar of Chinese culture and a cookbook author and restaurant consultant, introduced FOOD & WINE readers to the simple, earthy cuisine of the Hakka people of southeast China.

One 3½- to 4-pound chicken, preferably free-range, rinsed and patted dry
1½ tablespoons Chinese rice wine or dry sherry
5 quarter-size slices of fresh ginger, lightly smashed
2 scallions, lightly smashed and cut into 1½-inch lengths
5 cilantro sprigs, plus additional cilantro leaves for garnish
1 star anise pod
1 tablespoon Rose Dew Liqueur or extra-dry vermouth
4½ pounds kosher salt
Cilantro leaves, for garnish
Hakka Dipping Sauces (recipe follows), for serving

1. Rub the cavity of the chicken with the wine and stuff with the ginger, scallions, cilantro sprigs and star anise. Place the chicken, breast up, on a rack and brush the outside with the liqueur. Let the chicken stand in a cool, airy place until the skin is dry to the touch, about 2 hours.

2. Truss the chicken with kitchen string. Set the chicken on a single layer of cheesecloth that is long enough to be wrapped around the chicken and tied. Pull the ends of the cheesecloth up and tie them together on top of the chicken breast with kitchen string. The chicken should be tightly wrapped in a neat ball.

3. Pour the kosher salt into a large heavy stockpot or spun-steel wok that will hold the chicken snugly. Turn the heat to moderately high and stir the salt frequently until it is very hot to the touch, about 10 minutes. Carefully pour all but 1 inch of the salt (about 6 cups) into a heatproof bowl. Set the chicken in the pot, breast up, and cover completely with the reserved hot salt. Cover the pot, reduce the heat to moderate and cook the chicken undisturbed on top of the stove for 1½ hours. Check for doneness by brushing off the salt and piercing a thigh with a sharp knife. If the juices are still pink, re-cover with salt and continue to cook for another 15 to 30 minutes before checking again.

4. Push the salt aside and carefully remove the chicken, holding it by the knotted cheesecloth; try not to tilt the chicken and spill the juices. Set on a large platter and remove the cheesecloth and the trussing strings. Discard the salt. Carve the chicken or use a cleaver to chop it Chinese-style into bite-size pieces. Serve the chicken hot or at room temperature, garnished with cilantro leaves and accompanied by the dipping sauces.

HAKKA DIPPING SAUCES
CHILI SAUCE
1 tablespoon hot water
1 tablespoon Chinese chili sauce
1 teaspoon unseasoned Japanese rice vinegar
½ teaspoon sugar
GARLIC SAUCE
2 tablespoons unseasoned Japanese rice vinegar
1 tablespoon plus 1 teaspoon minced garlic
1 tablespoon sugar
GINGER SAUCE
1 tablespoon (packed) minced fresh ginger
2 tablespoons peanut oil
¼ teaspoon kosher salt

1. MAKE THE CHILI SAUCE: In a small glass or stainless-steel bowl, combine the water with the chili sauce, vinegar and sugar and stir to dissolve the sugar. Let stand for at least 15 minutes and stir before serving.

2. MAKE THE GARLIC SAUCE: In a small glass or stainless-steel bowl, combine the vinegar, garlic and sugar; stir to dissolve the sugar. Let stand for at least 15 minutes and stir the sauce before serving.

3. MAKE THE GINGER SAUCE: Put the ginger in a small heatproof bowl. Heat the oil in a small saucepan until it sends up a wisp of smoke and then pour it over the ginger and stir. Stir in the kosher salt. Serve warm or at room temperature. —*Barbara Tropp*

Spanish Chicken and Rice with Sprouts and Chorizo

4 SERVINGS

2 teaspoons olive oil
4 skinless chicken breast halves on the bone, halved crosswise
Salt and freshly ground pepper
One 6-inch chorizo (about 3 ounces), halved lengthwise and sliced crosswise ¼ inch thick

Provençal Herb and Lemon Roasted Chicken

1 **medium onion, finely chopped**
2 **serrano chiles, minced**
1 **garlic clove, minced**
2 **cups large bean sprouts (½ pound), such as chickpea, lentil or green pea**
1 **cup medium-grain rice, such as Valencia**
One 35-ounce can peeled Italian **tomatoes—seeded, chopped and drained**
2 **cups chicken stock (p. 117) or canned low-sodium broth**
2 **bay leaves**
1 **scallion, thinly sliced**

1. Preheat the oven to 350°. In a large enameled cast-iron casserole or Dutch oven, heat the oil. Season the chicken breasts with salt and pepper and cook over moderate heat, turning once, until the chicken is lightly golden on both sides. Transfer the chicken breasts to a plate. Add the chorizo to the casserole and cook over moderate heat, stirring, until just brown, about 1 minute. Add the onion, chiles and garlic to the casserole and cook, stirring, until the vegetables are soft, about 2 minutes. Stir the bean sprouts and rice into the casserole and toss to coat. Add the tomatoes, stock, bay leaves and 1 teaspoon of salt to the casserole and bring to a boil. Return the chicken breasts to the casserole.

2. Cover the casserole and bake for about 15 minutes, or until the chicken breasts are cooked through. Transfer the chicken breasts to a plate and cover with aluminum foil. Stir the scallion into the rice, cover and bake for about 5 more minutes, or until the liquid is absorbed and the rice is tender. Let the rice stand for 5 minutes. Discard the bay leaves. Spoon the rice onto a platter, top with the chicken breasts and serve. —*Grace Parisi*

ONE SERVING Calories 525 kcal, Total Fat 13.7 gm, Saturated Fat 4.3 gm
WINE With its chorizo and serrano chiles, this spicy chicken dish needs a clean, crisp Spanish white wine, such as the 1996 Torres Viña Sol or the 1996 Montecillo Viña Cumbrero Rioja Blanco.

Roasted Salt-Brined Turkey with Giblet Gravy with, CLOCKWISE FROM TOP, Corn Bread—Pecan Dressing (p. 291), Pole Beans Cooked in Smoky Pork Stock (p. 309), Sweet Potato Casserole (p. 335) and Spicy Collard Greens (p. 306).

Roasted Salt-Brined Turkey with Giblet Gravy

12 SERVINGS

Soaking a turkey overnight in salted water produces an especially moist and well-flavored bird. Careful attention to basting the turkey, especially during the last hour of roasting, also contributes to its juiciness.

BRINE

1 cup plus 2 tablespoons kosher salt
1 gallon cold water

thanksgiving buffet game plan

For a happy Thanksgiving, do most of the work in advance. Many dishes in the menu at right can be made ahead and reheated, if needed.

Two weeks ahead
Make the Smoky Pork Stock • Spritz Cookies • Blackberry Cordial

One week ahead
Make the Cheese Straws • Benne Wafers • Shrimp Paste • Roasted Beets in Gingered Syrup • Lane Cake

Two days ahead
Make the Southern Corn Bread • Cranberries with Orange Zest and Port

One day ahead
Make the Silken Turnip and Potato Soup • Pole Beans Cooked in Smoky Pork Stock • Spicy Collard Greens • Egg Custard • *Brine the turkey* • *Start the* Giblet Gravy, Corn Bread Dressing, Sweet Potato Casserole *and* Ambrosia

Big day
Prepare the Oysters on the half shell • Roasted Salt-Brined Turkey with Giblet Gravy • Corn Bread Dressing • Sweet Potato Casserole • Deviled Eggs • Cloverleaf Rolls • Ambrosia

One 12-pound free-range turkey—neck, wing tips, heart and gizzard reserved for gravy

TURKEY

6 tablespoons unsalted butter, softened
¼ cup fresh orange juice
2 tablespoons fresh lemon juice
1 tablespoon dried thyme
1 teaspoon kosher salt
¾ teaspoon freshly ground pepper
1 large onion, quartered
2 celery ribs, cut into 2-inch lengths
1 bunch of thyme sprigs (2 ounces)
4 sage sprigs
4 garlic cloves, unpeeled
3 bay leaves
6 thick slices of bacon
1 quart chicken stock (p. 117) or canned low-sodium broth
Giblet Gravy (recipe follows), for serving

1. BRINE THE TURKEY: In a large stockpot, dissolve the kosher salt in the cold water. Add the turkey and refrigerate for 12 to 24 hours. Remove the turkey from the brine and pat dry inside and out with paper towels.

2. ROAST THE TURKEY: Preheat the oven to 325°. In a small glass or stainless-steel bowl, blend the butter with the orange juice, lemon juice, thyme, kosher salt and pepper. Rub the turkey inside and out with the seasoned butter. Fill the turkey cavity with the onion, celery, thyme sprigs, sage sprigs, garlic and bay leaves and then truss the turkey tightly. Transfer the turkey to a rack set in a roasting pan. Arrange the bacon slices over the turkey breast and pour 2 cups of the stock into the roasting pan.

3. Roast the turkey in the oven for 45 minutes and then baste with 1 cup of the stock. Roast the turkey for 1½

hours longer, basting it with the pan juices every 20 minutes. Add the remaining 1 cup of stock to the pan and then roast the turkey for about 1 hour and 50 minutes longer, basting it every 15 minutes with the pan juices. The turkey is done when an instant-read thermometer inserted into the thickest part of the thigh registers 170°; if the bacon is very dark, remove it from the turkey breast. Transfer the turkey to a carving board, cover loosely with aluminum foil and let rest for at least 20 minutes.

4. Pour the roasting juices into a glass measure or bowl and skim off the fat. Strain the juices into the Giblet Gravy and then reheat the gravy if necessary. Carve the turkey and serve it with the gravy. ➤

Roasted Salt-Brined Turkey
with Giblet Gravy with,
FROM LEFT TO RIGHT ACROSS THE TABLE,
Sweet Potato Casserole (p. 335),
Roasted Beets in Gingered
Syrup (p. 319), Spicy Collard
Greens (in back; p. 306),
Cranberries with Orange Zest
and Port (p. 360), Pole Beans
Cooked in Smoky Pork Stock (p. 309),
Deviled Eggs (p. 25), Corn Bread–
Pecan Dressing (p. 291) and
Cloverleaf Rolls (p. 289).

GIBLET GRAVY

MAKES ABOUT 6 CUPS

1 stick plus 2 tablespoons
  (5 ounces) unsalted butter
Reserved turkey neck, wing tips,
  heart and gizzard, neck cut
  crosswise into ½-inch pieces
1 carrot, coarsely chopped
1 celery rib, coarsely chopped
1 small onion, coarsely chopped
Salt
3 parsley stems
3 black peppercorns
3 whole cloves
1 bay leaf
½ teaspoon dried thyme
4 cups chicken stock (p. 117) or
  canned low-sodium broth
3 cups water
1 cup dry white wine
½ cup all-purpose flour
Reserved turkey pan juices
3 tablespoons brandy
Freshly ground pepper

1. In a large saucepan, melt 2 tablespoons of the butter. Add the turkey

neck pieces, wing tips, heart and gizzard and cook over moderate heat until well-browned all over, about 10 minutes. Add the carrot, celery and onion and season with salt. Cook, stirring often, until the vegetables start to brown, about 5 minutes. Add the parsley stems, peppercorns, cloves, bay leaf and thyme to the saucepan and cook for 5 minutes longer. Add the stock, water and wine and bring to a simmer. Skim the broth and reduce the heat to low. Cover the pan partially and simmer until the giblets are very tender, about 2 hours.

2. Strain the broth; reserve the neck and giblets. Remove the meat from the neck, discarding the skin and bones. Finely chop the neck meat and giblets. If you have more than 6 cups of broth, simmer to reduce it to 6 cups.

3. In a medium saucepan, melt the remaining 1 stick of butter. Stir in the flour and cook over moderately high heat, stirring constantly, until the roux turns deep brown, about 8 minutes. Gradually whisk in the 6 cups of broth until smooth. Simmer the gravy over low heat, stirring often, until no floury taste remains, about 5 minutes.

4. Add the reserved neck meat and giblets, the turkey pan juices and the brandy. Season with salt and pepper and simmer for 5 minutes longer. Pour into a gravy boat and serve hot.

—Edna Lewis and Scott Peacock

MAKE AHEAD Prepare the gravy through Step 3 a day ahead. Refrigerate it and the meats separately.

Roasted Turkey with Sausage-Apple Stuffing, with Mashed Potatoes with Mascarpone (p. 337) and Pan-Roasted Brussels Sprouts with Pancetta (p. 314).

Roasted Turkey with Sausage-Apple Stuffing

8 SERVINGS

Make sure the turkey is at room temperature when it goes into the oven; otherwise it will take longer to roast.

One 12-pound turkey, wing tips, neck, heart and gizzard reserved
Salt and freshly ground pepper
4 tablespoons unsalted butter, softened
2 tablespoons vegetable oil
1 medium onion, quartered
1 large celery rib, cut into thirds
¾ cup dry white wine
6 cups canned low-sodium chicken broth or water
2 canned plum tomatoes, halved and seeded
3 parsley sprigs
2 thyme sprigs
1 bay leaf
¼ cup plus 2 tablespoons water
⅓ cup all-purpose flour
2 tablespoons port or Madeira (optional)
Sausage-Apple Stuffing (recipe follows)

1. Preheat the oven to 475°. Rinse the turkey inside and out and pat dry. Season the cavity with salt and pepper and set the bird on a rack in a roasting pan large enough to let air circulate all around. Rub the softened butter over the breast and legs and season with salt and pepper. Roast the turkey in the top third of the oven for about 30 minutes, or until beginning to brown. Reduce the oven temperature to 375°, cover the turkey loosely with aluminum foil and continue roasting, basting often, for about 2½ hours, or until an instant-read thermometer inserted into the thickest part of the thigh registers 175°. Transfer to a serving platter, cover again with foil, and let stand for at least 20 minutes before carving.

2. Meanwhile, cut the turkey neck and gizzard in half. Heat the oil in a medium saucepan and add the neck, gizzard, heart and wing tips. Cook over moderately high heat, stirring occasionally, until browned and crisp, about 7 minutes. Stir in the onion and celery and cook until golden. Add the wine and boil until reduced by half, about 7 minutes. Add the chicken broth and bring to a boil. Stir in the tomatoes, parsley, thyme and bay leaf and cook over very low heat until reduced to 3½ cups, about 1 hour. Strain the turkey stock into a bowl; reserve 1½ cups for the stuffing.

3. In a small bowl, mix the water with the flour until smooth. Remove the rack from the roasting pan and spoon off the fat. Set the pan over 2 burners over high heat. Add the remaining 2 cups of turkey stock and bring to a boil, scraping up any brown bits from the bottom of the roasting pan. Whisk in the flour paste and cook until the gravy thickens and then add the port. Strain the gravy into a sauceboat. Carve the turkey and serve with the gravy and Sausage-Apple Stuffing.

SAUSAGE-APPLE STUFFING
MAKES ABOUT 10 CUPS
If possible, buy the sausage from a butcher shop that makes its own—you can ask the butcher to sell you a pound without the casings and save yourself a few minutes of prep work.

4½ tablespoons unsalted butter
6 celery ribs, finely chopped
3 medium onions, finely chopped
1½ pounds sweet Italian sausage, removed from the casings and crumbled
9 cups cubed (1 inch) day-old Italian bread (about 1 large loaf)
36 pitted prunes, coarsely chopped (about 10 ounces)
3 medium Golden Delicious or Granny Smith apples—peeled, cored and coarsely chopped

12-step dinner plan

1. Chop all the parsley for the meal, about one cup. Peel seven onions needed for the menu.
2. Prepare and roast the turkey, basting occasionally.
3. Make the stock and leave it simmering.
4. Make and refrigerate the cassata.
5. Make the turkey stuffing.
6. Prepare the ingredients for the brussels sprouts.
7. Prepare the ingredients for the squash.
8. Prepare the ingredients for the mashed potatoes.
9. Assemble the antipasto platter.
10. Bake the stuffing and squash; cook the brussels sprouts and potatoes.
11. Make the gravy.
12. Mash the potatoes. Serve Thanksgiving dinner. Unmold and garnish the cassata while the dishes are being cleared.

Cornish Hens with Pomegranate and Lemon

⅓ cup finely chopped flat-leaf
    parsley
¼ cup finely chopped sage
1½ teaspoons salt
¾ teaspoon freshly ground pepper
¾ teaspoon freshly grated nutmeg
4 large eggs, lightly beaten
1½ cups reserved turkey stock

I. Preheat the oven to 425° and generously butter 2 medium baking dishes that are at least 2 inches deep. Melt the 4½ tablespoons butter in a large skillet. Add the celery and onions and cook over moderate heat until the vegetables are softened, about 5 minutes. Add the sausage and cook, stirring, just until it loses its pink color, about 7 minutes.

2. In a large bowl, toss the bread with the prunes, apples, parsley and sage. Add the sausage mixture; season with the salt, pepper and nutmeg. Add the eggs and the reserved turkey stock and mix well. Divide the stuffing between the prepared baking dishes. Cover with aluminum foil and bake for 20 minutes. Remove the foil and bake for about 10 minutes longer, or until heated through and browned on top. Let cool slightly before serving. —*Nancy Verde Barr*

MAKE AHEAD The stuffing without the eggs and turkey stock can be refrigerated overnight; the final ingredients should be added just before baking the turkey.

Cornish Hens with Pomegranate and Lemon

4 SERVINGS

Sparkling ruby pomegranate seeds give these Cornish hens a burst of tartness. Allow time for the hens to marinate overnight.

½ **cup extra-virgin olive oil**
Zest of 1 lemon, cut into thin strips
1 **teaspoon ancho chile powder**
**Four 1¼-pound Cornish hens, legs
    tied together with kitchen string**

¼ cup pine nuts
Salt and freshly ground black pepper
¼ cup plus 1 tablespoon minced
    onion
1 tablespoon minced garlic
1 tablespoon finely grated fresh
    ginger
⅓ cup pomegranate seeds (see
    Note)
¼ cup fresh lemon juice
2 teaspoons ground cumin
½ teaspoon ground coriander
¼ teaspoon cayenne pepper
2 cups chicken stock (p. 117) or
    canned low-sodium broth
2 tablespoons honey

I. Combine the oil, lemon zest and ½ teaspoon of the chile powder in a small bowl. Put 2 Cornish hens in each of 2 large resealable plastic bags. Add half of the marinade to each bag, seal the bags and rub the marinade all over the hens. Refrigerate overnight.

2. Preheat the oven to 350°. Spread the pine nuts on a baking sheet. Toast for 3 to 4 minutes, or until the pine nuts are lightly browned.

3. Raise the oven temperature to 375°. Remove the hens from the bags, scraping off any excess marinade; pour the marinade into a bowl. Season the hens inside and out with salt and black pepper.

4. Heat 1 tablespoon of the marinade in a heavy skillet. Add 2 of the hens and cook over high heat, turning once, until golden and crisp, about 3 minutes per side. Transfer the Cornish hens to a large roasting pan, breast side up. Repeat with 1 more tablespoon of the marinade and the remaining hens; set the skillet aside.

5. Roast the Cornish hens for about 50 minutes, or until the juices run clear when the thighs are pierced with a knife. Transfer the hens to a platter and let rest for 15 minutes. Pour the pan juices into a bowl and skim off the fat.

6. Pour off all but 2 tablespoons of the fat from the skillet and set it over moderately high heat. Add the onion, garlic and ginger and cook just until softened, about 2 minutes. Add the pomegranate seeds, lemon juice, pine nuts, cumin, coriander, cayenne and the remaining ½ teaspoon of chile powder. Cook, scraping up any brown bits, until the liquid is nearly evaporated, about 2 minutes. Add the stock and honey and bring to a boil. Cook until reduced to ¾ cup, about 12 minutes. Add the reserved pan juices. Transfer the Cornish hens to plates, spoon the sauce on top and serve.

—*Matthew Kenney*

NOTE To remove the seeds from a pomegranate, cut off the crown of the fruit. Score the skin in quarters. Transfer the pomegranate to a bowl of cold water. Working in the water, peel off the skin and remove the seeds from the membranes; discard the skin and the membranes as you go. Drain the pomegranate seeds.

WINE Look for the 1996 Michel Tête Beaujolais-Villages. The juicy quality of this Beaujolais will enhance the taste of the game hens.

Grilled Cornish Hens with Bacon and Mustard

4 SERVINGS ✻

A savory blend of mustard, bacon and garlic rubbed under the skin of the Cornish hens gives these birds a quick flavor boost. The hens are cooked under a brick (or a cast-iron skillet) so that they lie flat. This technique has the added advantage of making the birds cook quickly and evenly.

2 **strips of bacon, coarsely
    chopped**
2 **large garlic cloves, smashed**
2 **tablespoons Dijon mustard**
2 **teaspoons thyme leaves**
Cayenne pepper

Grilled Cornish Hens with Bacon and Mustard

Roasted Quail with Grapes, Foie Gras and Armagnac

2 SERVINGS

The flavors of southwestern France are highlighted in a quick and easy recipe. It will serve four as a first course.

- 4 ounces mousse de foie gras (see Note), softened
- ½ cup Armagnac
- 2 tablespoons golden raisins
- 4 partially boned quail

Salt and freshly ground pepper

- 1 tablespoon duck fat (see Note)
- 1 pound seedless green grapes, stemmed
- ½ cup duck stock or chicken stock (p. 117)

1. In a bowl, combine the mousse de foie gras with 1 teaspoon of the Armagnac and the raisins. Refrigerate until firm, about 10 minutes. Spoon into the quail cavities. Flatten the quail slightly and, using toothpicks, close the cavities. Season with salt and pepper.

2. Preheat the broiler with a rack 8 inches from the heat. In a skillet, melt the duck fat over high heat. Add the quail and half of the grapes. Brown the quail, about 2 minutes per side. Transfer to a broiler pan, breasts up.

3. Add the remaining Armagnac and the stock to the skillet and cook over high heat until the liquid is slightly reduced and the grapes are soft, about 3 minutes. Transfer to a blender and puree. Return the sauce to the skillet, add the remaining grapes and cook over high heat until the sauce is reduced by half, about 3 minutes.

4. Meanwhile, broil the quail for about 4 minutes, or until just pink at the bone. Transfer to a platter and remove the toothpicks. Add any accumulated quail juices to the sauce and pour it over the quail.   —*Ariane Daguin*

NOTE Mousse de foie gras and duck fat are available by mail order from D'Artagnan, 800-327-8246.

- 2 large Cornish game hens (about 1½ pounds each), backbones removed

Salt and freshly ground black pepper

1. Light a grill. In a mini-processor, combine the bacon, garlic, mustard, thyme and a large pinch of cayenne and process to a coarse paste.

2. Lay the Cornish hens, skin side up, on a work surface. Press down firmly on the breastbones to flatten the hens. Using your fingers, carefully loosen the skin over the breasts and spread the bacon stuffing under the skin. Season the hens with salt and black pepper.

3. Lay the hens on the grill, skin side down. Set an aluminum foil–wrapped brick or a cast-iron skillet on each hen and grill over a medium-low fire for about 25 minutes, or until the skin is deeply browned and crisp. Check occasionally so that the hens don't burn. Turn the birds, replace the bricks and grill for about 25 minutes longer, or until the thighs are cooked through and the skin is crisp.

4. Transfer the hens to a platter, cover with aluminum foil and let rest for 10 minutes. Halve the birds lengthwise and serve.   —*Jan Newberry*

Roasted Quail with Grapes, Foie Gras and Armagnac

Duck Breasts with Sour Cherries, with Saffron Rice Pilaf (p. 341).

Duck Breasts with Sour Cherries

12 SERVINGS

When organizing your dinner, plan to make the rice pilaf first because it can stand while you prepare the duck.

2 cups red wine

¾ cup dried sour cherries (4 ounces)

2 tablespoons extra-virgin olive oil

12 skinless Pekin duck breast halves (5 ounces each)

Salt and freshly ground pepper

½ pound shiitake mushrooms, stems removed, caps thinly sliced

6 shallots, thinly sliced

1 cup water

1 tablespoon plus 1 teaspoon honey mustard

Saffron Rice Pilaf (p. 341)

1. Preheat the oven to 250°. In a small saucepan, combine the wine and dried cherries and simmer over low heat for 3 minutes. Set aside.

2. In each of 2 large skillets, heat 1 tablespoon of oil. Season the duck breasts on both sides with salt and pepper. Add 6 duck breasts to each skillet and cook over moderately high heat until well browned and medium

222

rare, about 4 minutes per side. Transfer the duck breasts to a baking sheet, cover with aluminum foil and keep warm in the oven.

3. Add half the mushrooms and shallots to each skillet, cover and cook over low heat, stirring once, until they are browned, about 4 minutes. Uncover and add ½ cup of water to each skillet. Simmer over moderately high heat, scraping up any brown bits from the skillets, until the water has reduced by half, about 4 minutes. Add half of the cherry-and-wine mixture to each skillet and simmer until reduced by one-third, about 3 minutes. Scrape the contents of 1 skillet into the other. Stir in the honey mustard and season with salt and pepper.

4. Remove the duck breasts from the oven and pour any accumulated juices into the sauce. Cut the duck breasts crosswise into ¼-inch-thick slices and arrange them on a warmed platter. Pour any carving juices into the sauce. Reheat the sauce briefly and pour it over the duck. Serve at once with the Saffron Rice Pilaf.   —*Marcia Kiesel*
ONE SERVING Calories 209 kcal, Total Fat 3 gm, Saturated Fat .3 gm
WINE A red, such as the 1991 Quinta do Carvalhinho Bairrada Reserva from Portugal or 1989 Cune Imperial Gran Reserva Rioja from Spain.

Roasted Duck with Licorice-Merlot Sauce

8 SERVINGS
Normand Laprise, a Canadian chef, chooses Barhary duck from Canada to make this recipe; Muscovy is a more readily available alternative. Neither is particularly fatty. In the sauce, he uses licorice pastilles, which can be found at specialty food stores.

 3 tablespoons honey
12 kumquats, halved lengthwise and seeded

1½ cups dry red wine, such as Merlot
 ¼ cup chicken stock (p. 117) or canned low-sodium broth
 8 small black licorice jelly beans
 2 pounds celery root—quartered, peeled and cut into 2-inch chunks
 1 large Idaho potato, peeled and cut into 2-inch chunks
Salt
 5 tablespoons cold unsalted butter
 1 tablespoon imported hazelnut oil
Freshly ground pepper
 6 large Muscovy duck breasts, with skin (about ½ pound each)

1. In a medium saucepan, simmer the honey over moderate heat for 1 minute. Add the kumquats and cook until softened, about 3 minutes. Strain the honey into a medium saucepan; reserve the kumquats separately.

2. Add the wine and stock to the honey; cook over moderate heat until reduced to ½ cup, about 15 minutes. Add the jelly beans. Remove from the heat and let stand until the sauce has a nice licorice flavor, about 5 minutes. Discard the jelly beans.

3. Preheat the oven to 350°. In a large saucepan, cover the celery root and potato chunks with water and add 1 teaspoon of salt. Boil over moderately high heat until tender, about 30 minutes. Drain the vegetables; return them to the saucepan and shake over high heat to dry out. Transfer the celery root and potato to a food processor and puree until smooth. Wipe out the saucepan and return the puree to it. Stir in 3 tablespoons of the butter and the hazelnut oil. Season with salt and pepper, cover and keep warm.

4. Heat a large skillet. Using a sharp knife, score the duck breast skin in a cross-hatch pattern. Season the duck

breasts with salt and pepper and add 3 to the skillet, skin side down. Cook over moderate heat until the skin is deep brown and crisp, about 5 minutes; spoon off the fat once or twice. Turn the breasts and cook until browned on the bottom, about 2 minutes. Transfer the breasts to a baking sheet, skin side down, pour off the fat from the skillet and repeat with the remaining breasts. Bake the duck in the oven for about 6 minutes, or until medium rare. Transfer to a carving board, skin side up, cover loosely with aluminum foil and let rest for 5 minutes.

5. Bring the licorice sauce just to a boil. Remove from the heat and whisk in the remaining 2 tablespoons of butter; season with salt and pepper. Thinly slice the duck breasts crosswise and arrange the slices on 8 large plates. Spoon the sauce around the duck and top with the honeyed kumquats. Spoon the celery root puree alongside the duck and serve.   —*Normand Laprise*
WINE A full-bodied, balanced California Merlot, such as Robert Sinskey.

Roasted Duck with Licorice-Merlot Sauce

Cassoulet D'Artagnan

kosher salt and the remaining herbs and spices. Put the duck legs in a large bowl and rub them with the spices. Add the clove-studded garlic. Set a plate on top of the duck legs and then put a large can on the plate. Refrigerate the duck legs for at least 12 and up to 24 hours.

2. Using a dry towel, wipe the salt mixture off the duck legs. In an enameled cast-iron casserole, melt the duck fat. Add the duck legs; they should be submerged. Cook the duck legs over very low heat until the meat is tender, about 1½ hours. Using tongs, transfer the legs to a ceramic crock, or crocks if the confit is to be used gradually. Pour the duck fat over the legs to cover them completely. Let cool. When the fat is solid, refrigerate.

—*André Daguin*

NOTE Duck fat is available by mail order from D'Artagnan, 800-327-8246.

WINE The fattiness here calls for the tannic contrast of a young, vigorous Médoc wine from Bordeaux—ideally, a 1994 Château Grand-Puy Ducasse or Château Branaire-Ducru.

Cassoulet D'Artagnan

8 SERVINGS

1½ pounds navy or Great Northern beans, rinsed and picked over
½ pound unsmoked bacon or pancetta, in one piece
6 ounces fresh pork rind or fat back, in one piece, rinsed well
10 garlic cloves, peeled
2 medium onions, halved
1 carrot, coarsely chopped
Bouquet garni made of 1 thyme sprig, 1 bay leaf, 3 celery leaves, 5 parsley sprigs, 5 whole cloves and 10 black peppercorns, wrapped in cheesecloth and tied
10 cups water
½ pound duck gizzard confit (see Note)

Duck Leg Confit

4 SERVINGS

The duck leg confit should be allowed to mellow in the refrigerator for a minimum of two weeks, and it keeps for up to four months. Duck leg confit can be pan-fried over moderate heat until the skin is crisp and the meat is heated, about five minutes per side. Serve the duck leg confit with garlicky sautéed potatoes.

10 garlic cloves
10 whole cloves
4½ tablespoons kosher salt
2 teaspoons freshly ground pepper
1½ teaspoons dried thyme
1½ teaspoons crushed dried rosemary
1 bay leaf, broken
¼ teaspoon ground nutmeg
¼ teaspoon cinnamon
¼ teaspoon ground allspice
¼ teaspoon ground cloves
4 whole duck legs (2½ pounds)
28 ounces duck fat (see Note)

I. Pierce each of the garlic cloves with a whole clove. In a bowl, combine the

4 confit duck legs (opposite page, or see Note)

Three 7-ounce containers duck-and-veal demiglace (see Note), dissolved in 3 cups of water

2 large tomatoes—peeled, seeded and chopped

Kosher salt and freshly ground pepper

4 D'Artagnan duck and Armagnac sausages (see Note), halved crosswise

½ pound French garlic sausage, cut into 8 slices

¼ cup duck fat (see Note), melted

1. Cover the beans with water and soak overnight. Drain the beans. Put them in a large enameled cast-iron casserole with the bacon, pork rind, garlic, 1 onion, the carrot and bouquet garni. Cover with the water and bring to a boil. Simmer over low heat, stirring often, until the beans are barely tender, about 1 hour. Drain and return to the casserole, discarding the onion and bouquet garni.

2. Add the remaining onion and the gizzard confit, duck legs, demiglace mixture and tomatoes; bring to a boil. Add a pinch each of kosher salt and pepper and simmer over low heat until the gizzards and legs are tender when pierced with a fork, about 15 minutes.

3. Drain the bean mixture in a colander set over a bowl; reserve 5 cups of the cooking liquid. Discard the bacon and pork rind. Remove the duck legs and cut each in half at the joint. Season the beans with 1 teaspoon of kosher salt and a few grindings of pepper.

4. Preheat the oven to 325°. Place half of the bean mixture in the casserole. Add the duck legs, duck sausages and garlic sausage and cover with the remaining beans. Add the reserved cooking liquid and drizzle the duck fat over the top. Cover and bake for about 2 hours, or until hot and bubbling.

5. Increase the oven temperature to 400°. Uncover the casserole and bake for about 20 minutes, or until the top is browned. Let the cassoulet stand for about 15 minutes before serving.

—*Ariane Daguin*

MAKE AHEAD The cassoulet can be prepared through Step 4. Let cool and refrigerate for up to 3 days. Return to room temperature before proceeding.

NOTE Duck gizzard confit, duck leg confit, duck-and-veal demiglace, duck and Armagnac sausages and duck fat are all available by mail order from D'Artagnan, 800-327-8246.

WINE The classic match is an inky-dark red wine from southwest France, such as the 1993 Chapelle Laurette Madiran. Or serve a feisty St-Estèphe, such as the 1994 Château Meyney.

Duck Stew in Red Wine

6 SERVINGS

This hearty stew substitutes duck for the classic hare, so that it remains full of rich flavor but without the gamy taste. You can have your butcher cut each duck into eight pieces, but be sure to get the backs and necks for the sauce.

2 ducks, preferably Muscovy (about 3½ pounds each)

Salt and freshly ground pepper

10 shallots, thinly sliced

5 carrots, thinly sliced

2 yellow onions, cut into ½-inch chunks

7 celery ribs, thinly sliced crosswise

20 black peppercorns, crushed

8 juniper berries

2 bay leaves

9 thyme sprigs

2 bottles full-bodied red wine, such as Syrah

3 tablespoons olive oil

1 head of garlic, halved crosswise, plus 1 peeled clove

4 tablespoons unsalted butter

¼ cup all-purpose flour

1 tablespoon tomato paste

12 small cipolline or pearl onions, peeled

1 cup chicken stock (p. 117) or canned low-sodium broth

¼ teaspoon sugar

6 ounces slab bacon, sliced ⅓ inch thick and cut crosswise into ¼-inch strips

6 ounces chanterelles or other wild mushrooms, cut into pieces if large

1 tablespoon finely chopped chives or flat-leaf parsley

1. Remove the legs from the ducks and cut them into drumsticks and thighs. Split each of the breasts down the center and then cut them in half crosswise through the bones. Cut off and discard as much of the carcass fat as possible. Chop the back and neck bones into 2 or 3 pieces. Season the duck pieces and the reserved bones with salt and pepper.

2. Arrange the duck pieces and bones in a large, deep stainless-steel roasting pan. Scatter the shallots, carrots, yellow onions, celery, peppercorns, juniper berries, bay leaves and 8 of the thyme sprigs on top. Pour the red wine over the meat and bones, cover with plastic wrap and refrigerate overnight. Turn the duck and bones in the marinade a few times.

3. Preheat the oven to 425°. Remove the duck pieces and bones from the marinade and pat dry. Strain the marinade in a colander; reserve the liquid and vegetables separately.

4. In a large skillet, heat 2 tablespoons of the oil. Add the drained vegetables and the head of garlic, season with salt and pepper and cook over high heat until the liquid evaporates and the vegetables start to brown. Reduce the heat to moderate and cook, stirring

Duck Stew in Red Wine

often, until the vegetables are evenly browned, about 8 minutes. Remove from the heat.

5. In a very large, wide enameled cast-iron casserole, melt 2 tablespoons of the butter in the remaining 1 tablespoon of oil. Sprinkle the duck pieces and bones with 2 tablespoons of the flour and cook them in batches until the duck is very richly browned all over. Reduce the heat to low if necessary to avoid burning and transfer each batch to a plate as it's done.

6. Return all of the duck to the casserole and stir in the tomato paste, coating the bones with it. Sprinkle with the remaining 2 tablespoons of flour and stir to lightly brown the flour. Add the vegetables from the skillet and the reserved marinade and bring to a simmer. Cover with a round of parchment paper and a lid and braise in the oven for 1¼ hours; skim off the fat every 20 minutes or so.

7. Meanwhile, in a small saucepan, combine the cipolline onions with the stock, sugar, 1 tablespoon of butter and the remaining thyme sprig and garlic clove. Season with salt and pepper. Cover with a round of parchment paper and simmer over low heat until the onions are tender, about 20 minutes. Remove from the heat.

8. Pour 2 inches of water into a small saucepan, add the bacon and bring to a boil; drain and pat dry.

9. In a large skillet, melt the remaining 1 tablespoon of butter over moderate heat. Add the bacon and cook, tossing, until lightly browned. Add the chanterelles, season with salt and pepper and cook, stirring occasionally, until tender, about 8 minutes.

10. When the duck is done, transfer the drumsticks, thighs and breasts to a serving bowl. Strain the contents of the casserole through a coarse strainer set over a large bowl, pressing on the solids to extract as much liquid as possible; discard the solids. Skim the fat from the sauce.

11. Add ¼ cup of water to the casserole and bring to a boil over high heat, scraping up any brown bits from the bottom. Add the onion cooking liquid and boil until thickened. Add to the sauce and season with salt and pepper. Pour the sauce over the duck and garnish with the onions, bacon and mushrooms. Sprinkle with the chives and serve. —*Daniel Boulud*

MAKE AHEAD The stew and the garnishes can be prepared up to 1 day ahead and refrigerated separately. Reheat thoroughly before serving.

SERVE WITH Buttered noodles or mashed potatoes.

WINE This hearty yet refined dish needs an equally refined wine, not an over-exuberant one that will overwhelm it. The 1994 Horton Vineyards Mourvèdre from Virginia and the 1997 Augustus Cabernet Sauvignon from Spain are well-balanced, not too alcoholic wines with fine *terroir* character.

CHAPTER 8 pork veal

Corsican-Style Pork Chops (p. 235)

Pork and Mushroom Ragout

Pork and Mushroom Ragout

4 SERVINGS

Portobellos add substance but their black gills can darken the stew and make it look unappetizing. To prevent this, remove the gills with a spoon before chopping the mushrooms.

- 2 cups chicken stock (p. 117) or canned low-sodium broth
- ½ cup dried porcini mushrooms (about 1 ounce)
- 2 tablespoons olive oil
- 1½ pounds pork tenderloin, trimmed of all visible fat and cut into 1-inch cubes

Salt and freshly ground pepper
- 1 medium onion, finely chopped
- 4 garlic cloves, minced
- 1 teaspoon minced sage
- 1⅔ pounds fresh Portobello mushrooms, caps and stems cut into ½-inch pieces
- ½ cup dry white wine

One 28-ounce can whole peeled tomatoes, drained and coarsely chopped
- 1 tablespoon tomato paste
- ¼ cup finely chopped flat-leaf parsley

1. Bring the stock to a boil in a small saucepan. Remove from the heat and add the dried porcini. Cover and let steep for 20 minutes. Drain the porcini, pressing down on them to extract as much liquid as possible. Reserve the liquid and discard the porcini.

2. Heat 1 tablespoon of the oil in a large enameled cast-iron casserole. Season half of the pork with salt and pepper and cook in a single layer over high heat, turning once, until browned, about 4 minutes. Transfer the meat to a plate. Repeat with the remaining oil and pork. Add the onion, garlic, sage, 1½ teaspoons of salt and ½ teaspoon of pepper to the casserole and cook over moderate heat, stirring often, until the onion softens, about 5 minutes.

Stir in the Portobello pieces and cook until their volume is reduced by two-thirds, about 10 minutes.

3. Add the wine, raise the heat to high and boil until reduced by half, about 3 minutes. Stir in the tomatoes and tomato paste. Pour in the reserved mushroom liquid, stopping when you reach the grit at the bottom. Bring to a boil, reduce the heat to moderately low and simmer for 20 minutes.

4. Add the pork and its juices to the casserole and simmer gently until the pork is just cooked through, about 5 minutes. Season with salt and pepper. Remove from the heat, stir in the chopped parsley and serve.

—Jan Newberry

ONE SERVING Calories 420 kcal, Total Fat 14.7 gm, Saturated Fat 3.5 gm
WINE The savory flavors of this mushroom-packed meat dish call for a light Italian red with its own earthy flavors. Go for a Chianti Classico, such as the 1995 Badia a Coltibuono or the 1993 Monsanto Riserva.

Grilled Pork Tenderloins with Jamaican Spices

4 SERVINGS

Butterflying pork tenderloins—slicing them almost in half lengthwise and spreading them open—helps the meat cook faster and creates a larger surface area for the spice marinade to penetrate.

- 3 garlic cloves, smashed
- 2 tablespoons fresh lime juice
- 2 tablespoons extra-virgin olive oil
- 2 tablespoons thyme leaves
- 1 large shallot, minced

One 1-inch piece of fresh ginger, minced
- ½ teaspoon cinnamon

Grilled Pork Tenderloins with Jamaican Spices

Pork Medallions with Crushed Nut and Sage Sauce, served with Warm Mixed Greens (p. 305).

½ teaspoon freshly grated nutmeg
½ teaspoon ground allspice
½ teaspoon ground coriander
½ teaspoon salt
½ teaspoon freshly ground pepper
Two 1-pound pork tenderloins,
    butterflied

1. Light a grill. In a bowl, combine the garlic, lime juice, olive oil, thyme, shallot, ginger, cinnamon, nutmeg, allspice, coriander, salt and pepper. Add the pork and turn until well coated with the spice mixture. Let stand for 15 to 20 minutes.

2. Grill the pork over a medium-hot fire or in a preheated grill pan for about 10 minutes per side, or until an instant-read thermometer registers 140° for medium.

3. Transfer the pork to a platter and cover loosely with aluminum foil. Let it rest for 5 minutes and then slice the pork and serve.   *—Jan Newberry*

Spicy Simmered Tofu

4 SERVINGS

This silky tofu in a thick, spicy sauce is traditionally made with a little pork, but the dish is also delicious without meat. Made with one tablespoon of chile paste, the tofu is medium-hot.

2 tablespoons peanut or
   vegetable oil
4 garlic cloves, minced
3 scallions, cut into 1½-inch
   lengths
¼ pound boneless pork tenderloin,
   shoulder or butt, thinly sliced
   against the grain (optional)
1 tablespoon minced fresh ginger
1 tablespoon or more Hot Chile
   Paste (p. 117)

3 tablespoons soy sauce
1 pound firm tofu, cut into ½-inch
   cubes and patted dry
½ cup chicken or vegetable broth
½ teaspoon salt
1 tablespoon cornstarch mixed
   with 1 tablespoon cold water

1. Set a large wok over high heat until it is very hot. Add the oil and swirl to coat the wok. When the oil is hot, add the garlic and scallions and stir-fry for 30 seconds. Add the pork, ginger and Hot Chile Paste and stir-fry for 30 seconds, pressing the meat and scallions against the side of the wok. Add the soy sauce to the wok and stir-fry for 30 seconds.

2. Add the tofu, broth and salt. Bring to a vigorous boil and then lower the heat and simmer for 4 minutes. Add the cornstarch mixture and stir-fry over high heat until the sauce thickens and becomes clear, about 20 seconds. Transfer the tofu to a shallow bowl and serve hot, warm or at room temperature, with a small ladle.

   —Jeffrey Alford and Naomi Duguid

WINE A light but intensely fruity Pinot Noir—served cool—will balance the heat of this tofu dish. Stick with West Coast examples, such as the 1996 Carneros Creek Fleur de Carneros from California or the 1996 Firesteed from Oregon.

Pork Medallions with Crushed Nut and Sage Sauce

4 SERVINGS ✳

Pork is one of the most popular meats of the Basque country. Walnuts are a local product, and cooks on the Spanish side of the border often make nut sauces like this one.

⅓ cup walnuts
⅓ cup whole almonds
1 small garlic clove
½ teaspoon coriander seeds
¼ cup plus 2 tablespoons olive oil

2 pork tenderloins (about ¾ pound each), well trimmed

Kosher salt and freshly ground pepper

½ cup dry white wine

1 tablespoon finely chopped shallot

8 sage leaves

½ cup veal stock, chicken stock (p. 117) or canned low-sodium broth

1. Preheat the oven to 300°. In a food processor, combine the walnuts, almonds, garlic and coriander seeds and add ¼ cup of the oil. Pulse just until the mixture resembles a coarse pesto.

2. Cut the tenderloins into ¾-inch-thick medallions; season with kosher salt and pepper. In a large skillet, heat the remaining 2 tablespoons of oil. Add half the medallions and sauté over moderately high heat until well browned and just cooked through, 2 to 3 minutes per side. Transfer to a large plate and keep warm in the oven. Repeat with the remaining medallions.

3. Add the wine and shallot to the skillet and cook over moderately high heat, scraping up any brown bits from the bottom of the pan. Add the sage leaves and boil until the wine is reduced by half, about 3 minutes.

4. Add the stock and the nuts to the pan; stir until warmed through. Season with kosher salt and pepper. Transfer the pork to large plates, drizzle with the sauce and serve. —*Gerald Hirigoyen*

Pork Tenderloin with Lentils and Mustard Sauce

4 SERVINGS

Fried shallots add crunch and sweetness to this comforting main course.

⅓ cup plus 3 tablespoons extra-virgin olive oil

2 large shallots, thinly sliced

1 cup Vertes du Puy lentils (about ½ pound), picked over

3½ cups chicken stock (p. 117) or canned low-sodium broth

1 bay leaf

½ teaspoon dried thyme

⅓ cup coarsely chopped flat-leaf parsley

Salt and freshly ground pepper

1½ pounds pork tenderloin, cut into 8 pieces

⅓ cup dry white wine

2 tablespoons Dijon mustard

1. In a small skillet, heat ⅓ cup of the oil. Add the shallots; cook over moderately high heat, stirring frequently, until golden brown and crisp, about 5 minutes. Using a slotted spoon, transfer the fried shallots to paper towels to drain; reserve the shallot oil.

2. In a medium saucepan, cover the lentils with 2¾ cups of the stock and bring to a boil over high heat. Add the bay leaf and thyme, cover and simmer over low heat until the lentils are tender, about 30 minutes. Drain the lentils and return them to the saucepan; discard the bay leaf. Stir in the parsley and the reserved shallot oil and season with salt and pepper. Cover and keep warm.

3. Meanwhile, in a large heavy skillet, heat 1 tablespoon of the oil until almost smoking. Flatten each piece of pork tenderloin slightly with the palm of your hand and season on both sides with salt and pepper. Working in batches if necessary, add the flattened pork to the skillet and cook over moderately high heat until well browned and just cooked through, about 4 minutes per side. Transfer the pork to a plate and keep warm in a low oven.

4. Add the wine to the skillet and bring to a boil. Cook, stirring, until reduced by half, about 2 minutes. Add ½ cup of the stock, the mustard and the remaining 2 tablespoons of oil. Boil, whisking constantly, for 1 minute. Remove from the heat.

5. Stir the remaining ¼ cup of stock into the lentils and bring to a simmer over moderately high heat. Spread the lentils on a platter, arrange the pork on top and drizzle with the mustard sauce. Garnish with the crisp shallots and serve at once. —*Jan Newberry*

NOTE Try a pungent extra-virgin olive oil to accent the mustard sauce.

WINE The savory combination of mustard and wine turns this pork dish toward medium-weight red wine. A 1994 Bordeaux, such as the Château Prieuré-Lichine or the Château Langoa Barton, has just the right contrasting balance of fruit and tannin.

Sweet and Hot Habanero Pork

4 SERVINGS

3 habanero or Scotch Bonnet chiles—2 thinly sliced, 1 minced

1 large garlic clove, minced

One 1-inch piece of fresh ginger, peeled and minced

2 tablespoons plus 1 teaspoon olive oil

Two 8- to 10-ounce pork tenderloins

Salt and freshly ground pepper

2 shallots, thinly sliced

½ cup Riesling Kabinett or other dry fruity white wine

2 tablespoons Sauternes or other sweet wine

2 tablespoons unsalted butter

1. In a small bowl, combine the minced habanero with the garlic, ginger and 1 teaspoon of the oil. Rub the mixture all over the pork, cover and refrigerate for 6 hours or overnight.

2. Scrape the chile rub from the pork; season the meat with salt and pepper. In a large skillet, heat the remaining 2 tablespoons of oil. Add the tenderloins, cover and cook over moderate heat, turning occasionally, until browned all over and cooked through, about 16 minutes. Transfer the pork to a cutting board and let rest for 5 minutes. ➤

3. Add the shallots and sliced habaneros to the skillet, cover and cook over low heat until wilted, about 3 minutes. Uncover and raise the heat to high. Add the Riesling and cook until reduced by half, about 2 minutes. Add the Sauternes and remove from the heat. Swirl in the butter and season with salt and pepper.

4. Carve the pork into thick slices and arrange on plates. Spoon the habanero sauce on top and serve.—*Marcia Kiesel*

WINE Sweet wines are wonderful antidotes to heat and spice. To tame the fire in this dish, as well as complement the pork, try the 1995 Château Suduiraut or the 1989 Château Guiraud Sauternes.

Pork Chops with Lemon Butter

4 SERVINGS ✻

- 1 teaspoon vegetable oil
- 4 thin-cut, bone-in pork loin chops (about 1¼ pounds)

Salt and freshly ground pepper
- 1 tablespoon unsalted butter
- 1 garlic clove, minced
- 2 tablespoons drained capers
- 1 tablespoon fresh lemon juice
- 1 tablespoon chopped chives (optional)

1. Heat the oil in a large nonstick skillet. Lightly season the pork chops with salt and pepper and cook over high heat until browned, 3 to 4 minutes. Turn the chops; sear until just cooked through, about 2 minutes; transfer to a platter.

2. Add the butter and garlic to the skillet and stir over moderate heat until the garlic softens, about 1 minute. Stir in the capers, lemon juice and chives. Spoon the lemon butter sauce over the chops and serve. —*Jan Newberry*

WINE An aromatic Viognier.

Pan-Roasted Pork Chops with Madeira Sauce

4 SERVINGS

The highly acclaimed chef Kevin Taylor updates his pork chop and apples with luxurious morels at the Denver Art Museum's Palettes restaurant.

- 2 tablespoons extra-virgin olive oil
- 1 tablespoon thyme leaves
- 2 teaspoons minced garlic

Four 1-inch-thick pork loin chops (8 to 10 ounces each)
- 20 small dried morels (about 1½ ounces)
- 3 tablespoons unsalted butter
- 3 Granny Smith apples—peeled, cored and cut into 8 wedges each
- 1 tablespoon sugar
- ¾ cup Madeira
- ¼ cup brandy
- 1 cup chicken stock (p. 117) or canned low-sodium broth

Salt and freshly ground pepper

1. Combine the oil, thyme and garlic on a large plate. Add the pork chops and turn to coat in the seasoned oil. Let stand at room temperature for 2 hours.

2. Meanwhile, cover the dried morels with warm water and let soak until

Pork Chops with Lemon Butter

softened, about 20 minutes. Drain, rinse under running water and pat dry.

3. Melt 1 tablespoon of the butter in a large skillet. Add the apples, sprinkle with the sugar and cook over moderate heat, turning occasionally, until tender and caramelized, about 20 minutes. Transfer the apples to a plate.

4. Return the skillet to high heat, add the Madeira and brandy and cook until reduced by half. Add the morels and stock and cook until the stock is reduced by half, about 7 minutes. Stir in the apples and remove from the heat.

5. Preheat the oven to 375°. Heat a large ovenproof skillet until almost smoking. Season the pork chops with salt and pepper and cook over moderately high heat until deep golden and crusty, 4 to 5 minutes. Turn the pork chops, transfer the skillet to the oven and roast the chops for about 6 minutes, or until cooked through. Transfer to a platter.

6. Set the skillet over high heat. Add the apple and morel sauce and cook, scraping up any browned bits, until slightly reduced, about 2 minutes. Stir in the remaining 2 tablespoons of butter and season with salt and pepper. Set the pork chops on 4 large plates, spoon the apple and morel sauce on top and serve. —*Kevin Taylor*

Pan-Roasted Pork Chops with Madeira Sauce

Corsican-Style Pork Chops

4 SERVINGS

The pork chops need to soak in the brine for at least twenty-four hours.

Kosher salt
- 3 tablespoons sugar
- 1 cup hot water
- 3 cups cold water
- 1 teaspoon dried thyme
- 1 teaspoon crushed juniper berries
- ½ teaspoon cracked coriander seeds
- ½ teaspoon cracked peppercorns
- ¼ teaspoon dried sage
- 2 bay leaves, crumbled

Four 1¼-inch-thick center-cut pork rib chops
- 1½ tablespoons extra-virgin olive oil

Freshly ground pepper
- 1 cup chicken stock (p. 117) or canned low-sodium broth
- 2 tablespoons dry white wine
- 1 cup tomato sauce
- ¼ cup orange juice
- 1 garlic clove, smashed
- 8 cracked green olives, pitted and coarsely chopped
- 2 teaspoons each of finely chopped basil, mint and flat-leaf parsley

1. In a large stainless steel bowl or plastic container, combine ¼ cup of kosher salt with the sugar and hot water and stir until dissolved. Add the cold water, thyme, juniper berries, coriander seeds, peppercorns, sage and bay leaves. Put the chops in the brine, cover and refrigerate for 24 to 48 hours, turning them occasionally.

2. Discard the brine. Pick any whole spices off the pork chops and discard. Pat the chops dry with paper towels.

3. Heat the oil in a large deep skillet until it shimmers. Add the pork chops and cook over high heat, turning once, until browned, about 6 minutes. Transfer the chops to a plate and season with kosher salt and pepper. ➤

Corsican-Style Pork Chops, with Squash and Potato Gratin (p. 316).

4. Pour off the fat from the skillet. Add the stock and the wine and bring to a boil, scraping up any bits that are stuck to the pan with a wooden spoon. Cook until reduced by half, about 3 minutes. Add the tomato sauce, orange juice and garlic and simmer for 5 minutes.

5. Return the pork chops to the skillet, turn to coat with the sauce and bring to a boil. Cover tightly and cook over low heat until the pork is tender and cooked through, about 10 minutes. Transfer the chops to a platter, cover and keep warm.

6. Add the olives to the sauce and cook over high heat until reduced to about 1 cup. Stir in the herbs and pour the sauce over the pork chops.

—Paula Wolfert

Cider-Glazed Pork Roast with Apples and Cabbage

4 SERVINGS

 4 ounces lean bacon, cut into
  ½-inch pieces
 2 tablespoons vegetable oil
1½ pounds boneless pork loin roast
Salt and freshly ground pepper
 ½ cup Reduced Cider
  (recipe follows)
 2 firm red apples, such as
  Winesap, cored and cut
  crosswise into ½-inch-thick
  rings
 1 medium onion, coarsely
  chopped
 ¾ pound napa cabbage, sliced
  crosswise ½ inch thick (4 cups)
 2 teaspoons cider vinegar
 1 teaspoon thyme leaves

1. Preheat the oven to 350°. In a large enameled cast-iron casserole or Dutch oven, cook the bacon over moderate heat until lightly browned, about 5 minutes. Using a slotted spoon, transfer the bacon to a plate.

2. Add 1 tablespoon of the oil to the casserole. Season the pork with salt

Cider-Glazed Pork Pork Roast with Apples and Cabbage

and pepper and add the roast to the casserole, fat side down. Cook over moderately high heat, turning occasionally, until browned all over, about 8 minutes.

3. Transfer the casserole to the oven and roast the pork for 15 minutes. Spoon ¼ cup of the Reduced Cider over the meat and roast for 15 minutes longer, or until an instant-read thermometer inserted in the thickest part of the meat registers 135°. Transfer the roast to a cutting board, cover loosely with aluminum foil and let stand for 10 minutes.

4. Increase the oven temperature to 425°. Dip the apple rings in the juices in the casserole and arrange them on a baking sheet. Roast the apple rings for about 10 minutes, or until they are browned on the bottom. Turn the apple rings and roast them for 5 minutes

longer, or until they are well glazed.

5. Meanwhile, add the remaining 1 tablespoon of oil to the casserole. Add the onion. Cook over moderately low heat, stirring occasionally, until the onion is golden brown, about 5 minutes. Add the napa cabbage, vinegar, thyme leaves and the remaining ¼ cup of Reduced Cider and cook over moderately high heat, stirring, until the cabbage is wilted and the pan juices have reduced to a glaze, about 4 minutes. Season the cabbage with salt and pepper. Slice the pork roast and serve with the apple rings and glazed cabbage.

SERVE WITH Mashed potatoes.
WINE The 1995 Marcel Deiss Alsace Pinot Gris Bergheim from France or the 1996 Lingenfelder Grosskarlbacher Osterberg Riesling Spätlese from Germany.

Real Barbecue

REDUCED CIDER

MAKES ABOUT 2 CUPS

At L'Etoile, in Madison, Wisconsin, Odessa Piper uses Reduced Cider as a base for some of her sauces. It can also be added to salad dressings to give them a heartier flavor. Don't use sparkling cider in this recipe.

1 gallon apple cider

In a large saucepan, boil the cider over high heat until reduced to 1 quart, about 1½ hours. Reduce the heat to moderate and simmer until reduced to the consistency of maple syrup, about 45 minutes. Let the cider cool completely and then store in a tightly sealed jar in the refrigerator. It will keep indefinitely. —*Odessa Piper*

Real Barbecue

10 SERVINGS

Despite the mystique created by pit masters, barbecuing is easy to do in the backyard with a charcoal grill. The trick is using wood chips, soaked in cold water for an hour and then drained, to generate smoke and indirect heat so that the meat doesn't burn after hours of cooking.

One 5- to 6-pound piece of pork shoulder, or 8 pounds of country ribs, or one 5- to 6-pound beef brisket with at least ¼ inch layer of fat
Salt and freshly ground pepper or a favorite rub
Assorted barbecue sauces

1. Light about 50 coals in a chimney starter and rake them into 2 piles on either side of the grill. Let the coals burn down to glowing embers. Set a 10-inch foil drip pan in the center of the grill bottom. Scatter 2 cups of soaked wood chips over the coals and set the grill in place. Every hour, add 20 fresh coals and 1 cup of soaked chips.

2. Season the meat with salt and pepper. **For the pork shoulder:** Set the meat in the center of the grill rack. Cover the grill and smoke-cook until tender, 6 to 7 hours. **For the ribs:** Set the racks of ribs, slightly overlapping, in the center of the grill rack. Cover the grill and smoke-cook until tender, about 2 hours total; turn and rotate the ribs every 20 minutes. **For the brisket:** Do not use a drip pan. Put the meat in a foil pan set in the center of the grill rack. Cover the grill and smoke-cook until tender, 6 to 7 hours; turn the brisket once an hour.

3. Transfer the meat to a cutting board and let cool for 15 minutes. To serve, shred the pork shoulder meat with your fingers; cut the ribs between the bones; thinly slice the brisket across the grain. Accompany with barbecue sauces. —*Steven Raichlen*

Braised Pork and Dried Corn Stew with Chiles

4 SERVINGS

Posole and hominy are both forms of dried corn, but hominy always has its hulls removed. This satisfying dish combines tender pork with chewy dried corn and a squeeze of tart lime. Posole must soak overnight, so be sure to plan accordingly.

1½ cups dried yellow posole (about ½ pound)
3 quarts water
2½ pounds bone-in pork shoulder in 1 piece
1 large ancho chile
1 large onion, coarsely chopped
3 large garlic cloves, coarsely chopped
Salt
3 medium poblano chiles
Lime wedges, for serving

1. Cover the posole with water and let soak overnight. Drain the posole and transfer to a large enameled cast-iron

Braised Pork and Dried Corn Stew with Chiles

casserole. Add 3 quarts of water and the pork and bring to a simmer over moderate heat, skimming occasionally.

2. Meanwhile, in a small skillet, toast the ancho chile over moderate heat until blistered and pliable, about 2 minutes per side. Rinse the chile and discard the stem and seeds. Tear the chile into large pieces and add it to the posole along with the onion and garlic. Simmer over low heat for 1½ hours. Add a large pinch of salt and continue simmering, stirring occasionally, until the posole and pork are tender, about 3 hours.

3. Remove the pork from the stew. Cut the meat from the bone and discard any fat and gristle. Cut the pork into 2-inch chunks, return it to the stew and keep warm over low heat.

4. Roast the poblano chiles over a gas flame or under a broiler until charred all over. Put them in a bowl; cover with plastic wrap. Let steam for 5 minutes.

Pork Adobo

Remove the charred skins, stems and seeds and finely chop the poblanos. Add the poblanos to the pork stew, season the stew with salt and simmer for 10 minutes. Serve the pork stew with lime wedges.   —*Marcia Kiesel*

MAKE AHEAD The stew can be refrigerated for up to 3 days.

WINE The sweet corn, mild pork and roasted chiles create a warm, spicy, earthy dish whose flavors need only a basic California Chardonnay to provide a refreshing contrast. Look for a full-flavored bottling, such as the 1997 Amberhill or the 1996 Sebastiani.

Giambotta of Mixed Greens with Pork Spareribs

4 TO 6 SERVINGS ★★★ 1986

In this Italian-style stew, all of the ingredients cook together at a gentle boil, yielding a rustic one-pot dish that is much more than the sum of its parts. Have the butcher cut the spareribs for you.

- 1 head of garlic, cloves peeled and crushed (about 15 cloves)
- 1 tablespoon Hungarian hot paprika
- 1 teaspoon salt
- ½ teaspoon coarsely ground pepper
- ½ cup plus 1 tablespoon extra-virgin olive oil
- One 2½-pound slab of pork spareribs, sawed across the bones into thirds and trimmed of excess fat
- 1 small rutabaga—peeled, cut into eighths and sliced crosswise ½ inch thick
- 1 pint tiny white pearl onions, peeled
- 1½ cups water
- 2 tablespoons white wine vinegar
- 2 bay leaves
- ½ teaspoon (loosely packed) saffron threads, crushed

- 3 pounds mixed greens, such as kale, escarole, Swiss chard, mustard or broccoli rabe, stemmed and coarsely shredded
- 1 large sweet potato—peeled, halved lengthwise and sliced crosswise ¼ inch thick
- 2 pounds spinach, stemmed and coarsely shredded

1. In a small bowl, combine the garlic, paprika, ½ teaspoon of the salt and the pepper; add 1 tablespoon of the oil and mash to a paste. Rub the paste on the ribs. Cover and let marinate at room temperature for 1 to 2 hours, or refrigerate overnight for a more garlicky flavor.

2. In a large enameled cast-iron casserole, combine the sliced rutabaga, pearl onions, water, vinegar, bay leaves and saffron with the remaining ½ cup of oil and ½ teaspoon of salt. Add half of the mixed greens, cover and cook over high heat until the greens wilt, 2 to 3 minutes. Add the remaining greens and cook, tossing, until wilted.

3. Cut the ribs into 2- to 3-rib pieces and add them to the casserole. Cover and cook over moderately high heat, maintaining a slow boil and stirring occasionally, until the ribs and the rutabaga are tender, about 1 hour.

4. Scatter the sweet potato slices over the giambotta and cook, stirring occasionally, until softened, 10 to 15 minutes. Discard the bay leaves. Add the spinach and cook, stirring, until just wilted, about 1 minute. Serve hot.
    —*Anne Disrude*

Pork Adobo

12 SERVINGS

Adobo, the national dish of the Philippines, starts out as a garlicky and tangy stew. The meat is then removed from the casseroles and fried until crisp, and the cooking liquid is reduced to make the richly flavored sauce.

12 pounds country-style pork ribs (not the loin), each rib cut in half crosswise

6 cups rice vinegar

3 cups soy sauce

6 heads of garlic, separated into unpeeled cloves

Freshly ground black pepper

2 large red bell peppers

Vegetable oil, for frying

½ cup crushed unsalted peanuts (optional)

Steamed rice, for serving

1. In each of 2 large enameled cast-iron casseroles, combine half of the ribs, vinegar, soy sauce and garlic. Season with black pepper and bring to a simmer. Cook over low heat, skimming occasionally, until the ribs are cooked through, about 30 minutes.

2. Using a slotted spoon, transfer the ribs to a platter, leaving the garlic behind. Continue to simmer the cooking liquid in the 2 casseroles until the garlic is tender, about 30 minutes; let cool. Remove the garlic cloves and peel them and then add to the ribs.

3. Remove the fat from the cooking liquid. Pour the liquid into a medium saucepan and boil until reduced to 2 cups, about 15 minutes.

4. Roast the red peppers directly over a gas flame or under a broiler, turning, until charred all over. Transfer to a large bowl, cover with plastic wrap and let stand for 10 minutes to loosen the skins. Peel the peppers, discarding the cores, ribs and seeds; cut the flesh into long thin strips.

5. In a large skillet, heat 2 tablespoons of oil. Add as many of the ribs as will fit without crowding and fry over moderate heat until deeply browned, about 4 minutes. Transfer to paper towels to drain. Repeat with the remaining ribs, adding more oil as needed.

Barbecued Rib Roast of Pork, with Yellow Tomato, Watermelon and Arugula Salad (p. 86), Red, White and Blue Potato Salad (p. 94) and Seven-Vegetable Slaw with Citrus Dressing (p. 91).

6. Add the garlic cloves to the skillet and fry, stirring, until browned and crisp, about 5 minutes. Arrange the ribs and garlic on a warmed platter. Scatter the peanuts and red pepper strips on top of the ribs and serve. Pass the reduced cooking liquid and the rice separately. —*Marcia Kiesel*

MAKE AHEAD The adobo can be prepared through Step 2 up to 2 days ahead; refrigerate the liquid and ribs separately.

WINE This spicy dish requires a not-quite-dry white to provide a refreshing flavor background. Look for the 1996 Bonny Doon Pacific Rim Riesling or the 1996 Jekel Johannisberg Riesling, both from California.

Barbecued Rib Roast of Pork

10 SERVINGS

2½ tablespoons ancho chile powder

2½ tablespoons Hungarian sweet paprika

2½ tablespoons dried thyme

1½ teaspoons salt

½ teaspoon cayenne pepper

1 large garlic clove, minced

1 bone-in pork rib roast, chine bone removed (about 6½ pounds)

2 tablespoons vegetable oil

2 tablespoons maple syrup

1 cup chicken stock (p. 117), canned low-sodium broth or water

Chile-Spiked Barbecue Sauce (p. 351)

1. In a small bowl, combine the ancho chile powder with the paprika, thyme, salt, cayenne and garlic.

2. Set the pork roast, meaty side up, on a rack in a flameproof roasting pan. Combine the oil and maple syrup in a small bowl and rub the mixture all over the roast. Generously coat the meat with the spice mix and let stand at room temperature for about 1 hour.

3. Preheat the oven to 375°. Roast the pork in the lower third of the oven for about 1 hour and 10 minutes, or until an instant-read thermometer inserted in the center of the roast registers 140°. Let the roast stand for 15 minutes. Carve by cutting between the bones. Arrange the chops on a large platter.

4. Pour off the fat from the roasting pan. Set the pan over high heat, add the stock and the meat juices from the platter and boil, scraping up any brown bits from the bottom of the pan, until reduced to ⅓ cup. Add the meat juices to the Chile-Spiked Barbecue Sauce. Serve the roast with the barbecue sauce on the side. —*Brendan Walsh*

WINE Pinot Noir's lighter acids and bright berry character make it great for the summer. The 1995 Cosentino

Modern Choucroute

Napa is hard to find but worth the effort. Another fine choice is the extremely elegant and complex 1995 Steele Bien Nacido Vineyard.

Modern Choucroute

12 SERVINGS

- 3 pounds kale, stemmed
- 2 tablespoons olive oil
- 6 medium carrots, thinly sliced
- 3 medium onions, thinly sliced
- 5 pounds sauerkraut, lightly rinsed and squeezed dry
- 12 juniper berries
- ½ teaspoon caraway seeds
Salt and freshly ground pepper
Twelve 6- to 8-ounce smoked pork chops (see Note)
- 12 mild white sausages, such as bockwurst (2 pounds)
- 1 pound cooked garlic sausage or kielbasa, cut into 12 pieces
- 1 bottle Riesling

1. Preheat the oven to 350°. In a large pot of boiling salted water, cook the kale until just tender, about 4 minutes. Drain in a colander; rinse under cold water. Squeeze dry and chop coarsely.
2. In a large deep casserole, heat the oil. Add the carrots and onions. Cook over moderate heat, stirring occasionally, until softened but not browned, about 7 minutes. Add the kale; cook, stirring, until heated through, about 3 minutes. Add the sauerkraut, juniper and caraway and mix. Season with salt and pepper. Remove from the heat.
3. Generously butter a roasting pan. Arrange the chops in a single layer. Spread the sauerkraut mixture over the chops and tuck in the white and garlic sausages. Pour the Riesling over all and cover tightly with aluminum foil. Bake the choucroute for about 2 hours, or until piping hot throughout. Serve at once. —*Marcia Kiesel*
NOTE If you can't find smoked pork chops locally, you can order them

from O. Ottomanelli & Sons, 212-675-4217. Or substitute 12 top-quality frankfurters and tuck them in with the other sausages.
SERVE WITH Boiled red potatoes with butter and parsley.
WINE A dry Riesling from Alsace.

Lentil Salad with Knockwurst

MAKES 6 SERVINGS

Be sure to cook the lentils for this unusual salad only until they are just tender because they will continue to cook slightly as they cool in the aromatic cooking liquid.

- 5 flat-leaf parsley sprigs, stems reserved and leaves coarsely chopped
- 1 leek, green part only
- 1 bay leaf
- 1 pound Vertes du Puy lentils (2 cups), rinsed and picked over
- 1 large yellow onion, halved lengthwise
- 1 celery stalk, halved crosswise
- 1 large carrot, halved crosswise
- 2 quarts of cold water
- 1 pound cooked knockwurst, casing removed, sausage sliced ¼ inch thick
- 1 small red onion— thinly sliced, rinsed in cold water and patted dry
- 1 garlic clove, minced
- 2 tablespoons red wine vinegar
- 1½ tablespoons Dijon mustard
Salt and freshly ground white pepper
- 3 tablespoons extra-virgin olive oil

1. Tie the parsley stems, leek green and bay leaf together with kitchen string. Put the herb bundle in a large saucepan and add the lentils, onion, celery, carrot and water and bring just to a boil. Reduce the heat and simmer, skimming frequently, until the lentils are just tender, about 30 minutes. Remove from the heat and let the lentils cool to room temperature.

2. Drain the lentils. Pick out and discard the herb bundle and vegetables. In a large bowl, toss the lentils with the chopped parsley, knockwurst, red onion and garlic. In a small bowl, whisk together the vinegar and mustard. Season with salt and white pepper and then whisk in the oil until blended. Pour the dressing over the lentils and serve. —*Daniel Boulud*
MAKE AHEAD The cooked lentils can be refrigerated for up to 2 days. Bring to room temperature before proceeding.
WINE A dry, elegant white with citrus flavors and good acidity would marry well with this rustic dish. Either the 1996 Hermann J. Weimer Johanisberg Riesling from New York State or, from Italy, the 1996 Venica Vignis White Table Wine are good possibilities.

Creamy Ham and Leek Gratin

4 SERVINGS

- 4 cups water
- 6 medium leeks, white and tender green, split lengthwise
- ½ cup dry white wine
- 1 bay leaf
Salt
- 1 cup heavy cream
- 1 large shallot, thinly sliced
- 1 tablespoon fresh lemon juice
Freshly ground pepper
- 6 ounces baked smoked ham, cut into 2-by-½-inch matchsticks
- ⅔ cup unsalted pistachios (about 3 ounces), coarsely chopped
- 2 tablespoons unsalted butter, melted

1. In a large skillet, bring the water to a boil. Add the leeks, wine, bay leaf and a large pinch of salt and simmer over moderate heat until the leeks are tender, about 25 minutes. Using a slotted spoon, transfer the leeks to a plate, keeping them intact. Add the cream and shallot to the cooking liquid and

Ham and Gruyère French Toast Sandwiches

¼ cup maple syrup

One 3-inch cinnamon stick

⅔ cup milk

2 large eggs, beaten

Eight ½-inch-thick hand-cut slices
from a loaf of white bread

Dijon mustard

6 ounces sliced Gruyère cheese

½ pound thickly sliced smoked ham

1 to 2 tablespoons unsalted
butter

1. In a medium saucepan, combine the apple slices, water, maple syrup and cinnamon stick and bring to a boil. Simmer over moderately low heat, stirring occasionally, until the apples are tender, about 6 minutes. Using a slotted spoon, transfer the apples to a bowl and let cool to room temperature.

2. In a bowl, whisk the milk and eggs. Spread 4 slices of the bread with mustard. Top with half of the cheese, the ham and then the remaining cheese.

3. In a large skillet, melt 1 tablespoon of the butter over low heat. Dip the bottoms of the 4 topped bread slices in the beaten egg mixture until just saturated and transfer to the skillet. Dip the remaining slices of bread on 1 side only and place them, soaked side up, on the sandwiches. Cover the skillet and cook over moderately low heat until the bread is browned on the bottom, about 3 minutes. Turn the sandwiches, adding more butter to the skillet if necessary. Cover; cook until the second side is browned and the cheese is melted, about 3 minutes longer. Transfer the sandwiches to a cutting board and let stand for 5 minutes. Cut in half and serve with the apples.   —*Jesse Cool*

MAKE AHEAD The apples can be refrigerated in the poaching liquid for up to 1 day; drain just before using.

SERVE WITH Steamed or sautéed mustard greens.

WINE The smoky, salty ham and the sweet, nutty Gruyère are perfectly

simmer over moderate heat until reduced to 1¼ cups, about 6 minutes. Add the lemon juice and season with salt and pepper.

2. Preheat the oven to 500°. Arrange the leeks, cut side up, and the ham in a large gratin dish. Pour the cream sauce evenly over the leeks and ham. In a small bowl, combine the pistachios and melted butter and scatter over the leeks. Bake in the upper third of the oven for about 8 minutes, or until golden brown on top. Serve piping hot.   —*Marcia Keisel*

MAKE AHEAD The recipe can be prepared through Step 1 and refrigerated overnight.

WINE Salty ham and oniony leeks stand up beautifully to the sweetness of Sauternes, and the cream sauce and the pistachio crust underscore the wine's rich texture. Try the 1990 Château de Rayne Vigneau or the 1990 Château de Malle.

Ham and Gruyère French Toast Sandwiches

4 SERVINGS

Dive into this delectable sandwich with a knife and fork or pick it up with your hands, providing there are plenty of napkins. You can tuck the maple apples in with the ham and cheese or serve the fruit on the side, along with a spicy mustard or horseradish sauce.

2 Granny Smith apples—peeled,
cored and thinly sliced

1 cup water

complemented by the contrasting fruity, tart character of a dry or off-dry Riesling, such as the 1995 Bonny Doon Pacific Rim from California or the 1996 Richter Wehlener Sonnenuhr Kabinett from Germany.

Seared Veal Medallions with Herbed Wasabi Butter

4 SERVINGS

Fiery wasabi-spiked butter makes a luxurious glaze for the tender veal. It can be topped with reconstituted *hijiki* seaweed instead of nori. Chef Tetsuya Wakuda serves the veal with a refreshing cucumber and pickled ginger salad at his restaurant, Tetsuya's, in Sydney. The sea urchin roe adds a briny complexity to the butter.

2½ tablespoons wasabi powder (ground Japanese horseradish)

2 tablespoons warm water

1 stick (4 ounces) unsalted butter, softened

2 ounces fresh sea urchin roe (optional)

1 tablespoon light soy sauce

2 teaspoons fresh lemon juice

2 tablespoons finely chopped chives

2 teaspoons finely chopped tarragon

½ teaspoon finely chopped thyme

Pinch of cayenne pepper

Salt and freshly ground white pepper

Eight 3-ounce veal medallions

2 tablespoons olive oil

One 8-inch-square sheet of nori (pressed seaweed), cut with scissors into 4-by-½-inch strips (optional)

1. In a small bowl, mix the wasabi powder with the warm water to make a paste. In a medium bowl, blend the butter with the wasabi paste, sea urchin roe, soy sauce, lemon juice, chives, tarragon, thyme and cayenne. Season with salt and white pepper.

Seared Veal Medallions with Herbed Wasabi Butter

Scrape the butter onto a sheet of wax paper and wrap, shaping the butter into a 1-inch-thick log. Let stand at room temperature.

2. Preheat the broiler. Brush the veal on both sides with 2 teaspoons of the oil and season with salt and white pepper. In a large skillet, heat the remaining 1 tablespoon plus 1 teaspoon of oil. Add half of the veal to the skillet and pan-fry over high heat until well browned and lightly pink in the center, about 2 minutes per side. Transfer the veal to a rimmed baking sheet and then pan-fry the remaining medallions.

3. Top each veal medallion with ½ tablespoon of the wasabi butter and broil 4 inches from the heat for 1 to 2 minutes, basting with the juices and butter and rotating the pan until the meat is golden brown and glazed. Transfer to plates and top each medallion with an additional 1 teaspoon of the wasabi butter. Garnish with the nori strips and serve at once.

—*Tetsuya Wakuda*

MAKE AHEAD The wasabi butter can be refrigerated for up to 3 days or frozen for up to 1 month.

WINE Wasabi and wine don't usually pair well, but the layered flavors in this dish work beautifully with a medium-weight wine that has up-front fruit flavors, such as the 1996 Coldstream Hills Pinot Noir from Australia or the 1996 Domaine Rémi Jobard Premier Cru Les Vignes Rondes Monthélie Rouge from France.

Roasted Veal Loin with Rosé Pan Sauce

4 SERVINGS ✳

This recipe will make more than you can eat, so use the leftover meat in sandwiches.

  1 tablespoon vegetable oil
One 2-pound boneless veal loin, trimmed and tied
Salt and freshly ground pepper
  ¾ cup rosé wine
  1 tablespoon finely chopped tarragon
  1 tablespoon unsalted butter

Roasted Veal Loin with Rosé Pan Sauce

1. Preheat the oven to 375°. Heat the oil in a large ovenproof skillet. Season the veal with salt and pepper and cook over moderately high heat until browned all over, about 7 minutes. Put the skillet in the oven and roast the veal for about 45 minutes, or until the meat is just slightly pink in the center and reaches 130° on an instant-read thermometer. Transfer the veal to a cutting board, cover loosely with aluminum foil and let rest for 5 minutes before slicing.

2. Set the skillet over high heat and pour in the rosé. Cook, scraping up any browned bits from the pan, until the sauce is reduced to ⅓ cup, about 6 minutes. Whisk in the tarragon and butter. Transfer the sauce to a small bowl and serve with the veal.

—*Jan Newberry*

SERVE WITH Orzo with parsley.
WINE A rich Chardonnay will suit the sweet, tender meatiness of the veal, but a Pinot Noir or red Burgundy will add more complexity and underscore the fruitiness of the rosé sauce. Consider the 1995 Sterling Vineyards Winery Lake Pinot Noir from California or the 1995 Chandon de Briailles Savigny-les-Beaune Burgundy.

Wine-Braised Veal Shanks

6 SERVINGS

These luscious, melt-in-your-mouth veal shanks are brushed with their sauce and glazed in the oven just before serving.

  2 tablespoons vegetable oil
Six 1-pound veal shanks, tied
Salt and freshly ground pepper
  3 ounces finely chopped bacon
  1 tablespoon unsalted butter
  1 cup chopped onion
  ⅓ cup chopped carrot
  ⅓ cup chopped celery
  ¼ cup sliced shallots
  2 large garlic cloves, minced
  2 tablespoons all-purpose flour
  2 cups dry white wine
  3½ cups chicken stock (p. 117) or canned low-sodium broth
  3 bay leaves
  2 thyme sprigs
  1 sage sprig

1. Preheat the oven to 325°. Heat the oil in a large enameled cast-iron casserole. Season the veal shanks with salt and pepper and cook over moderately high heat until well browned, about 4 minutes per side. Transfer to a plate.

2. Add the bacon and butter to the casserole and cook slowly over low

menu

Arugula and Chanterelle Salad with Vacherin Croutons (p. 79)

1995 ALBERT BOXLER
GRAND CRU RIESLING
SOMMERBERG

—

Wine-Braised Veal Shanks (p. 246)

Butternut Squash, Swiss Chard and Apple Risotto (p. 343)

1995 DANIEL CHAUVEAU
CHINON PALLUS

—

Chestnut and Armagnac-Poached Prune Tarts (p. 393)

1987 GIARD CALVADOS
LE PERTYER

Wine-Braised Veal Shanks

heat until the bacon fat has been rendered, about 3 minutes. Add the onion, carrot, celery, shallots and garlic and cook, stirring, until softened but not browned, about 5 minutes. Increase the heat to moderately high and whisk in the flour. Cook, whisking, for 2 minutes. Gradually whisk in the wine and simmer for 4 minutes. Add the stock and bring to a boil.

3. Return the veal shanks to the casserole and add the bay leaves, thyme and sage. Season lightly with salt and pepper. Cover and bake for 2 hours, or until the veal is very tender. Transfer the shanks to a plate and cover with aluminum foil to keep warm. Increase the oven temperature to 500°.

4. On top of the stove, boil the cooking liquid until it is very flavorful, about 12 minutes. Strain the liquid into a medium saucepan and skim the fat from the surface. Season the sauce with salt and pepper.

5. Dip each veal shank into the sauce and place it on a baking sheet. Roast the veal shanks on the top rack of the oven until they are nicely glazed,

about 5 minutes. Reheat the sauce if necessary. Set a veal shank in the center of each of 6 plates, spoon the sauce on top and serve.

—*Eleven Madison Park, New York City*

MAKE AHEAD The recipe can be prepared through Step 3; refrigerate the shanks in the cooking liquid for up to 2 days. Reheat before proceeding.

WINE Look for the 1995 Daniel Chauveau Chinon Pallus.

CHAPTER 9 beef lamb

Roast Beef with Shallot Confit and Port Wine Sauce (p. 253)

Sparks's Sautéed Filet Mignon with Yellow Tomato Vinaigrette

Sparks's Sautéed Filet Mignon with Yellow Tomato Vinaigrette

4 SERVINGS ♛

Katy Sparks is chef at Quilty's in New York City. She recommends constantly basting filet mignon with melted butter while it is cooking to keep the meat juicy.

- 1 stick (4 ounces) unsalted butter, softened
- ¼ cup coarsely chopped basil, ¼ cup finely shredded leaves, plus basil sprigs for garnish
- 3½ tablespoons capers
- ¾ teaspoon finely grated lemon zest
- ¾ teaspoon minced garlic
- Salt and freshly ground pepper
- 2 medium yellow tomatoes— cored, seeded and finely chopped
- ⅓ cup finely chopped red onion
- 2 tablespoons extra-virgin olive oil
- 2 teaspoons rice vinegar
- 1 teaspoon finely grated orange zest
- 2 saffron threads, crushed
- 2 tablespoons canola oil
- Four 7-ounce filet mignon steaks, about 1¾ inches thick
- 1 pound grilled asparagus, for serving (optional; see Note)

1. In a food processor, blend the butter with the coarsely chopped basil, 2 tablespoons of the capers, the lemon zest and the garlic until almost smooth. Season with salt and pepper and transfer to a small bowl.

2. In a bowl, toss the tomatoes with the onion, olive oil, vinegar, orange zest and saffron. Season the tomato vinaigrette with salt and pepper.

3. Heat the canola oil in a large heavy skillet until almost smoking. Season the steaks, add them to the skillet and cook over high heat until well browned on all sides, about 10 minutes. Transfer to a platter and pour off the fat from the skillet. Return the steaks to the skillet and add the basil butter. Lower the heat to moderately high and cook the steaks, basting them continuously with the butter sauce, 6 to 8 minutes for medium rare. Remove the pan from the heat, return the steaks to the platter and cover loosely with aluminum foil. Add the remaining 1½ tablespoons of capers and the shredded basil to the skillet.

4. Arrange the grilled asparagus on 4 large plates and spoon the tomato vinaigrette alongside. Set the sautéed steaks on the vinaigrette and spoon the caper butter sauce on top. Garnish the steaks with the basil sprigs and serve at once. —*Katy Sparks*

NOTE To grill asparagus, toss lightly with oil, season with salt and pepper and cook on a grill or in a grill pan over moderate heat for about 3 minutes.

WINE A *premier cru* Burgundy is full-flavored enough to work with the meat as well as the caper butter.

Grilled Beef Tenderloin with Tortilla Española

6 SERVINGS

Argentineans love beef. So great is their respect for this noble meat that no Argentinean would ever dream of marinating it or of seasoning it with anything other than salt. Still, two condiments are commonly served with grilled meats: a gutsy parsley-garlic sauce called chimichurri and a robust relish called salsa criolla. The former is a cross between pesto and vinaigrette, made with fragrant fresh flat-leaf parsley and a nose-blasting dose of garlic. Salsa criolla combines tomatoes, onions and peppers. A typical Argentinean steak house would serve baked potatoes or french fries. Las Naszarenas, in Buenos Aires, also offers a pan-fried potato-onion frittata called Tortilla Española.

- Six 7-ounce beef tenderloin steaks (1½ inches thick)
- Coarse sea salt
- Tortilla Española (recipe follows)
- Chimichurri Sauce (p. 352)
- Salsa Criolla (p. 358)

Light a grill; for best flavor, toss a few soaked oak chips onto the fire. Alternatively, preheat a grill pan and oil it lightly. Generously season the steaks with sea salt and grill over a hot fire for about 8 minutes per side for medium rare. Let the steaks stand for 3 minutes and then serve with wedges of Tortilla Española and bowls of Chimichurri Sauce and Salsa Criolla.

WINE The jalapeño and the garlic in the chimichurri add noticeable heat to the grilled meat. Look for a Merlot with enough fruit to tolerate the spice, such as the 1995 Bodegas Weinert from Argentina or, from California, the 1995 Tessera or the 1995 Franciscan.

TORTILLA ESPANOLA

6 SERVINGS

The traditional way to make Tortilla Española is to deep-fry the potatoes and pan-fry the tortilla, but boiling the potatoes and finishing the tortilla in the oven makes less of a mess and also reduces the overall fat in the dish. Tortilla Española can be served warm or at room temperature.

- 2 pounds Yukon Gold potatoes, peeled and sliced ¼ inch thick
- Salt
- ¼ cup olive oil
- 2 large onions, halved lengthwise and thinly sliced crosswise
- 6 large eggs
- Freshly ground pepper

1. In a large saucepan, cover the potatoes with cold water, add 1 teaspoon of salt and bring to a boil over high heat. Reduce the heat to moderate and simmer until the potatoes are just tender, about 7 minutes. Drain the potatoes

and rinse under cold running water to stop the cooking; drain again. Spread the potato slices on paper towels and pat dry.

2. Preheat the oven to 400°. In a heavy 12-inch ovenproof skillet, heat 2 tablespoons of the oil. Add the onions and cook over moderate heat, stirring often, until golden brown, 10 to 15 minutes.

3. In a large bowl, lightly beat the eggs. Gently stir in the potatoes and onions and season the mixture generously with salt and pepper.

4. Heat the remaining 2 tablespoons of oil in the skillet. Add the egg mixture and cook over moderate heat undisturbed until the bottom of the tortilla is lightly browned, about 2 minutes. Transfer the skillet to the oven and bake the tortilla for about 20 minutes, or until the eggs are set and the

potatoes are very tender. Remove the tortilla from the oven and let it cool for 5 minutes.

5. Loosen the tortilla from the pan by running the tip of a knife around the edge. Place a round platter over the pan and invert. Cut the tortilla into wedges and serve. —*Steven Raichlen*

MAKE AHEAD The recipe can be prepared through Step 2 up to 6 hours before serving.

Wine-Braised Beef Fillet with Cherry Tomatoes

4 SERVINGS

- ¼ cup extra-virgin olive oil
- 3 shallots, minced
- 1 medium carrot, finely chopped
- 1½ ounces fatty prosciutto, finely chopped
- 24 large cherry tomatoes
- 1 tablespoon minced sage

One 2-pound trimmed beef-tenderloin roast
Freshly ground pepper
Salt

- 6 ounces porcini or shiitake mushrooms, stemmed and quartered
- 2 medium tomatoes—peeled, seeded and chopped
- 1¼ cups dry red wine
- 1 cup beef stock or canned low-sodium broth
- 2 tablespoons unsalted butter

1. In a large skillet, heat the oil. Add the shallots, carrot and prosciutto, cover and cook over low heat, stirring once or twice, until the shallots are softened but not browned, about 6 minutes.

2. Blanch the cherry tomatoes in boiling water just until the skins loosen, about 10 seconds. Drain in a colander and rinse under cold running water. Peel the tomatoes and cut them in half crosswise. Scoop out the seeds and pat the tomatoes dry.

3. Rub the sage all over the roast and season with pepper. Push the vegetable mixture to the side of the skillet. Add the roast. Cook over high heat until the roast is well-browned all over, about 12 minutes. Season the roast with salt and stir in the mushrooms and tomatoes. Add ¾ cup of the wine and boil for 3 minutes. Add the stock and bring to a simmer. Cover and simmer gently over low heat, turning the meat once or twice, about 25 minutes for rare. Transfer the roast to a carving board and cover loosely with aluminum foil.

4. Add the remaining ½ cup of wine to the skillet and boil over high heat for 5 minutes. Transfer the mixture to a food processor and puree until smooth. Return the puree to the skillet and bring to a simmer over moderate heat. Add the cherry tomatoes, season with salt

Grilled Beef Tenderloin with Tortilla Española

and pepper and cook for 2 minutes. Remove the sauce from the heat and swirl in the butter.

5. Thinly slice the meat and arrange on 8 dinner plates. Spoon some of the cherry-tomato sauce over the meat and serve at once. Pass any remaining sauce separately. —*Umberto Creatini*

Beef Tenderloin with Red Pepper–Walnut Sauce

4 SERVINGS ✳

A toaster oven with convection heat cuts the cooking time of this roast by a third and the circulating hot air browns the meat evenly. If you're using a standard toaster oven or a conventional oven, adjust the roasting time accordingly.

½ cup walnuts (about 2 ounces)
One 2-pound beef-tenderloin roast
Salt and freshly ground black pepper
One 12-ounce jar roasted red
    peppers, drained and coarsely
    chopped
2 tablespoons finely chopped basil
1 serrano or other small hot chile,
    seeded and minced
1 tablespoon extra-virgin olive oil
1 teaspoon fresh lemon juice
¼ teaspoon ground cumin

1. Preheat a convection toaster oven to 450°. On a small pie plate, toast the walnuts for about 3 minutes, or until they are fragrant and lightly browned. Let cool slightly and then coarsely chop the walnuts.

2. Season the beef with salt and black pepper and roast in the toaster oven for about 35 minutes for medium rare, or until an instant-read thermometer inserted in the center of the meat registers 125° to 130°. Transfer to a work surface, cover loosely with aluminum foil and let stand for about 10 minutes.

3. Meanwhile, in a small bowl, combine the red peppers, walnuts, basil, chile, oil, lemon juice and cumin and

season with salt and black pepper. Carve the roast into thick slices and serve with the red pepper sauce.

—*Jan Newberry*

WINE Serve a mildly tannic Merlot with this rich meat dish—either a Bordeaux blend, such as the 1994 Mouton Cadet Réserve, or a South African example, such as the 1996 Glen Carlou.

Roast Beef with Shallot Confit and Port Wine Sauce

8 SERVINGS

SHALLOT CONFIT

½ pound shallots, sliced ¼ inch
    thick
1 cup dry red wine
½ cup ruby port
1 thyme sprig
1 teaspoon sugar

ROAST BEEF

¼ cup vegetable oil
4 ounces unstemmed shiitake
    mushrooms, coarsely chopped
1 small onion, coarsely chopped
1 small carrot, coarsely chopped
1 small celery rib, coarsely
    chopped
3 garlic cloves, coarsely chopped
2 sage leaves
1 rosemary sprig
1 thyme sprig
1½ cups dry red wine
½ cup ruby port
4 cups beef stock or canned broth
Two 2-pound beef-tenderloin roasts,
    preferably center cut
Salt and freshly ground pepper
2 tablespoons cold unsalted
    butter

1. MAKE THE SHALLOT CONFIT: Preheat the oven to 350°. Combine all of the ingredients in a small shallow baking dish. Cover with aluminum foil and bake for 1 hour. Uncover and continue baking for about 30 minutes longer, or until the shallots are tender and the liquid has almost completely

Wine-Braised Beef Fillet with Cherry Tomatoes

menu

Marchese Nicolò Incisa Della Rocchetta served this menu to guests—with, of course, the famed super-Tuscan Sassicaias that he produces. Other super-Tuscans that you might try: Tignanello, Ornellaia, Solaia, Sassolloro and Fontalloro.

Autumn Vegetable Sauté with Sausage and Mint (p. 330)

1993 SASSICAIA

—

Curly Pasta with Spinach and Chickpeas (p. 122)

—

Wine-Braised Beef Fillet with Cherry Tomatoes (p. 252)
Swiss Chard Sformatino (p. 306)

1988 SASSICAIA

—

Arugula, Mushroom and Walnut Salad (p. 78)

—

Ricotta Tortes with Zabaglione (p. 436)

Caramelized Chocolate-Chestnut Custards (p. 429)

1979 SASSICAIA

Roast Beef with Shallot Confit and Port Wine Sauce, with Buttery Sautéed Potatoes (p. 337), Mixed Mushrooms with Garlic (p. 313) and green beans.

evaporated. Let cool to room temperature. Discard the thyme sprig. Raise the oven temperature to 400°.

2. MAKE THE ROAST BEEF: Heat 2 tablespoons of the oil in a large saucepan. Add the mushrooms, onion, carrot, celery, garlic, sage, rosemary and thyme and cook over moderately low heat, stirring occasionally, until the vegetables start to brown, about 12 minutes. Raise the heat to high, add the wine and port and boil until the liquid is reduced to ¼ cup, about 10 minutes.

3. Add the beef stock to the saucepan and bring to a boil. Reduce the heat to low and simmer until reduced to 2 cups, about 30 minutes. Strain the sauce into a saucepan, pressing on the solids to extract as much liquid as possible from them.

---

menu

Foie Gras Terrine with Caramelized Apples (p. 65)

Lobster Bisque with Armagnac (p. 112)

1995 ZIND HUMBRECHT WINTZENHEIM GEWURZTRAMINER

Roast Beef with Shallot Confit and Port Wine Sauce (p. 253)

Buttery Sautéed Potatoes (p. 337)

Mixed Mushrooms with Garlic (p. 313)

Braised Savoy Cabbage with Bacon (p. 307)

1995 LOUIS JADOT BEAUNE BOUCHEROTTES

Poached Pears with Mascarpone Cream and Chocolate Sauce (p. 423)

Hazelnut Butter Cookies (p. 398)

1996 QUADY ESSENSIA

---

4. Season the tenderloins with salt and pepper. Heat the remaining 2 tablespoons of oil in a large ovenproof skillet over moderately high heat. Set the roasts in the skillet, smooth side down, and brown them on all sides, about 12 minutes in all. Turn the roasts smooth side up and spread the shallot confit on top. Transfer the skillet to the oven and roast the tenderloins for about 30 minutes, or until an instant-read thermometer registers 125° for rare. Transfer the roasts to a carving board, cover loosely with aluminum foil and let rest for 10 minutes.

5. Set the skillet over high heat and cook until the pan juices sizzle. Whisk in the reserved port sauce and simmer for 3 minutes. Remove the skillet from the heat and whisk the butter into the sauce, 1 tablespoon at a time, until blended. Season the sauce with salt and pepper and pour it into a gravy boat. Carve the roasts and serve with the port sauce.

—*The Point, Lake Saranac, New York*

WINE Roast beef and caramelized shallots, buttressed by mushrooms, potatoes, and cabbage, have sweet, earthy flavors that perfectly showcase a flavorful red Burgundy. Among various possibilities, consider the 1995 Louis Jadot Beaune Boucherottes or the 1995 Marquis d'Angerville Volnay Champans. The 1996 Acacia Carneros and the 1995 Robert Mondavi Carneros are West Coast Pinot Noir alternatives.

MAKE AHEAD The shallot confit can be refrigerated for up to 1 week. The port sauce can be made through Step 3 and refrigerated separately for up to 3 days.

Glazed Beef Tenderloin with Curried Vegetables

12 SERVINGS

Roasted beef tenderloin, served cold, is a great make-ahead dish for a picnic.

BEEF

3 tablespoons soy sauce
2 tablespoons pure maple syrup
2 large shallots, minced
2 teaspoons curry powder
Two 2½-pound beef-tenderloin roasts
2 tablespoons vegetable oil
Salt

VEGETABLES

1½ pounds sugar snap peas
2 pounds fresh lima beans, shelled (about 2 cups)
2½ tablespoons curry powder
4 teaspoons mustard seeds
⅔ cup pure olive oil
6 tablespoons white wine vinegar
3 large garlic cloves, minced
2 teaspoons finely grated lemon zest
1½ teaspoons kosher salt
4 bunches red radishes, quartered
4 cucumbers—peeled, halved lengthwise, seeded and sliced 1 inch thick
½ cup snipped chives

1. PREPARE THE BEEF: Preheat the oven to 500°. In a large glass baking dish, combine the soy sauce, maple syrup, shallots and curry powder. Add the tenderloins and rub the soy mixture all over.

2. In an ovenproof skillet, heat the oil until almost smoking. Season the tenderloins with salt, add to the skillet and cook over moderately high heat until browned, about 15 minutes. Transfer the skillet to the oven and roast the meat for about 20 minutes, or until it reaches 125° on an instant-read thermometer for medium rare. Transfer the roasts to a cutting board and let stand until cooled.

3. PREPARE THE VEGETABLES: In a pot of boiling salted water, cook the sugar snaps for 1 minute. Using a slotted spoon, transfer them to a colander set under cold running water;

ABOVE: **Beef Braciole Skewers with Bread and Lemons.** TOP: **Glazed Beef Tenderloin with Curried Vegetables.**

drain, pat dry and transfer to a large bowl. Repeat with the lima beans, cooking them until just tender, about 4 minutes; add them to the peas.

4. In a small skillet, toast the curry powder over low heat, stirring, for 2 minutes; transfer it to a plate. Add the mustard seeds to the skillet and cook for 2 minutes; transfer the mustard seeds to another plate.

5. In a small glass or stainless-steel bowl, combine the curry powder, oil, vinegar, garlic, zest and kosher salt.

6. Cut each roast into ¼-inch-thick slices. Add the radishes, cucumbers,

chives, mustard seeds and ½ cup of the curry vinaigrette to the sugar snaps and lima beans and toss. Serve the beef with the vegetables and pass the remaining vinaigrette separately.

—*Marcia Kiesel*

MAKE AHEAD The roasted beef and the cooked peas and beans can be refrigerated separately overnight.

Beef Braciole Skewers with Bread and Lemons

12 SERVINGS

Braciole is the Italian name for beef rolls stuffed with cheese and herbs and then sautéed and simmered, or grilled.

2½ cups fresh bread crumbs
1 cup finely diced Provolone cheese (3½ ounces)
½ cup plus 2 tablespoons freshly grated Parmesan cheese (1½ ounces)
3 tablespoons finely chopped parsley
3 small garlic cloves, minced
2 shallots, minced
2½ teaspoons finely grated lemon zest
2½ teaspoons minced rosemary
Kosher salt and freshly ground pepper
⅓ cup extra-virgin olive oil, plus ½ cup for brushing
3¼ pounds beef eye of round, cut crosswise into 36 slices (1½ ounces each) and pounded into 6-by-4-inch rectangles
3 lemons, halved lengthwise, then thickly sliced crosswise
1 baguette, top and bottom crusts cut off, sliced 1 inch thick
Grilled Lemon Vinaigrette (recipe follows)

1. In a bowl, combine the bread crumbs, cheeses, parsley, garlic, shallots, lemon zest and rosemary with 1½ teaspoons kosher salt and ½ teaspoon pepper. Mix in ⅓ cup of the oil.

2. Set a slice of beef on a work surface with the long side facing you. Spread 1½ tablespoons of the filling along the bottom third of the slice. Roll the meat around the filling into a tight log, folding in the sides as you go. Repeat with the remaining meat and filling to make 36 rolls.

3. On each of twelve 12-inch skewers, thread 1 lemon slice, 1 bread slice, 1 lemon slice and 1 beef roll; repeat 2 more times. Generously brush the skewers with the remaining ½ cup of oil and season with salt and pepper.

4. Light a grill or preheat the broiler. Grill or broil the skewers until the bread is crusty brown and the meat is pink in the center, about 2 minutes per side. Serve hot with the Grilled Lemon Vinaigrette.

GRILLED LEMON VINAIGRETTE

MAKES ABOUT 1½ CUPS

3 large lemons, halved lengthwise, then cut crosswise ½ inch thick
1 cup extra-virgin olive oil
2 teaspoons kosher salt

Light a grill or preheat the broiler. Grill or broil the lemon slices until charred on both sides. Transfer them to a large coarse strainer set over a bowl. Using a wooden spoon, crush all of the juice from the lemons; discard the skins and seeds. Stir the oil and kosher salt into the lemon juice. —*Marcia Kiesel*

Steak Frites

6 SERVINGS

People throughout France sit down regularly to a meal of deceptive simplicity and universal appeal: steak and french fries. It might seem like the world's easiest dish (after all, it requires only two main ingredients), but the steak must be meaty and juicy, the potatoes buttery and crisp, and both must arrive at the table piping hot. Here's an uptown version, fea-

Steak Frites

turing rib eye and a dollop of creamy Roquefort butter. The French would pan-fry the steaks, but grilling gives meat a wonderful flavor. The *frites* get their meltingly soft interior and crisp crust from a two-step frying process: the first at a lower temperature to cook them through, and then the second at higher heat to crisp them.

Six ½-pound rib-eye steaks
  4 tablespoons unsalted butter, at room temperature, plus 1½ tablespoons, melted
Freshly ground pepper
  1 ounce Roquefort cheese, at room temperature
  4 large baking potatoes
Peanut oil, for deep-frying
Coarse sea salt

1. Brush the steaks with the melted butter and season with pepper; let the steaks come to room temperature.

2. In a small bowl, beat the 4 tablespoons of butter with the Roquefort until blended.

3. Peel the potatoes and slice lengthwise ¼ inch thick. Cut the slices into ¼-inch-wide sticks and soak in ice water for 15 minutes.

4. In a deep-fryer or a large saucepan, heat 2 inches of oil to 325°. Drain the potato sticks and then blot them completely dry. Divide the potatoes into 4 batches and fry each batch until the potatoes are cooked through but not browned, 4 to 6 minutes. Using a slotted spoon, transfer the fried potatoes to paper towels to drain.

5. Light a grill. Generously season the steaks with sea salt and grill over a hot fire for 4 to 6 minutes per side for medium rare. Alternatively, pan-fry the steaks over moderately high heat for about 4 minutes per side.

6. Reheat the oil to 375°. Fry the potatoes until crisp and golden brown, 1 to 2 minutes per batch. Using a slotted spoon, transfer the potatoes to fresh paper towels to drain. Top each steak with a spoonful of Roquefort butter and serve the potatoes on the side.
—*Steven Raichlen*

MAKE AHEAD The potatoes can stand at room temperature for up to 4 hours after their preliminary frying.

Rib-Eye Steaks with Ancho Chile Cream Sauce
4 SERVINGS ✳
Cookbook author Georgeanne Brennan makes her version of the classic green peppercorn steak sauce with an ancho chile, which adds a sweet heat.

  1 small ancho chile—stemmed, seeded and halved lengthwise
  ¼ teaspoon cumin seeds
  ⅔ cup light cream
  ¼ teaspoon dried oregano
Freshly ground pepper
Salt

Four ½-pound rib-eye steaks, about ⅜ inch thick
  ½ cup water

1. Heat a small heavy skillet. Using a spatula, press the chile into the skillet, skin side down, and toast over moderately high heat until beginning to blister, 1 to 2 minutes. Transfer to a plate. Add the cumin seeds to the skillet and toast just until fragrant, about 30 seconds. Add to the chile.

2. Using a pair of kitchen shears, cut the chile into small pieces and transfer to a saucepan. Add the cumin, cream, oregano and ⅛ teaspoon pepper. Bring to a boil and simmer over moderate heat, stirring, until reduced to about ½ cup, 6 to 8 minutes. Strain the sauce, return it to the saucepan and keep warm.

3. Sprinkle 2 large cast-iron skillets with a scant ¼ teaspoon salt each and heat until almost smoking. Add the steaks and cook over high heat until browned, about 1½ minutes per side for medium rare. Transfer the steaks to dinner plates. Add ¼ cup of water to each skillet, scraping up any brown bits, and cook until the liquid in each skillet is reduced to 1 tablespoon. Pour the pan drippings into the cream sauce, spoon over the steaks and serve.
—*Georgeanne Brennan*

WINE These rich rib-eye steaks call for a deeply flavored California Cabernet Sauvignon. Among a wealth of possibilities, consider the 1994 E. & J. Gallo Estates or the 1994 St. Francis Reserve.

Teriyaki Beef and Sweet Potato Packets
6 SERVINGS
Grill the steak about twenty minutes after the sweet potatoes start to bake.

  ⅔ cup soy sauce
  ½ cup mirin
  ½ cup sake

⅓ cup sugar

4 scallions, minced

Four ¼-inch-thick slices of fresh
   ginger, smashed

4 garlic cloves, smashed

1 tablespoon plus 2 teaspoons
   Asian sesame oil

1½ pounds sirloin steak in 1 piece,
   cut about 1 inch thick

Salt and freshly ground pepper

Sweet Potato Packets
   (recipe follows)

1. In a saucepan, combine the soy sauce, mirin, sake, sugar, scallions, ginger, garlic and 2 teaspoons of the sesame oil. Bring to a boil over moderate heat and cook until reduced to 1¼ cups, 8 to 10 minutes. Strain the sauce into a small bowl.

2. Light a grill or preheat the broiler. Brush the steak with the remaining 1 tablespoon of sesame oil and season generously with salt and pepper. Grill or broil the steak, basting with some of the sauce, for 4 to 5 minutes per side for medium rare. Let rest for 5 minutes and then thinly slice on the diagonal and serve with the potato packets. Pass the remaining sauce separately.

WINE The acerbic qualities of such classic Bordeaux as the 1995 Château Coufran and the 1994 Château Grand-Puy Ducasse mirror the saltiness of the soy sauce.

SWEET POTATO PACKETS

6 SERVINGS

The sweet potatoes can also be baked in parchment paper; simply pleat the edges of the paper instead of crimping. Be careful when opening the packets at the table—they will be full of steam.

3 tablespoons sesame seeds

6 tablespoons unsalted butter

2 sweet potatoes (¾ pound each),
   peeled and sliced crosswise
   ¼ inch thick

Teriyaki Beef and Sweet Potato Packets

3 tablespoons soy sauce

2 garlic cloves, thinly sliced

3 scallions, cut into 1-inch lengths

Salt and freshly ground pepper

1. Preheat the oven to 350°. In a small skillet, toast the sesame seeds over moderate heat, stirring, until fragrant and golden, about 2 minutes.

2. Set out six 16-by-12-inch sheets of aluminum foil, shiny side down, with the shorter edges facing you. Spread about 1 teaspoon of the butter in the center of the bottom half of each sheet. Mound the sweet potatoes on the buttered areas and sprinkle with the sesame seeds, soy sauce, garlic and scallions. Season the sweet potatoes with salt and pepper and dot with the remaining butter.

3. Fold over the top of the foil to enclose the potatoes and crimp the edges to seal. Slide the 6 packets onto 2 large baking sheets and bake for 30 minutes, reversing the pans halfway through, until the packets are puffed and the potatoes are tender. Transfer to plates and serve.

—*Steven Raichlen*

MAKE AHEAD The packets can be assembled up to 6 hours before baking.

Cowboy Steaks with Onions and Yuca Fries

6 SERVINGS

Southeast meets Southwest in this paean to the T-bone steak, the favorite cut of beef in the American West, and to yuca, a starchy root vegetable that's popular from Brazil to Miami. The steak is dusted with a fiery blend of chile powder, cumin and cayenne pepper before grilling and then topped with the sweet charred onions. Keep the steaks warm while you fry the yuca.

- 1½ **tablespoons pure chile powder**
- 1 **teaspoon cayenne pepper**
- 1 **teaspoon ground cumin**
- 1 **teaspoon dried oregano**
- **Coarse salt and freshly ground black pepper**
- 6 **T-bone steaks, cut ¾-inch thick (about 1 pound each)**
- 2 **large onions, sliced crosswise ½ inch thick**
- 2 **tablespoons vegetable oil**
- **Yuca Fries, for serving (recipe follows)**

1. In a small bowl, combine the chile powder, cayenne, cumin and oregano with 1 tablespoon of coarse salt and 1 teaspoon of black pepper. Rub the steaks with the spice mixture and arrange on a platter. Let them come to room temperature.

2. Light a grill or preheat a grill pan and oil it lightly. Brush the onions with the oil and season with coarse salt and black pepper. Grill over a hot fire until nicely charred, about 8 minutes.

3. Grill the steaks over the hot fire for 4 to 5 minutes per side for medium rare. Transfer to plates and top with the onions. Serve Yuca Fries on the side.

WINE The chili rub and the charred onions both give the steaks a spiciness that calls for an equally spicy California Zinfandel. Look for such peppery, fruity examples as the 1996 Quivira or the 1995 Cline.

YUCA FRIES

6 SERVINGS

The fries here are a Latino version of french fries. When buying yuca, look for firm heavy roots with unblemished waxed skins; avoid any with soft spots, cracks, mold or an unpleasant aroma. The flesh should be pure white—do not use yuca with brown spots or grayish or bluish veins.

- 2 **pounds firm, unblemished yuca, peeled and cut into 2-by-½-inch sticks**
- 1 **cup cold water**
- **Canola oil, for deep-frying**
- **Salt**

1. In a large saucepan of lightly salted boiling water, cook the yuca for 10 minutes. Add the 1 cup of cold water to the saucepan and bring back to a boil. (The cold water tenderizes the yuca.) Continue to cook the yuca until tender, about 5 minutes longer. Drain and refresh under cold running water; drain again and pat thoroughly dry. Check for stringy fibers and pull them out.

2. In a deep-fryer or medium saucepan, heat 2 inches of oil to 350°. Divide the yuca into 4 batches and fry each batch until golden brown, 2 to 4 minutes. Using a slotted spoon, transfer the yuca to paper towels to drain. Sprinkle with salt and serve at once.

—*Steven Raichlen*

MAKE AHEAD The boiled yuca can be refrigerated for up to 2 days before deep-frying.

Seared Flank Steak with Salsa Verde

4 SERVINGS

- ⅔ **cup flat-leaf parsley leaves**
- 1 **garlic clove, minced**
- 6 **anchovy fillets**

Cowboy Steaks with Onions and Yuca Fries

2 tablespoons drained capers

1 teaspoon red wine vinegar

½ cup plus 1 tablespoon
extra-virgin olive oil (see Note)

Salt and freshly ground pepper

1 pound flank steak

I. In a food processor or blender, pulse the parsley, garlic, anchovies, capers and vinegar until coarsely chopped. With the machine on, slowly pour in ½ cup of the oil; mix just until blended.

2. In a large nonstick skillet, heat the remaining 1 tablespoon of oil until almost smoking. Season the flank steak and add it to the skillet. Cook the flank steak over moderately high heat until it is well seared outside and still pink inside, 5 to 6 minutes per side for medium rare. Transfer the steak to a cutting board and let stand for 5 minutes. Carve the steak across the grain into thin slices. Serve the sliced flank steak with the salsa verde.

—Jan Newberry

NOTE A peppery or pungent extra-virgin olive oil gives the steak's salsa verde an edge.

WINE The beef's piquant sauce calls for a red with sufficient fruity intensity. A hearty Shiraz from Australia is ideal: look for the 1994 Thomas Mitchell or the 1996 Rosemount.

Papaya-Marinated Steak

6 SERVINGS

The flank steak here is first lightly coated with a rub and then marinated between papaya skins, which act as a tenderizer.

2 scallions, minced

1 tablespoon English dry mustard

1 teaspoon minced thyme leaves

¾ teaspoon freshly ground pepper

¼ teaspoon ground ginger

One 1¾-pound flank steak

Skins of 2 ripe medium papayas, halved lengthwise, with ⅛ inch of the flesh left on

Seared Flank Steak with Salsa Verde

2 tablespoons vegetable oil, for brushing

Kosher salt

Malay Onion Sambal (p. 360)

I. In a small bowl, combine the scallions, dry mustard, thyme, pepper and ginger. Rub the mixture evenly on both sides of the flank steak.

2. Put 2 of the papaya skin halves in a glass baking dish, flesh side up. Add the flank steak and top it with the remaining 2 papaya skin halves, flesh side down; the papaya skins should cover the surface of the flank steak.

Cover and refrigerate the flank steak for 1 to 1½ hours.

3. Light a grill or preheat the broiler. Discard the papaya skin halves and then lightly oil both sides of the flank steak. Season the flank steak with kosher salt. Grill or broil the flank steak, turning it once, for about 10 minutes, or until the meat is medium rare. Thinly slice the flank steak across the grain on the diagonal. Serve the sliced flank steak hot with Malay Onion Sambal.

—Jenna Holst

Michael's Flank Steak Hoagies with Coffee Barbecue Sauce

Michael's Flank Steak Hoagies with Coffee Barbecue Sauce

6 SERVINGS

According to Michael Lomonaco, the executive chef at Manhattan's Windows on the World, these hoagies are perfect for a tailgate party. The coffee-flavored barbecue sauce is reminiscent of the red-eye gravy that Southerners favor with their biscuits and country ham. Be sure to allow time for the steak to marinate overnight.

1 teaspoon cumin seeds
¼ cup plus 2 tablespoons olive oil
2 tablespoons honey
1 tablespoon cider vinegar
1 tablespoon finely chopped garlic
1 tablespoon ancho chile powder
1 tablespoon freshly ground black pepper
1 teaspoon ground coriander
½ teaspoon cayenne pepper
2 pounds flank steak (about ¾ inch thick)
6 Italian rolls, halved lengthwise
Coarse salt
2 cups shredded iceberg lettuce
2 to 3 jalapeños—halved, seeded and thinly sliced
1 cup Coffee Barbecue Sauce (recipe follows)

1. In a small skillet, toast the cumin seeds over moderate heat until fragrant, 2 to 3 minutes. Let cool and then grind coarsely in a mortar or spice mill.
2. In a shallow glass baking dish, combine ¼ cup of the oil with the honey, vinegar, garlic, chile powder, black pepper, coriander, cayenne and ground cumin. Add the flank steak, turn to coat with the marinade, cover and refrigerate overnight.
3. Light a grill or heat a grill pan. Brush the cut sides of the rolls with the remaining 2 tablespoons of olive oil and lightly toast them on the grill.
4. Remove the steak from the marinade and season with coarse salt. Grill for 3 to 4 minutes per side for medium rare. Transfer to a carving board, cover loosely with aluminum foil and let rest for 5 minutes.
5. Spread the lettuce on the rolls and top with the jalapeños. Slice the meat across the grain and then set it on the jalapeños. Spoon the Coffee Barbecue Sauce on the meat and serve at once.

COFFEE BARBECUE SAUCE

MAKES ABOUT 3 CUPS

This java-flavored sauce cooks more quickly than most barbecue sauces.

1 cup ketchup
¾ cup (packed) dark brown sugar
½ cup brewed espresso
¼ cup red wine vinegar
1 medium onion, coarsely chopped
3 jalapeños, halved and seeded
2 garlic cloves, crushed
2 tablespoons molasses
2 tablespoons dry mustard powder, mixed with 1 tablespoon water
2 tablespoons Worcestershire sauce
2 tablespoons ground cumin
2 tablespoons ancho chile powder

Combine all of the ingredients in a medium saucepan and bring to a boil. Simmer over low heat for 20 minutes and let cool. Transfer the sauce to a blender or food processor and puree until smooth. —*Michael Lomonaco*
MAKE AHEAD The barbecue sauce can be refrigerated for up to 2 weeks.

Grilled Skirt Steak with Chimichurri

6 SERVINGS

Chimichurri, an assertive blend of garlic, parsley, vinegar and crushed red pepper, is Argentina's national steak sauce. In fact, it turns up throughout Latin America—at roadside barbecue stalls and in pricey steak palaces, as far south as Tierra del Fuego and as far north as Miami. Here it is paired with well-marbled, full-flavored skirt steak, a cut of meat much loved by Miami's Latinos. Don't be alarmed by the seemingly enormous quantity of garlic: it tastes wonderful, and the parsley acts as a breath freshener.

- 1 large bunch flat-leaf parsley (about 4 ounces), large stems discarded
- 10 garlic cloves, coarsely chopped
- 1 medium carrot, coarsely grated
- 1 cup extra-virgin olive oil
- 1/3 cup distilled white vinegar
- 1/4 cup water
- 1 teaspoon dried oregano
- 1/2 to 1 teaspoon crushed red pepper

Kosher salt and freshly ground black pepper

- 2 pounds skirt steak

1. In a food processor, finely chop the parsley and garlic. Add the carrot, oil, vinegar, water, oregano, crushed red pepper to taste, 1 teaspoon of kosher salt and 1/2 teaspoon of black pepper and process until blended.

2. Light a grill or preheat the broiler. Generously season the skirt steak with kosher salt and black pepper. Grill over a hot fire or broil for about 4 minutes per side for medium rare. Serve the steak with the chimichurri on the side. —Steven Raichlen

WINE Grilled beef points to a substantial red wine, but the sharp sauce narrows the choice to one with a youthful bite of its own. Go for a Chilean Cabernet, such as the 1996 Montgras Reserva or the 1994 Cousino Macul Antiguas Reserva.

Coriander Beef with Tortillas

4 SERVINGS ✷

The beef's spicy poaching broth can be reserved and used as the base for a hearty black bean soup.

- 3 cups water
- 1 small onion, coarsely chopped
- 6 fresh cilantro stems, plus 1/4 cup coarsely chopped cilantro
- 1 garlic clove, smashed
- 1 large jalapeño, thickly sliced
- 1 tablespoon coriander seeds, crushed, plus 1 1/2 teaspoons whole seeds
- 1/2 teaspoon whole black peppercorns

Salt

- 1 pound skirt steak
- 2 tablespoons fresh lime juice
- 1/4 teaspoon freshly ground pepper
- 1/4 cup plus 1 tablespoon vegetable oil
- 6 large romaine lettuce leaves, shredded
- 1 ripe Hass avocado, sliced
- 3 medium radishes, sliced
- 2 scallions, white and tender green, cut into 1/2-inch pieces

Warm corn tortillas, for serving

Hot sauce, for serving

1. In a Dutch oven, combine the water, onion, cilantro stems, garlic, jalapeño, crushed coriander, whole peppercorns and 1/2 teaspoon of salt and bring to a boil. Cut the steak in halves or thirds to fit in the Dutch oven. Add the meat to the pot and simmer over moderately low heat until tender, about 25 minutes. Transfer the meat to a plate and let cool slightly; thinly slice the meat across the grain. Reserve the broth if desired.

2. Meanwhile, in a small skillet, toast the whole coriander seeds until they are fragrant, about 3 minutes. Transfer the toasted seeds to a spice grinder or mortar and grind to a powder. Put the ground coriander in a small glass or stainless-steel bowl and whisk in the lime juice, 1/2 teaspoon of salt and the freshly ground pepper. Whisk in the oil until combined.

3. Line a platter with the romaine. Toss the sliced meat with 1/3 cup of the dressing and the chopped cilantro. Mound the meat on the lettuce and garnish with the avocado, radishes and scallions. Drizzle the remaining dressing on top and serve with warm tortillas and hot sauce. —Jan Newberry

WINE The slightly sweet coriander is a minor note next to the meatiness of the steak and the tartness of the vinaigrette. A full-flavored Zinfandel, such as the 1996 Alderbrook Old Vine Old Clone or the 1995 Haywood Winery Los Chamizal Vineyard, would wrap nicely around this dish.

Grilled Beef Onglet with Tomato-Onion Panade

6 SERVINGS

Onglet, also called hanger steak, is becoming increasingly available at American butcher shops; if you can't find it, use skirt steak instead.

- 2 pounds onglet or skirt steak
- 1 1/2 teaspoons coarse sea salt

Olive oil

Tomato-Onion Panade (recipe follows)

1. Rub the onglet all over with the sea salt and refrigerate overnight. Bring the onglet to room temperature before grilling it.

2. Light a grill or preheat a grill pan. Lightly rub the onglet with oil and grill the steak over a hot fire until nicely charred, 3 to 5 minutes per side for medium rare, depending on the thickness of the meat. Transfer the onglet to a carving board and let rest for 5

minutes. Thinly slice the onglet across the grain and serve the steak hot with the Tomato-Onion Panade.

WINE Consider a bright, full-flavored Rhône red, such as the 1995 Château du Trignon Gigondas, or a California Syrah with good fruit, such as the 1996 Unalii.

TOMATO-ONION PANADE

6 SERVINGS

This is one of Zuni restaurant's many summertime variations on *panade à l'oignon,* a dense, rich gratin of onion, bread and Gruyère cheese. Chef Judy Rodgers first made it when she was the lunch chef at Chez Panisse and she was relying on Richard Olney's *Simple French Food,* whose recipes, she says, "made it look like I already knew how to cook."

- 3 pounds sweet yellow onions, such as Vidalia, thinly sliced
- ½ cup plus 2 tablespoons olive oil
- 12 garlic cloves, slivered

Sea salt

- 1 pound stale Tuscan-style white bread, sliced ½ inch thick
- 20 basil leaves
- 1 pound ripe tomatoes, sliced ¼ inch thick
- ½ cup freshly grated Parmigiano-Reggiano cheese

About 2 cups lightly salted chicken stock

Grilled Beef Onglet with Tomato-Onion Panade

I. In a bowl, toss the onions with ¼ cup of the oil. Transfer the onions to a large, heavy saucepan or enameled cast-iron casserole and cook over moderate heat, stirring often, until beginning to color slightly, about 7 minutes. Add the garlic and season with sea salt. Reduce the heat to low and cook, stirring occasionally, until the onions are very tender, about 1 hour and 20 minutes.

2. Preheat the oven to 250°. Brush the bread slices on both sides with ¼ cup of the oil and sprinkle with sea salt. Line the bottom of a 2-quart ceramic or glass baking dish with a layer of bread. Spread one-fourth of the onions over the bread, followed by 5 of the basil leaves and one-fourth of the tomato slices. Sprinkle with 2 tablespoons of the cheese. Continue layering in this fashion, ending with tomato slices and cheese.

3. Gradually pour 2 cups of the stock around the edge of the panade, allowing the panade to absorb the stock as you pour. Drizzle the remaining 2 tablespoons of oil over the top.

4. Cover the panade loosely with aluminum foil and bake for 1 hour, or until bubbling. Uncover and increase the oven temperature to 375°. Continue baking for about 30 minutes longer, or until the panade is golden brown on top. Let rest for at least 10 minutes before serving it directly from the baking dish. It should be silky and juicy beneath the crust; if it seems dry, add a little more stock and bake for 10 minutes longer.   —*Judy Rodgers*

MAKE AHEAD The panade can be made 6 hours ahead through Step 3.

Korean Beef Ribs

6 SERVINGS ★★★ 1988

Linda Burum and Linda Merinoff wrote a wonderful article on Asian-style ribs for FOOD & WINE that included this

Korean Beef Ribs

recipe. The short ribs are sliced across the bones so that each piece of meat has three small pieces of bone. The ribs are available precut at Asian markets and some supermarkets.

 5 pounds flanken-style beef ribs, cut ½ inch thick
 ⅓ cup sake
 ¼ cup granulated sugar
 1 cup soy sauce
 7 large garlic cloves, minced
 4 scallions, white and tender green, minced
 3 tablespoons (packed) dark brown sugar
 ½ teaspoon Asian sesame oil
 1⅓ cups water
 2 tablespoons vegetable oil
 ¼ teaspoon freshly ground pepper

1. In a large glass or ceramic baking dish, rub the ribs all over with the sake and granulated sugar. Cover and let stand for 10 to 15 minutes.

2. Meanwhile, in a medium bowl, combine the soy sauce, garlic, scallions, brown sugar and sesame oil. Add the water and stir until the sugar dissolves. Stir in the vegetable oil and pepper. Pour this marinade over the ribs and turn to coat evenly. Cover and refrigerate overnight. Let the ribs return to room temperature before cooking.

3. Preheat the broiler. Broil the ribs about 3 inches from the heat until browned, about 6 minutes on each side. Serve the ribs as is, or cut them between the bones for smaller pieces.

—*Linda Burum and Linda Merinoff*

Braised Short Ribs with Whole Grain Mustard

8 SERVINGS

These succulent, twice-cooked short ribs need to marinate overnight in red wine before braising; plan accordingly.

 1 bottle full-bodied red wine, such as Côtes du Rhône
 2 medium carrots, coarsely chopped
 1 large leek, white and tender green, coarsely chopped
 5 garlic cloves, coarsely chopped
 4 parsley sprigs
 2 thyme sprigs

Sake-Marinated Beef Ribs

1 bay leaf
8 beef short ribs (about 5½ pounds), trimmed of excess fat
Salt and freshly ground pepper
½ cup all-purpose flour, for dredging
¼ cup vegetable oil
1 quart rich veal stock, or one 6½-ounce container demiglace diluted in 3 cups of water (see Note)
2 tablespoons grainy mustard

1. In a large saucepan, bring the wine to a boil over moderately high heat. Remove from the heat and add the carrots, leek, garlic, parsley and thyme sprigs and bay leaf. Let the marinade cool. Spread the short ribs in a large shallow baking dish in a single layer. Pour the marinade over the ribs, cover and refrigerate overnight.

2. Preheat the oven to 300°. Remove the short ribs from the marinade. Strain the marinade, reserving the liquid and vegetables separately. Discard the herb sprigs and bay leaf.

3. Season the ribs with salt and pepper and dredge them in the flour. In a large skillet, heat 2 tablespoons of the oil until almost smoking. Add half of the ribs and cook over moderately high heat until well browned, about 4 minutes per side. Transfer the ribs to a large roasting pan. Brown the remaining ribs in the remaining 2 tablespoons of oil and add them to the roasting pan in a single layer.

4. Pour off all but 1 tablespoon of fat from the skillet. Add the reserved vegetables and cook over high heat until beginning to brown, about 4 minutes. Spoon the vegetables over the ribs. Add the marinade to the skillet and bring to a boil. Pour the marinade over the ribs and add the veal stock. Cover with aluminum foil and bake for about 3 hours, or until the meat is very tender and almost falling off the bone.

Transfer the ribs to a large baking dish. Leave the oven on.

5. Strain the cooking juices into a large saucepan and skim the fat from the surface. Boil over high heat until reduced to 2 cups, about 15 minutes. Whisk in the mustard; season with salt and pepper. Pour over the ribs.

6. Return the ribs to the oven and bake for 30 minutes. Let cool slightly before serving. —*Joseph and Thomas Keller*

MAKE AHEAD The short ribs can be prepared through Step 5 and refrigerated for up to 2 days. Let return to room temperature before baking.

NOTE Veal-and-duck demiglace is available by mail order from D'Artagnan, 800-327-8246.

WINE The big, meaty flavors of the braised short ribs match the complex dark fruit character of the 1995 Pahlmeyer red Bordeaux Blend. An alternative: the 1994 Ridge Geyserville, a Zinfandel blend; its extracted dark jammy fruit and hints of smoke and leather suit the braised meat and tender vegetables.

Sake-Marinated Beef Ribs

8 SERVINGS

Have your butcher cut the beef ribs across the bone for you; this makes for manageable pieces of meat. Remember to allow time for the ribs to marinate overnight.

8 meaty beef short ribs (8 pounds), cut crosswise into 2-inch lengths
3 cups sake (rice wine)
2 large onions, thinly sliced
2 medium carrots, finely chopped
1 celery rib, finely chopped
24 green olives, pitted
1 tablespoon ground coriander
1 teaspoon minced garlic
1 teaspoon finely grated fresh ginger
1 teaspoon ground turmeric
1 teaspoon curry powder
½ teaspoon cayenne pepper
Pinch of saffron threads
Salt and freshly ground white pepper
2 cups short-grain rice (about 14 ounces)
2 tablespoons soy sauce
1 tablespoon mascarpone cheese
2 tablespoons chopped flat-leaf parsley

1. Spread the ribs in an even layer in a large glass or ceramic baking dish. Pour 2 cups of the sake over the ribs, cover and let marinate overnight in the refrigerator.

2. Preheat the oven to 350°. Drain the marinated ribs. In a large roasting pan, toss the ribs with the onions, carrots, celery, olives, coriander, garlic, ginger, turmeric, curry powder, cayenne, saffron and the remaining 1 cup of sake; season with salt and white pepper. Cover with aluminum foil and roast, turning the ribs halfway through cooking, for about 3 hours, or until the meat is very tender; skim the fat occasionally. Season the ribs with salt and white pepper.

3. Meanwhile, bring a large saucepan of salted water to a boil. Add the rice and boil over moderate heat until tender, about 17 minutes. Drain the rice and return it to the saucepan. Stir in the soy sauce and mascarpone.

4. Spoon the rice into 4 bowls. Spoon the short ribs and sauce over the rice, garnish with the parsley and serve.
—*Tetsuya Wakuda*

MAKE AHEAD The beef ribs can be refrigerated for 3 days. Rewarm them on the stove.

WINE The dry but sweet sake marinade calls for a soft, generous red wine without too much tannin. Consider the 1996 Rosemount Estate South Eastern Cabernet Sauvignon from Australia or the 1995 Markham Napa Valley Merlot.

Sunflower Seed–Crusted Lamb Loin, with Cauliflower Puree (p. 314) and peas and beans.

Black Truffle Hamburgers with Watercress Salad

4 SERVINGS ✳

Jeremiah Tower, chef and co-owner of San Francisco's legendary Stars, recommends using two truffles to flavor his indulgent burgers. To infuse the burgers with a deeper truffle flavor, refrigerate them for up to eight hours before cooking.

- 1 pound coarsely ground sirloin (not extra-lean)
- One to two 2-inch fresh black truffles, peeled and coarsely chopped
- 2 teaspoons pure olive oil
- Salt and freshly ground pepper
- 4 English muffins, halved and toasted
- 2 large bunches of watercress, tough stems discarded
- 2½ tablespoons untoasted walnut oil
- 1 tablespoon fresh lemon juice

1. In a bowl, gently combine the sirloin and truffle and shape into 4 thick burgers. Set the burgers on a plate, cover with plastic wrap and let stand at room temperature for 30 minutes.

2. In a large heavy skillet, heat the olive oil until shimmering. Season the burgers with salt and pepper and cook over high heat until browned, about 3 minutes per side for medium rare. Set the burgers on the toasted English muffins.

3. Toss the watercress with the walnut oil and lemon juice. Season the salad with salt and pepper and serve with the burgers.   —*Jeremiah Tower*

WINE This upscale burger needs a gutsy red with earthy, truffly flavors of its own, such as the 1995 Stags' Leap Winery Petite Syrah from California or the 1995 Penfolds Shiraz-Mourvèdre-Grenache from Australia.

Sunflower Seed–Crusted Lamb Loin

8 SERVINGS

Alan Tardi, chef and owner of the restaurant Follonico in New York City, serves lamb with a lavender and balsamic vinegar dressing for a unique flavor combination.

2 **well-trimmed boneless lamb loins (¾ pound each)**
Salt and freshly ground pepper
1 **large egg white, lightly beaten**
1 **cup raw sunflower seeds (3½ ounces), finely chopped**
1 **tablespoon all-purpose flour**
2 **tablespoons pure olive oil**
Lavender Balsamic Vinaigrette (recipe follows)

1. Preheat the oven to 400°. Season the lamb loins with salt and pepper and brush lightly with the egg white. On a plate, toss the sunflower seeds with the flour. Roll the lamb loins in the sunflower seeds until evenly and thoroughly coated.

2. Heat the oil in a large nonstick skillet. Add the lamb loins and cook over moderately high heat, turning with a spatula, until the sunflower seed crust is browned all over, about 2 minutes. Transfer the lamb loins to a rimmed baking sheet and roast for about 7 minutes for medium rare. Carve each loin into 12 slices.

3. Arrange 3 lamb medallions on each of 8 warmed dinner plates. Drizzle some of the Lavender Balsamic Vinaigrette around each portion of lamb and serve at once.

WINE This strongly flavored dish begs for a concentrated, earthy wine with an aroma of dried violets: L'Ecole No 41 Merlot from Washington State, a Ridge Zinfandel from California or a red from the southern Rhône Valley, such as a Gigondas or a Côtes du Rhône Villages.

LAVENDER BALSAMIC VINAIGRETTE
MAKES ABOUT 1 CUP

1 **teaspoon lavender or wildflower honey**
1½ **cups balsamic vinegar**
1 **tablespoon fresh lavender leaves**
2 **tablespoons extra-virgin olive oil**
Salt and freshly ground pepper
1 **teaspoon fresh lavender flowers**

In a medium saucepan, cook the honey over moderate heat until bubbling. Add the vinegar and lavender leaves and simmer over moderately low heat until reduced to ¾ cup, 8 to 10 minutes. Strain and let cool slightly. Whisk in the oil and season with salt and pepper. Add the lavender flowers just before serving. —*Alan Tardi*

Rack of Lamb with a Mustard and Herb Crust

8 SERVINGS

The great twist here is that the mustard and herbs are added after the lamb is grilled, so the flavors stay vibrant.

Two 1½-pound racks of lamb (8 chops each), ribs scraped clean
Freshly ground pepper
¼ **cup extra-virgin olive oil**
2 **tablespoons minced rosemary**
Salt
⅓ **cup Dijon mustard**
⅓ **cup minced herbs, such as parsley, mint, chives and tarragon**

1. Season the lamb racks with pepper. In a large shallow dish, combine the oil with the rosemary. Add the lamb and turn to coat. Cover and refrigerate for at least 1 hour or overnight.

2. Light a grill or preheat the oven to 500°. Season the lamb racks with salt and grill them, fat side down, until the fat is browned and very crisp, about 5 minutes. Turn the lamb racks and move

them away from the coals (if necessary, push the coals to one side). Cover and grill for about 10 minutes, turning, until an instant-read thermometer inserted into the meat registers 130° for medium rare. Alternatively, heat a large ovenproof skillet. Add the lamb racks, fat side down, and cook over moderately high heat until well browned, about 8 minutes. Turn the lamb racks and lightly brown the other meaty side, about 3 minutes. Transfer the lamb racks to a rimmed baking sheet and roast in the oven for about 10 minutes, or until an instant-read thermometer inserted into the meat registers 130° for medium rare. Transfer the

menu

Warm Figs with Feta and Basil
(p. 21)

Grilled Oysters with
Fennel Butter (p. 27)

Chicken Drumettes
with Romesco Sauce (p. 197)

1995 RAVENSWOOD SONOMA
OLD VINES ZINFANDEL

———

Spinach Salad with Prosciutto,
Portobellos and Cheese Fondue
(p. 77)

1996 RAVENSWOOD DICKERSON
VINEYARD ZINFANDEL

———

Rack of Lamb with a Mustard
and Herb Crust (p. 269)

Giant Lima Beans with Chives
(p. 309)

1996 RAVENSWOOD
MONTE ROSSO VINEYARD
ZINFANDEL

———

Preserved Lemon
and Apricot Cake (p. 367)

1997 RAVENSWOOD LATE HARVEST
GEWURZTRAMINER

Rack of Lamb with a Mustard and Herb Crust, with Giant Lima Beans with Chives (p. 309).

lamb racks to a cutting board and let stand for 5 minutes.

3. Brush the lamb racks generously with the mustard and pat the herbs on top. Carve the lamb racks into 8 double chops. Serve at once.

—*Tony Najiola*

Slow-Roasted Lamb in Rich Miso Sauce

4 SERVINGS

Delicate white miso (a paste made from fermented soybeans) mixed with a nugget of pungent blue cheese makes a rich sauce for these juicy lamb racks. Don't substitute one of the more strongly flavored darker misos; it will be overpowering.

- 1 cup chicken stock (p. 117) or canned low-sodium broth
- ⅓ cup Japanese white or light miso (about 3½ ounces)
- 2 tablespoons soft mild blue cheese, such as Saga Blue
- 1 teaspoon soy sauce
- 1 teaspoon mirin (sweet rice wine)

Two 2-pound racks of lamb (8 chops each), trimmed of fat, ribs scraped clean

Salt and freshly ground white pepper

- 3 tablespoons grapeseed oil or vegetable oil
- 1 medium red bell pepper, thinly sliced
- 2 large bunches of arugula, large stems discarded
- 1 tablespoon minced chives
- 1 teaspoon black sesame seeds

1. Preheat the oven to 450°. In a medium saucepan, bring the stock to a simmer over moderate heat. Stir in the miso until dissolved. Add the blue cheese and stir until dissolved. Add the soy sauce and mirin and simmer for 1 minute, stirring constantly. Strain the sauce into a clean saucepan.

2. Season the lamb with salt and white pepper. In a large ovenproof skillet,

heat 2 tablespoons of the oil until almost smoking. Set the lamb racks in the skillet, fat side down, and sear them over high heat until they are nicely browned, about 5 minutes. Turn the racks over and brown the bottoms, about 3 minutes. Transfer the skillet to the oven and roast the lamb racks for about 25 minutes for medium rare, or until an instant-read thermometer inserted in the thickest part of the meat registers 130°. Transfer the lamb racks to a cutting board, cover them loosely with aluminum foil and let them rest for 10 minutes.

3. Meanwhile, in a medium skillet, heat the remaining 1 tablespoon of oil. Add the red pepper and cook over moderately high heat until barely tender, about 2 minutes. Add the arugula and stir until just wilted. Season with salt and white pepper.

4. Reheat the sauce and season with salt and white pepper. Transfer the arugula mixture to 4 large plates. Carve the racks into individual chops and arrange 4 on each plate. Spoon about ¼ cup of the miso–blue cheese sauce over and around the meat. Sprinkle with the chives and black sesame seeds and serve at once.

—*Tetsuya Wakuda*

WINE Pick a spicy, full-flavored wine to match the blue cheese–enriched miso sauce. A Shiraz, such as the 1996 Hamilton Old Vines Reserve, is a traditional match for lamb in Australia. A French southern Rhône blend, such as the 1995 Château des Tours Vacqueyras, works equally well.

Mixed Grill with Sicilian Lemon Salad and Almond Mint Salsa

8 SERVINGS

LEMON SALAD

- 4 lemons
- ¼ cup plus 2 tablespoons extra-virgin olive oil

- 1 teaspoon sea salt
- 1 teaspoon freshly ground pepper

MIXED GRILL

- 8 small Portobello mushrooms (about 1½ pounds), stemmed
- ⅓ cup finely chopped red onion
- 2 anchovies, rinsed and mashed to a paste
- ¼ cup balsamic vinegar
- ¼ cup dry Marsala wine
- 8 chicken sausages (about 1¼ pounds)

Two 3-pound lamb racks (8 bones each)—trimmed, ribs scraped clean and racks cut into individual chops

Sea salt and freshly ground pepper

- 3 large bunches arugula, large stems discarded

Almond Mint Salsa (p. 358)

1. PREPARE THE LEMON SALAD: Using a small sharp knife, remove the peel and bitter white pith from the lemons; thinly slice the lemons crosswise. Transfer to a bowl, toss with the oil, sea salt and pepper and let stand for 20 minutes. ➤

Mixed Grill with Sicilian Lemon Salad and Almond Mint Salsa

271

2. PREPARE THE MIXED GRILL: Meanwhile, light a grill or preheat the broiler. Set the mushrooms in a large shallow dish, gill side up. In a small bowl, combine the onion, anchovies, vinegar and Marsala. Pour the marinade over the mushrooms; let stand at room temperature for 20 minutes.

3. Grill the mushrooms over a medium-high fire or broil them for about 15 minutes, turning, until tender and lightly charred. Transfer the mushrooms to a large platter, cover loosely with aluminum foil and keep warm. Prick the sausages all over with a fork and grill or broil for 10 to 15 minutes, turning, until cooked through. Add the sausages to the platter. Season the lamb chops with sea salt and pepper and grill for about 3 minutes per side for medium

rare. Arrange the lamb chops on the platter. Mound the arugula on the platter, pile the lemon salad alongside and serve with Almond Mint Salsa.

—*Mario Batali*

Leg of Lamb Kebabs with Pomegranate Glaze

8 SERVINGS

Boneless leg of lamb, now widely available, is a succulent choice for kebabs.

- 4 garlic cloves, minced
- 1½ tablespoons coarse salt
- ½ teaspoon ground coriander
- ½ teaspoon ground cardamom
- ¼ teaspoon paprika
- 4 pounds boneless leg of lamb, trimmed, cut into 1½-inch cubes
- 3 tablespoons olive oil

- 6 medium red bell peppers, cut into 1½-inch squares
- 2 medium white onions, cut into 1½-inch squares
- 2 tablespoons sugar
- 3 tablespoons rice wine vinegar
- 1 cup chicken stock (p. 117) or canned low-sodium broth
- ¼ cup pomegranate molasses (see Note)
- 1 serrano or jalapeño chile, seeded and finely chopped
- 1 tablespoon arrowroot dissolved in 1 tablespoon water

I. Light a grill or preheat the broiler. In a large shallow bowl, combine the garlic, coarse salt, coriander, cardamom and paprika. Add the lamb and olive oil; rub to coat the meat with the spice mixture. Thread the lamb, red peppers

Leg of Lamb Kebabs with Pomegranate Glaze, with Israeli Couscous and Corn Salad (p. 97) and Grilled Beans (p. 309).

and onions onto long metal skewers, alternating the meat and vegetables.

2. In a small saucepan, melt the sugar over moderate heat until it caramelizes, about 4 minutes. Add the vinegar and boil for 1 minute. Add the stock, pomegranate syrup and chile and boil until reduced to ¾ cup, about 8 minutes. Stir in the dissolved arrowroot.

3. Grill the kebabs over very high heat or broil, turning frequently, for 2 minutes. Move the kebabs to a cooler part of the grill or further from the broiler and brush them all over with the glaze. Grill or broil the kebabs for about 8 minutes, turning once, until the meat is slightly pink inside. Arrange the kebabs on a platter and drizzle with the remaining glaze. Serve at once.
—*Christer Larsson*

NOTE Pomegranate molasses is available at Middle Eastern groceries.

Dried Apricot and Lamb Sosaties

8 SERVINGS

Lamb *sosaties*, South African lamb kebabs, are the national favorite, but beef, pork and chicken *sosaties* are also common. The meat or poultry is marinated in a spicy curry sauce and then grilled until crisp on the outside but still moist and tender inside. The dish has its roots in Malay cuisine (*sosatie* comes from the Malay words *sate,* meaning spiced sauce, and *sesate,* meaning skewered meat).

½   **cup strained apricot jam**
⅓   **cup white wine vinegar or**
     rice wine vinegar
¼   **cup water**
2½ **tablespoons curry powder**
2   **garlic cloves, minced**
2   **teaspoons kosher salt**
2   **teaspoons ground coriander**
1½ **teaspoons minced fresh ginger**
4   **whole cloves**
4   **allspice berries**

Dried Apricot and Lamb Sosaties

1   **bay leaf**
½   **teaspoon ground cumin**
¼   **teaspoon freshly ground pepper**
1½ **pounds trimmed boneless leg**
     of lamb, cut into 1-inch cubes
24 **dried apricots (about 7 ounces)**
Boiling water

1. In a medium saucepan, combine the jam, vinegar, water, curry powder, garlic, kosher salt, coriander, ginger, cloves, allspice, bay leaf, cumin and pepper. Bring to a boil and then simmer over low heat for 5 minutes. Let the marinade cool completely.

2. Put the lamb in a large glass baking dish, add the marinade and toss to coat evenly. Cover and refrigerate for 2 hours, tossing the meat 2 or 3 times.

3. In a small heatproof bowl, cover the apricots with boiling water. Let plump for 1 hour; drain before using. Soak eight 8-inch bamboo skewers in water.

4. Thread the lamb cubes and apricots onto the skewers, using 3 apricots per skewer. Return the skewers to the marinade for up to 2 hours.

5. Light a grill or preheat the broiler. Grill or broil the lamb skewers for 12 to 15 minutes, basting and turning them occasionally, until the lamb is still slightly pink inside. Serve the lamb *sosaties* at once. —*Jenna Holst*

MAKE AHEAD The marinade can be refrigerated, covered, for up to 1 day.

Tangy Lamb Stew with Lettuce and Scallions

8 SERVINGS

The cooking time for this stew is only thirty minutes because tender leg of lamb cooks more quickly than other cuts. Serve the stew with french fries or steamed rice, which will soak up the delicious juices.

3 tablespoons olive oil

3 pounds trimmed boneless leg of lamb, cut into 1-inch chunks

Salt and freshly ground pepper

1 cup dry white wine

12 medium scallions, finely chopped

2 tablespoons unsalted butter

2 cups water

2 large heads Romaine lettuce (2½ pounds), cut crosswise into ½-inch-wide strips

3 large eggs

⅔ cup fresh lemon juice

2 tablespoons cornmeal mixed with 2 tablespoons water

2 tablespoons chopped dill

½ pound feta cheese, sliced

1. In a large enameled cast-iron casserole, heat 1 tablespoon of the oil. Season the lamb with salt and pepper. Add one-third of the meat to the casserole and brown it over moderately high heat; transfer to a plate. Repeat with the remaining oil and lamb in 2 batches.

2. Discard the fat from the casserole. Add the wine and boil until reduced by half, about 5 minutes. Return all the

Tangy Lamb Stew with Lettuce and Scallions

meat to the casserole along with any accumulated juices. Add the scallions and butter and season with salt and pepper. Add the water and lettuce and bring to a boil. Simmer the stew over low heat until the lamb is tender, about 30 minutes, pressing down occasionally to submerge the greens.

3. Meanwhile, in a medium glass or stainless-steel bowl, lightly beat the eggs. Beat in the lemon juice, cornmeal slurry and dill and then gradually beat in ¼ cup of the hot cooking liquid. Add the egg mixture to the casserole and cook, stirring constantly, until the sauce thickens; do not boil or the eggs will curdle. Serve hot with feta cheese. —*Fany Boutari*

MAKE AHEAD The stew can be prepared through Step 2 and refrigerated for up to 2 days.

WINE The 1992 Boutari Grande Reserve Naoussa.

Chile-Rubbed Lamb Steaks

4 SERVINGS ✳

Boneless lamb steaks, cut from the meaty sirloin or leg, grill beautifully and quickly because the meat is relatively

---

healthy stew tips

Fortify the broth by adding some polenta or rice; the thicker the stew, the richer it will seem. Or stir in coarsely chopped vegetables, such as meaty mushrooms or beans, to make the stew chunkier.

Don't try to make a totally fat-free stew. Sautéing the aromatics, and sometimes the meat, in just a little oil or butter improves the flavor dramatically.

Be sure not to overcook the meat, poultry or shellfish. The fastest way to ruin the taste of a stew is to toughen up the lean protein.

---

lean. The lamb here is flavored with a chile-accented rub that's mixed with just a bit of olive oil to balance the spices.

½ teaspoon cumin seeds
1 tablespoon ancho chile powder
½ teaspoon salt
¼ teaspoon oregano
⅛ teaspoon cinnamon
1 tablespoon olive oil
Four ½-pound lamb sirloins or boneless lamb leg steaks, about 1 inch thick

1. Light a grill. In a small skillet, toast the cumin seeds over moderate heat until fragrant, about 1 minute. Let cool slightly and then transfer to a mortar or spice grinder and grind to a powder. In a small bowl, combine the ground cumin with the chile powder, salt, oregano and cinnamon. Stir in the oil and then rub the spice paste into the lamb steaks.

2. Light a grill or preheat a grill pan. Grill the lamb over a medium-hot fire or in a grill pan over moderately high heat for about 5 minutes per side, or until an instant-read thermometer inserted in the thickest part of the meat registers 125° for medium rare. Transfer the lamb to a cutting board, cover with aluminum foil and let rest for 5 minutes before serving.

—*Jan Newberry*

Spiced Lamb Steaks and Chickpea "Fries"

6 SERVINGS

This dish bridges two continents: Africa and Europe. Lamb is the preferred meat for grilling in North Africa—served sizzling off the fire at outdoor stalls and casual restaurants. The seasoning here is a Tunisian spice mix called *tabil*. Rubbing toasted caraway and hot pepper flakes on the meat gives a unique flavor. As for the "fries," they're

actually strips of chickpea flour dough cut to look like french fries.

1 tablespoon coriander seeds
1 tablespoon cumin seeds
1 tablespoon caraway seeds
1 tablespoon crushed red pepper
1 tablespoon coarse sea salt
2 tablespoons vegetable oil
Six ½-pound lamb steaks cut from the leg
Chickpea "Fries" (recipe follows)

1. Put the coriander, cumin and caraway seeds in a small dry skillet and toast over moderate heat until fragrant, about 3 minutes. Transfer the spices to a bowl and let cool. In a spice mill, grind the toasted spices to a fine powder with the red pepper and sea salt. Put the ground spices in a bowl and stir in the oil.

2. Light a grill or preheat a grill pan and oil it lightly. Rub the lamb with the spice paste and grill over a hot fire for 5 minutes per side for medium rare. Transfer to plates and serve with the Chickpea "Fries."

WINE The pointed, inky concentration of such Syrah-based wines as the 1994 Château Fortia Châteauneuf-du-Pape from France and the 1996 Wynns Coonawarra Estate Shiraz from Australia will echo the spicy coriander, cumin and caraway rub.

CHICKPEA "FRIES"

6 SERVINGS

French fry–shaped fritters made from a chickpea flour dough are popular on both sides of the Mediterranean. In Provence they're called *panisses*. You wouldn't find garlic in the traditional recipe, but it flavors the dough beautifully. Chickpea flour has a wonderful flavor that is simultaneously toasty, nutty and earthy. It's available at Indian grocery stores (where it's called *besan*) and health food stores. The dough needs to chill overnight.

Spiced Lamb Steaks and Chickpea "Fries"

2 cups chickpea flour (about
½ pound)

2 tablespoons minced parsley

1 garlic clove, minced

½ teaspoon freshly ground pepper

Salt

2⅓ cups water

Vegetable oil, for frying

1. In a heavy medium saucepan, combine the chickpea flour with the parsley, garlic, pepper and 1 teaspoon of salt. Whisk in the water in a thin stream until a smooth paste forms. Boil the mixture over moderately high heat, whisking constantly, until very thick, about 5 minutes. Beat with a wooden spoon until smooth.

2. Scrape the chickpea dough into a 12-by-7½-inch baking dish and then smooth the surface. Let the dough cool to room temperature. Press a piece of plastic wrap directly on the dough and refrigerate for at least 6 hours or overnight.

3. In a medium skillet, heat 2 inches of oil to 350°. Unmold the chickpea dough onto a cutting board. Cut it in half lengthwise and then slice crosswise into ½-inch-wide sticks. Fry the chickpea sticks in 2 batches until golden brown, 2 to 3 minutes. Using a slotted spoon, transfer the fries to paper towels to drain. Sprinkle with salt and serve at once.

—*Steven Raichlen*

Jerked Leg of Lamb

12 SERVINGS

The wonderful jerked lamb at the Blue Lagoon Restaurant in Port Antonio, Jamaica, was the inspiration for this dish. For the best flavor, marinate the meat overnight.

2½ tablespoons whole allspice
berries

One 2-inch piece of cinnamon
stick

2 teaspoons black peppercorns

2 whole cloves

⅓ cup soy sauce

1 small onion, chopped

4 garlic cloves, chopped

2 large scallions, chopped

2 tablespoons vegetable oil

2 tablespoons dark rum

1 tablespoon thyme leaves

1 teaspoon salt

1 teaspoon freshly grated nutmeg

6 pounds boneless leg of lamb—
trimmed, cut into 3 equal
pieces and butterflied for
even thickness

1. In a medium skillet, combine the allspice berries, cinnamon stick, black peppercorns and whole cloves and cook over moderate heat until lightly toasted, about 1 minute. Transfer the toasted spices to a plate and let cool and then grind them to a powder in a spice grinder.

2. In a food processor, combine the soy sauce, onion, garlic, scallions, oil, rum, thyme, salt, nutmeg and ground spices and process to a paste. In a large shallow dish, coat the lamb with the marinade. Cover and refrigerate overnight.

3. Light a grill or preheat a broiler. Grill the leg of lamb over a moderately high flame or broil it for about 10 minutes per side for medium rare, rotating and turning the meat for even cooking. Transfer the leg of lamb to a cutting board and let it stand, loosely covered with aluminum foil, for 10 minutes. Carve the jerked leg of lamb across the grain and serve at once.

—*Marcia Kiesel*

WINE The intense marinade gives spice to the lamb, narrowing the wine choice to a red with a pronounced pepperiness. Something fruity would be welcome also. The solution? A fruity, spicy California Zinfandel, such as the 1996 Rabbit Ridge or the 1996 Alderbrook O.V.O.C.

Roasted Leg of Lamb with Gravy

12 SERVINGS

When it comes to cooking a bone-in leg of lamb, buy the short leg, also called a frenched leg or three-quarter leg. It has an intact sirloin section, with most of the hipbone, or aitchbone, removed, leaving a leg that has a classic look and will fit in most roasting pans. Choice-grade lamb is best since it's less fatty and usually younger than prime. Ask your butcher to remove the tailbone and the rest of the hipbone to facilitate carving, and also have him trim off any excess fat. For a nice overall shape, have the butcher tie the meat together where the hipbone was. Painting the entire roast with a mustard and garlic coating gives the meat an excellent flavor and obviates the need for basting.

1 cup Dijon mustard

4 large garlic cloves, pureed,
plus 2 large unpeeled cloves,
smashed

2 tablespoons soy sauce

1 teaspoon ground dried
rosemary

Jerked Leg of Lamb, with Cabbage and Green Bean Salad (p. 90) and Grilled Plantains, Pineapple and Chayotes (p. 327).

½ cup light olive oil or vegetable
    oil
One 6- to 7-pound short leg of
    choice lamb, fat trimmed to
    ¹⁄₁₆ inch, the roast tied
½ cup coarsely chopped carrots
½ cup coarsely chopped onions
1½ cups lamb or beef stock or
    canned low-sodium beef broth
2 tablespoons tomato sauce
Salt and freshly ground pepper

1. In a small bowl, whisk the mustard with the pureed garlic, soy sauce and rosemary. Gradually whisk in the oil until creamy. Set ¼ cup of the mixture aside and coat the lamb with the rest. Let the lamb stand at room temperature for several hours.

2. Preheat the oven to 350°. Set the coated lamb, fat side up, on a rack in a shallow flameproof roasting pan and cook in the lower third of the oven for 20 minutes. Scatter the carrots and onions and the smashed garlic in the pan and reduce the oven temperature to 325°. Continue roasting for about 1 hour and 40 minutes longer. The lamb will be done when an instant-read thermometer inserted in the thickest part of the meat registers 140° for pink meat. Transfer the lamb to a carving board or platter; let rest for 20 minutes. Remove all the strings before carving.

3. Meanwhile, spoon off all but 1 tablespoon of the fat from the roasting pan. Set the pan over 2 burners, add the stock and tomato sauce and bring to a boil over moderate heat, stirring and scraping up any brown bits from the bottom of the pan. Strain the sauce into a small saucepan, pressing hard on the solids to extract all the liquid. Whisk in the reserved mustard and garlic mixture and bring to a simmer. Season with salt and pepper and serve hot.   —*Julia Child*

WINE Red Bordeaux is the classic match for leg of lamb.

Braised Lamb Shanks with Peppers and Garlic

4 SERVINGS ★★★ **1986**

Jeremiah Tower was the chef at Chez Panisse in the early Seventies. He introduced this dish at Stars in San Francisco, which he opened in 1984.

4 lamb shanks (about 1 pound
    each)
1¼ teaspoons salt
1 teaspoon freshly ground black
    pepper
36 garlic cloves (from 3 heads)—
    24 peeled, 12 unpeeled
6 bay leaves
6 thyme sprigs plus 1 tablespoon
    thyme leaves
3½ cups chicken stock (p. 117) or
    canned low-sodium broth
1 large red bell pepper, cut into
    ¼-inch strips
1 large yellow bell pepper, cut into
    ¼-inch strips
1 tablespoon unsalted butter

1. Preheat the oven to 300°. Season the lamb with 1 teaspoon of the salt and ½ teaspoon of the black pepper

Roasted Leg of Lamb with Gravy

Braised Lamb Shanks with Peppers and Garlic

2. In an enameled cast-iron casserole just large enough to hold the lamb shanks, combine the shanks with the unpeeled garlic cloves, bay leaves and thyme sprigs. Cook the shanks over moderate heat until evenly browned, about 15 minutes. Cover the casserole and roast the shanks for 2 hours, or until very tender, turning every 20 minutes. Remove from the oven and let stand, covered, for 20 minutes.

3. Remove the lamb shanks and set them aside. Add the stock to the casserole and bring to a boil over high heat, scraping up any brown bits from the bottom with a wooden spoon. Continue boiling, skimming frequently, until reduced to 2 cups, about 10 minutes.

4. Strain the stock and return it to the casserole. Add the peeled garlic cloves and simmer gently until tender, about 20 minutes. Return the lamb to the casserole and add the red and yellow peppers and thyme leaves. Cover and cook until the peppers are tender, about 10 minutes.

5. Using a slotted spoon, transfer the lamb shanks to warm serving plates. Stir the butter into the sauce and season with the remaining ¼ teaspoon of salt and ½ teaspoon of black pepper. Spoon the sauce over and around the shanks and serve. —*Jeremiah Tower*

Lamb Shanks with Beans, Butternut Squash and Gremolata

2 SERVINGS

At Mel's Bar & Grill in Denver, executive chef Ben Davis wilts fresh spinach in the hot sauce in Step 7.

- 3 tablespoons olive oil
- 2 lamb shanks (1 pound each)

Salt and freshly ground pepper

- 8 garlic cloves, 6 unpeeled, 2 minced
- 3 celery ribs, coarsely chopped
- 2 carrots, coarsely chopped
- 1 large onion, coarsely chopped
- ¼ cup tomato paste
- 2 cups dry red wine
- 4 cups chicken stock (p. 117) or canned low-sodium broth

One 3-inch strip of orange zest

- 1½ pounds butternut squash, peeled and cut into 1-inch cubes
- 2 tablespoons chopped parsley
- 2 teaspoons finely grated lemon zest
- ⅔ cup cooked cannellini beans

1. Heat 2 tablespoons of the oil in a large enameled cast-iron casserole. Season the lamb shanks with salt and pepper, add them to the casserole and brown well on all sides, about 8 minutes. Transfer the shanks to a plate.

2. Preheat the oven to 350°. Add the unpeeled garlic cloves, celery, carrots and onion to the casserole. Cook over moderate heat, stirring occasionally, until golden brown, about 8 minutes. Add the tomato paste and cook, stirring, until glossy, about 2 minutes. Add the wine; boil over high heat until the liquid is very syrupy, about 15 minutes.

3. Return the shanks to the casserole and add the stock and orange zest. Bring to a simmer. Cover the casserole and braise the shanks in the oven for about 2 hours, or until the meat is very tender; turn the shanks from time to time as they cook.

4. Meanwhile, on a large rimmed baking sheet, toss the squash with the remaining 1 tablespoon of oil. Season with salt and pepper and bake in the oven (along with the lamb) for about 1 hour, or until tender.

5. In a small bowl, mix the minced garlic with the parsley and lemon zest. Set the gremolata aside.

6. Remove the shanks from the oven and transfer to a plate. Pass the sauce through a coarse strainer, pressing hard on the vegetables. Skim the fat from the surface of the sauce.

7. Return the sauce to the casserole, season with salt and pepper and bring to a boil over moderately high heat. Add the lamb shanks and squash; simmer just until warmed through. Add the cannellini beans, cover and remove from the heat. Let stand for a few minutes to allow the flavors to blend.

8. Spoon the vegetables and sauce into 2 large shallow bowls and set the lamb shanks on top. Garnish with the gremolata and serve.

—*Mel's Bar & Grill, Denver*

MAKE AHEAD With the exception of Step 5, the recipe can be prepared through Step 6 and refrigerated for up to 2 days.

WINE The 1994 Domaine le Sang des Cailloux Vacqueyras—a deep, rich, full-bodied Rhône red—is the perfect mate for this lamb.

Sula and Stuffed Tandoori Potatoes

4 SERVINGS

Sula (sometimes written *sule*) is the traditional barbecue of Rajasthan, the northwest Indian province that includes the Thar (Indian) Desert. It's unique in several ways. First, the type of meat: traditionally game is used, though we've suggested lamb as well. Second, the cut of meat: unlike the chunks or ground meat used for grilling elsewhere in India, *sula* is made from thin broad escalopes that are threaded onto skewers. Third, the heat source: it's customarily done on a hibachi-like grill. And finally, the seasoning: a piquant mixture of yogurt, ginger, garlic and lemon juice with a touch of heavy cream and a blast of cayenne pepper.

- 6 garlic cloves

One 2-inch piece of fresh ginger, peeled and coarsely chopped

- 1 cup plain whole milk yogurt
- ⅓ cup heavy cream
- 1 tablespoon fresh lemon juice
- 1 teaspoon cayenne pepper
- 1 teaspoon freshly ground black pepper
- 1 teaspoon garam masala or ground coriander
- ½ teaspoon caraway seeds
- 2 pounds boneless leg of lamb or venison in large trimmed pieces, sliced across the grain ¼ inch thick

Salt

Stuffed Tandoori Potatoes (recipe follows)

1. In a mini-processor, combine the garlic and ginger and puree until fairly smooth. Transfer to a medium glass or stainless-steel bowl and stir in the yogurt, cream, lemon juice, cayenne, black pepper, garam masala and caraway seeds. Add the meat and turn to coat. Let marinate at room temperature for 1 to 2 hours.

2. Light a grill or preheat a grill pan and oil it lightly. Using a rubber spatula, scrape some of the marinade off the meat. Thread the lamb onto 2 parallel skewers, keeping the meat slices as flat as possible. Season the meat with the salt and grill over a hot fire until browned, about 3 minutes per side. Serve the lamb hot with the tandoori potatoes.

WINE Indian spices can unravel the flavors of heavy reds, so pick a light, fruity wine that can be served cool, such as Beaujolais-Villages, as a refreshing foil to the spicy meat and rich potatoes. Among the top examples are the 1997 Georges Duboeuf and the 1997 Louis Jadot.

STUFFED TANDOORI POTATOES

6 SERVINGS

12 small red-skinned potatoes (about 2 pounds)

Salt

2 tablespoons vegetable oil

1 medium onion, finely chopped

1 garlic clove, minced

½ teaspoon cumin seeds

½ teaspoon turmeric

½ teaspoon cayenne pepper

2 cups finely shredded green cabbage

1 medium tomato, seeded and finely chopped

2 tablespoons coarsely chopped cashews

2 tablespoons finely chopped cilantro

½ cup grated Gouda or mild Cheddar cheese

Freshly ground black pepper

2 tablespoons melted butter

1. In a medium saucepan, cover the potatoes with cold water, add salt and bring to a boil. Cover and simmer over moderate heat until the potatoes are just tender throughout, 10 to 15 minutes. Drain in a colander, rinse under cold running water and drain again; pat thoroughly dry.

2. When the potatoes are cool, cut ½ inch off the top of each; reserve the caps. With a melon baller, scoop the insides of the potatoes into a bowl, leaving a ¼-inch-thick shell. Coarsely mash the potatoes in the bowl; reserve the shells and caps.

3. Preheat the oven to 400°. In a large skillet, heat the oil with the onion, garlic, cumin seeds, turmeric and cayenne. Cook over moderate heat, stirring frequently, until the onion begins to brown, about 5 minutes. Add the mashed potatoes, cabbage, tomato and cashews and cook, stirring, for 2 minutes. Cover and cook over low heat, stirring occasionally, until the vegetables are very tender, 10 to 15 minutes. Stir in the cilantro. Remove from the heat and stir in the cheese. Season generously with salt and black pepper.

4. Using a teaspoon, stuff the potato shells with the filling and cover with the reserved caps. Set the potatoes in a baking dish and brush with the melted butter. Bake for about 20 minutes, or until lightly browned and heated through. Serve hot or warm.

—*Steven Raichlen*

MAKE AHEAD The stuffed potatoes can be refrigerated overnight. Bring to room temperature before baking.

CHAPTER 10 bread pizza

A Shrimp, Tomato and Basil "Pizza" (p. 300).

Braided Challah

Braided Challah

MAKES 2 LARGE LOAVES

Here is a basic challah recipe, followed by directions for making twisted and braided rolls. There is also a variation baked in a loaf pan and one with raisins and cinnamon. A generous sprinkling of coarse salt or of seeds, such as poppy or sesame, can add another layer of flavor to the already delectable challah. Use 1 teaspoon of coarse salt, or 1 tablespoon of poppy or sesame seeds, topping the dough after the second egg glazing.

- 2 packages active dry yeast
- ½ cup lukewarm water (105° to 110°)
- ⅓ cup sugar, plus a pinch
- 1 stick (4 ounces) unsalted butter, thinly sliced, plus 2 tablespoons, melted
- 1 cup warm milk
- 1 tablespoon honey
- 2½ teaspoons salt
- 4 extra-large eggs, at room temperature, plus 1 extra-large egg beaten with 1 extra-large egg yolk and 1 tablespoon water, for glazing

About 6 cups bread flour

Cornmeal, for dusting

1. In a small bowl, dissolve the yeast in the lukewarm water with the pinch of sugar and let stand until creamy and starting to bubble. In a medium saucepan, combine the sliced butter and the milk. Warm over low heat just until the butter melts. Stir in the remaining ⅓ cup of sugar and the honey and salt. Pour the milk mixture into a large bowl and then stir in the dissolved yeast and the 4 eggs.

2. Stir in just enough of the flour, ½ cup at a time, to form a dense dough that doesn't stick to the side of the bowl. Turn the dough out onto a lightly floured surface and knead until smooth and elastic, adding only as much flour as necessary to keep the dough from sticking.

3. Brush a large bowl with 1½ tablespoons of the melted butter. Transfer the dough to the buttered bowl; brush the top with the remaining ½ tablespoon of melted butter. Cover the bowl with plastic wrap and a kitchen towel and let rise in a warm, draft-free spot until doubled in bulk, about 2 hours.

4. Punch down the dough and then cover and let rise until doubled in bulk again, about 1¼ hours.

5. Line 2 large rimmed baking sheets with parchment paper and sprinkle the paper with cornmeal. On a lightly floured work surface, divide the dough in half. Cover one half with plastic wrap and divide the other half into 3 equal pieces. Using lightly floured hands, roll each piece into a 10-inch-long rope with tapered ends.

6. Arrange the 3 ropes side by side pointing toward you and just touching. Starting in the middle and working toward your body, braid the ropes together, bringing the outside ropes over the center one. Pinch the ends to seal and tuck them under. Turn the loaf around and repeat with the other half, this time braiding the outer ropes under the center one. Seal the ends, tuck them under and transfer the loaf to a prepared baking sheet; gently plump the loaf with your hands. Repeat with the remaining dough. Cover the loaves with kitchen towels and let them rise for 35 minutes.

7. Preheat the oven to 375°. Brush the loaves with the egg glaze. Let stand uncovered for 10 minutes and then brush again with the glaze. Bake the loaves in the upper and lower thirds of the oven, switching the pans halfway through baking, for 35 to 45 minutes, or until they are golden, feel light when lifted and sound hollow when tapped on the bottom. Loosely cover the loaves with aluminum foil if they become too brown during baking. Transfer the loaves to a rack and let them cool thoroughly before slicing.

MAKE AHEAD The dough can be prepared through Step 3 and refrigerated up to 2 days before proceeding.

INDIVIDUAL BRAIDED CHALLAH ROLLS

MAKES 16 ROLLS

Follow the recipe for Braided Challah through Step 3. Refrigerate the dough in the covered bowl until chilled. Transfer the dough to a lightly floured work surface and divide the dough into 16 equal pieces. Divide 1 piece into thirds and roll each third into a 6-inch rope. Braid the ropes, tuck the ends under the roll and transfer to the prepared baking sheet; shape the remaining rolls. Cover loosely with a kitchen towel and let rise for 35 minutes. Glaze twice, as directed in the Braided Challah recipe, and bake the rolls at 375° for 25 to 30 minutes, or until golden. Let the rolls cool on a rack.

INDIVIDUAL TWISTED CHALLAH ROLLS

MAKES 16 ROLLS

Follow the recipe for Braided Challah through Step 3. Refrigerate the dough in the covered bowl until chilled. Transfer the dough to a lightly floured work surface and divide into 16 pieces. Divide 1 piece in half and roll each half into a 6-inch rope. Twist the ropes together, elongating them slightly. Put your thumb down on 1 end of the roll and twist the other end to tighten. Pinch and tuck the ends under the roll and transfer to the prepared baking sheets; shape the remaining rolls. Cover loosely with a kitchen towel and let rise for 35 minutes. Glaze twice, as directed in the Braided Challah recipe, and bake the rolls at 375° for 25 to 30 minutes, or until golden. Let the rolls cool on a rack.

A sandwich made with Loaf Pan Challah.

LOAF PAN CHALLAH

MAKES THREE 8-BY-4-INCH
LOAVES

Follow the recipe for Braided Challah through Step 4. Generously butter three 8-by-4-inch loaf pans and sprinkle them with cornmeal. Punch down the dough, turn it out onto a lightly floured surface and divide it into 3 equal pieces. Flatten 1 piece of dough gently with your hand and roll it out to a 10-by-8-inch rectangle. Starting from the short end, roll the dough into a snug log. Pinch the ends well to seal. Set the loaf, seam side down, in 1 of the prepared loaf pans. Repeat with the remaining dough. Cover and let rise for 35 minutes, and then glaze the tops twice, as directed in the Braided Challah recipe. Bake at 375° for 30 to 35 minutes, or until golden. Turn the loaves out and let cool on a rack.

RAISIN CHALLAH WITH A CINNAMON SWIRL

MAKES THREE 8-BY-4-INCH
LOAVES

Follow the recipe for Braided Challah through Step 4, adding 1 cup each of golden and dark raisins to the milk and butter before warming in Step 1. Follow the directions for shaping Loaf

Pan Challah, omitting the cornmeal. Combine ¾ cup of sugar with 1½ tablespoons of cinnamon in a small bowl; before rolling up the dough, sprinkle each piece with ¼ cup of the cinnamon-sugar. Let the dough rise and then glaze twice. Bake the challah and let cool on a rack.   —*Lauren Groveman*

Challah French Toast

MAKES 4 SERVINGS
A wonderfully decadent way to start the day is with French toast made with rich homemade challah. It's also a great use for leftover challah.

  3 extra-large eggs
½ cup milk
½ teaspoon cinnamon
½ teaspoon pure vanilla extract
Pinch of freshly grated nutmeg
Four ¾-inch-thick slices of Braided
        Challah (p. 285), Loaf Pan
        Challah (recipe at left) or Raisin
        Challah with a Cinnamon Swirl
        (recipe above)
2½ tablespoons unsalted butter
Warm pure maple syrup, for serving

1. In a medium shallow baking dish or bowl, beat the eggs with the milk, cinnamon, vanilla and nutmeg until blended. Working with 1 challah slice at a time, soak the bread in the egg mixture, turning several times.

2. Meanwhile, melt the butter in a large heavy skillet until bubbling. Add 2 of the soaked challah slices. Cook until golden brown on the bottom, about 2 minutes. Turn and cook until golden brown on the second side, about 2 minutes longer. Repeat with the remaining egg-soaked challah. Serve hot with maple syrup. —*Lauren Groveman*

Bacon, Onion and Walnut Kugelhopf

10 SERVINGS
Alsatian bakers traditionally make this rich bread in hand-painted earthenware

molds, but steel, nonstick aluminum or glass molds are fine too.

  4 slices of bacon, cut crosswise
      into ¼-inch strips
  1 small onion, finely chopped
¾ cup lukewarm milk
¼ cup sugar
  1 teaspoon active dry yeast
  1 large egg
  1 teaspoon salt
2⅔ cups all-purpose flour
1½ sticks (6 ounces) unsalted
      butter, at room temperature—
      11 tablespoons cut into small
      pieces, 1 tablespoon melted
⅔ cup coarsely chopped walnuts
      (about 3 ounces)
17 whole almonds

1. In a medium skillet, cook the bacon slices over moderate heat, stirring, until they are lightly browned, about 7 minutes. Using a slotted spoon, transfer the bacon to paper towels. Add the onion to the skillet and cook, stirring, until softened but not browned, about 5 minutes; using a slotted spoon, transfer to paper towels.

2. In a standing mixer fitted with a paddle, combine the milk, sugar and yeast and let stand for 5 minutes. Add the egg and salt and beat at medium speed until blended. Gradually add the flour and continue beating until the dough is elastic, about 4 minutes. Gradually add the 11 tablespoons of softened butter, beating until the dough comes cleanly off the side of the bowl, about 8 minutes. At low speed, beat in the bacon, onion and walnuts until they are evenly distributed throughout the dough. Cover the bowl with plastic wrap and let the dough rise at warm room temperature until doubled in bulk, 2 to 3 hours.

3. Generously butter a 9-inch kugelhopf mold or fluted tube pan and set the almonds in the indentations in the bottom. Punch down the dough, shape

it into a ball and make a hole in the middle. Set the ring of dough in the mold; cover and let rise until it almost reaches the top of the mold, about 1 hour.

4. Preheat the oven to 375°. Bake the kugelhopf for about 40 minutes, or until golden brown. Transfer to a rack and let stand for 10 minutes and then unmold. Brush with the melted butter while still warm and serve at room temperature. —*Pierre Hermé*

MAKE AHEAD The unbuttered kugelhopf can be wrapped in aluminum foil and stored at room temperature for 1 day; don't use the melted butter.

Walnut Bread

MAKES TWO 8-INCH LOAVES

This whole wheat bread studded with toasted walnuts is delectable with Foie Gras Terrine with Caramelized Apples (p. 65) or served with an assortment of cheeses after dinner.

- 2 cups walnuts (about ½ pound)
- 1 tablespoon plus 1 teaspoon active dry yeast
- 1½ cups lukewarm water (105° to 115°)
- 4 tablespoons unsalted butter, melted
- 1 large egg, lightly beaten
- 2 teaspoons salt
- 2½ cups all-purpose flour
- 2½ cups whole wheat flour

1. Preheat the oven to 350°. Spread the walnuts on a baking sheet and toast for about 8 minutes, or until deeply browned. Let cool.

2. In a large bowl, sprinkle the yeast over the water; let stand until foamy. Stir in the butter, egg and salt. Add the all-purpose flour, whole wheat flour and walnuts, stirring until the dough becomes stiff. Scrape the dough onto a lightly floured surface and knead until a smooth dough forms. Transfer the dough to a lightly oiled large bowl, cover with plastic wrap and let stand

Braided Challah (p. 285) can be turned into Raisin Challah with a Cinnamon Swirl.

in a warm place until doubled in bulk, about 1½ hours.

3. Punch the dough down and cut it in half. Knead each half briefly and shape into 6-inch rounds. Set the rounds on a large, lightly oiled baking sheet about 4 inches apart. Let stand until the rounds are almost doubled in volume and hold an impression when lightly pressed, about 30 minutes.

4. Preheat the oven to 375°. Bake the loaves in the center of the oven for about 50 minutes, or until they are nicely browned and sound hollow when tapped on the bottom. Transfer to a rack to cool completely before slicing. —*The Point, Lake Saranac, New York*

MAKE AHEAD The loaves can be frozen for up to 2 weeks.

Garlic, Herb and Cheese Pot Bread

MAKES 1 10-INCH ROUND LOAF

Pot bread, or *potbrood,* is traditionally served at *braais,* or South African spit roasts. It was once baked in a cast-iron Dutch oven set directly in the hot ash-gray coals, with more coals piled on the lid. Today, most South Africans bake the bread in a conventional oven.

- 2 cups warm water (105° to 115°)
- 1 tablespoon active dry yeast
- 1 tablespoon sugar
- 2½ tablespoons olive oil
- 5¾ cups unbleached all-purpose flour
- 2 teaspoons salt
- 1½ tablespoons minced garlic
- ½ cup minced flat-leaf parsley

2 tablespoons minced scallion
greens

2 teaspoons minced rosemary

1½ cups coarsely grated sharp
Cheddar cheese (4½ ounces)

ı. In a bowl, combine the water, yeast and sugar and let stand until foamy, 5 to 8 minutes. Stir in 2 tablespoons of the oil.

2. In a large bowl, combine the flour and the salt and make a well in the center. Pour in the yeast mixture and stir well with a wooden spoon. Turn the dough out onto a lightly floured work surface and knead until it is smooth and satiny, about 7 minutes. Shape the dough into a ball and transfer it to a lightly oiled bowl; turn the dough ball to coat it evenly with oil. Cover the bowl with a damp kitchen towel and let the dough rise in a warm place until it is doubled in bulk, about 1½ hours.

3. Punch down the dough and knead it briefly while it is still in the bowl. Turn the dough out onto a lightly floured work surface and knead again until smooth, 2 to 3 minutes. Return the dough to the bowl and let rest, uncovered, for 20 minutes.

4. Meanwhile, in a small skillet, heat the remaining ½ tablespoon of olive oil. Add the garlic and cook over moderate heat, stirring occasionally, until softened but not browned, 1 to 2 minutes; set aside. In a small bowl, combine the parsley, scallion greens and rosemary.

5. Generously grease a 2½-quart round cast-iron casserole or a 10-inch skillet. Cut off a ½-cup-size piece of dough. Using a lightly floured rolling pin, roll the small piece of dough into a 10- to 12-inch round. Fit the dough round in the bottom and 1 inch up the side of the prepared casserole. Roll out the remaining dough to a 22-by-15-inch rectangle.

6. Spread the garlic evenly over the dough, leaving a 1-inch border. Sprinkle the herb mixture on the dough; spread the cheese evenly on top. Starting with a long side, roll the dough into a log. Cut 1 inch off each end and discard. Cut the log crosswise into 8 equal slices. Set 1 slice on its side in the center of the dough-lined casserole and arrange the remaining 7 slices around it. Let the dough rise, uncovered, until it is about 3 inches high, 1 to 1½ hours.

7. Preheat the oven to 350°. Bake the bread for 50 to 60 minutes, or until it is golden brown on top. Run a knife around the edge of the casserole to loosen the bread and then turn it out onto a rack. Using a clean kitchen towel, turn the bread right side up and let cool for 10 to 15 minutes before slicing. —*Jenna Holst*

MAKE AHEAD The baked bread can be wrapped and frozen for 1 week.

Rye Berry Bread

MAKES 2 ROUND 9-INCH LOAVES
Thinly sliced, toasted or not, this dense, hearty whole-grain bread is wonderful topped with smoked salmon, sour cream and chopped onions, or with bitter orange marmalade. Allow time for the sponge to sit overnight.

SPONGE

3 cups whole wheat flour,
preferably organic

3 cups water

1 teaspoon active dry yeast

BREAD

1 cup whole rye berries (about
6 ounces)

3 cups water

Kosher salt

4 cups whole grain rye flour,
preferably organic

1 cup whole wheat flour,
preferably organic

2 teaspoons caraway seeds

Cornmeal, for dusting

ı. MAKE THE SPONGE: In a large bowl, mix the whole wheat flour with the water and yeast until blended. Cover and let stand overnight at room temperature.

2. MAKE THE BREAD: In a medium saucepan, cover the rye berries with the water, add a large pinch of kosher salt and bring to a boil. Cover and simmer over low heat until the rye berries are tender, about 45 minutes. Drain and let cool to room temperature.

3. Add the rye berries to the sponge. Using a wooden spoon, stir in the rye flour, whole wheat flour, caraway seeds and 1 tablespoon plus 1 teaspoon of kosher salt. When the dough becomes too stiff to mix, scrape it out onto a floured work surface. Using a dough scraper, lightly knead the dough, adding any leftover flour, until the dough forms a cohesive but sticky mass. Transfer the dough to a clean bowl. Cover and let stand in a cool place until the dough increases in volume by two-thirds and holds an impression when lightly pressed, about 2 hours.

4. Scrape the dough out onto a lightly floured surface. Using floured hands, briefly knead the dough. Cut it in half and shape each half into a 7-inch round. Sprinkle a large peel or rimless baking sheet generously with cornmeal. Transfer the loaves to the sheet, leaving about 3 inches between them. Let stand in a cool place until the dough is well risen and holds a slight impression when lightly pressed, about 1 hour.

5. Set a pizza stone or baking tiles on the bottom shelf of the oven. Preheat the oven to 350° for 30 minutes. Slide the loaves onto the preheated stone or bake on the baking sheet for 30 minutes. Reduce the oven temperature to 325° and continue baking for about 45 minutes, or until the loaves are nicely risen and browned; they

should sound hollow when tapped on the bottom. Transfer the loaves to a rack to cool for at least 4 hours before slicing. —*Marcia Kiesel*

MAKE AHEAD The bread can be refrigerated for up to 10 days.

Cloverleaf Rolls

MAKES 2½ DOZEN

These elegant rolls made with a potato starter are an heirloom recipe Edna Lewis inherited from her mother. Be sure to allow time for the starter to stand overnight.

    1   medium baking potato
        (½ pound), peeled and cut into
        1-inch dice
    3   cups water
About 5½ cups plus 6 tablespoons
        all-purpose flour
    3   tablespoons sugar
    1   envelope active dry yeast
    1   cup milk, scalded and cooled
    2   large eggs, lightly beaten
    7   tablespoons unsalted butter,
        melted
    2   tablespoons lard or solid
        vegetable shortening, melted
        and cooled
    1   tablespoon salt

1. In a medium saucepan, cover the potato with the water and bring to a boil. Cook until the potato is just beginning to fall apart, about 15 minutes. Drain the potato, reserving 1 cup of the cooking liquid. Pass the potato through a ricer into a large bowl. Add the reserved potato water and let cool slightly. Stir in 6 tablespoons of the flour, the sugar and the yeast, cover the bowl with a kitchen towel and let stand overnight in a draft-free place.

2. Uncover the starter; it should be foamy, and smell slightly fermented. Add the milk, eggs and 2½ cups of the flour and stir until incorporated. Stir in 1 tablespoon of the butter, 2 tablespoons of the lard and the salt. Add the

remaining 3 cups of flour, 1 cup at a time, and stir vigorously to form a silky, slightly soft dough that pulls away from the bowl as you stir, about 8 minutes.

3. Transfer the dough to a lightly oiled bowl and turn to coat. Cover the bowl with plastic wrap and let the dough rise until doubled in bulk, about 1½ hours.

4. Gently deflate the dough by turning it in the bowl several times. Cover the bowl and let the dough rise again until doubled, about 40 minutes.

5. In a small bowl, combine the remaining 6 tablespoons of melted butter and 2 tablespoons of melted lard. Punch down the dough and divide it into 5 equal pieces. Cut each piece of dough into 18 equal pieces. Roll each piece into a ball; dip the balls in the melted butter and place 3 balls in each cup of a muffin pan. Continue to form the rolls, working with 1 large piece of dough at a time. Brush the tops of the rolls with some of the melted butter and lard and set aside in a draft-free spot until risen just beyond the rims of the muffin cups, about 1½ hours.

6. Preheat the oven to 425°. Bake the rolls in the lower and middle thirds of the oven for 15 minutes. Remove the rolls from the oven and brush liberally with the butter and lard. Return the rolls to the oven and bake for 5 to 6 minutes longer, or until golden all over. Serve warm or at room temperature.

—*Edna Lewis and Scott Peacock*

MAKE AHEAD The dough can be made through Step 4, gently deflated again, and then refrigerated overnight, covered.

Crisp Poppy and Sesame Lavash

MAKES 6 LARGE LAVASH

    1   envelope active dry yeast
    1½ cups lukewarm water
        (105° to 115°)
    3¼ cups all-purpose flour

Crisp Poppy and Sesame Lavashes

    1   tablespoon honey
    1   tablespoon light brown sugar
    1¼ teaspoons salt
    2   tablespoons poppy seeds
    1   tablespoon sesame seeds
    1   large egg, lightly beaten

1. In the bowl of a standing mixer fitted with a dough hook, dissolve the yeast in the water. Stir in 2 cups of the flour and the honey and brown sugar. Beat on medium speed for 1 minute. Cover with a kitchen towel and let stand for 1 hour.

2. On low speed, gradually beat the remaining 1¼ cups of flour and the salt into the sponge. Knead the dough at medium speed for 5 minutes. Cover and let stand at room temperature until doubled in bulk, about 2 hours.

3. Preheat the oven to 475°. Lightly oil 3 large baking sheets. In a small bowl, combine the poppy and sesame seeds. Transfer the dough to a lightly floured surface and shape into a log. Cut the dough into 6 equal pieces. Working with 1 piece at a time and keeping the rest covered and refrigerated, roll out the dough round on a lightly floured work surface to a 14-by-9-inch rectangle; if the dough seems too elastic, let it relax for a minute. Transfer the dough rectangle to an oiled baking

289

sheet, brush lightly with the beaten egg and sprinkle with 1½ teaspoons of the seeds.

4. Bake the lavash in the upper third of the oven for 8 to 10 minutes, or until crisp and golden brown in patches. Slide onto a rack and let cool completely. Meanwhile, roll out and bake the remaining lavash, oiling the baking sheets as necessary. Serve the lavash, breaking it into pieces at the table.

—*Christer Larsson*

MAKE AHEAD The lavash can be wrapped well and kept at room temperature for 1 day.

Skillet Pita Breads

MAKES 16 PITAS

1 envelope active dry yeast
2½ cups lukewarm water
   (105° to 115°)
3 cups all-purpose flour
1 tablespoon olive oil
1 tablespoon salt
3 cups whole wheat flour

1. In the bowl of a standing mixer fitted with a dough hook, dissolve the yeast in the lukewarm water. Let stand, stirring, until foamy, about 5 minutes. Add the all-purpose flour and mix on low speed for 1 minute. Cover the bowl with a kitchen towel and let stand for 1 hour.

2. Add the oil and salt to the sponge and gradually beat in the whole wheat flour on low speed. Increase the speed to high and knead until the dough is smooth, about 3 minutes. Cover and let stand until the dough has doubled in bulk, 1½ to 2 hours.

3. Divide the dough into 16 equal pieces and cover with a dish towel. On a lightly floured work surface, roll out each piece to a 7-inch round, about ⅛ inch thick. Stack the rounds between sheets of plastic wrap and cover with a dish towel.

4. Heat 2 lightly oiled cast-iron skillets. Place 1 dough round in each skillet and cook over moderately high heat for 20 seconds. Turn and cook until big bubbles appear in the pitas, about 1 minute. Turn again and cook until the pitas puff, 1 to 2 minutes longer. Wrap the pitas in a towel and keep warm while you cook the rest. Lightly oil the skillet as needed. Serve the pitas warm.

—*Christer Larsson*

Pal Appam

MAKES ABOUT 15 PANCAKES

Appam are bowl-shaped rice pancakes cooked on one side only in a curved iron pan. They are typically served with a coconut milk curry. Even if you can't duplicate the distinctive form, the sweet, yeasty flavor of this recipe is authentic.

4 teaspoons sugar
½ teaspoon active dry yeast
2½ cups warm water
¼ cup cream of rice cereal
2 cups rice flour
½ cup plus 2 tablespoons
   milk
1 teaspoon salt

1. In a small bowl, combine 1 teaspoon of the sugar and the yeast with ¾ cup of the water and let stand until frothy, about 10 minutes. Meanwhile, in a small saucepan, bring 1 cup of the water to a boil. Add the cream of rice; return to a boil. Reduce the heat to low. Cook, stirring, until thick, about 1 minute. Remove from the heat and let cool.

2. In a large bowl, combine the rice flour and 2 teaspoons of the sugar. Add the cream of rice, the yeast mixture and the remaining ¾ cup of water; whisk to form a thick batter. Cover the bowl with plastic wrap and let stand at room temperature until the batter has doubled in bulk and smells pleasantly sour, 8 hours or overnight.

3. Whisk the milk, salt and the remaining 1 teaspoon of sugar into the batter.

Heat an 8- to 10-inch nonstick skillet. Pour ¼ cup of the batter into the center of the skillet; it should sizzle and spread out quickly, forming a thin lacy pancake. (If the batter is too thick, thin it with a bit of milk.) Cover and cook over moderate heat on 1 side only until well browned on the bottom and dry on the surface, 2 to 3 minutes. Eat immediately or transfer to a platter and keep warm until all the Pal Appam are cooked. —*Maya Kaimal*

Dosas

MAKES ABOUT 16 DOSAS

Lacy pancakes made of urad dhal—a pulse, or dried edible legume seed—and rice are a mainstay of the South Indian diet. The batter needs to ferment. Since that takes place more readily in a tropical climate, yeast has been added here to speed up the process, but it is still important to keep the batter in a warm place.

½ cup split urad dhal, without
   skin (3½ ounces; see Note)
2 cups warm water
¼ teaspoon active dry yeast
1 cup rice flour
½ teaspoon salt
½ cup plain yogurt
1 tablespoon vegetable oil
1 tablespoon Asian sesame oil

1. Rinse the split urad dhal in several changes of water and then soak it for 4 hours. Drain before using.

2. In a food processor, combine the dhal with ½ cup of the water and pulse until finely ground.

3. In a large bowl, mix the yeast with 2 tablespoons of the water and let stand until foamy, about 10 minutes. Add the ground dhal, rice flour, salt and ¾ cup of the water and whisk until a smooth, thick batter forms. Cover loosely with plastic wrap and let stand in a warm place until foamy and doubled in bulk, 12 to 18 hours. Add the yogurt and the

remaining ½ cup plus 2 tablespoons of water to make a pourable batter.

4. In a small bowl, combine the vegetable and sesame oils. Heat a 10-inch cast-iron skillet over moderately low heat. Dip a paper towel in the oil and carefully wipe the inside of the skillet. Using a ladle, stir the batter and pour ¼ cup into the center of the skillet. Working quickly, spread the batter out evenly to make an 8-inch pancake; move the back of the ladle in a spiral motion from the center. Fill in any large holes with a little extra batter. When the top looks dry and the underside has browned, about 1 minute, turn the dosa and cook until lightly browned, about 30 seconds. Transfer to a platter and continue making dosas, wiping the skillet with oil each time. Serve the dosas as soon as possible.

—*Maya Kaimal*

NOTE Split urad dhal is available at Indian groceries and from these two mail-order sources: Kalustyan's, 212-685-3451, and Patel Brothers, 562-402-2953.

MAKE AHEAD The recipe can be prepared through Step 3 and refrigerated, covered, for up to 2 days.

SERVE WITH Red Coconut Chutney (p. 359) and Kerala Sambar (p. 327).

Corn Bread–Pecan Dressing

12 SERVINGS

Baking the dressing outside the bird reduces the risk of overcooking the turkey while attempting to fully cook the dressing. Whether you baste the dressing during baking or not is up to you, depending on how dry or moist you like it. Use the freshest pecans; they have the sweetest flavor and will enhance your dressing greatly. And be sure to dry your corn bread overnight.

Southern Corn Bread (recipe follows)

3 cups pecan halves (11 ounces)

8 thick slices of slab bacon

1 stick plus 2 tablespoons unsalted butter (5 ounces), 4 tablespoons melted

3 cups coarsely chopped onions

3 cups coarsely chopped celery

3 large shallots, minced

1½ tablespoons rubbed sage

1 tablespoon dried thyme

6 large eggs, beaten

1¾ cups chicken stock (p. 117) or canned low-sodium broth

Salt and freshly ground pepper

1. Break the corn bread into large pieces, scatter on a baking sheet and let dry overnight.

2. Preheat the oven to 400°. On a rimmed baking sheet, toast the pecans for about 10 minutes, or until nicely browned and fragrant. Transfer to a plate to cool. Reduce the oven temperature to 325°.

3. In a large skillet, cook the bacon in 6 tablespoons of the butter until very crisp, about 10 minutes; reserve the bacon for another use. Add the onions, celery, shallots, sage and thyme and cook over low heat until the vegetables are tender, about 25 minutes.

4. Tear the corn bread into 1½-inch pieces and place in a large bowl. Top with the cooked vegetable mixture and the pecans and toss well. Stir in the melted butter, the eggs and 1 cup of the stock. Season with 1½ teaspoons of salt and 1 teaspoon of pepper and mix well.

5. Butter a large shallow baking dish and add the corn bread dressing. Cover with aluminum foil and bake for 30 minutes. Uncover and baste the dressing with 6 tablespoons of the remaining stock. Bake for 10 minutes longer and then baste with the remaining 6 tablespoons of stock. Bake for 20 minutes longer, or until golden brown on top and heated through.

MAKE AHEAD The recipe can be prepared 1 day ahead through Step 2.

SOUTHERN CORN BREAD

MAKES ONE 10-INCH CORN BREAD

4 tablespoons unsalted butter

3 cups white cornmeal, preferably stone-ground

2 teaspoons cream of tartar

2 teaspoons salt

1 teaspoon baking soda

3 cups buttermilk

4 large eggs, beaten

1. Preheat the oven to 450°. Put the butter in a 10-inch cast-iron skillet and melt the butter in the oven.

2. Meanwhile, in a large bowl, mix the cornmeal with the cream of tartar, salt and baking soda. Add the buttermilk and eggs and stir to blend.

3. Remove the skillet from the oven and swirl to coat with butter. Pour the melted butter into the batter and stir just until incorporated. Scrape the batter into the hot skillet and bake for about 35 minutes, or until it is crusty around the edge and springy to the touch. Invert the corn bread onto a rack and let cool completely.

—*Edna Lewis and Scott Peacock*

MAKE AHEAD The corn bread can be stored in the refrigerator for 2 days.

"Festival"

MAKES 24 PIECES

According to legend, these light Jamaican corn bread fritters got their name because eating them is fun—like a festival.

1 cup all-purpose flour

½ cup cornmeal

1½ tablespoons sugar

¾ teaspoon salt

¼ teaspoon baking powder

⅛ teaspoon baking soda

¾ cup water

2 teaspoons vegetable oil, plus more for frying

1. In a bowl, combine the flour, cornmeal, sugar, salt, baking powder and baking soda. Add the water and the 2

teaspoons of oil and stir gently with a wooden spoon until the dough is thoroughly blended. Cover the dough with plastic wrap and let it stand at room temperature for 1 hour.

2. In a medium saucepan, heat 1 inch of oil to 350°. Using well-oiled hands, roll tablespoon-size pieces of the dough about 3 inches long. Flatten each piece of dough slightly and then drop it into the hot oil. If the dough sticks to your hands, just peel it off; don't worry about the shape. Fry 3 or 4 of the fritters at a time until they are golden brown, about 2 minutes per side. Using a slotted spoon, transfer the fritters to a rack set over a baking sheet to drain. Adjust the heat if necessary to keep the oil at 350°. Serve the hot fritters immediately.

—*Marcia Kiesel*

Sweet Potato Biscuits

Sweet Potato Biscuits

MAKES 1 DOZEN BISCUITS

Sweet potato makes these biscuits dense, sweet and moist. Delicious with roasted or grilled meats—or simply slathered with butter and honey—they're a must for holiday tables.

1⅔ **cups unbleached all-purpose flour**

1 **tablespoon light brown sugar**

2½ **teaspoons baking powder**

½ **teaspoon salt**

6 **tablespoons cold unsalted butter, cut into pieces**

1 **sweet potato (10 ounces)— baked, peeled and pureed**

¼ **cup cold half-and-half**

2 **tablespoons sesame seeds**

1. Preheat the oven to 425°. Line a baking sheet with parchment paper.

2. In a bowl, combine the flour, brown sugar, baking powder and salt. Cut in the butter with a pastry blender until the mixture resembles coarse crumbs. Stir in ¾ cup of the pureed sweet potato and the half-and-half and mix just until the dough comes together.

3. Turn the dough out onto a lightly floured work surface and knead gently 6 to 8 times, just until the dough holds together. Roll or pat the dough into an 8-inch square about ¾ inch thick. Sprinkle the dough with the sesame seeds and pat them in. Using a sharp knife, cut the dough into 12 squares. Arrange the biscuits ½ inch apart on the prepared sheet and bake for 15 to 18 minutes, or until they are golden brown. Serve the biscuits hot.

—*Beth Hensperger*

Sun-Dried Tomato Biscuits with Sausage Gravy

4 SERVINGS

When topped with a hearty gravy like the meaty one here, these large biscuits make a complete meal. They can also be cut smaller and served without the gravy in lieu of bread.

BISCUITS

2 **cups all-purpose flour**

1 **tablespoon baking powder**

1 **tablespoon sugar**

¾ **teaspoon salt**

1 **stick (4 ounces) cold unsalted butter, cut into small pieces**

½ **cup buttermilk**

¼ **cup minced red onion**

1 **large egg, lightly beaten**

2 **tablespoons finely chopped sun-dried tomatoes (oil-packed)**

GRAVY

¾ **pound breakfast sausage, casings discarded**

½ **medium onion, finely chopped**

2 **tablespoons finely chopped flat-leaf parsley**

1 **tablespoon finely chopped sage**

Salt and freshly ground pepper

1 tablespoon olive oil

½ pound mushrooms, thinly sliced

1 large leek, white and tender green, thinly sliced

⅓ cup all-purpose flour

2½ cups chicken stock (p. 117), canned low-sodium broth or milk

I. MAKE THE BISCUITS: Preheat the oven to 400° and lightly grease a baking sheet. In a large bowl, combine the flour, baking powder, sugar and salt. Using a pastry blender or 2 knives, cut the butter into the flour until it resembles small peas. In a small bowl, combine the buttermilk, onion, egg and sun-dried tomatoes. Stir the buttermilk mixture into the flour just until incorporated. Transfer the dough to a well-floured surface and knead 2 or 3 times.

2. Pat or roll the dough into a 7-inch square, about ¾ inch thick. Cut the dough into 4 squares and place on the prepared baking sheet. Reduce the oven temperature to 375° and bake on the center rack of the oven for about 25 minutes, or until the biscuits are golden on the bottom and cooked through.

3. MAKE THE GRAVY: In a medium bowl, combine the sausage with the onion, 1 tablespoon of the parsley, the sage and a generous pinch each of salt and pepper. Scoop walnut-size balls of the sausage mixture onto a large plate. In a large skillet, heat the oil. Add the sausage balls; cook over moderately high heat until browned all over, about 5 minutes, and then drain in a strainer set over a bowl.

4. Pour ¼ cup of the fat back into the skillet. Add the mushrooms and leek and cook over moderately high heat, stirring occasionally, until softened, about 5 minutes. Stir in the flour; cook, stirring, until lightly golden, about 2 minutes. Gradually stir in the stock

Sun-Dried Tomato Biscuits with Sausage Gravy

and cook over moderately low heat, stirring occasionally, until thickened, about 5 minutes. Return the sausage balls to the skillet and heat through. Season with salt and a generous pinch of pepper and stir in the remaining 1 tablespoon of parsley.

5. Split the biscuits in half and set the bottoms on 4 dinner plates. Top with the sausage gravy and biscuit tops.

—*Jesse Cool*

MAKE AHEAD Freeze the biscuits for up to 1 week; reheat in a 350° oven.

WINE Serve these gravy-soaked biscuits with a tart Tuscan red, such as the 1994 Contini Bonacossi Trefiano Carmignano or the 1995 Banfi Rosso di Montalcino.

Warm Yam Scones

MAKES 12 SCONES

One 7-ounce yam or sweet potato

⅓ cup sugar

2 tablespoons canola oil

1 large egg

1 teaspoon finely grated orange zest

½ teaspoon pure vanilla extract

1½ cups all-purpose flour

1½ teaspoons baking powder

1 teaspoon cinnamon

½ teaspoon ground ginger

¼ teaspoon ground cardamom

¼ teaspoon salt

1 tablespoon maple syrup

Warm Yam Scones

1. Preheat the oven to 375°. Prick the yam with a fork and bake for about 45 minutes, or until it is very soft. Alternatively, microwave the yam. Let cool and then peel and mash the yam until smooth. Set aside ¾ cup. Leave the oven on.

2. Coat a large baking sheet with oil or vegetable oil cooking spray. In a bowl, combine the ¾ cup cooked yam with the sugar, oil, egg, orange zest and vanilla. In a medium bowl, whisk together the flour, baking powder, cinnamon, ginger, cardamom and salt. Stir the dry ingredients into the yam mixture just until combined. Divide the dough in half.

3. Working on a lightly floured surface, pat each half into a 6-inch round. Cut each round into 6 wedges and brush the tops with the maple syrup. Arrange the wedges on the prepared baking sheet and bake for about 20 minutes, or until golden and cooked through. Serve warm.

—*Betsy Nelson and Jim Kyndberg*

ONE SCONE Calories 123 kcal, Total Fat 2.9 gm, Saturated Fat .3 gm

Cranberry Date Scones

MAKES 12 SCONES

These buttermilk scones with sugar-crusted tops are full of fall fruits.

- 3 cups unbleached all-purpose flour
- ½ cup sugar
- Grated zest of 1 large orange
- 1 tablespoon baking powder
- ½ teaspoon baking soda
- ½ teaspoon salt
- 1½ sticks (6 ounces) cold unsalted butter, cut into small pieces
- 1 heaping cup fresh or frozen cranberries (5 ounces)
- ½ cup chopped pitted dates
- 1 cup cold buttermilk
- 2 tablespoons sugar mixed with ⅛ teaspoon each cinnamon, allspice and mace, for sprinkling

1. Preheat the oven to 400°. Line a 15-by-12-inch baking sheet with parchment paper.

2. In a medium bowl, combine the flour, the ½ cup of sugar, the orange zest, baking powder, baking soda and salt. Cut in the butter until the mixture resembles coarse crumbs. Add the cranberries and dates and toss. Stir in the buttermilk until a stiff dough forms.

3. Turn the dough out onto a lightly floured work surface and knead gently just until the dough comes together. Divide in half and pat each piece into a 7-inch round about ¾ inch thick. Sprinkle the tops with the spiced-sugar mixture. Cut each round into 6 wedges.

4. Arrange the wedges ½ inch apart on the prepared baking sheet. Bake in the middle of the oven for 20 to 25 minutes or until golden brown. Serve warm.

—*Beth Hensperger*

Sour Cream Berry Muffins

MAKES 8 LARGE MUFFINS

Enjoy these cakey, ginger-laced muffins all year long; they were developed with frozen berries specifically in mind.

- 2 cups unbleached all-purpose flour
- 2 teaspoons baking powder
- ½ teaspoon baking soda
- ½ teaspoon salt
- 6 tablespoons unsalted butter, at room temperature
- ¾ cup sugar
- 1¼ cups sour cream
- 2 large eggs
- 2 cups unsweetened frozen blueberries, raspberries or blackberries (from a 12-ounce package)
- 3 tablespoons minced crystallized ginger

1. Preheat the oven to 375°. Coat 8 large muffin cups (3¼-inch diameter) with cooking spray.

2. In a large bowl, combine the flour, baking powder, baking soda and salt. In another bowl, beat the butter with ½ cup of the sugar until fluffy. Beat in the sour cream and eggs. Add the dry ingredients and stir just until evenly moistened; do not overmix. The batter will be very thick.

3. Spoon 3 tablespoons of the batter into each of the prepared muffin cups. Sprinkle with half of the frozen berries and crystallized ginger. Spoon another 3 tablespoons of batter on top and sprinkle with the remaining berries. Top with the remaining batter and sprinkle the muffins with the remaining ¼ cup of sugar and the remaining crystallized ginger.

4. Bake in the middle of the oven for about 35 minutes, or until the tops are golden brown and springy to the touch and a cake tester inserted into the center comes out clean. Let the muffins cool in the pan for 5 minutes before turning out. Serve warm.

—*Beth Hensperger*

MAKE AHEAD Let the muffins cool completely and then freeze in a resealable plastic bag for up to 1 month.

Maple Corn Bread with Pecans and Vanilla Currants

MAKES ONE 9-INCH CORN BREAD
A wedge of corn bread studded with corn kernels and nuts, spread with sweet butter and drizzled with maple syrup is delicious at breakfast.

- ¼ cup currants
- 1 tablespoon pure vanilla extract
- 1 cup finely ground yellow cornmeal, preferably stone-ground
- 1 cup unbleached all-purpose flour
- 1 teaspoon cream of tartar
- ½ teaspoon baking soda
- ½ teaspoon salt
- 2 large eggs
- 1 cup buttermilk
- ¼ cup pure maple syrup
- 6 tablespoons unsalted butter, melted, or ⅓ cup corn oil
- ¾ cup frozen yellow or white corn kernels
- ¼ cup chopped pecans

1. In a small bowl, toss the currants with the vanilla. Cover and let the currants stand at room temperature for 2 hours or overnight.

2. Preheat the oven to 375°. Coat a 9-inch-square baking pan with oil or vegetable oil cooking spray.

3. In a large bowl, combine the cornmeal, flour, cream of tartar, baking soda and salt. In a medium bowl, whisk the eggs and then whisk in the buttermilk and maple syrup. Add the egg mixture to the dry ingredients and pour the melted butter on top. Stir just until the batter is thoroughly blended and then fold in the currants, corn kernels and pecans.

4. Pour the batter into the prepared pan. Bake in the middle of the oven for 30 to 35 minutes, or until the bread is golden around the edges and the top feels firm when gently pressed. Let cool in the pan for 10 minutes before serving.   —Beth Hensperger

Pumpkin Bread

MAKES ONE 9-INCH LOAF
Let this delectable, spicy sweet bread cool before slicing. You can rewarm and butter the slices before serving

- 1½ cups all-purpose flour
- 1½ teaspoons cinnamon
- 1 teaspoon baking soda
- 1 teaspoon salt
- 1 teaspoon ground ginger
- ½ teaspoon freshly grated nutmeg
- ¼ teaspoon ground cloves
- ¼ teaspoon baking powder
- 6 tablespoons unsalted butter, softened
- 1½ cups light brown sugar
- 2 large eggs
- 1 cup canned unsweetened pumpkin puree
- 1 teaspoon pure vanilla extract
- ⅓ cup milk

1. Preheat the oven to 350°. Butter a 9-by-5-inch loaf pan; line the bottom with wax paper. In a bowl, sift together the flour, cinnamon, baking soda, salt, ginger, nutmeg, cloves and baking powder.

2. In a large bowl, beat the butter until creamy. Gradually add the brown sugar and beat for 4 minutes. Beat in the eggs, 1 at a time. Beat in the pumpkin puree. Stir the vanilla into the milk. Beat the dry ingredients into the pumpkin mixture in 3 additions at low speed, alternating with the milk mixture.

3. Spread the batter in the prepared pan. Bake for about 1 hour, or until a toothpick inserted in the center comes out clean. Let the loaf cool in the pan for 10 minutes and then turn it out onto a rack to cool.   —Rori Spinelli
MAKE AHEAD The bread can be wrapped well and stored at room temperature for up to 3 days.

Cranberry Date Scones

Banana Nut Bread

Spiced Brown Sugar Carrot Bread

MAKES TWO 8-BY-4-INCH LOAVES

Here is a moist, deep brown carrot-flecked bread with a very crisp crust.

- 3 cups unbleached all-purpose flour
- 2 teaspoons cinnamon
- 1½ teaspoons baking powder
- 1½ teaspoons baking soda
- 1 teaspoon crushed cardamom seeds
- ½ teaspoon salt
- 4 large eggs
- 1½ cups packed light brown sugar
- ½ cup granulated sugar
- 1 cup canola oil
- 1 teaspoon pure vanilla extract

Grated zest of 1 lemon
- 2½ cups shredded carrots (about 14 ounces)

1. Preheat the oven to 350°. Coat two 8-by-4-inch loaf pans with vegetable oil cooking spray or grease and lightly flour the pans.

2. In a medium bowl, combine the flour, cinnamon, baking powder, baking soda, cardamom and salt.

3. In a large bowl, beat the eggs with the brown and granulated sugars until smooth. Add the oil in a thin stream, beating at high speed until the batter has doubled in volume, about 2 minutes. Beat in the vanilla and lemon zest. Fold in the carrots. Beat in the dry ingredients at low speed in 3 batches, mixing well between additions.

4. Pour the batter into the prepared pans, filling them two-thirds full. Bake in the middle of the oven for 50 minutes to 1 hour, or until a cake tester inserted into the center of the loaves comes out clean. Let the loaves cool in the pans for 10 minutes before turning them out onto a rack to cool completely. —*Beth Hensperger*

MAKE AHEAD The bread can be wrapped tightly in plastic and stored at room temperature for up to 3 days or frozen for up to 2 months.

Banana Nut Bread

MAKES ONE 9-BY-5-INCH LOAF

If you like, you can make this banana bread regularly and have backup loaves in the freezer. It's a great way to use up overripe bananas. The nuts are toasted just enough to remove their raw edge before being added to the batter.

- ¾ cup coarsely chopped walnuts (3 ounces)
- 1¼ cups unbleached all-purpose flour

1 teaspoon baking soda
½ teaspoon cinnamon
½ teaspoon salt
1 cup sugar
2 large eggs
½ cup canola oil
3 medium overripe bananas, mashed (1¼ cups)
1 teaspoon pure vanilla extract

1. Preheat the oven to 350°. Coat a 9-by-5-inch loaf pan with oil or vegetable oil cooking spray. Spread the walnuts in a pie pan and toast in the oven for 5 to 8 minutes, or until fragrant; let cool.

2. In a medium bowl, whisk the flour with the baking soda, cinnamon and salt. In another bowl, combine the sugar, eggs and oil and beat at high speed until light-colored and creamy. Add the bananas and vanilla; beat until smooth. Stir in the dry ingredients until thoroughly blended. Fold in the nuts.

3. Pour the batter into the prepared pan and bake in the middle of the oven for 50 to 60 minutes, or until the top is springy and a cake tester inserted in the center comes out clean. Let the loaf cool in the pan for 10 minutes before turning it out onto a rack to cool completely. —*Beth Hensperger*
MAKE AHEAD The bread can be wrapped tightly in plastic and refrigerated for up to 5 days or frozen for up to 2 months.

Dried Apricot–Pecan Bread
MAKES TWO 7¼-BY-3½-INCH LOAVES
When chopping dried apricots, lightly oil the knife blade to prevent sticking.

1 cup sugar
1 cup boiling water
3 tablespoons unsalted butter
1½ cups dried apricots (10 ounces), coarsely chopped
2 cups unbleached all-purpose flour

1½ teaspoons baking soda
½ teaspoon salt
1 cup chopped pecans (4 ounces)
½ cup whole-wheat pastry flour (see Note)
2 large eggs
½ cup fresh orange juice

1. In a large bowl, combine the sugar, boiling water and butter. Stir to dissolve the sugar and then add the apricots. Set aside for 1 hour.

2. Preheat the oven to 350°. Coat two 7¼-by-3½-inch loaf pans with cooking spray or grease and flour the pans.

3. In a large bowl, combine the unbleached flour, baking soda and salt. Stir in the warm apricot mixture. Sprinkle the pecans and whole-wheat pastry flour over the batter. Add the eggs and orange juice and beat just until the ingredients are blended and the fruit and nuts are evenly distributed.

4. Pour the batter into the prepared pans and let stand for 15 minutes. Bake the loaves in the middle of the oven for 55 to 60 minutes, or until the tops are firm, the loaves pull away from the sides of the pan and a cake tester inserted into the centers comes out clean. Turn the loaves out onto a rack and let cool completely.
—*Beth Hensperger*
NOTE Whole-wheat pastry flour is available at most health-food stores and specialty shops.
MAKE AHEAD The bread can be wrapped tightly in plastic and refrigerated for up to 5 days or frozen for up to 2 months.

Herb and Onion Pizzettes
MAKES 16 PIZZETTES
Feel free to top these pizzettes with whatever ingredients you happen to have on hand; they're delicious with anchovies, sun-dried tomatoes, olives and cheese.

About 2½ cups unbleached all-purpose flour
1 envelope active dry yeast
1 cup lukewarm water (105° to 115°)
Salt
About ⅓ cup extra-virgin olive oil
1 medium red onion, very thinly sliced
3 tablespoons finely chopped flat-leaf parsley
1 teaspoon finely chopped rosemary
1 teaspoon finely chopped thyme
Freshly ground pepper

1. In a large bowl, combine ¼ cup of the flour with the yeast and ¼ cup of the water. Let stand in a warm place until foamy, about 30 minutes. Stir in 2¼ cups of the flour, the remaining ¾ cup of water and 1 teaspoon of salt to form a soft dough. Scrape the dough onto a lightly floured work surface and knead until silky and elastic, about 5 minutes; add just enough flour to keep the dough from sticking. Transfer the dough to a lightly oiled bowl, cover and let rise until it is doubled in bulk, about 1 hour.

2. Punch down the dough, cover and let rise for 30 minutes longer. Turn the dough out onto the work surface and divide it into 16 pieces. Let the dough pieces rest for 10 minutes before shaping them into rounds.

3. Meanwhile, set a pizza stone or baking tiles on a rack in the bottom third of the oven and then preheat the oven to 500°.

4. Roll out or stretch 4 pieces of dough into 5-inch rounds. Set the rounds on a lightly floured pizza peel or baking sheet and brush with a little of the oil. Scatter some of the onion, parsley, rosemary and thyme on top and season with salt and pepper. Slide as many pizzettes as will fit onto the pizza stone in the oven and bake for about 7

An Herb and Onion Pizzette, with Cherry Tomato Salad (p. 88).

minutes, or until the pizzettes are golden and crisp. Cut the pizzettes into wedges and serve them hot. Continue making the pizzettes in batches with the remaining ingredients.

—*Melissa Kelly*

MAKE AHEAD The dough can be prepared through Step 1 and refrigerated overnight.

Twin Pissaladières

MAKES TWO 8-INCH TARTS

The word *pissaladière* comes from *pissala,* a salted-fish concoction from Nice that's used as a savory topping for bread dough or pastry. This recipe is meant as a jumping-off point—let your own tastes dictate the toppings.

DOUGH

½ teaspoon active dry yeast

About ¼ cup lukewarm water (105° to 110°)

About 1½ cups unbleached all-purpose flour

1 large egg, beaten

2 tablespoons extra-virgin olive oil

TOPPING

1½ pounds onions, thinly sliced

3 garlic cloves, thinly sliced

2 tablespoons extra-virgin olive oil

8 large plum tomatoes—4 peeled, seeded and chopped, 4 sliced crosswise ¼ inch thick

Sea salt and freshly ground pepper

8 whole salt-packed anchovies (see Note), rinsed and filleted, or 16 oil-packed anchovy fillets, drained

20 Niçoise or Gaeta olives, halved and pitted

Basil leaves, torn

1. **MAKE THE DOUGH:** In a small bowl, stir the yeast into the water and set aside until foamy, about 5 minutes. Put 1½ cups of the flour in a large bowl and make a well in the center. Add the egg and olive oil to the well and start to incorporate the flour. As you mix, stir in the dissolved yeast. Continue mixing until a supple bread dough forms; you may need to add a little more flour or water as you mix.

2. Transfer the dough to a lightly floured work surface and knead for a few minutes, until silky smooth. Transfer the dough to a lightly oiled bowl, cover lightly with plastic wrap and set aside while you make the topping.

3. **MAKE THE TOPPING:** In a heavy saucepan or casserole, cook the onions and garlic in the olive oil over low heat, stirring often, until thoroughly softened and lightly golden, about 20 minutes. Add the chopped tomatoes and cook, stirring often, until the mixture is very thick, about 15 minutes. Season with sea salt and pepper and let cool.

4. Preheat the oven to 400°. Divide the dough into 2 pieces and roll each piece out to an 8-inch round about ¼ inch thick. (The rounds need not be regular in shape; in fact, irregularity is part of the charm.) Transfer each round to a lightly oiled cookie sheet.

5. Pinch around the edges of the dough to make very slightly raised borders. Spread the onion mixture over both dough rounds. On 1 tart, arrange the anchovy fillets in a lattice pattern and set the olives within the squares. On the other tart, scatter the sliced tomatoes and basil. Sprinkle both tarts with sea salt and pepper and bake in the center of the oven for about 25 minutes, or until the crusts are golden around the edges and the toppings are bubbling and beginning to brown. Cut into wedges and serve hot or at room temperature.

—*Nancy Harmon Jenkins*

NOTE Salt-packed anchovies are available at Greek and Italian markets, and their flavor and texture are worth the extra fuss. Rinse under running water and then separate each into 2 fillets, discarding the spine and any fins or tail pieces.

MAKE AHEAD The dough and the onion topping can be refrigerated separately overnight. Let both come to room temperature before assembling the tarts.

Arthur Schwartz's Pizza Marinara

MAKES FOUR 10-INCH PIZZAS

Arthur Schwartz, author of *Naples at Table: A Cook's Tour of Campania,* published by HarperCollins, says you may not be able to make *perfect* Neapolitan pizza at home, but you can make *very good* pizza. Don't worry if you can't form an even round; the taste of the dough is what counts.

DOUGH

1 envelope active dry yeast

1½ cups warm water

About 4 cups unbleached all-purpose flour

1½ teaspoons salt

TOPPING

20 canned peeled Italian plum tomatoes—seeded, finely chopped and drained well

2 teaspoons minced garlic

1 teaspoon dried crumbled
  oregano

6 tablespoons extra-virgin
  olive oil

1 teaspoon salt

1. MAKE THE DOUGH: In a 2-cup
glass measure, dissolve the yeast in
1 cup of the water. Stir in ½ cup of the
flour, cover and let stand until doubled
in bulk, about 30 minutes.

2. In a large bowl, combine 3½ cups
of the flour with the salt. Stir the yeast
mixture and add it to the bowl along
with the remaining ½ cup of warm
water; stir until the dough masses
together. Gather the dough into a ball
and turn it out onto a lightly floured
work surface. Knead until smooth and
elastic, about 10 minutes, adding just
enough flour to keep the dough from
sticking. Shape the dough into a ball
and transfer it to a lightly oiled bowl.
Cover and let rise until doubled in bulk,
about 1 hour.

3. Set a pizza stone or baking tiles in
the bottom of the oven and preheat to
500° for 30 minutes.

4. Punch down the dough. Divide it
into 4 pieces and roll each piece into
a ball. On a lightly floured surface, roll
or stretch 1 ball of dough into a 10-
inch round and transfer it to a floured
pizza peel or flat cookie sheet; keep
the rest of the dough covered with a
kitchen towel.

5. TOP THE PIZZA: Evenly cover
the dough with one-fourth of each of
the ingredients in the order given,
leaving a small border all around. Slide
the pizza onto the stone and bake for
about 8 minutes, or until the crust is
tinged with brown. Serve immediately.
Repeat to make the remaining pizzas.

—*Arthur Schwartz*

MAKE AHEAD The dough for the
pizzas can be refrigerated overnight or
frozen in individual plastic bags for up
to 2 weeks.

Dandelion Green and Shiitake Calzones

Dandelion Green and Shiitake Calzones

MAKES TWO 10-INCH CALZONES
You can use the leftover dandelion
stems in Pasta with Dandelion Stems
(p. 97). If you do not have a pizza
stone or baking tiles, bake the calzones on a single baking sheet. This
recipe can also be made into two
twelve-inch pizzas.

3 tablespoons extra-virgin olive
  oil, plus more for brushing

¼ pound shiitake mushrooms,
  stems discarded, caps sliced
  ⅜ inch thick

2 large garlic cloves, thinly sliced

1 pound young dandelion greens,
  stems removed

2 tablespoons water

Salt and freshly ground pepper

1 pound store-bought pizza dough,
  divided in half

½ pound shredded imported
  Fontina cheese

2 tablespoons freshly grated
  Parmesan cheese

1. Set a 16-by-14-inch pizza stone or
baking tiles on the bottom shelf of the
oven and preheat to 500° for at least
30 minutes. Meanwhile, in a large skillet, heat 2 tablespoons of the oil. Add
the shiitakes and cook over moderately high heat, stirring occasionally,
until beginning to brown, about 4 minutes. Add the garlic and cook, stirring
often, until lightly browned, about 3
minutes. Transfer the mushrooms and
garlic to a plate.

2. In the same skillet, heat 1 tablespoon of oil. Add the dandelion greens
and 1 tablespoon of the water and
cook, stirring, until wilted, about 4
minutes. Return the mushrooms and
garlic to the skillet, add the remaining

1 tablespoon of water and cook until the liquid is absorbed and the greens are al dente. Season with salt and pepper and transfer to a plate.

3. On a lightly floured surface, roll or stretch the dough to form two 10-inch rounds. Assemble 1 calzone at a time: transfer 1 dough round to a well-floured rimless cookie sheet. Sprinkle one-quarter of the Fontina on half of the dough, leaving a 1-inch border. Top with half of the dandelion mixture and another quarter of the Fontina. Fold the dough over to enclose the filling and press the edges together; crimp to seal. Using a toothpick, poke a hole in the top. Brush the calzone

with oil and sprinkle with 1 tablespoon of the Parmesan. Repeat with the remaining ingredients on a second rimless cookie sheet.

4. Jiggle the cookie sheets to release the calzones and slide them onto the pizza stone. Bake for about 11 minutes, or until the calzones are crisp and the filling is bubbling through the holes. Transfer to a rack. Cut the calzone in half and serve hot. —*Grace Parisi*

MAKE AHEAD The dandelion mixture can be cooked up to 1 day ahead and refrigerated.

WINE A straightforward, medium-bodied Bordeaux, such as the 1995 Michel Lynch Merlot, or a deeper

Médoc, such as the 1994 Château de Pez, would offer a pleasantly astringent contrast.

Shrimp, Tomato and Basil "Pizzas"

MAKES SIX 5½-INCH
PHYLLO PIZZAS

In these pretty and fragrant little pies, sheets of prepared phyllo replace the usual crust. The recipe, by Eric Ripert, the executive chef and co-owner of Le Bernardin in New York City, has been adapted from *Le Bernardin Cookbook,* published by Doubleday.

¼ cup extra-virgin olive oil

3 large garlic cloves, minced

A Shrimp, Tomato and Basil "Pizza."

2 large shallots, minced

7 medium tomatoes (about 2¼ pounds)—peeled, seeded and chopped

1 tablespoon tomato paste

1 large thyme sprig plus ¾ teaspoon thyme leaves

¼ teaspoon minced rosemary

Salt and freshly ground pepper

5 sheets phyllo dough

7 tablespoons unsalted butter— 6 melted, 1 softened

1¾ pounds medium shrimp— shelled, halved lengthwise down the back and deveined

¼ teaspoon saffron threads

1 tablespoon finely shredded basil

1. Preheat the oven to 375°. In a large saucepan, heat 2 tablespoons of the oil. Add the garlic and shallots and cook over moderately high heat until softened but not browned, about 3 minutes. Add the tomatoes, tomato paste, thyme sprig, rosemary and a generous pinch each of salt and pepper. Cook over moderate heat, stirring occasionally, until thick, about 20 minutes. Discard the thyme.

2. Meanwhile, line a baking sheet with parchment paper. On a work surface, brush 1 phyllo sheet with some of the melted butter and top with a second phyllo sheet. Continue brushing and layering the phyllo to make a stack of 5 sheets. Using a 5½-inch plate as a guide, cut out 6 stacked phyllo rounds. Transfer the rounds to the prepared baking sheet and cover with a sheet of parchment paper. Bake the phyllo rounds for about 12 minutes, or until they are crisp and golden. Discard the top paper.

3. Using the same plate, cut out 12 parchment paper rounds and brush 6 of them with the softened butter. Arrange the shrimp on the buttered paper rounds, cut side up, in a radial pattern,

overlapping them slightly. Cover with the remaining paper rounds and refrigerate until chilled, or for up to 3 hours.

4. Preheat the oven to 550°. Working quickly, spoon ¼ cup of the tomato sauce over each phyllo base. Remove the top paper from each shrimp round and invert it onto 1 of the phyllo bases. Remove the remaining paper rounds and then sprinkle the shrimp with the saffron and thyme leaves and season with salt and pepper. Drizzle with the remaining 2 tablespoons of oil and bake for about 7 minutes, or until the shrimp are pink and cooked through. Garnish with the basil and serve immediately. —*Eric Ripert*

MAKE AHEAD The "pizzas" can be made through Step 2 up to 1 day in advance. Store the phyllo rounds in an airtight container; refrigerate the sauce.

Charlie's Wood-Grilled Tailgate Pizza

MAKES TWO 15-INCH PIZZAS
Charlie Palmer, chef at Aureole in New York City, has dreamed up a pizza with three kinds of cheese, artichoke hearts, wild mushrooms and prosciutto.

3 cups all-purpose flour

¾ cup semolina flour

Two ¼-ounce packages of active dry yeast

Salt

1½ cups warm water

3 tablespoons olive oil

1 tablespoon honey

1 pound shiitake mushrooms, stems discarded, caps sliced ½ inch thick

Freshly ground pepper

Two 6.5-ounce jars of oil-packed artichoke hearts, drained

½ pound thinly sliced prosciutto

½ pound thinly sliced Fontina

½ pound thinly sliced smoked mozzarella

¼ cup freshly grated Parmesan

1. In a large bowl, combine the flours, yeast and 1 teaspoon of salt. In a small bowl, whisk together the water, 1 tablespoon of the oil and the honey and then stir the liquid into the dry ingredients. Scrape the dough out onto a lightly floured work surface and knead until smooth. Shape the dough into a ball and transfer to a lightly oiled bowl. Cover with plastic wrap and let rise until doubled in bulk, about 30 minutes.

2. Preheat the oven to 500°. Punch down the dough and divide it in half. On a lightly floured surface, roll out 1 piece of dough to a 15-inch round, about ¼ inch thick. Transfer to a large pizza pan or baking sheet. Repeat with the second piece of dough. Bake the dough for about 6 minutes, or until just dry and set.

3. Light a grill or leave the oven on. On a small baking sheet, toss the mushrooms with the remaining 2 tablespoons of oil and season with salt and pepper. Spread the mushrooms in an even layer. Set the baking sheet on the grill, cover with the lid and cook the mushrooms over a hot fire, or roast in the oven for about 3 minutes, or until softened.

4. Top the pizza crusts with the mushrooms, artichoke hearts, prosciutto, Fontina, smoked mozzarella and Parmesan. Slide 1 pizza onto the grill and cook over a medium hot fire, or bake in the oven for about 5 minutes, rotating the pizza as necessary, until the cheese is melted and the bottom is browned and crisp. Using 2 large spatulas, return the pizza to the pizza pan, cut into wedges and serve at once while you cook the second pizza.

—*Charlie Palmer*

CHAPTER 11 vegetables

Hot and Spicy Cucumbers (p. 311)

Stir-Fried Chinese Greens

Stir-Fried Chinese Greens

4 SERVINGS

Choy sum—sometimes called Chinese broccoli or flowering cabbage—is a small green-stemmed Chinese vegetable similar to broccoli rabe, with a few yellow flowers. It's good when stir-fried until bright green and still a little crunchy. You can find it at Asian produce markets and some large supermarkets, or substitute another Asian green, such as bok choy.

½ cup chicken or vegetable broth
1 tablespoon oyster sauce
1 tablespoon Chinese cooking wine, dry white wine or dry sherry
1 tablespoon soy sauce
¼ teaspoon sugar
¼ teaspoon salt
1 tablespoon peanut oil or vegetable oil
3 scallions, cut into 1-inch lengths
1 tablespoon minced garlic
1 teaspoon minced fresh ginger
1 pound choy sum, sliced crosswise at 3-inch intervals, thickest stalks halved lengthwise
1 teaspoon cornstarch mixed with 1 tablespoon cold water

1. In a small bowl, combine the broth with the oyster sauce, wine, soy sauce, sugar and salt.

2. Set a large wok over high heat. When it's hot, add the oil and swirl to coat. After 20 seconds, add the scallions, garlic and ginger and stir-fry for 30 seconds. Add the choy sum and stir-fry for 2 minutes; press it against the wok and then stir and press again. Add the broth mixture and bring to a boil; cover and simmer for 3 minutes. Add the cornstarch mixture and continue stir-frying until the sauce thickens, about 15 seconds. Transfer the greens to a small platter and serve hot.

—Jeffrey Alford and Naomi Duguid

Warm Mixed Greens

4 SERVINGS ✺

Use kale, escarole, collards, Swiss chard, and mustard and beet greens, but keep in mind kale and collards will take slightly longer to cook.

3 tablespoons unsalted butter
2 tablespoons extra-virgin olive oil
2 pounds mixed braising greens, trimmed and coarsely chopped
2 tablespoons water
Kosher salt and freshly ground pepper

In a large heavy saucepan, melt the butter in the oil. Add the greens and water and season with kosher salt and pepper. Cover and cook over high heat until wilted and tender, 2 to 3 minutes. Drain the greens and keep warm until serving. *—Gerald Hirigoyen*

Wilted Spinach with Shallot Vinaigrette

8 SERVINGS

In this recipe it's important to start with spinach leaves that are completely dry. Although the leaves cook slightly, they shouldn't release liquid or they'll dilute the dressing.

½ cup olive oil
¼ cup plus 2 tablespoons cider vinegar
2 shallots, minced
¼ teaspoon freshly ground pepper
Salt
4 pounds spinach—stemmed, cleaned and spun dry

In a small glass or stainless-steel bowl, combine the oil, vinegar, shallots, pepper and ¾ teaspoon of salt. Set a large enameled cast-iron casserole over high heat. When the casserole is very hot, add the vinaigrette and bring to a boil. Add the spinach to the casserole in large handfuls, tossing constantly with tongs until the leaves are partially wilted before adding the next batch.

stir-frying tips

Begin with a large enough wok—at least 16 inches in diameter—that's made to hold high heat and to distribute it evenly. We like Chinese spun-steel woks; look for one with a long wooden handle for maximum maneuverability.

Have all your ingredients prepared, measured and set out near the stove before you begin.

Preheat the wok.

Swirl the oil around the hot wok to heat the oil thoroughly before adding any other ingredients.

Don't overload the wok. For proper stir-frying, the food has to come into direct contact with the pan; if there's too much in the pan, the contents will stew, not sizzle. If necessary, cook the food in two batches.

Keep the ingredients moving; use a firm metal spatula with a long wooden handle to lift, turn and press ingredients against the side of the hot wok.

Rinse out the wok under hot, running water, scrubbing it thoroughly. Dry at once.

When most of the spinach is wilted, after about 4 minutes, remove the casserole from the heat. Season the wilted spinach with salt and then transfer it to a bowl and serve at once.

—Mark Gottwald

Spring Spinach and Garlic Frittata

8 SERVINGS

1 cup fine fresh bread crumbs
5 tablespoons unsalted butter, 4 of them melted
1 dozen large eggs
½ cup milk
Kosher salt and freshly ground pepper
1 tablespoon olive oil
3 garlic cloves, thinly sliced
1 pound fresh spinach, large stems trimmed

1   teaspoon fresh lemon juice
½   pound mesclun
1   tablespoon aged sherry vinegar
1   tablespoon extra-virgin olive oil

1. Preheat the oven to 350°. Spread the bread crumbs on a rimmed baking sheet and bake for about 5 minutes, or until lightly toasted. Transfer to a bowl and stir in the 4 tablespoons of melted butter. Leave the oven on.

2. In a large bowl, whisk the eggs with the milk and season with kosher salt and pepper. In a large cast-iron or nonstick ovenproof skillet, melt the remaining 1 tablespoon of butter in the olive oil and then swirl the pan to coat the bottom and side. Add the garlic to the skillet and cook over low heat, stirring occasionally, until golden, about 4 minutes. Add the spinach and stir with tongs until it is slightly wilted. Drain off any liquid, spread the spinach evenly in the pan and sprinkle with the lemon juice.

3. Pour the egg mixture over the spinach and cook over moderately low heat until the bottom begins to set, about 4 minutes. Sprinkle the top of the frittata with the buttered bread crumbs and transfer the pan to the oven. Bake for 15 to 20 minutes, or until the frittata is just set.

4. In a large salad bowl, toss the mesclun with the vinegar and extra-virgin olive oil and season with kosher salt and pepper. Loosen the frittata with a spatula and slide it out onto a large plate. Alternatively, cut the frittata into wedges in the pan. Serve the frittata warm or at room temperature with the mesclun salad.

—*Clifford Harrison and Anne Quatrano*

MAKE AHEAD The frittata can stand at room temperature for up to 1 hour.

WINE The grassy flavor of the 1996 Sanford Santa Barbara Sauvignon Blanc will provide balance for the fresh spinach and rich eggs.

Swiss Chard Sformatino

8 SERVINGS

A sformatino is a mold made of pureed vegetables. Leftovers should be no problem: they're wonderful sliced and fried in butter.

1   cup fine dry bread crumbs
2   pounds Swiss chard, stemmed and rinsed
⅔   cup milk
4   tablespoons unsalted butter
¾   cup freshly grated Parmigiano-Reggiano cheese (2½ ounces)
Salt and freshly ground pepper

1. Preheat the oven to 350°. Butter a 1-quart soufflé dish or deep baking dish. Add 2 tablespoons of the bread crumbs and shake the crumbs around the inside of the dish to coat it completely.

2. Heat a large skillet. Add the Swiss chard in 2 batches and cook over moderately high heat, stirring, until wilted. Transfer to a colander and rinse under cold running water; squeeze dry. Transfer the chard to a food processor and pulse until very finely chopped.

3. In a small saucepan, heat the milk until bubbles appear around the edge. In a medium saucepan, melt the butter over moderate heat. Add the remaining bread crumbs and stir to coat. Gradually pour in the milk, stirring, until the mixture is thick. Remove from the heat and stir in the chard and the cheese. Season with salt and pepper and scrape into the prepared dish.

4. Bake the sformatino for about 30 minutes, or until set. Invert onto a large plate and cut into 8 wedges. Serve hot.

—*Umberto Creatini*

Endive Gratin

6 SERVINGS

In this typical Lyonnais gratin, cooked endives are browned in bacon fat and then broiled under a blanket of cheese. If Tomme de Savoie cheese isn't available, use twice as much of the Gruyère.

6   large Belgian endives, outer leaves removed
4   cups chicken stock (p. 117), vegetable stock or water
Juice of 1 lemon
1   teaspoon salt
2   ounces bacon, cut into ½-inch pieces
4   ounces Tomme de Savoie cheese, grated (1½ cups)
4   ounces Gruyère cheese, grated (1½ cups)

1. Put the endives in a deep skillet that will hold them comfortably in a single layer. Add the stock, lemon juice and salt. Cover the endives with a round of parchment paper, make a small hole in the center of the paper and bring to a boil. Reduce the heat and simmer, turning occasionally, until the endives are very tender when pierced, about 30 minutes. Remove the endives as they are done and pat thoroughly dry.

2. Preheat the broiler. In the same skillet, cook the bacon over moderately high heat until it is lightly browned, about 3 minutes. Add the endives to the skillet, reduce the heat to moderate and cook, turning occasionally, until the endives are evenly browned, about 10 minutes.

3. Transfer the endives and bacon to a gratin dish and sprinkle with the grated cheeses. Broil the gratin for about 5 minutes, turning the dish to brown the cheese evenly. Serve immediately.

—*Daniel Boulud*

MAKE AHEAD The gratin can be prepared through Step 2 and refrigerated overnight. Reheat the endives before proceeding.

Spicy Collard Greens

12 SERVINGS

The important thing to watch for when buying greens is that the leaves have no yellow or discolored areas. When preparing this dish, you can control the level of spiciness by adding more or less of the crushed red pepper.

- 2 quarts Smoky Pork Stock (recipe follows)
- 6 pounds collard greens, stems and ribs removed, leaves cut into 1-inch wide ribbons
- ½ cup plus 2 tablespoons olive oil
- 3 medium onions, coarsely chopped
- 1½ tablespoons minced garlic
- 1½ teaspoons crushed red pepper
- Salt and freshly ground black pepper
- Two 28-ounce cans whole peeled tomatoes, drained

1. In a large enameled cast-iron casserole, bring the pork stock to a boil. Add the collard greens and cook over moderately high heat until tender, 30 to 40 minutes. Drain the greens, reserving the liquid.

2. Wipe out the casserole. Add the oil and onions and cook over moderate heat until the onions are translucent, 5 to 6 minutes. Add the garlic, crushed red pepper and ½ teaspoon each of salt and black pepper. Cook, stirring, for 1 minute. Add the tomatoes and 3 cups of the reserved cooking liquid and simmer over moderately low heat until the tomatoes begin to break down, about 15 minutes. Add the collard greens and cook until they are heated through, about 5 minutes.

MAKE AHEAD The greens can be prepared 1 day ahead and reheated.

SMOKY PORK STOCK
MAKES 4 QUARTS
If you can't find ham hocks from genuine dry-cured hams, use an excellent-quality smoked country bacon.

- One 2-pound smoke-cured pork shoulder hock, or 2 pounds sliced lean smoked country bacon, cut into 1-inch pieces
- 4½ quarts water

Put the bacon and the water in a stockpot and bring to a boil. Cover and cook over moderate heat for 2 hours; the pork stock will be intensely flavored. Strain the pork stock, let cool and then refrigerate for several hours. Discard the fat before using the pork stock.

—*Edna Lewis and Scott Peacock*
MAKE AHEAD The pork stock can be refrigerated for several days or frozen for 1 month. Be sure to cover it tightly to avoid flavoring everything else in the refrigerator.

Braised Savoy Cabbage with Bacon
8 SERVINGS
- 1½ pounds Savoy cabbage— quartered, cored, trimmed and cut into 1½-inch-thick wedges
- 4 slices smoked bacon, coarsely chopped
- 4 tablespoons unsalted butter
- Salt and freshly ground pepper
- 2 teaspoons finely shredded sage
- ½ cup water

1. In a large pot of boiling water, cook the cabbage until almost tender, about 8 minutes. Drain and refresh the cabbage under cold running water.

2. In a large enameled cast-iron casserole, cook the bacon over low heat until the fat is rendered and the bacon is slightly crisp, about 6 minutes. Add the butter; stir until melted. Arrange the cabbage wedges in the casserole in an even layer, season with salt and pepper and sprinkle with the sage. Cover with a round of parchment paper and simmer for 10 minutes. Add the water, cover again with the paper and simmer until the cabbage is tender and the liquid is flavorful, about 20 minutes more. Season with salt and pepper and serve.

—*The Point, Lake Saranac, New York*
MAKE AHEAD The braised cabbage can be refrigerated overnight; rewarm before serving.

Snow Peas with a Hint of Pork
4 SERVINGS
The bright-green pea pods should retain a little crispness when stir-fried. To prepare, wash them thoroughly and then work your way through the pile one by one, snapping off the stem end and pulling off the string that runs along the edge.

- 1 tablespoon Chinese cooking wine, dry white wine or dry sherry
- 1 tablespoon soy sauce
- ¼ pound boneless pork tenderloin, shoulder or butt, thinly sliced
- ½ pound snow peas
- 1 tablespoon peanut oil or vegetable oil
- 3 scallions, cut into ½-inch lengths
- 2 garlic cloves, minced
- ½ cup chicken broth
- ½ teaspoon sugar
- ½ teaspoon salt
- 1 teaspoon cornstarch mixed with 1 teaspoon cold water

1. In a small glass or stainless-steel bowl, combine the wine and soy sauce. Add the pork and stir to coat. Let stand at room temperature for at least 30 minutes and up to 1 hour.

2. In a medium saucepan of boiling water, cook the snow peas until bright green, about 1 minute. Drain the snow peas, refresh under cold running water and drain again.

3. Set a large wok over high heat until it is very hot. Add the oil and swirl to coat. When the oil is hot, add the scallions and garlic and stir-fry for 30 seconds. Add the pork and any remaining marinade and stir-fry until the meat changes color, 1 to 2 minutes. Add the snow peas and stir-fry for 30 seconds. Add the broth, sugar and salt, cover and cook for 1 minute. Add the cornstarch mixture and cook, stirring occasionally, until the sauce thickens, 1 to

2 minutes. Remove the wok from the heat, transfer the snow peas to a platter and serve hot.

—*Jeffrey Alford and Naomi Duguid*

WINE Stir-fried pork and scallions add a rich flavor to this dish that is easily balanced by the round, fruity smoothness of a California Chardonnay. Among the possibilities, consider the 1996 Trefethen or the 1996 Kistler Sonoma.

Summer Pea Casserole

8 SERVINGS

- 2 cups shelled fresh lima beans (from about 2 pounds), or 10 ounces frozen baby lima beans
- ½ pound sugar snap peas, stringed
- 1 cup shelled fresh English or sweet peas (from 1 pound), or 1 cup frozen petite peas
- 1 cup snow peas (about 4 ounces), strings removed
- 4 tablespoons unsalted butter
- ½ cup chicken stock (p. 117) or canned low-sodium broth
- 2 cups finely shredded romaine lettuce (about one-half head)

Salt and freshly ground pepper

1. In a large saucepan of salted boiling water, blanch the lima beans and all of the peas separately until crisp-tender, about 20 minutes for fresh lima beans, 5 minutes for sugar snaps and fresh English peas and 2 minutes for snow peas and frozen limas; frozen petite peas will not need to be blanched. Rinse the beans and peas well with cold water after cooking. Drain, shaking off the excess water, and transfer to a large bowl.

2. Melt the butter in a large saucepan. Add the stock and cook over high heat until reduced by half, about 4 minutes. Add the beans, peas and romaine lettuce and cook, stirring, until the lettuce is wilted and the peas are heated through. Season with salt and pepper and serve at once. —*Sascha Lyon*

Braised Peas with Dill

12 SERVINGS

It may seem that cooking peas for more than a few minutes would destroy their flavor, but this long-simmered dish is not to be missed. Try this cooking method with other vegetables, such as green beans or shredded leafy greens. You'll be surprised how much flavor long cooking can coax out of vegetables.

- ⅔ cup olive oil
- 3 medium red onions, finely chopped

Five 10-ounce boxes frozen peas

- 6 cups water
- ¼ cup chopped dill

Salt and freshly ground pepper

Heat the oil in a large saucepan. Add the onions and cook over moderate heat, stirring occasionally, until softened but not browned, about 5 minutes. Add the frozen peas, water and dill and season with a large pinch each of salt and pepper. Bring to a boil and then simmer over moderate heat until the water has evaporated and the peas are very tender, about 45 minutes. Serve the braised peas hot.

—*Fany Boutari*

MAKE AHEAD The peas can be refrigerated for up to 1 day.

Summer Pea Casserole

Grilled Beans

8 SERVINGS

- 2 pounds mixed green beans and yellow wax beans
- 2½ tablespoons olive oil

Salt and freshly ground pepper

- 1 medium red onion, thinly sliced

Light a grill or preheat the oven to 450°. In a bowl, toss the beans with the oil and season with salt and pepper. Grill, arranging the beans across the slats, or roast on a baking sheet, turning with tongs every 5 minutes, for about 15 minutes, or until tender and lightly browned. In a large bowl, toss the beans with the onion and serve warm. —*Christer Larsson*

Roasted Green Beans with Garlic

4 SERVINGS ★★★ 1995

Oven-blasted vegetables became popular in the Nineties. This recipe from the very talented cookbook author Nancy Verde Barr, applying the technique to green beans, was a first for FOOD & WINE.

- 1 pound green beans, tender tips left on
- ¼ cup extra-virgin olive oil
- 3 garlic cloves, smashed
- 3 thyme sprigs, halved

Salt and freshly ground pepper

- 3 anchovy fillets, mashed
- 2 to 3 teaspoons fresh lemon juice

Finely grated zest of 1 lemon

1. Preheat the oven to 450°. In a large baking dish, toss the green beans with the oil, garlic and thyme; season with salt and pepper. Spread the beans in a single layer and roast, tossing occasionally, until they are tender and lightly browned, about 15 minutes.

2. Discard the thyme sprigs; transfer the beans to a bowl. Add the anchovies, lemon juice and lemon zest and toss well to coat. Serve warm or at room temperature. —*Nancy Verde Barr*

Pole Beans Cooked in Smoky Pork Stock

12 SERVINGS

Pole beans, or broad beans, are slightly flat, hardy green beans that are eaten for their pods. They should be crisp and bright when you buy them. Avoid overly mature beans with tough looking pods and be sure to remove the strings from both sides before cooking. The beans benefit from being cooked at least two hours in advance and then allowed to mellow in their cooking liquid.

- 2 quarts Smoky Pork Stock (p. 307)
- 2½ pounds pole beans or large green beans, strings removed

Salt and freshly ground pepper

In a large saucepan, bring the Smoky Pork Stock to a boil. Add the beans, pushing them down into the stock, and return to a boil. Cover and simmer until tender, 30 to 45 minutes for true pole beans. Drain the beans and season with salt and pepper. Serve hot.

—*Edna Lewis and Scott Peacock*

MAKE AHEAD The beans can be cooked 1 day ahead and reheated in the stock before serving.

Giant Lima Beans with Chives

8 SERVINGS

- ¾ pound dried large lima beans, soaked overnight
- 3 quarts water
- 1 small onion studded with 3 whole cloves
- 5 whole black peppercorns
- 1 thyme sprig
- 1 bay leaf

Salt

- 2 tablespoons extra-virgin olive oil

Freshly ground pepper

- 2 tablespoons minced chives

1. Drain the beans and put them in a saucepan. Add the water, onion, peppercorns, thyme and bay leaf. Bring to a boil and then simmer over low heat until tender, about 1 hour. Season with salt. Drain the beans and discard the peppercorns, thyme and bay leaf.

2. In a large skillet, heat the oil. Add the beans and cook over moderately high heat, stirring, for 2 minutes. Season with salt and pepper, sprinkle with the chives and serve. —*Tony Najiola*

Three-Minute Bean Sprouts

4 SERVINGS

These delicious bean sprouts should come to the table piping hot and still slightly crisp. The Chinese often cut off the ends of the sprouts before cooking, but that's optional.

- 1 tablespoon peanut oil
- 2 scallions—halved crosswise, finely julienned and cut into 2-inch lengths
- ½ pound bean sprouts

Scant ½ teaspoon salt

- ½ teaspoon soy sauce
- ½ teaspoon rice vinegar
- ½ teaspoon Asian sesame oil

Set a wok over high heat until it's very hot. Add the peanut oil. When it's very hot, add the scallions and bean sprouts and stir-fry vigorously for 1 minute, tossing and pressing the vegetables against the side of the hot wok. Add the salt and stir-fry for 1 minute. Add the soy sauce and vinegar and stir-fry for 30 seconds to 1 minute longer. Transfer the sprouts to a plate and drizzle with the sesame oil. Toss the sprouts gently and serve immediately.

—*Jeffrey Alford and Naomi Duguid*

Golden Fried Cardoon

4 SERVINGS

Cardoons have a distinctive rich artichoke flavor with a hint of lemon.

- 2 quarts water
- 2 tablespoons white vinegar
- 4 large cardoon ribs (1 pound), ends and leaves trimmed

Hot and Spicy Cucumbers

2 large egg yolks beaten with
   1 tablespoon water

1 large egg, beaten

1 cup homemade dry
   bread crumbs

¼ cup freshly grated Parmesan
   cheese

Salt and freshly ground pepper

Vegetable oil, for frying

Lemon wedges

ı. In a large glass or stainless-steel bowl, combine the water and vinegar. Using a vegetable peeler, remove the tough outer strings of the cardoon ribs. Cut the ribs into 2-inch lengths, adding them to the vinegar water as you work. Drain the cardoon, transfer to a large saucepan of lightly salted water and boil until very tender, about 30 minutes. Drain and pat dry; let cool.

2. In a shallow bowl, combine the egg yolk mixture and the egg. In another bowl, toss the bread crumbs with the Parmesan cheese, ½ teaspoon of salt and ⅛ teaspoon of pepper. Dip the cardoon in the egg mixture and then dredge in the bread crumbs, pressing to help the crumbs adhere. Shake off any excess crumbs and set the cardoon on a wax paper–lined tray.

3. In a medium skillet, heat ½ inch of oil over moderately high heat. When the oil is very hot, add the cardoon, 5 or 6 pieces at a time. Fry until golden and crisp, about 1½ minutes per side. Transfer the fried cardoon to a wire rack set over a baking sheet. Sprinkle lightly with salt and serve the cardoon hot or at room temperature with lemon wedges.   —*Grace Parisi*

Hot and Spicy Cucumbers

4 SERVINGS

- 1 tablespoon soy sauce
- ¼ teaspoon salt
- ¼ teaspoon sugar
- 1 tablespoon peanut oil
- 1 tablespoon minced garlic
- 1 heaping teaspoon minced fresh ginger
- About 1 teaspoon Hot Chile Paste (p. 117)
- 2 European cucumbers—peeled, halved, seeded and sliced crosswise 1 inch thick

In a small bowl, combine the soy sauce, salt and sugar. Six minutes before serving, set a wok over high heat. When it's very hot, add the oil and swirl to coat. Add the garlic, ginger and chile paste and stir-fry for 15 seconds. Add the cucumbers and stir-fry for 2 minutes. Pour the soy sauce mixture into the wok and stir-fry until the cucumbers are softened but still slightly crisp in the center, 2 to 3 minutes. Transfer the cucumbers to a plate and serve hot or at room temperature.

—*Jeffrey Alford and Naomi Duguid*

Roasted Asparagus with Olive Oil and Lemon

4 SERVINGS

- 1½ **pounds medium asparagus, peeled**
- 3 **tablespoons extra-virgin olive oil (see Note)**
- **Salt and freshly ground pepper**

- 1 **tablespoon fresh lemon juice**
- 1 **teaspoon finely grated lemon zest**

Preheat the oven to 450°. In a baking dish, drizzle the asparagus with half of the oil and season with salt and pepper. Roast for about 15 minutes, or until tender when pierced with a knife. Drizzle the asparagus with the remaining oil and the lemon juice and zest. Serve hot.   —*Jan Newberry*

N O T E A nutty or buttery extra-virgin olive oil partners well with this lemon-accented asparagus.

Oven-Dried Tomatoes in Herbed Oil

MAKES ABOUT 1 CUP

- ½ **cup extra-virgin olive oil**
- **Oven-Dried Tomatoes (recipe follows)**
- 1 **rosemary sprig**
- 1 **thyme sprig**
- 1 **small garlic clove, halved**
- 1 **basil sprig**

In a medium saucepan, warm the oil over low heat. Add the tomatoes, rosemary, thyme and garlic; cook over very low heat for 30 minutes. Transfer the mixture to a large heatproof bowl and let cool completely and then add the basil. Store in a sealed jar, refrigerated, for up to 1 day.

OVEN-DRIED TOMATOES

MAKES ABOUT 1 CUP

Drying tomatoes dramatically intensifies their flavor and sweetness.

- 1 **pound red and yellow cherry tomatoes, halved**

Preheat the oven to 200°. Lightly oil 2 large racks and set them over 2 large baking sheets or line 2 large baking sheets with parchment paper. Set the tomato halves on the racks and bake for 2 hours, rotating the sheets for even drying. Reduce the oven temperature to 150° and bake for 3 hours

Oven-Dried Tomatoes in Herbed Oil

virgins defined

The label Most American markets carry two types of olive oil, one labeled Pure and one labeled Extra-Virgin. Pure olive oil is produced from bruised or otherwise defective olives; the oil is then stripped of unacceptable aromas and flavors. Extra-virgin oil is produced by crushing healthy olives as quickly as possible after harvest—within twenty-four to forty-eight hours—to retain the olives' complex flavors.

The flavors Extra-virgin oil should have a balance of flavors that are fruity, bitter and pungent—the back-of-the-throat pepperiness characteristic of oil from fresh olives. Like fine estate wines, the best oils vary considerably in flavor. You may prefer one oil for salads, another for sautés and a third to garnish a delicate fish. I keep at least three or four on hand at any given time.

The olives Olives may be picked at all stages of ripeness, with colors from thoroughly green to green streaked with amethyst to the rich, glossy black of mature olives. In general, the younger the olives at harvest, the more the oil will exhibit a pleasing roughness, with mature olives giving a smoother, sweeter oil.

The shelf-life Stored in a cool, dark place, extra-virgin oils should last two years.

ABOVE: **Pan-Roasted Brussels Sprouts with Pancetta.** TOP: **Zucchini "Noodles."**

Cauliflower Puree

6 SERVINGS

- 1 small cauliflower (1½ pounds), cut into 1-inch florets
- 1 pound large Yukon Gold potatoes, peeled and cut into ½-inch dice
- 3 tablespoons heavy cream

Salt and freshly ground pepper

In a large saucepan, cover the cauliflower and potatoes with water; bring to a boil. Reduce the heat to moderately low, cover partially and cook until tender, about 25 minutes. Drain very well and return to the saucepan. Add the cream and mash by hand until smooth. Season with salt and pepper and serve. —*Alan Tardi*

MAKE AHEAD The puree can be refrigerated for up to 6 hours.

Pan-Roasted Brussels Sprouts with Pancetta

8 SERVINGS

Use salt sparingly here (the pancetta is already salty), but don't eliminate it altogether: it draws the juices from the shallots and adds to the flavor of the dish.

- ½ pound thickly sliced pancetta, cut into ¼-inch dice
- 8 large shallots, quartered

Salt and freshly ground pepper

- 2 pounds brussels sprouts, quartered
- ½ cup white wine vinegar

In a large deep skillet, cook the pancetta over moderate heat until it is slightly crisp and the fat is rendered, 8 to 10 minutes. Stir in the shallots, season with salt and pepper and cook until golden, about 10 minutes. Add the brussels sprouts and vinegar and bring to a boil. Reduce the heat to low. Cover the pan; cook until the sprouts and shallots are tender and the pan is almost dry, 10 to 12 minutes. Transfer the sprouts to a bowl and keep warm until serving. —*Nancy Verde Barr*

Zucchini "Noodles"

4 SERVINGS

Choose small, firm zucchini with few seeds for this dish. The "noodles" are just barely cooked in olive oil—it's more like they're simply steeped and warmed in it—so they stay crisp and flavorful.

- 3 tablespoons extra-virgin olive oil
- 1½ teaspoons thyme leaves
- 1 teaspoon minced garlic
- 1½ pounds small zucchini, finely julienned

Salt and freshly ground pepper

- 2 tablespoons minced parsley
- 1 tablespoon fresh lemon juice

In a large skillet, warm the oil. Add half the thyme and all the garlic and cook over moderate heat for 1 minute. Add the zucchini and cook, stirring occasionally, until it just begins to lose its crunch, about 5 minutes; season with salt and pepper as it cooks. Transfer the zucchini to a bowl and toss with the parsley, lemon juice and remaining thyme. Season with salt and pepper and serve warm.   —*Eberhard Müller*

Zucchini and Goat Cheese Frittata

4 SERVINGS

- 8 large eggs
- 1 cup half-and-half
- Salt and freshly ground pepper
- 1 tablespoon plus 1 teaspoon olive oil
- 2 cups Oven-Dried Zucchini (recipe follows)
- 4 ounces fresh goat cheese, in small pieces
- 1 teaspoon chopped dill

1. Preheat the broiler. In a large bowl, beat the eggs with the half-and-half. Season lightly with salt and pepper.
2. In a heavy 9-inch ovenproof skillet, warm the oil over moderately high heat. When the oil is almost smoking, pour in the egg mixture. Reduce the heat to moderately low. Scatter the zucchini over the egg mixture. Dot the egg mixture with the goat cheese and sprinkle with the dill. Cover and cook until the eggs are almost set, about 12 minutes.
3. Broil the frittata for about 2 minutes, or until the eggs are set. Cut into wedges and serve hot or warm.
SERVE WITH A green salad with pumpkin seed–oil vinaigrette and sourdough bread.
WINE The 1996 Hiedler Grüner Veltliner Langenloiser Thal from Austria.

OVEN-DRIED ZUCCHINI

MAKES ABOUT 4 CUPS
Drying not only concentrates the flavor of delicate summer squash, it gives it a more substantial texture and also makes the squash easier to store, since dried zucchini takes up less space. Dry enough of the squash in the fall to last all winter long; you can add it to soups, pastas and egg dishes.

- 5 pounds zucchini, coarsely grated
- 2½ teaspoons salt

1. Preheat the oven to 250°. On a work surface, toss the zucchini with the salt. Divide the zucchini between 2 large colanders set in the sink. Set plates directly on the zucchini and weight them down with canned goods. Let the zucchini drain for 15 minutes. Squeeze out the excess water, spread the zucchini on a triple layer of paper towels and blot as dry as possible.
2. Lightly oil 2 large rimmed baking sheets. Spread the zucchini evenly in the pans and bake for 2 hours, stirring the zucchini a few times, or until it reduces in volume by two-thirds but is still moist. Let cool completely. Transfer 1- or 2-cup portions of the zucchini to sturdy plastic bags or airtight containers and freeze for up to 6 months; defrost before using. —*Odessa Piper*

Zucchini Flower Fritters

MAKES 24 FRITTERS
For large fritters, use male flowers (the ones that grow on the stems rather than on the zucchini); for small ones, use the female. Wash the flowers first to remove any dirt and then drain and pat them dry.

- 1⅓ cups all-purpose flour
- 4 large egg whites
- 1 cup chilled dry white wine

Zucchini Flower Fritters

Oven-Roasted Butternut Squash with Marsala

½ teaspoon baking powder

3 cups canola oil, for deep-frying

24 zucchini flowers, pistils removed

Salt

Basil or lettuce leaves, for garnish

1. In a large bowl, combine 1 cup of the flour with the egg whites, wine and baking powder; mix with a fork until a lumpy batter forms. Let stand at room temperature for 1 hour.

2. In a large skillet, heat the oil to 400°. Lightly dredge 1 zucchini flower at a time in the remaining ⅓ cup of flour and dip it in the batter. Fry in batches of 6, turning occasionally, until lightly browned all over, 2 to 3 minutes. Using a slotted spoon, transfer the fritters to a wire rack. Season the fritters with salt and serve immediately, garnished with basil leaves. —*Ed Giobbi*

MAKE AHEAD The fritters can be made 3 hours ahead and recrisped on a rack set on a baking sheet in a 425° oven for 3 to 4 minutes.

WINE The mildness of the fritters needs little more than the lively contrast of a clean, lean Italian Pinot Grigio, such as the 1997 Bollini or the 1997 Barone Fini.

Butternut Squash with Cardamom and Cinnamon

8 SERVINGS

Butternut squash are so plentiful all throughout South Africa that farm stands sell them in sacks of fifteen or so. A favorite ingredient in side dishes and soups, the squash are typically curried or scented with sweet spices.

One 3-pound butternut squash— peeled, seeded and cut into 1-inch cubes

6 cardamom pods, crushed with the back of a knife

6 whole cloves

Three 3-inch cinnamon sticks, broken in half

3 bay leaves

1½ tablespoons unsalted butter

Malay Chile Jam (p. 361), warmed

Salt

In a medium bowl, toss the butternut squash with the cardamom, cloves, cinnamon sticks and bay leaves. Bring water to a boil in a large steamer, add the spiced butternut squash, cover and steam until the squash is tender, about 15 minutes. Discard the spices. Transfer the steamed squash to a bowl and add the butter and 3 tablespoons of chile jam. Season the squash with salt and toss gently. Serve extra chile jam on the side. —*Jenna Holst*

Oven-Roasted Butternut Squash with Marsala

8 SERVINGS

Most supermarkets carry peeled and sliced butternut squash in the late fall. If you are unable to find it, buy a large squash, cut it into large pieces and then remove the skin with a vegetable peeler.

3 tablespoons olive oil

3 pounds butternut squash, peeled and cut into ¾-inch dice

3 medium onions, coarsely chopped

1 tablespoon finely chopped thyme

½ teaspoon freshly grated nutmeg

Salt and freshly ground pepper

1 cup dry Marsala

3 tablespoons finely chopped flat-leaf parsley

Preheat the oven to 425°. Spread the oil in a large metal baking dish. Add the butternut squash, onions, thyme, nutmeg and a generous pinch each of salt and pepper; toss to coat. Roast the vegetables for 20 to 25 minutes, or until the squash and onions are tender and lightly browned. Transfer the vegetables to a serving bowl and set the pan over high heat. Add the Marsala and cook until reduced to a glaze, about 15 minutes. Pour the Marsala over the vegetables, sprinkle with the parsley and toss well. Keep warm until serving. —*Nancy Verde Barr*

Squash and Potato Gratin

8 SERVINGS

2 garlic cloves, crushed

2 tablespoons chopped flat-leaf parsley

2 tablespoons finely shredded mint

¾ teaspoon salt

½ teaspoon freshly ground pepper

1 butternut squash (1⅓ pounds)—quartered, peeled, seeded and sliced crosswise ⅛ inch thick

⅔ cup freshly grated Pecorino cheese (3 ounces)

½ cup tomato sauce

¼ cup fresh ricotta or small curd cottage cheese

1½ pounds red potatoes, peeled and sliced ⅛ inch thick

1¼ cups whole milk

2 tablespoons fresh bread crumbs

1 tablespoon extra-virgin olive oil

1. Preheat the oven to 350°. Generously oil a 2-quart earthenware dish.

2. In a small bowl, combine the garlic with the parsley, mint, salt and pepper. In a large bowl, combine the butternut squash, Pecorino, tomato sauce, ricotta and half of the garlic-herb mixture. In another bowl, combine the potatoes with the remaining garlic-herb mixture.

3. Spread half of the potatoes in the prepared gratin dish in an even layer. Cover with the squash mixture and then top with the remaining potatoes. Pour the milk over the potatoes, sprinkle the top with the bread crumbs and drizzle with the oil.

4. Bake the gratin for about 40 minutes, or until the potatoes are just tender and the liquid is bubbling. Raise the heat to 400° and bake the gratin for 30 minutes longer, until the top is deep golden and most of the liquid has been absorbed. Let the gratin rest for 15 minutes before serving.

—*Paula Wolfert*

Oven-Roasted Squash

8 SERVINGS

Eight 11-ounce golden acorn squash or pumpkins, top quarters and seeds discarded

4 tablespoons unsalted butter, melted

5 medium unpeeled shallots

Two 2½-pound butternut squash or sugar pumpkins, halved lengthwise and seeds discarded

Salt and freshly ground pepper

3 tablespoons heavy cream (optional)

1½ teaspoons finely chopped thyme, plus thyme sprigs for garnish (optional)

1. Preheat the oven to 425°. Cut a thin slice from the base of each acorn squash and set upright on a baking sheet. Brush the tops with 1 tablespoon of the melted butter. Wrap the shallots loosely in aluminum foil.

2. Brush the cut sides of the butternut squash with 1 tablespoon of the melted butter and then season with salt and pepper. Set the butternut squash with the cut side down on another baking sheet.

3. Roast the butternut squash for about 50 minutes, or until the squash is tender. Roast the acorn squash and the shallots for about 40 minutes, or until the shallots are soft and the squash is golden. Keep the acorn squash warm, but let the butternut squash and the shallots cool slightly. Squeeze the soft shallots from their skins. Coarsely chop the shallots and then transfer them to a bowl.

4. Scoop the butternut squash from their skins. Add the butternut squash to the shallots and mash them both with the remaining 2 tablespoons of melted butter, the heavy cream and the chopped thyme. Season the mixture with salt and pepper. Spoon the mixture into the acorn squash and garnish with thyme sprigs, if you like. Serve the stuffed acorn squash warm.

—*Rori Spinelli*

Oven-Roasted Squash

Carrot Shallot Puree

Carrot Shallot Puree

MAKES ABOUT 1½ CUPS

- 1 pound carrots, thickly sliced
- 1 large shallot, minced
- 1 tablespoon extra-virgin olive oil

Salt

Freshly grated nutmeg

1. In a medium saucepan, cover the carrots with water and simmer over moderate heat until tender, about 20 minutes. Drain, reserving the liquid.
2. In a small skillet, sauté the shallot in the oil over moderately low heat until it is softened, about 7 minutes. Transfer the sautéed shallot to a food processor along with the carrots and ⅓ cup of the carrot cooking liquid and process until smooth. Transfer the puree to a bowl. Season the puree with salt and freshly grated nutmeg and serve. —*Grace Parisi*

Braised Carrots with Thyme

6 SERVINGS

- 2 tablespoons unsalted butter
- 1½ pounds carrots, peeled and sliced ¼ inch thick on the diagonal
- 2 garlic cloves, thinly sliced
- 2 thyme sprigs

Salt and freshly ground pepper
- 1¾ cups chicken stock (p. 117) or canned low-sodium broth

1. Preheat the oven to 375°. In a large ovenproof skillet, melt the butter over moderately low heat. Add the carrots, garlic and thyme and season with salt and pepper. Cook, tossing frequently, until the carrots are tender but not browned, about 10 minutes. Add the stock, bring to a boil and remove from the heat.
2. Cover the carrots with a round of parchment paper and cover the skillet with a lid. Braise the carrots in the oven for about 30 minutes, or until they are very tender. Discard the thyme sprigs and serve. —*Daniel Boulud*

MAKE AHEAD The cooked carrots can be refrigerated for up to 1 day. Gently reheat the carrots in their liquid before serving.

Carrot and Orange Sambal

MAKES ABOUT 2 CUPS

In Malaysia and South Africa, a sambal can be eaten as a tangy side dish, a condiment or a small salad.

- 2 medium navel oranges
- 6 medium carrots, coarsely grated
- 3 tablespoons fresh lemon juice
- 3 tablespoons fresh orange juice
- 1½ tablespoons sugar
- ½ teaspoon salt
- ⅛ teaspoon ground coriander
- 3 tablespoons chopped cilantro

Using a sharp knife, peel the oranges, removing all of the bitter white pith. Cut in between the membranes to release the orange sections; coarsely chop the sections. In a bowl, combine the carrots with the lemon juice, orange juice, sugar and salt and mix thoroughly. Stir in the orange sections and coriander. Let the sambal stand at room temperature for 30 minutes. Sprinkle the sambal with the cilantro before serving. —*Jenna Holst*

Roasted Beets with Capers

4 SERVINGS

Be picky about the beets you buy; they're as delicate as corn. Look for small ones and dress the red, white and gold varieties separately so that their colors don't blend. When the leaves are tender and fresh, they add a lovely acidic dimension to the salad.

- 2 cups kosher salt
- 12 small beets of mixed colors if possible (about 2 pounds), tops trimmed, 12 small leaves reserved and minced
- 3 tablespoons extra-virgin olive oil
- 1 tablespoon red wine vinegar
- 1 tablespoon drained capers
- 1 tablespoon minced chives

Salt and freshly ground pepper

I. Preheat the oven to 425°. Spread the kosher salt in a small roasting pan and set the beets on top. Transfer to the oven and roast for about 50 minutes, or until the beets are tender when pierced. Let cool for 20 minutes.

2. While the beets are still warm, peel and cut them into wedges. In medium bowls, combine each color of beet and their leaves with some of the oil, vinegar, capers and chives. Season with salt and pepper, toss and then serve together.   —*Eberhard Müller*

Roasted Beets in Gingered Syrup

12 SERVINGS

Baking the beets rather than boiling them intensifies their flavor. The beets must marinate overnight, so plan accordingly.

- 2 pounds medium beets
- 2 tablespoons vegetable oil

Freshly ground pepper

- 2 cups cider vinegar
- 2 cups sugar

One 2-inch piece of fresh ginger, peeled and thinly sliced

- 4 whole cloves

- 1 bay leaf
- ½ teaspoon salt

I. Preheat the oven to 325°. Put the beets in a large roasting pan. Drizzle with the oil and sprinkle with pepper. Cover with a sheet of parchment paper and then with a double thickness of aluminum foil, sealing tightly. Bake for 1 to 1½ hours, or until the beets are tender when pierced. Remove from the oven and let cool, covered.

2. Meanwhile, in a medium stainless steel saucepan, combine the vinegar, sugar, ginger, cloves, bay leaf and salt. Simmer over low heat until syrupy, about 20 minutes. Strain the syrup and let cool to room temperature.

3. Peel the beets. Thickly slice them or cut into ½-inch wedges. Transfer the beets to a large bowl and pour the

ABOVE: **Carrot and Orange Sambal.**
TOP: **Roasted Beets with Capers.**

syrup on top. Cover and refrigerate overnight. Serve the beets chilled or warm, in the syrup.

—Edna Lewis and Scott Peacock

MAKE AHEAD The beets can be refrigerated in their syrup for 1 week.

Keralan Stir-Fried Beets

4 SERVINGS

Thoren, as this dish is called in Kerala, South India, is made of finely chopped vegetables stir-fried with grated coconut and spices. The ingredients are added to the pan in rapid succession, so have everything prepped and measured before you begin.

- 1 cup finely grated dried unsweetened coconut
- 2 garlic cloves, crushed
- 1 serrano or Thai chile, cut in half lengthwise
- 1 teaspoon salt
- 1 teaspoon ground cumin
- ¼ teaspoon cayenne pepper
- ¼ teaspoon turmeric
- ⅓ cup water
- 2 tablespoons vegetable oil
- 1 teaspoon mustard seeds

keralan menuspeak

Many restaurants in the United States that bill themselves as South Indian serve popular vegetarian snacks from neighboring Tamil Nadu rather than dishes from the state of Kerala. To identify authentic Keralan food on a menu, look for the word *Malabar,* Kerala's coast, or these dishes:

Appam Rice flour pancakes

Aviyal Mixed vegetables in a grated coconut sauce

Fish molee Fish prepared with coconut milk and vinegar

Konju pappas A curry made with shrimp and coconut milk

Lamb fry or **chicken fry** Dry spiced meat curries

- 2 whole dried red chiles
- 10 curry leaves, or 2 bay leaves
- 1 tablespoon long-grain rice
- 4 large beets (about 2 pounds), peeled and coarsely grated

1. In a small bowl, combine the coconut, garlic, serrano chile, salt, cumin, cayenne and turmeric with the water. Set aside.

2. In a large wok, warm the oil over moderately high heat. Add the mustard seeds, dried red chiles and curry leaves and cover. When the mustard seeds begin to pop, add the rice and stir until the rice just turns opaque, about 5 seconds. Add the beets and cook over moderate heat, stirring occasionally, until barely softened. Add the coconut mixture and cook, stirring occasionally, until the beets are just tender, about 5 minutes. Serve the beets at once. —Maya Kaimal

Roasted Chioggia Beets with Feta

8 SERVINGS

Chioggia beets, which show off their pretty white and pink rings when sliced, are a sweet accent to tangy feta.

- ½ cup raspberry vinegar
- 3 tablespoons honey
- 1 medium shallot, minced

Kosher salt

Coarsely cracked black pepper

- ¼ cup grapeseed oil
- 8 small beets (about 2½ pounds), washed and trimmed
- 1 tablespoon unsalted butter, cut into small bits
- 4 ounces feta cheese, thinly sliced (see Note)

Handful of spicy baby greens, such as mizuna, for garnish

1. Preheat the oven to 350°. In a medium bowl, whisk together ¼ cup of the raspberry vinegar, 1½ tablespoons of the honey, the shallot, ½ teaspoon of kosher salt and ½ teaspoon of black

pepper. Whisk in the grapeseed oil until emulsified.

2. Arrange the beets so they fit snugly in a single layer in a deep baking dish. Add enough water to barely cover the beets and then add the remaining ¼ cup of vinegar and 1½ tablespoons of honey and the butter. Season with salt and pepper. Cover with aluminum foil and bake for 50 to 60 minutes, or until the beets are tender when pierced with a knife. Let cool slightly.

3. Drain and peel the beets and slice them ¼ inch thick. Add the beet slices to the honey dressing and let cool for up to 4 hours.

4. To serve, arrange half of the beet slices on 8 small plates and cover with the feta. Top with the remaining beet slices and drizzle each serving with about 1 tablespoon of the dressing. Garnish with the greens and serve.

—Clifford Harrison and Anne Quatrano

NOTE Use the least salty feta you can find. Creamy Bulgarian feta is an especially good choice here. If you can only find salty feta cheese, just soak it in milk and water overnight to mellow the salty edge.

MAKE AHEAD The roasted beets can be refrigerated for up to 1 day. Let return to room temperature before proceeding.

Skillet Ramp Gratin

4 SERVINGS ★★★ 1997

Test Kitchen associate Grace Parisi developed this rustic gratin using ramps, or wild leeks, which have pink-hued bulbs and broad dark green leaves. The gratin is equally delicious made with fat scallions or young and tender leeks, both of which will require a little more cooking than the ramps.

- 2 tablespoons unsalted butter
- ½ cup fresh bread crumbs made from French or Italian bread
- ½ cup grated Gruyère cheese

Roasted Chioggia Beets with Feta

Miso-Glazed Burdock with Red Lettuces

1. Preheat the oven to 350°. Brush a large shallow baking sheet with ½ tablespoon of the oil. Spread the onion wedges on the baking sheet, drizzle with 1½ tablespoons of the oil and season with salt and pepper. Cover the onions with aluminum foil and bake for about 25 minutes, or until they are soft but not brown.

2. Heat 1½ tablespoons of the oil in a large skillet. Add the scallions and season with salt and pepper. Cover and cook the scallions over high heat, stirring frequently, until they are tender but still green, about 5 minutes. Transfer the scallions to a bowl.

3. Heat the remaining 1½ tablespoons of oil in the skillet. Add the red onions and cook over moderate heat, stirring often, until soft but not colored, about 25 minutes. Stir in the vinegar and cook until nearly evaporated, about 1 minute. Add the port and cook for 1 minute longer.

4. Just before serving, combine the cooked onions and scallions in the skillet and rewarm over moderate heat. Transfer the onion ragout to a bowl and serve. —*Sascha Lyon*

MAKE AHEAD The recipe can be prepared through Step 3 up to 1 day ahead; refrigerate the different onions separately.

Miso-Glazed Burdock with Red Lettuces

4 SERVINGS

Raw burdock is tough and fibrous, so be sure to use a sharp knife to slice it. The lemon in the cooking water keeps the burdock white.

¼ cup walnut halves
½ lemon
4 cups water
1 tablespoon plus 2 teaspoons sugar
Salt
½ pound burdock (2 roots)

¾ pound ramps, trimmed and washed well
Salt and freshly ground white pepper
⅔ cup heavy cream

1. Melt 1 tablespoon of the butter in a large ovenproof skillet. Add the bread crumbs and toast over high heat, stirring occasionally, until lightly golden, about 2 minutes. Transfer the bread crumbs to a plate to cool and then toss them with the Gruyère cheese.

2. Turn on the broiler. Cook the remaining 1 tablespoon of butter in the skillet until just brown. Add the ramps and cook over high heat until limp and lightly golden, 3 to 4 minutes. Season with salt and white pepper, add the cream and cook until bubbling, about 1 minute. Remove from the heat and sprinkle the bread crumbs over the ramps. Broil for about 30 seconds, or until lightly browned and bubbling. Serve immediately. —*Grace Parisi*

Three-Onion Ragout

8 SERVINGS

Here is a versatile side dish that goes with grilled or roasted poultry, pork or meaty fish.

¼ cup plus 1 tablespoon extra-virgin olive oil
2 large Vidalia or other sweet onions, cut into 16 wedges each
Salt and freshly ground pepper
2 bunches of scallions, cut into 1½-inch lengths
2 medium red onions, halved and sliced ¼ inch thick
2 tablespoons red wine vinegar
2 tablespoons port

2 tablespoons plus 1 teaspoon
rice-wine vinegar

1 tablespoon dark or red miso

3 tablespoons peanut oil

Freshly ground pepper

10 loosely packed cups torn
red lettuces, such as Lolla Rosa,
Red Oak and Red Leaf
(not radicchio)

1. Preheat the oven to 400°. Spread the walnut halves in a pie pan and toast them for about 6 minutes, or until they're fragrant.

2. Squeeze the lemon into a medium saucepan and add the water, 1 tablespoon of the sugar and a pinch of salt. Peel the burdock under cool running water. Cut the burdock into ¼-inch slices on a sharp diagonal, adding the slices to the lemon water as you work. Bring the water to a boil and cook the burdock slices over moderately high heat until they are al dente, about 30 minutes. Drain the burdock slices and let them cool slightly. Stack the burdock slices and then cut them into thin matchsticks.

3. Return the burdock matchsticks to the saucepan. Add the remaining 2 teaspoons of sugar, 1 teaspoon of the vinegar and 1 teaspoon of the miso. Cook the burdock over moderately high heat, stirring, until glossy, about 2 minutes. Transfer the burdock to a plate and let cool.

4. In a small glass or stainless-steel bowl, whisk the remaining 2 tablespoons of vinegar with the remaining 2 teaspoons of miso until the miso is dissolved. Whisk in the oil and season the dressing with salt and pepper.

5. In a large salad bowl, toss the lettuces, walnuts and burdock. Add the dressing, toss again and serve immediately. —*Grace Parisi*

MAKE AHEAD The recipe can be prepared through Step 3 up to 1 day in advance.

Creamy Salsify with Horseradish

4 SERVINGS

The surprise in this side dish is that the sweet, subtle flavor of black salsify is brilliantly complemented by the judicious addition of pungent horseradish.

1 gallon water

2 tablespoons white vinegar

2¼ pounds black salsify

Salt

3 tablespoons heavy cream

2 tablespoons unsalted butter

¾ teaspoon finely grated
horseradish root

Freshly ground white pepper

Parsley leaves, for garnish

1. In a large bowl, combine 2 quarts of the water with the vinegar. Peel the salsify under cool running water. Cut the roots into 4-inch lengths, adding them to the vinegar water as you work. Drain the salsify, transfer to a medium saucepan and add 2 quarts of fresh water and a generous pinch of salt. Bring to a boil and cook over moderately high heat until tender, 8 to 10 minutes.

2. Drain the salsify, reserving 3 tablespoons of the cooking water. In a food processor, combine the salsify and the reserved cooking water with the cream, butter and horseradish and puree until smooth. Season with salt and white pepper. Work the puree through a fine sieve and serve hot, sprinkled with parsley. —*Grace Parisi*

MAKE AHEAD The puree can be refrigerated for up to 1 day.

Jerusalem Artichoke and Sweet Potato Gratin

6 SERVINGS

I used to avoid Jerusalem artichokes, or sunchokes, because they were so annoying to peel. Now I enjoy them unpeeled, scrubbed with a stiff vegetable brush.

all in the family

The diverse Compositae family includes plants that are both familiar—artichokes, endive, radicchio—and unfamiliar. Here are some ideas for using some of the less known members on its family tree, as well as classic and new ways to prepare the more mundane ones.

Black salsify Peeled and boiled, then pureed, sautéed, gratinéed or roasted

Burdock Peeled and boiled, then sautéed, pickled or pureed

Cardoons Peeled, blanched and gratinéed; braised; fried; sautéed in butter

Chicory and **Escarole** Sautéed with garlic; shredded in soups and pastas

Dandelions Wilted in salads, with bacon; sautéed with garlic and crushed red pepper

Endive and **Radicchio** Grilled or sautéed; shredded in pastas and risottos

Jerusalem artichokes (sunchokes) Raw in salads; roasted; pureed; gratinéed

Romaine lettuce Shredded in soups and stir-fries; braised with peas and cured ham

Sunflower seeds Raw in breads and muffins; toasted and salted for snacks; sprinkled on salads and vegetables

Tarragon Raw in salad dressings and omelets; added to seafood and chicken dishes and tartar sauce

1 tablespoon unsalted butter

1 leek, white and tender green,
thinly sliced

¼ cup homemade dry bread
crumbs

2 tablespoons freshly grated
Gruyère cheese

1 pound Jerusalem artichokes,
thinly sliced crosswise

Salt and freshly ground pepper

1 medium sweet potato
(about ½ pound), peeled
and thinly sliced crosswise

¾ cup heavy cream

1. Preheat the oven to 350°. Using 1 teaspoon of the butter, grease a 9-

Jerusalem Artichokes with Sweet Potato Gratin

Stewed Winter Vegetables

8 SERVINGS

Wait till you try this combination—parsnips and carrots for sweetness, turnips for depth of flavor, shallots and leeks for interest and delicious little potatoes for satisfaction.

  8 medium shallots, peeled
2½ tablespoons unsalted butter
Salt and freshly ground pepper
  8 medium parsnips, peeled and cut into 2-inch lengths
  4 large turnips, peeled and quartered
  4 medium carrots, cut into 2-inch lengths
  2 large leeks, halved lengthwise and cut crosswise into 2-inch pieces
2½ cups chicken stock (p. 117) or canned low-sodium broth
  1 thyme sprig
½ pound small purple or red-skinned potatoes

1. Preheat the oven to 350°. Put the shallots on a large piece of aluminum foil and top with ½ tablespoon of the butter. Season with salt and pepper and seal the shallots in the foil. Bake for about 30 minutes, or until tender.

2. In a large saucepan, combine the parsnips, turnips, carrots, leeks, stock, thyme and the remaining 2 tablespoons of butter. Bring to a boil over moderately high heat and then reduce the heat to low and add a pinch each of salt and pepper. Cover and simmer, stirring occasionally, until the vegetables are tender, about 20 minutes. Discard the thyme sprig.

3. In a medium saucepan, cook the potatoes in boiling salted water until tender, about 10 minutes. Drain the potatoes and cut them into 2-inch cubes. Add the potatoes and roasted shallots to the vegetable stew, season with salt and pepper and serve.

—*Joseph and Thomas Keller*

inch glass pie plate and a 12-inch square of aluminum foil.

2. In a medium skillet, melt 1 teaspoon of the butter. Add the leek and cook over moderately high heat until softened but still green, about 2 minutes. Transfer the leek to a plate.

3. Melt the remaining 1 teaspoon of butter in the skillet and add the bread crumbs. Cook, stirring, until coated and lightly browned. Transfer the crumbs to a plate and toss with the Gruyère.

4. Layer half of the Jerusalem artichoke slices in the prepared pie plate and season with salt and pepper. Cover with half of the leek slices and half of the sweet potato slices, reserving the nicest slices for the top. Season with salt and pepper. Repeat with the remaining Jerusalem artichokes, leek and sweet potato and then pour the cream evenly over the top.

5. Cover the pie plate with the aluminum foil, buttered side down, and bake for 30 minutes, or until bubbling and the vegetables are just tender. Remove the foil and bake for 20 minutes, or until lightly browned. Sprinkle the bread crumbs on top and bake for 20 minutes longer, or until golden. Let the gratin stand for 15 minutes before serving. —*Grace Parisi*

Stewed Winter Vegetables, with Braised Short Ribs with Whole Grain Mustard (p. 265).

Spicy Corn Stew

Spicy Corn Stew

4 SERVINGS

It's poetic license to call something that cooks so briefly a stew, but whatever you choose to call it, this is the answer when you've had your fill of plain corn on the cob. Fresh corn and cilantro are critical.

    3 tablespoons unsalted butter
    1 small onion, coarsely chopped

One 3-ounce piece of slab bacon
    ½ cup white wine, preferably
       Riesling
    2 garlic cloves, chopped
    1 large jalapeño, minced
    2 cups chicken stock (p. 117) or
       canned low-sodium broth
    6 ears fresh corn, shucked
       and kernels cut from the cobs,
       cobs reserved

    1 cup halved cherry tomatoes
    ¼ cup finely chopped cilantro, plus
       4 cilantro sprigs
    1 tablespoon fresh lime juice
Salt and freshly ground pepper

ı. In a large deep skillet, melt 2 tablespoons of the butter over moderate heat. Add the onion and the bacon and cook, stirring, until the onion is softened but not browned, about 5 minutes. Add the wine and boil over moderately high heat, stirring occasionally, until reduced by half, about 1½ minutes. Add the garlic and jalapeño and cook, stirring constantly, for 1 minute. Add the stock and corn cobs and cook until the liquid is reduced by half, about 10 minutes. Discard the corn cobs.

2. Add the corn to the skillet and simmer over moderate heat, stirring frequently, until tender, about 15 minutes. Remove the bacon.

3. Swirl the remaining 1 tablespoon of butter into the cooked corn. Stir in the tomatoes, finely chopped cilantro and lime juice and season with salt and pepper. Ladle the stew into bowls, garnish with the cilantro sprigs and serve hot. —*Eberhard Müller*

Grilled Plantains, Pineapple and Chayotes
12 SERVINGS

Chayote is a roughly pear-shaped pale green vegetable with a crisp texture. Like zucchini, these squash are at their sweetest when small.

- 6 ripe (black) plantains, peeled and sliced lengthwise ⅓ inch thick
- 6 chayotes—halved lengthwise, pitted and sliced lengthwise ¼ inch thick
- ⅓ cup olive oil

Salt

One large ripe pineapple—peeled, halved lengthwise, cored and sliced crosswise ½ inch thick

Light a charcoal grill or preheat a grill pan. Brush the plantain and chayote slices generously with the oil and season the chayotes with salt. Grill the plantains and chayotes, along with the pineapple, over moderately high heat for 3 to 4 minutes per side, or until tender and lightly charred. Serve hot or warm. —*Marcia Kiesel*

Lentils with Thyme
8 SERVINGS

- 1 pound lentils, picked over and rinsed
- 8 cups water
- 1 garlic clove, minced
- 1½ tablespoons finely chopped thyme
- 2 tablespoons unsalted butter
- 1 tablespoon extra-virgin olive oil
- 2 medium carrots, finely chopped
- 1 medium onion, finely chopped
- 1 large celery rib, finely chopped

Salt and freshly ground pepper

1. In a large saucepan, combine the lentils with the water, garlic and 1 tablespoon of the thyme and bring to a boil. Cover partially; simmer over low heat until tender, about 45 minutes. Drain and transfer to a bowl to cool.

2. In a medium skillet, melt the butter in the oil. Add the carrots, onion and celery; cook over moderate heat until tender. Season with salt and pepper and the remaining ½ tablespoon of thyme. Stir the vegetables into the lentils. Season with salt and pepper. Serve at room temperature. —*Mark Gottwald*

Mixed Dhal Vada
MAKES ABOUT 30 VADA

Freshly fried *vada,* or fritters, made with two kinds of ground dhal, are served at teatime in southern India. Dhal is a pulse, or edible legume seed that has been dried.

- ½ cup split urad dhal (3½ ounces; see Note)
- ½ cup thoor dhal or yellow split peas (3½ ounces; see Note)
- 2 tablespoons water
- ¾ cup finely chopped onion
- ¼ cup chopped cilantro
- 2 teaspoons minced fresh ginger
- 1 serrano or Thai chile, minced
- ½ teaspoon ground cumin
- ¼ teaspoon cayenne pepper
- ⅛ teaspoon asafetida (see Note)

Salt

Vegetable oil, for deep-frying

1. Rinse the dhals separately in several changes of water and then soak them for 4 hours. Drain before using. In a food processor, combine the dhals with the water and pulse until finely ground but not pureed. Transfer the dhals to a medium bowl and add the onion, cilantro, ginger, serrano chile, cumin, cayenne and asafetida and 1¼ teaspoons of salt.

2. In a wok, heat 2 inches of oil to 325°. Scoop scant tablespoons of the vada batter onto a wax paper–lined plate and flatten slightly. Slide 5 or 6 patties at a time into the hot oil and cook, turning once, until deep golden brown, about 5 minutes. Using a slotted spoon, transfer the fritters to paper towels to drain. Sprinkle with salt and serve at once. —*Maya Kaimal*
NOTE Split urad dhal, thoor dhal and asafetida are available at Indian groceries and from these two mail-order sources: Kalustyan's, 212-685-3451, and Patel Brothers, 562-402-2953.
SERVE WITH Sweet small bananas and milky tea.

Kerala Sambar
4 SERVINGS

Adding the distinctive mustard seed, curry leaf and dried red chile seasoning at the end gives this vegetable curry the stamp of Kerala, in southern India.

- ½ cup thoor dhal or yellow split peas (3½ ounces; see Note), rinsed in several changes of water
- 3¼ cups water
- ¼ teaspoon turmeric
- 2 tablespoons vegetable oil
- ¼ teaspoon fenugreek seeds
- ⅛ teaspoon asafetida (see Note)
- ¼ pound okra, trimmed
- 1 medium boiling potato, peeled and cut into ¾-inch dice

1 medium tomato, coarsely
chopped

1 medium onion, coarsely
chopped

¼ cup cilantro leaves

1 serrano or Thai chile, cut in half
lengthwise

2 teaspoons ground coriander

1½ teaspoons salt

½ teaspoon ground cumin

¼ teaspoon tamarind concentrate
(see Note), dissolved in
1 tablespoon boiling water

⅛ teaspoon cayenne pepper

⅛ teaspoon freshly ground black
pepper

¼ teaspoon mustard seeds

8 curry leaves, or 2 bay leaves

1 dried red chile

½ teaspoon fresh lemon juice

1. In a small saucepan, combine the dhal with 1¼ cups of water and ⅛ teaspoon of the turmeric and bring to a boil. Cover and cook over low heat until soft, about 30 minutes (45 minutes for yellow split peas). Partially mash the dhal with a potato masher.

2. Meanwhile, in a large saucepan, heat 1 tablespoon of the oil. Add the fenugreek seeds and asafetida and cook over moderately high heat until fragrant and lightly colored, about 1 minute. Add the okra, potato, tomato, onion, cilantro, serrano chile, coriander, salt, cumin, the remaining ⅛ teaspoon of turmeric, dissolved tamarind, cayenne and black pepper along with the remaining 2 cups of water and bring to a boil. Reduce the heat to moderately low and simmer until the potatoes are tender, about 18 minutes. Add the mashed dhal and simmer 10 minutes longer.

3. In a small skillet, heat the remaining 1 tablespoon of oil. Add the mustard seeds, curry leaves and dried red chile. Cover and cook over moderately high heat until the mustard seeds have

popped for a few seconds and then stir into the vegetable and dhal mixture. Add the lemon juice and serve.

—*Maya Kaimal*

NOTE Thoor dhal, asafetida and tamarind concentrate are available at Indian groceries and from these two mail-order sources: Kalustyan's, 212-685-3451, and Patel Brothers, 562-402-2953.

MAKE AHEAD The recipe can be prepared through Step 1 a day ahead.

Thoor Dhal with Tomato and Onion

4 SERVINGS

Thoor dhal is a kind of legume seed, which looks like a flat, beige split pea. Its rich, earthy taste makes it popular in the southern Indian state of Kerala. Finish the dish by adding the classic Keralan seasoning blend of dried red chiles, mustard seeds and curry leaves, sizzled together in oil.

1 cup thoor dhal (7 ounces; see
Note)

¼ teaspoon turmeric

2½ cups water

2 serrano or Thai chiles, cut in half
lengthwise

1 small onion, thinly sliced

1 teaspoon minced garlic

1 teaspoon minced fresh ginger

1 tomato, coarsely chopped

1¼ teaspoons salt

2 tablespoons vegetable oil

½ teaspoon mustard seeds

10 curry leaves, or 2 bay leaves

2 dried red chiles

1. In a medium saucepan, combine the thoor dhal and turmeric with the water and bring to a boil. Cover and cook over low heat until tender but not mushy, about 30 minutes. Add the serrano chiles, onion, garlic and ginger; simmer until the onion is softened, about 5 minutes. Add the tomato and salt and simmer until the tomato is softened.

2. In a small skillet, combine the oil, mustard seeds, curry leaves and dried red chiles. Cover and cook over moderately high heat until the seeds pop. Stir the spices into the dhal and serve.

—*Maya Kaimal*

NOTE Thoor dhal is available at Indian groceries and from these mail-order sources: Kalustyan's, 212-685-3451, and Patel Brothers, 562-402-2953.

SERVE WITH Boiled rice.

Cranberry Beans and Pea Shoots in Sherry-Hazelnut Vinaigrette

4 SERVINGS

Fresh cranberry beans, which are sold almost everywhere from July through September, are a revelation. They can be cooked until tender without losing their shape. As for the pea shoots, the smaller the better. Be sure that the hazelnut oil is fresh and made from unroasted nuts.

3 pounds fresh cranberry
beans, shelled

3 cups chicken stock (p. 117) or
canned low-sodium broth

One ¼-pound piece of slab bacon
(optional)

1 medium onion, quartered

4 thyme sprigs

2 garlic cloves, crushed

¼ cup unroasted hazelnut oil

2 tablespoons sherry vinegar

1 tablespoon Dijon mustard

Salt and freshly ground pepper

2 cups small pea shoots
(about 3 ounces)

1. In a medium saucepan, combine the cranberry beans with the chicken stock, bacon, onion, thyme and garlic. Partially cover and cook over moderate heat until the cranberry beans are tender, 20 to 30 minutes. Drain the cranberry beans, reserving 2 tablespoons of the stock. Pick out and discard the bacon, onion, thyme and

Cranberry Beans and Pea Shoots in Sherry-Hazelnut Vinaigrette

Autumn Vegetable Sauté with Sausage and Mint

garlic. Transfer the cranberry beans to a bowl set in a larger bowl of ice water and refrigerate until chilled, about 1 hour, or omit the ice water and refrigerate the cranberry beans overnight.

2. In a large glass or stainless-steel bowl, combine the oil, vinegar, mustard and the 2 tablespoons of reserved stock. Season the vinaigrette with salt and pepper. Toss the pea shoots with a little of the vinaigrette and transfer them to a platter. Add the cranberry beans to the remaining vinaigrette and toss until they are coated. Spoon the cranberry beans onto the pea shoots and serve.

—*Eberhard Müller*

Stewed Flageolets with Thyme
4 SERVINGS ♛

- 1 cup dried flageolets or dried baby lima beans (about 6 ounces), picked over and rinsed
- 4 cups water
- ½ cup finely chopped onion
- 1 tablespoon minced garlic
- 1 tablespoon olive oil
- 1 medium tomato—peeled, seeded and finely chopped
- 1 quart Chicken Stock (p. 117)
- Salt and freshly ground white pepper
- 1 small Idaho potato, peeled and cut into ½-inch dice
- 2 teaspoons minced thyme
- 2 tablespoons unsalted butter

1. Soak the flageolets in 4 cups of water for 24 hours. Discard any beans that float; drain the beans.

2. In a medium saucepan, cook the onion and garlic in the oil over moderate heat, stirring, until softened, about 5 minutes. Add the tomato and cook just until it starts to break down, about 3 minutes. Add the stock and beans and bring to a boil. Reduce the heat to moderately low, cover partially and cook until the beans are tender and the liquid is slightly thickened, about 1½ hours; add water if the beans are dry. Season with salt and white pepper.

3. Add the potato and thyme and cook until the potato is tender, about 20 minutes. Stir in the butter and season with salt and white pepper.

—*Anne Kearney*

MAKE AHEAD The cooked beans can be refrigerated overnight; rewarm before serving, adding a little water.

Autumn Vegetable Sauté with Sausage and Mint
8 SERVINGS

Together, the beans, the mushrooms and the other ingredients create a play of tastes and textures that is unusual and completely delicious. The dried beans must be soaked overnight before cooking.

- ½ cup dried cannellini beans (3½ ounces)
- 5 cups water
- 2 pounds fava beans, shelled and peeled
- 1½ pounds small chanterelle or button mushrooms, stems removed and reserved
- 1 bunch of spearmint—¼ cup whole small leaves, ¼ cup chopped leaves, stems reserved
- 2 large shallots, minced, skins reserved
- ¼ cup plus 2 tablespoons extra-virgin olive oil

1 pound fresh Italian sausage,
casings removed, meat formed
into 1-inch balls

⅓ cup dry white wine

Salt and freshly ground pepper

1. In a bowl, cover the cannellini beans with water and let soak overnight. Drain the beans and transfer to a medium saucepan. Add 5 cups of water and bring to a boil. Simmer over low heat, stirring occasionally, until tender, about 1 hour. Drain the cannellini beans in a colander set over a bowl; reserve the cooking water.

2. Cook the fava beans in boiling salted water until tender, 3 to 5 minutes. Drain the favas in a colander set over a medium saucepan. Add the reserved cannellini bean cooking water to the fava water and stir in the mushroom stems, mint stems and shallot skins. Simmer over low heat until reduced to 2 cups, about 20 minutes; strain.

3. In a large skillet, heat 2 tablespoons of the oil. Add the mushrooms and shallots and cook over moderate heat, stirring, until the mushrooms are lightly browned, about 5 minutes. Push the mushroom mixture to the side and add the sausage balls in an even layer. Cook until browned, about 3 minutes per side. Add the chopped mint and the wine and cook until the wine evaporates. Add the cannellini and fava beans and their cooking liquid. Cook over high heat until the liquid is reduced by half, about 10 minutes.

4. Remove the skillet from the heat and let stand for 5 minutes. Season the vegetable sauté with salt and pepper. Spoon the vegetable sauté onto 8 plates and scatter the mint leaves over the top. Drizzle with the remaining ¼ cup of oil and serve.

—*Umberto Creatini*

MAKE AHEAD The sauté can be prepared through Step 2 and refrigerated for up to 1 day.

Sweet Potato Scallops with Caramelized Onion (p. 336)

Escarole Torta with Sweet Potato Hash Brown Crust

Escarole Torta with Sweet Potato Hash Brown Crust

MAKES ONE 10-INCH TORTA

Here, hash browns pressed into a kind of crust serve as a base for a torta.

1½ pounds sweet potatoes, peeled and coarsely grated
1 medium yellow onion, grated
Salt
2½ tablespoons all-purpose flour
Freshly ground pepper
Freshly grated nutmeg
1 tablespoon olive oil, plus more for brushing
1 medium red onion, coarsely chopped
2 garlic cloves, minced
4 cups chopped escarole
6 large eggs, beaten
1½ cups grated provolone cheese (6 ounces)
1 cup milk
1½ tablespoons chopped oregano

I. Preheat the oven to 400°. In a colander set in the sink, combine the sweet potatoes, yellow onion and ¾ teaspoon of salt. Let drain for 15 minutes and then squeeze out the excess liquid. Transfer the mixture to a bowl. Add the flour and a pinch each of pepper and nutmeg; toss well. Press the mixture into a generously oiled 10-inch pie plate, pushing it up the side and onto the rim to form a crust; brush lightly with oil. Bake the crust for about 25 minutes, or until slightly crisp; cover the rim with aluminum foil if it browns too quickly.

2. Meanwhile, in a medium skillet, heat 1 tablespoon of the oil. Add the red onion and garlic and cook over moderate heat until softened but not browned, about 3 minutes. Add the escarole; cook, stirring occasionally, until wilted, about 3 minutes. Transfer the escarole to a colander set in the sink and press out as much liquid as possible; let cool slightly.

3. In a medium bowl, beat the eggs with 1 cup of the provolone cheese and the milk and oregano. Add the wilted escarole and season with salt and pepper. Pour the mixture into the sweet potato crust and sprinkle the remaining cheese on top.

4. Reduce the oven temperature to 375°. Bake the torta for about 45 minutes, or until the center is set; cover it loosely with aluminum foil if it browns too quickly. Let stand for 5 minutes before serving. —Jesse Cool

SERVE WITH Sliced ham and thick slices of bread with apple butter.

WINE This quichelike dish is rich and cheesy with a touch of sweetness, an ideal match for a round fruity California Chardonnay. Try the 1996 Sanford or the 1995 Raymond Reserve.

Sweet Potato Casserole

12 SERVINGS

Sweet potatoes and pecans are major fall crops in the deep South, and this casserole is a staple on holiday tables there. Buttery and sweet, it makes a wonderful addition to a savory meal. Serve it with roasted turkey and dressing, along with spicy collard greens.

SWEET POTATOES

5 pounds small sweet potatoes (about 10)
1 stick (4 ounces) unsalted butter, cut into pieces
⅔ cup granulated sugar
½ cup light brown sugar
½ cup honey
2 teaspoons pure vanilla extract
1¾ teaspoons salt
¾ teaspoon freshly grated nutmeg
3 large eggs, lightly beaten
2½ cups hot milk

TOPPING

1 cup all-purpose flour
1 cup light brown sugar
½ teaspoon cinnamon
½ teaspoon freshly grated nutmeg
¼ teaspoon salt
1 stick (4 ounces) unsalted butter, cut into ½-inch dice and chilled
1 cup (4 ounces) coarsely chopped pecans

I. MAKE THE SWEET POTATOES: Preheat the oven to 350°. Spread the sweet potatoes on a rimmed baking sheet and bake for about 1½ hours, or until tender. Let the sweet potatoes cool slightly, about 10 minutes, and then peel them.

2. In a large bowl, beat the hot sweet potatoes on low speed and then beat in the butter. Add the granulated sugar, brown sugar, honey, vanilla, salt and nutmeg and beat until blended. Add the eggs and beat on medium speed for 2 minutes. Reduce the speed to low and gradually add the hot milk to the sweet potatoes.

3. Preheat the oven to 375°. Butter a 13-by-9-by-2 inch baking dish and then pour in the pureed sweet potatoes. Spread the sweet potatoes in an even layer.

4. MAKE THE TOPPING: In a large bowl, rub together the flour, brown sugar, cinnamon, nutmeg and salt. Add the butter and rub or cut it in until the mixture resembles coarse meal. Stir in the pecans.

5. Sprinkle the topping evenly over the pureed sweet potatoes and bake for 1 to 1¼ hours, until the topping turns golden brown and crisp. If the topping browns too quickly around the edge before the center is crisped, cut a large hole in the center of a sheet of aluminum foil and rest the sheet on the baking dish while the casserole finish baking. Serve the casserole hot. —Edna Lewis and Scott Peacock

MAKE AHEAD The pureed sweet potatoes and the topping can be refrigerated separately for up to 1 day. Bring them to room temperature before proceeding.

Sweet Potato Scallops with Caramelized Onion

Sweet Potato Scallops with Caramelized Onion

4 SERVINGS

Select long slender sweet potatoes that will make perfect round scallops when sliced crosswise.

- 3 sweet potatoes (1½ pounds)
- 2 tablespoons vegetable oil

Salt and freshly ground pepper

- 1 large onion, thinly sliced

1. In a saucepan, cover the sweet potatoes with water and boil over high heat until just tender, about 12 minutes. Drain the sweet potatoes and let cool. Peel and slice the sweet potatoes crosswise 1 inch thick.

2. In a medium skillet, heat 1 tablespoon of the vegetable oil. Add half of the sweet potato slices to the skillet and cook over moderately high heat until well browned, about 3 minutes per side. Transfer the sweet potato slices to a plate and season them with salt and pepper. Repeat with the remaining 1 tablespoon of oil and sweet potato slices.

3. Add the onion to the skillet, cover and cook over low heat, stirring occasionally, until softened and browned, about 8 minutes. Season with salt and

pepper, scatter over the sweet potatoes and serve. —*Marcia Kiesel*

WINE This wine-friendly side dish could be happily paired with a nonvintage sparkling wine, for example the Zardetto Prosecco from Italy. The onions make it an especially good match with the fruity 1996 or 1997 Georges Duboeuf Beaujolais.

Crisp Garlic Yukon Gold Potatoes

8 SERVINGS

¼ cup extra-virgin olive oil
Salt and freshly ground pepper
2 pounds small Yukon Gold potatoes, halved
6 medium garlic cloves, thinly sliced
2 tablespoons finely chopped flat-leaf parsley

1. Preheat the oven to 400°. Brush a baking sheet with 1 tablespoon of the oil and sprinkle with salt and pepper. Arrange the potatoes on the baking sheet, cut side down; bake for 45 minutes, or until crisp and golden brown. Transfer the potatoes to a bowl.

2. Heat the remaining 3 tablespoons of oil in a large skillet. Add the garlic and cook over moderately low heat, stirring, until crisp and lightly browned; do not let the garlic get too brown or it will be bitter. Pour the garlic and oil over the potatoes, add the parsley and toss. Season with salt and pepper and serve at once. —*Sascha Lyon*

Buttery Sautéed Potatoes

8 SERVINGS

You don't have to take the time to cut your potatoes into perfect ovals; simply peel and quarter them.

6 medium russet potatoes, quartered
¼ cup pure olive oil
1 stick (4 ounces) unsalted butter
Salt and freshly ground pepper

1. Using a paring knife, peel each potato quarter lengthwise and shape it into a long oval.

2. Heat the oil in a large skillet. Add the potatoes and cook over moderate heat until browned on all sides, about 15 minutes. Add the butter and cook over moderately low heat, turning often, until tender, about 10 minutes longer. Season the potatoes with salt and pepper. Using a slotted spoon, transfer the sautéed potatoes to a large bowl and serve at once.

—*The Point, Lake Saranac, New York*

MAKE AHEAD The sautéed potatoes can stand at room temperature for up to 8 hours. Rewarm in a 400° oven.

Creamed Potatoes with Tomatoes

8 SERVINGS

3 pounds Idaho potatoes
1½ cups milk
1 cup heavy cream
4 scallions, thinly sliced
2 plum tomatoes, seeded and finely chopped
Salt and freshly ground white pepper

1. Preheat the oven to 350°. Bake the potatoes for about 1 hour, or until they are tender.

2. In a large saucepan, warm the milk and heavy cream. Halve the potatoes and scoop the flesh into the saucepan. Mash over low heat until creamy. Stir in the scallions and tomatoes and season with salt and white pepper Serve at once.

—*Joseph and Thomas Keller*

Mashed Potatoes with Mascarpone

8 SERVINGS

Using small unpeeled boiling potatoes saves a great deal of time; the skins of Yukon Golds are particularly tender. If you don't like the skins, use larger baking potatoes, peeled and quartered.

3 pounds small Yukon Gold or Yellow Finn potatoes, scrubbed
2 bunches of scallions, white and tender green, cut into ½-inch pieces
2 teaspoons salt
1½ cups mascarpone cheese (about ¾ pound), at room temperature
¼ cup finely chopped flat-leaf parsley
Freshly ground white pepper

1. Put the potatoes and scallions in a large saucepan and add enough water to cover by 1 inch. Add the salt, cover and bring to a boil. Reduce the heat and simmer the potatoes until tender when pierced, about 20 minutes.

2. Drain the potatoes, reserving 1 cup of the cooking water. Return the potatoes to the saucepan and coarsely mash by hand. Add the mascarpone and parsley; add a little of the cooking water if the potatoes are too stiff. Season with salt and white pepper and serve at once. —*Nancy Verde Barr*

Golden Mashed Potatoes with Morels and Baked Eggs

4 SERVINGS

These oniony mashed potatoes are wonderful morning or night. The recipe is a great way to use up leftovers, but fresh mashed potatoes make a fluffier dish.

½ cup dried morels (½ ounce)
½ cup boiling water
1½ pounds Yukon Gold potatoes, peeled and cut into 2-inch chunks
6 garlic cloves, peeled
¼ cup extra-virgin olive oil
1 large onion, coarsely chopped
¾ cup heavy cream
Salt and freshly ground pepper
4 large eggs
½ cup freshly grated Asiago or Parmesan cheese
1 tablespoon minced chives

1. Preheat the oven to 375°. In a heat-proof bowl, cover the morels with the boiling water and let stand for about 15 minutes to soften. Drain the morels, reserving the water; rinse and coarsely chop the morels.

2. Meanwhile, in a large saucepan, cover the potatoes and garlic with water and boil over high heat until tender, about 15 minutes. Drain the potatoes and garlic and return them to the pan. Dry over moderately high heat, shaking the pan for about 1 minute. Work the potatoes and garlic through a ricer or mash by hand in a large bowl.

3. In a large skillet, heat the oil. Add the onion; cook over low heat, stirring often, until soft and golden, about 15 minutes. Add the morels and ¼ cup of the cream and simmer for 2 minutes. Add the onion mixture to the potatoes with the remaining ½ cup of heavy cream and the reserved mushroom water; season with salt and pepper.

4. Spoon the potatoes into a buttered shallow 1½-quart baking dish. Make 4 shallow indentations in the potatoes and break an egg into each. Sprinkle the cheese over all. Bake for about 12 minutes, or until the egg whites are set and the yolks are softly cooked. Garnish with the chives and serve at once. —*Jesse Cool*

SERVE WITH A spinach, bacon and mushroom salad.

WINE By themselves, eggs don't particularly complement wine, but this mushroom-and-onion-rich recipe is more than wine-friendly. It needs a light red whose acidic tartness and fresh fruitiness can contrast with the buttery tastes. A California Gamay, such as the 1997 Beringer Gamay Beaujolais, would be perfect. Serve it slightly cool to enhance its fruit.

MAKE AHEAD The recipe can be prepared through Step 2 up to 6 hours before serving.

Potato-Apple Galette with Horseradish Cream

4 SERVINGS

 5 medium Yukon Gold potatoes, peeled
Kosher salt
 1 medium Fuji or Granny Smith apple, peeled and cored
 1 medium onion, finely chopped
2½ tablespoons extra-virgin olive oil
 1 tablespoon finely chopped sage
Freshly ground pepper
 1 tablespoon minced chives
Horseradish Cream (recipe follows)

1. Preheat the oven to 400°. Coarsely grate 4 of the potatoes into a colander. Toss with 1 tablespoon of kosher salt and let drain for 5 minutes. Using your hands, squeeze out as much liquid as possible and transfer the grated potatoes to a bowl. Grate the apple and add it to the grated potatoes. Add the onion, 1 tablespoon of the oil and the sage; toss well. Season with pepper.

2. Using a sharp knife or a mandoline, slice the remaining potato ¼ inch thick. In a 10-inch nonstick ovenproof skillet, heat 1 tablespoon of the oil. Arrange the potato slices in the skillet in concentric circles. Season with kosher salt and pepper. Cook over moderate heat, pressing down on the potatoes with a spatula a few times, until brown around the edges, about 5 minutes.

3. Spoon the grated potato mixture into the skillet, pressing firmly to make a neat cake. Transfer the skillet to the oven and bake for about 35 minutes, or until browned and crisp on the bottom. Invert the cake onto a flat plate. Add the remaining ½ tablespoon of oil to the skillet. Slide the potato cake back into the skillet and cook over moderately low heat until nicely browned on the bottom, about 5 minutes. Slide the cake onto a cutting board and top with the chives. Cut into 4 wedges and serve with the Horseradish Cream.

MAKES ABOUT 1 CUP
 1 cup crème fraîche or sour cream
 ¼ cup freshly grated horseradish root or drained prepared horseradish
 1 tablespoon fresh lemon juice
Salt and freshly ground pepper

In a bowl, combine the crème fraîche, horseradish and lemon juice; season with salt and pepper. —*Maria Helm*

MAKE AHEAD The cream can be refrigerated for up to 3 days.

Potato-Cheese Gratin with Tarragon

8 SERVINGS

At the restaurant Cena in New York City, chef Normand Laprise sometimes serves this gratin crowned with a pair of ruffly homemade potato chips. The recipe calls for aged balsamic vinegar, but if you don't have this, you can cook down regular balsamic to concentrate the flavor: boil three tablespoons over low heat until reduced to four teaspoons.

 8 medium red or fingerling potatoes (about 1½ pounds)
 1 shallot, minced
 ⅓ cup extra-virgin olive oil
Salt and freshly ground pepper
 40 tarragon leaves
 4 ounces Comté or Gruyère cheese, cut into eight 2½-inch-square slices
 1 tablespoon plus 1 teaspoon aged balsamic vinegar

1. Preheat the broiler. In a large saucepan of boiling salted water, cook the potatoes until just tender, about 20 minutes. Drain and let cool and then cut each into neat ⅓-inch-thick slices.

2. On an oiled baking sheet, arrange each potato into a round of slightly overlapping slices. Sprinkle each of the rounds with a little of the shallot

Potato-Cheese Gratin with Tarragon

and 2 teaspoons of oil; season with salt and pepper. Arrange 5 tarragon leaves on each round and top with 1 slice of cheese. Broil the rounds, rotating the pan, for about 2 minutes, or until the cheese is bubbly but not browned.

3. Carefully transfer the potato rounds to plates using a metal spatula. Sprinkle ½ teaspoon of the balsamic vinegar around the potato on each plate and serve at once. —*Normand Laprise*

Potato Gratin with Parmesan and Caramelized Onions

4 SERVINGS 🌷

1½ **pounds Yukon Gold potatoes**
1 **teaspoon canola oil**
1 **teaspoon olive oil**
2 **medium onions, thinly sliced**
1 **small garlic clove, minced**
¼ **teaspoon minced rosemary**
¼ **teaspoon minced sage**
¼ **teaspoon minced thyme**

Salt and freshly ground pepper
Vegetable oil cooking spray
½ cup freshly grated Parmesan cheese (about 2 ounces)
3 large egg whites, plus 2 large whole eggs
¾ cup skim milk
3 tablespoons nonfat dry milk
⅛ teaspoon freshly grated nutmeg

1. In a steamer basket, steam the potatoes until they are tender, about

339

20 minutes. Let the potatoes cool slightly and then peel and cut them into ¼-inch-thick slices.

2. Meanwhile, heat the canola oil and olive oil in a medium skillet. Add the onions and cook over moderately high heat, stirring occasionally, until softened and just beginning to brown, about 5 minutes. Reduce the heat to moderately low and cook, stirring, until the onions are caramelized, about 15 minutes; add 1 to 2 tablespoons of water if the skillet is dry. Stir the garlic, rosemary, sage and thyme into the skillet and season the mixture with salt and pepper.

3. Preheat the oven to 350°. Coat a 9-inch deep-dish pie pan with vegetable oil cooking spray. Arrange half of

Herbed Lemon Rice

the potato slices in the pie pan, overlapping them slightly, and season with salt and pepper. Top the potato slices with the onion mixture and half of the Parmesan cheese. Cover with the remaining potato slices.

4. In a bowl, combine the egg whites, whole eggs, skim milk, dry milk and nutmeg and season them with salt and pepper. Pour the custard mixture over the potatoes and sprinkle the remaining Parmesan cheese on top. Bake the gratin for about 45 minutes, or until the custard is set and the top is golden. Let the gratin rest for 10 minutes before serving.

—*Betsy Nelson and Jim Kyndberg*

ONE SERVING Calories 321 kcal, Total Fat 8.8 gm, Saturated Fat 3.4 gm

Rice-Bowl Rice

MAKES ABOUT 6 CUPS

Rice-Bowl Rice is plain white Chinese rice. Notice that no salt or oil is added during cooking; all the flavor comes from *cai*—the dishes eaten with the rice, such as Beef and Lettuce Congee (p. 116), Soupy Chicken with Mushrooms (p. 190) or Stir-Fried Chinese Greens (p. 305).

2 cups white Chinese rice or Thai jasmine rice

2¼ cups cold water

Put the rice in a heavy medium saucepan that is at least 8 inches in diameter. Rinse the rice thoroughly under cold running water, rubbing it between your fingers, until the water is clear; drain well. Add the 2¼ cups of water and bring to a vigorous boil over high heat. Cover tightly, reduce the heat to very low and cook without peeking for 14 minutes. Remove from the heat; lift the lid to release steam and replace it immediately. Let the rice stand for 10 minutes to firm up the starches. Serve straight from the pan, using a moistened wooden rice paddle or a shallow wooden spoon.

—*Jeffrey Alford and Naomi Duguid*

Herbed Lemon Rice

2 SERVINGS 🌺 🌷

1½ teaspoons olive oil

½ small onion, minced

½ cup long-grain rice

1 bay leaf

½ teaspoon finely grated lemon zest

1 cup chicken stock (p. 117) or canned low-sodium broth

2 tablespoons dry white wine

1 tablespoon fresh lemon juice

½ teaspoon salt

2 teaspoons finely chopped tarragon

1. Preheat the oven to 350°. Heat the oil in a casserole. Add the onion and cook over moderate heat, stirring, until softened, about 5 minutes. Add the rice, bay leaf and lemon zest and cook, stirring, until the rice is well coated.

2. Add the stock, wine, lemon juice and salt and bring to a boil. Cover and bake in the oven for about 20 minutes, or until the rice is tender and has absorbed the liquid. Fluff the rice with a fork and discard the bay leaf. Stir the tarragon into the rice and serve.

—*Ferdinand Metz*

ONE SERVING Calories 120 kcal, Total Fat 2.3 gm, Saturated Fat 0.5 gm

Saffron Rice Pilaf

12 SERVINGS

- 1 tablespoon extra-virgin olive oil
- 1 large onion, chopped
- One 3-inch cinnamon stick, broken into 4 pieces
- ½ teaspoon loosely packed saffron threads
- 3 cups long-grain rice
- 6 cups chicken stock (p. 117) or canned low-sodium broth
- 1 teaspoon salt

Freshly ground pepper

Preheat the oven to 375°. In a large enameled cast-iron casserole, heat the oil. Add the onion, cinnamon and saffron and cook over moderate heat, stirring, until the onion is softened but not browned, about 5 minutes. Add the rice and stir for 1 minute to coat the rice with the oil. Add the stock, salt and a pinch of pepper and bring to a boil over high heat. Simmer for 2 minutes, stirring occasionally. Cover, transfer to the oven and bake the rice for 15 minutes. Remove the casserole from the oven and let the rice stand, covered, for up to 30 minutes. Fluff the rice with a fork before serving it.

—*Marcia Kiesel*

ONE SERVING Calories 221 kcal, Total Fat 4.6 gm, Saturated Fat 1 gm

Yellow Rice with Raisins

Yellow Rice with Raisins

8 SERVINGS

This slightly sweet rice pilaf is flavored with citrus zest and spices and tinted yellow with turmeric.

- 3¾ cups water
- 2 cups long-grain rice
- 3 cardamom pods
- ½ cinnamon stick
- One 1-inch piece of tangerine or orange zest, white pith removed
- 1 teaspoon salt
- ½ teaspoon turmeric
- 3 tablespoons unsalted butter
- ½ cup sliced almonds (about 2 ounces)
- ½ cup raisins (about 3 ounces)
- 3 tablespoons sugar

I. In a medium saucepan, combine the water with the rice, cardamom, cinnamon stick, tangerine zest, salt and turmeric. Stir well and bring to a boil. Cover and cook over very low heat until the liquid is absorbed and the rice is tender, 15 to 17 minutes. Remove the tangerine zest. ➤

Fresh Tomato Risotto with Basil

2. Meanwhile, in a large saucepan, melt the butter over moderate heat. Add the almonds and cook, stirring, until golden, about 2 minutes. Stir in the raisins and sugar and remove from the heat. Add the rice to the mixture and stir gently to combine. Transfer to a bowl and serve.   *—Jenna Holst*

Fresh Tomato Risotto with Basil

4 SERVINGS

- 5   cups hot homemade meat broth (see Note)
- 4   tablespoons butter
- ⅓   cup chopped onion
- 1   tablespoon vegetable oil
- 1½   pounds firm ripe tomatoes—peeled with a vegetable peeler, seeded and cut into ½-inch pieces

Salt and freshly ground pepper

- 1½   cups carnaroli, arborio or vialone nano rice (about 10 ounces)
- ½   cup freshly grated Parmigiano-Reggiano cheese
- 10   basil leaves, cut into very thin strips

risotto tips

Use imported Italian rice of one of the following varieties: carnaroli, arborio or vialone nano. Carnaroli is the most expensive and it's not as readily available as arborio, but it makes the best risotto.

Use a heavy heat-retaining pan, such as enameled cast-iron.

Use a wooden spatula with a straight edge to stir the risotto.

Use broth as the cooking liquid; do not use stock, because it imparts too strong a taste. Meat broth, which is good for all non-seafood risottos, is simply water in which fresh meat has been boiled—the more meat and the fewer bones the better. You can also use the blanching water from any vegetables in the risotto or the strained water from soaking dried mushrooms. Use plain water, not fish stock, for seafood risotto. If using clams or mussels, you can add their filtered juices.

Keep the cooking liquid simmering in a separate pan nearby.

Finish off the risotto as you began. If you started with butter, remove the risotto from the heat when it is done and swirl in more butter and grated Parmigiano. If you started with olive oil, stir in a thin stream of extra-virgin olive oil at the end.

1. In a medium saucepan, bring the broth to a boil; keep the broth at a simmer over low heat.

2. Meanwhile, put 2 tablespoons of the butter with the onion and oil in a large saucepan. Cook over moderate heat, stirring occasionally, until the onion turns pale gold. Add the tomatoes and a pinch each of salt and pepper. Cook, stirring occasionally, for 10 minutes.

3. Add the rice and stir to thoroughly coat the grains. Add ½ cup of the simmering broth to the rice and stir constantly until most of the liquid has been absorbed, adjust the heat if necessary to maintain a simmer. Gradually add more broth, ½ cup at a time, and cook, stirring the rice constantly to prevent it from sticking to the pan at any time. The rice is done when it is firm but tender, without a chalky center.

4. Add the remaining 2 tablespoons of butter, the cheese and the basil and stir for 1 minute longer. Season the risotto with salt and pepper and serve at once. —*Marcella Hazan*

NOTE In place of meat broth, you can use 1 beef bouillon cube dissolved in 5 cups of boiling water or ¾ cup of canned beef broth diluted with 4¼ cups of water.

WINE A clean, crisp Italian Pinot Grigio is just what this creamy but tomato-intense risotto needs for contrast. Among various possibilities are the 1996 Tieffenbrunner or the 1996 Santa Margherita.

Butternut Squash, Swiss Chard and Apple Risotto

6 SERVINGS

- ¼ cup Vertes du Puy lentils
- 1 cup ½-inch dice peeled butternut squash
- 6 cups chicken stock (p. 117) or canned low-sodium broth
- 3 tablespoons unsalted butter
- 2 tablespoons olive oil
- 2 tablespoons minced bacon
- 2 large garlic cloves, minced
- 1 small shallot, minced
- 2 cups arborio rice
- 1 cup dry white wine
- 1 cup finely shredded Swiss chard
- ½ cup ½-inch dice peeled Granny Smith apple
- ¼ cup freshly grated Parmesan cheese

- 1 tablespoon chopped sage leaves
- Salt and freshly ground pepper

1. In a medium saucepan of boiling water, cook the lentils until tender, about 15 minutes; drain and set aside. In another saucepan, steam the squash in a steamer basket until just tender, about 4 minutes. Transfer the squash to a plate.

2. In a medium saucepan, bring the stock to a boil; keep it at a bare simmer over very low heat. In a large saucepan, melt 1 tablespoon of the butter in the oil over moderate heat. Add the bacon, garlic and shallot and cook until softened, about 3 minutes. Add the rice and stir to coat thoroughly. Add the wine and simmer until almost evaporated, about 4 minutes. Stir in one-third of the simmering stock and cook, stirring constantly, until the stock is almost entirely absorbed; repeat with the remaining stock. The risotto should be creamy with just-tender rice grains after 20 minutes.

3. Add the lentils, squash, Swiss chard and apple to the risotto. Stir in the Parmesan, sage and the remaining 2 tablespoons of butter. Season the risotto with salt and pepper and serve it immediately.

—*Eleven Madison Park, New York City*

Curried Fried Rice with Beef Jerky

4 SERVINGS

Beef jerky made without additives is best. If you're not a jerky fan, substitute smoked ham.

- 1 cup long-grain rice, rinsed and drained
- 1½ cups water, plus 2½ cups boiling water
- 3 ounces beef jerky, cut into 1-inch pieces
- 1 large dried tree ear mushroom, or 4 dried shiitake mushrooms
- 1½ tablespoons vegetable oil

- 1 small onion, finely chopped
- ½ small sweet potato, cut into ½-inch dice, or 1 medium carrot, cut into ½-inch slices
- One 1-inch piece of fresh ginger, peeled and minced
- 1½ teaspoons curry powder
- ½ cup toasted whole almonds
- 1 tablespoon soy sauce
- Salt
- 1 scallion, thinly sliced

1. In a medium saucepan, combine the rice with the 1½ cups of water and bring to a boil. Cover and cook over low heat for 12 minutes. Remove the rice from the heat and let stand, covered, for 5 minutes. Uncover, fluff the rice and let cool completely.

2. Meanwhile, in a medium bowl, pour 2 cups of the boiling water over the beef jerky. Cover and let stand until the beef jerky is pliable, about 30 minutes. Drain the beef jerky and then coarsely chop it.

3. In a small bowl, cover the tree ear mushroom with the remaining ½ cup of boiling water and let stand until softened, about 10 minutes. Drain and chop the tree ear into 1-inch pieces; if using shiitakes, discard the stems and chop the caps.

4. Heat the oil in a large skillet. Add the onion, sweet potato and ginger and cook over low heat, stirring, until the onion is softened, about 4 minutes. Add the curry powder and cook, stirring, until fragrant, about 2 minutes. Raise the heat to high and add the beef jerky, tree ear mushroom and almonds. Stir-fry until heated through. Add the rice and the soy sauce and stir-fry to break up the rice and heat it through. Season the rice with salt. Stir the scallion into the rice and serve.

—*Marcia Kiesel*

MAKE AHEAD The recipe can be prepared through Step 3 up to 1 day in advance. Refrigerate the cooked rice and the chopped beef jerky and tree ear mushroom separately.

WINE For this curried rice dish, stick with sparkling wine, such as the non-vintage Mumm Cuvée Napa from California, or play off the red-pepper notes of the curry powder with a crisp California Sauvignon Blanc, such as the 1996 Murphy-Goode Reserve Fumé II.

Curried Fried Rice with Beef Jerky

Wild Rice Spoon Bread

8 SERVINGS

1⅓ cups organic wild rice
   (6 ounces)
1 quart water
Salt
4 tablespoons unsalted butter
1 medium onion, coarsely chopped
1 large scallion, coarsely chopped
1 quart milk
½ cup fine yellow cornmeal
6 large eggs, separated
¼ cup freshly grated Parmesan cheese
1½ teaspoons baking powder

I. Butter a 13-by-9-inch baking dish. In a medium saucepan, cover the wild

rice with the water, add a pinch of salt and bring to a boil. Cover and simmer over low heat, stirring occasionally, until just tender, about 20 minutes. Drain the rice.

2. Preheat the oven to 350°. Melt 1 tablespoon of the butter in a large skillet. Add the onion and cook over moderate heat until lightly browned and just tender, about 4 minutes. Stir in the scallion and wild rice. Season lightly with salt and spread in the prepared baking dish.

3. In a medium saucepan, bring the milk to a simmer. Gradually whisk in the cornmeal. Whisk over moderately low heat until thickened and bubbling, about 5 minutes. Scrape the mixture into a large bowl and let stand, stirring often, until warm. Whisk in the remaining 3 tablespoons of butter, the egg yolks and Parmesan, 1½ teaspoons of salt and the baking powder.

4. In a large bowl, beat the egg whites to firm peaks. Using a rubber spatula, stir one-quarter of the whites into the cornmeal mixture and then fold in the remaining whites until a few white streaks remain. Scrape the spoon bread over the wild rice. Bake in the center of the oven for about 30 minutes, or until puffed and golden. Let the spoon bread rest for 5 minutes before serving. —*Marcia Kiesel*

MAKE AHEAD The recipe can be prepared through Step 2 and refrigerated overnight.

Lemon Tabbouleh with Red Pepper

4 SERVINGS

Start the tabbouleh a day ahead so the bulgur has time to soak.

- 1 **cup bulgur (about 6 ounces)**
- 1½ **cups boiling water**
- ½ **cup fresh lemon juice**
- 1 **medium red bell pepper, finely chopped**

Wild Rice Spoon Bread

- 1 **cup finely chopped scallions**
- 1 **cup finely chopped flat-leaf parsley**
- ¼ **cup olive oil**
- 1 **teaspoon salt**
- ½ **teaspoon freshly ground black pepper**

Put the bulgur in a medium bowl and stir in the boiling water. Let the bulgur stand for 15 minutes and then add the lemon juice. Cover and let plump overnight at room temperature. Stir in the red pepper, scallions, parsley, oil, salt and black pepper. Serve the tabbouleh at room temperature.

—*Matthew Kenney*

MAKE AHEAD The tabbouleh can be refrigerated overnight. Let return to room temperature before serving.

Parmesan Barley Cake

8 SERVINGS

This tasty barley cake can be served cut into wedges or, if you prefer a more rustic approach, scoop out portions with a serving spoon.

Parmesan Barley Cake

8 cups water
1 tablespoon unsalted butter
1 medium onion, finely chopped
2 cups pearl barley (about
   14 ounces), rinsed
1½ cups freshly grated Parmesan
   cheese (about 4½ ounces)
Salt and freshly ground pepper
¼ cup vegetable oil

I. Bring the water to a boil in a medium saucepan; cover and keep warm over low heat. Melt the butter in a large saucepan, add the onion and cook over low heat, stirring, until translucent, about 8 minutes.

2. Add the barley to the onion and cook over moderate heat, stirring, until thoroughly coated with butter, about 2 minutes. Add 2 cups of the hot water; simmer, stirring often, until the water has evaporated, about 10 minutes. Repeat the process with the remaining water, adding 2 cups at a time. Remove from the heat. Stir in 1 cup of the Parmesan and season with salt and pepper. Spread the barley on a baking sheet, cover with plastic and let cool.

3. Line a 10-inch cake pan with plastic wrap, allowing a 6-inch overhang. Using a rubber spatula, spread half of the barley evenly in the cake pan. Sprinkle with the remaining ½ cup of Parmesan and cover with the remaining barley; smooth the surface. Cover the barley cake with the overhanging plastic wrap and refrigerate until firm, at least 4 hours or overnight.

4. Heat the oil in a 10-inch nonstick skillet. Working quickly, unwrap the barley cake and gently lift it from the pan using the plastic wrap. Invert the barley cake onto an unrimmed baking sheet, discard the plastic wrap and slide the cake into the skillet. Cook over moderate heat until the barley cake is heated through and very brown and crisp on the bottom, about 15 minutes. Set a large serving plate over the skillet and invert the barley cake onto it. Serve the barley cake cut into wedges. —*Joseph and Thomas Keller*

WINE The clean, clear fruit flavors of the 1995 Pahlmeyer Merlot are sensational paired with the savory, Parmesan-accented barley cake.

MAKE AHEAD The cake can stand at room temperature for up to 4 hours. Rewarm in a 350° oven.

African-Spiced Black Barley with Okra and Tomatoes

6 SERVINGS
Ethiopian black barley, a darker variety of pearl barley, is currently being cultivated in Arizona and California. The grain splits open to reveal a bright white center. You can also use pearl barley or red rice in this dish; neither will need as long a cooking time.

1¼ cups black barley (about
   ½ pound)
3½ tablespoons vegetable oil
1 medium onion, finely chopped
2 medium tomatoes, peeled and
   coarsely chopped
1 large garlic clove, minced
½ teaspoon ground cumin
½ teaspoon ground coriander
¼ teaspoon cinnamon
¼ teaspoon cayenne pepper
Pinch of ground cloves
1 cup water
1 pound small okra, stems
   trimmed
Salt

I. In a medium saucepan, cover the barley with water and bring to a boil. Cover and simmer over low heat, stirring occasionally, until the barley has split and is tender but still slightly chewy, about 45 minutes. Drain the barley and transfer to a bowl.

2. Wipe out the saucepan and heat 1½ tablespoons of the oil in it. Add the onion and cook over moderately low heat, stirring, until tender, about 5 minutes. Add the tomatoes and cook over moderate heat until their juices thicken, about 4 minutes. Add the garlic and cook until fragrant, about 2 minutes. Add the cumin, coriander, cinnamon, cayenne and cloves and cook, stirring, until fragrant, about 3 minutes. Add the barley and the water, cover and simmer over low heat until the flavors are nicely blended, about 4 minutes.

3. In a large skillet, heat the remaining 2 tablespoons of oil until almost smoking. Add the okra and cook, turning once, until browned, about 6 minutes. Season with salt and stir into the barley. Season the barley with salt and serve hot. —*Marcia Kiesel*

MAKE AHEAD The recipe can be prepared through Step 2 and refrigerated for up to 2 days. Bring back to a simmer before proceeding.

WINE This spice-rich vegetable stew warrants an equally spicy red with a texture to match. A California Zinfandel, such as the 1996 Ridge Sonoma Station or the 1996 Turning Leaf, is just the ticket, particularly if this stew accompanies a hearty meat dish.

African-Spiced Black Barley with Okra and Tomatoes

CHAPTER 13 sauces
dips condiments

Classic Swiss Cheese Fondue (p. 357)

Spicy Tomato Sauce

Spicy Tomato Sauce

MAKES ABOUT 2½ CUPS

Not only does this sauce taste good, but cooking the tomatoes actually enhances their nutritional benefits. Lycopene, the substance that turns tomatoes red, is liberated by cooking. Studies have linked lycopene to lowered rates of heart disease, prostate cancer and colon cancer. This sauce will coat one pound of pasta.

2 pounds tomatoes, peeled and halved

3 tablespoons extra-virgin olive oil

½ cup thinly sliced Vidalia onion

2 large garlic cloves, thinly sliced

½ teaspoon crushed red pepper

Salt

1 tablespoon minced basil

½ tablespoon minced mint

1. Scoop the seeds from the tomatoes into a strainer set over a bowl and press on the seeds to extract as much juice as possible. Coarsely chop the tomatoes and add them to the juice.

2. Heat the oil in a large skillet until shimmering. Add the onion and cook over moderately high heat, stirring, until softened and just brown, about 5 minutes. Stir in the garlic and cook for 1 minute. Add the tomatoes with their juice and the crushed red pepper. Season with salt and cook, stirring, until thickened, about 20 minutes. Stir in the basil and mint and serve.

—*Grace Parisi*

Mustard Barbecue Sauce

MAKES ABOUT 1½ CUPS

In the southern part of North Carolina (and in a few parts of South Carolina and Florida), barbecue just isn't barbecue unless it's served with a lurid yellow sauce made from honey, vinegar and cheap ballpark-style mustard. If you come from tomato-sauce country, the notion might be off-putting, but mustard barbecue sauce quickly becomes addictive. Shredded pork shoulder is the meat of choice here.

¾ cup honey

½ cup yellow mustard

¼ cup distilled white vinegar

Salt and freshly ground pepper

Combine the honey, yellow mustard and white vinegar in a heavy medium saucepan and bring to a boil. Simmer the sauce over moderate heat, stirring occasionally, until it is slightly thickened, about 5 minutes. Season the sauce with salt and pepper. Let the sauce cool completely. Transfer the cooled barbecue sauce to a jar.

—*Steven Raichlen*

MAKE AHEAD The sauce can be refrigerated for up to 1 month.

North Carolina Vinegar Barbecue Sauce

MAKES ABOUT 1½ CUPS

A piquant mix of vinegar and crushed red pepper, with just a little sugar to cut the acidity, is a favorite condiment in North Carolina, particularly the northwestern corner. The barbecued meat is always pork, and it's shredded or finely chopped, not sliced. Put the pork and vinegar sauce together on a bun and you have one damnably delectable barbecue sandwich.

¾ cup cider vinegar

½ cup water

½ cup thinly sliced onion

1½ teaspoons sugar

1½ teaspoons crushed red pepper

1 teaspoon salt

¼ teaspoon freshly ground black pepper

Combine the cider vinegar, water, sliced onion, sugar, crushed red pepper, salt, and black pepper in a jar and then stir the sauce until the sugar and salt are completely dissolved.

—*Steven Raichlen*

MAKE AHEAD The sauce can be refrigerated for up to 1 week.

Texas-Style Barbecue Sauce

MAKES ABOUT 1½ CUPS

Texans take a bold approach to barbecue sauce, adding little or no sugar but plenty of vinegar and chile hellfire. Here, I've replicated the sauce from the legendary Sonny Bryan's Smokehouse in Dallas. No, it's not the actual sauce served there—I know better than to ask a pit master to part with his recipe. Still, this is everything a Texas barbecue sauce should be, and there isn't a barbecued brisket in creation that wouldn't be proud to wear it.

1½ cups water

¾ cup ketchup

½ cup cider vinegar

¼ cup Worcestershire sauce

2 tablespoons pure chile powder

1 tablespoon sweet paprika

1 tablespoon mustard

1 tablespoon fresh lemon juice

½ teaspoon crushed red pepper

½ teaspoon freshly ground black pepper

½ teaspoon brown sugar

¼ teaspoon liquid smoke

Combine all of the ingredients in a large heavy saucepan and bring to a boil. Cook the sauce over moderately high heat, stirring frequently, until it is thick and richly flavored, about 30 minutes. Let the barbecue sauce cool completely and then transfer it to a jar. Refrigerate the sauce for at least 2 days. Warm the sauce before using (Texans customarily serve their barbecue sauce warm). —*Steven Raichlen*

MAKE AHEAD The sauce can be refrigerated for up to 1 month.

Chile-Spiked Barbecue Sauce

MAKES ABOUT 2 CUPS

1½ teaspoons vegetable oil

1 medium onion, chopped

1 teaspoon chopped garlic

¼ cup bourbon

½ cup cider vinegar

2½ tablespoons brown sugar

1½ canned chipotle chiles in adobo sauce, stemmed

¾ teaspoon whole-grain mustard

¾ teaspoon ancho chile powder

½ bay leaf

Pinch of ground allspice

1 cup chicken stock (p. 117) or canned low-sodium broth

¾ cup chili sauce

½ cup canned plum tomatoes

Salt and freshly ground pepper

1. Heat the oil in a medium saucepan. Add the onion and cook over moderate heat, stirring, until browned, about 10 minutes. Add the garlic and cook for 2 minutes and then add the bourbon and simmer for 2 minutes longer. Stir in the vinegar, brown sugar, chipotle chiles, mustard, ancho chile powder, bay leaf and allspice and bring to a boil. Cover and cook over low heat for 30 minutes.

Grappa-Fontina Sauce atop baked potatoes.

2. Add the stock, chili sauce and tomatoes, cover partially and cook over low heat until reduced by half, about 1 hour. Remove from the heat and let cool. Discard the bay leaf. Transfer the sauce to a blender and puree until smooth. Season with salt and pepper.

—*Brendan Walsh*

MAKE AHEAD The barbecue sauce can be refrigerated for up to 1 week.

B.B.'s Lawnside Spicy Apple Cider Barbecue Sauce

MAKES ABOUT 1½ CUPS

When most people think of barbecue sauce, Kansas City style is what they have in mind: sweet, spicy, tomatoey, thick enough to stick to barbecued ribs (the stock-in-trade of Kansas City pit masters) and versatile enough to accompany pork, beef, even chicken— in short, just what Lindsay Shannon serves at B.B.'s Lawnside. His sweet, suave barbecue sauce owes its fruity finish to the addition of apple cider.

1½ cups ketchup

⅔ cup apple cider

2 tablespoons Worcestershire sauce

1 tablespoon sulphured molasses

1 tablespoon cider vinegar

1 tablespoon soy sauce

1 tablespoon dark brown sugar

1 tablespoon granulated sugar

1 teaspoon cayenne pepper

½ teaspoon freshly ground black pepper

½ teaspoon celery seeds

½ teaspoon cinnamon

Pinch of ground cloves

Combine all of the ingredients in a heavy medium saucepan and bring to a boil. Gently simmer over low heat, stirring frequently, until thick, about 30 minutes. Let cool completely and then transfer to a jar. —*Steven Raichlen*

MAKE AHEAD The sauce can be refrigerated for up to 1 month.

Chimichurri Sauce

MAKES ABOUT 2 CUPS

This parsley and garlic sauce is all you need to serve beef Argentinean style. It's easy to make, but be sure to use fresh parsley and high-quality olive oil. The jalapeño isn't strictly traditional— Argentineans like crushed red pepper—but it adds grassy flavor and fire.

1 cup coarsely chopped flat-leaf parsley

½ cup coarsely chopped red bell pepper

8 garlic cloves, coarsely chopped

1 to 2 jalapeños, seeded and coarsely chopped

1 cup extra-virgin olive oil

⅓ cup water

⅓ cup white wine vinegar

1 teaspoon salt

1 teaspoon dried oregano
½ teaspoon freshly ground black pepper

In a food processor, combine the parsley, red pepper, garlic and jalapeños and pulse until minced. Add the oil, water, vinegar, salt, oregano and black pepper and process to blend. Transfer the sauce to a bowl and serve.

—*Steven Raichlen*

MAKE AHEAD The sauce can be refrigerated for several days, but it's at its best when it's freshly made.

Grappa-Fontina Sauce

MAKES ABOUT ⅔ CUP

Grappa, the high-powered Italian spirit made from what remains of the grapes after they have been pressed for wine, adds a fruity punch to this luxurious cheese sauce.

½ cup heavy cream
1 tablespoon unsalted butter
½ cup freshly grated Parmesan cheese
¼ cup shredded Fontina cheese
1 tablespoon grappa
Salt

1. In a small saucepan, bring the cream to a simmer over low heat. Stir in the butter until melted and then whisk in the Parmesan until smooth. Add the Fontina and cook, whisking, until the cheese is melted and the sauce is smooth, about 3 minutes.

2. Remove from the heat, stir in the grappa and season the sauce lightly with salt. Serve warm.

—*Marcia Kiesel*

MAKE AHEAD The sauce can be kept at room temperature for up to 6 hours. To serve, whisk over low heat to rewarm.

SERVE WITH Twice-baked potatoes; cooked mild greens, such as spinach or Swiss chard; fresh fettuccine or pappardelle; broccoli; soft or fried polenta.

Caviar and Leek Sauce over salmon.

Caviar and Leek Sauce

MAKES ABOUT 1 CUP

2 tablespoons unsalted butter
2 medium leeks with 3 inches of green, split lengthwise and thickly sliced crosswise
½ cup dry white wine
¾ cup sour cream, at room temperature
1 ounce caviar (about 2 tablespoons), preferably osetra
1 teaspoon fresh lemon juice
Salt and freshly ground pepper

1. Melt the butter in a medium saucepan. Add the leeks and cook over low heat, stirring, until they are softened but not browned, about 7 minutes. Add the wine and simmer until it is reduced to 2 tablespoons, about 4 minutes.

2. Remove the sauce from the heat; stir in the sour cream and then the caviar. Add the lemon juice and season with salt and pepper. —*Marcia Kiesel*

MAKE AHEAD The recipe can be prepared though Step 1 up to 6 hours in advance and kept at room temperature. Rewarm before finishing.

SERVE WITH Pan-fried or poached salmon or halibut steaks, mahimahi or tilefish fillets; pan-roasted chicken breasts; baked potatoes; fresh pasta; steamed asparagus or artichokes.

Yogurt and Mint Sauce

MAKES ABOUT 1½ CUPS

Use this mango-studded yogurt sauce on salmon or as a dip for Crisp Poppy and Sesame Lavash (p. 289) and Skillet Pita Breads (p. 290).

- ¾ cup goat's milk or whole cow's milk yogurt
- 1 tablespoon honey
- 1 tablespoon coarsely chopped cilantro
- 1 tablespoon coarsely chopped mint
- ¼ teaspoon ground cumin
- ¼ teaspoon ground coriander
- ½ medium mango, finely chopped (about ½ cup)

In a medium bowl, combine the yogurt, honey, cilantro, mint, cumin and coriander. Stir in the mango. Chill in the refrigerator before serving.

—*Christer Larsson*

MAKE AHEAD The sauce can be refrigerated overnight; stir in the mango before serving.

Lobster Butter

MAKES ABOUT ¾ CUP

Serve this delicious butter on corn, grilled seafood or steamed potatoes.

- 1 stick (4 ounces) unsalted butter, softened

Tomalley and roe from 8 lobsters (½ cup)

Salt and freshly ground pepper

1. In a small saucepan, melt 1 tablespoon of the butter over moderately high heat. Add the tomalley and roe and cook, stirring constantly with a fork, until the tomalley turns light green and the roe turns bright red, about 3 minutes. Remove from the heat and mash the tomalley and roe to a paste. Transfer to a bowl and let cool to room temperature.

2. Blend in the remaining 7 tablespoons of butter to make a smooth spread and season it with salt and pepper. Serve the butter at once or refrigerate it for up to 2 days.

—*Mark Gottwald*

Avocado "Butter"

MAKES 1 CUP 🌸

High in fat but rich in nutrients, Avocado "Butter" tastes like a refined guacamole. You need only a bit for a big flavor payoff.

- 2 tablespoons minced chives
- 2 tablespoons minced capers
- 2 tablespoons fresh lemon juice
- 1 tablespoon finely chopped tarragon
- ½ teaspoon kosher salt
- ¼ teaspoon freshly ground pepper
- 1 large Hass avocado, coarsely chopped

1. In a mini-processor, combine the chives and capers, lemon juice, tarragon, kosher salt and pepper and pulse until finely chopped. Add the avocado and process until smooth.

2. Transfer the avocado mixture to a small bowl and press a piece of plastic directly onto the top of it. Refrigerate the avocado mixture for up to 2 days before using it.

—*Robbin Haas*

ONE TABLESPOON Calories 27 kcal, Total Fat 2.4 gm, Saturated Fat .4 gm

SERVE WITH Grilled chicken or fish, or on a sandwich.

Classic Aïoli

MAKES ABOUT 1⅔ CUPS

The recipe below is for traditional aïoli, which is made with uncooked egg yolks. If you prefer to avoid raw eggs, Aïoli-Style Mayonnaise (right) is a delicious variation made with commercially prepared mayonnaise.

- 8 plump garlic cloves, chopped

Coarse sea salt

- 3 large egg yolks, at room temperature
- 1 cup extra-virgin olive oil

- 2 tablespoons fresh lemon juice, plus more to taste
- ½ cup vegetable oil

1. In a mortar, pound the garlic cloves with 1 teaspoon of sea salt until a thick paste forms. Scrape the mixture into a glass or stainless steel bowl, stir in the egg yolks and let stand for 5 minutes.

2. Set the bowl on a damp kitchen towel (to hold it steady) and begin whisking in the olive oil a few drops at a time. Slowly add ½ cup of the olive oil, whisking constantly; as the aïoli begins to thicken, add the oil in a thin stream. When the aïoli is very thick, add 2 teaspoons of the lemon juice. Gradually whisk in another ¼ cup of the olive oil and then 2 more teaspoons of the lemon juice. Whisk in the remaining ¼ cup of olive oil. Add the 2 remaining teaspoons of lemon juice; whisk in the vegetable oil. When all of the vegetable oil has been incorporated, season with lemon juice and sea salt to taste.

—*Nancy Harmon Jenkins*

MAKE AHEAD The aïoli can be covered tightly and refrigerated overnight. Serve chilled.

Aïoli-Style Mayonnaise

MAKES ABOUT 1½ CUPS

- 8 garlic cloves, chopped

Sea salt

- 1¼ cups mayonnaise, at room temperature
- ½ cup plus 2 tablespoons extra-virgin olive oil
- 1 tablespoon fresh lemon juice

In a mortar, pound the garlic cloves to a paste with 1 teaspoon of sea salt. Scrape the paste into a bowl and add the mayonnaise. Gradually whisk in the oil. Stir in the lemon juice and season with sea salt.

—*Nancy Harmon Jenkins*

MAKE AHEAD The mayonnaise can be tightly covered and refrigerated overnight. Serve chilled.

Cilantro-Orange Dressing

MAKES ABOUT ½ CUP

Serve the dressing with Moroccan-Spiced Crab Cakes (p. 179), with plain grilled or broiled fish fillets or on a spinach salad.

- ½ cup fresh orange juice
- 1 teaspoon cumin seeds
- ½ cup lightly packed cilantro leaves
- 1 tablespoon fresh lemon juice
- ¼ cup canola oil

Salt

Cayenne pepper

1. In a saucepan, boil the orange juice over moderately high heat until reduced to 2 tablespoons, about 8 minutes. Let cool and then transfer to a blender.

2. Meanwhile, in a small dry skillet, toast the cumin seeds over moderate heat, shaking the pan occasionally, until fragrant, about 2 minutes. Grind the cumin in a mortar with a pestle or in a spice grinder.

3. Add the cumin to the blender along with the cilantro and lemon juice and blend until smooth. With the blender on, add the oil in a thin, steady stream. Season with salt and cayenne.

—Matthew Kenney

MAKE AHEAD The dressing can be refrigerated for up to 4 hours. Let it return to room temperature before serving.

Roasted Pumpkin Seed Oil Vinaigrette

MAKES ABOUT ½ CUP

Because Austrian roasted pumpkin seed oil, a current favorite in American restaurant kitchens, becomes acrid when heated, it's best not to cook it.

- ¼ cup fresh orange juice
- 2 tablespoons soy sauce
- 1 tablespoon plus 1 teaspoon roasted pumpkin seed oil (see Note)

- 2 teaspoons white wine vinegar
- 1 teaspoon minced jalapeño
- 1 garlic clove, minced
- ½ teaspoon minced fresh ginger

Pinch each of salt and freshly ground pepper

Combine all of the ingredients in a bowl. —Marcia Kiesel

NOTE Roasted pumpkin seed oil is available at specialty food stores.

MAKE AHEAD The vinaigrette can be refrigerated overnight. Serve at room temperature.

SERVE WITH Grilled shrimp; shrimp or vegetable dumplings; chicken salad; avocado-tomato salad; boiled rice noodles.

Cucumber Yogurt Dip

Cucumber Yogurt Dip

MAKES ABOUT 1½ CUPS

This *tzatziki* is quite garlicky. For a milder flavor, use only one garlic clove.

- 1 European cucumber—peeled, halved lengthwise and seeded
- 1 cup whole-milk yogurt
- 2 garlic cloves, finely grated
- 1 tablespoon extra-virgin olive oil
- ¼ teaspoon fresh lemon juice

Salt

Dill sprigs

Cucumber spears, for serving

Coarsely grate the cucumber onto a kitchen towel. Pat the cucumber in the towel to remove the juices and then transfer it to a bowl. Stir in the yogurt and garlic. Add the oil and lemon juice. Season with salt. Refrigerate the dip

Classic Swiss Cheese Fondue

until chilled, at least 1 hour and up to 8 hours. Top with dill sprigs and serve with cucumber spears. —*Fany Boutari*

Eggplant Dip

MAKES ABOUT 4 CUPS

Adding a little mayonnaise to the traditional *melitzanosalata*—a blend of roasted eggplant, olive oil and lemon juice—makes the dip unusually creamy.

2 large eggplants (3 pounds total)
1 small onion, minced
2 large garlic cloves, minced
½ cup extra-virgin olive oil
¼ cup fresh lemon juice
3 tablespoons mayonnaise
Salt and freshly ground pepper
Pita bread, cut into triangles

I. Preheat the oven to 475°. Prick the eggplants all over with a fork and set

them on a large baking sheet. Roast for 30 minutes, or until the eggplants are charred and very soft. Let cool slightly and then peel. Coarsely chop the eggplant pulp, transfer it to a strainer set over a bowl and let drain for 30 minutes; press to release any remaining liquid.

2. Finely chop the eggplant and transfer to a bowl. Add the onion and garlic

and then gradually stir in the oil and lemon juice until incorporated. Stir in the mayonnaise and season with salt and pepper. Serve the dip with pita.

—*Fany Boutari*

MAKE AHEAD The dip can be refrigerated for up to 8 hours.

WINE The 1996 Boutari Santorini.

Grilled Eggplant Dip

MAKES ABOUT 3 CUPS

A goat cheese garnish gives a tangy edge to this smoky eggplant dip. Serve it with Crisp Poppy and Sesame Lavash (p. 289), Skillet Pita Breads (p. 290) or just plain pitas.

- 2 medium eggplants (about 2 pounds total)
- 2 garlic cloves, finely chopped
- 2 tablespoons tahini
- 1 tablespoon fresh lemon juice
- 1 tablespoon plain yogurt

Salt and freshly ground pepper
- 4 ounces soft goat cheese
- 1 to 2 tablespoons coarsely chopped flat-leaf parsley

I. Light a grill or preheat the broiler. Pierce the eggplant in several places with a fork and grill over a medium-low fire or broil as far from the heat as possible for 20 to 30 minutes, turning occasionally, until the eggplants are tender throughout when pierced. Let cool slightly.

2. Halve the eggplants lengthwise and scoop their flesh into a food processor. Add the garlic, tahini, lemon juice and yogurt and pulse to combine; season the eggplant with salt and pepper. Transfer the eggplant dip to a serving bowl and refrigerate it until chilled, about 1 hour. Top the eggplant dip with the goat cheese, sprinkle it with the chopped parsley and serve.

—*Christer Larsson*

MAKE AHEAD The eggplant dip can be refrigerated overnight.

Tapenade

MAKES ABOUT 1⅓ CUPS

The best olives to use for a proper tapenade are naturally the ones Provençal cooks use: black Niçoise. In a pinch, however, any top-quality black olives can be combined with capers and anchovies to make this rustic dip or spread.

- 1½ cups Niçoise olives (10 ounces), pitted and coarsely chopped
- ¼ cup drained capers
- ¼ cup drained tuna
- 2 oil-packed anchovy fillets, coarsely chopped
- ½ cup extra-virgin olive oil
- 1 teaspoon Cognac (optional)

Freshly ground pepper
Grilled or toasted bread, for serving

In a food processor, combine the olives with the capers, tuna and anchovies. Pulse until a coarse puree forms. With the machine on, gradually add the oil until it is incorporated. Transfer the mixture to a bowl and then stir in the Cognac. Season with freshly ground pepper and serve with grilled bread.

—*Nancy Harmon Jenkins*

MAKE AHEAD The Tapenade can be refrigerated for up to 2 days. Bring to room temperature before serving.

Anchoïade

MAKES ABOUT 1 CUP

This Provençal puree of anchovies with garlic and olive oil can be spread on toast or served as a dip. Don't worry if some bones remain in the anchovies—just think of them as added calcium.

- 10 whole salt-packed anchovies (see Note)—rinsed, filleted and coarsely chopped, or 20 oil-packed anchovy fillets, drained and coarsely chopped
- 4 garlic cloves, coarsely chopped
- 2 tablespoons unsalted butter, at room temperature
- ½ cup extra-virgin olive oil
- 1½ teaspoons aged red-wine vinegar

Freshly ground pepper
Grilled or toasted bread, for serving

In a food processor, combine the anchovies with the garlic and pulse until pureed. Blend in the butter. Transfer the mixture to a bowl and stir in the oil, a few tablespoons at a time, until incorporated. Stir in the vinegar and season with pepper. To serve, spread the anchovy mixture on the grilled bread or put it out in a bowl alongside the toasts. —*Nancy Harmon Jenkins*

NOTE Salt-packed anchovies are available at Greek and Italian markets, and their flavor and texture are worth the extra fuss. Rinse under running water and then separate each into 2 fillets, discarding the spine and any fins or tail pieces.

MAKE AHEAD The Anchoïade can be prepared up to 4 hours ahead; keep it at room temperature.

Classic Swiss Cheese Fondue

8 SERVINGS

Steamed red-skinned potato chunks, grilled or toasted Tuscan bread cubes and pear slices are great for dipping into the melted cheese. Be sure to stir the fondue as you dip.

- 1 garlic clove, halved
- 1 pound Gruyère cheese, grated
- ½ pound Emmentaler cheese or other Swiss cheese, grated
- 1 cup dry white wine
- 1 tablespoon plus 1 teaspoon cornstarch
- 1 teaspoon fresh lemon juice
- 1½ tablespoons kirsch

Freshly ground pepper
Freshly grated nutmeg

Rub the inside of a cheese fondue pot or medium enameled cast-iron casserole with the garlic clove; discard the garlic. In the fondue pot, combine the grated cheeses with the wine, cornstarch and lemon juice and cook over moderate heat, stirring occasionally, until the cheeses begin to melt, about 5 minutes. Add the kirsch and a generous pinch each of pepper and nutmeg. Continue to cook the fondue, stirring occasionally, until it is creamy and smooth, about 10 minutes; don't overmix or overcook the fondue or it will get stringy. Serve at once.

—Melissa Kelly

Roasted Pepper, Almond and Cilantro Pesto

MAKES ABOUT 2 CUPS

The pesto dip goes well with Paprika Chips (p. 18) or simple toasted slices of baguette.

One 12-ounce jar roasted red peppers, drained
½ cup cilantro leaves
1 tablespoon tomato paste
1 tablespoon sherry vinegar
2 teaspoons fresh lemon juice
1½ teaspoons minced garlic
1¼ teaspoons kosher salt
½ teaspoon hot or sweet paprika
½ teaspoon chili powder
¼ teaspoon cayenne pepper
1 cup coarsely ground blanched almonds (4 ounces)

In a food processor or blender, combine the roasted red peppers with the cilantro, tomato paste, vinegar, lemon juice, garlic, kosher salt, paprika, chili powder and cayenne pepper and pulse until the roasted peppers and cilantro are finely chopped. Scrape down the side of the bowl and process until the pesto is smooth. Add the ground almonds and pulse until combined. Transfer the pepper and almond pesto to a bowl and serve.

—Mary Barber and Sara Corpening

MAKE AHEAD The pesto can be refrigerated for up to 2 days. Return to room temperature before serving.

Fresh Tomato Salsa

MAKES ABOUT 1 CUP

¾ pound tomatoes, coarsely chopped
3 tablespoons coarsely chopped flat-leaf parsley
3 tablespoons coarsely chopped mint
1 serrano or jalapeño chile, seeded and minced
1 garlic clove, minced
2 tablespoons fresh lime juice
2 tablespoons olive oil
Salt

In a medium bowl, stir together the tomatoes, parsley, mint, jalapeño and garlic. Stir in the lime juice and oil and season the salsa with salt.

—Christer Larsson

Salsa Criolla

MAKES ABOUT 3 CUPS

This colorful tomato, onion and pepper relish is another traditional accompaniment for grilled meats throughout South America.

1 pound ripe tomatoes, seeded and cut into ¼-inch dice
1 medium onion, cut into ¼-inch dice
1 small green bell pepper, cut into ¼-inch dice
3 tablespoons chopped flat-leaf parsley
3 tablespoons extra-virgin olive oil
2 tablespoons red wine vinegar
1 teaspoon dried oregano
Salt and freshly ground black pepper

In a medium bowl, combine the tomatoes, onion, green pepper, parsley, oil, vinegar and oregano. Just before serving, season generously with salt and black pepper. —Steven Raichlen

MAKE AHEAD The salsa can be prepared up to 4 hours ahead, but should be seasoned just before serving.

Almond Mint Salsa

MAKES ABOUT 2 CUPS

Serve the salsa with mixed grills or toss it with macaroni or any tubular pasta, adding a little of the pasta cooking water to thin out the sauce so that it will coat the macaroni well.

1 cup blanched almonds (about 6 ounces)
1 cup (packed) mint leaves
½ cup green olive paste
½ cup extra-virgin olive oil
¼ cup fresh orange juice
½ teaspoon crushed red pepper
Salt

In a blender, combine the almonds, mint, olive paste, oil, orange juice and crushed red pepper and blend until smooth. Transfer to a bowl and season with salt. —Mario Batali

Walnut and Yogurt Chutney

MAKES 2 CUPS

In Kashmir, India, this garlicky, nutty, chile-spiked chutney is often served alongside highly spiced meat dishes, but it also makes a tasty dip for fresh vegetables. This version is adapted from Neela Paniz's Bombay Cafe Cookbook, published by Ten Speed Press.

2 cups walnut halves or pieces (½ pound)
3 green serrano chiles, ends trimmed
2 garlic cloves, halved
About 1 cup plain yogurt
½ teaspoon salt

In a food processor, combine the walnuts, serrano chiles and garlic cloves and process until the mixture has the consistency of chunky peanut butter. Blend in half of the yogurt and the salt. Add the remaining yogurt to give the chutney a thinner consistency.

—Maya Kaimal

MAKE AHEAD The prepared chutney can be refrigerated, covered, for up to 2 days.

Red Coconut Chutney

MAKES ABOUT ¾ CUP

Here is a variation on the standard white coconut chutney usually served with Dosas (p. 290). A dried red chile is ground up with the coconut, coloring it pale red.

- 1 dried red chile, stemmed
- ½ cup water
- ½ cup plus 2 tablespoons finely grated dried unsweetened coconut
- 1 tablespoon finely chopped shallot
- 1 tablespoon plain yogurt
- ½ teaspoon finely chopped serrano or Thai chile
- ½ teaspoon minced fresh ginger
- ½ teaspoon fresh lemon juice
- ½ teaspoon salt
- 1 tablespoon vegetable oil
- ¼ teaspoon mustard seeds
- 4 curry leaves, or 1 bay leaf

I. In a small saucepan, combine the dried red chile with the water and bring to a boil. Remove from the heat and let stand for 10 minutes. Drain the red chile, reserving the liquid. In a blender, combine the red chile with the coconut, shallot, yogurt, serrano chile, ginger, lemon juice, salt and enough of the reserved chile soaking liquid to make the thick mixture just pourable.

2. In a large skillet, heat the oil. Add the mustard seeds and curry leaves, cover and cook over moderately high heat until the mustard seeds begin to pop. Stir in the coconut mixture and remove from the heat. Transfer the chutney to a serving bowl. Serve the chutney at room temperature.

—*Maya Kaimal*

MAKE AHEAD The chutney can stand at room temperature for up to 3 hours. In fact, a bit of a wait will let the flavors develop and meld together.

what's in a fruit?

Here's how 140-gram servings of the ten most nutritious fruits stack up in terms of the percentage of Daily Value, or the FDA's recommended daily intake, of a few key nutrients.

	Vitamin A	Vitamin C	Other Significant Nutrients
1. **Kiwi** (2 medium)	4.90%	230.00%	Vitamin E 17.4%, Folate 13.3%
2. **Papaya** (½ small)	7.95%	144.20%	Vitamin E 17.4%, Folate 13.3%
3. **Cantaloupe** (¼ medium)	90.27%	98.46%	
4. **Strawberry** (8 large)	.76%	132.30%	
5. **Mango** (½ large)	109.03%	64.63%	Vitamin B1 5.4%
6. **Lemon** (2½ small)	.81%	123.66%	
7. **Orange** (1 medium)	5.74%	124.13%	Folate 10.6%, Vitamin B1 8.1%
8. **Red Currant** (1⅓ cups)	3.36%	95.66%	
9. **Mandarin Orange** (2 small)	25.76%	71.86%	Vitamin B1 9.8%, Folate 7.1%
10. **Avocado** (¾ medium)	17.14%	18.43%	Folate 21.7%

Mango Chutney

MAKES ABOUT 4 CUPS

- 6 ripe mangoes, peeled and chopped
- 3 cups sugar
- 1 cup cider vinegar
- ½ cup dried currants
- ¼ cup crystallized ginger, chopped
- 2 garlic cloves, minced

Put all ingredients in a large pot. Bring to a boil. Reduce the heat and simmer for 1 hour, stirring frequently. Ladle the hot chutney into sterilized jars.

—*Allegra Goodman*

Strawberry-Mango Salsa

4 SERVINGS 🌸

Compound the nutritional benefits of strawberries and mangoes (see chart above) by combining the two.

- 1 cup diced strawberries
- ½ cup diced mango
- ¼ cup diced yellow bell pepper
- 2 tablespoons fresh lime juice
- 1 tablespoon minced chives
- 1 tablespoon chopped cilantro
- 1 tablespoon olive oil
- 1 tablespoon red-wine vinegar
- 1 teaspoon minced fresh chile

Salt and freshly ground black pepper

Combine all the ingredients in a bowl; refrigerate for 1 hour. Serve cold or at room temperature. —*Oliver Saucy*

SERVE WITH Grilled chicken, fish, shellfish or pork.

ONE SERVING Calories 59 kcal, Total Fat 3.6 gm, Saturated Fat .5 gm

Dried Plum and Garlic Compote

MAKES ABOUT 1½ CUPS

This sweet and sour condiment can be served with flat breads or with grilled lamb or pork.

- 1 cup moist pitted prunes (about 6 ounces), quartered
- ¾ cup chicken stock (p. 117) or canned low-sodium broth
- 1 medium onion, coarsely chopped
- 3 garlic cloves, thinly sliced lengthwise
- 2 tablespoons red wine vinegar
- 1 dried red chile

Salt

In a medium saucepan, combine the prunes, chicken stock, onion, garlic, vinegar and chile; bring to a boil over moderate heat. Reduce the heat to low and simmer, stirring occasionally, until the mixture thickens, about 15 minutes, and then discard the chile. Season the compote with salt and serve warm or at room temperature.

—*Christer Larsson*

MAKE AHEAD The compote can be refrigerated for up to 3 days. Let return to room temperature before serving.

Cranberries with Orange Zest and Port

MAKES ABOUT 4½ CUPS

An unusual way of cooking the cranberries takes advantage of their affinity for the flavor of port. The cranberries are rendered perfectly done but not mushy, resulting in a relish that sparkles like a dish of jewels.

Cranberries with Orange Zest and Port

1 cup port
6 cups fresh cranberries (1½ pounds), picked over and rinsed
1½ cups sugar
2 tablespoons finely chopped orange zest
¼ teaspoon salt

In a large skillet, bring the port to a boil over high heat. Add the cranberries and cook, stirring, until they begin to pop, about 5 minutes. Add the sugar, orange zest and salt and cook, stirring, until the sugar dissolves and the mixture returns to a simmer, 3 to 5 minutes. Let cool before serving.

—*Edna Lewis and Scott Peacock*

MAKE AHEAD Store the cranberries at room temperature for up to 2 days.

Caperberry Gremolata

MAKES ABOUT ⅓ CUP

Thumbnail-size caperberries are what remain after the petals of the flowers of the caper bush have dropped off; capers themselves are the brined or pickled flower buds.

2 garlic cloves, minced
3 tablespoons coarsely chopped flat-leaf parsley
2 tablespoons caperberries (see Note), finely chopped, or salt-packed capers, rinsed
1½ tablespoons finely grated lemon zest
1 teaspoon finely grated orange zest
2 teaspoons fresh lemon juice

Combine all of the ingredients in a small bowl and let stand until the flavors develop, at least 20 minutes.

—*Marcia Kiesel*

NOTE Caperberries are available at specialty food stores.

MAKE AHEAD The gremolata can be kept refrigerated in a covered bowl for up to 5 days.

SERVE WITH Grilled, sautéed or roasted tuna steaks, halibut steaks or fillets, pork loin or shrimp; pan-roasted chicken breasts (stuff about 1 tablespoon under the skin of each of 4 chicken breasts).

Malay Onion Sambal

MAKES ABOUT 1½ CUPS

The onions in this condiment are salted and then rinsed, a process that both softens them and removes any bitter juices. Serve this with Papaya-Marinated Steak (p. 261) or with any grilled steak or chop. The flavors in the sambal are at least as good with lamb and pork as they are with beef.

3 medium onions, quartered lengthwise and very thinly sliced
3 tablespoons kosher salt

A pan-fried chicken breast stuffed with Caperberry Gremolata.

¼ cup cider vinegar

2½ tablespoons strained apricot
jam

2½ tablespoons minced mint,
cilantro or a mix of both

1 medium-hot fresh red chile,
seeded and minced

I. Set a colander in the sink. Add the
onions and kosher salt; rub the salt
into the onions and squeeze them

gently for a few minutes. Rinse the
onions thoroughly under cold running
water and then drain well and pat dry.
2. In a small bowl, combine the vinegar and apricot jam. Stir in the onions
and mint. Add the chile and serve.
—*Jenna Holst*

MAKE AHEAD The sambal can be
prepared through Step 1 up to 1 day
ahead.

Malay Chile Jam

MAKES ABOUT ½ CUP

This chile jam is a wonderful accompaniment to bread and sharp cheeses
and can be made with almost any
medium-hot chile. (Do not use the
very hot habanero or Scotch bonnet
chiles.) Green chiles are fine, but red
chiles produce a spectacular color.
Wear thin latex or rubber gloves when

handling chiles to prevent any skin irritation, and remember to keep the gloves away from your face and especially your eyes.

- 1 small onion, quartered and thinly sliced
- ½ cup sugar
- ⅓ cup minced seeded medium-hot chiles, such as jalapeños or serranos
- ¼ cup minced red bell pepper
- ¼ cup water
- ¼ lemon, cut into 2 wedges

Large pinch of salt

Kiwi Raita

Combine all of the ingredients in a medium saucepan and bring to a boil. Cook over moderate heat, stirring often, until the chile jam thickens and registers 210° on a jelly thermometer, about 12 minutes. Discard the lemon wedges and pour the chile jam into a clean jar or container. Refrigerate the chile jam for up to 2 weeks. Warm the chile jam slightly in the jar set in a saucepan of gently simmering water before serving it.   —*Jenna Holst*

Kiwi Raita

ABOUT 1½ CUPS

Kiwi takes the place of the traditional cucumber in this just slightly sweet version of the lightly spiced Indian yogurt condiment.

- ½ teaspoon black mustard seeds
- ½ teaspoon cumin seeds
- ¼ teaspoon coriander seeds
- 2 kiwis, peeled and coarsely chopped
- ½ cup plain low-fat yogurt
- ¼ cup low-fat sour cream
- ¼ cup finely chopped onion
- ½ tablespoon coarsely chopped cilantro
- ⅛ teaspoon pure red chile powder or crushed red pepper

Salt

1. In a dry skillet, combine the mustard, cumin and coriander seeds and toast over moderate heat, stirring, until fragrant, about 3 minutes. Coarsely grind the toasted seeds in a spice grinder or mortar.

2. In a bowl, combine all but 1 tablespoon of the kiwi with the yogurt, sour cream and onion. Stir in the ground spices, cilantro and chile powder and season with salt. Cover and refrigerate until cold. Garnish with the reserved kiwi and serve.   —*Norman Van Aken*

SERVE WITH Spicy lamb or chicken.
ONE SERVING Calories 66 kcal, Total Fat 1.8 gm, Saturated Fat 1 gm

Chilean Mushroom Crumbs

MAKES ABOUT 3 CUPS

Dried Chilean wild mushrooms, sometimes known as Chilean porcini, are smokier than most other dried mushrooms. If you can't find them, use dried Polish or European porcini, which are widely available; they are also smoky and flavorful.

 2 cups dried Chilean wild mushrooms (about 1 ounce); see Note
 1 cup boiling water
 2 tablespoons unsalted butter
 1 tablespoon pure olive oil
 2 small shallots, minced
 2 medium garlic cloves, minced
 2½ tablespoons dry Marsala
 1½ cups coarse fresh bread crumbs
 1 teaspoon finely chopped thyme
Salt and freshly ground pepper

I. In a small bowl, cover the dried mushrooms with the boiling water and let stand until softened, about 20 minutes. Drain, reserving 2 tablespoons of the liquid; be sure it doesn't contain any grit. Press any excess liquid from the mushrooms, coarsely chop them and transfer to a plate.

2. In a large skillet, melt the butter in the oil. Add the shallots and cook over moderate heat, stirring occasionally, until wilted, about 2 minutes. Add the chopped mushrooms and garlic and 2 tablespoons of the Marsala and cook, stirring frequently, until the Marsala is slightly reduced, about 2 minutes. Add the bread crumbs and continue cooking, stirring frequently, until completely blended, about 3 minutes.

3. Scrape the crumb mixture into a large skillet and stir in the remaining ½ tablespoon of Marsala and the thyme. Season the crumb mixture with salt and pepper and then toast over moderately high heat, stirring, until the crumbs are lightly browned and crisp, about 5 minutes. —Marcia Kiesel

NOTE Chilean wild mushrooms, or porcini, are available at gourmet food stores or by mail order from Marché aux Delices (888-547-5471).

MAKE AHEAD The crumbs can be refrigerated for up to 3 days.

SERVE WITH Pan-roasted chicken breasts (stuff about ½ cup under the skin of each of 6 chicken breasts) or pork chops (press ½ cup of the crumbs onto each of 6 pork chops); pasta, such as spaghetti, rigatoni or fusilli (toss the crumbs with the cooked pasta, adding a little pasta cooking water, butter, Marsala and Parmesan cheese).

CHAPTER 14 cakes tarts cookies

Cinnamon-Sugar Cookies (p. 397)

Preserved Lemon and Apricot Cake

Preserved Lemon and Apricot Cake

MAKES ONE 10-INCH CAKE

Because this crumbly cake isn't overly sweet, it's nice for breakfast as well as dessert.

PRESERVED LEMONS

 1 cup sugar
 1 cup water
 2 lemons, scrubbed and sliced ⅛ inch thick

APRICOT CAKE

 ½ cup Late Harvest Gewürztraminer or other dessert wine
 1 cup coarsely chopped dried apricots (about ½ pound)
 1 cup sliced almonds (3 ounces)
1¾ cups all-purpose flour
1½ teaspoons baking powder
 11 tablespoons unsalted butter, softened
 ½ cup plus 3 tablespoons sugar
 3 large eggs

Whipped cream, for serving

I. MAKE THE PRESERVED LEMONS: In a saucepan, combine the sugar and water and stir over moderate heat until the sugar dissolves. Add the lemon slices and simmer over low heat until the syrup becomes quite thick, about 20 minutes. Let cool to room temperature. Set aside 12 of the nicest lemon slices; finely chop the rest and reserve the syrup.

2. MAKE THE APRICOT CAKE: Preheat the oven to 350°. Butter a 10-inch round cake pan. In a small saucepan, warm the wine. Add the apricots and soak for 30 minutes. Meanwhile, spread the almond slices on a rimmed baking sheet and toast in the oven for about 7 minutes, or until they are golden brown; leave the oven on. Transfer the almonds to a plate to cool. Sift the flour with the baking powder.

3. In a large bowl, using an electric mixer on high speed, beat the butter with the sugar until light and fluffy, about 8 minutes. Add the eggs, 1 at a time, beating well between each addition. On medium speed, gradually blend in half of the flour mixture. Add the chopped preserved lemons and the apricots with their soaking liquid and mix lightly. Gently blend in the remaining flour mixture. Using a rubber spatula, fold in the almonds.

4. Scrape the batter into the prepared pan, smoothing the surface. Arrange the reserved lemon slices on top and bake the cake in the center of the oven for about 40 minutes, or until a toothpick inserted into the center comes out clean. Let the cake cool in the pan. Transfer the cake to a plate, lemons up, and generously brush the top with the reserved lemon syrup. Using a serrated knife, carefully cut the cake into thick wedges and serve with whipped cream. —*Tony Najiola*

Lemony Polenta Cake

MAKES ONE 9-INCH CAKE

Extra-virgin olive oil and sugar combine to put a crisp sweet crust on this crumbly treat. The cool simplicity of the unsweetened cream nicely complements the tangy cake.

 2 cups all-purpose flour
 ¼ cup polenta
 ½ teaspoon baking soda
 ½ teaspoon salt
 ½ cup extra-virgin olive oil (see Note)
 2 tablespoons fresh lemon juice
 1 tablespoon pure vanilla extract
 2 large eggs
 1 cup granulated sugar
 1 tablespoon finely grated lemon zest
 1 cup heavy cream
 1 teaspoon confectioners' sugar

I. Preheat the oven to 325°. Butter a 9-inch springform pan. Sift together the flour, polenta, baking soda and

salt. In a small bowl, combine the oil, lemon juice and vanilla.

2. In a large bowl, beat the eggs with the granulated sugar at medium speed until thick, about 3 minutes. Gradually beat in the oil mixture and the lemon zest. Gently fold in the dry ingredients just until blended.

3. Scrape the batter into the prepared pan and bake for about 50 minutes, or until the center springs back when lightly pressed. Let the cake cool on a wire rack for 5 minutes. Remove the side and let cool completely.

4. In a medium bowl, whip the heavy cream to soft peaks. Transfer the cake to a serving plate and sift the confectioners' sugar over the top. Serve with the whipped cream. —*Jan Newberry*

NOTE Make the cake with a buttery extra-virgin olive oil; do not use a pungent oil.

WINE This soft, mildly sweet polenta cake needs a slightly sweet wine, such as a chilled glass of fruity Italian Moscato, to add the desired flourish to the dessert. Look for the 1996 Bera Moscato d'Asti or the 1996 Vietti Moscato Cascinetta.

Polenta Pound Cake with Elderflower Crème Anglaise

MAKES ONE 10-BY-5-INCH CAKE

The dense pound cake is flavored with orange-flower water, a fragrant distillate that is made from bitter-orange blossoms.

 3 cups all-purpose flour
 1 cup polenta
 ½ teaspoon salt
 2 cups sugar
 3 sticks (¾ pound) unsalted butter, softened
 6 large eggs
 ½ cup orange-flower water (see Note)
 1 tablespoon finely grated orange zest

Polenta Pound Cake with Elderflower Crème Anglaise

Elderflower Crème Anglaise (recipe
   follows), for serving
Mixed fresh berries, for serving

1. Preheat the oven to 325°. Butter
and flour a 2-quart loaf pan (10-by-5-
by-3 inches). In a bowl, sift together
the flour, polenta and salt.

2. In a standing electric mixer fitted
with the paddle, beat the sugar and
the butter at medium speed until light
and fluffy. Add the eggs to the butter
mixture, 1 at a time, beating just until
each is incorporated. Add the orange-
flower water and orange zest and beat
until blended. Mix in the dry ingredients at low speed until thoroughly
moistened, scraping the side and bottom of the bowl as necessary.

3. Spread the batter in the prepared
pan and smooth the surface. Bake in
the center of the oven for about 2
hours, or until a toothpick inserted in
the center of the cake comes out
clean. Let the cake cool in the pan for
10 minutes and then turn it out onto
a wire rack to cool completely.

4. Slice the cake and serve it with
the Elderflower Crème Anglaise and
fresh berries.

NOTE Orange-flower water is available at Middle Eastern groceries and
specialty food shops.

MAKE AHEAD The cake can be
wrapped in plastic and stored in an
air-tight container for several days.

WINE Look for something cold and
sparkling. No wine is quite as refreshing with dessert as a Moscato d'Asti;
the Santo Stefano from Ceretto and
the Nivole from Michele Chiarlo are a
cut above the rest.

ELDERFLOWER CREME ANGLAISE
MAKES ABOUT 3½ CUPS

   1 **cup heavy cream**
   1 **cup milk**
   6 **large egg yolks**
   1 **cup elderflower concentrate**
      (see Note)

1. In a large saucepan, heat the cream
and milk until beginning to steam. Set
a heatproof medium bowl in a large
bowl of ice. In another bowl, whisk the
egg yolks with the elderflower concentrate until smooth. Gradually whisk
in the hot cream.

2. Return the mixture to the saucepan
and cook over moderate heat, stirring
gently with a wooden spoon, until the
custard coats the back of the spoon,
about 6 minutes; do not let it boil.
Strain the custard into the bowl in the
ice bath and let cool completely, stirring often.   —Alan Tardi

NOTE Elderflower concentrate, made
in England from elderflowers and
lemons, is available by mail from
Mushrooms & More, 914-232-2107.

MAKE AHEAD The sauce can be refrigerated for up to 1 day.

Orange Chiffon Cake with Rhubarb Jam

MAKES ONE 10-INCH CAKE

This airy orange-infused dessert has the texture of a rich chiffon cake.

JAM

- ½ cup sugar
- ¼ cup fresh orange juice
- 1 pound rhubarb, trimmed and thickly sliced
- 2 teaspoons finely grated orange zest

CAKE

- 1½ cups cake flour
- 1 tablespoon baking powder

Pinch of salt

- 6 large eggs at room temperature, separated
- 1¾ cups sugar
- 2 tablespoons finely grated orange zest
- ⅓ cup vegetable oil
- ½ cup fresh orange juice

Pinch of cream of tartar

I. MAKE THE JAM: In a heavy saucepan, bring the sugar and orange juice to a boil over moderately high heat, stirring. Add three-quarters of the rhubarb and the orange zest and simmer, stirring, until the rhubarb is softened and slightly thickened, about 5 minutes. Add the remaining rhubarb and cook until just tender, about 2 minutes. Let cool.

2. MAKE THE CAKE: Preheat the oven to 375°. In a bowl, sift together the flour, baking powder and salt. In a large bowl, beat the egg yolks with 1½ cups of the sugar and the orange zest on high speed until light and fluffy, about 3 minutes. Gradually beat in the oil. Working in batches, alternately fold in the flour mixture and the orange juice, beginning and ending with the flour mixture.

3. In a large bowl, beat the egg whites with the cream of tartar until very soft peaks form. Add the remaining ¼ cup of sugar and beat until firm, glossy peaks form. Fold one-third of the whites into the cake batter until incorporated and then fold in the remaining whites just until blended.

4. Scrape the batter into a 10-inch tube pan with a removable bottom and lightly smooth the top. Tap the pan once to release any air pockets. Bake the cake in the bottom third of the oven for about 30 minutes, or until the top springs back when lightly pressed. Invert the cake pan onto a jar and let cool in the pan.

5. Run a thin metal knife between the cake and the side of the pan to loosen. Invert the cake onto a cake plate and serve with the rhubarb jam.

—*Joseph and Thomas Keller*

Spice Cake with Orange Curd and Meringue Frosting

MAKES ONE 8-INCH CAKE

The unadorned spice cake layers, which need to stand overnight to develop their flavor, are delicious on their own. Filling the layers with the Orange Curd and frosting them with the

Orange Chiffon Cake with Rhubarb Jam

orange-scented Meringue Frosting makes this cake extraordinary.

2½ cups sifted cake flour

1 teaspoon baking powder

½ teaspoon baking soda

½ teaspoon cinnamon

½ teaspoon ground ginger

¼ teaspoon freshly grated nutmeg

¼ teaspoon salt

⅛ teaspoon ground cloves

1 cup buttermilk, at room temperature

1 teaspoon pure vanilla extract

1½ sticks (6 ounces) unsalted butter, softened

1 cup (packed) light brown sugar

½ cup granulated sugar

3 large eggs, at room temperature

Orange Curd (recipe follows)

Meringue Frosting (recipe follows)

1. Preheat the oven to 350° and position a rack in the lower third. Butter and flour two 8-by-2-inch round cake pans. Sift the flour with the baking powder, baking soda, cinnamon, ginger, nutmeg, salt and cloves onto a sheet of wax paper. Combine the buttermilk and vanilla in a small pitcher.

2. In a standing electric mixer fitted with a paddle attachment, beat the butter at medium speed until creamy. Add the brown sugar and granulated sugar and beat until light and fluffy, about 4 minutes, stopping once to scrape down the bowl. Add the eggs, 1 at a time, beating well after each addition. Beat in the flour mixture at low speed in 3 batches, alternating with the buttermilk mixture, just until the batter is smooth; stop the mixer occasionally to scrape down the bowl.

3. Divide the batter evenly between the pans. Transfer the pans to the oven and bake for 30 to 35 minutes, or until the cakes begin to shrink from the sides. Let the cakes cool for 10 minutes and then turn each out onto a rack, invert onto another rack and let

cool completely. Wrap each cake in plastic and store at room temperature overnight.

4. Cut a ¼-inch notch in the side of each cake; this will allow you to line up the layers when assembling the cake. Using a long serrated knife, cut each cake layer in half horizontally and set on a work surface, cut side up.

5. Center 1 bottom cake layer on a platter and spread ½ cup of the Orange Curd on top, leaving a ½-inch border around the edge. Cover with its top cake layer, cut side down, taking care to line up the notches. Spread the tops and sides of both cakes with ½ cup Orange Curd, leaving a ½-inch border. Repeat with the remaining cake and curd, ending with a cake layer. Spread the top and side with the Meringue Frosting.

WINE The citrus in this light, airy spice cake is a natural match for the tartness of Champagne. Because of the cake's sugariness, a sweeter extra-dry cuvée works better than an austere nonvintage brut. Look for Mumm Extra Dry or Moët & Chandon White Star.

ORANGE CURD

MAKES ABOUT 1⅔ CUPS

3 large eggs

2 large egg yolks

½ cup sugar

¼ cup fresh orange juice

2 tablespoons fresh lemon juice

2 teaspoons finely grated orange zest

2 teaspoons finely grated lemon zest

1 stick (4 ounces) cold unsalted butter, cut into tablespoons

In a small heavy saucepan, whisk together the eggs and the egg yolks. Whisk in the sugar and then whisk in the orange juice, lemon juice, orange zest and lemon zest. Add the butter

and whisk constantly over moderately low heat until the mixture thickens, about 8 minutes; do not let it boil. Immediately strain the curd into a bowl. Press plastic wrap directly on the surface of the curd and cut 6 small steam vents in the plastic. Refrigerate the curd overnight; it can be refrigerated for up to 1 week.

MERINGUE FROSTING

MAKES ABOUT 3 CUPS

Make the frosting shortly before assembling the cake.

⅔ cup plus 2 tablespoons sugar

¼ cup water

3 large egg whites

⅛ teaspoon cream of tartar

2 teaspoons finely grated orange zest

1 teaspoon pure vanilla extract

1. In a small saucepan, combine the ⅔ cup of sugar with the water and stir over low heat until the sugar dissolves. Using a brush dipped in cold water, wash down any sugar crystals from the side of the saucepan. Boil the sugar syrup without stirring over moderately high heat until the syrup reaches 240° on a candy thermometer, about 7 minutes.

2. Meanwhile, in the bowl of a standing electric mixer fitted with the whisk, beat the egg whites with the cream of tartar at medium-high speed until the whites hold soft peaks. Add the remaining 2 tablespoons of the sugar and beat until the egg whites are firm. With the machine on, drizzle the boiling sugar syrup down the side of the mixing bowl, avoiding the whisk, and beat at low speed for 3 minutes until stiff, glossy peaks form when the whisk is lifted. Beat in the orange zest and the vanilla and then let the frosting cool for 10 minutes. Use the Meringue Frosting as soon as possible.

—Flo Braker

Spice Cake with Orange Curd and Meringue Frosting

ABOVE: Caramelized Apple Upside-Down Spice Cake.
LEFT: Apple Muffin Cakes.

Apple Muffin Cakes

MAKES 6 LARGE OR 12 SMALL CAKES

Deborah Madison, the consulting chef at the O'Keeffe Cafe in Santa Fe's Georgia O'Keeffe Museum, got her inspiration for these delectable fruit-filled muffins from a recipe found in *A Painter's Kitchen,* by Margaret Wood. Apples are one of the few fruits that are grown successfully in northern New Mexico; here they're bound with just a little batter before they're baked in muffin tins.

¾ cup coarsely chopped pecans (about 3 ounces)

1½ cups all-purpose flour

1 teaspoon baking soda

½ teaspoon cardamom

⅛ teaspoon salt

1 stick (4 ounces) unsalted butter, softened

¾ cup granulated sugar

1 large egg

3 tablespoons yogurt or low-fat buttermilk

2 medium Granny Smith apples— peeled, cored and cut into ¾-inch dice

Confectioners' sugar (optional), for dusting

1. Preheat the oven to 325°. Butter 6 large or 12 regular-size muffin cups. Line the bottoms of the cups with wax paper and brush them with butter. Spread the pecans on a baking sheet and toast for about 8 minutes, or until fragrant. Transfer the pecans to a plate and let cool.

2. In a bowl, sift together the flour, baking soda, cardamom and salt. In another bowl, beat the butter until creamy. Add the granulated sugar to the butter and beat until light and fluffy. Beat in the egg and yogurt. Stir in the dry ingredients until fully incorporated and then fold in the apples and pecans.

3. Spoon the cake batter into the prepared muffin cups and bake for about 40 minutes for large cakes and 30 minutes for regular cakes, or until the apples are tender and a toothpick inserted into the center of the cakes comes out clean. Let the cakes cool in the pan for 5 minutes. Invert the cakes onto a rack, remove the wax paper and then turn the cakes right side up and let them cool completely. Dust the muffin cakes with confectioners' sugar before serving, if desired.

—*Deborah Madison*

Caramelized Apple Upside-Down Spice Cake

MAKES ONE 10-INCH CAKE

TOPPING

- 6 tablespoons unsalted butter
- 5 Fuji or Granny Smith apples (about 2½ pounds)—peeled, cored and cut into 6 wedges each
- ¼ cup brandy
- 1 cup sugar

CAKE

- ½ cup plus 2 tablespoons buttermilk
- 3 large egg yolks
- 1 teaspoon pure vanilla extract
- 1 cup cake flour
- ¾ cup sugar
- ½ cup all-purpose flour
- 1¾ teaspoons baking powder
- ½ teaspoon baking soda
- ½ teaspoon freshly grated nutmeg
- ½ teaspoon ground cinnamon
- ½ teaspoon ground cloves
- ¼ teaspoon salt
- 6 tablespoons unsalted butter, softened

Vanilla ice cream, for serving

I. MAKE THE TOPPING: Butter a 10-inch cake pan. Melt the 6 tablespoons butter in a large skillet. Add the apple wedges in an even layer and cook over moderately low heat, turning halfway through cooking, until golden brown, about 8 minutes. Add the brandy and simmer until the alcohol cooks off, about 3 minutes. Add the sugar and cook, stirring occasionally, until the apples are browned and the sugar caramelizes to a deep gold, about 12 minutes.

2. Using a slotted spoon, transfer the cooked apple wedges to the prepared cake pan and arrange them in concentric circles. Pour the caramel over the apple wedges.

3. MAKE THE CAKE: Preheat the oven to 350°. In a medium bowl, mix the buttermilk with the egg yolks and vanilla. In a large bowl, combine the cake flour, sugar, all-purpose flour, baking powder, baking soda, nutmeg, cinnamon, cloves and salt. Using an electric mixer, beat in the butter. Gradually add the buttermilk mixture, beating on low speed until well blended.

4. Scrape the batter over the apple wedges in the pan and smooth the top. Bake for about 30 minutes, or until a cake tester inserted in the center of the cake comes out clean. Let the cake cool until warm and then invert onto a large plate. Cut the cake into wedges and serve with the vanilla ice cream. —*Maria Helm*

MAKE AHEAD The cake can stand at room temperature for up to 5 hours.

Corn Cake with Dried Cranberries

MAKES ONE 8- OR 9-INCH CAKE

Serve this subtly sweet, fruit-studded skillet cake at breakfast, as a snack or even as a rustic dessert.

- 1 cup all-purpose flour
- ½ cup stone-ground cornmeal
- 3 tablespoons (packed) light brown sugar

Pinch of salt

- 2 tablespoons coarsely chopped dried cranberries
- 1 large egg, lightly beaten
- ¾ cup milk
- 2 tablespoons vegetable oil

Softened unsalted butter, for serving

Maple syrup, for serving

I. In a bowl, stir together the flour, cornmeal, brown sugar and salt. Stir in the dried cranberries. In another bowl, mix the beaten egg with the milk and 1 tablespoon of the oil. Pour the egg mixture into the dry ingredients and stir gently just until combined; do not overmix.

2. In an 8- or 9-inch skillet, heat ½ tablespoon of the oil until shimmering. Scrape the batter into the skillet, smoothing the surface. Cover partially and cook over moderately low heat until the corn cake has browned on the bottom and bubbles have formed on the surface, about 5 minutes. Using a large metal spatula, transfer the corn cake to a dinner plate. Add the remaining ½ tablespoon of oil to the skillet. Gently invert the corn cake into the skillet, partially cover and cook until the cake is just cooked through and the top springs back when lightly pressed, about 5 minutes longer. Serve the corn cake hot, with butter and maple syrup. —*Marcia Kiesel*

Cranberry-Almond Cake with Raspberry Coulis

MAKES ONE 9-BY-2-INCH CAKE

At the Fine Arts Restaurant in The Museum of Fine Arts in Boston, Jim Dodge accents his elegant *financier,* or French almond cake, with cranberries to add a refreshing tartness. Serve the cake with the Raspberry Coulis or with fresh raspberries.

CAKE

- ½ cup sliced almonds (about 2 ounces)
- 2 cups confectioners' sugar, plus 1 tablespoon, for dusting
- 1 cup all-purpose flour
- 1 teaspoon kosher salt
- 9 large egg whites
- 2 sticks (½ pound) unsalted butter, melted and cooled
- 2 tablespoons Chambord or framboise
- 1 teaspoon almond extract
- 1 teaspoon finely grated lemon zest
- 1½ cups fresh or frozen cranberries

COULIS

- 1 pint fresh raspberries
- 2 tablespoons granulated sugar
- 2 tablespoons fresh lemon juice or water

Cranberry-Almond Cake with Raspberry Coulis

I. MAKE THE CAKE: Preheat the oven to 350°. Butter and flour a 9-by-2-inch round cake pan. Spread the almonds on a small rimmed baking sheet and toast for about 4 minutes, or until golden. Transfer to a work surface and let cool. Crush the almonds with a rolling pin until very fine, but with a few larger pieces remaining. Transfer to a bowl and add the 2 cups of confectioners' sugar, the flour and kosher salt.

2. In a large bowl, beat the egg whites until firm peaks form. Fold in the dry ingredients, a handful at a time, until no streaks of flour remain. In a large glass measuring cup, combine the butter, Chambord, almond extract and lemon zest. Pour about one-quarter of the butter mixture down the side of the bowl; gently fold into the batter

until blended. Fold in the remaining butter mixture in 3 batches, pouring each down the side of the bowl. Fold in the cranberries and spread the batter in the prepared pan.

3. Bake the cake for about 35 minutes, or until golden and the top springs back when lightly pressed. Sift the remaining 1 tablespoon of confectioners' sugar over the cake and bake for 5 minutes longer. Let the cake cool in the pan for 10 minutes. Invert the cake onto a wire rack and then turn it right side up on a serving plate and let cool to room temperature.

4. MAKE THE COULIS: In a food processor or blender, puree the raspberries with the granulated sugar and lemon juice. Strain the puree into a bowl. Serve the cake with the raspberry coulis.   —*Jim Dodge*

Mantuan Crumb Cake
MAKES ONE 10-INCH CAKE

In the Italian Renaissance city of Mantua, a cake called *sbrisolona,* which tastes like a sandy almond cookie, is typical. Here's the version from the Trattoria dei Martini in Mantua.

- ½ **pound blanched whole almonds**
- 1 **cup sugar**
- 1¾ **cups sifted all-purpose flour**
- 1¼ **cups cornmeal**
- **Finely grated zest of 1 lemon**
- 2 **large egg yolks**
- ½ **teaspoon pure vanilla extract**
- 2 **sticks (½ pound) cold unsalted butter, cut into ½-inch pieces**

I. Preheat the oven to 375°. Generously butter a 10-inch fluted tart pan with a removable bottom.

2. In a food processor, combine the blanched whole almonds with ¼ cup of the sugar and pulse until the nuts are finely ground. Add the flour, cornmeal, lemon zest and the remaining ¾ cup of sugar to the food processor and pulse to combine. Add the egg yolks and the vanilla and pulse until blended. Add the butter and process just until incorporated and the dough resembles coarse crumbs.

3. Pour ¾ of the crumbs into the prepared tart pan, distributing them evenly; lightly pack the crumbs. Pinch small handfuls of the remaining crumbs together to form almond-size clumps and scatter them on top, pressing very gently. Bake the crumb cake for 40 minutes, or until it is deep golden and just brown around the edge. Cover the crumb cake with aluminum foil and then bake for 10 minutes longer, until it is dry in the center. Transfer the crumb cake to a rack and let it cool before unmolding. Break the crumb cake into rough chunks to serve.

—*Sandra Martini*

WINE 1990 Isole e Olena Vin Santo or 1997 Saracco Moscato d'Asti

Almond Blitztorte

MAKES ONE 8-INCH CAKE 🌷

CAKE

Butter-flavored cooking spray

⅓ cup plus ¼ cup sliced almonds

1¼ cups sifted cake flour

1¼ teaspoons baking powder

⅛ teaspoon salt

2 large eggs, separated

2 tablespoons vegetable oil

1 teaspoon vanilla extract

1 teaspoon almond extract

¾ cup granulated sugar

¼ cup skim milk, warmed

4 large egg whites, at room temperature

¼ teaspoon cream of tartar

1 cup plus 1 tablespoon superfine sugar

1 teaspoon cinnamon

FILLING

1 cup plain low-fat yogurt, drained for 4 hours

3 tablespoons seedless raspberry jam

1 pint fresh raspberries

1. MAKE THE CAKE: Preheat the oven to 350°. Coat two 8-inch cake pans with butter-flavored cooking spray and line the bottoms with wax paper or parchment paper. Coat the paper with cooking spray and dust lightly with flour.

2. In a pie plate, toast ¼ cup of the almonds for about 8 minutes, or until fragrant. Let the nuts cool slightly and then finely chop. In a bowl, sift together the flour, baking powder and salt.

3. In a medium bowl, using an electric mixer, beat the egg yolks with the oil and the vanilla and almond extracts until blended. Add ½ cup of the granulated sugar and beat until pale yellow. Gradually beat in the warm milk on low speed; increase the speed to medium and beat for 1 minute.

4. In a clean bowl, beat 2 of the egg whites until foamy. Gradually add the remaining ¼ cup of granulated sugar and beat until stiff peaks form. Fold in the finely chopped almonds. Alternate folding the beaten egg whites and the dry ingredients into the egg yolk mixture. Divide the batter evenly between the prepared pans; smooth the tops.

5. In a clean bowl, beat the remaining 4 egg whites with the cream of tartar until foamy. Gradually add 1 cup of the superfine sugar and beat until stiff. Spread half of the meringue evenly over each pan of cake batter.

6. Combine the remaining 1 tablespoon of superfine sugar with the cin-namon and sprinkle over the meringue. Sprinkle the ⅓ cup of sliced almonds over 1 of the cakes. Bake the cakes for about 30 minutes, until the meringue is lightly colored and crisp. Let cool on wire racks for 10 minutes. Run a knife around the sides of the pans. Turn the cakes out onto plates and then invert them onto a rack to cool completely.

7. PREPARE THE FILLING: Combine the thickened yogurt with the raspberry jam.

8. Set the cake layer without almonds on a large plate, with the meringue

Almond Blitztorte

Toasted Almond Raspberry Cake

side down. Spread the raspberry and yogurt filling on the cake and arrange most of the raspberries on top of it in a single layer. Cover the raspberries with the second layer of the cake, meringue side up. Top the cake with the remaining raspberries and serve.

—*Susan G. Purdy*

ONE SERVING (SERVES 10)
Calories 300 kcal, Total Fat 7.3 gm, Saturated Fat 1.2 gm

Toasted Almond Raspberry Cake

MAKES ONE 10-INCH CAKE ✳

Anyone who has ever tried to beat eight egg whites with a hand mixer can appreciate the benefits of a standing electric mixer. Not only does your wrist get a rest, having your hands free makes following directions like "gradually add the sugar" far easier than it is when you have a beater in one hand and a bowl in the other.

nuts and nutrition

Anyone promoting fat-packed nuts as health food would have to be, well, crazy. Right? Not so fast. A growing body of scientific evidence is giving nuts (the seeds or dried fruits of trees) new respectability. Here's the scoop.

Q: Can nuts reduce the risk of heart disease?

A: This association was first detected six years ago in a large-scale study at Loma Linda University in California. Researchers examined the diet records of more than 31,000 Seventh-Day Adventists (who eat a varied, predominantly vegetarian diet) and found that those who ate nuts often—five or more times a week—were half as likely to have a fatal heart attack as Adventists who rarely

or never ate nuts. Scientists at several institutions (including Loma Linda, the University of Florida at Gainesville and the University of Hawaii, Honolulu) are showing that incorporating two to three ounces of walnuts, peanuts or macadamias each day into a low-fat diet can reduce "bad" LDL cholesterol that can clog arteries.

Q: How do nuts control cholesterol?

A: No one knows for sure. There may be a correlation with their rich stores of cholesterol-busting mono- and polyunsaturated fats and soluble and insoluble fiber. Some nuts, especially walnuts, are also good sources of heart-healthful Omega-3 fatty acids. In addition, government researchers have recently discovered that peanuts contain resveratrol, a beneficial component of red wine. One ounce of

peanuts delivers nearly half the resveratrol of an ounce of red wine. Experts say other nuts probably contain resveratrol, too.

Q: Are there more benefits to nuts?

A: Plenty. Whether you eat them raw, roasted, stir-fried or toasted, nuts are nuggets of concentrated nutrients. Ounce for ounce, peanuts and almonds provide about as much protein as red meat, yet without any cholesterol. And they're packed with vitamins and minerals. One-third cup of shelled peanuts, for example, supplies 20 percent of the recommended Daily Value for folate and niacin, 6 percent for iron and zinc, 8 percent for thiamin and 14 percent for magnesium. Some nuts are surprisingly rich in calcium; one-third cup of almonds has as much

1 cup whole almonds (about 5 ounces)
1½ cups sugar
1 cup all-purpose flour
¼ teaspoon salt
1 stick (4 ounces) unsalted butter
2 tablespoons Cognac or brandy
2 teaspoons pure vanilla extract
8 large egg whites
½ pint raspberries, plus more for garnish
Whipped cream, for garnish

1. Preheat the oven to 350°. Butter a 10-inch springform pan. Spread the almonds on a rimmed baking sheet and toast for about 7 minutes, or until fragrant; let cool completely. Transfer to a food processor, add ¾ cup of the sugar and pulse until finely ground. Pour into a bowl and stir in the flour and salt.

2. In a small saucepan, cook the butter over moderate heat until lightly browned, 3 to 4 minutes. Let cool slightly; stir in the Cognac and vanilla.

3. Using a standing electric mixer, beat the egg whites until they form very soft peaks. Gradually add the remaining ¾ cup of sugar and continue beating until the whites hold soft peaks. Fold the almond mixture and browned butter alternately into the egg whites in 3 batches. Gently fold in the raspberries.

4. Pour the batter into the prepared pan. Bake for about 50 minutes, or until the cake is golden and just beginning to pull away from the side. Let cool slightly on a rack and then remove the side of the pan and let cool completely. Transfer the cake to a large plate and serve with whipped cream and fresh berries. —*Jan Newberry*

MAKE AHEAD The cake can stand at room temperature for up to 8 hours.

WINE Lightly sweet Italian Moscato d'Asti is a perfect partner for this dessert. Try the 1997 Ceruto Santo Stefano or the 1997 Bera

Lane Cake

MAKES ONE 9-INCH CAKE
A certain Mrs. Lane created her rich and delicious raisin, pecan and coconut confection in Alabama in the late nineteenth century. The cake will improve in flavor if you assemble it a week ahead.

CAKE
3½ cups cake flour
2 teaspoons cream of tartar
2 teaspoons baking soda
¼ teaspoon salt
1 cup milk, at room temperature
1 teaspoon pure vanilla extract
2 sticks (½ pound) unsalted butter, softened
2 cups sugar
8 large egg whites, at room temperature

FILLING
12 large egg yolks
1½ cups sugar
1½ sticks (6 ounces) unsalted butter, melted and cooled

---

calcium as one-quarter cup of milk. Nuts are also rich in phytochemicals (including resveratrol and quercetin, one of the beneficial components of tea); scientists believe these plant compounds may help prevent cancer.

Q: But what about all the fat and calories in nuts?

A: On average, nuts weigh in at about 180 calories and 18 grams of fat per handful (or one-third cup), on a par with potato chips. It doesn't make much difference if you eat them fresh from the shell or oil-roasted—nuts absorb very little fat in the roasting process.

What does matter, however, is how many nuts you eat. Work your way through a small bowl of cocktail nuts at a bar and you can consume nearly 720 calories and 72 grams of fat. For this reason, nutritionists generally advise eating no more than two tablespoons, or roughly half an ounce, per day. "That's enough to get the nutritional benefits of nuts without overdosing on fat and calories," says Lenore Hodges, director of nutritional services at Florida Hospital in Orlando.

Still, nuts may not be as bad for the waistline as most people think. "In the Loma Linda study, subjects who ate nuts regularly actually weighed less than subjects who avoided nuts," observes Richard Mattes, professor of foods and nutrition at Purdue University in West Lafayette, Indiana. The reason, he believes, is that nuts are highly satiating. "We don't know if it's the mix of fatty acids, the type of protein or the fiber, but nuts seem to fill people up before they overeat," he says.

Q: How is the fat taken out of "reduced-fat" nuts?

A: Nut processors won't reveal their defatting secrets. But food technology professors, who will talk, say the defatting probably involves placing the nuts in a pressurized chamber, which literally squeezes the oil out of them. The procedure removes nearly 50 percent of the fat and 15 percent of the calories.

Another newfangled peanut is expected to hit supermarkets in a year or two. Researchers at the University of Florida recently cultivated a hybrid variety that produces peanuts with as much monounsaturated fat as olive oil. In one study, daily 1- to 2½-ounce doses helped 20 post-menopausal women lower their LDL cholesterol by 12 percent in six months. —*Julia Califano*

1½ cups (6 ounces) finely chopped pecans

1½ cups (10½ ounces) finely chopped raisins

1½ cups freshly grated coconut

½ cup bourbon

1½ teaspoons pure vanilla extract

¼ teaspoon salt

I. MAKE THE CAKE: Preheat the oven to 325°. Butter three 9-inch round cake pans and line the bottoms with parchment paper. Butter the parchment paper and dust with flour, tapping out the excess.

2. Sift the flour, cream of tartar, baking soda and salt into a medium bowl.

In a small pitcher, combine the milk and vanilla. In a large bowl, beat the butter on medium speed until creamy. Slowly add the sugar and beat until light and fluffy, scraping down the side of the bowl. On low speed, alternately add the dry ingredients and the milk mixture in 3 batches. Beat the batter until smooth, scraping down the side of the bowl as necessary.

3. In another bowl, using clean beaters, beat the egg whites until they form soft peaks. Stir one-third of the whites into the batter to lighten it. Using a rubber spatula, fold in the remaining egg whites until no white streaks remain.

4. Pour the batter into the prepared cake pans and smooth the tops. Tap the pans lightly on a work surface to release any air bubbles. Bake the cakes on the middle and lower racks of the oven for about 30 minutes, shifting the pans halfway through, until the tops spring back when pressed lightly and a toothpick inserted in the center comes out with a few moist crumbs attached. Let cool in the pans for 5 minutes and then invert the cakes onto a wire rack to cool completely. Peel off the parchment paper.

5. MAKE THE FILLING: In a large saucepan, combine the egg yolks and sugar and stir until smooth. Add the melted butter to the egg mixture and cook over moderate heat, stirring, until it is thick enough to coat the back of a spoon, about 6 minutes; do not let it boil. Stir in the pecans, raisins and coconut and cook for about 1 minute. Add the bourbon, vanilla and salt and let the filling cool to lukewarm.

6. Place a cake layer on a serving plate, right side up, and spread it with 1¼ cups of the filling. Repeat with a second cake layer and another 1¼ cups of filling. Top with the last cake layer and frost the cake with the remaining filling. Let the cake cool completely before serving.

—*Edna Lewis and Scott Peacock*
MAKE AHEAD Refrigerate the cake in a tightly covered container for up to 1 week. Serve at room temperature.

Lane Cake

Celebration Cake with Coconut, Pecans and Chocolate

MAKES ONE 9-INCH CAKE
Here's a variation on German chocolate cake with white layers and a rich, bittersweet chocolate frosting.

2 cups cake flour

1 cup all-purpose flour

1 tablespoon plus 1 teaspoon baking powder

½ teaspoon salt
1 cup plus 2 tablespoons milk
1 tablespoon pure vanilla extract
1 stick (4 ounces) unsalted butter, softened
2 cups sugar
4 large eggs

Coconut Pecan Filling (recipe follows)
Chocolate Frosting (recipe follows)

1. Preheat the oven to 350° and position 2 racks in the middle and lower thirds. Line the bottoms of three 9-inch round cake pans with parchment or wax paper. In a medium bowl, whisk the cake flour and all-purpose flour with the baking powder and salt. Combine the milk and vanilla in a small pitcher.

2. In a large bowl, using an electric mixer, beat the softened butter at medium speed until creamy. Add the sugar and beat until the mixture resembles moist sand, about 3 minutes. Beat in the flour mixture at low speed in 3 batches, alternating with the milk mixture, stopping the mixer occasionally to scrape down the side of the bowl. Add the eggs to the batter, 1 at a time, beating at medium speed between additions.

3. Divide the cake batter evenly among the prepared cake pans and bake for about 25 minutes, or until the layers are light golden and a toothpick inserted into the center of the cake comes out clean. Let the cakes cool in the pans for 10 minutes. Turn each of the cakes out onto a rack and then peel off the parchment paper. Invert the cakes onto another rack and let them cool completely.

4. Center a cake layer on a platter and spread one-third of the Coconut Pecan Filling over the top, leaving a ½-inch border at the edge. Set a second cake layer on top of the first layer and spread another third of the filling on top. Cover with the third cake layer.

Celebration Cake with Coconut Pecans and Chocolate

Spread the top and side of the cake with the Chocolate Frosting. Spread the remaining Coconut Pecan Filling over the frosting on the top, leaving a 1-inch border.

MAKE AHEAD The unfrosted cake layers can be wrapped in plastic and stored at room temperature for up to 1 day or frozen for up to 1 month.

WINE The sweetness of this decadently delicious cake would overwhelm most dessert wines, but a sweet cream sherry from Spain, such as Harvey's Bristol Cream, can match the sugariness and will also echo the coconut, pecan and chocolate flavors.

COCONUT PECAN FILLING

MAKES ABOUT 3 CUPS

1⅔ cups sweetened shredded coconut
⅔ cup coarsely chopped pecans (2½ ounces)
6 large egg yolks
½ cup granulated sugar
½ cup (packed) dark brown sugar
1 cup evaporated milk
2 tablespoons cornstarch
Pinch of salt
1 teaspoon pure vanilla extract
¾ cup heavy cream
⅔ cup coarsely chopped semisweet chocolate (4 ounces)

1. Preheat the oven to 350°. Spread the coconut and pecans on separate baking sheets and bake for about 7 minutes, or until golden and fragrant; let cool.

2. In a large heavy saucepan, whisk the egg yolks with the granulated sugar and dark brown sugar. Stir in the milk, cornstarch, salt and 1 cup of the coconut and cook over moderate heat, stirring constantly with a wooden spoon, until puddinglike, about 6 minutes. Strain the custard, pressing hard on the coconut. Discard the coconut and let the custard cool. Stir in the vanilla and refrigerate until cold.

3. Whip the cream until it holds firm peaks. Fold the cream into the custard and then fold in the chocolate, pecans and the remaining coconut.

CHOCOLATE FROSTING
MAKES ABOUT 2 CUPS

1 cup heavy cream
8 ounces bittersweet chocolate, chopped
4 tablespoons unsalted butter, softened

In a medium saucepan, heat the cream until bubbles appear around the edge; remove from the heat. Add the chocolate and stir until melted. Stir in the butter until smooth. Let the frosting cool and then beat with a wooden spoon until slightly thickened.
—*Emily Luchetti*

Chocolate Mousse Cake with Raspberry Sauce
MAKES ONE 8-INCH CAKE

A recipe originally clipped from *The New York Times* lends itself well to a Valentine's Day interpretation.

2 sticks (½ pound) unsalted butter
6 ounces semisweet chocolate, cut into pieces
2 ounces unsweetened chocolate
5 large eggs, separated

3 large egg yolks
1 cup plus 2½ tablespoons granulated sugar
1½ pints raspberries
2 tablespoons fruit liqueur (optional)
About 1 tablespoon confectioners' sugar
Mint sprigs, for garnish

1. Preheat the oven to 325°. Butter an 8-inch springform pan and set it on a baking sheet.

2. In a bowl set over a saucepan with 1 inch of simmering water, combine the butter with the semisweet and unsweetened chocolate. Stir until the chocolate is melted, about 6 minutes; let cool.

3. In a medium bowl, beat the egg whites until stiff peaks form. In another bowl, beat 1 cup of the granulated sugar with the egg yolks until thickened and pale, about 3 minutes. Stir the chocolate mixture into the egg yolks and then stir in half of the egg whites. Using a spatula, fold in the remaining egg whites.

4. Pour the batter into the prepared pan and bake for 50 minutes, or until the cake is well risen and cracked in a few places. Transfer the cake to a rack and let stand for 10 minutes. Run a knife between the side of the pan and the cake and then remove the side and let the cake cool completely.

5. In a food processor, puree 1 pint of the raspberries with the remaining 2½ tablespoons of granulated sugar and the liqueur; strain to remove the seeds.

6. Cut a heart-shaped template from a piece of stiff paper large enough to cover the cake. Place the outside of the template on the cake and sift the confectioners' sugar over the top; carefully remove the template. Run a knife under the cake and transfer it to a cake plate. Alternatively, cut the cake into wedges and serve on individual

plates. Garnish with the mint, the remaining ½ pint of raspberries and the raspberry sauce. Pass the additional sauce on the side.   —*Alice Harper*

MAKE AHEAD The cake and sauce can be refrigerated for up to 1 day. Serve cold or at room temperature.

WINE The 1988 Château Rieussec Sauternes.

Chocolate Cake l'Ansecoy
MAKES ONE 10-BY-5-INCH CAKE

This loaf cake filled with chocolate mousse is easy to make but looks special. Note that you'll need an oversize loaf pan and that the cake has to firm up in the freezer for several hours or overnight.

CAKE

1½ cups all-purpose flour
¾ cup unsweetened cocoa powder
2 teaspoons baking powder
1 teaspoon baking soda
½ teaspoon salt
1½ sticks (6 ounces) unsalted butter, softened
1½ cups sugar
3 large eggs
¾ cup water

FILLING

2 cups heavy cream
4 large egg yolks
1 cup sugar
12 ounces bittersweet chocolate, chopped
3 large egg whites

1. MAKE THE CAKE: Preheat the oven to 350°. Butter and flour a 10-by-5-by-4-inch loaf pan. In a medium bowl, sift the flour with the cocoa powder, baking powder, baking soda and salt. In a large bowl, beat the butter until creamy. Add the sugar and beat until light and fluffy. Add the eggs, 1 at a time, beating for 1 minute between additions. Add the dry ingredients and beat at low speed, scraping down the side of the bowl. Add the water in a

thin stream and beat until the batter is silky and fluffy. Scrape the batter into the loaf pan and smooth the top. Bake for 1 hour and 5 minutes, or until a toothpick inserted into the center of the cake comes out clean. Let the cake cool in the pan for 10 minutes before transferring it to a rack to cool completely. Clean the loaf pan.

2. MAKE THE FILLING: In a saucepan, combine 1 cup of the cream with the egg yolks and ½ cup of the sugar. Cook over moderately low heat, stirring constantly, until the custard coats the back of the spoon, about 10 minutes. Remove from the heat. Add the chocolate; gently stir until melted and smooth. Let cool to room temperature.

3. In a medium bowl, whip the remaining 1 cup of cream until firm; chill. In a large bowl, beat the egg whites to soft peaks. Gradually add the remaining ½ cup of sugar. Beat until firm, glossy peaks form. Fold the egg whites into the chocolate mixture and then fold in the whipped cream. Refrigerate the chocolate mousse.

4. Line the loaf pan with plastic wrap, leaving at least 6 inches of overhang all around. Using a long serrated knife, slice off the top of the cake so that you have a neat rectangular loaf. Cut the loaf horizontally into five ½-inch-thick slices. Line the bottom of the loaf pan with the bottom slice of cake and line the 2 long sides with 2 more slices. Cut 1 of the remaining slices to fit the short ends and wedge the pieces into the pan. Gently press all the edges together. Pour the mousse into the loaf pan; top with the remaining cake slice. Fold up the plastic wrap and freeze the cake until firm, at least 5 hours or preferably overnight. Meanwhile, eat the cake scraps.

5. Let the cake stand at room temperature for 15 minutes before unwrapping and unmolding; then cut it into

1-inch-thick slices. Transfer the slices to plates and serve right away or let stand at room temperature until thawed. —*Sylvia Fernandez*

WINE A sweet fortified wine, such as the Mas Amiel Spéciale 10-Year-Old Maury, with its notes of cocoa and coffee, is a good match for the chocolate cake.

Silky Chocolate Cake with Espresso Ganache

MAKES ONE 9-INCH CAKE
The thin layer of frosting on this sophisticated chocolate dessert doesn't overwhelm the cake's superfine texture.

- 1 cup plus 2 tablespoons unsweetened Dutch-process cocoa
- 1⅓ cups boiling water
- 4 large egg yolks
- 2 large eggs, lightly beaten
- 1 tablespoon pure vanilla extract

- 3 cups plus 2 tablespoons sifted cake flour
- 2 cups sugar
- 1 tablespoon plus 1 teaspoon baking powder
- 1 teaspoon salt
- 2½ sticks (10 ounces) unsalted butter, softened

Espresso Ganache (recipe follows)

1. Preheat the oven to 350° and position 2 racks in the middle and lower thirds. Butter three 9-inch round cake pans and line the bottoms with parchment or wax paper. Butter and flour the parchment.

2. In a medium bowl, whisk the cocoa with the boiling water until smooth; let cool to room temperature. In a small bowl, combine the egg yolks, eggs and vanilla with one-fourth of the cocoa mixture.

3. In a standing electric mixer, stir together the flour, sugar, baking powder

Chocolate Mouse Cake with Raspberry Sauce

Deep Chocolate Sour Cream Pound Cake

and salt. Add the butter and remaining cocoa mixture and mix at low speed just until the dry ingredients are moistened. Scrape down the side of the bowl and beat at medium speed until light and smooth. Add the egg mixture in 3 batches, beating for 20 seconds between additions.

4. Divide the batter evenly among the cake pans. Smooth the tops and bake for about 25 minutes, or until a toothpick inserted in the center of each cake comes out clean. Let the cakes cool in the pans for 10 minutes and then turn each out onto a rack and peel off the parchment paper. Invert the cakes onto another rack and let cool completely.

5. Center a cake layer on a platter and spread ¾ cup of the ganache over the top. Set a second cake layer on top of the first and spread ¾ cup more filling on top. Cover with the third cake layer and spread the top and side with the remaining ganache.

WINE A fruity late-bottled vintage port, such as the 1991 Quinta do Noval or the 1991 Sandeman, would stand up to the bittersweet chocolate and coffee flavors of this cake.

ESPRESSO GANACHE

MAKES 3 CUPS

This frosting is just like the chocolate and cream mixture found in truffles.

- **18** ounces bittersweet chocolate, broken into ¾-inch pieces
- **1¾** cups plus 2 tablespoons heavy cream
- **1½** teaspoons instant espresso powder
- **1½** tablespoons Kahlúa

Put the chocolate in a heatproof bowl. In a small saucepan, heat the cream until bubbles appear around the edge; remove from the heat. Add the espresso powder and stir to dissolve. Pour the hot cream over the chocolate and let stand for 1 minute. Stir the chocolate until melted and smooth. Stir in the Kahlúa. Let the ganache stand at room temperature until firm enough to spread. —*Rose Levy Beranbaum*

Basque Chocolate Cake with Cherry Preserves

MAKES ONE 9-INCH CAKE ✳

- **12** tablespoons unsalted butter
- **5½** ounces bittersweet chocolate
- **3** large eggs
- **¾** cup sugar

- **⅓** cup all-purpose flour
- **¾** cup black cherry preserves
Crème fraîche, for serving

1. Preheat the oven to 375° and then lightly butter and flour a 9-inch round cake pan.

2. In a heavy medium saucepan, combine the butter and the chocolate. Melt over moderate heat, stirring frequently, until smooth, about 4 minutes. Remove the chocolate mixture from the heat and let cool slightly.

3. In a medium bowl, using an electric mixer, beat the eggs with the sugar at high speed until thick and pale, about 3 minutes. Add the flour and beat at low speed just until combined. Fold in one-third of the melted chocolate and then gently fold in the remaining chocolate; do not overmix.

4. Pour the batter into the prepared pan and bake for 30 to 35 minutes, or until a toothpick stuck into the center of the cake comes out clean. Invert the cake onto a rack and let cool.

5. Meanwhile, in a saucepan, warm the cherry preserves over moderate heat. Cut the cake into wedges and serve with the cherry preserves and crème fraîche. —*Gerald Hirigoyen*

Deep Chocolate Sour Cream Pound Cake

MAKES ONE 10-INCH CAKE

This intensely chocolate cake benefits from three glazings with sugar syrup. The glaze keeps the cake moist, and the extra sweetness complements the chocolate.

- **2¼** cups self-rising cake flour
- **¾** cup unsweetened cocoa
- **¾** teaspoon baking soda
- **2** sticks (½ pound) unsalted butter, softened
- **2** cups sugar
- **3** large eggs
- **1** teaspoon pure vanilla extract
- **1** cup sour cream

2 ounces bittersweet or semisweet chocolate, cut into ¼-inch pieces

½ cup water

Decadent Soft Chocolate Cream (recipe follows)

Softly whipped cream, for serving

1. Preheat the oven to 325°. Lightly butter a 10-inch loaf pan and line the bottom with parchment or wax paper; butter the paper.

2. In a medium bowl, whisk together the flour, cocoa and baking soda. In a large bowl, using an electric mixer, beat the butter with 1 cup of the sugar at medium speed until blended. Add the eggs, 1 at a time, beating well after each addition. Add the vanilla. On low speed, alternately beat in the sour cream and the dry ingredients in 3 batches. Add the chocolate pieces and beat just until combined. Scrape the batter into the prepared pan and bake for about 1 hour and 10 minutes, or until a toothpick inserted into the center comes out with only a few moist crumbs attached. Let the cake cool on a rack for 15 minutes and then unmold and let cool right side up.

3. In a small saucepan, combine the remaining 1 cup sugar with the water; simmer for 5 minutes, stirring to dissolve the sugar. Brush a thin layer of the glaze over the cake and let set. Brush the cake with the glaze 2 more times, allowing it to dry between glazings.

4. Cut the cake into ¾-inch-thick slices and serve with the Decadent Soft Chocolate Cream and whipped cream.

MAKE AHEAD The cake can be wrapped well and kept at room temperature for 1 day.

DECADENT SOFT CHOCOLATE CREAM
MAKES ABOUT 4½ CUPS

5 large egg yolks

¼ cup sugar

½ pound milk chocolate, melted

2 tablespoons unsalted butter, melted

2 cups heavy cream

1. In a medium heatproof bowl, combine the egg yolks and sugar. Set the bowl over a saucepan of barely simmering water and stir until the egg yolk mixture is hot to the touch. Remove the bowl from the heat and, using an electric mixer, beat the egg yolks until doubled in volume. Add the chocolate and beat on low speed just until incorporated; the mixture will stiffen. Beat the butter into the chocolate mixture. Add 2 tablespoons of the heavy cream and beat on medium speed until smooth.

2. In another medium bowl, whip the remaining heavy cream until stiff peaks form. Beat one-quarter of the whipped cream into the warm chocolate mixture and then fold in the remaining whipped cream. Pour the soft chocolate cream into a serving bowl and refrigerate until it is firm, preferably overnight. —*Sascha Lyon*

MAKE AHEAD The chocolate cream can be refrigerated for 3 days.

Chocolate-Nut Cassata

MAKES ONE 10-BY-6-INCH CAKE

Cassata is a traditional Sicilian dessert of liqueur-soaked cake layered with a chocolate-and-nut-studded ricotta filling; it is often coated with marzipan. You can buy small marzipan decorations in Italian markets and in some supermarkets. Many Sicilians frost the cake with chocolate icing or serve it with chocolate sauce.

One 10-by-6-inch pound cake (about 15 ounces)

1½ **pounds whole milk ricotta, preferably fresh**

¾ **cup confectioners' sugar**

¼ **cup plus 2 tablespoons orange liqueur**

1 **teaspoon pure vanilla extract**

¾ **pound finely chopped bittersweet chocolate, or** 1½ **cups high-quality chocolate chips, chopped**

¼ **cup candied orange peel, chopped**

½ **cup coarsely chopped walnuts**

½ **cup water**

½ **cup granulated sugar**

½ **cup sweetened cocoa powder**

1. Shave the browned top, bottom and sides from the pound cake and discard the shavings. Cut the cake horizontally into 4 even slices.

2. Push the ricotta through a sieve into a large bowl. Sift the confectioners' sugar over the ricotta and beat it in along with 2 tablespoons of the orange liqueur and the vanilla. Fold in the chopped chocolate, candied orange peel and walnuts.

3. In a small saucepan, heat the water with the granulated sugar until the sugar dissolves. Remove from the heat; stir in the remaining ¼ cup of orange liqueur. Line a 10-by-6-inch loaf pan with plastic wrap, allowing 6 inches of overhang all around. Brush 1 side of

Chocolate-Nut Cassata

Mozart

1 cake slice with the orange syrup and set it, dry side down, in the loaf pan. Spread one-third of the ricotta filling over the cake in the pan. Brush both sides of a second cake slice with orange syrup and set it in the pan. Cover with another third of the ricotta filling, another brushed cake slice and the remaining ricotta. Brush the last cake slice only on 1 side and set it on the ricotta, dry side up. Cover with the plastic wrap and refrigerate for at least 1 hour.

4. Invert the cake onto a platter and discard the plastic. Sift the cocoa on top. Cut the cake into 1-inch slices and serve. —*Nancy Verde Barr*
MAKE AHEAD The cassata can be refrigerated for up to 3 days.

Mozart

MAKES ONE 9-INCH CAKE
For this grand chocolate cake, layers of cinnamon-almond pastry are filled with apple-flecked chocolate mousse.
PASTRY
- 2 sticks plus 5 tablespoons (10½ ounces) unsalted butter, softened

- ½ cup plus 2 tablespoons confectioners' sugar
- ½ cup plus 1 tablespoon finely ground blanched almonds
- 3 hard-boiled large egg yolks, cooled to room temperature and pressed through a fine sieve
- 2 teaspoons cinnamon
- ¼ teaspoon salt
- 1 tablespoon dark rum
- 2½ cups all-purpose flour
- ¼ teaspoon baking powder

MOUSSE
- 1 large Granny Smith apple— peeled, cored and cut into ¼-inch dice
- ¼ cup sugar
- ⅛ teaspoon cinnamon
- 1 tablespoon unsalted butter
- 2 tablespoons dark rum
- ⅓ cup heavy cream
- 1 cinnamon stick, broken in half
- 8 ounces bittersweet chocolate, coarsely chopped
- 6 large egg whites, at room temperature

GARNISHES
- 2 ounces bittersweet chocolate, at room temperature, shaved with a vegetable peeler
- ¼ Granny Smith apple
- 1 teaspoon lemon juice
- 2 teaspoons apple or quince jelly
- 3 cinnamon sticks

1. MAKE THE PASTRY: Cream the butter in a food processor. Add the confectioners' sugar, ground almonds, egg yolks, cinnamon and salt and process until smooth. Add the rum and pulse to blend. Add the flour and baking powder and pulse to blend. Transfer the dough to a floured work surface and gather into a ball. Cut the dough into thirds; pat each piece into a 6-inch disk and wrap separately in plastic. Refrigerate for at least 2 hours and up to 2 days. Let the dough soften slightly before rolling it out.

2. Preheat the oven to 350°. Line 3 baking sheets with parchment paper. On a lightly floured surface, roll 1 disk of the dough into a 10-inch round. Using the bottom of a springform pan as a guide, cut out a 9-inch round. Carefully transfer the round to a parchment-lined baking sheet and chill for 30 minutes. Repeat with the remaining disks of dough. Prick the rounds all over with a fork and then bake them one at a time for 20 to 25 minutes, or until lightly browned. Transfer the pastry to a rack and let cool completely.

3. MAKE THE MOUSSE: In a bowl, combine the apple with 1 tablespoon of the sugar and the cinnamon. In a large heavy skillet, melt the butter over moderately high heat. Add the apple and cook over high heat, stirring, until lightly crusted and tender but not mushy, 3 to 5 minutes. Add the rum, carefully ignite it and stir the apple to coat. Transfer to a plate and let cool to room temperature.

4. In a small saucepan, heat the cream with the cinnamon stick until bubbles appear around the edge. Remove from the heat, cover and let steep for 10 minutes. Meanwhile, melt the chocolate in a metal bowl set over a saucepan of simmering water. Remove from the heat. Strain the hot cream over the chocolate and discard the cinnamon stick. Gently stir until smooth and let cool until tepid.

5. In a bowl, beat the egg whites until very foamy. Gradually add the remaining 3 tablespoons of sugar, beating until stiff glossy peaks form. Using a large rubber spatula, fold one-quarter of the beaten whites into the chocolate. Fold in the remaining whites and then fold in the apple.

6. Set 1 cinnamon pastry round in the bottom of a 9-inch springform pan and spread half of the chocolate mousse on top. Cover with a second cinnamon pastry round, pressing gently. Spread the rest of the mousse over the top and cover with the last pastry round. Refrigerate for at least 30 minutes and up to 8 hours.

7. GARNISH THE CAKE: Remove the side of the pan and pat a thin layer of chocolate shavings against the side of the cake. Cut 5 thin slices from the apple and rub with the lemon juice. Fan the apple slices on the cake. In a small saucepan, melt the apple jelly over moderately high heat and brush a thin layer over the apples. Garnish with the cinnamon sticks and serve.

—*Pierre Hermé*

Goat Cheese Cake with Mixed Berries

MAKES ONE 9-INCH CAKE

Goat cheese gives a twist to traditional cheesecake and adds a savory element to this not-too-sweet dessert.

- 11 ounces mild fresh goat cheese, softened
- ¾ cup granulated sugar
- 1½ teaspoons fresh lemon juice
- 1 teaspoon minced lemon zest
- 1 teaspoon pure vanilla extract
- 6 large eggs, separated
- 3 tablespoons all-purpose flour
- 3 cups mixed fresh berries, such as blueberries, raspberries and quartered strawberries (see Note)

Confectioners' sugar, for dusting

I. Preheat the oven to 350°. Butter a 9-inch round cake pan. Dust with granulated sugar, pouring off the excess.

2. In a medium bowl, combine the goat cheese with the granulated sugar, lemon juice, lemon zest and vanilla; beat at medium speed until smooth. Beat in the egg yolks, 2 at a time, incorporating them completely before adding the next batch. Beat in the flour at low speed.

3. In another bowl, using clean beaters, beat the egg whites until firm but not dry. Beat one-third of the whites into the goat cheese mixture and then gently fold in the remaining whites. Spoon the batter into the prepared pan and bake for about 40 minutes, or until a skewer inserted in the center of the cake comes out clean. Transfer to a wire rack to cool completely.

4. Invert the goat cheese cake onto a large plate. Arrange the berries on top and sift confectioners' sugar over all. Cut the cake into wedges and serve.

—*Emily Luchetti*

MAKE AHEAD The cake can be wrapped well and stored at room temperature for 1 day.

NOTE To make a fruit sauce for the cake, lightly crush the raspberries and blueberries with 1 tablespoon of sugar and set aside for 10 minutes. Garnish the cake with additional whole berries.

Goat Cheese Cake with Mixed Berries

Skee's Cheese Pie

MAKES ONE 9-INCH PIE

Patricia Beard, a cousin of FOOD & WINE editor in chief Dana Cowin, passed on this recipe for their grandmother's delicious cheese pie.

- 16 zwieback, crushed to coarse crumbs
- 6 tablespoons unsalted butter, melted
- 2 tablespoons sugar
- 1½ teaspoons cinnamon

FILLING

- 1½ pounds cream cheese, at room temperature
- 1 cup sugar
- 3 large eggs, at room temperature
- 1 teaspoon pure vanilla extract
- 1 pint sour cream, at room temperature

I. MAKE THE CRUST: Preheat the oven to 350°. Mix the zwieback, butter, sugar and cinnamon together in a

CAKES, TARTS & COOKIES

Strawberry Tart

FILLING

- 2 large egg yolks
- 1 cup milk
- 3 tablespoons sugar
- 3 tablespoons all-purpose flour
- ½ teaspoon pure vanilla extract

Pinch of salt

- 2 tablespoons heavy cream
- 2 pints strawberries, hulled

1. MAKE THE PASTRY: In a food processor, combine the flour, butter, sugar and egg; pulse just until the dough begins to come together. Turn the pastry out onto a lightly floured surface and pat it into a 6-inch disk. Wrap in plastic and refrigerate for at least 1 hour or overnight.

2. Preheat the oven to 350°. On a lightly floured surface, roll out the pastry into a 12-inch round. Fit the dough without stretching it into a 9-by-¾-inch fluted tart pan with a removable bottom. Trim the overhang to ¾ inch. Fold in the overhang and press it against the side to reinforce it. Prick the bottom several times with a fork and refrigerate until firm. Bake the shell for about 25 minutes, or until the dough is golden and cooked through. Let the shell cool completely on a wire rack before filling.

3. MAKE THE FILLING: In a medium saucepan, combine the egg yolks with 3 tablespoons of the milk, the sugar, flour, vanilla and a pinch of salt and then whisk until smooth. In a small saucepan, bring the remaining milk to a simmer.

4. Gradually whisk the hot milk into the egg yolk mixture. Cook the pastry cream over moderate heat, whisking constantly, until it boils and thickens like pudding, about 4 minutes. Strain the pastry cream through a fine sieve set over a bowl. Whisk in the heavy cream. Press a piece of plastic wrap directly on the pastry cream to prevent a skin from forming. Let cool

medium bowl. Press the crumbs over the base and 1 inch up the side of a 9-inch springform pan and refrigerate while you prepare the filling.

2. MAKE THE FILLING: In a large bowl, beat the cream cheese and sugar until smooth. Beat the eggs into the cream cheese mixture, one at a time. Beat in the vanilla and sour cream until blended. Pour the filling into the crust and set the pan on a baking sheet. Bake on the middle shelf of the oven for 50 minutes, or until the edge of the pie is set but the middle

still jiggles slightly. Let the pie cool and then refrigerate overnight. Serve the pie cold.   —*Patricia Beard*

Strawberry Tart

MAKES ONE 9-INCH TART

PASTRY

- ¾ **cup plus 2 tablespoons all-purpose flour**
- 6 **tablespoons cold unsalted butter, cut into ½-inch pieces**
- 2 **tablespoons sugar**
- 2 **tablespoons beaten egg (see Note)**

slightly and then refrigerate until thoroughly chilled, at least 2 hours.

5. Unmold the pastry shell and carefully transfer it to a platter. Vigorously beat the cold pastry cream until smooth and spread it evenly in the pastry shell. Arrange the strawberries in the tart, tips up, in tight concentric circles. Refrigerate the tart for 1 to 4 hours before serving.

—*Betsy Bernardaud*

NOTE First beat 1 large egg in a small bowl and then measure out 2 tablespoons.

MAKE AHEAD The recipe can be prepared through Step 4 up to 1 day ahead. Wrap the pastry shell in aluminum foil and store it at room temperature.

Blueberry Lemon Soufflé Pie

MAKES ONE 9-INCH PIE ★★★ **1994**

Peggy Cullen is the owner of Lucky Star Sweets, a candy company in New York City. She's also a pie-making queen, and this sophisticated and unusual summer pie is one of FOOD & WINE's favorites.

FLAKY PIE SHELL

- 1 cup plus 2 tablespoons all-purpose flour
- ¾ teaspoon salt
- ¾ teaspoon sugar
- 3½ tablespoons cold vegetable shortening, cut into ½-inch dice
- 3 tablespoons cold unsalted butter, cut into ½-inch dice
- 3 tablespoons ice water

FILLING

- 3 cups blueberries, picked over
- 6 tablespoons granulated sugar
- 3 large eggs, separated
- ¼ cup plus 3 tablespoons superfine sugar
- ¼ cup plus 3 tablespoons fresh lemon juice

Grated zest of 2 lemons

- ⅛ teaspoon salt

I. MAKE THE FLAKY PIE SHELL: In a food processor, combine the flour, salt and sugar and pulse until mixed. Add the shortening and butter and pulse until the mixture resembles coarse meal with some pieces the size of small peas. Drizzle the ice water evenly over the mixture and pulse 8 to 12 times, until the dough forms small clumps.

2. Turn the dough out onto a work surface. Using the heel of your hand, gently press the dough onto the surface with a few quick strokes. Pat the dough into a disk, wrap in plastic and refrigerate for at least 4 hours.

3. On a lightly floured surface, pat the dough out to a 6-inch round and then roll it out to an 11-inch round. Transfer the dough to a 9-inch pie pan and press it into the pan without stretching. Fold the overhang under itself and crimp decoratively. Chill the shell for at least 30 minutes.

4. Preheat the oven to 450°. Line the pie shell with aluminum foil, making sure to cover the crimped edge, and fill with pie weights or dried beans. Bake in the center of the oven for 20 minutes, or until the edges are lightly golden. Remove the foil and weights and bake the shell for 12 to 15 minutes longer, until golden brown all over. Let cool. Reduce the oven temperature to 400°.

5. MAKE THE FILLING: In a saucepan, toss the blueberries with the granulated sugar and cook over moderately high heat, stirring occasionally, until the juices just begin to bubble, 3 to 5 minutes; do not overcook or the berries will burst. Drain the blueberries in a stainless steel strainer set over a bowl; reserve the juices.

6. In a medium bowl, using an electric mixer, beat the egg yolks with ¼ cup of the superfine sugar until thick and pale, about 2 minutes. Gradually beat in the lemon juice and then the zest.

Transfer the mixture to a saucepan and cook over low heat, stirring, until thickened, about 8 minutes; do not boil. Scrape into a bowl and let cool.

7. In another bowl, using clean beaters, beat the egg whites until foamy. Add the salt and beat until soft peaks form. Add the remaining 3 tablespoons of superfine sugar, ½ tablespoon at a time, beating well after each addition. Beat at high speed until the whites are firm and glossy, about 20 seconds longer. Using a rubber spatula, stir one-fourth of the beaten egg whites into the lemon curd; fold in the remaining whites in three additions.

8. Spoon the blueberries into the baked pie shell and drizzle 2½ tablespoons of the reserved juices over them. Mound the soufflé mixture over the berries and gently spread it so it touches the pie shell all around. Bake the pie in the middle of the oven for about 15 minutes, or until the top is nicely browned. Transfer the pie to a rack to cool slightly. —*Peggy Cullen*

Individual Quince Tartes Tatins with Sheep's Milk Ice Cream

MAKES EIGHT 4-INCH TARTS

Poached quinces have a delicate sweetness and rosy color, making them a fine alternative to apples in this version of the classic French dessert. To remove the quinces' tough centers, cut the peeled fruit into wedges and then remove the cores with an apple corer or small biscuit cutter. The fruity poaching liquid can be reduced to a syrup and served as a topping for vanilla ice cream.

- 1½ plus 1⅓ cups sugar
- 1 vanilla bean, split lengthwise, seeds scraped out
- 6 cups water
- 6 large quinces—peeled, cut into 12 wedges each and cored
- 4 tablespoons unsalted butter

An Individual Quince Tarte Tatin with Sheep's Milk Ice Cream.

CAKES, TARTS & COOKIES

½ cup golden raisins (optional)

2 pounds frozen puff pastry, preferably all butter, thawed but still cold

Sheep's Milk Ice Cream (recipe follows) or vanilla ice cream, for serving

1. In a large saucepan, combine 1½ cups of the sugar with the vanilla bean and seeds and the water. Cook over high heat, stirring, until the sugar dissolves, about 8 minutes. Add the quince wedges and bring just to a boil. Reduce the heat to low, cover and simmer until tender, about 2 hours; occasionally submerge the quinces in the poaching liquid. Let the quinces cool in the liquid.

2. Preheat the oven to 375°. Melt the butter in a medium skillet. Sprinkle the remaining 1⅓ cups of sugar over the butter and cook over moderate heat, without stirring, until the sugar just begins to brown around the edges, about 2 minutes. Cook, stirring gently, until the caramel turns dark golden, 6 to 8 minutes. Immediately pour the caramel into eight 4-inch-wide ramekins (1⅓-cup capacity). Swirl the caramel in the ramekins to coat the bottoms.

3. Remove the quinces from the liquid with a slotted spoon and arrange 9 wedges in each ramekin in overlapping circles. Scatter the raisins on top.

4. On a lightly floured surface, roll out the puff pastry ⅛ inch thick. Using a large biscuit cutter, cut eight 4-inch rounds from the pastry; make two 1-inch slits in the center of each. Top the quinces with the dough rounds and bake for about 45 minutes, or until the crust is golden and the juices are bubbling. Let cool slightly and then invert onto plates. Serve with the ice cream.

MAKE AHEAD The quinces can be refrigerated in their liquid up to 3 days; drain just before using. The baked tarts can stand at room temperature for up to 8 hours; reheat in a 325° oven for 10 minutes before unmolding.

SHEEP'S MILK ICE CREAM
MAKES ABOUT 1½ QUARTS

1½ cups sheep's milk or whole milk

½ cup (packed) light brown sugar

1 vanilla bean, split lengthwise, seeds scraped out

Pinch of salt

7 large egg yolks

¼ cup granulated sugar

2¼ cups heavy cream

1. In a medium saucepan, combine the milk, brown sugar, vanilla bean and seeds and salt. Cook over moderately low heat, stirring occasionally, until it is steaming, about 8 minutes; do not let it boil. Remove from the heat and keep warm. Discard the vanilla bean.

2. Meanwhile, in a bowl, whisk the egg yolks with the granulated sugar until thick and pale. Whisk in half the warm milk mixture and then whisk in the rest. Return to the saucepan and cook, stirring frequently, until the custard thickens slightly and coats the back of a spoon, 8 to 10 minutes. Stir in the cream. Strain into a bowl; chill thoroughly. Transfer to an ice cream maker and freeze according to the manufacturer's instructions. —*Melissa Kelly*

Pear Galette

MAKES ONE 9-INCH TART ★★★ 1987

This lustrous free-form pear tart is from FOOD & WINE's resident baker, Test Kitchen director Diana Sturgis. It's especially good warm, served with crème fraîche or vanilla ice cream.

1 cup all-purpose flour

1 tablespoon sugar

½ teaspoon salt

7 tablespoons unsalted butter— 5 tablespoons cut into small pieces and chilled, 2 tablespoons melted

1 egg

1 teaspoon milk

2 tablespoons apricot preserves, strained

2 large Bosc pears

½ teaspoon very hot water

1. Preheat the oven to 425°. In a medium bowl, toss the flour with 1 teaspoon of the sugar and the salt. Cut in the cold butter until the mixture resembles fine crumbs.

2. In a small bowl, beat the egg with the milk. Sprinkle 2 tablespoons of the beaten egg over the flour mixture and stir. Working quickly, gather the dough into a smooth mass, squeezing the dough gently. Transfer the dough to a lightly floured surface and pat it into a 5-inch disk. Wrap in wax paper and refrigerate until firm but not hard, about 30 minutes.

3. On a lightly floured surface, roll out the dough to a 9½-inch round, turning it clockwise an inch or two each time you roll to maintain an even shape. Transfer the dough to a heavy flat baking sheet. Fold up ¼ inch of the edge of the dough to form a neat rim. Using a knife, score the rim in a decorative pattern. Brush the rim with a little of the remaining beaten egg. Brush 1 tablespoon of the apricot preserves over the bottom of the dough and refrigerate while you prepare the pears.

4. Peel, quarter and core the pears. Slice each of the pear quarters lengthwise into 5 thin wedges. Arrange all but 6 of the pear wedges on the dough in a spoke pattern, overlapping the wedges slightly. Cut the remaining pear wedges and arrange them in the center of the tart to form a decorative rose. Brush all of the pear wedges with the melted butter and then sprinkle them with the remaining 2 teaspoons of sugar.

5. Bake the galette in the middle of the oven for 25 to 30 minutes, or until

Maple-Glazed Pear and Hazelnut Tarts

the pears are tender and the pastry is crisp and golden. Carefully slide the galette onto a rack to cool slightly.

6. Stir the hot water into the remaining 1 tablespoon of apricot preserves and brush on the pears. Serve the galette at room temperature.

—*Diana Sturgis*

Maple-Glazed Pear and Hazelnut Tarts

MAKES FOUR 7-INCH SQUARE TARTS

⅓ cup hazelnuts

Vegetable oil cooking spray

6 sheets of phyllo dough, plus extra in case of tearing

¼ cup maple syrup

2 ripe Anjou or Bartlett pears

1. Preheat the oven to 350°. In a small pie plate, toast the hazelnuts for about 7 minutes, or until fragrant. Transfer to a kitchen towel and rub off the skins; let the nuts cool completely. In a mini-processor, pulse the nuts until finely ground.

2. Coat 2 large nonstick baking sheets with cooking spray. Cut the phyllo sheets into 7-inch squares; you should have 12 squares. Lay a phyllo square on a work surface, brush lightly with

maple syrup and sprinkle with a scant ½ teaspoon of the hazelnuts. Repeat to make 2 more layers and set the 3-layer square on a baking sheet. Repeat to make 3 more 3-layer phyllo-hazelnut squares.

3. Peel, halve and core the pears. Cut each half into 6 lengthwise slices. Set a pear half on each phyllo square, fanning out the slices. Drizzle the pears with the remaining maple syrup and sprinkle with the remaining hazelnuts.

4. Bake the tarts on the upper and middle racks of the oven for about 35 minutes, or until they are golden and crisp and the pears are caramelized; switch the pans halfway through cooking. Serve the tarts warm.

—*Jim Kyndberg and Betsy Nelson*

ONE SERVING (1 TART) Calories 201 kcal, Total Fat 3.5 gm, Saturated Fat .4 gm

Banana Tartlets

MAKES SIX 4-INCH TARTLETS

Florian Bellanger, the pastry chef at Le Bernardin, stirs the rum into the hot caramel carefully, as it tends to spatter.

PASTRY

2 cups all-purpose flour

¼ cup sugar

Pinch of salt

1 stick plus 2 tablespoons (5 ounces) unsalted butter, cut into small pieces and chilled

1 large egg

1 tablespoon water

FILLING

4 tablespoons unsalted butter

8 bananas (2½ pounds), 4 mashed

3 tablespoons honey

¼ cup fresh lemon juice

Pinch of freshly grated nutmeg

¾ cup heavy cream

1 tablespoon confectioners' sugar

½ cup granulated sugar

¼ cup light rum

1. MAKE THE PASTRY: In a food processor, combine the flour, sugar and salt and pulse to blend. Add the butter and pulse until the mixture resembles coarse meal. In a small bowl, beat the egg with the water and then add it to the processor and pulse until combined. Transfer the dough to a work surface and gather into a ball. Divide the dough into 6 equal pieces and flatten each piece into a 4-inch disk. Wrap each disk in plastic and refrigerate for 30 minutes or up to 1 day.

2. Preheat the oven to 350° and lightly butter six 4-by-1-inch ring molds or tartlet pans with removable bottoms. If using ring molds, line a baking sheet with parchment paper. On a lightly floured work surface, roll the pastry disks into ⅛-inch-thick rounds and gently ease them into the molds. Trim off any overhang. Bake the pastry shells for about 30 minutes, or until golden all around and cooked through. Let cool completely before unmolding.

3. MAKE THE FILLING: Melt 2 tablespoons of the butter in a medium skillet. Add the 4 mashed bananas and the honey and cook over moderately high heat, stirring, until hot to the touch and very smooth, about 2 minutes. Add 2 tablespoons of the lemon juice and the nutmeg and transfer the puree to a bowl to cool completely. In a medium bowl, whip the heavy cream with the confectioners' sugar until firm. Fold the puree into the whipped cream and refrigerate.

4. Up to 1 hour before serving, slice the remaining 4 bananas ⅓ inch thick and toss with the remaining 2 tablespoons of lemon juice. Melt the remaining 2 tablespoons of butter in a medium skillet. Add the granulated sugar and cook over moderate heat, stirring, until an amber caramel forms, about 5 minutes. Remove the skillet from the heat and at arm's length, add

Banana Tartlets

Chestnut Armagnac-Poached Prune Tarts

the rum. Stir until smooth. Add the sliced bananas and stir to coat with the caramel.

5. Spoon the banana cream into the pastry shells and arrange the caramelized banana slices decoratively on top. Transfer the tartlets to dessert plates. Spoon any leftover caramel sauce over the bananas and onto the plates and serve. *—Sylvia Fernandez*
WINE The 1997 Domaine des Bernardins Muscat de Beaumes-de-Venise has a sweetness and lychee perfume that are lovely with the creamy banana flavors.

Chestnut and Armagnac-Poached Prune Tarts
MAKES SIX 4-INCH TARTS

¾ pound frozen puff pastry, preferably all butter
¼ cup plus 2 tablespoons sweetened chestnut puree
1½ cups water
¼ cup Armagnac
2 tablespoons sugar
½ vanilla bean, split lengthwise
2 cups pitted prunes (½ pound)
½ cup dried cranberries
Crème fraîche, for serving

I. Line a baking sheet with parchment paper. If necessary, roll out the puff pastry ¼ inch thick. Using a biscuit cutter, stamp out six 4-inch puff pastry rounds; transfer to the prepared baking sheet. Spread 1 tablespoon of the chestnut puree over each pastry round to within ½ inch of the edge. Freeze the rounds.

2. Preheat the oven to 400°. In a medium saucepan, combine the water, Armagnac, sugar and vanilla bean and bring to a simmer. Add the prunes and poach over moderately low heat until plumped, 15 to 20 minutes. Remove the prunes to a plate. Add the cranberries to the poaching liquid and cook until plumped, about 5 minutes.

Fig Caramel Tart with Raspberry Sorbet

Remove to a plate. Simmer the poaching liquid until it reduces to a syrup, about 3 minutes. Strain the syrup.

3. Arrange the prunes and cranberries on the tartlets and brush with some of the syrup. Bake for 25 minutes, or until the pastry is well browned on the bottom and cooked through. Let cool slightly. Brush with the remaining syrup, spoon a dollop of crème fraîche onto each tartlet and serve.
—Eleven Madison Park, New York City
WINE Look for the 1987 Calvados Huard Le Pertyer.

Fig Caramel Tart with Raspberry Sorbet
MAKES EIGHT 4-INCH TARTS
PASTRY

1¾ cups all-purpose flour
⅓ cup sugar
Pinch of salt
1 stick (4 ounces) unsalted butter, cut into small pieces and chilled
1 large egg
3 tablespoons milk
FILLING
1½ cups sugar
½ cup water

6 tablespoons unsalted butter, cut
into 6 pieces

12 fresh Black Mission figs, halved
Raspberry Sorbet (recipe follows),
for serving

1. MAKE THE PASTRY: In a bowl, combine the flour, sugar and salt. Using a pastry cutter or 2 knives, cut in the butter until the mixture resembles coarse meal. Beat the egg with the milk and add to the bowl. Stir gently just until a dough forms. Divide the dough in half and shape each half into a disk. Wrap the disks in plastic and refrigerate until thoroughly chilled, at least 4 hours or overnight.

2. On a lightly floured surface, roll out 1 disk of dough to a 12-inch round. Cut out four 4-inch rounds and arrange on a baking sheet. Repeat with the remaining dough. Cover with plastic and freeze until firm, for up to 3 days.

3. MAKE THE FILLING: Preheat the oven to 375°. Arrange eight 4- to 5-inch gratin dishes on 2 baking sheets. In a saucepan, boil the sugar and water over moderate heat until deep amber, about 10 minutes. Remove the caramel from the heat and stir in the butter until smooth.

4. Pour 2 tablespoons of the caramel into each gratin dish and add 3 fig halves, cut side down. Set a frozen disk of dough on each dish to cover the figs. Bake for about 40 minutes, or until the dough is golden and the caramel is bubbly. Carefully unmold the tarts onto plates, pastry side down. Top each with a scoop of Raspberry Sorbet and serve.

WINE A spicy Late Harvest California Gewürztraminer, such as De Loach.

RASPBERRY SORBET

MAKES ABOUT 1 QUART

2½ pints raspberries

1¼ cups sugar

1 teaspoon fresh lemon juice

In a blender, puree half of the raspberries with half of the sugar and lemon juice until smooth. Strain the puree into a bowl and then repeat with the remaining ingredients. Freeze the sorbet in an ice cream maker according to manufacturer's instructions. Transfer the sorbet to a container and store in the freezer for up to 3 days.
—Normand Laprise

Bittersweet Chocolate Tart

MAKES ONE 9-INCH TART ★★★ **1991**
Exquisitely elegant, this tart is from Joël Robuchon, who would bake it to order at his three-star Paris restaurant, Jamin. It's relatively easy to make, it's beautiful and the chocolate plays wonderfully against the delicate sweet pastry. It's also very rich, so offer your guests slender slices.

PASTRY SHELL

1 plump vanilla bean

1 large egg yolk, at room temperature

½ cup confectioners' sugar, sifted

2 tablespoons whole blanched almonds

¾ cup all-purpose flour, sifted

Pinch of salt

5 tablespoons unsalted butter, at room temperature

FILLING

¾ cup heavy cream

⅓ cup milk

7 ounces imported bittersweet chocolate, grated or finely chopped

1 large egg, lightly beaten

½ teaspoon unsweetened cocoa powder, for sifting

1. MAKE THE PASTRY SHELL: Flatten the vanilla bean and cut it in half lengthwise. With a small spoon, scrape the seeds into a small bowl. Add the egg yolk and stir to blend.

2. In a food processor, combine the sugar and almonds and process until

the nuts are finely ground. Add the flour and salt and process to blend. Add the butter and process just until the mixture resembles coarse crumbs. Add the egg yolk mixture and pulse just until the dough begins to hold together. Do not overprocess—the dough should not form a ball. Gently pat the dough into a disk, handling it as little as possible. Wrap the dough in wax paper and refrigerate until well chilled, at least 1 hour or overnight.

3. Butter the bottom and side of a 9-inch fluted tart pan with a removable bottom. On a lightly floured surface, roll out the dough to an 11-inch round. Transfer the dough to the prepared pan and gently press the dough against the side, allowing about ½ inch to hang over the rim. Prick the bottom of the dough all over with a fork. Refrigerate until well chilled, at least 1 hour.

4. Preheat the oven to 375°. Set the tart pan on a cookie sheet and bake in the middle of the oven for about 5 minutes, until the pastry just begins to firm up. Remove from the oven and, with a sharp knife, carefully cut off and discard the overhanging pastry to make a smooth, even rim. Return the shell to the oven and bake for about 15 minutes longer, until the pastry is well browned all over. Transfer to a rack and let cool completely before filling. Leave the oven on.

5. MAKE THE FILLING: In a medium saucepan, bring the cream and milk to a simmer. Remove from the heat. Add the chocolate; stir until melted. Let cool to lukewarm and then whisk in the egg until thoroughly blended.

6. Pour the custard in the pastry shell; bake in the middle of the oven for 12 to 15 minutes, or until the filling is almost set but still trembling in the center. Transfer to a wire rack to cool. Sift the cocoa over the tart. Serve warm or at room temperature. *—Joël Robuchon*

Bittersweet Chocolate Tart

Meringue Cookies

MAKES ABOUT 4 DOZEN COOKIES

- 4 large egg whites, at room temperature

Pinch of salt

- 1 cup granulated sugar

1. Preheat the oven to 200°. Line 2 large baking sheets with parchment paper. In a metal or glass bowl, using an electric mixer, beat the egg whites with the salt at low speed until frothy. Increase the speed to high and beat until the whites hold firm peaks. Beat in the granulated sugar, 1 tablespoon at a time, until the whites are stiff and glossy, 5 to 6 minutes.

2. Spoon or pipe tablespoon-size mounds of the meringue onto the prepared baking sheets, spacing them 2 inches apart. Bake the meringues for about 3 hours; they should be quite pale and should be dry and crisp throughout. Let the meringues cool overnight in the turned-off oven.

—*Peggy Knickerbocker*

Kourambiedes

MAKES 3 DOZEN COOKIES

Beating the butter until very fluffy—a good ten minutes—makes these Greek shortcakes especially light.

- 2 sticks (½ pound) unsalted butter, softened
- 1 large egg yolk
- 2 tablespoons brandy
- 1 teaspoon pure vanilla extract
- 2 cups all-purpose flour
- ¾ cup confectioners' sugar, plus more for coating
- ½ teaspoon baking powder
- ⅛ teaspoon ground cloves

Pinch of salt

1. In a large bowl, using a handheld electric mixer, beat the butter at high speed until it is light and fluffy, about 10 minutes. Add the egg yolk, brandy and vanilla to the butter and beat until smooth.

2. Sift the flour with ¾ cup of the confectioners' sugar, the baking powder, cloves and salt. Add the dry ingredients to the butter mixture in 3 batches, beating at low speed just until smooth. Scrape the dough onto a large sheet of plastic wrap or wax paper and roll into a rough 2-inch log. Wrap and refrigerate until firm, at least 30 minutes or up to 3 days.

3. Preheat the oven to 325°. Line 2 heavy baking sheets with parchment paper. Unwrap the dough and roll it into a perfect cylinder. Cut it into 3 equal pieces. Slice each piece crosswise into 12 cookies and arrange them on the prepared baking sheets about 1 inch apart.

4. Bake the cookies on the top and middle racks of the oven for 20 minutes, or until golden on the bottom; shift the sheets from top to bottom halfway through baking. Let the cookies cool slightly on the sheets, about 15 minutes.

5. Pour confectioners' sugar into a large shallow bowl. Add the warm cookies in batches and heavily coat the tops and sides. Transfer the cookies to a sheet of wax paper that has been dusted with confectioners' sugar and let cool.   —*Grace Parisi*

MAKE AHEAD The cookies can be stored in an airtight tin between layers of wax paper for up to 2 weeks.

Liar's Cookies

MAKES ABOUT 5 DOZEN COOKIES

There's no use lying about whether you've eaten these crisp anise-flavored cookies, called *bugie* in Italian: the dusting of confectioners' sugar, which inevitably lands on your clothes, will give you away. You'll need a pasta machine to roll the dough out as thin as possible.

- 2½ cups all-purpose flour
- 2 tablespoons granulated sugar
- ½ teaspoon baking powder
- ¼ teaspoon salt
- 2 large eggs
- 1 stick (4 ounces) unsalted butter, melted and cooled slightly
- ¼ cup fresh orange juice
- 1½ tablespoons brandy
- ½ teaspoon pure vanilla extract
- ¾ teaspoon aniseeds
- 1 quart peanut or vegetable oil, for deep frying
- 2 cups confectioners' sugar

1. Sift the flour with the granulated sugar, baking powder and salt onto a large sheet of wax paper.

2. In the bowl of a standing electric mixer fitted with a paddle, beat the eggs with the butter, orange juice, brandy, vanilla and aniseeds at low speed until well blended. Add the dry ingredients all at once and beat until the dough clumps around the paddle, about 1 minute. Turn the dough out onto a floured surface and knead it into a smooth ball; flatten slightly. Wrap the dough in plastic and refrigerate it until chilled, at least 2 hours or overnight.

3. Divide the dough into 8 equal pieces. Keeping the dough well dusted with flour, crank 1 piece of the dough through the widest setting of a pasta machine 3 times. Pass the dough through successively narrower settings until it is almost thin enough to see through. Cut the dough into 2-inch-wide strips and then cut the strips on the diagonal at 2-inch intervals to form diamonds. Using a metal spatula, transfer the cookies to a baking sheet lined with parchment paper and cover with plastic wrap to prevent them from drying out. Repeat with the remaining cookie dough.

4. In a deep fryer, preheat the oil to 375°. Fry the cookies, 6 at a time, turning once, until they are golden, about 1 minute. Transfer the cookies

to paper towels to drain. Sift confectioners' sugar over the hot cookies; wait a few minutes and then dust the cookies well a second time.

—*Michael Chiarello*

MAKE AHEAD The cookies will keep for up to a week in tightly sealed tins. Pack them loosely between sheets of wax paper that have been dusted with confectioners' sugar. Dust the cookies again with confectioners' sugar before serving.

Spritz Cookies

MAKES ABOUT 6 DOZEN COOKIES

Refrigerating these rich and buttery cookies before baking them helps them hold their shape, but it's not essential.

- 2 sticks (½ pound) unsalted butter, softened
- ½ cup superfine sugar
- 1 large egg yolk
- ½ teaspoon pure vanilla extract
- ½ teaspoon pure almond extract
- 1¾ cups all-purpose flour

I. In a large bowl, beat the butter until creamy. Add the sugar and beat until light and fluffy. Add the egg yolk and vanilla and almond extracts and beat until blended. Stir in the flour, ¼ cup at a time, until incorporated.

2. Preheat the oven to 375°. Press the dough through a cookie press into 2-inch-long S shapes onto ungreased baking sheets. Bake the cookies in the upper and middle third of the oven for 12 to 15 minutes, or until they are golden on the bottom and lightly browned around the edges. Let the cookies cool on the baking sheet for 3 minutes before transferring them to a rack to cool completely. If the cookies stick to the baking sheet, return them to the oven to soften for 1 minute.

—*Edna Lewis and Scott Peacock*

MAKE AHEAD The cookies can be layered between sheets of wax paper

in an airtight container and stored at room temperature for 1 week or frozen for several weeks.

Sugar Cookies

MAKES ABOUT 6½ DOZEN COOKIES

With their greater proportion of butter to sugar, these cookies are more tender and less crumbly than most sugar cookies. You can serve them golden brown as they come from the oven— but if you have artistic talent, here is your chance to show it off. Besides using the colored sugar and sprinkles suggested here, you can stamp these cookies with decorative designs before baking and stencil, ice and glaze them afterward.

- 4 large egg yolks
- 3 tablespoons heavy cream
- 3½ cups all-purpose flour
- 1 cup granulated sugar
- 2½ sticks (10 ounces) cold unsalted butter, cut into 1-inch pieces
- 2 teaspoons water

Colored sugar and sprinkles, for decorating

I. In a small bowl, whisk 2 of the egg yolks with the cream. In a standing electric mixer, combine the flour and sugar. Add the butter and beat at low speed until the mixture resembles crumbs, 2 to 3 minutes. Add the cream mixture in a slow steady stream, beating at low speed until the ingredients are just combined. Divide the dough into 4 equal pieces, shape into 6-inch disks and wrap in plastic. Refrigerate until chilled, at least 2 hours or overnight. Let the dough stand at room temperature for 10 minutes before rolling it out.

2. Preheat the oven to 350°. Line several baking sheets with parchment paper. On a lightly floured surface, roll out 1 piece of the dough ⅛ inch thick. Using cookie cutters, cut out shapes

A Sugar Cookie.

and transfer them to the prepared baking sheets.

3. In a small bowl, beat the remaining 2 egg yolks with the water. Lightly brush the cookies with the egg wash and sprinkle with colored sugar and sprinkles. Bake for 16 to 18 minutes, or until pale golden. Transfer the cookies on the parchment paper to a rack to cool. Line the cookie sheets again and repeat with the remaining dough.

—*Gerry Moss*

MAKE AHEAD The baked cookies will keep for up to 1 week in tightly sealed tins. Pack between sheets of wax paper.

Cinnamon-Sugar Cookies

MAKES ABOUT 5 DOZEN COOKIES

- 1¼ cups all-purpose flour
- ¼ teaspoon baking soda

Large pinch of salt

- 1 stick (4 ounces) unsalted butter
- ¾ cup granulated sugar
- ½ cup (lightly packed) light brown sugar
- 1 large egg
- 1 teaspoon pure vanilla extract
- 2½ tablespoons cinnamon

I. Sift together the flour, baking soda and salt. Using an electric mixer, in a large bowl, beat the butter with ¼ cup of the granulated sugar and the brown

397

sugar at medium speed until combined. Add the egg and vanilla and beat until pale. Stir in the dry ingredients just until combined. Divide the dough into thirds, shape into 6-inch logs and wrap in plastic. Refrigerate or freeze until firm.

2. Preheat the oven to 350°. In a small bowl, combine the remaining ½ cup of granulated sugar with the cinnamon and spread on a flat plate. Unwrap the logs and then roll them in the cinnamon sugar until thoroughly coated. Rewrap the logs and refrigerate or freeze until firm.

3. Slice the cookie dough logs ¼ inch thick. Arrange the slices 1 inch apart on 2 large cookie sheets and bake for 18 to 20 minutes, or until golden. Transfer the cookies to a rack to cool and then bake the remaining cookies. Serve the cookies when they have cooled. —*Sascha Lyon*

MAKE AHEAD The cookie dough logs can be frozen for up to 2 weeks. The baked cookies can be kept in an airtight container for up to 2 weeks.

Almond Butter Tuiles

MAKES ABOUT 2½ DOZEN COOKIES

Traditionally, *tuiles* have a curved shape, but these crisp cookies taste just as good if you leave them flat.

- ½ cup sliced almonds (about 1½ ounces)
- 2 large egg whites
- 6½ tablespoons sugar
- 5 tablespoons unsalted butter, melted and cooled
- ¼ teaspoon pure vanilla extract
- ⅓ cup all-purpose flour

1. Preheat the oven to 350°. Spread the almonds in a pie plate and bake for about 5 minutes, or until the almonds are toasted. Let the almonds cool and then coarsely crumble them with your fingers.

2. Butter 2 large heavy cookie sheets. In a medium bowl, whisk the egg whites with the sugar and almonds just until combined. Stir in the butter and vanilla and then stir in the flour.

3. Drop rounded tablespoons of the batter onto the cookie sheets, about 3½ inches apart. Using the back of the spoon, spread the batter evenly into 3-inch rounds. Bake for about 13 minutes, or until golden. Using a metal spatula, quickly transfer the cookies to a rack or drape them over rolling pins or glasses until cool. Repeat with the remaining batter. —*Emily Luchetti*

Hazelnut Butter Cookies

MAKES ABOUT 64 COOKIES

Serve these delectably crisp nut cookies with Poached Pears with Mascarpone Cream and Chocolate Sauce (p. 423) or on their own with coffee.

- 1 cup hazelnuts (about 5 ounces)
- ¼ cup granulated sugar, plus more for sprinkling
- 2 sticks (½ pound) unsalted butter, softened
- 1½ cups confectioners' sugar, sifted
- 2 large eggs, separated
- 1 teaspoon pure vanilla extract
- 2½ cups all-purpose flour
- 1 teaspoon cinnamon
- ½ teaspoon salt

1. Preheat the oven to 400°. Spread the nuts on a rimmed baking sheet; toast in the oven for about 10 minutes, or until deeply browned. Let cool slightly, transfer to a kitchen towel and rub vigorously to remove the skins. Let the nuts cool completely and then transfer them to a food processor with the ¼ cup of granulated sugar. Process just until the hazelnuts are finely ground.

2. In a large bowl, cream the butter with the confectioners' sugar. Beat in the egg yolks and vanilla. Stir in the ground nuts, flour, cinnamon and salt

to make a smooth dough. Pat the dough into a disk, wrap in plastic and refrigerate until firm, about 2 hours.

3. Divide the dough in half and refrigerate 1 half. On a lightly floured surface, roll out the other half to a 12-inch square. Cut the dough into sixteen 3-inch squares. Cut the squares on the diagonal to form 2 triangles each. Arrange the triangles about 1 inch apart on baking sheets and refrigerate until well chilled, about 15 minutes.

4. Preheat the oven to 350°. In a small bowl, lightly beat the egg whites. Brush the cookies with the whites and sprinkle with granulated sugar. Bake in the center of the oven for about 15 minutes, or until golden. Let stand on the sheets until firm and then transfer to a rack to cool. Repeat with the remaining dough.

—*The Point, Lake Saranac, New York*

MAKE AHEAD The cookie dough can be refrigerated for up to 2 days or frozen for up to 1 month. The baked cookies can be kept in an airtight container for up to 2 days.

Maple Pecan Cookies

MAKES ABOUT 3½ DOZEN COOKIES

Buttery and subtly maple-flavored, these cookies are like the best pecan sandies you've ever tasted. The recipe can easily be doubled or tripled.

- 2 sticks (8 ounces) unsalted butter, softened
- ½ cup granulated sugar
- 1 large egg yolk
- 2 tablespoons pure maple syrup
- ½ teaspoon pure vanilla extract
- 2 cups all-purpose flour
- 1¼ cups pecans, coarsely chopped (4½ ounces)

1. In a medium bowl, beat the butter with an electric mixer until pale and creamy, about 3 minutes. Gradually beat in the sugar until well blended. ➤

Cinnamon-Sugar Cookies

A Maple-Pecan Cookie, with Liar's Cookies (p. 396).

rolled-cookie tips

Some tactics to help make perfect cookies from rich, thinly rolled dough:

Use cold unsalted butter. Room-temperature butter becomes greasy when whipped, making greasy cookies.

Cut the dough in half or in quarters before wrapping and chilling it. Small amounts of dough are easier to roll out.

Don't arrange cookies of different sizes on the same baking sheet. It takes less time to bake smaller cookies than it does to bake larger ones.

Press the cutting edge of cookie cutters into a small mound of flour if the cutters are sticking to the dough.

Refrigerate or slightly freeze cookies prior to baking. They will hold their shape better during cooking.

Let baking sheets cool before reusing them. Clean and regrease them if needed.

—Gerry Moss

2. In a small bowl, whisk the egg yolk with the maple syrup and vanilla. Drizzle the mixture into the butter, beating at low speed until incorporated.

3. Using a wooden spoon, stir in the flour and pecans. Divide the dough in half and shape into 2 disks. Wrap each disk in plastic and refrigerate until chilled, at least 2 hours or overnight. Let the dough stand at room temperature for 10 minutes before rolling it out.

4. Preheat the oven to 325°. Roll out each disk of dough ¼ inch thick between 2 sheets of wax paper. Cut the dough into 2-inch rounds and transfer to baking sheets lined with parchment paper. Bake for 20 to 25 minutes, or until golden. Transfer the cookies to wire racks to cool.   *—Gerry Moss*

MAKE AHEAD The cookie dough can be frozen for up to 1 month. The cookies will keep for up to 1 week stored in tightly sealed tins.

Ginger-Almond Cookies

MAKES ABOUT 4 DOZEN ✳

These tempting cookies are quick to throw together, and they bake less than twenty minutes, but you do have allow time for the cookie dough to chill.

½ cup whole almonds (3 ounces), toasted
¼ cup plus 2 tablespoons sugar
1 cup all-purpose flour
2 teaspoons ground ginger
Salt
1 stick (4 ounces) unsalted butter, at room temperature
1 teaspoon pure vanilla extract

I. In a food processor, combine the almonds with 3 tablespoons of the sugar; process to a coarse powder. Transfer to a bowl and stir in the flour, ginger and a pinch of salt.

2. In a large bowl, beat the butter with the remaining 3 tablespoons of sugar and the vanilla until well blended. Add the flour mixture to the bowl and beat until combined.

3. Divide the dough in half and shape each half into a 6-inch-long log. Wrap each log in plastic and chill until firm, at least 3 hours or for up to 3 days.

4. Preheat the oven to 350° and line 2 cookie sheets with parchment paper. Slice the dough logs ¼ inch thick and arrange the slices 1 inch apart on the prepared cookie sheets. Bake the cookies for about 18 minutes, or until golden on the bottoms and edges; shift the pans halfway through baking. Slide the parchment with the cookies onto wire racks and let the cookies cool completely before serving.

—*Jan Newberry*

MAKE AHEAD The ginger cookies can be kept in an airtight container for up to 3 days.

Pistachio-Apricot Biscotti

MAKES 40 BISCOTTI

The dried apricots here, along with the raisins, add another dimension to the typical biscotti—a satisfying extra sweetness and chewiness.

Butter-flavored cooking spray

About 2 cups sifted all-purpose flour

1½ **teaspoons baking powder**

¼ **teaspoon salt**

½ **cup shelled unsalted pistachios, very coarsely chopped (about 2½ ounces)**

⅓ **cup coarsely chopped dried apricots**

¼ **cup golden raisins**

½ **cup plus 2 tablespoons sugar**

2 **tablespoons unsalted butter, softened**

2 **large eggs, at room temperature**

1 **teaspoon pure vanilla extract**

¼ **teaspoon pure almond extract**

I. Preheat the oven to 350°. Lightly coat a cookie sheet with butter-flavored cooking spray. In a medium bowl, whisk 2 cups of the flour with the baking powder and salt. In a small bowl, toss the pistachios, apricots and raisins with 2 tablespoons of the flour mixture.

2. In a large bowl, beat the sugar and butter until combined. Beat in the eggs, 1 at a time, and then mix in the vanilla extract and almond extract. Blend in the flour mixture on low speed. Stir in the pistachios and dried fruits just until incorporated.

3. Gather the dough into a ball; if it's sticky, work in a little more flour. Divide the dough in half. On a lightly floured surface, shape each piece into a 13-inch log. Set the logs 2 inches apart on the cookie sheet and gently flatten the logs until they are ¾ inch thick.

4. Bake the logs for about 20 minutes, or until they are golden on top and a toothpick inserted in the centers comes out clean. Let the logs cool for 10 minutes. Reduce the oven temperature to 300°.

5. Using a serrated knife, slice the warm logs diagonally into ½-inch-thick slices. Arrange the slices on their sides on the cookie sheet; if necessary, use a second cookie sheet. Bake the biscotti for about 20 minutes, or

Ginger-Almond Cookies

until they are crisp and golden. Transfer the biscotti to a rack to cool.

—*Susan G. Purdy*

ONE BISCOTTO Calories 60 kcal, Total Fat 1.8 gm, Saturated Fat .5 gm

MAKE AHEAD The biscotti can be kept in an airtight container for 3 days.

Brown Sugar Granola Biscotti

MAKES ABOUT 3 DOZEN BISCOTTI

Bake these cookies at home and pack them for camping. They're excellent for snacks while hiking and they're also good for breakfast. Using a granola with raisins adds a pleasant chewiness.

1 **cup all-purpose flour**

⅔ **cup (packed) light brown sugar**

1 **teaspoon finely grated lemon zest**

401

Brown Sugar Granola Biscotti

1 teaspoon coarsely chopped aniseeds

¾ teaspoon baking powder

Salt

5 tablespoons cold unsalted butter, cut into small pieces

2 large cold eggs, lightly beaten

1 teaspoon pure vanilla extract

2 cups granola, large pieces broken up

1. In a food processor, combine the flour, sugar, lemon zest, aniseeds, baking powder and a pinch of salt and pulse a few times to blend. Add the butter; pulse just until incorporated. Add the eggs and vanilla to the food processor and process just until combined. Scrape the dough into a medium bowl and stir in the granola. Cover and refrigerate until firm, about 30 minutes.

2. Preheat the oven to 350°. Lightly butter a baking sheet. Quarter the chilled dough, shape it into four 6-by-1-inch logs and then flatten each log into a rectangular shape. Transfer the logs to the prepared baking sheet and bake them for about 20 minutes, or until golden brown and almost firm. Let the logs cool on the baking sheet for 5 minutes.

3. Transfer the logs to a work surface with a metal spatula. Using a serrated knife and a gentle sawing action, slice the logs crosswise ½ inch thick. Arrange the biscotti on their sides on the baking sheet and bake for about 12 minutes, or until they are very firm and beginning to brown. Transfer the biscotti to a rack to cool completely and then store in an airtight container.

—*Marcia Kiesel*

MAKE AHEAD The biscotti can be kept at room temperature in an airtight container for up to 1 week or frozen for up to 2 weeks.

Chocolate-Walnut Biscotti

MAKES ABOUT 4 DOZEN BISCOTTI

1 cup walnut halves (about 4 ounces)

4½ cups all-purpose flour

1 tablespoon baking powder

½ teaspoon salt

2 sticks (½ pound) unsalted butter, softened

1½ cups sugar

4 large eggs

1 tablespoon pure vanilla extract

5½ ounces bittersweet chocolate, cut into ½-inch chunks (about 1 cup)

1. Preheat the oven to 400°. Toast the walnuts for about 8 minutes, or until golden brown. Let the nuts cool and then coarsely chop them. Lower the oven temperature to 325°.

2. In a large bowl, sift together the flour, baking powder and salt. In another large bowl, cream the butter with the sugar. Beat in the eggs, 1 at a time, blending thoroughly after each addition. Add the vanilla. Gradually stir in the flour mixture and then fold in the walnuts and the chocolate until just blended. Divide the dough into 4 pieces and shape each piece into a 12-inch log. Set the logs on 2 lightly buttered baking sheets and refrigerate until chilled, at least 30 minutes.

3. Bake the logs of dough for about 20 minutes, or until they are firm and starting to brown. Transfer the logs to a rack and let them cool slightly. Lower the oven temperature to 250°. Using a serrated knife, cut the logs crosswise diagonally, ½ inch thick. Set the biscotti on their sides on the baking sheets and bake them for about 15 minutes, or until the biscotti are golden brown. Let the biscotti cool before serving.

—*Clifford Harrison and Anne Quatrano*

MAKE AHEAD The biscotti can be stored in an airtight container for up to 3 days.

Marie Gachet's Pillow

MAKES ABOUT 24 WEDGES

This puffy tea pastry comes from the recipe book of Marie Gachet, whose father was Vincent van Gogh's friend and physician.

¾ cup all-purpose flour

¾ cup mascarpone (about 6 ounces)

2 to 3 tablespoons raw brown sugar (see Note)

1. In a medium bowl, stir the flour into the mascarpone. Turn the dough onto a work surface and knead just until smooth. Pat the dough into a 6-inch square and transfer to a plate. Cover and refrigerate the dough until cold, 30 minutes to 1 hour.

2. Preheat the oven to 450°. On a lightly floured surface, roll out the dough to a 15-by-12-inch rectangle. Wrap the dough around the rolling pin and unroll onto a large baking sheet. Sprinkle the dough evenly with the brown sugar. Bake for 10 to 12 minutes, or until the pastry is puffed and golden brown and the sugar is caramelized in places. Cut the pastry in half crosswise and then into wedges. Serve hot from the oven.

—*Anne Daguin*

NOTE Raw brown sugar is available at health food stores.

Coconut Clusters

MAKES 2 DOZEN CLUSTERS

Serve this sugary confection with cups of strong espresso.

1 cup sugar
1 cup water
One 7-ounce package sweetened
   shredded coconut
Salt
½ teaspoon pure vanilla extract
Freshly grated nutmeg, for sprinkling

1. Lightly oil a large baking sheet. In a medium saucepan, combine the sugar and water and boil over high heat, stirring occasionally, until the sugar dissolves. Add the coconut and a pinch of salt and cook over moderate heat, stirring, until the syrup has evaporated and the coconut has a light, somewhat crystallized coating, about 20 minutes. Stir in the vanilla.

2. Working quickly, scrape the coconut mixture onto the prepared baking sheet and spread it into a 10-by-9-inch rectangle; let cool to room temperature. Sprinkle a little nutmeg over the top. Using a large knife, cut the rectangle into 24 pieces and serve.

—Marcia Kiesel

MAKE AHEAD The clusters can be made up to 6 hours ahead.

CHAPTER 15 fruit desserts

Almond Berry Cakes (p. 412)

Strawberries in Champagne Jelly

Strawberries in Champagne Jelly

6 SERVINGS ★★★ **1994**

Lindsey Shere, pastry chef at Chez Panisse and owner of the Downtown Bakery and Creamery in the San Francisco Bay area, has a wonderful way with desserts. This barely set, sparkling homemade jelly will be a revelation.

- 3¼ teaspoons unflavored powdered gelatin
- 1 cup water
- ¾ cup plus 3 tablespoons sugar
- 1 bottle dry Champagne
- 1 pint strawberries, hulled and thinly sliced lengthwise

1. In a medium saucepan, sprinkle the gelatin over the water and let soften until no dry spots are visible, about 5 minutes. Melt the gelatin over low heat, stirring with a wooden spoon just until no lumps remain; do not overcook. Remove from the heat and stir in ¾ cup plus 2 tablespoons of the sugar until thoroughly dissolved. Stir in the Champagne. Pour the gelatin into a shallow bowl or plastic container, cover and refrigerate until set, at least 6 hours or overnight.

2. To assemble, toss the strawberries with the remaining 1 tablespoon of sugar. Scramble the gelatin with a fork. Alternate layers of the gelatin and the strawberries in glass bowls. Drizzle a little juice from the berries over the top and serve cold.   *—Lindsey Shere*

Chilled Strawberry Champagne Soup

4 SERVINGS

- 1 pint ripe strawberries, hulled
- ¼ cup sugar, plus more to taste
- 2 tablespoons fresh orange juice
- 2 tablespoons Champagne
  Yogurt Lime Sorbet (recipe follows), or 1½ cups lime sorbet

1. In a blender, combine the strawberries, ¼ cup of the sugar and the orange juice and puree until smooth. Transfer the puree to a bowl, cover and refrigerate until chilled, at least 2 hours and up to 6 hours. Add more sugar if necessary.

2. Stir the Champagne into the soup and pour into 4 bowls. Top with a small scoop of sorbet and serve.

YOGURT LIME SORBET

MAKES ABOUT 1½ CUPS

This tangy and tart sorbet makes a refreshing contrast to the sweet fruit soup; add more sugar to the sorbet if you want to serve it alone. Since it loses its creamy texture if it's frozen ahead, the best plan is to serve the sorbet just after it's made.

- 1 cup plain whole-milk yogurt
- ½ cup fresh lime juice
- 3 tablespoons sugar
- 1 teaspoon finely grated lime zest

In a small bowl, whisk together the yogurt, lime juice, sugar and lime zest. Refrigerate until the yogurt is cold, about 1 hour. Transfer the yogurt mixture to an ice cream maker and freeze according to manufacturer's directions. Serve at once.   *—Gray Kunz*

Lemon Granita with Strawberries in Rosemary Syrup

4 SERVINGS

Sweet rosemary-scented syrup makes an unusual foil for the tart lemon ice.

GRANITA

- 2½ cups water
- 1 cup sugar
- 1 cup fresh lemon juice (about 6 large lemons)

STRAWBERRIES

- 1 cup water
- ½ cup sugar
- 1 rosemary sprig
- 1 cinnamon stick
- 2 pints strawberries, hulled and sliced

1. MAKE THE GRANITA: In a medium saucepan, combine the water and sugar and bring to a boil, stirring until the sugar is completely dissolved. Remove from the heat and let cool. Stir in the lemon juice. Pour the syrup into a 13-by-9-inch metal baking pan and freeze for at least 2 hours, stirring the granita with a fork every 20 minutes to give it a nice, granular consistency.

2. MAKE THE STRAWBERRIES: Meanwhile, in a medium saucepan, combine the water, sugar, rosemary and cinnamon and bring to a boil. Simmer over moderately high heat for 10 minutes. Let cool completely and then strain into a medium bowl. Add the strawberries and macerate for 1 hour.

3. Serve the lemon granita in shallow bowls with the sliced strawberries on the side.   *—Marta Braunstein*

MAKE AHEAD The granita can be frozen for up to 3 days.

ONE SERVING Calories 355 kcal, Total Fat .6 gm, Saturated Fat 0 gm

Lemon Sabayon with Strawberries

4 SERVINGS

Here's a dessert for people who like to finish a meal with something that's sweet but not heavy.

- 2 pints strawberries, hulled and halved
- ¼ cup sugar
- 1 teaspoon finely chopped mint
- ¼ cup fresh lemon juice
- 3 large egg yolks
- 2 tablespoons Grand Marnier
- ½ teaspoon pure vanilla extract

1. In a bowl, toss the strawberries with 1 tablespoon of the sugar and the mint. Fill a large bowl halfway with ice cubes and water and then set a medium bowl in the water.

2. In a large stainless steel bowl, combine the lemon juice, egg yolks, Grand Marnier, vanilla and the remaining 3 tablespoons of sugar. Set the bowl over a saucepan containing 1½ inches of simmering water and whisk constantly until the egg mixture is light and thick enough to leave a ribbon trail when the whisk is lifted, about 10 minutes.

3. Pour the sabayon into the medium bowl set in ice water and whisk until cool, about 5 minutes. Spoon the sabayon into parfait glasses and serve with the strawberries. —*Allen Susser*

MAKE AHEAD The strawberries can be prepared up to 1 hour ahead.

ONE SERVING Calories 167 kcal, Total Fat 4.4 gm, Saturated Fat 1.2 gm

Lemon Sabayon with Strawberries

Grilled Strawberries

4 SERVINGS ✳

Grilling on a skewer is an unexpected and surprisingly delicious way to prepare strawberries.

  24 whole strawberries
  ½ cup confectioner's sugar
Vanilla ice cream, for serving

Light a grill. Dust the strawberries with confectioners' sugar and then thread them onto skewers. Cook the berries over a medium-hot fire for about 3 minutes per side, or until slightly browned and warmed through. Slice and serve over vanilla ice cream.—*Jan Newberry*

Strawberry Biscuits with Honey and Crème Fraîche

8 SERVINGS

 1½ pints medium strawberries, hulled and sliced
  ¼ cup plus 2 teaspoons sugar
  2 cups all-purpose flour
  2 tablespoons baking powder
  1 teaspoon kosher salt
  1 stick (4 ounces) cold unsalted butter, cut into ½-inch pieces
  2 large eggs
  ½ cup buttermilk
  1 cup crème fraîche
  ¼ cup clover honey
  4 mint leaves, finely shredded

1. Preheat the oven to 400°. In a medium bowl, toss the strawberries with 2 teaspoons of the sugar and let stand at room temperature.

2. Butter a large baking sheet. In a food processor, combine the flour, baking powder, kosher salt and the remaining ¼ cup of sugar; pulse until blended. Add the butter and pulse until the mixture resembles coarse meal. In a small bowl, mix the eggs with the buttermilk and add to the dry ingredients; pulse just until the dough comes together.

3. On a lightly floured surface, gently knead the dough until smooth and then roll it out to a large square 1 inch thick. Using a 1½-inch round pastry cutter, cut out 16 biscuits; reroll the scraps if necessary. Arrange the biscuits on the baking sheet and bake in the upper third of the oven for about 15 minutes, or until golden. Transfer the biscuits to a rack and let cool for 15 minutes.

4. Cut the biscuits in half and set 2 bottom halves on each plate. Top the biscuit bottoms with strawberries, the biscuit tops and a dollop of crème fraîche. Drizzle the biscuits with honey and any accumulated strawberry juice. Garnish the biscuits with the mint leaves and serve.

—*Clifford Harrison and Anne Quatrano*

Fresh Berry Shortcakes

10 SERVINGS

SHORTCAKES

3¾ cups all-purpose flour

½ cup plus 1 tablespoon sugar

2 tablespoons baking powder

½ teaspoon finely grated orange zest

Pinch of salt

½ vanilla bean, split lengthwise

1½ sticks (6 ounces) cold unsalted butter, cut into tablespoons, plus 2 tablespoons, melted

1½ cups cold heavy cream

FILLING

½ vanilla bean, split lengthwise

¼ cup sugar

2 pints strawberries, halved

¼ cup cold heavy cream

1 tablespoon pure vanilla extract

I. MAKE THE SHORTCAKES: Preheat the oven to 400°. In a large bowl, sift the flour with ½ cup of the sugar and the baking powder. Add the orange zest and salt and scrape the seeds from the vanilla bean into the bowl. Cut in the 1½ sticks of butter until the mixture resembles coarse meal. Add the cream and mix until a dough forms.

2. On a lightly floured surface, roll out the dough to a ¾-inch thickness. Using a 2-inch round biscuit cutter, stamp out 10 rounds. Set the rounds on a baking sheet and refrigerate for at least 15 minutes and up to several hours.

3. Brush the rounds with the melted butter and sprinkle the remaining 1 tablespoon of sugar on top. Bake the shortcakes for about 20 minutes, or until golden all over. Transfer the shortcakes to a rack and let cool for at least 15 minutes.

4. MAKE THE FILLING: Scrape the seeds from the vanilla bean into a small bowl and stir in 3 tablespoons of the sugar. Add the strawberries and toss. Refrigerate for 1 hour.

5. In a medium bowl, whip the cream with the remaining 1 tablespoon of sugar and the vanilla extract. Cut the shortcakes in half and set the bottom halves on plates. Top each shortcake bottom with a dollop of the whipped cream and a large spoonful of strawberries. Cover the strawberries with the shortcake tops and serve the shortcakes at once. —*Brendan Walsh*

MAKE AHEAD The shortcakes can be baked up to 4 hours ahead.

Buttery Almond Cakes with Strawberry Compote

12 SERVINGS

1 stick plus 2 tablespoons unsalted butter

1¼ cups whole blanched almonds (6½ ounces)

1¾ cups confectioners' sugar

¾ cup all-purpose flour

Salt

5 large egg whites

⅛ teaspoon pure almond extract

¼ cup pine nuts

Strawberry Compote (recipe follows)

I. Preheat the oven to 450°. Generously butter a 12-cup mini-muffin pan (¼-cup size). In a medium saucepan, cook the butter over low heat until fragrant and browned, about 8 minutes; let cool completely. Spread the almonds on a rimmed baking sheet and toast in the oven for about 5 minutes, or until light brown; transfer to a plate and let cool completely.

2. In a mini-processor, finely grind the almonds; watch carefully so they don't form a paste. Pass the ground almonds through a coarse sieve to remove any large pieces and to fluff them up. Return the almonds to the sieve, add the confectioners' sugar, flour and ¼ teaspoon of salt and sift together into a large bowl.

3. In a large stainless steel bowl, whip the egg whites with a pinch of salt until

Strawberry Biscuits with Honey and Crème Fraîche

they hold very soft peaks. Stir the butter and the almond extract into the almond mixture and then fold in the egg whites until just combined.

4. Spoon the batter into the prepared muffin cups, filling each two-thirds of the way; sprinkle with the pine nuts. Bake for 8 minutes. Reduce the oven temperature to 400° and bake for 8 minutes longer, or until the centers of the cakes have risen to form points and spring back when touched. Run a small knife around the cakes and remove them from the pan while still hot. Let the cakes cool completely on a rack. Serve with the compote.

MAKE AHEAD The almond cakes can be stored in an airtight container for up to 1 day.

Buttery Almond Cakes with Strawberry Compote

STRAWBERRY COMPOTE

12 SERVINGS

- 3 quarts strawberries, halved if large
- ¼ cup pure maple syrup
- 3 tablespoons Grand Marnier

In a large bowl, toss the strawberries with the maple syrup and the Grand Marnier. Let the compote stand at room temperature, stirring often, for at least 1 hour or refrigerate for up to 4 hours. —*Marcia Kiesel*

Raspberries in Maraschino

6 SERVINGS

Macerate the raspberries for at least one hour.

- 1½ pints ripe raspberries
- 6 tablespoons Maraschino liqueur
- 6 mint sprigs

Cookies, for serving (optional)

In a medium bowl, gently toss the raspberries with the liqueur. Refrigerate for at least 1 hour and up to 4 hours. Spoon the berries into 6 goblets and garnish with the mint sprigs. Serve with cookies. —*Ed Giobbi*

Cornmeal and Raspberry Soufflés

4 SERVINGS

The lovely texture of these individual soufflés comes from cornmeal and the refreshing juiciness comes from the raspberries that are baked inside.

- 1¼ cups skim milk
- 1 long strip of orange zest
- 1½ teaspoons unsalted butter, softened
- ¼ cup sugar, plus more for dusting
- 3 tablespoons cornmeal
- ⅓ cup fresh orange juice
- 3 large egg whites
- ½ pint fresh raspberries

1. In a medium saucepan, combine the skim milk and orange zest and bring to a simmer over moderately high heat. Remove the saucepan from the heat, cover and let the infused milk steep for 30 minutes. Discard the orange zest.

2. Meanwhile, preheat the oven to 400°. Coat four 1-cup ramekins with the butter and dust lightly with sugar. Return the milk to a simmer. Add 2 tablespoons of the sugar and then stir in the cornmeal in a thin stream. Stir in the orange juice and simmer over moderately low heat, stirring constantly, until the mixture is soft and creamy, about 10 minutes. Transfer the mixture to a medium bowl and stir to cool slightly.

3. In a large bowl, beat the egg whites until foamy. Gradually beat in the remaining 2 tablespoons of sugar until soft peaks form. Stir one-quarter of the beaten whites into the cornmeal mixture until combined. Gently fold in the remaining egg whites just until incorporated. Gently fold in the raspberries. Divide the soufflé batter among the prepared ramekins. Set the ramekins in a medium baking dish and add enough hot water to the dish to reach halfway up the sides of the ramekins. Transfer the baking dish to the oven and bake for about 25 minutes, or until the soufflés have risen and are golden but still soft in the center. Transfer the ramekins to plates and serve the soufflés at once. —*Ferdinand Metz*

ONE SERVING Calories 157 kcal, Total Fat 1.9 gm, Saturated Fat 1 gm

---

light soufflés

You can use the tricks here to lighten any fruit soufflé:

Use skim milk to make the soufflé base.

Try a little flour, cornstarch or even cornmeal instead of using egg yolks as a thickener.

Fold in berries to add a refreshing texture to finished soufflés.

Raspberries in Maraschino

Star-Spangled Fools

10 SERVINGS

This traditional English dessert—a combination of fruit and cream—is perfect for our own Fourth of July when made with red raspberries and blueberries.

- 1 pint blueberries
- ½ cup sugar
- ¼ cup blueberry jam
- 2 tablespoons Kirsch or raspberry liqueur
- 1 pint raspberries
- ¼ cup red raspberry jam
- 3½ cups cold heavy cream
- ½ vanilla bean, split lengthwise

Boy holding a Star-Spangled Fool.

1. In a small saucepan, crush ½ cup of the blueberries with 2 tablespoons of the sugar. Cook over moderate heat until the berry juices are released, about 5 minutes. Stir in the blueberry jam and cook until warmed through. Strain the mixture into a bowl, pressing hard on the solids. Add 1 tablespoon of the Kirsch and let cool.

2. Rinse out the saucepan and add ½ cup of the raspberries and 2 tablespoons of the sugar; crush together. Cook over moderate heat until the berry juices are released. Add the raspberry jam and cook until warmed through. Strain the mixture into a bowl, pressing hard on the solids. Add the remaining 1 tablespoon of Kirsch and let cool.

3. In a medium bowl, whip 2 cups of the heavy cream. Gently fold half of the whipped cream into the blueberry mixture and the other half into the raspberry mixture. Refrigerate the fools.

4. In a bowl, combine the remaining 1½ cups of heavy cream with the remaining ¼ cup of sugar. Scrape the seeds from the vanilla bean into the bowl and whip together.

5. Spoon the blueberry fool into 10 stemmed glasses, followed by the vanilla cream and then the raspberry fool; gently tap the glasses between layers. Top with the remaining blueberries and raspberries and serve the fools immediately. —*Brendan Walsh*

Almond Berry Cakes

MAKES EIGHT 4½-INCH CAKES

The almond flour, or almond meal, that gives these cakes their unique flavor is available at specialty food shops.

- 2 cups almond flour (7 ounces)
- 2 cups confectioners' sugar
- ⅔ cup all-purpose flour
- 1 stick (4 ounces) unsalted butter, softened
- 5 large eggs, at room temperature
- 2 tablespoons dark rum
- 2 cups fresh blueberries

1. Preheat the oven to 350°. Grease eight shallow 4½-inch ramekins or foil tart pans and set them on 2 baking sheets. In a bowl, sift the almond flour with the sugar and all-purpose flour.

2. In a large bowl, beat the butter until it is creamy. On low speed, gradually beat in half of the dry ingredients. Beat in 1 egg and then beat in one-fifth of the remaining dry ingredients; repeat until all the eggs and dry ingredients are incorporated. Add the rum and beat at medium speed for 2 minutes. Spoon the cake batter into the

Almond Berry Cakes

Prune Flan with Orange Salad, with Vin d'Oranges (p. 446).

prepared ramekins, spreading it evenly. Sprinkle the blueberries on top.

3. Bake the cakes in the upper and lower thirds of the oven for about 30 minutes, or until they are golden and firm. Let the cakes cool slightly. Unmold and serve the cakes warm or at room temperature. —*Mark Gottwald*

Red Currant Yogurt Soufflés
4 SERVINGS

Fresh red currants are available at farmers' markets in the early summer. Use a fork to comb the fresh currants from their stems.

- ¼ cup plus 3 tablespoons granulated sugar
- 1 pint red currants, stemmed
- 2 tablespoons water
- 1 teaspoon grated orange zest
- 1 teaspoon grated lemon zest
- Vegetable oil cooking spray
- ½ cup plain low-fat yogurt
- 2½ tablespoons all-purpose flour
- 2 teaspoons pure vanilla extract
- 2 large egg whites
- Confectioners' sugar

1. Preheat the oven to 425°. In a small saucepan, combine ¼ cup of the granulated sugar with the currants, water, orange zest and lemon zest. Cook over low heat for 5 minutes and then boil over moderate heat until the mixture starts to thicken, about 8 minutes. Strain the sauce through a fine sieve, pressing hard on the solids to extract the juices. Boil the sauce down to ⅓ cup, about 5 minutes. Let cool.

2. Lightly coat four 5-ounce ramekins with vegetable oil cooking spray. In a medium bowl, stir together the currant sauce, yogurt, flour and vanilla.

3. In a separate medium bowl, beat the egg whites until they hold soft peaks and then gradually beat in the remaining 3 tablespoons of granulated sugar until the whites are stiff but not dry. Fold half of the egg whites into the yogurt-currant mixture with a whisk and then gently fold in the remaining egg whites using a rubber spatula. Spoon the mixture into the prepared ramekins until it just reaches the top.

4. Transfer the ramekins to a baking sheet and bake on the lowest rack of the oven for about 12 minutes, or until the soufflés are well risen and light brown on top. Dust the tops of the soufflés with confectioners' sugar and serve at once. —*Marta Braunstein*
ONE SERVING Calories 174 kcal, Total Fat .6 gm, Saturated Fat .3 gm

Mandarin Orange Terrine
4 SERVINGS

Tart and sweet, solid and jiggly, this gelatin for grown-ups is a perfect combination of contrasting textures and flavors.

- 8 large mandarin oranges
- 1 cup water
- ½ cup sugar
- 1 inch of fresh ginger, peeled and thinly sliced
- ½ vanilla bean, split lengthwise
- 2 tablespoons Triple Sec or other orange liqueur
- 1 envelope unflavored gelatin
- Fresh mint leaves, for garnish

1. Peel the oranges with a sharp knife, making sure to remove the bitter white pith. Working over a strainer set over a bowl, cut between the membranes to release the segments. Remove the seeds and then drain the orange segments on a paper towel–lined platter. Squeeze the juice from the membranes into the bowl; reserve the juice. Refrigerate the oranges for 2 hours.

2. In a small saucepan, combine the water, sugar, ginger and vanilla bean and bring to a boil. Reduce the heat to moderately low and simmer for 10 minutes. Stir the Triple Sec and gelatin into the reserved orange juice and then add it to the ginger syrup, stirring to dissolve the gelatin. Bring just to a boil, strain the syrup through a fine sieve and let cool to room temperature. Stir in the orange segments.

3. Line a 7½-by-3½-by-2½-inch loaf pan with plastic wrap, leaving plenty of extra plastic overhanging on all sides. Pour in the oranges and syrup and lightly tap the pan to release any air bubbles. Cover loosely with the overhanging plastic and refrigerate until firm, at least 3 hours or overnight. Uncover and invert onto a plate. Remove the plastic. Cut the terrine in half crosswise and then halve each piece on the diagonal to form 4 triangles. Transfer to plates, garnish with mint leaves and serve. —*Allen Susser*
ONE SERVING Calories 214 kcal, Total Fat .4 gm, Saturated Fat 0 gm

Prune Flan with Orange Salad
6 SERVINGS

- ⅓ plus ½ cup sugar
- 12 plump prunes, pitted
- 1½ cups whole milk
- 1 vanilla bean, halved lengthwise
- 3 large eggs
- 3 navel oranges
- 1 teaspoon orange liqueur

1. In a small saucepan, cook ⅓ cup of the sugar over moderate heat, stirring constantly with a wooden spoon, until a dark caramel forms, about 5 minutes. Immediately pour the caramel into the bottom of an 8-by-1-inch ring mold. Arrange the prunes on the caramel, spacing them evenly. Let cool completely.

2. In another small saucepan, combine the milk with 3 tablespoons of the sugar. Scrape the seeds from half of the vanilla bean; add the seeds and the scraped vanilla bean half to the milk and bring to a boil.

3. Meanwhile, in a medium bowl, vigorously whisk the eggs with 3 tablespoons of the sugar until the mixture turns pale. Gradually whisk in the hot milk. Strain the custard into a bowl and let cool.

4. Preheat the oven to 325°. Set the caramel-lined mold in a small roasting pan and pour in the custard. Set the pan in the oven. Add enough hot water to the pan to reach halfway up the side of the mold. Bake for about 50 minutes, or until the flan is just set and a knife inserted into the custard comes out clean. Let cool in the water bath for 10 minutes and then transfer the ring mold to a rack and let cool to room temperature. Refrigerate the flan for at least 2 hours.

5. Meanwhile, using a sharp knife, peel the oranges; be sure to remove all the bitter white pith. Working over a bowl, cut in between the membranes to release the orange segments. Scrape the seeds from the remaining vanilla bean half into the oranges. Toss gently with the orange liqueur and the remaining 2 teaspoons of sugar.

6. To unmold the flan, bring ½ inch of water to a boil in a large skillet. Carefully set the ring mold in the skillet, leave for 1 minute and then remove the mold and wipe the bottom dry. Using a small knife, gently free the flan from the mold. Tilt the mold; if the caramel doesn't seep out, return the mold to hot water and repeat.

7. Place a serving platter on top of the ring mold and invert the flan onto the platter. Tap the mold lightly and lift it off. Spoon the orange salad into the center of the flan. Slice the flan and serve with the oranges and caramel sauce. —*Daniel Boulud*
MAKE AHEAD The baked flan can be refrigerated in the mold for 2 days.

Ambrosia

12 SERVINGS
Ambrosia is a traditional Southern fruit salad and an absolutely essential part of the Southern holiday meal. It is imperative that you use freshly grated coconut and the very best oranges. Sweeten sparingly and add just enough sherry to enhance, not overwhelm, the dish. A fine Ambrosia is far greater than the sum of its parts. Sadly, today you find many versions made with canned fruit cocktail, maraschino cherries and marshmallows. This recipe is the real deal.

12 **large navel oranges**
2½ **cups freshly grated fresh coconut (1 medium coconut)**
3 **tablespoons sugar**
3 **tablespoons cream sherry**
¼ **teaspoon salt**

1. Using a sharp knife, peel the navel oranges, removing all the bitter white pith. Working over a bowl, cut in between the membranes to release the orange sections. Squeeze the juice from the membranes over the oranges in the bowl.

2. Two to four hours before serving, stir in the coconut, sugar, sherry and salt. —*Edna Lewis and Scott Peacock*
MAKE AHEAD The recipe can be prepared through Step 1 a day ahead.

Candied Oranges

MAKES 32 PIECES
These succulent candied oranges can be served on their own as a sweet or chopped and used in other desserts.

8 **medium navel oranges, preferably organic, quartered lengthwise**
Water
5½ **cups granulated sugar**
¼ **cup light corn syrup**

1. In a large saucepan, cover the orange quarters with water and bring the water to a boil. Reduce the heat; simmer for 30 minutes. Using a slotted spoon, transfer the orange quarters to a baking sheet that has been lined with parchment paper.

2. Pour the water out of the saucepan. Put 4 cups of the sugar with the corn syrup and 2 cups of fresh water into the saucepan and bring to a boil over moderately high heat. Stir constantly until the sugar is dissolved. Add the oranges and cook over low heat, stirring once or twice, until they begin to look glassy, about 1½ hours.

3. Raise the heat to high and boil vigorously for 7 minutes; the rinds will begin to look translucent. Remove from the heat and let the oranges cool in the syrup. Using a slotted spoon, transfer the oranges to a baking sheet lined with parchment paper. Let stand uncovered overnight or until tacky to the touch. Reserve the cooking syrup.

4. Bring the syrup to a boil over high heat. Add the oranges and boil for 10 minutes. Let cool completely in the syrup. Using a slotted spoon, transfer the oranges, skin side down, to a rack. Let stand until tacky.

5. Put the remaining 1½ cups sugar in a paper bag, add the oranges and shake until well coated. Dry on a baking sheet lined with parchment paper; sugar them again if they still seem moist. Let stand uncovered overnight or for several days. —*Margaret Braun*
MAKE AHEAD The oranges can be stored in an airtight container for up to 1 month.

Crispy Hats with Plums and Raisins

4 SERVINGS
You can increase or decrease the sugar depending on how sweet your plums are. The recipe comes from *The French Culinary Institute's Salute to Healthy Cooking* (Rodale Press).

4 **sheets phyllo dough**
4 **teaspoons unsalted butter, melted**
2 **tablespoons confectioners' sugar**

A Crispy Hat with Plums and Raisins.

Vegetable oil cooking spray

- ½ cup water
- ¼ cup raisins
- 4 large Italian prune plums, pitted and cut into 8 wedges each
- 2 to 3 tablespoons granulated sugar
- 1 tablespoon rum
- 1 pint plum or passion fruit sorbet (optional)

1. Preheat the oven to 350°. Coat the outside of four 4-ounce custard cups with vegetable oil cooking spray and invert the custard cups on a large baking sheet lined with parchment paper.

2. Spread 1 sheet of phyllo on a work surface; keep the remaining sheets covered with a kitchen towel. Lightly brush the phyllo with some of the butter. Fold the dough in half crosswise; lightly brush again with butter and sift ½ tablespoon of the confectioners' sugar over the dough. Drape the phyllo, sugared side down, over a custard cup and carefully mold it to the side; let the extra phyllo drape onto the baking sheet. Repeat to form the remaining "hats." Bake the hats for 10 minutes, or until crisp and golden. Let them cool thoroughly.

3. In a small saucepan, bring the water to a boil. Remove from the heat, add the raisins and let plump for 10 minutes. Drain and pat dry. In a medium bowl, toss the plums with the raisins.

4. Set a small heavy saucepan over moderately high heat. When the pan is very hot but not smoking, add the granulated sugar and cook, stirring, until lightly caramelized, about 3 minutes. Add the plums and raisins and cook for 2 minutes. Stir in the rum; carefully ignite it with a long match and then cook over moderate heat, stirring frequently, until the plums are almost soft, about 3 minutes. Remove the plums from the heat and let them cool slightly.

5. Unmold the phyllo hats and set on plates. Fill the hats with the warm plum mixture and top with the sorbet, if using. Serve immediately.

—Jacques Pépin, Alain Sailhac, André Soltner and Jacques Torres

ONE SERVING (INCLUDING SORBET) Calories 330 kcal, Total Fat 8 gm, Saturated Fat 3 gm

BELOW: **Plum Clafoutis.**

BOTTOM: **Roasted Plum and Kataifi Shortcakes.**

Plum Clafoutis

8 SERVINGS

Small local plums are not the only fruit that can be used in this recipe; you can use cherries, which are actually the traditional French choice, or even peaches. Cherries should be pitted, small plums halved and pitted, and peaches halved, pitted and cut into thin slices.

- 1 tablespoon unsalted butter
- 1 pound fresh fruit, such as Mirabelle plums, halved and pitted, or cherries, pitted
- ⅓ cup all-purpose flour
- 2 tablespoons cornstarch

Salt

- ¼ cup plus 1 tablespoon sugar
- 3 large eggs, lightly beaten
- ¾ cup whole milk
- ½ cup heavy cream or half-and-half
- 1 teaspoon pure vanilla extract

1. Preheat the oven to 400°. Use the butter to coat a shallow 2-quart glass or ceramic baking dish. Arrange the fruit in the dish, cut side up.

2. In a small bowl, stir together the flour, cornstarch and a pinch of salt. In a medium bowl, whisk ¼ cup of the sugar with the eggs, milk, cream and vanilla until smooth. Whisk in the dry ingredients until smooth. Pour the batter evenly over the fruit and bake for about 30 minutes, or until set and beginning to brown around the edge. Remove from the oven.

3. Preheat the broiler. Sprinkle the clafoutis with the remaining 1 tablespoon of sugar. Broil as close to the heat as possible for about 1 minute, or until the sugar is caramelized; serve immediately.   —Annie Romana

Roasted Plum and Kataifi Shortcakes

6 SERVINGS

Kataifi is a phyllo-like dough that is made into fine threads by being passed through a sieve onto a hot griddle. As for the plums, roasting can bring out the flavor of even the least-promising specimens.

SHORTCAKES

- 4 ounces kataifi (see Note), thawed
- 4 tablespoons unsalted butter, melted and cooled
- 1 tablespoon sugar
- 1 teaspoon cinnamon

FILLING

- ¼ cup water
- ¼ cup granulated sugar
- 2 tablespoons fresh lime juice
- 4 firm plums, each cut into 8 wedges
- 1 tablespoon unsalted butter, melted

⅔ cup ricotta cheese (5 ounces), pressed through a fine sieve

2 tablespoons confectioners' sugar, plus more for dusting

1 cup heavy cream

1. MAKE THE SHORTCAKES: Preheat the oven to 375°. Butter a large baking sheet. On a work surface, gently fluff and separate the strands of the kataifi. Sprinkle with half of the butter and the sugar and cinnamon; toss gently to coat. Keep covered loosely with plastic wrap as you shape the rounds.

2. Using a 3-inch ring mold or a large biscuit cutter, shape ⅓ cup of the kataifi into a 3-inch round on the baking sheet. Dip a pastry brush into the remaining butter and tamp down the dough; remove the ring mold. Repeat with the remaining kataifi and butter to make 12 rounds, spacing them evenly on the baking sheet. Bake for about 15 minutes, or until golden.

3. MAKE THE FILLING: In a saucepan, combine the water with 3 tablespoons of the granulated sugar and the lime juice and bring to a boil. Cook, stirring, until the sugar dissolves.

4. Increase the oven temperature to 450°. In a large bowl, toss the plums with the remaining 1 tablespoon of granulated sugar and the butter. Spread the plums in a roasting pan and roast for about 15 minutes, or until caramelized.

5. In a medium bowl, combine the ricotta with the 2 tablespoons of confectioners' sugar and 2 tablespoons of the lime syrup. Whip the cream until it holds stiff peaks. Fold into the ricotta.

6. Set 6 of the kataifi rounds on 6 dessert plates. Top with all but 6 of the plum wedges, most of the ricotta cream and then the remaining 6 kataifi rounds. Garnish each shortcake with a dollop of the remaining ricotta cream and a plum wedge. Drizzle with the remaining lime syrup and dust with

Vanilla Gelato with Peaches in Balsamic Vinegar

confectioners' sugar. Serve the shortcakes immediately.   —*Grace Parisi*

NOTE Kataifi is available at Middle Eastern markets and by mail order from Adriana's Caravan, 800-316-0820.

MAKE AHEAD The recipe can be prepared through Step 3 up to 1 day ahead. Store the kataifi rounds at room temperature in an airtight container between layers of wax paper. Refrigerate the lime syrup. Bring the syrup to room temperature before continuing.

Vanilla Gelato with Peaches in Balsamic Vinegar

8 SERVINGS

Pouring vinegar over fruit is one of the secrets of the kitchens of Modena, the Italian city where balsamic vinegar originated.

2 cups heavy cream

2 cups whole milk

1 cup plus 2 tablespoons sugar

5 large eggs

1 teaspoon pure vanilla extract

8 ripe peaches or nectarines, thinly sliced

¼ cup balsamic vinegar

¾ teaspoon freshly ground pepper

1. In a medium saucepan, combine the cream, 1 cup of the milk and 1 cup of the sugar. Warm over moderate heat, stirring, just until steaming.

2. In a large bowl, whisk the eggs and the remaining 1 cup of milk until smooth. Slowly pour in the hot cream mixture, whisking constantly, until combined. Return the mixture to the saucepan; cook over moderate heat, stirring constantly, until it coats the back of a wooden spoon, about 8 minutes. Strain the custard into a bowl and refrigerate until chilled.

3. Stir the vanilla extract into the custard, transfer to an ice cream maker and freeze according to the manufacturer's instructions. Pack the vanilla gelato into a chilled container and freeze until firm.

4. In a bowl, combine the peaches with the vinegar, pepper and 2 tablespoons of sugar and let stand for 10 minutes. Divide the peaches and their juices among 8 bowls and top with scoops of the gelato. —*Mario Batali*

MAKE AHEAD The vanilla gelato can be kept in the freezer to 2 days.

Peach Croustade

MAKES ONE 10½-INCH CROUSTADE

This jam-and-fruit tart and the fig one that follows were made with luscious homemade preserves that are among the most mouth-watering items in the Provençal pantry. Using preserves like

BELOW: **Peach Croustade.** BOTTOM: **Fig Croustade.**

these, with their bright fruit flavors, will enhance a simple croustade.

Buttery Pastry (recipe follows)
½ cup peach preserves
1 pound ripe peaches, pitted and cut into ½-inch wedges
¼ cup skinless almonds
1 tablespoon unsalted butter, cut into small pieces
1 tablespoon sugar

Preheat the oven to 400°. Bake the frozen pastry tart shell for 12 minutes, or until the pastry is dry. Spread the peach preserves in the shell and then arrange the peaches on top. Scatter the almonds around the peaches. Dot with the butter and sprinkle with the sugar. Bake the croustade in the center of the oven for about 40 minutes, or until the pastry is nicely browned and the preserves are bubbling. Transfer the croustade to a rack to cool. Unmold, cut the croustade into wedges and serve.

BUTTERY PASTRY

MAKES ONE 10½-INCH TART SHELL

This simple, flaky pastry comes from cookbook author Lydie Marshall.

1 cup all-purpose flour
1 stick (4 ounces) unsalted butter
1 tablespoon sugar
Salt
2 to 3 tablespoons cold water

1. In a food processor, combine the flour, butter, sugar and a pinch of salt. Pulse until the mixture resembles coarse meal and transfer to a bowl. Add 2 tablespoons of the cold water and toss gently with a fork; add up to 1 more tablespoon of water if the dough seems dry. Gather the dough into a ball and flatten slightly. Wrap in wax paper and refrigerate for at least 1 hour.

2. On a lightly floured surface, roll out the dough to a 12-inch round. Fit the dough into a 10½-inch fluted tart pan

with a removable bottom. Trim the edge and prick the bottom. Freeze the shell for at least 30 minutes before baking. —*Nancy Harmon Jenkins*

MAKE AHEAD The frozen shell can be wrapped in plastic and kept in the freezer for up to 1 month.

Fig Croustade

MAKES ONE 10½-INCH CROUSTADE

Preserves from Provence are ideal here, but the recipe will be delicious made with any good fig preserves.

Buttery Pastry (recipe above)
1 cup black fig preserves
16 ripe black figs, halved crosswise
1 tablespoon unsalted butter, cut into small pieces
1 tablespoon sugar

Preheat the oven to 400°. Bake the frozen pastry tart shell for 12 minutes, or until the pastry is dry. Spread the fig preserves over the bottom of the shell. Arrange the figs in the shell, cut side up. Dot with the butter and sprinkle with the sugar. Bake the croustade in the center of the oven for about 40 minutes, or until the pastry is nicely browned and the preserves are bubbling. Transfer the croustade to a rack to cool. Unmold, cut into wedges and serve. —*Nancy Harmon Jenkins*

Fruit Soup with Caramel Meringues

8 SERVINGS

MERINGUES
⅔ cup plus ½ cup sugar
½ cup water
8 large egg whites, at room temperature

FRUIT SOUP
1½ cups sugar
3 tablespoons fresh lemon juice
1 quart water
4 large ripe Comice pears— peeled, cored and halved

Fruit Soup with a Caramel Meringue.

3 tablespoons pear eau-de-vie
1 cup fresh pineapple chunks
2 kiwis, halved and thinly sliced
½ pint blueberries
½ pint raspberries

I. MAKE THE MERINGUES: In a small saucepan, dissolve ½ cup of the sugar in ¼ cup of the water over low heat. Raise the heat to moderate and boil until the syrup is caramelized to a golden brown, about 10 minutes. Carefully stir in the remaining ¼ cup of

water until incorporated and divide the caramel syrup evenly among eight ½-cup ramekins or custard cups.

2. In a large clean bowl, beat the egg whites on low speed until frothy. Continue beating on high speed until the whites form soft peaks. Beat in the remaining ⅔ cup of sugar, 1 tablespoon at a time, just until the whites form stiff peaks. Swirl the caramel in the ramekins to line the bottoms and then spoon in the meringue. Smooth

the tops and arrange the ramekins in a large roasting pan.

3. Put the roasting pan in the oven. Add ½ inch of hot water to the pan and bake for 30 minutes, or until the meringues are set and the tops are browned. Remove the ramekins from the water bath and let cool on a rack. Cover and refrigerate until chilled, about 4 hours.

4.MAKE THE FRUIT SOUP: In a medium saucepan, combine the sugar, lemon juice and water. Bring to a simmer over moderate heat, stirring to dissolve the sugar. Add the pears and simmer until tender when pierced, about 20 minutes. Let the pears cool in the liquid.

5. In a food processor, puree the pears with the eau-de-vie, adding about ½ cup of the poaching liquid to make a souplike consistency; reserve the remaining poaching liquid. Refrigerate the pear puree until it is chilled, about 2 hours.

6. Unmold the caramel meringues onto individual rimmed plates and then pour the pear puree around the meringues. Add the pineapple chunks, kiwi slices, blueberries and raspberries to the reserved pear poaching liquid to moisten them and then transfer the fruit to a strainer to drain. Arrange the fruit around the meringues and serve.

—*Georges Perrier*

MAKE AHEAD The desserts can be made 2 hours ahead and refrigerated.
ONE SERVING Calories 392 kcal, Total Fat .7 gm, Saturated Fat .1 gm

Poached Pears with Mascarpone Cream and Chocolate Sauce, with Hazelnut Butter Cookies (p. 398).

Poached Pears with Mascarpone Cream and Chocolate Sauce

8 SERVINGS

    2 cups sugar
    2 cups dry white wine
    2 cups water
Zest strips from ½ orange
Zest strips from ½ lemon
    1 cinnamon stick, broken in half
    1 vanilla bean, split lengthwise
    8 ripe Bartlett pears, peeled
    ½ cup mascarpone
    ½ cup heavy cream
Bittersweet Chocolate Sauce
        (recipe follows)

1. In a large saucepan, combine the sugar, wine, water, orange and lemon zests, cinnamon stick and vanilla bean and bring to a boil, stirring to dissolve the sugar. Set the pears in the syrup, stems up, and simmer over moderately low heat, setting them upright if they roll around, until tender when pierced with a knife, about 20 minutes. Using a slotted spoon, transfer the pears to a dish to cool.

2. Strain the syrup into a medium saucepan. Boil over moderate heat until the syrup thickens to the consistency of maple syrup and registers 220° on a candy thermometer, about 10 minutes. Let cool to room temperature and then refrigerate until chilled.

3. In a small bowl, whisk ¼ cup of the reduced syrup into the mascarpone and chill. Using an apple corer or a teaspoon, core the pears all the way through.

4. In a large bowl, beat the cream until stiff peaks form. Fold in the chilled mascarpone mixture. Spoon the mascarpone cream into a pastry bag fitted with a medium star or plain tip. Stand the pears on a platter and pipe the mascarpone cream into their centers.

5. Spoon a heaping tablespoon of the chocolate sauce onto each of 8 dessert plates. Set the pears on the sauce and spoon a little more sauce over each pear. Pipe the remaining mascarpone cream around the pears and serve.

MAKE AHEAD The pears can be prepared through Step 4 and refrigerated for up to 1 day; refrigerate the remaining mascarpone cream in the pastry bag.

WINE This dessert has a sweet intensity best matched by an equally penetrating dessert wine—a Muscat de Beaumes-de-Venise from France, such as the 1995 Georges Duboeuf or the nonvintage Prosper Maufoux, or a Muscat-based California wine, such as the 1996 Quady Essensia.

BITTERSWEET CHOCOLATE SAUCE

MAKES ABOUT 1 CUP

Cocoa powder gives this luscious sauce its bittersweet edge.

    ½ cup heavy cream
    3 tablespoons unsweetened cocoa powder, preferably Dutch process
    4 ounces semisweet chocolate, finely chopped
    ½ teaspoon pure vanilla extract

In a small saucepan, bring the heavy cream to a simmer. Whisk in the cocoa powder until smooth. Remove from the heat, add the chocolate and let stand until melted. Whisk in the vanilla extract and serve the sauce warm.

—The Point, Lake Saranac, New York

MAKE AHEAD The sauce can be refrigerated for up to 2 days. Rewarm over low heat, stirring frequently.

Honey-Poached Quinces

12 SERVINGS

Firm fruit like Bosc pears or Golden Delicious apples can be prepared similarly; poach them for thirty minutes.

    12 cups water
    ¾ cup sugar
    ½ cup mild honey
    ⅓ cup fresh lemon juice
Zest strips from 1 lemon removed with vegetable peeler
    12 medium quinces (6 ounces each)—peeled, quartered and cored
    ¼ cup chopped almonds
    1 cup whole milk yogurt, for serving
Kourambiedes (p. 396), for serving

1. In a large pot, combine the water with the sugar, honey, lemon juice and lemon zest and bring to a boil, stirring occasionally, until the sugar dissolves. Add the quinces and return to a boil. Cover partially and cook over low heat until tender, about 2 hours. Remove the quinces with a slotted spoon. Boil the syrup until it is reduced to 4 cups, about 20 minutes. Return the quinces to the syrup while it cools.

2. Meanwhile, in a small heavy skillet, toast the almonds over moderate heat, stirring constantly, until golden, 6 to 8 minutes. Transfer to a plate to cool. Serve the quinces at room temperature or chilled, with their syrup and the yogurt, sprinkled with the almonds. Pass the Kourambiedes separately.

—Grace Parisi

MAKE AHEAD The poached quinces can be refrigerated in the honey syrup for up to 3 days.

Baked Rhubarb Compote with Crème Fraîche

4 SERVINGS ✳

    1 pound rhubarb, stalks peeled
    ½ cup sugar
    ¼ teaspoon freshly grated lemon zest
    2 teaspoons unsalted butter, cut into small pieces
Crème fraîche or sour cream, for serving

Preheat the oven to 350°. Butter a 1-quart shallow baking dish. If the rhubarb stalks are very wide, cut them

Lemony Corn and Fruit Salad

lengthwise into ½-inch strips. Cut all of the stalks crosswise into 1½-inch lengths. Toss the rhubarb with the sugar and lemon zest and spread in the prepared baking dish. Dot with the butter. Cover and bake for about 30 minutes, or until the rhubarb is tender when pierced but still holds its shape. Serve warm or at room temperature with crème fraîche. —*Alice Waters*

WINE Try a refreshing dessert wine, such as the 1996 Pecota Moscato d'Andrea.

Lemony Corn and Fruit Salad

10 SERVINGS

While this dessert may not be something to attempt on a work night, it's eminently doable when broken down into components, most of which can be prepared ahead.

LEMON CREAM

- 1⅓ cups sugar
- 4 large eggs
- ¾ cup fresh lemon juice
- Finely grated zest of 3 lemons
- 2 sticks plus 5 tablespoons (10½ ounces) unsalted butter, cut into small pieces and softened
- 2 teaspoons unflavored gelatin
- ¼ cup cold water
- 1 cup plain whole-milk yogurt
- 1⅓ cups heavy cream

WHITE CHOCOLATE ROUNDS

- 9 ounces white chocolate, finely chopped

STRAWBERRY COULIS

- 1 pint strawberries, hulled
- ¼ cup sugar
- ¼ cup orange–passion fruit juice (optional)
- ¼ cup guava nectar (optional)
- 3 tablespoons lemon juice
- Pinch of freshly ground pepper

SALAD AND GARNISH

- ½ medium pineapple—peeled, cored and cut into ¼-inch dice (2 cups)

- 2 medium Granny Smith apples— peeled, cored and cut into ¼-inch dice
- One 10-ounce package frozen corn kernels, thawed
- Red currants or whole strawberries, for garnish

I. MAKE THE LEMON CREAM: In a large metal bowl, using an electric mixer, beat 1 cup of the sugar with the eggs, lemon juice and lemon zest. Set the bowl over a saucepan of simmering water and beat the mixture until it is thick enough to leave a trail when the whisk is lifted, about 15 minutes. Let cool slightly and then strain into a blender. Gradually add the butter, blending at high speed until the cream is light and perfectly smooth, about 5 minutes. Scrape down the side of the container as needed. Transfer the cream to a bowl, cover and refrigerate for up to 2 days.

2. In a small saucepan, sprinkle the gelatin over the water and let stand for 5 minutes. Cook over low heat, stirring, until the gelatin dissolves. In a large bowl, combine the gelatin mixture with 2 tablespoons of the yogurt and the remaining ⅓ cup of sugar. Mix in the remaining yogurt and the cold lemon cream. Lightly whip the heavy cream and fold it into the lemon cream. Refrigerate, covered, for at least 1 hour and up to 1 day.

3. MAKE THE WHITE CHOCO- LATE ROUNDS: Melt the chocolate in a medium metal bowl set over a saucepan of simmering water, stirring until smooth. Line 2 baking sheets with parchment paper. Using an offset spatula, spread half of the chocolate evenly over each sheet. Chill until almost set, 5 to 10 minutes. Using a 4-inch round biscuit cutter, stamp out 10 rounds. Return the baking sheets to the refrigerator and chill again to firm up the chocolate, at least 15 minutes.

4. MAKE THE STRAWBERRY COULIS: Combine all of the ingredients in a blender; blend until pureed. Transfer to a bowl, cover and refrigerate for up to 1 hour.

5. MAKE THE FRUIT SALAD AND GARNISH: In a bowl, combine the pineapple, apples and corn and toss to mix.

6. For each dessert, set a 4-inch dessert ring or empty 12-ounce tuna fish can with the ends removed in the center of a soup or dessert plate and pack it halfway with fruit salad. Fill the ring to the top with the lemon cream. Lift off the ring. Carefully peel a white chocolate round off the parchment paper and set it on top. Spoon some of the coulis around the plate and garnish the coulis with the currants. Serve immediately. —*Pierre Hermé*

CHAPTER 16 other desserts

Almond Pudding (p. 430)

Caramelized Chocolate-Chestnut Custards

Caramelized Chocolate-Chestnut Custards

8 SERVINGS

The chestnut in these custards is actually chestnut flour, which has a smoky aroma and a mild flavor. The chestnut flour thickens the custards; when they are cooked slowly, at 300°, they have the smoothest, silkiest texture imaginable. If you like, when serving add chocolate sauce to the plates.

1⅔ cups sugar
⅓ cup water
2 cups heavy cream
1 cup milk
3 ounces milk chocolate, coarsely chopped
8 large egg yolks
½ cup plus 2 tablespoons imported Italian chestnut flour (2 ounces; see Note), sifted
½ cup unsweetened cocoa powder

1. Preheat the oven to 300°. In a small saucepan, combine ⅔ cup of the sugar with the water and boil over moderate heat, swirling the pan a few times, until a deep amber caramel forms, about 10 minutes. Working quickly, divide the caramel among eight ½-cup ramekins. Set the ramekins in a large roasting pan that holds them with room to spare.

2. In a medium saucepan, heat the cream and milk until bubbles appear around the edge. In a heatproof bowl set over a pan of simmering water, melt the chocolate, stirring a few times with a wooden spoon. Remove the bowl from the pan.

3. In a large bowl, whisk the egg yolks with the remaining 1 cup of sugar until blended. Whisk in the chestnut flour and cocoa. Gradually whisk in the warm cream mixture and then the melted chocolate. Pour the chocolate mixture through a fine sieve into the ramekins, filling them almost to the top. Carefully pour enough hot water into the roasting pan to reach halfway

up the sides of the ramekins. Cover the pan tightly with aluminum foil. Bake in the center of the oven for about 2 hours and 45 minutes, or until the custards are just set but still a bit wobbly in the center. Transfer the ramekins to a rack to cool to room temperature. Cover the custards with plastic wrap and refrigerate for at least 8 hours or up to 3 days.

4. Run a small, thin knife around the edge of each ramekin. Top each with a dessert plate and invert to release the custard and caramel sauce. Serve chilled. —*Umberto Creatini*

NOTE Chestnut flour is available at health food stores and Italian markets.

Chocolate Flan

12 SERVINGS

Smooth and rich, with a slightly bitter caramel taste, this flan in a ring is a wonderful make-ahead dessert, since it needs to chill overnight.

1¾ cups sugar
2 tablespoons fresh lemon juice
4 cups milk
6 ounces bittersweet or semisweet chocolate, coarsely chopped
8 large eggs
½ teaspoon pure vanilla extract
¼ teaspoon cinnamon

1. Preheat the oven to 300°. In a heavy medium saucepan, combine 1 cup of the sugar with the lemon juice. Stir with a wooden spoon over moderate heat until the sugar dissolves and then cook, stirring occasionally, until the sugar turns deep brown, about 10 minutes. Pour the hot caramel into an 8-cup metal ring mold; holding the mold carefully by the rim, tilt the mold to coat the interior with the caramel. If needed, use a wooden spoon to push the caramel up the side.

2. In a heavy medium saucepan, combine the milk with the remaining ¾ cup

of sugar. Cook over moderate heat, stirring occasionally, until the sugar dissolves. Add the chocolate, cover and remove the pan from the heat. Set aside until the chocolate is melted. Stir.

3. In a medium bowl, lightly beat the eggs. Gradually whisk in the hot milk mixture, vanilla and cinnamon until thoroughly combined. Strain the custard into a large glass measure and then pour it into the ring mold. Cover the flan loosely with aluminum foil and set the mold in a baking dish or roasting pan. Pour in enough hot water to reach halfway up the side of the mold. Bake the flan in the center of the oven for about 1 hour and 10 minutes, or until it is set but still jiggly in the center. Remove the mold from the baking dish. Let the flan cool to room temperature and then refrigerate it overnight. Run a small sharp knife around the side of the ring mold, cover with a large rimmed plate and invert. Cut the flan into wedges and serve.

—*Marcia Kiesel*

MAKE AHEAD The flan can be refrigerated for up to 2 days.

Egg Custard

12 SERVINGS

Simple, smooth and subtle, this nutmeg-scented custard comforts as no exotic and complicated dessert can.

6 large eggs
¾ cup sugar
¼ teaspoon salt
4½ cups milk
½ teaspoon pure vanilla extract
¼ teaspoon freshly grated nutmeg

1. Preheat the oven to 300°. In a large bowl, beat the eggs. Add the sugar and salt and stir until dissolved. Stir in the milk, vanilla and nutmeg. Strain the mixture and pour it into twelve 4-ounce custard cups.

2. Set the cups in a large roasting pan and place in the oven. Pour 1 inch of

ABOVE: **Egg Custard.** TOP: **Panna Cotta and Saba.**

hot water into the roasting pan and bake the custards for about 30 minutes, or until just set. Remove the custards from the waterbath when cool enough to handle. Serve the custards warm, at room temperature or chilled.
—*Edna Lewis and Scott Peacock*
MAKE AHEAD The custards can be refrigerated overnight.

Panna Cotta and Saba
10 SERVINGS
Judy Rodgers, chef at Zuni in San Francisco, flavors this panna cotta—literally cooked, cooked cream—with bitter almonds, which she gets from the San Joaquin valley. If you can find bitter almonds, you'll need only five to flavor the cream, and you won't need the almond extract. Saba is a Trebbiano grape syrup from Modena, Italy.

 1 cup almonds (5 ounces)
 1 quart heavy cream, preferably not ultrapasteurized
 2 cups milk
Pinch of sea salt
 1 tablespoon unflavored gelatin
 ½ cup sugar
 ¾ teaspoon pure almond extract
Saba (see Note), for drizzling

1. Preheat the oven to 350°. In a pie pan, toast the almonds for about 10 minutes, until fragrant. Chop the nuts.
2. In a large saucepan, combine the almonds with the cream, 1½ cups of the milk and the sea salt and bring just to a simmer. Remove from the heat and let steep for 15 minutes. Strain the liquid through a fine sieve.
3. In a saucepan, sprinkle the gelatin over the remaining ½ cup of milk. Let stand until the gelatin is soft, 2 to 3 minutes. Add the sugar and warm over moderate heat, stirring, until the gelatin is completely dissolved, about 1 minute. Add the gelatin mixture to the cream and let cool. Stir in the almond extract. Pour into ten ½-cup ramekins. Cover and refrigerate overnight.
4. To unmold, run a knife around the edge of each panna cotta, top with an inverted plate and flip. Give the mold 1 quick tap and lift off the ramekin. Drizzle 1 to 2 teaspoons of Saba over and around each panna cotta and serve at once.   —*Judy Rodgers*
NOTE Saba is available at specialty food store or by mail order from Zingerman's Deli, 888-636-8162.
MAKE AHEAD The panna cotta can be refrigerated for up to 3 days.
WINE The 1994 Topaz Late Harvest Sauvignon-Semillon from the Napa Valley is worth seeking out. Or try the 1993 Maculan Torcolato from Italy.

Almond Pudding
6 SERVINGS
The signature component of this lightly sweet pudding is almond flour, which is available at health food stores. (So is the rice flour.) Or you can substitute two ounces of finely ground blanched almonds for the almond flour, which will give the pudding a coarser texture.

 3 cups milk
 ¼ cup rice flour
 ½ cup sugar
 ½ cup almond flour
 ¼ cup unsalted pistachios or sliced almonds, lightly crushed (optional)

1. In a medium bowl, combine ½ cup of the milk with the rice flour. In a medium saucepan, combine the remaining 2½ cups of milk, the sugar and the almond flour and bring the mixture to a boil over moderate heat. Stir one-quarter of the boiling milk mixture into the dissolved rice flour; add this mixture to the pan and bring to a boil, stirring frequently. Reduce the heat to low and simmer, stirring frequently, for 30 minutes.
2. Pour the pudding mixture into a bowl. Press a piece of plastic wrap directly onto the surface of the pudding to prevent the formation of a skin and refrigerate until chilled. Scoop the pudding into stemmed glasses and sprinkle with the crushed nuts.
—*Christer Larsson*
MAKE AHEAD The pudding can be refrigerated overnight.

Coconut Red Rice Pudding
6 SERVINGS
Colusari red rice (grown near Colusa, California) is medium-grained and brightens from brown to light burgundy when cooked.

 4 cups water
 1¼ cups red rice (½ pound; see Note)

Almond Pudding

Mocha Fudge Pudding

Salt

One 13.5-ounce can unsweetened
    coconut milk

1 cup heavy cream

½ vanilla bean, split

½ cup sugar

I. In a medium saucepan, combine the
water and red rice and bring to a boil.
Add a large pinch of salt, cover and
cook over low heat until tender, about
20 minutes. Uncover and simmer, stirring occasionally, over moderately low
heat for 10 minutes. Add the coconut
milk and simmer until the liquid becomes very thick, about 35 minutes.

2. Meanwhile, in a small saucepan,
combine the cream and vanilla bean
and bring to a simmer. Cook for 3 minutes. Remove from the heat, cover
and let steep for 20 minutes. Scrape
the seeds from the vanilla bean into
the cream; discard the bean.

3. Stir the sugar into the cream mixture until dissolved. Stir the cream
mixture into the rice and let stand,
covered, for 30 minutes. Serve warm.
                              —*Marcia Kiesel*

NOTE Red rice is available at health
food stores and by mail from Gold
Mine Natural Food Co., 800-475-3663;

Indian Harvest, 800-294-2433 and
SoHo Provisions, 212-334-4311.

MAKE AHEAD The rice pudding can
be refrigerated overnight. Reheat the
pudding gently before serving.

Mocha Fudge Pudding

4 SERVINGS ✳

This extra rich, trufflelike dessert was
inspired by a recipe from Ann Hodg-
man's book *Beat That!,* published by
Chapters. The pudding is so good, you'll
want to make enough for seconds.

½ **cup heavy cream**

1 **tablespoon instant espresso
    powder**

6 **ounces bittersweet chocolate,
    coarsely chopped**

¼ **cup sugar**

1 **large egg**

1 **teaspoon pure vanilla extract**

Pinch of salt

Lightly sweetened whipped cream,
    for serving

I. Combine the cream and espresso
powder in a small saucepan and bring
to a boil over high heat, stirring.

2. Meanwhile, in a food processor,
combine the chocolate and sugar and
pulse until the chocolate is finely

ground. Add the egg, vanilla and salt;
pulse to a paste. With the machine on,
add the hot cream mixture in a steady
stream. Blend until smooth and silky,
about 1 minute. Transfer the pudding to
4 small dessert bowls or large ramekins
and chill until set, about 1 hour. Serve
with whipped cream. —*Jan Newberry*
MAKE AHEAD The pudding can be
refrigerated overnight.

Vanilla Ice Milk and
Espresso Parfaits

8 SERVINGS

Refreshing and flavorful, this dessert
layers sweet eggless ice milk with a
potent espresso syrup.

1 quart milk

2 cups sugar

1 tablespoon pure vanilla extract

2 cups brewed espresso

Lightly sweetened whipped cream,
    for serving

Cinnamon, for garnish

I. In a medium saucepan, combine
the milk with 1 cup of the sugar and
stir over moderate heat until the sugar
dissolves. Pour the milk into a large
bowl and let cool to room temperature. Add the vanilla and refrigerate
until chilled. Freeze the ice milk in an
ice cream maker according to the manufacturer's instructions.

2. In a medium saucepan, boil the
espresso with the remaining 1 cup of
sugar over moderately high heat until
reduced to about 1½ cups, about 10
minutes. Pour the syrup into a bowl
and let cool to room temperature.

3. Scoop the ice milk into Champagne
flutes and drizzle with espresso syrup.
Garnish each serving of ice milk with a
dollop of whipped cream and a pinch
of cinnamon.   —*Anne Quatrano*
MAKE AHEAD The vanilla ice milk
can be frozen for up to 1 day. The espresso syrup can be refrigerated for
up to 3 days.

Prune Ice Cream with Armagnac

MAKES ABOUT 4 CUPS

The ice cream recipe has been adapted from André Daguin's book *Foie Gras, Magret, and Other Good Food from Gascony,* published by Random House.

1¼ cups pitted prunes (7 ounces)
½   cup Armagnac
2   cups milk
½   cup sugar
4   large egg yolks

1. In a small saucepan, combine the prunes with the Armagnac, cover and simmer over low heat until the prunes are soft, about 5 minutes. Remove the pan from the heat and set aside, covered, until cool. Transfer the prunes and Armagnac to a food processor and puree them.

2. In a heavy medium saucepan, combine the milk with ¼ cup of the sugar. Cook over moderate heat, stirring, until bubbles appear around the edge. Remove from the heat.

3. In a heatproof bowl, whisk the egg yolks with the remaining ¼ cup of sugar until the eggs are pale and thick. Gradually whisk in the hot milk mixture. Pour the egg and milk mixture back into the saucepan and cook it over moderate heat, whisking constantly, until the custard reaches 175° on a candy thermometer, about 5 minutes. Immediately pour the custard into a heatproof bowl and stir often until cooled to room temperature. Cover the custard and refrigerate until well chilled.

4. Add the prune puree to the custard, transfer to an ice cream maker and freeze according to the manufacturer's instructions. Pack the ice cream into a chilled container and freeze.

—*André Daguin*

MAKE AHEAD The ice cream can be frozen for up to 3 days.

Caramelized Pumpkin Trifle

8 SERVINGS

½   cup sugar
3   tablespoons cornstarch
⅛   teaspoon salt
2   cups half-and-half
1   teaspoon cinnamon
1   tablespoon pure vanilla extract
Pumpkin Bread (p. 295), or one 1½-pound loaf of gingerbread, sliced ¼ inch thick
Candied Pumpkin (recipe follows)
Softly whipped cream, for garnish
2   tablespoons finely chopped candied ginger, for garnish
Mint sprigs, for garnish

Prune Ice Cream with Armagnac

1. In a bowl, whisk together the sugar, cornstarch and salt. Whisk in ⅓ cup of the half-and-half. In a heavy medium saucepan, combine the remaining 1⅔ cups of half-and-half with the sugar mixture and the cinnamon. Cook over moderate heat, stirring constantly, until the pudding thickens and comes to a boil. Remove from the heat and stir for 1 minute. Stir in the vanilla. Transfer the pudding to a bowl and press plastic wrap on the surface. Refrigerate until chilled.

2. Arrange one-third of the Pumpkin Bread slices in a large glass bowl or divide them among 8 serving glasses,

Caramelized Pumpkin Trifle

overlapping them slightly. Spread one-third of the cinnamon pudding evenly on top. Top with one-third of the Candied Pumpkin with its syrup. Repeat the layering process two times. Garnish the trifle with a few dollops of whipped cream, the candied ginger and mint sprigs.

MAKE AHEAD The pudding can be refrigerated overnight.

CANDIED PUMPKIN
MAKES ABOUT 3 CUPS

- 4 tablespoons unsalted butter
- 3 cups diced (1/2-inch) sugar pumpkin or butternut squash
- 1/3 cup sugar
- 3/4 cup maple syrup
- 1 tablespoon minced fresh ginger
- 1/2 teaspoon cinnamon

Melt the butter in a large heavy skillet. Add the pumpkin and cook over moderately low heat, stirring occasionally, until tender, about 20 minutes. Stir in the sugar until dissolved. Stir in the maple syrup, ginger and cinnamon and remove from the heat. Let cool and refrigerate until chilled, at least 2 hours or overnight. —*Rori Spinelli*

Baked Phyllo with Vanilla Cream
8 SERVINGS

This golden, flaky dessert is filled with a pastry cream that has been thickened with Cream of Wheat.

- 1 1/3 cups milk
- 1 cup granulated sugar
- 2/3 cup 10-minute Cream of Wheat
- 2 sticks (1/2 pound) plus 2 teaspoons unsalted butter
- 2 large egg yolks
- 1 tablespoon pure vanilla extract
- 12 sheets phyllo dough (see Note)
- 1/2 cup confectioners' sugar

1. In a medium saucepan, combine the milk, sugar and Cream of Wheat and cook over moderate heat, stirring, until the mixture begins to thicken, about 10 minutes. Stir in the 2 teaspoons of butter and let cool slightly. Beat in the egg yolks and vanilla until smooth. Cover and refrigerate until chilled, at least 1 hour and up to 1 day.

2. Preheat the oven to 350°. In a small saucepan, melt the remaining 2 sticks of butter. Spread 1 sheet of phyllo on a work surface and brush with some of the melted butter. Cover with a second sheet, brush with more butter and continue until you have a stack of 6 buttered sheets. Repeat with the remaining phyllo and as much of the butter as necessary, to make 2 stacks.

3. For each phyllo stack, spoon half of the vanilla cream filling evenly across a long side, leaving a 1/2-inch border at the ends. Roll up the phyllo stacks around the filling to form 2 rolls, brushing the dough with butter as you roll. Pinch the ends and transfer the rolls, seam side down, to a large baking sheet. Bake for about 30 minutes, or until the phyllo is lightly browned. Let cool completely on the baking sheet and then sift the confectioners' sugar over the tops. Trim off the ends. Slice each roll into 8 pieces and serve. —*Fany Boutari*

NOTE Phyllo dough is available in 1-pound packages (18 to 24 sheets) in the freezer section of most supermarkets. Thaw it overnight in the refrigerator before using, or it may crack.

WINE The nonvintage Boutari Samos.

Pistachio Baklava
MAKES ABOUT 2 DOZEN PIECES

- 1 pound shelled unsalted pistachios (about 3 1/3 cups)
- 1 1/2 cups sugar
- 2 sticks (1/2 pound) unsalted butter, melted
- 12 sheets of phyllo dough (about 1/2 pound)
- 1/2 cup water

phyllo and its relatives

These flour-and-water doughs start out virtually alike and then each is pressed or rolled into a thin pastry sturdy enough to hold hefty fillings.

Phyllo (or filo) Rolled or stretched very thin. Used in Greek and Turkish pastries such as *tiropita* and baklava.

Kataifi Made into fine threads by pressing the dough through a sieve onto a hot griddle. Sweetened with sugar syrup and used in Greek and Turkish pastries.

Yufka Rolled slightly thicker than phyllo; often fried to make the Turkish savory pastries called *sigara borek*.

- 1/2 cup honey
- 1/2 teaspoon cinnamon

1. Preheat the oven to 400°. Butter a 13-by-9-inch glass baking dish. In a food processor, pulse the pistachios with 1/2 cup of the sugar just until the nuts are finely ground. Transfer to a medium bowl and stir in half the butter.

2. Stack the phyllo sheets and cut them in half crosswise. Set a half sheet of phyllo in the prepared baking dish and brush lightly with some of the remaining melted butter. Repeat with 11 more half sheets of phyllo, buttering each sheet; don't worry if the pastry tears a little. Cover the remaining phyllo with a towel.

3. Spread the pistachio mixture evenly on the phyllo in the baking dish. Top with the remaining phyllo sheets, buttering each sheet as above. Drizzle any remaining butter over the top. Using a sharp knife, make diagonal slices 1 1/2 inches apart all the way through the baklava; slice similarly in the opposite direction to make a diamond pattern. Bake for about 20 minutes, or until evenly browned on top.

4. Meanwhile, in a small saucepan, combine the remaining 1 cup of sugar with the water and bring to a boil over

moderate heat, stirring to dissolve the sugar; remove from the heat. Stir in the honey and cinnamon. Pour the syrup evenly over the baklava when it first comes out of the oven. Let cool completely before serving.

—Christer Larsson

MAKE AHEAD The baklava can be refrigerated for 3 days. Let return to room temperature before serving.

Ricotta Tortes with Zabaglione
8 SERVINGS

The only tricky part of making this great simple-to-assemble dessert is having eight ring molds or their equivalent on hand.

Ricotta Tortes with Zabaglione

Eight ½-inch-thick slices pound cake (12 ounces)
¼ cup Galliano or Southern Comfort
¾ cup pine nuts (4 ounces)
¾ cup golden raisins (4 ounces)
16 ounces fresh whole-milk ricotta cheese (2½ cups)
¼ cup wildflower honey
2 tablespoons heavy cream
Zabaglione (recipe follows)

1. Preheat the oven to 350°. Using eight 3-by-2-inch ring molds or 8-ounce pineapple-ring cans with both ends removed, cut a round from each cake slice. Set the molds on a baking sheet. Without removing the mold, brush the top of each cake round with ½ tablespoon of Galliano.

2. In a pie plate, toast the pine nuts for about 7 minutes, or until they are golden brown. In a small heatproof bowl, cover the raisins with boiling water and let stand until softened, about 5 minutes. Drain the raisins and pat dry.

3. In a large bowl, combine the ricotta, honey, heavy cream, pine nuts and raisins. Spoon ½ cup of the ricotta mixture into each mold and spread to form an even layer. Cover and refrigerate until firm, at least 2 hours or overnight.

4. Set a torte on each plate and carefully lift off the mold. Spoon 3 tablespoons of Zabaglione around each torte and serve.

ZABAGLIONE
8 SERVINGS

Zabaglione is also delicious served on its own or as a sauce for fresh fruit.

3 large egg yolks
½ cup Galliano or Southern Comfort
¼ cup sugar

In a stainless steel bowl, combine the egg yolks, Galliano and sugar. Set the bowl over a saucepan with 1 inch of gently simmering water and whisk constantly until the mixture is pale golden, thick and fluffy, about 4 minutes. Do not overcook or the eggs will scramble. Serve at once.

—Umberto Creatini

Maple-Nut Granola
8 SERVINGS

Feel free to try unusual grains, like buttery Kamut and hard-grained spelt, both of which are available at health food stores.

Vegetable oil cooking spray
½ cup maple syrup
2 tablespoons canola oil
1 teaspoon pure vanilla extract

1 teaspoon finely grated orange
zest

¼ teaspoon cinnamon

2 cups rolled oats

1 cup rolled barley flakes

½ cup rolled Kamut flakes

½ cup rolled spelt flakes

½ cup sliced almonds

¼ cup unsalted roasted
sunflower seeds

1 cup coarsely chopped mixed
dried fruit (about 5 ounces)

Preheat the oven to 350°. Lightly coat
a 13-by-9-inch roasting pan with cooking spray. In a bowl, combine the maple
syrup, oil, vanilla, orange zest and cinnamon. Stir in the oats, barley, Kamut,
spelt and almonds. Spread the granola
in an even layer in the prepared pan.
Bake for about 30 minutes, stirring
every 5 minutes, until toasted and
golden. Let cool; stir in the sunflower
seeds and dried fruit.

—*Jim Kyndberg and Betsy Nelson*

MAKE AHEAD The granola can be
stored in an airtight container for up to
1 week or frozen for up to 1 month.

ONE SERVING Calories 346 kcal,
Total Fat 11 gm, Saturated Fat 1 gm

SERVE WITH Fresh fruit and skim
milk or nonfat yogurt.

Cream of Wheat Halvah

12 SERVINGS

Halvah, a sweet dessert, takes many
different forms throughout the Mediterranean, the Middle East and India.
This version is molded and its texture
falls somewhere between that of a
pudding and a cake.

1 stick (4 ounces) unsalted butter

⅓ cup slivered almonds (about
1½ ounces)

1½ cups 10-minute Cream of Wheat
(about 10 ounces)

1½ cups milk

1½ cups water

1¼ cups granulated sugar

Cream of Wheat Halvah

2 teaspoons confectioners' sugar

½ teaspoon cinnamon

1. In a heavy medium saucepan, melt
the butter over moderate heat. Add
the almonds and cook until lightly colored, about 5 minutes. Using a slotted
spoon, transfer the almonds to a plate.
Add the Cream of Wheat to the saucepan and cook, stirring constantly, until
lightly browned, about 10 minutes.

2. In a second medium saucepan,
combine the milk, water and granulated sugar. Cook over moderate heat,
stirring to dissolve the sugar, until bubbles appear around the edge. Gradually add the hot milk mixture to the
Cream of Wheat and whisk over low
heat until smooth and thick, about 5

minutes. Remove from the heat and
stir in the almonds. Cover with a towel
and let stand for 20 minutes.

3. Spoon the mixture into a 9½-inch
ring mold and smooth the surface. Let
stand until cool. Cover and refrigerate
until cold. To serve, invert the halvah
onto a large platter. Sift the confectioners' sugar and cinnamon over the
top and serve. —*Fany Boutari*

MAKE AHEAD The halvah can be
prepared up to1 day ahead.

CHAPTER 17 beverages

Pineapple Cosmopolitans (p. 444)

Sparkling Citrusade

Sparkling Citrusade

MAKES 2 QUARTS

- ⅔ cup superfine sugar
- 1½ cups fresh orange juice
- 1½ cups fresh tangerine or grapefruit juice
- ½ cup fresh lemon juice
- ¼ cup fresh lime juice
- 1 quart sparkling water
- 8 mint sprigs

Ice

Lime, lemon or orange slices, for garnish

In a large pitcher, stir the sugar into the fruit juices until dissolved. Add the sparkling water and mint. Add ice, stir and pour into tall glasses. Garnish with the fruit slices.

—Clifford Harrison and Anne Quatrano

Pineapple-Mango Juice

4 SERVINGS ✳

This tropical fruit drink combines fresh pineapple and mango juice and a spicy hit of ginger. For an adult version, add a shot of vodka. For a kid's treat, freeze the juice in ice pop molds or small paper cups, positioning a wooden stick in the center when the juice begins to solidify.

- 1 large pineapple (about 3 pounds)—peeled and cored, 1 slice reserved, the rest cut into chunks
- 3 large ripe mangoes (about 3 pounds total), cut into large chunks

One 2-inch piece of fresh ginger

- 1 teaspoon pure vanilla extract

Crushed ice, for serving

Using a juice extractor, juice the pineapple chunks, mangoes and ginger into a large glass measuring cup. Whisk in the vanilla extract. Cut the reserved pineapple slice into 4 pieces. Serve the Pineapple-Mango Juice over crushed ice, garnished with the pieces of pineapple. —Jan Newberry

Strawberry Pineapple Batido

1 SERVING

The most common *batidos*—and those most typical of juice bars in Central America—are made with fresh fruit.

- 1 cup crushed ice
- ½ cup coarsely chopped strawberries, plus 1 whole strawberry, for garnish
- ½ cup coarsely chopped pineapple
- 3 tablespoons pineapple juice
- 1 tablespoon sweetened condensed milk
- 1 tablespoon sugar
- 1 teaspoon lime juice

Combine the crushed ice, chopped strawberries, pineapple, pineapple juice, condensed milk, sugar and lime juice in a blender and blend until smooth. Pour into a tall glass, garnish with the whole strawberry and serve.

—Steven Raichlen

Mango Banana Batido

1 SERVING

- 1 cup crushed ice
- 1 medium mango, coarsely chopped
- 1 small very ripe banana, coarsely chopped
- 1 tablespoon sweetened condensed milk
- 1 teaspoon lime juice

Combine the crushed ice, mango, banana, condensed milk and lime juice in a blender; blend until smooth. Serve in a tall glass. —Steven Raichlen

Puffed Wheat Batido

1 SERVING

Unusual and nutritious, this drink is a Cuban concoction that tastes like very sweet puffed wheat cereal.

- 1 cup unsweetened puffed wheat
- ½ cup skim milk
- ½ cup crushed ice
- 1 tablespoon sweetened condensed milk
- 1 tablespoon honey

Salt

Combine the puffed wheat, skim milk, crushed ice, condensed milk, honey and a pinch of salt in a blender and blend until smooth. Serve in a tall glass. —Steven Raichlen

Pink Grapefruit Slush

1 SERVING 🌷

- ⅔ cup fresh pink grapefruit juice
- 1 ripe medium banana
- ½ cup crushed ice
- 1 teaspoon honey

Combine the grapefruit juice, banana, crushed ice and honey in a blender and puree until smooth.

—Betsy Nelson and Jim Kyndberg

ONE SERVING Calories 182 kcal, Total Fat .7 gm, Saturated Fat .2 gm

Kiwi Crush

1 SERVING 🌷

The small black seeds of the kiwi add a peppery kick. To avoid them, halve two kiwis and scoop out the center cores.

- 1 ripe medium banana
- 1 medium kiwi, peeled
- ⅓ cup fresh orange juice
- ½ cup crushed ice

Combine the banana, kiwi, orange juice and crushed ice in a blender and puree until smooth.

—Betsy Nelson and Jim Kyndberg

ONE SERVING Calories 190 kcal, Total Fat 1 gm, Saturated Fat .2 gm

Raspberry Rush

1 SERVING 🌷

You can add a little honey to sweeten this smoothie. If you don't like the texture of raspberry seeds, first puree the fruit with the milk and then strain and process the puree with the ice.

- 1 ripe medium banana
- ¾ cup fresh or frozen raspberries
- ½ cup skim milk
- ½ cup crushed ice

Combine all of the ingredients in a blender and puree until smooth.

—Betsy Nelson and Jim Kyndberg

ONE SERVING Calories 189 kcal, Total Fat 1.1 gm, Saturated Fat .4 gm

Pear-Ginger Smoothie

1 SERVING

Carrot juice gives this drink its orange color and lots of vitamin A.

- 1 ripe Anjou or Bartlett pear— peeled, cored and chopped
- ¼ cup fresh carrot juice
- ¼ cup skim milk
- ½ teaspoon finely grated fresh ginger
- ½ cup crushed ice

Combine all of the ingredients in a blender and puree until smooth.

—Betsy Nelson and Jim Kyndberg

ONE SERVING Calories 145 kcal, Total Fat .9 gm, Saturated Fat .1 gm

Blueberry Smoothie

1 SERVING

- 1 ripe medium banana
- ¾ cup fresh or frozen blueberries

Hot Cocoa

- ¼ cup nonfat vanilla yogurt
- ¾ cup skim milk

Pinch of cinnamon

- ½ cup crushed ice

Combine all of the ingredients in a blender and puree until smooth.

—Betsy Nelson and Jim Kyndberg

ONE SERVING Calories 281 kcal, Total Fat 1.3 gm, Saturated Fat .4 gm

Prune-Apple Smoothie

1 SERVING

Rich and satisfying, this drink packs in lots of fiber as well as fruity flavor.

- 3 pitted prunes
- ¾ cup apple cider or apple juice
- ¼ cup nonfat vanilla yogurt
- ⅛ teaspoon cinnamon
- ½ teaspoon pure vanilla extract

Pinch of freshly grated nutmeg

- ½ cup crushed ice

In a small bowl, cover the prunes with hot water and let stand until plump, about 15 minutes. Drain the prunes and let cool. In a blender, combine the prunes with the apple cider, yogurt, cinnamon, vanilla, nutmeg and crushed ice and puree until smooth.

—Betsy Nelson and Jim Kyndberg

ONE SERVING Calories 205 kcal, Total Fat .4 gm, Saturated Fat .1 gm

Peach Ice Cream Sodas

4 SERVINGS

Almond Butter Tuiles (p. 398) make an excellent accompaniment to these special sodas.

- 1¼ pounds ripe peaches—peeled, pitted and sliced
- 1½ cups seltzer or soda water
- ½ teaspoon fresh lemon juice

About ¼ cup sugar

Pinch of salt

- 4 scoops of vanilla ice cream
- 1 cup fresh raspberries

1. In a food processor, puree the peach slices until smooth. In a bowl, combine the peach puree with 1 cup of the seltzer, the lemon juice and ¼ cup of sugar; add more sugar if desired. Stir in the salt.

2. Place 1 scoop of vanilla ice cream and ¼ cup of raspberries into each of 4 tall glasses. Pour in the peach mixture and then top with the remaining seltzer.

—Emily Luchetti

Hot Cocoa

MAKES ABOUT 10 CUPS

Gerry Moss is pastry chef at Tre Vigne in St. Helena, California. The secret to his cocoa is infusing the hot milk with strips of orange zest. After that, two kinds of top-quality chocolate—cocoa and bittersweet bar chocolate—are whisked in.

- 2 quarts milk
- 1 cinnamon stick
- 2 strips of orange zest
- 1 cup unsweetened cocoa powder, sifted
- ¾ cup sugar
- 2 cups heavy cream
- ½ pound bittersweet chocolate, chopped

1. In a large saucepan, combine the milk, cinnamon stick and orange zest and cook over moderately high heat until bubbles appear around the edge. Remove from the heat, cover and let steep for at least 30 minutes and up to 2 hours.

2. Remove and discard the cinnamon stick and orange zest. Whisk the cocoa and sugar into the infused milk until thoroughly blended. Add the cream and bittersweet chocolate and cook over moderate heat, whisking constantly, until the cocoa is smooth. Serve piping hot.   *—Gerry Moss*

Moroccan Mint Tea

6 SERVINGS

- 1 tablespoon plus 1 teaspoon Chinese green tea
- 5 cups boiling water

FRONT TO BACK: **Kiwi Crush (p. 441)**, **Raspberry Rush (p. 441)**, **Pear-Ginger Smoothie (p. 442)**, **Blueberry Smoothie (p. 442)**, **Prune-Apple Smoothie (p. 442)** and **Pink Grapefruit Slush (p. 441)**.

Herbed Tomato Juice

Herbed Tomato Juice

10 SERVINGS

This liquified version of gazpacho is so intense that a small cup will suffice for each guest.

2 medium bunches of mint, stems discarded, plus additional whole sprigs, for garnish

10 sugar cubes

I. In a large teapot, cover the tea with 1 cup of the boiling water to rinse the leaves and warm the pot. Quickly pour off the water, leaving the tea in the pot.
2. Bring the remaining 4 cups of water to a rolling boil. Pack the mint leaves and sugar cubes into the teapot and add the boiling water. Let steep for 5 minutes before pouring the tea into heatproof glasses or cups. Garnish the tea with mint sprigs and serve.
—FOOD & WINE Test Kitchen

1½ pounds ripe tomatoes, quartered

¼ cup plus 2 tablespoons extra-virgin olive oil

1 tablespoon plus 1 teaspoon red wine vinegar

2 teaspoons thyme leaves

2 teaspoons coarsely chopped tarragon

1 small garlic clove, minced

1½ teaspoons sherry vinegar

Pinch of cayenne pepper

Salt and freshly ground black pepper

I. In a food processor, combine the tomatoes, oil, red wine vinegar, thyme, tarragon, garlic, sherry vinegar and cayenne; process until smooth. Season lightly with salt and black pepper and transfer to a bowl. Refrigerate for at least 1 hour and up to 1 day.
2. Just before serving, strain the tomato juice through a fine sieve, pressing on the tomatoes. Season again with salt and black pepper. Whisk the juice until frothy and then pour into small cups and serve. *—Frédérick Hermé*

Pineapple Cosmopolitans

8 SERVINGS

Pretty and pink, these Cosmopolitans have a hit of fresh pineapple. The pineapple and vodka need to stand for three days, so plan ahead.

2 cups (1 pound) coarsely chopped ripe pineapple

2 cups vodka

1 cup cranberry juice

1 tablespoon fresh lime juice

3 cups crushed ice

Lime slices, for garnish

I. In a large jar, combine the pineapple and vodka. Cover; let stand at room temperature until the vodka is well flavored with pineapple, about 3 days.
2. Strain the vodka through a fine sieve into a pitcher. Add the cranberry and lime juices and the crushed ice and stir well. Strain into chilled martini glasses. Serve garnished with lime slices.
—Mary Barber and Sara Corpening

Chez Es Saada's Palmyra

2 SERVINGS

The Palmyra cocktail is a specialty of the restaurant Chez Es Saada on the Lower East Side of Manhattan.

3½ ounces vodka (7 tablespoons)

⅓ cup fresh lime juice, plus 2 lime slices, quartered

¼ cup simple syrup (see Note)

6 mint sprigs, coarsely chopped, plus 2 long sprigs

Ice

In a cocktail shaker, mix the vodka, lime juice, simple syrup and chopped mint and strain into 2 glasses filled with small ice cubes. Garnish with the lime slices and mint sprigs and serve.
NOTE To make the simple syrup, simmer 1 cup of sugar and 1 cup of water

Pineapple Cosmopolitans

in a saucepan over moderate heat, stirring, until clear, about 1 minute. Let cool. A batch (about 1½ cups) will keep in the refrigerator for up to 1 month.

—*Chez Es Saada, New York City*

Desert Sun

1 SERVING

This zingy cocktail was created for New York City's Blue Water Grill.

- 3 ounces Stolichnaya vodka
- 1 ounce Grand Marnier
- 1 ounce orange juice

Splash of lime juice
Ice
Grenadine

In a cocktail shaker, combine the vodka, Grand Marnier, citrus juices and ice. Shake and strain into a martini glass. Finish with a splash of grenadine and serve. —*Summaiya Peterman*

Vin d'Oranges

MAKES 6 CUPS

A festive aperitif, this flavored wine is also perfect with dessert. The wine must stand for at least forty days to be at its best, so plan accordingly.

- ½ cup sugar
- ¼ cup water
- 5 cups white or rosé wine
- 1 cup kirsch
- ½ vanilla bean—split, seeds scraped and reserved
- 2 navel oranges
- ½ lemon

I. In a small saucepan, combine the sugar and water and bring to a boil. Pour the sugar syrup into a large heat-

Rum Punch

proof bowl. Let cool, and then stir in the wine, kirsch and the vanilla bean and seeds.

2. Slice the oranges and the lemon half crosswise ¼ inch thick. Cut the fruit slices into small triangles. Put the fruit in a large carafe and pour in the wine mixture. Cover and refrigerate for 40 days.

3. Before serving, strain the flavored wine through a double layer of cheesecloth. —*Daniel Boulud*

Plum Wine Spritzer

12 SERVINGS

Enjoy this fragrant and refreshing drink before dinner.

Ice
- 3 cups Japanese plum wine
- 3 cups sparkling water
- 12 tablespoons lime juice (from about 4 limes)
- 1 lime, cut into ¼-inch-thick slices

Fill 12 white-wine glasses with ice. Into each glass, pour ¼ cup of Japanese plum wine, ¼ cup of sparkling water and 1 tablespoon of lime juice. Stir, garnish the spritzer with slices of lime and serve. —*Marcia Kiesel*

Rum Punch

MAKES 10 CUPS

An intensely fruity rum punch gives a dinner party a kick start.

- 3 cups water
- 1 pint passion fruit sorbet, melted

One 12-ounce can frozen orange juice concentrate, thawed

One 12-ounce can frozen pineapple juice concentrate, thawed

- 1¼ cups white rum
- ¾ cup golden rum
- ¼ cup plus 2 tablespoons grenadine
- 3 tablespoons fresh lime juice
- ½ teaspoon freshly grated nutmeg

Ice

In a large punch bowl or pitcher, combine the water with the sorbet, orange and pineapple juice concentrates, white and golden rums, grenadine, lime juice and nutmeg. Fill 6 tall glasses with ice, pour in the punch and serve. —*Sylvia Fernandez*

MAKE AHEAD The punch can be refrigerated for up to 4 hours.

Blackberry Cordial

MAKES 1 QUART

The South has a long tradition of fruit wines, liqueurs and cordials. This one is made from the region's favorite berry. Be sure to seek out Ceylon cinnamon: most other cinnamons are too harsh and can spoil the flavor. It's fine to use frozen berries. The cordial must sit for at least two weeks for proper flavors to develop.

- 4 cups blackberries
- 3 cups bottled water
- 4 whole cloves
- 3 black peppercorns
- 3 cardamom pods, lightly crushed
- 2 cinnamon sticks, broken into 2-inch pieces
- 1 bay leaf
- 1 cup light brown sugar
- 1¼ cups Cognac or other brandy

1. In a medium saucepan, combine the blackberries with the bottled water, cloves, peppercorns, cardamom, cinnamon sticks and bay leaf and bring just to a boil. Cook over low heat for 30 minutes, gently crushing the blackberries against the side of the saucepan. Strain the blackberries through a fine sieve into a heatproof bowl without pressing on the berries. Stir the brown sugar into the berry juice until dissolved. Let cool.

2. Stir in the Cognac and pour the cordial into bottles. Seal the bottles tightly and store in a cool dark place for at least 2 weeks before serving.

—*Edna Lewis and Scott Peacock*

Chez Es Saada's Palmyra

Guide to Special Recipes

The recipes marked with symbols throughout the book are listed here so that
you can quickly locate all the dishes of a particular type.

☀ Quick Recipes

p. 51

p. 115

Healthy Recipes

p. 93

p. 170

★★★ THRU ★★★
1978 **1998**

20 Best Recipes

p. 407

p. 154

Best New Chefs

p. 86

index

Page numbers in **boldface** indicate photographs

INDEX

Y

Z

contributors

Jeffrey Alford and **Naomi Duguid** are the authors of *Flatbreads and Flavors: A Baker's Atlas* (William Morrow) and *Seductions of Rice* (Artisan). They are working on a book about the cuisines of the Mekong, to be published by Artisan in 2000.

Oliver Altherr was named one of FOOD & WINE's Best New Chefs in 1998. He is the chef at Hoku's in Honolulu.

Ann Chantal Altman is a chef, a food writer and a cooking teacher at Peter Kump's New York Cooking School in New York City.

Mary Corpening Barber and **Sara Corpening** are co-owners of Thymes Two Catering in San Francisco. Their most recent book is *Wraps: Easy Recipes for Handheld Meals* (Chronicle). *Cocktail Food* and *Smoothies II* are due from Chronicle in 1999 and 2000, respectively.

Nancy Verde Barr is a cookbook author and food writer. She is the author of *We Called It Macaroni* (Knopf) and the soon to be released *Simply Italian.*

Mario Batali is the chef/owner of Pó and Babbo in New York City and the host of *Molto Mario* and *Mediterranean Mario* on the Food Network. He is the author of *Mario Batali Simple Italian Food: Recipes from My Two Villages* (Clarkson Potter).

Patricia Beard is a contributing writer for *Elle, Mirabella* and *Town & Country.*

Florian Bellanger is the executive pastry chef at Le Bernardin in New York City.

Rose Levy Beranbaum is the author of *The Cake Bible* and *Rose's Christmas Cookies* (both from William Morrow). Her most recent book is *The Pie and Pastry Bible* (Scribner).

Betsy Bernardaud is married to Michel Bernardaud, a member of the fifth generation of the famous French Limoges porcelain makers.

Paul Bertolli is the chef/owner of Oliveto in Oakland, California.

Vera Bini is the chef at the restaurant Aquila Nigra in Mantua, Italy.

Daniel Boulud is the chef at Café Boulud and Restaurant Daniel in New York City. He is the author of *Cooking with Daniel Boulud* (Random House) and the upcoming *Café Boulud Cookbook.*

Fany Boutari is the matriarch of the family that owns Boutari & Son, Greece's oldest and most prestigious wine producer.

Flo Braker, a baking teacher, is the author of *The Simple Art of Perfect Baking* (Chapters) and the forthcoming revised and updated edition of *Sweet Miniatures,* to be published by Chronicle.

Marta Braunstein is pastry chef at Smith & Wollensky in Miami Beach.

Georgeanne Brennan is a cookbook author whose latest books are *Holiday Pumpkins* (Smithmark Publishing) and *In the French Kitchen Garden* (Chronicle).

Linda Burum is a food writer and teacher based in Santa Monica, California. She is the author of *Asian Pasta* (Addison-Wesley), *A Guide to Ethnic Food in Los Angeles* (HarperCollins) and the Zagat guide to the Los Angeles marketplace. Her book *Ethnic Cooking American Style* is due out this year.

Michael Chiarello is the chef/owner of Tra Vigne restaurant in St. Helena, California. His books, co-authored with Penelope Wisner, include both *Flavored Vinegars* and *Flavored Oils* and the upcoming *Season by Season at Tra Vigne,* all published by Chronicle.

Julia Child is the author of nine classic cookbooks. Her latest television series, which will air on PBS in the fall of this year, is *Julia and Jacques: Cooking at Home,* co-hosted with Jacques Pépin. The series will have a companion book.

Paul Chung, a self-taught chef, specializes in the recipes of his Jamaican-Chinese heritage.

Alfonso Contrisciani is the chef/proprietor of Opus 251 at the Philadelphia Art Alliance and the executive chef at Circa Restaurant, also in Philadelphia.

Jesse Cool has contributed to many major magazines. Her books include *Tomatoes. A*

Country Garden Cookbook, Onions: A Country Garden Cookbook and *Breakfast in Bed* (all HarperCollins).

Umberto Creatini is the chef at the Sassicaia vineyards in Bogheri, Italy.

Peggy Cullen is a New York City–based pastry chef, candy maker and food writer.

Danielle Custer, one of FOOD & WINE's Best New Chefs in 1998, is the executive chef and general manager at Laurels in Dallas. She is working on a book entitled *Spice Line.*

André Daguin is a cookbook author and chef in Gasgony, France. He has published two books in France and is also the author of *Foie Gras, Maigret, and Other Good Food from Gascony,* published in the United States by Random House.

Anne Daguin and **Hermann Van Beeck** are pastry cooks who specialize in old and historic recipes without any additives or chemicals.

Ariane Daguin, a native of Gascony, is co-owner of D'Artagnan, a New Jersey–based distributor of fresh duck and game products and a line of prepared pâtés and entrées.

Arnaud Daguin owns the Michelin-starred Les Platanes restaurant in Biarritz, France.

Anne Disrude is a food stylist and recipe developer based in New York City.

Jim Dodge is the consulting chef at the Fine Arts Restaurant in The Museum of Fine Arts in Boston.

Sylvia Fernandez is a native of St. Vincent, in the British West Indies. She cooks on the island of Mustique for Maguy Le Coze, co-owner of Le Bernardin in New York City.

Massimo Ferrari is a cooking teacher and restaurant consultant. He is the owner of Al Bersagliere in Goito, Italy.

Mark Franz is the chef and co-owner of Farallon in San Francisco.

Trey Foshee was named one of FOOD & WINE's Best New Chefs in 1998. He is the executive chef at the Sundance Resort in Sundance, Utah.

Edward Giobbi is a food writer and artist. He is the author of *Italian Family Cooking* (Random House), *Eat Right, Eat Well—The Italian Way* and *Pleasures of the Good Earth* (both from Knopf).

Allegra Goodman grew up on the island of Oahu, in Hawaii, and is the author of *Kaaterskill Falls* (Dial Press) and *The Family Markowitz* (Pocket Books).

Mark Gottwald is the chef/owner of Ships Inn on Nantucket and Ellie's Restaurant in Vero Beach, Florida.

Lauren Groveman is the owner of Lauren Groveman's Kitchen, a cooking school in Larchmont, New York. The author of *Lauren Groveman's Kitchen: Nurturing Food for Family & Friends* (Chronicle), she is a contributor to the *Baking With Julia* TV show and book.

Robbin Haas is the chef at the restaurant Bex in Boca Raton, Florida.

Alan Harding is the chef/owner of the restaurant Patois in Brooklyn.

Alice Harper, an avid amateur cook, teaches techniques of microsurgery in New York City.

Marcella Hazan is a renowned Italian cookbook author and teacher whose books include *Essentials of Classic Italian Cooking* (Knopf) and *Marcella Cucina* (HarperCollins).

Lee Hefter was named one of FOOD & WINE's Best New Chefs in 1998. He is the chef at Spago Beverly Hills.

Maria Helm, the chef of PlumpJack Cafe in San Francisco, was named one of FOOD & WINE's Best New Chefs in 1996. She is developing the culinary program at Robert Sinskey Vineyards in Napa, California.

Beth Hensperger is a cookbook author and food writer whose books include *The Bread Bible, Beth's Basic Bread Book, Bread for All Seasons* and *Baking Bread* (all Chronicle). *The Pleasure of Whole Grain Breads* (Chronicle) and *The Baker's Apprentice* (Ten Speed Press) are due out this year.

Pierre Hermé is a fourth-generation pastry chef. In 1997 he was elected Pastry Chef of the Year in France. He is a consultant to restaurants around the world. His first book in the United States was *Desserts by Pierre Hermé* (Little, Brown); *Chocolate by Pierre Hermé* will be published in 2000.

Gerald Hirigoyen is chef/co-owner of Fringale and Pastis restaurants in San Francisco. He was named one of FOOD & WINE's Best New Chefs in 1994. He is the author of *Bistro* (Sunset) and, with his wife, Cameron, *The Basque Kitchen* (HarperCollins), due out this year.

Jenna Holst is a writer, culinary-event producer, teacher and consultant. Her most recent book is *Stews* (Macmillan). *The Complete Idiot's Guide to Soups,* also to be published by Macmillan, is due out this year. She is researching and writing a book on South African food and wine.

Madhur Jaffrey is a food writer, cooking teacher, chef, food consultant and television personality as well as an actress. Her newest book is *Madhur Jaffrey's World Vegetarian,* which will be published by Clarkson Potter.

Nancy Harmon Jenkins divides her time between Camden, Maine, and Cortona, Italy. Her latest cookbook is *Flavors of Puglia* (Broadway Books). She is working on two books, one on olive oil and one about key Mediterranean ingredients.

Maya Kaimal is a food writer based in New York City. Her first book, *Curried Flavors: Family Recipes From South India* (Abbeville Press), was published in 1996. She is working on her second book, tentatively entitled *The Kerala Kitchen,* due out in 2000 from HarperCollins.

Anne Kearney was named one of America's Best New Chefs of 1998 by FOOD & WINE. She is the chef/proprietor of Peristyle, a small American bistro serving Louisiana-French contemporary fare, located in New Orleans.

Thomas and **Joseph Keller**, of the French Laundry in Yountville, California, and The Woodbox Inn in Nantucket, Rhode Island, respectively, are teaming up to open a classic French bistro in Yountville.

Melissa Kelly is the chef at the Old Chatham Sheepherding Company Inn in Old Chatham, New York.

Matthew Kenney is a chef/restaurateur in New York City. The author of *Matthew Kenney's Mediterranean Cooking* (Chronicle), he has another book in the works.

Marcia Kiesel is the associate director of FOOD & WINE's test kitchen and a co-author of *Simple Art of Vietnamese Cooking* (Simon & Schuster).

Peggy Knickerbocker is a food writer and cooking teacher based in San Francisco. She is the author of *Olive Oil: From Tree to Table* (Chronicle) and *Rose Pistola: A North Beach Cookbook,* due out this year from Broadway Books.

Gray Kunz is a chef, restaurateur and kitchen designer. His first cookbook, *Elements of Taste,* with Peter Kaminsky, will be published by Viking this year.

Emeril Lagasse, the chef and owner of Emeril's, NOLA and Delmonico Restaurant and Bar in New Orleans and Emeril's New Orleans Fish House in Las Vegas, hosts two cooking shows on the Food Network. His latest book is *Emeril's TV Dinners* (William Morrow).

Normand Laprise is the chef at Cena in New York City.

Christer Larsson is the chef/owner of Christer's, an upscale restaurant, and Knödel, a take-out sausage spot, both located in New York City.

Edna Lewis and **Scott Peacock** are the authors of *Coming Together to Cook,* to be published by Knopf this year.

Jeem Han Lock is the executive chef at Wild Ginger in Seattle. In 1997 he received the James Beard Foundation Award for Best Chef of the Northwest Region.

Michael Lomonaco is the executive chef and culinary director of Windows on the World in New York City. He is the host of *Michael's Place* on the Food Network and the co-author of *The '21' Cookbook* (Doubleday). He is working on two books on contemporary American food and cooking, to be published in 2000.

Emily Luchetti is the executive pastry chef at Farallon Restaurant in San Francisco and the author of *Four-Star Desserts* (HarperCollins).

Sascha Lyon is the sous-chef at the restaurant Balthazar in New York City.

Sirio Maccioni is the owner of Le Cirque 2000 in New York City.

Deborah Madison is the author of *Vegetarian Cooking for Everyone* (Broadway Books), *The Savory Way* and *The Greens Cookbook* (both from Bantam).

Lucie Romana Martin lives with her family in Ampus, a small in town in the Haut-Var region of Provence.

Zarela Martinez is the chef at Zarela in New York City and the author of *The Food and Life of Oaxaca* (Macmillan).

Sandra Martini is chef/owner of the restaurant Trattoria dei Martini in Mantua, Italy.

Rosario Salas McNish is the chef/owner of the restaurant Las Molas in Miami.

Linda Merinoff is a food writer and cookbook author based in Los Angeles and New York City.

Ferdinand Metz is the president of the Culinary Institute of America, in Hyde Park, New York, and St. Helena, California.

Rene Michelena was named one of FOOD & WINE's Best New Chefs in 1998. He is the chef at La Bettola in Boston.

Gerry Moss is the pastry chef at Tra Vigne, Michael Chiarello's restaurant in St. Helena, California.

Eberhard Müller is chef and part owner at Lutèce in New York City.

Tony Najiola is the executive chef at Ravenswood in Sonoma, California.

Betsy Nelson and **Jim Kyndberg** are, respectively, head of food operations and chef at Organica restaurant at the Aveda Spa Retreat in Osceola, Wisconsin.

Jan Newberry, a cookbook editor, food writer and FOOD & WINE columnist, lives in Oakland, California.

Charlie Palmer, chef and owner of Aureole in New York City, is the author of *Great American Food* (Random House).

Neela Paniz is a chef, restaurateur and cooking teacher. Her book, *The Bombay Café Cookbook,* was published in 1998 by Ten Speed Press.

Grace Parisi is the recipe tester-developer for FOOD & WINE. She is the author of *Summer/Winter Pasta* (William Morrow).

Jacques Pépin is a master chef, TV personality, food columnist, cooking teacher and contributor to FOOD & WINE. He is the author of numerous books and the co-host, with Julia Child, of *Julia and Jacques: Cooking at Home,* airing on PBS in the fall of this year.

Guillermo Pernot was named one of FOOD & WINE's Best New Chefs in 1998. He is the chef at Vega Grill in Philadelphia.

Georges Perrier is the chef/owner of the restaurant Le Bec-Fin in Philadelphia. He is the author of *Georges Perrier: Le Bec-Fin Recipes,* published by Running Press.

Summaiya Peterman has developed drink recipes for bars all over New York City.

Charles Phan is the chef/owner of The Slanted Door in San Francisco.

Odessa Piper is the chef/owner of L'Etoile in Madison, Wisconsin. She is working on a book of L'Etoile recipes and philosophy entitled *Spirit of Place.*

Susan G. Purdy teaches baking across the country. She is the author of *Let Them Eat Cake* and *Have Your Cake and Eat It, Too* (both William Morrow). She is working on a book about classic old-fashioned home baking.

Anne Quatrano and **Clifford Harrison** are the chef/owners of Bacchanalia and Floataway Cafe in Atlanta. They are collaborating on *Sundays at Summerland Farms,* a collection of seasonal menus.

Steven Raichlen, a food writer and syndicated columnist, is the founder of Cooking in Paradise, on St. Barthélemy. He is the author of *The Barbecue! Bible, Miami Spice* (both Workman) and *Healthy Latin Cooking* (Rodale). He has two upcoming books in his High-Flavor, Low-Fat series: *Mexican Cooking* and *Jewish Cooking* (both Viking).

Eric Ripert is the co-owner and executive chef of Le Bernardin in New York City. He is the co-author, with Maguy Le Coze, of *Le Bernardin Cookbook: Four Star Simplicity* (Doubleday).

Joël Robuchon owned the restaurants Jöel Robuchon and Jamin, which received the highest Michelin rating. He is the author of numerous books published in France and his recipes are featured in *Simply French,* published in the United States by Hearst.

Judy Rodgers is the chef at Zuni Café in San Francisco.

Michael Romano is the chef of Union Square Cafe and the author of *The Union Square Cafe Cookbook*, published by HarperCollins. He is currently working on his second book.

Nadia Santini is the chef at Dal Pescatore in Canneto sull'Oglio, Italy.

Shirley Sarvis is a food writer and winery consultant who is based in San Francisco.

She conducts wine-tasting seminars across the United States.

Oliver Saucy is the chef at Café Maxx in Pompano Beach, Florida.

Chris Schlesinger is the chef/owner of East Coast Grill & Raw Bar in Boston. His most recent book is *License to Grill* (William Morrow).

Arthur Schwartz is a radio personality and the author of four cookbooks, the latest of which is *Naples at Table: Cooking in Campania* (HarperCollins).

Lindsey Shere, a former pastry chef at Chez Panisse, is part owner of the Downtown Bakery and Creamery in Healdsburg, California. She is the author of *Chez Panisse Desserts* (Random House).

Lydia Shire is the chef and owner of the restaurants Biba and Pignoli in Boston.

Jane Sigal is a senior editor at FOOD & WINE and the author of *Backroad Bistros, Farmhouse Fare* (Doubleday) and *Normandy Gastronomique* (Abbeville).

Alexander Smalls is a restaurateur based in New York City. He is the author of *Grace the Table* (HarperCollins), which is a memoir-cookbook.

Peggy Smith is the owner of Tomales Bay Foods in Point Reyes, California.

Katy Sparks was named one of FOOD & WINE's Best New Chefs in 1998. She is the chef at Quilty's in New York City.

Rori Spinelli is a professional cook and a freelance food stylist who is based in New York City.

Diana Sturgis is the test kitchen director at FOOD & WINE magazine.

Allen Susser is the owner of Allen's 2 Go, a gourmet market in Aventura, Florida. He is the author of *The Great Citrus Book,* published by Ten Speed Press, and *Alan Susser's New World Cuisine and Cookery,* published by Doubleday.

Judith Sutton is a cook/pastry chef, food writer, cookbook editor and food consultant based in New York City.

Michael Symon was named one of America's Best New Chefs of 1998 by FOOD & WINE. He is the chef at the restaurant Lola in Cleveland.

Romano Tamani is the chef/owner of Ristorante Ambrasciata in Quistello, Italy. He has published two cookbooks in Italian.

Alan Tardi is the chef/owner of Follonico restaurant in New York City. He also writes about food and wine.

Kevin Taylor is a chef and restaurateur in Denver. His restaurants there include Palettes in the Denver Art Museum, Brasserie Z, Kevin Taylor and Jou Jou.

Laurent Tourondel was named one of FOOD & WINE's Best New Chefs in 1998. He is the chef at the restaurant Palace Court in Las Vegas.

Jeremiah Tower is a restaurateur based in San Francisco. He is the owner of Stars and the author of *Jeremiah Tower's New American Classics,* published by Harper-Collins. His new book, *Stars Cookbook,* will be published in 2000.

Barbara Tropp is a consulting chef, cooking teacher and Asian tour guide. She is the author of both *The Modern Art of Chinese Cooking,* published by Hearst, and *China Moon Cookbook,* published by Workman.

Tom Valenti is the chef at Butterfield 81 in New York City.

Norman Van Aken is the award-winning chef and owner of Norman's in Miami. He is the author of *Norman's New World Cuisine* (Random House), *Feast of Sunlight* (Harvard Common Press) and *The Great Exotic Fruit Book* (Ten Speed Press). He is currently working on a project for PBS.

Theodora van den Beld is the chef and owner of Theoz Restaurant & Bar, Yakima Grill and Theoz/Baci Catering, all of which are in Seattle.

Tetsuya Wakuda is the chef at Tetsuya's, in Sydney, Australia. His first cookbook will be published this year.

Brendan Walsh is the chef at the Elms Restaurant and Tavern in Ridgefield, Connecticut.

Nancy Walters developed an award-winning recipe for white chili that was included in *John Madden's Ultimate Tailgating* (Viking).

Alice Waters, one of America's leading activists in the fields of organic and sustainable agriculture, is the owner and chef of Chez Panisse restaurant in Berkeley, California. Her books include *Chez Panisse Vegetables, Fanny at Chez Panisse,* both published by HarperCollins, and the upcoming *Chez Panisse Cafe Cookbook.*

Joanne Weir is a cooking teacher and the author of *You Say Tomato,* published by Broadway Books.

Paula Wolfert is the author of *Couscous and Other Good Food from Morocco, Mediterranean Cooking, The Cooking of Southwest France, The Cooking of the Eastern Mediterranean* and *Mediterranean Grains and Greens,* all published by Harper-Collins, and *Mostly Mediterranean,* published by Penguin. She is at work on *Cooking Mediterranean—Slow and Easy.*

We also would like to thank the following restaurants for their contributions to this cookbook:

Aquila Nigra, Mantua, Italy; **Chez Es Saada,** New York City; **Eleven Madison Park,** New York City; **Mel's Bar & Grill,** Denver; **The Point,** Lake Saranac, New York

photo credits

William Abranowicz: back cover—top right, 68, 89, 108, 202, 274, 282, 300, 355, 391, 437, 446; **Quentin Bacon:** front cover, 10, 21, 30, 44, 76, 130, 132, 135, 140, 143, 146, 160, 164, 174, 176, 180, 189, 191, 208, 223, 264, 270, 277, 292, 295, 315, 339, 352, 353, 361, 366, 393, 411, 421, 430 (top), 447; **Andrè Baranowski:** 46, 78, 129, 211, 242, 372 (top), 385; **Fernando Bengochea:** 240; **Bill Bettencourt:** 23 (bottom), 28, 122, 168, 207, 222, 272, 290, 298, 348, 356, 388, 426, 431; **Beatriz Da Costa:** back cover—top left, bottom right, 45, 55, 80, 81, 82, 88, 90, 152, 155 (left), 157, 206, 221, 224, 228, 235, 236, 247, 265, 279, 299, 322, 324, 372 (bottom), 374, 392, 395, 406; **Reed Davis:** 15, 33, 54, 64, 83, 99, 100, 104, 106, 115, 116, 117, 149, 167, 199, 204, 232, 234, 239, 244, 252, 257, 259, 260, 276, 293, 308, 332, 334, 336, 344, 345, 347, 364, 371, 376, 379, 382, 386, 399, 401, 402; **Miki Duisterhof:** 40, 49, 63, 86 (bottom), 95, 155 (right), 241, 321, 409, 412, 418 (top), 420, 440; **Gentl & Hyers:** 48, 58, 67, 79, 87, 96, 118, 123, 124, 148, 163, 186, 250, 253, 330, 428, 436; **Noelle Hoeppe:** 433; **Matthew Hranek:** 16, 34, 38, 52, 56, 72, 102, 111, 113, 139, 172, 179, 184, 195, 200, 216, 218, 248, 254, 256 (top), 262, 314 (bottom), 316, 325, 346, 369, 383, 384, 404, 410, 413, 422, 424, 444; **Geoff Lung:** 51, 61, 245, 266; **Rita Maas:** 318, 350; **Maura McEvoy:** 19, 93, 110, 112, 212, 214-215, 226, 284, 286, 287, 360, 378, 414, 430 (bottom); **Michael McLaughlin:** 169, 342; **Minh & Wass:** 196, 256 (bottom); **Michael Mundy:** 31, 75, 158, 177, 381; **Amy Neunsinger:** 59, 418 (bottom); **Oriani & Origone:** 134, 142, 312; **Daniel Proctor:** 43, 60, 114, 230, 246, 432; **Maria Robledo:** 70, 74, 109, 159, 197, 294, 390, 417, 443; **Victor Schrager:** 14, 317, 434; **Zubin Shroff:** 127, 136, 144, 171, 261; **Evan Sklar:** 92, 151, 162, 170, 302, 304, 310, 362, 408; **Laurie Smith:** 238; **Ann Stratton:** 121, 154, 192, 237, 311, 375; **Luca Trovato:** 128; **Simon Watson:** back cover—bottom left, 17, 18, 20, 22, 23 (top), 24, 25, 26, 27, 29, 35, 36, 107, 126, 268, 273, 319 (bottom), 341, 368, 438, 445; **Jonelle Weaver:** 12, 13, 50, 53, 84, 86 (top), 94, 105, 120, 198, 220, 231, 271, 278, 314 (top), 319 (top), 326, 329, 340, 397, 400, 419, 442.